CONTENTS

SECTION TWO

Austria

SECTION THREEE

England

SECTION FOUR

France

SECTION FIVE

Interlude: The High Plateau

SECTION SIX

United States of America

SECTION SEVEN

General Developments

FOREWORD

by Edward Rothstein

Music Critic, *The New Republic*

THE YEAR BEFORE *Liberace's death, I went on a pilgrimage to a mini-mall not far from the Las Vegas strip to visit the Liberace Museum—Nevada's third most popular tourist attraction, after gambling and the Hoover Dam. It was a small building stocked with all the outfits, rhinestones and glitz one might have expected from the pop pianist, including a painting of his mother, opulent gifts from royalty and an extravagantly decorated Rolls-Royce. But the heart of the collection was the display of the embossed and encrusted pianos of the entertainer's flamboyant concert life, and, intermingled among them, their pianistic ancestors—a Pleyel on which (it was claimed) Chopin had played, a Bösendorfer once played by Liszt and other instruments linked to virtuosos of times gone by.*

These latter pianos did not find their place among jewels and mink by accident. Liberace was, quite self-consciously, a kitschy imitation of the virtuoso, a Las Vegas Liszt whose success was linked to the qualities that made nineteenth-century pianists such imposing figures, including picturesque mannerisms, magnetic personas and intimate relationships to the middle-class public and the repertoire it craved. The piano was as essential to him as to his predecessors; more than any ermine robe or studded ring, it was Liberace's primary symbol, and its fate seemed peculiarly outlined in this progress from Chopin's Pleyel to Liberace's raffish Baldwin.

I might not have been aware of the implications of all these connections had Arthur Loesser not shown, in this book, that the piano was more than just an ordinary contraption constructed out of 10,000 pieces of wood, hide, metal and cloth. The evolution of the piano, its rise and its fall, is one of the epic stories of modern times, and Loesser was the first to grant it that scope and range. So despite the casual title, this book is not just a folksy collection of anecdotes about pianos and their players for the hobbyist and amateur. Despite Arthur Loesser's easy-going style, despite his cultivated enthusiasm for the byways of musical history, despite his affection for human ingenuity in all its variety and despite his delight in music ranging from the most vulgar to the most profound, this is not just a "popular history."

But Loesser does tell the story of this instrument in a popular fashion—and it turns out to be a gripping narrative. First invented in Italy by Bartolomeo Cristofori during the early eighteenth century, the instrument was born as a "clavicembalo col piano e forte"—a keyboard instrument that could play both soft and loud. But if it was in Italy, the country of song, that the piano originated, it was in the housebound north that it most strongly took root. And it was as an instrument of the home that the piano began to work its wiles. Tracing its triumphant advance, Loesser moves easily from country to country, taking examples and evidence culled from literature, newspapers, music manuscripts, popular accounts and scholarship, evidence unavailable elsewhere and amassed during the seven years in which he wrote this book.

By 1847, Loesser notes, an instrument that had been a novelty just fifty years before had become central to musical life: there were 180 piano makers in Paris alone, along with 60,000 instruments; in England 300 piano firms were producing more than 20,000 instruments a year. The instrument also made its way across the ocean, where families such as Chickering and Steinway so spectacularly advanced its design that the American piano became a world standard. By 1910 the United States was the world's largest piano manufacturer, with 300 companies producing more than 350,000 pianos yearly. From being an upper-crust instrument that Beethoven cursed for its easily broken strings, it had become a mammoth iron-framed harp in elaborate furniture casings, played in every parlor and hall.

The triumph of this instrument is easily told. What is less easily explained is why the piano was so important, and what its presence meant for the cultures it touched. And here Loesser's tale becomes more intricate. He shows that in its construction, in its teaching, in its performance, in its place in the home, the piano was as much an expression of a society's dreams and style as was the music it played. Moreover, it was not just an occasional accompanist to that world; it was its central voice.

It became, for example, the social anchor of the middle-class home. Lessons were required of every eligible maiden and bachelor. Etiquette books explained how a woman should play for an admirer and how a courtship should be carried out at the keyboard. The piano's singing voice was well suited to domestic expressions of passion and of social aspiration, as well as to the more public aesthetic achievements of the classical repertoire. The discipline of playing the instrument also meant that these passions were controlled and shaped. The piano was not just a seducer, it was also a moral guide; it played the Mephisto Waltz *but also* The Maiden's Prayer. *The study of the piano was necessary—one journal asserted—for the proper "formation of character."*

The instrument was also inseparable from developments in nineteenth-century commerce and technology. The manufacturers were all middle-class family firms making instruments for middle-class families. Their innovation, labor, craftsmanship and obsession—their "industry"—matched the industry of the teachers who turned out method after method for their equally industrious pupils. As Loesser shows, in fact, the piano stood at the crossroads of commerce, art and society in nineteenth-century Europe; it migrated to other societies around the world with similar aspirations. There was even something religious about the keyboard; it was both an icon and an altar. "I crucify, like a good Christ, the flesh of my fingers," wrote the pianist Hans von Bülow of his practicing. In response, listeners gathered around the piano in devotion and celebration both at the hearth and in the hall. Like the music it played, the piano spanned high and low, the private and the public, comprehending the spirit of an age.

There is no other book about the instrument—or, for that matter, about nineteenth-century European music culture—that captures so much and captures it so nearly whole. Like the social theorist, Loesser takes society seriously and finds it represented in music and its instruments. But he does not reduce society to theoretical abstraction, nor does he slight the texture of ordinary human life; he respects and never mocks its ambitions and trials. Like the music historian, he insists on the significance of the detail—the works that were played, the number of pianos manufactured, the technological advances in the instrument—but these are used to construct a portrait that lies beyond the reach of strict scholarship. Like the popularizer, he never presumes too much, but at the same time he never condescends and rarely oversimplifies. And like the performing artist he was, he treats the great music of the repertoire with respect and awe, but is not above taking pleasure in the reams of pop sheet music that accompanied nineteenth-century domestic life. Of course there are longueurs in Loesser's tale, arguments I would question, issues I wish he had explored more deeply; but I would still sooner consult Arthur Loesser than any other authority on the history of the instrument.

This is partly because Loesser, who died in 1969 at the age of 74, drew on what Jacques Barzun calls a "large fund of general culture and miscellaneous reading." His German-Jewish father did not consider the New York schools sufficiently rigorous and had the prodigious child pianist tutored at home, in French, Latin and, of course, music. Later educated at Columbia University, the City College of New York (where he studied zoology) and the Institute of Musical Art (now the Juilliard School), Loesser became an accomplished pianist and accompanist, touring the United States, Asia and Australia, and appearing regularly with the violinist Mischa Elman. In 1926 he moved to Cleveland, where he joined the piano faculty of the Cleveland Institute of Music. His house became a salon for Cleveland's musical life. Loesser loved music in all its forms (including the songs of his half-brother, Frank, best known for Guys and Dolls*). He was a dedicated teacher and performer and lecturer, became an important music critic in Cleveland and counted as friends such figures as Jascha Heifetz and Arthur Rubinstein. He even anticipated the fashions of later decades in his early love for Romantic piano exotica and the music of ragtime. Like the instrument he writes about, Loesser's captivating voice—as performer, critic, raconteur and lover of music—represents a style and culture that have by now faded into obscurity.*

As Loesser approaches the end of his story, there is a sense of regret and sorrow evident in that voice as he chronicles the passing of an era. For beginning with the later 1920s the piano entered a decline—a decline that may have quickened to a plunge. First came the player piano, whose automatic mechanisms offered, as one advertisement put it, "perfection without practice." By 1923 it represented 56 percent of all pianos made. Then came the phonograph and the radio, permanently undoing the piano culture. There were 295 piano makers in the United States in 1922; there were 81 in 1929. Then the Depression knocked out many of the remaining manufacturers, leaving the names of once great pianos as mere trademarks attached to unworthy shells. Loesser notes that, as social habits changed, virtuosos on the instrument no longer inspired the awe they once did, and a "prudishness" in programing took over. Loesser titled his penultimate chapter "The Dusk of the Idol."

Now, nearly two generations later, that dusk has passed into night. In 1954, when Loesser was writing, it was still true that piano-vocal arrangements of popular songs and songs from shows regularly sold 100,000 copies. It was still true that most children were expected to learn to play the instrument. And it was still true that the piano was a standard participant in popular musical performance. Loesser's final description now seems dated, but he knew where things were headed:

> *In the family, the piano competes manfully with the washing machine and the station wagon for the installment dollar, and rather more weakly with gardening, photography, and canasta for hobby time. As a source of passive musical enjoyment, it has been all but snuffed out by the phonograph, the radio, and the television set. . . .*

Let us complete the picture. Whereas in 1909 U.S. piano factories made 364,545 pianos, in 1989 only about 165,000 pianos were sold here, less than two-thirds of them made domestically. The 295 piano manufacturers in the United States in 1911 have decreased to fewer than 10, with even fewer making pianos using the standards and craftsmanship of earlier eras and most diversifying into the manufacture of clocks, furniture, even circuit boards. European manufacturers have suffered as well, while the Japanese piano industry has boomed, as if replicating earlier middle-class ideals of industry and devotion, expanding into countries that once barely had contact with European musical culture.

Meanwhile, the "electronic piano" that Loesser presciently wondered about in 1954 has nearly displaced the traditional instrument (now labeled "acoustic"), with U.S. sales of 4 million in 1989 alone. Many of these instruments provide the social benefits in our popular culture that the piano once did: a certification of belonging, a means for entering preferred circles, a source of pleasure shared with one's peers. But contemporary popular culture makes far fewer demands on skills and literacy than did the classical tradition. Moreover, whereas the piano was a fixed musical anchor in the home, the new keyboards are deliberately portable, not really home instruments at all. They are an extension of a youth-oriented commercial music culture whose very origins are based on opposition to the bourgeois social life that nurtured the piano. And they are musically unable to imitate the very "soft–loud" expression that was the essence of the "piano-forte."

Of course, as Loesser notes, the piano will never become obsolete. It remains essential to our concert life and appears prodigiously on our stages. But its current role is primarily to replay the music of its nineteenth-century maturity; the keyboard music of this century is generally treated as an appendix to a tale already completed. Moreover, playing the piano is no longer expected of every aspiring citizen. There is no longer a consensus about its importance; the home has become incidental to music rather than its center; concert halls have become little more than museums mounting the same exhibitions; and most of our pianists seem content with becoming mechanisms, not transcending them. Even musical amateurism has declined.

So there is little doubt that Loesser's tale is reaching a sad conclusion. The piano, in fact, has become little more than a shadow of the phenomenon Loesser describes, a wraith on display. It has always conferred sophistication and prestige—attributes caricatured in Liberace's instruments and in modern advertisements—but it was also once concerned with the connection between spiritual and material aspirations, the home and the community, the earthly and the ethereal. The piano was really about a culture's notion of transcendence. But it is doubtful whether the instrument itself can transcend its present place in our culture, when it has so lost its aura and its power. The piano still lives, we are tempted to insist after reading Loesser. But may it rest in peace.

Summer 1990

PREFACE

by Jacques Barzun

Our century's self-conscious interest in culture and society has produced valuable attempts to retell the Western past with the aid of such organizing principles as technological change, art collecting, and—in a humorous but informative vein—the modes and means of sanitary plumbing. It was left to Mr. Arthur Loesser, a pianist and musician as well as a musical journalist, to hit upon an idea which seems obvious now that he has given it body and form, but which had not occurred to anyone before, despite its patently rich possibilities.

Taking the piano as a "center" for writing the social history of the last three hundred years was an inspired idea. It combines all the virtues and advantages: the piano being a creation and plaything of men, its story leads us into innumerable biographies; being a boxful of gadgets, the piano has changed through time and improved at ascertainable moments and places, and every Western land has both contributed and succumbed to it. Indeed, for the last century and a half the piano has been an institution more characteristic than the bathtub—there were pianos in the log cabins of the frontier, but no tubs. As a result of this ubiquity, the identification of piano with music took such deep root as to constitute a superstition. We are only now emancipating ourselves from it, and it is thus doubly fitting that we should review its origin and spread.

All this Mr. Loesser must have seen at a glance when his great idea struck him, and his work proves that he also perceived how in itself the piano is a perfect symbol of Western civilization in modern times. I suggested with undue scorn a moment ago that the piano is a gadget; it is in fact a machine. More than any other music-making contrivance until the advent of radio, its growth has paralleled that of technology. There is something of the power loom in the ultimate "grand" of the nineteenth century, and a fair likeness between note-spinning virtuosos and cotton-spinning magnates.

Again, the piano is the social instrument par excellence. It is drawing-room furniture, a sign of bourgeois prosperity, the most massive of the devices by which the young are tortured in the name of education and the grown-up in the name of entertainment. It is a rallying point for the convivial when letting off spirituous fumes through song, and for the amorous conducting a romance with the aid of romances. At the same time, too, the piano is the individualist's instrument for nursing the illusion that he is a host in himself. With bare hands and intermittent foot he can unleash quasi-symphonic storms and discharge the tensions induced by a world increasingly populated and oppressive, a world in which standardization and noise-making power jointly increase, the inevitable concomitants of machinery—including the piano.

But this summary is not the tale itself, and we cannot really be said to know what the conclusion stands for until we have read Mr. Loesser's admirably balanced and leisurely account. In the hands of a less versatile writer, the story might have left deplorable gaps or pitched into impassable technicalities. A breathless narrator would have choked on his own learning and given us vertigo instead of pleasurable instruction. Just think: in his progress from country to country and from age to age, the historian must tell us how the piano grew out of its various keyboard ancestors; he must explain the mechanism, the manufacture, and the playing of all these hybrids; he must describe the music and its patrons, the cost and arrangement of their diversions, and the economics of their lives. Equally his concern are the printing and publishing of music, and the tastes and fads, reputations and charlatanisms of an industry which culminates in vulgar idolatry as well as high art. These in turn, as Mr. Loesser shows, reflect the image of the great intellectual and political movements, from the Reformation, which lies just behind his starting point in 1648, to twentieth-century democracy and totalitarianism. Almost his last words connect the rise of Hitler and the failures of American banks with the nadir of piano manufacture and the victory of air-borne music.

Nothing that is or was relevant is too slight for his notice; nothing that can entice the imagination of the curious and the thoughtful is too impalpable for him to convey. He evokes (without solving) the mystery of how four-hand duets were played at one keyboard when hoop-skirts were wider than the instrument, and he knows how to sum up what is not at all mysterious: "The lyrichord, the musical glasses, and the guitar earned but short rides on the wheel of time; the pianoforte was the object that fulfilled the needs of a longer day. It had expression; playing it required only a slight adaptation of an existing skill; and it was expensive enough to be socially desirable."

We do not of course expect Mr. Loesser to rewrite the history of the

French Revolution or tell us "all about Chopin." But wherever we test him he gives us the grateful feeling that he has seen and thought for himself. He may err in judgment—as I think he does whenever he deals with Rousseau—but the mistake, if it is one, does not matter, because it is part of a considered whole which in turn rests upon first-hand impressions. Mr. Loesser has undoubtedly fingered and examined all the types of instruments he speaks of; he has studied illustrations and exploited foreign sources; played or read the music, good and bad, which has adorned or compromised the costly apparatus which is his theme. In a word, Mr. Loesser is a good craftsman in research.

But he could never have made a book, in seven years or in seventeen, if he had not started with a large fund of general culture and miscellaneous reading. No amount of research into the lives of baroque organists would suggest an analogy of their trios with Leibniz's "windowless monads." No degree of conscientious reading about the eighteenth century would lead a man to characterize Richardson's novels as "viscous." Mr. Loesser, it is clear, is a man of strong and vivid opinions, and they color his work. No one but a pedant would want it colorless.

His prevailing wind of doctrine, one may say, is the astringent. He prefers the aristocratic ideal to the bourgeois, polyphonic music to homophonic, art to trade, the individual to the mass, the definite and elegant to the atmospheric and passionate. These are temperamental choices which also help account for the sustained lucidity of his prose—no mean advantage when so much that is intricate in mechanics and sound, in costume and chronology, has to be imparted without tables, diagrams, or notation. Indeed, the author's power to convey the quality or purport of a piece is most unusual in an age when music is generally supposed to make us speechless. See how Mr. Loesser manages: "Variations now were made to open with a magniloquent introductory section containing a number of attention-raping chords and flourishes ranging over a good portion of the keyboard. A clever composer might also incorporate into these a sly anticipatory allusion to a measure or two of the tune to come. The bustle would subside, and a hold would be arranged upon a leading tone or chord, whereupon the simply attired melody would come forth, effectively set forth against the suspense just accumulated. In other words, the tune was made to 'make an entrance' in the best theatrical or operatic manner." A writer who always knows what he means will assume other writers carry meaning too. And so when Mr. Loesser quotes from foreign authors, his translation has point and character and sounds as if written in English. Thus his entire work is of a piece, free alike from witless gush and from hollow gravity.

But who am I to praise a performer in whose pages a colleague can learn innumerable lessons? It is much more modest and becoming to point out that Mr. Loesser's chapter titles do not come up to his own standards of expression and might even mislead the unwary. Let the intending reader sample the text rather than the Table of Contents. His eye is bound to fall upon such happy phrases as: "light music is a good lubricant"; "Vienna was built dense"; "musicians were invited to many salons *on terms of putative equality"; and even before he encounters such a problem as "the need of the thumb in strained digital situations," he will have been convinced that in order to know all and enjoy the exploration he must begin at the beginning. This is the spot where, having held a candle before the sun—or perhaps the herald's trumpet before the grand piano—we now leave the reader, confident that he is setting out on a memorable journey.*

ACKNOWLEDGMENTS

MY PROFOUND THANKS are due a number of persons and institutions that have helped me in the preparation of this work.

The staff of the Music Section of the Cleveland Public Library has placed me under permanent debt, through its courtesy and its eagerness to be of service, beyond the call of duty. To Barbara Penyak, its chief, I am under particular personal obligations for some important photostats obtained abroad. The others likewise: Luisa Heeth, Russell Hehr, and Irene Adamczak—all make me feel that I could never have written my book without them. Staff members of other divisions of this great library have also been signally helpful: I must especially mention Ella Frank, who was outstandingly successful in managing interlibrary loans.

The late lamented Albert Riemenschneider, Director of the Conservatory of Music of Baldwin-Wallace College, Berea, Ohio, will always be remembered by me with the most affectionate gratitude for making available to me the rare volumes of his Bach Library, at a time when it was his private uncatalogued treasure, kept under continual lock and key.

The staff of the Music Division of the Library of Congress has been notably generous and courteous in making its facilities available to me, and that of the Music Division of the New York Public Library has likewise provided indispensable assistance.

I wish further to thank the library of Western Reserve University, Dr. Lyon N. Richardson at its head, for the important privileges it has placed at my disposal. Moreover, the Western Reserve Historical Society as well as the Virginia Historical Society were both kind enough to supply several interesting items.

I have been much moved at observing the zest which John Hollander, his wife Anne Loesser Hollander (my daughter), and their friend Stephen Kitay Orgel put into the making of this book's index. I flatter myself that intellectual sympathy, more than family feeling, animated those young people in their achievement, invaluable to me.

My editor Henry W. Simon is the one who has kept me going, morally speaking, all these years. His quiet understanding patience seemed to imply a belief in me that I felt obligated to live up to.

It is impossible to convey the flavor of my grateful feelings toward my wife Jean Bassett Loesser, who stood by me loyally through the seven years during which I was pregnant with this work, and during which I suffered the anxieties, the tantrums, and the spells of morning sickness appropriate to that condition.

Cleveland, Ohio ARTHUR LOESSER

SECTION

ONE

Germany

1. EACH KEYBOARD HAS ITS PLACE

On October 24, 1648, the treaties of Westphalia were published. As the bells tolled the event, Johann Crüger composed a tune to Martin Rinkart's words:

Nun danket alle Gott
Mit Herzen, Mund und Händen,
Der grosse Dinge thut
An uns und allen Enden.

Now thank we all our God
With heart and hands and voices
Who wondrous things hath done
In whom His world rejoices.

—Translation by Catherine Winkworth

It was destined to become one of the most famous of Lutheran hymns.

There was good cause for thanksgiving. For thirty years Protestant and Catholic, Swedish, Austrian, French, and German soldiers of all kinds had killed, burned, raped, and pillaged their way through the German lands. They did it in the name of the Empire, of Gustav Adolf, of Cardinal Richelieu, in the name of Justification by Faith, and in the name of the Holy Ghost. The warring princes could not pay the thugs they had hired or shanghaied, so they urged them to "live off the country." More often they had lived off the towns, which gave better meat for scientific plundering. It was the towns especially that the war had degraded and impoverished.

Even without the war the Germanies would have been a backward portion of Christendom. In the great European commercial expansion of the sixteenth and seventeenth centuries Germany had taken little part. After the epoch-making voyages of Columbus and Da Gama the oceans became the great world trade routes; and it was the nations bordering on the Atlantic that had the opportunity and the capacity for taking advantage of them. It was the Spanish and the Portuguese, the French, the Dutch, and the English who planted colonies in the Americas and who traded with the Indies. In all this tremendous traffic of wealth, in the burgeoning of enterprise, and in the intellectual tingle that went with it the Germans had little active share.

The violence had ceased now, but generations of small, mean living were ahead. Germany was broken: irrevocably split down the middle religiously, and politically shattered into three hundred fragments. Some of these were sizable realms such as the Kingdom of Saxony or the Kingdom of Bavaria, but most were pint-sized principalities—"duodecimo states" they were contemptuously called later. Some had curious names that came unscrewed in the middle, such as Schwarzburg-Sondershausen, Oettingen-Wallerstein, or Schaumburg-Lippe. Each was headed by an absolute sovereign princelet, who owed a theoretical and ceremonial allegiance to a Holy Roman Emperor in Vienna, but who in practice did pretty much as he pleased with his domain. Each strutted about, affectionately coddling his ornamental army, his hunting apparatus, and his little orchestra.

A kind of cultural stasis marked the German latter seventeenth century. The propertied townspeople of Reformation times may have shown a trend toward an improvement in their social influence, but the war had humbled them and diminished their pretensions. The ancient European estates—nobility, citizenry, peasantry—had frozen into a sort of caste system. The noble lords of the land, as well as their landless relatives, looked down with distant disdain upon the burghers of the towns. Their very pronouns and verb-endings changed when they had to talk to those lower forms of life. But the burghers faithfully reflected the same distance and disdain when they in turn confronted peasants and menials.

The inflexible stratification of society was an unquestioned rule of life, an unassailable dogma for everybody. In schools and churches segregation of classes was an unbreachable canon. It would have been the height of indecency to think of baptizing the infant heir to a noble title in the water that had been used to besprinkle the young of a tradesman. There were even some who hopefully speculated that a divinely appointed separation of ranks would be continued in the blessed life beyond the grave. The three estates of society differed profoundly from one another, ethically. In their sense of values, their ideals, and their unthinking habits, the members of each group represented separate kinds of human beings. If we wanted to describe the difference by means of an oversimplified slogan, we might say that the nobility lived by authority and personal prestige; the peasantry by obedience and labor; while the middle classes lived by persuasion and special skills. Among these, the purely mental skills were judged far superior to the manual.

Many persons, even among those who were not the greatest beneficiaries of the prevailing social scheme, nevertheless found in it a certain peace of mind. It fulfilled their craving for order and symmetry. If everything in the world were dissected into readily distinguishable parts, neatly defined, classified, ranked, and labeled, why, everything could seem to be understood, controlled, and possessed; and the torment of uncertainty could appear to be evaded. One could behave better if one knew one's exact place in life; the universe could be grasped by a handy separation of God, nature, and man; and fencing or ballet dancing could be mastered by five or six tidily numbered "positions."

The Latin language was a particularly happy vehicle of this systematizing mentality. German intellectuals of the seventeenth century delighted in the multiplicity of its categories, its *accusativus cum infinitivo,* its *verba deponentia,* and its "epexegetical genitive." Latin was, of course, the common means of intercourse among the learned all over Europe, but the Germans drenched themselves in it with a particular devotion. In some schools the boys were urged, under threat of penalties, to eat their meals and play their games in Latin. Ability to handle its complexities made a man feel and act superior, besides also establishing a communion with remote demigods such as Julius Caesar and Tullius Cicero. In 1660, of all books published in Germany, those in Latin outnumbered those in German by four to one. But even the authors who wrote in German felt obliged to preserve their learned loftiness by interlarding every sentence with Latin words and phrases. Moreover, these Latin words were obliged to wear the insignia of their origin at all times; thus in German publications of the period bland lumps of Roman type bespot every page, sometimes every line, of the *schnörkel*ed black-letter of the vernacular.

The prevailing rationalism also possessed the Protestant clergy. The Lutheran revolt had petrified into a new orthodoxy. Not Christian conduct, not living faith, but purity of doctrine seemed to be the main concern of the preachers. God and His ways could be calculated and proved by clever deductions from His Scriptural revelations. "Aberrations from the true doctrine were considered to be chiefly errors in logical reasoning and were to be answered and cured only by means of the instruments of logic," says one historian aptly. Pettifogging theological disputes, displays of rhetoric and learning were the main content of many sermons. In 1664 a well-known theologian, Johann Christian Koenig, on his deathbed, preparing to meet his Maker, was less concerned with whether he had ever been guilty of pride, meanness, or hypocrisy, than with whether he could be assured that his teaching had never departed from the Augsburg Confession.

Inevitably the music of the period took on the general flavor of the atmosphere into which it was projected. There, too, intellectual principle tended to be more important than musical feeling as we understand it. Not that music was supposed to be devoid of emotion; but the passion for compartmentization, for mental consistency, had to be assuaged at all costs, regardless of what other effect the tones achieved. There was, for instance, the "doctrine of the affections" to which many musical thinkers of the period adhered. According to one phase of this idea, an emotion could be represented or symbolized—we cannot say "expressed"—by one or more appropriate types of musical figures or motives. The figures having been established at the beginning of a piece of music, consistency would require that the entire composition stick to them. There might be some more or less ingenious "treatment" of these motives, within limits, but unity of theme and movement had to be preserved, for logical reasons. All this explains the "monotony" that many a sincere nineteenth-century music lover felt in the presence of a work by Bach or Buxtehude.

Peasants and menials in those days had their own music, their simple songs and dances. They could not write it down for the most part, and the learned and the noble affected to treat it with the disregard they showed toward anything associated with the lower classes. Still, the lowly musical idiom must have been familiar to the higher burghers and even to the nobility—familiar enough to recognize and contemn. Class segregation was an ideal and a powerful convention, but it could not become a total physical reality. Through their own servants, or through casual contacts in field and street, the upper classes were exposed to the attractions of the vulgar tunes; just as a century later, in the American South, the music of the Negro slaves got its hold upon their white masters.

Of the kings and dukes, the greater and richer ones maintained their own opera establishments. These were very expensive, fancy luxuries, requiring incredibly complicated stage machinery; and their vocal departments were mostly staffed by Italians singing in the Italian language. The very foreignness of the institution gave it an added prestige: how great must a sovereign be who could command such marvelous imported extravagance! The opera texts themselves were an elaborate costumed flattery of the exalted personage who was paying for them. No one less than a Greek god, a Roman emperor, or a Babylonian potentate would do as the central character of the plot. An air of high-flown artifice exuded from these shows, and low-class people could be portrayed in them only in order to provide the relief of laughter.

Princelets who could not afford their own operas contented themselves with keeping little chamber orchestras. The music which these provided also had a strong foreign savor. Concertos and sonatas were based on Italian models, while the suites of courantes, minuets, and bourrées bore the stamp of France.

In particular the glamour of the French court, with Louis XIV at its head, had a dazzling effect upon these minor German princes. The *grand monarque* had everything, in their idea, that a ruler ought to have: absolute power, a vast domain, a huge, powerful army, and millions in money to advertise his magnificence. By aping the least of his ways, perhaps they could borrow a little of his splendor. Thus the rulers of Hanover, Württemberg, or Krähwinkel-Binsensumpf, together with their cousins and aunts, spoke bad French, wore French clothes and wigs, and even built *orangeries* à la Versailles. They tried hard to look like little Sun Kings.

Some of the opera and chamber music composed for these aristocratic palaces may have occasionally filtered down into the experience of a few of the burghers, through the grapevine of the professional musicians; but in general it was heard only by the invited guests of the noble lords. As for the merchants, doctors, and aldermen of the towns, their chief musical resource, if they were Protestants, was their church. The Lutheran churches did, indeed, in the late seventeenth century, make much of music. The simple, dignified traditional chorale melodies, often of popular origin, formed the essential musical phase of the service itself; but somehow, too, between the reading of the Gospel and the sermon, an elaborate musical performance developed, a sort of sacred concert known as the *cantata*. It included elaborations of the chorale of the day and might contain choruses, arias, ensembles, recitatives, or even purely instrumental interludes. Need we recall that Johann Sebastian Bach, a late-comer to this musical manifestation, devoted a great portion of his genius to it?

The North German communities set great store by this cantata of the week, this superadded musical enhancement of their worship. Indeed, it was the town council, as much as the church itself, that took responsibility for it, and helped to select and hire the singers and players. It reflected a fondness for oratorical ceremoniousness on the part of educated German burghers; and their propensity for declaiming pretentious verses at birthdays, wedding anniversaries, New Year's celebrations, installations of officers, and housewarmings was thereby translated into the calendar of the Lutheran church—music effectively substituting for the orotund voice in which the words were expected to be delivered. The cantata music was of a formalized complexity that gave it an air of importance; it abounded in fugues, polyphonic devices, and *da capo* arias. It was intended to have a flavor of learning, to be related to the theology and the *iura*—"law" we call it, not quite accurately—whose paradigms and principles were conned at the universities and which were regarded as the corpus of higher education. Latin-schoolboys were engaged as choristers, and university students with musical abilities often formed the string-instrument complement of the performing group. Cantata texts were in German; but Latin jargon seemed right for musical concepts, and there was an affinity of atmosphere between a *"tonus peregrinus"* or *"canon in motu contrario"* and a *"futurum exactum"* or *"coniugatio periphrastica."* Johann Beerens, writing in 1719, discussed the question of whether a composer *"necessario"* must have studied at a university and answered it decisively in the affirmative. Thus the cantata may be seen as a self-assertive exercise on the part of a German town's *"Honoratioren"*—the collective name given to those of its citizens who both owned the most property and belonged to the learned professions. Burghers as a class were unalterably inferior to nobles; but a citizen who could afford to have had himself soaked in Latin as a child, to become a *"studiosus"* and then maybe a *"Doctor Utriusque Iuris,"* could achieve a kind of urban and local aristocracy within his estate and thereby climb out on a balcony from which he could look down upon the smaller shopkeepers and handicraft pliers beneath him.

However, non-Latinizing residents—butchers, bakers, and blacksmiths, not to speak of drovers and housemaids—also went to church regularly. It appears that they sometimes complained that apart from the familiar chorale hymns the music was incomprehensively complicated, way over their heads. But no town councilor in his right mind would ever have entertained the outrageous, subversive thought of adapting the music to the lower or duller-witted members of the congregation. Enough, said one spokesman, that simple people realize that they are in the presence of a sacred exercise, whether they fully understand it or not; and besides, "God could not be praised artificially enough," that is, with the utmost expenditure of means and effort.

The instrument most suitable for artificial God-praising was the organ. It could sound both grand and intricate, like the Lord's own works. Moreover, the organist's hands did not, by vulgar muscular effort, themselves make the sounds they evoked; for his fingers merely released valves that permitted great numbers of air columns, mechanically and menially produced elsewhere, to pass through the pipes at his exclusive will and discretion. He was not a mere player, subject to the limitations of a human body, but rather a superpersonal operator, a commander and disposer of a thousand interacting sounds, a special image of the Lord himself. His right hand on one manual, his left on another, his feet busy on the pedal keys, he would often play a so-called "trio": three clearly drawn melodic lines, independent, congruous, and rigorously segregated; and if we wished to borrow the vocabulary of Leibniz, the age's most representative philosopher, we could call them three windowless monads building the best of all possible worlds by pre-established harmony.

The organist's fingers, as we have said, did not themselves make the tones which they called forth; neither directly nor by mechanical contrivance did the hands have any contact with the source of sound. Neither the volume nor the quality of the tone could be affected by any bodily impulse; neither crescendo, diminuendo, nor stress accent was possible. Pounding the keys or caressing them was quite useless—indeed, such procedures would have seemed disorderly and carnal to the musical devotees of the time. They had no interest even in a mechanically simulated crescendo, and the German organs of the period were not provided with a swell box. Clearness and evenness of tones were the desirable qualities in an instrument and in an executant. Changes of volume and quality could indeed be brought about, by the throwing in and out of "stops," that is, complete sets of pipes, each set differing from the others in timbre and loudness. All such changes, however, had to be made with a certain abruptness; they were calculated applications of variety, and the changes had to correspond with the formal divisions of the composition being played.

The other highly esteemed keyboard instrument of the late seventeenth century was the harpsichord. "Harpsichord" is the English name for it. The instrument came from Italy, where it was usually called *"clavicembalo"*; while in France it was called *"clavecin."* The Germans often used both the Italian and the French terms. This was its structure: strings, one to a tone, were stretched over a wooden sounding board in ascending order of pitch from left to right. The longer strings for the lower notes proceeding toward the shorter strings for the higher notes natually gave the instrument a roughly triangular or harplike shape. The Germans thought it rather resembled a bird's wing, so they sometimes called it a *"Flügel"* ("wing"). Often, however, space was economized and the strings were stowed away in a frame that was rectangular or pentangular in form, with the size of the case thus much reduced. In that case the instrument was often called a "spinet" (Italian *"spinetto,"* German *"Spinett,"* French *"épinette"*).

The harpsichord was provided with one key for each pitch, while into the further end of each key was inserted a wooden upright known as a jack. Into a gap at the top of the jack was built a small pivoting wooden tongue, hinged so as to swing in only one direction. Onto this tongue was fastened a small plectrum —a pick—made of either bird's quill or leather. When a key was pressed down, its jack rose, pushing the plectrum against its string from below; with further pressure the elastic plectrum gave way and passed beyond the string, plucking it and producing a tone. When the key was released, the jack dropped and the plectrum again lightly touched the string in its descent; but this time the one-way tongue-hinge came into play, swinging outward away from the string: by the time a springy bristle at the back of the tongue made it swing back into its original position, the plectrum had made the little journey around the string and again found itself underneath it. The plectrum's slight descending touch on the string had almost no force, and no second tone was produced; and anyway, a cloth damper at the top of each jack instantly silenced all residual vibration.

The tone quality of a harpsichord was clear and bright, and resembled most that of a guitar: in fact, an ample harpsichord composition sounded a little like an ensemble of guitars. The amount of force exerted by the player's finger could hardly affect the loudness of a harpsichord's tone. That is quite clear from the very nature of the tone-producing mechanism. For the loudness of a string's tone consists in the amplitude—that is, the transverse dimension—of its vibrations. The maximum amplitude of a plucked string is identical with the amount to which the plectrum had bent the string out of line when it plucked. In a harpsichord that distance must be a fixed quantity, dependent upon the length, mass, and elasticity of the plectrum. A plectrum of a given length, density, and elasticity—activated by a lever of fixed size, position, and radius of movement—can bend a string just so much, no more and no less. The force with which a key is pressed down can affect only the speed of the jack's rise; but, as we see, this is of almost no amplitude-producing moment. Moreover, attempts to produce a softer tone by pressing the key gently are equally of no avail, since the plectrum will not pass beyond the string, will not pluck, until it has slid past a certain point of its length; that point is determined by the plectrum's own intrinsic properties, upon which the speed of its rise can have practically no effect.

Thus all musical outlines on a harpsichord, while admirably clean and sharp, were inflexibly level in quantity of tone. Indeed, the sound had a stiff kind of charm, like the smile of a porcelain countess. The plectra against the strings made their tones, but their contacts and movements made a certain amount of scratching noise in addition. This could be interpreted pleasantly, and one German author of the time said that the harpsichord "lisped and rustled"—just as live countesses sometimes did.

Inevitably, however, the capacity for a certain amount of variety came to be demanded from this instrument, especially for occasions on which it was to be played alone. This variety was achieved by building large harpsichords with two, three, or even four complete sets of strings, strung above one another. Additional jacks for each complete set were inserted into each key. The additional sets of strings were often half the length, or double the length, of the fundamental strings, so that they could produce tones an octave above, or below, the basic tones. The strings and jacks pertaining to any one key were disposed not quite in line, so as not to interfere with each other. A set of knobs on the harpsichord's front board operated a mechanism whereby each entire set of jacks could be slightly shifted so as to engage its particular choir of strings. These shifts were called "stops," or "registers," by easy analogy with the organ. Any combination of these stops, of course, would produce a special pattern of string grouping. Thus on a large instrument the knobs could be so pulled as to permit one key to play a tone in two unisons, in or with upper or lower octaves, two octaves apart, or in three octaves at once. Two manuals had to be built into these elaborate harpsichords in order to make all these variations practical in execution.

Clearly, two strings make more sound than one, and four more than two; so that all these combinations resulted in differing levels of tonal volume. But differing tone-qualities could also be mechanically achieved on the harpsichord. It was possible, for example, to build a set of jacks that plucked, not a different set of strings, but the same set at a different point of their lengths. Furthermore, a lever could be constructed causing small pieces of leather to lean lightly against the strings and partially dampen them, thus letting the plectra pluck them with a dry, *pizzicato*-like quality. This type of device was known as a "buff stop" or "lute stop." The most complicated harpsichord, then, might have five, six, or seven stops distributed over its two keyboards; and these would involve a considerable number of permutations. The analogy with the organ is again clearly seen when we learn that the octave stops were given the same designation as their organ equivalents, namely: "four-foot," "eight-foot," and "sixteen-foot."

Pulling out stops, or pushing them in, requires an appreciable amount of time, and it was only rarely possible to interrupt the continuity of a composition for this purpose. In general, just as in the case of the organ, it was not considered seemly to alter the volume of tone except to mark the organic divisions of a piece of music, such as the sections of a fugue, the couplets of a rondeau, or the separate variations on an air. As with the organ, contrasts of tone and volume were in the nature of sharp terraces, not of inclines, curves, or salient points. Occasionally, short phrases, repeated literally, were played louder the first time and softer the second. These "echo" effects were much enjoyed, their simple symmetry pleasing both the ear and the mind. It is easy to see how neat, terracelike contrasts of tonal volume seemed proper to the taste of people who liked to classify and categorize.

German dukes and princes had introduced harpsichords into their little orchestras, as an Italian fashion, in the middle of the seventeenth century; and the instruments were used as harmonic binders and fillers in the ensemble of strings and winds. They were also employed in the opera, where they served as a minimal accompaniment to the "dry" recitatives with which the drama was propelled. To some extent they were also used as solo instruments. At first harpsichords were little affairs of three or four octaves at most. They were portable to a degree, readily movable boxes that could be set on stands or tables anywhere as desired. Toward the end of the seventeenth century many were built larger because of the stops; sometimes they reached a length of seven or eight feet and stood on their own built-in legs.

There was still another keyboard instrument in use in Germany, in many ways the most significant of all: it was called the "clavichord." It, too, was a stringed instrument, but its strings were to be struck, not plucked. It worked on the following curious principle: if a string be struck, and the striking implement stay in contact with the point of impact, then the string is unable to vibrate in its entire length, but must vibrate in the two segments into which the striking implement has divided it. We can get an idea of this principle if we watch how a violinist, without using his bow, sometimes idly drums on the strings of his finger board with the fingers of his left hand, making some kind of faint melody.

The clavichord was an open oblong box, across the longer dimension of which strings were stretched, in pairs, at a slight angle. The strings were not necessarily all of differing length and thickness. The keys were simple levers pivoting up and down on pins. Fixed into each key toward its farther end was a small upright triangular blade, usually made of brass, about ¾ inch high. The blade was fastened into the key by the triangle's apex, while its base, about ¼ inch long, faced upward, parallel to the key's length and at right angles to the strings. This blade was called a "tangent": it was its longer, upper edge which struck the string and at the same time divided it into two unequal lengths. The tangent thus simultaneously struck the string and stopped it, making the tone and determining its pitch in the same instant. Actually, when the tangent hit, both segments of the divided string vibrated; but the longer was the louder, and in addition, the shorter segments of the entire row of strings were usually dampened by having a ribbon of cloth wound in and around them. Since the tangents stayed in contact with the strings after hitting them, they tended to dampen the very vibrations which they had set in motion: they made a tone and crushed it all at once. Consequently the quality of a clavichord's tone was rather poor and its volume tiny.

Nevertheless, the instrument had certain advantages. The key and tangent were made together, in one rigid piece, and thus there was no need for extremes of precision in the adjustment of moving parts. Moreover, the clavichord was never provided with stops, that is, additional sets of strings and tangents. All this simplicity made for cheapness, which was indeed one of the instrument's primary recommendations. Furthermore, its maintenance was equally inexpensive: it had no quills that constantly needed sharpening and replacing.

Since the tangents determined the pitch by the precise spot on the string at which they struck, the same string might be used to make two, or even more, different pitches. The same string, for example, could sound A when struck by one tangent, and B-flat, half a tone higher, when struck by another a little further up. Of course, these two different tones could not be produced simultaneously. On this principle, a clavichord of, say, three octaves (that is, thirty-six semitones) might get along with only twenty-four strings, thus still further reducing the materials and labor required for its construction. These clavichords with sub-numerary strings were said to be *"gebunden"*—literally, "bound"—while the usual translation is "fretted." Only after the first quarter of the eighteenth century were clavichords made *"bundfrei,"* that is, with a separate string for each tangent.

The clavichord had one further advantage, which was appreciated more and more as the eighteenth century wore on. Where tone is produced by a direct stroke upon a string, as distinct from plucking it by means of a fixed lever, the speed and momentum of the blow does affect the amplitude of the string's vibration. Thus, the clavichord's tonal volume could, within small limits, be varied by the impulse of the player's fingers. The instrument was dynamically stroke-responsive, or touch-responsive, as we sometimes say, not quite accurately. Any really brisk attack upon the keys was too much for the tangent's fragile method of tone production and created little but jangling; however, within a narrow range—say, from what we should now call *pp* to *ppp*—the clavichord was capable of flexible shading, of gradual increase and decrease of volume.

It is a question whether this stroke-responsive, dynamically flexible capability of the clavichord was as yet truly esteemed during the seventeenth century; but certainly after 1740 that became its paramount virtue, as we shall see. Its sound was too faint to allow participation in an ensemble, or even to be heard in a room of any great size. Cheapness and compactness made it attractive to the middle classes during the poverty-stricken decades after the Thirty Years' War. It was generally thought of as an inferior member of the clavier family, the poor man's keyboard.

These, then, were the keyboard instruments of the Germany of 1700: the organ, the harpsichord, and the clavichord. Each had its own musical character, and each fitted into its own particular social atmosphere.

The organ's unparalleled manifoldness was most impressive, and it also carried all the prestige of an established church: it was generally judged "the king of instruments." The polyphonic, rationalist spirit of organ music formed an ideal which influenced musicians even when they composed for the harpsichord. We have seen how stops analogous with those on the organ were built into harpsichords; and to some extent music for the two instruments was interchangeable.

If the social associations of the organ were intellectual and lofty, those of the harpsichord were aristocratic and luxurious. We have stated that it belonged properly in royal operas and princely orchestras. In Italy it had long been a collector's object for wealthy nobles. To them it seemed not only a tool for creating art, but a work of art in itself. Duke Alfonso II of Modena, in 1598, had fifty-two such instruments, while a century later Prince Ferdinand de' Medici possessed at least forty. Charming paintings on the inside of the lid, cunning inlay work, and rare jewelry seemed appropriate decorations for those articles of *virtù*. Undoubtedly there were German lords who also indulged this hobby. To them the harpsichord further had an exhilarating foreign flavor, and they liked to impute to it an added value for having been the work of a French or Flemish maker. For example, it was said that, as early as 1680, the instrument maker Michael Mietcke, of Charlottenburg, near Berlin, was able to get three hundred thalers for one of his harpsichords when he pretended that it had been imported from Paris; but that he had to reduce his price to a mere sixty or eighty thalers after he admitted that his instruments were homemade.

We can also be pretty certain that harpsichords were to be found in the homes of certain of the wealthier burghers—such as those to whom rulers had granted valuable commercial monopolies, or such as the rich "senators" of "free" commercial cities like Hamburg or Lübeck. These influential, fundamentally middle-class people, having as yet no style of their own to believe in, mostly tended to imitate that of the aristocracy. In any case, we can be pretty certain that the two-manualed seven-foot instruments were relatively rare and that the trim spinets were the rule in all but the most ostentatious houses.

By contrast, the simple clavichord was an unpretentious German homemade product, a "folksy" thing. We hear of one occasionally in Italy, very, very rarely in England, and almost never in France: neither the Italians, the English, nor the French could bring themselves to find much satisfaction in its puny, solitary voice. To a German it would have seemed utterly wrongheaded, if not impossible, to import one from abroad.

We have referred to its cheapness. Figures for the earlier eighteenth century are hard to obtain; but if we may assume that the costs of materials relative to each other did not vary much during six or eight decades, then we may reasonably guess, on the basis of price lists from the latter part of the century, that a clavichord could be made and sold at about one third to one fourth the price that would have to be charged for a harpsichord of equivalent quality of workmanship. Fancy decorations, we can understand, were for the most part inappropriate to an object of such modest affinities. The clavichord's square, compact, homely lines were most frequently and most congruously set amidst the simple deal furniture of the small dwelling rooms afforded by schoolmasters, clergymen, cantors, and poor but musical petty officials.

Need we say that in 1700 keyboard instruments were made by individual craftsmen? If the masters did not work entirely single-handed, still they personally watched over and controlled the work of such few assistants as they had. Harpsichords and clavichords could not be bought at a "store" or at "warerooms": they were expressly made to the order, and often to the specification, of individual customers. Since the dawn of civilization it had seemed an obvious, unquestionable procedure that a person desiring to own a made object apply to a skilled maker to make it for him, and then compensate him for his work and his materials. Demand first, then sale, and finally production and delivery: that has always been the humanly natural progression. Only during the last hundred and fifty years or so has mankind speculated in the crazy custom of first making things on a vaguely huge scale and then trying to induce people to buy them.

It is unlikely that, before the middle of the eighteenth century, there was enough demand for harpsichords and clavichords in any one German region to occupy a craftsman exclusively with the making of them. Usually these instruments were a side line of organ builders or of cabinet makers. It was after 1740 that the demand grew to a point where building them could become an independent trade.

No people understood the respective qualities of the harpsichord and the clavichord—and later the pianoforte—better than did the Germans. In the later eighteenth century we come upon discourse after discourse accurately detailing the relative virtues of each of these musical instruments. Nevertheless, the Germans were in the habit of giving them all the indiscriminate name of "keyboard." "*Clavier*" is their word. The manuals of an organ were also frequently referred to as "*Claviere.*" It is rather astonishing to find this sloppiness of nomenclature on the part of people ordinarily given to an excessive making of subheadings. Inevitably the loose use of the word *Clavier* helped to confuse later generations. We may say that, as time proceeded, the word *Clavier* tended to become applied exclusively to the particular keyboard instrument most in the general consciousness and acceptance: after 1750 *Clavier* usually meant clavichord; after about 1815 it usually meant pianoforte. The word *Flügel,* which, as we have seen, designated a large-sized harpsichord during the eighteenth century, came to mean "grand piano" after the first decades of the nineteenth.

2. "FEELING" SEEMS BETTER THAN LOGIC

No PREVAILING moral atmosphere ever makes everyone happy. There are always persons whose native dispositions are not favored by the ideals of the society in which they live. It may happen that in some communities sizable minorities, perhaps even majorities, secretly hate the very things that are constantly held up to them as good and proper. Seventeenth-century Protestant Germany offered spiritual contentment for the landed, the learned, and the logical; but many others were at a disadvantage. In particular, considerable numbers of earnestly religious people were left dissatisfied. Those nice theological arguments, those artful Latin-studded pulpit orations, those magnificent polyphonic cantatas left thousands of good men and women out in the cold. Much of the official worship began to strike them—very respectfully at first—as pretentious, obscure claptrap. Moreover, during the long war, each of the conflicting armies had carried the insignia of some creed upon its banners; and each had inflicted endless misery on the people. Baptism and communion, it seemed, were not enough to make men good.

Something else was needed: a deep personal devotion to the highest things, to God, to the Saviour, to the Sacred Scriptures. One had truly to love the Lord with an intense personal feeling, one had to try to achieve a direct contact, a direct union with Him through emotional strength and concentration, in order to be able truly to partake of His blessing. To take the sacraments, to hear a sermon, to go to a church service on an appointed day, to mumble a thoughtless prayer at regular intervals—whilst taking care in any case to avoid the coarser sins—all this would impress God but little: for true regeneration, every human being must set up the priesthood of the Lamb in his own heart. Thousands of Germans, in the later seventeenth century, began to think thus.

This conviction took on the proportions of a considerable movement. It was not a new teaching revealed by an inspired prophet, but it was rather a frame of mind that arose simultaneously in large numbers of people. Influential preachers such as Philipp Jakob Spener helped to focus it and to hearten those who gave themselves to it. Proclaiming no new theology or doctrine, these religious enthusiasts in fact tended to make little of all doctrine; they called their attitude "The Faith of Piety." Their opponents, half in ridicule, called them "Pietists," and that name has stuck to them.

Union with God, suffusion by God: it was not a thing to be "proved" or to be "believed" passively—it could only be felt. It was a state of exaltation with which the Saviour rewarded His true lovers. Feeling was the main thing, doctrine was secondary. Unruly, indeed, was the vocabulary of the Pietist preachers: "The heart must burn," said one; "Just as a drunkard becomes full of wine, so must the congregation become filled with spirit," exhorted another; "In prayer one must not be ashamed and must stamp, shout, and beat," encouraged still another. To a heartfelt prayer the Lord might respond with a special message, an "illumination." Every happy combination of ideas, every moment of heightened awareness of truth or beauty that crossed their minds, these simple devotees regarded as a personal intervention of the Deity. The Bible verse whose meaning was understood after much pondering was "revealed" to them, and they "interpreted" their dreams in a meaningful religious, personal sense.

Pietists were only too eager to tell themselves and others about their emotional lives. Large numbers of Germans began to grovel in an amazed contemplation of their own mental states. They kept diaries full of attempts to clothe feelings in strong words. Many felt the need of keeping in touch with kindred spirits who had moved away to distant parts; and letters began to fly, highly charged with emotional verbiage. These were conned reverently, copied, and sent abroad further.

Only a few people have Latin and theology, but everybody has feelings. Pietism was good medicine for the unlearned: women, for example, were much drawn to it. Pietist preachers were all for women: they praised the female's abundant sensibility; they rejoiced publicly in the fact that congregations were more than half feminine; and they liked to point out that it was the women who remained at the Cross to the end, after all the apostles had run away.

If God were primarily responsive to "feeling," it must be that He cared for naked human souls, stripped of all accidents of birth or rank, or equipage of education. His grace might fall as readily upon the simplest washwoman or bootblack as upon the most powerful lord or the glibbest jurist. Inevitably, Pietism gave comfort to the lower classes. Comfort, we say, not ambition; for nothing in the cult of "feeling" tended to fire its devotees into subverting the existing social order. "Feeling" was a satisfactory end in itself, it seemed.

In fact, in time Pietism became rather respectable. Some people of noble birth embraced it; and there were even smaller princes who favored it, creating the curious spectacle of Pietist courts. The University of Halle became a center for the training of Pietist clergymen, developed into a focus of Pietist thought, and thus in turn had great influence on general education.

Pietism had no direct revolutionary intent, and so aroused little violent opposition; but that was why it was able within a few generations to modify profoundly the entire tone of German life. Those fervent letter writers and diarists, for example, who were so articulate about their "illuminations" and exaltations, helped to give vitality to the German language. The nobles might chatter their imitation French, the doctors might blow up their clouds of Latinistic jargon, but lower-middle-class Pietists would find the old home German talk the best for reveling in the bursts of their flaming hearts. They prepared the way for a marvelous German literature, soon to burgeon. Already in the 1710's, newly published books in German were equal in number to those printed in Latin. Slowly, as the eighteenth century grew up, Pietist proclivities and judgments of value began to infect large numbers of Germans, many of whom did not rightly share the Pietist religious notions. Even after Pietism began to decline as a purely religious manifestation, a propensity to wallow in wonderful sentiments crept over a good part of the nation. Little by little, simple people, heart throbs, the feminine mind, and the native language all went up higher and higher in the general esteem.

There was, naturally, a musical phase of this Pietist-inspired trend. In general, the Pietists refrained from emphasizing music. Any great indulgence in it would have seemed to them like the "setting the world on a level with the Saviour" of which they disapproved. Moreover, they were especially averse to complicated music in church services; for that they regarded as a vain distraction from worship, rather than an aid to it. Still, they had their hymns, artless tunes with which they celebrated their yearnings to be close to God. We may say that the spread of the Pietist frame of mind created a prejudice in favor of musical simplicity. An easy melody that "sprang from the heart" was worth more to God than any amount of praising Him "artificially," and thousands of people who did not regard themselves as Pietist fellow-travelers began to find these ideas comfortable to agree with.

By the end of the 1730's a number of well-educated voices were raised against musical complexity and polyphony. Johann Mattheson of Hamburg, for example, the son of an official, was a highly gifted musician and composer, and an early friend and colleague of Handel's. He was also a student of law and political science, and served in a diplomatic post for some time. Moreover, in 1715 he became canon and cantor (precentor) of the Hamburg Cathedral. We would expect his ideas to be rationalist and conservative. On the contrary! In 1739 he wrote:

> The ear often finds more delight in a single well-ordered voice which carries a clean melody in all its natural freedom, than in four-and-twenty; for in that case the same is so torn to pieces in distributing itself over them all, that one cannot tell what the whole thing is supposed to mean. The unadorned melody in its noble simplicity, clarity, and distinctness moves hearts in such a manner that it often surpasses all arts of harmony.

As the eighteenth century progressed, the general approach to music became deeply tinged with the emphasis on "feeling" encouraged by the Pietists. Eventually even learned writers, instead of thinking of music as "the unconscious arithmetic of the soul," as Leibniz called it—or as "a justifiable gratification of the senses," in Sebastian Bach's phrase—found themselves, as we have just seen, speaking of the power of music to "move" the feelings.

Consonant with this trend we find the homely clavichord the object of greater affectionate attention. Its capacity to make increases and decreases of volume directly at the player's stroke is seen more and more as an important virtue. Again we quote Mattheson, a passage from his *Das Neu-Eröffnete Orchestre,* published as early as 1713:

> Overtures, sonatas, toccatas, suites, etc., are brought out the best and the cleanest on a good clavichord, upon which one can express the art of singing much more intelligibly, with sustaining and softening, than upon the always alike strongly resonant harpsichords and spinnets. If anyone wishes to hear a delicate hand and a pure style, let him lead his candidate to a neat clavichord . . .

The stroke-responsive advantage of the clavichord will be better understood if we here bring up the fundamental question of the psychology of tonal intensity. I do not know whether in recent times human beings have been subjected to controlled laboratory experiments to determine the precise effects which increases and decreases in the volume of sounds have on the vasomotor system, the nervous system, or the electrical conductivity of the skin. Whatever modern scientific findings about these effects are, or will be, certain rough-and-ready correlations concerning them have always been accepted.

A rapid increase of sound is a strong nervous stimulant: it commands a quick general alertness and may also provoke a constriction of certain blood vessels, with accompanying pallor and intestinal stasis. An extremely vehement burst of sound may produce profound shock and even cause death. But a more gradual increase, such as the steady rumble of an approaching vehicle, or the nearing tramp of a parade of marching men, may arouse a vague impulse to go out and meet the sound before it has arrived, a pleasurable expectancy that may be evinced by a dilatation of the facial capillaries and a gentle moistening of the eyes. Certain it is, however, that any level of intensity, whatever powerful results it may have produced when first reached, soon loses its potency over the human body when prolonged for more than a short period. The nerves soon accustom themselves to any din, soft or loud, if it does not vary. It is the change of intensity rather than its absolute level that arouses the emotion. The more frequent the changes, the more restlessly the nerves and blood vessels are made to jump.

But if changes of sound intensity give people feelings, the changes of their own feelings in turn cause them to vary the intensity of the sounds they themselves produce. The acoustical intensity of human speech becomes greater or less with the nervous, vasomotor, and glandular changes that come under the head of emotion. Anger or joy often cause the voice to louden, discouragement and fatigue to soften. In their turn, these vocal alterations tend to transmit their corresponding emotion to those people—or animals—who feel themselves in communion with them. Clearly, all human beings are constantly expressing and communicating the most delicate shades of feeling by slight unpremeditated alterations in the loudness of their speech, as well as of their wordless ejaculations. Incidentally, the very words of many languages are unintelligible unless given their proper stress, their differential of loud and soft.

The spontaneous-seeming loudening and softening of human sounds is the very image of the affective aspect of the mind. The crescendo is a mounting anxiety, a sharpening desire; it is something that is going somewhere purposefully. The diminuendo is a relaxation, a resignation; is something that has been somewhere and is leaving, a yielding, a relief, a nostalgia. It is obvious that the crescendo and diminuendo, the brisk accent, the completely selective, completely flexible piano and forte are indispensable to music that aims to "move," to arouse e-motion. Everybody has taken this for granted for a long time. The dynamic of soft and loud is the chief element of what is generally called musical "expression."

In "expression" lies the unfailing musical appeal of the human voice. It is hard to imagine an individual who, feeling the impulse to sing, would do so with the total lack of expression intrinsic to the harpsichord or the organ. Possibly, certain eighteenth-century vocal virtuosos may have been so intent on getting their runs and trills fast and in tune that they neglected it; but in general the flow of tones made by the human voice is the archetype of all musical expression. That is what older writers were talking about when they extolled the voice over all instruments of their time; and that is why later writers, trying to praise the quality of a performance, could say nothing better than that the instrument could be made to "sing."

Once again we will quote Mattheson, from a paragraph written in defense of the clavichord. It appeared in his *Critica Musica* in 1725:

> That this agreeable instrument be called a hoarse clavichord is very shameful. Should I propose it to a candidate . . . my friend will advance the opinion of the English against mine, saying: "The greatest masters there hold that a pupil, in so far as he wants to learn thoroughly, must begin right away with quilled instruments, but must never play a clavichord." Those masters will forgive me magnanimously; I am not, and never will be, of their mind. My

reasons lie in *arte modulatoria,* in the art of singing. He who understands the one, will also understand the other, and will find it right.

By *ars modulatoria,* Mattheson clearly means the art of shading, of making smooth gradations of loud and soft; and he assimilates this skill to the vocal art.

Yet, one could imagine a German early-eighteenth-century rationalist looking with fishy-eyed skepticism at the growing vogue for "expression." What a cheap way of bullying the feelings, he might have said—almost animal. The essence of music, he might have continued, lies in the multifarious intrinsic relationships of the tones, the wonderful interplay of varying degrees of consonance and dissonance, the placing of cadences, the progressions from one key to another, the dispersion of melodic patterns, the transformation of themes. This primitive loudening and softening that people are tending to enjoy does, indeed, stir the feelings in a crude sort of way; but it therefore also helps to distract the mind from the real music. At that rate any childish babble, or even outright gibberish, could be made acceptable to insensitive ears, provided it were launched with this kind of low-plane direct assault on the nerves and blood vessels. Why, one could even compel some kind of excitement by crescendoing and diminuendoing mere noises—toneless scrapings and knockings—without making a single musical sound whatsoever!

The modernists of the time could have answered our hypothetical doctor thus: the intensity of a tone (that is, the amplitude of its vibration) is as much an organic part of the tone as its pitch (that is, its frequency) or its duration. Therefore, intensity constitutes an essential element of music, which music may neglect only to its loss. Music may truly be the unconscious mathematics of the soul, but it is also something more. A puerile succession of tones, uttered with expression, thereby becomes less puerile. A profound or witty musical phrase, rendered monotonously, thereby loses some of its meaning.

3. THE SUPER-CHOPPING-BOARD AROUSES MUCH "FEELING"; WHY NOT FIT IT WITH KEYS?

THE EARLY eighteenth century was a time ready for Pantaleon Hebenstreit. The man who bore this queer name turned up in Leipzig, Saxony, about 1697. He was a dancing master and, it was said, quite a vigorous violinist. These, however, were not his significant accomplishments; he became known more importantly for having worked startling improvements on the dulcimer.

The dulcimer is an old, old instrument, and it probably came from Asia. It consists essentially of a wooden board, near the two opposing edges of which a number of bridges are affixed. Across these bridges are stretched a number of strings of varying length and thickness, forming some kind of scale. The player makes his tones by hitting the strings with a couple of sticks held in the fists. The sticks may have knobbed ends, or they may be covered with a soft material to lessen any nonmusical noise. The instrument has never become obsolete: its vogue in Central and Eastern Europe is still unimpaired, for Hungarian and Rumanian gypsies are entertaining thousands with a modernized form of it this very minute. Commonly it is called *"czimbalom."*

Whatever the dulcimer's musical capacities may have been, its eighteenth century social affinities were decidedly low-class. We do not hear of it in ducal orchestras, it does not appear to have been employed in church services, and among the many contemporary treatises on the practice of music there seems to have been none on The Art of Playing the Dulcimer. On the other hand, there are credible accounts of its having been used in itinerant puppet shows. Dulcimers found their way into peasant houses, where they provided a rudimentary musical pleasure at no great effort of skill. They were pretty crude in those days, of small range, with barely a diatonic scale, not to speak of a chromatic one. The Germans usually called the instrument by the familiar-contemptuous name of *"Hackbrett"*—literally, "hacking-board"—meaning a block for chopping up sausage meat!

Pantaleon Hebenstreit, they said, during a period of unemployment in a village near the town of Merseburg, likewise in Saxony, was impressed by hearing a *Hackbrett* played in a tavern; stimulated by the possibilities of this form of music production, he had one made to his design, on a heroic scale. It was a double dulcimer, with two sounding boards, six feet long, four times the size of an ordinary one, and with strings of both gut and metal, some of them double- and triple-strung—about two hundred in all. The instrument had a range of at least five octaves, with a complete chromatic scale. Each of the two sticks with which Hebenstreit played it was covered on both ends with material of differing consistency, thus allowing for variety of tone quality. All in all, his super-sausage-board was a tone-producing tool of power and resonance unheard of among its kind.

Here was stroke-responsiveness with a vengeance. A strong, nimble man sending a couple of mallet heads straight down onto the unstopped strings, emitting anything from whacks to love-taps at any instant at his own wanton will, could make the instrument speak loud and soft, crescendo and diminduendo, in incalculably flexible alternations. Here was "feeling" for fair, the very image of the unruly flows and ebbs of the body's humors. Furthermore, cloth or leather, on gut or metal, one hand or both—all these gave many permutations of quality that multiplied the effects of the performance. Hebenstreit also liked to roll great billows of arpeggiated chords over the wide range of his instrument and to allow the full resonance of the undampened strings to die slowly on the listeners' ears. It was a new sensation at the time, and it seemed ravishing.

Hebenstreit astonished and delighted many people with his extraordinary playing; still, some of the social leaders of his region may not have known quite how to take this bumptious new plebeian musical manifestation. At any rate, we hear little of him at first. He seems to have judged rightly that a prophet has a better chance to be with honor outside his own country; thus, he decided upon a bold stroke: he would bid for the approval of the personage who, after God and the Pope, was the most exalted in all the universe, namely Louis XIV, the awesome King of France. In 1705 Pantaleon Hebenstreit made the long journey from Saxony to Paris and was successful in approaching the King. The Great Monarch was much charmed with this remarkable new music and showed him many signs of favor. Moreover, a performance which the musician gave before a small gathering in the house of the King's friend, the witty, vivacious Ninon de l'Enclos, was recounted by the Abbé de Chateauneuf, who was one of the company at the occasion. The Abbé first speaks of him as a "musical prodigy, all the more worthy of curiosity since he came from a country little given to bringing forth men of fire and genius." After describing the instrument and admiring the performer's execution, he tells of the effect produced on the listeners:

> He was granted an attention that was interrupted only by the applause that he received from all those who listened to him, according to the degree of sensitivity that each one had for music. Among the others, one could follow on *Leontium*'s [Mlle. de l'Enclos'] face the various movements and the different passions that the musician sought to express: for she found expression where we often found only harmony, and one could have said that for her every note was a feeling.

Pantaleon, stimulated by the famous lady's response, redoubled his efforts and never in his life was more inspired.

Finally the great Louis made a most flattering suggestion: that the musician name his unique instrument for himself. Hebenstreit did so, and the overgrown "chopping-block" thenceforth bore the dignified appellation of "pantaleon," or "pantalon," with a dazzling Sun King for a godfather.

Hebenstreit returned to Saxony, his repute and social position much enhanced. Presently the petty Duke of Eisenach gave him a position, in which, however, he was still expected to play violin. Again he traveled, to Vienna this time, where the pleased Holy Roman Emperor gave him a gold chain and a locket containing the imperial portrait. Finally, on May 11, 1714, the royal Saxon court at Dresden appointed him "Pantalonist" at the annual salary of twelve hundred thalers. This was an ample stipend, when we reflect that twenty years later Johann Sebastian Bach's entire income was seven hundred thalers, including his salary as cantor of Leipzig's leading choir school and all incidental fees for music at funerals, weddings, and similar occasions. With this high and mighty support, Pantaleon and his pantalon were now famous in the musical world, and he was universally praised and accepted. Listen to Johann Kuhnau, Bach's predecessor at St. Thomas' school, as he writes at length about the pantalon in a letter dated December 8, 1717:

> Especially when one strikes a bass tone, it sounds for a long time afterward, like one that is held upon an organ, and many *passages*

> and *resolutiones* of *dissonantia* may be absolved before it fades completely—to the great delectation of the feelings. . . . Nor does the harmony suffer by the pleasant after-humming of middle and upper voices, since even in the fastest things all notes are heard *distinctissime.* But when one arpeggiates in chords—which can be accomplished here in the fullest manner—and since also when one ceases, the sound diminishes little by little as if from afar, the delightful buzzing of the harmony goes right into the quick. [Kuhnau's own baroque syntax.]

It is rather touching thus to hear the devout old music director yield to the seduction of a colorful harmonic impurity. Kuhnau continues:

> The instrument has also this privilege and property ahead of the claviers: namely, that one can play it with *force* and then again *piano,* wherein consists a great *momentum dulcedinis et gratiae musicae.*

He then tells of a musical gathering that had taken place some years before between himself, Hebenstreit, and a certain Count Logi, who was a good lutenist. Logi played his instrument, Kuhnau performed on the clavichord, and:

> . . . at length Mons. Pantalon made his leaps, and after he had shown us his musical treasure in various kinds of preluding, improvising, fuguing, and all sorts of *caprices* with the bare sticks, he finally bound up the sticks with cotton and played a *partita.* At that the Count was quite beside himself; he led me out of his room and across the hall, listened from afar, and said: "I say, what is that? I have been in *Italia,* I have heard all the beauties there are *in musica,* but something like this has never yet come to my ears."

The awkwardness of these translations gives a mere faint reflection of the pretentious, involuted flavor of the Latinized, Frenchified original. Note also that the musician is now called *Monsieur Pantalon.*

Still, the pantalon had its disadvantages. It was cumbersome, as well as troublesome and expensive to keep in repair. They said it cost one hundred thalers—some even said two hundred thalers—a year to maintain. Besides, the thing was almost the only one of its kind, and Pantaleon's peculiar technique could hardly be duplicated, except perhaps by an inordinately industrious disciple or two. Saxony was full of Pantaleon's enraptured hearers, and it was clear that the notion of adapting the pantalonic hammer-principle to the familiar keyboard apparatus would sooner or later sprout in some Saxon head: instead of one hammer in each fist, why not four or five octaves' worth of finger-playable keys, each key operating a little hammer of its own?

The idea had already germinated in a French brain as early as 1716; for in February of that year a man named Marius had constructed several models of what he called a *"clavecin à maillets"* (that is, a "hammer harpsichord"), which he submitted to the Académie des Sciences. Is it not possible that Marius had heard Pantaleon in Paris or had at least heard his playing described? At any rate, the Académie praised Marius' designs politely and laid them on the shelf. They were not very practical, as we shall see.

The Saxon with the same bright scheme was Christoph Gottlieb Schröter, a studious, voluble young organist and musician of Leipzig. As early as his eighteenth year he was giving clavier lessons, and he tells how, after teaching his pupils to play with some expression on the clavichord, he became discouraged by the hopelessness of having them achieve a similarly "mannerly style," as he calls it, when they turned to the harpsichord. "Not long afterward," he continues, "I was granted the long-desired opportunity of hearing the world-famous virtuoso, Mr. Pantaleon Hebenstreit, upon his instrument," whereupon "I considered it certain that it would be possible for me to invent a keyboard instrument upon which one could play loud or soft at will." The intention was easy, the execution difficult, "since I had never yet whittled, sawed, planed, or joined anything." Schröter turned to a cousin, a young journeyman cabinetmaker, who after many trials made him "a double model on a long and narrow little box, which had an overall length of four feet and was six inches wide. In front and rear it had three keys. At one place the stroke upon the strings came from below, but at the other it came from above. Both kinds were as easy to play as an ordinary clavichord. On each of the models loud or soft sounds could be brought forth in differing degrees."

He goes on to say that certain Saxon court officials were much interested in his model, but that somehow in the course of official confusion and red tape the thing disappeared. He hints strongly that certain later makers of pianofortes appropriated his ideas. Schröter speaks of these events as having occurred between 1717 and 1721, but some of the claims which we have quoted were made twenty years—and others forty-five years—after that period.

By that time he was a disgruntled old pedant; but he speaks with an insistent sincerity, and the very imperfections of his diagrams are some evidence of his originality. Although he never made an instrument, we will do the best we can for him and call him a collateral originator of the idea of the pianoforte.

4. AN ITALIAN THOUGHT OF IT FIRST; HE CLEVERLY MADE HAMMERS REBOUND

SCHRÖTER and Marius did not realize it, but they were late. By the time they were groping at their little models, a number of well-working hammer-actioned, stringed keyboard instruments had already been made, in faraway Italy, by a man who had never had an opportunity of hearing Hebenstreit play.

We have previously mentioned Prince Ferdinand de' Medici, the owner of forty harpsichords and spinets. He was a son of the reigning Grand Duke of Tuscany, a remote collateral descendant of the Magnificent Lorenzo, and a well-meaning, music-loving aristocrat. Aristocrats live by authority: they deign to eat their own food, make their own love, ride their own horses, and perhaps fight their own duels—but most of everything else that they effect, they accomplish by commanding others: such is the essence of their lordliness. They do not, for instance, as a rule, themselves hang, dust off, repair, or catalogue the precious art works that they accumulate. So, Ferdinand hired a harpsichord maker named Bartolommeo Cristofori to come from his native Padua to Florence to take care of the princely musical instruments.

In 1709 the Marquis Scipione Maffei, gentleman and littérateur, visited Ferdinand with a view to elicit from him the use and prestige of his noble name—and perhaps a pinch of his vulgar cash—in support of a learned quarterly magazine to be published in Venice under the name of *Giornale de' Letterati d'Italia.* Maffei undoubtedly made Cristofori's acquaintance on this occasion, for two years later, when the *Giornale* had got as far as Volume V, it contained an article by Maffei describing what he calls a "*Nuova invenzione d'un gravicembalo col piano e forte*"—"New invention of a harpsichord with the soft and loud"—of which he named Cristofori as the ingenious constructor. *"Gravicembalo"* is a mere verbal corruption of *"clavicembalo."* (Many Italians have an antipathy toward pronouncing "cla" as an initial syllable.) Even educated persons laid little stress on syllabic exactitude in those days, and Maffei succeeds further in miscalling the hero of his piece: "Cristofali"!

Maffei's treatise is a remarkable little exposition: its fifteen small-format pages are a finely apt explanation of the new instrument's reason for coming into existence, a close analysis of its essential mechanical problems, and a shrewd estimate of the general nature of its musical function.

> Everyone who enjoys music knows that one of the principal sources from which those skilled in this art derive the secret of especially delighting their listeners is the alternation of soft and loud. This may come either in a theme and its response, or it may be when the tone is artfully allowed to diminish little by little, and then at one stroke made to return to full vigor—an artifice which has often been used, and with wonderful success, at the great concerts in Rome.
>
> Now of all this diversity and variation of tone, in which the bowed instruments excel among all others, the harpsichord is entirely deprived, and one might have considered it the vainest of fancies to propose constructing one in such a manner as to have this gift. Such a bold invention, nevertheless, has been no less cleverly thought out than executed, in Florence, by Mr. Bartolommeo Cristofali, a Paduan, a harpsichord player in the employ of His Serene Highness the Prince of Tuscany. He has thus far constructed three specimens, of the usual size of ordinary harpsichords, and they have been a complete success The bringing out of greater or lesser degree of sound depends upon the varying force with which the keys are pressed by the player; [and] by regulating this, may not only loud and soft be heard, but also gradations and diversity of sounds, as if it were a violoncello.

Maffei elucidates the new mechanism and appends a diagram. In place of quilled jacks as in the harpsichord, he says, the instrument is fitted with a register of hammers that activate the strings by striking them from below. Each hammer has a head covered with deer leather and hangs at the base of its shank from a round buckler that is capable of a swinging motion. The set of bucklers, in turn, is imbedded in a kind of rack, a separate unit. Each hammer has a small square downward protrusion arising near the base of its shank.

We continue our description according to the diagram. The key, when pressed down by the finger, operates another lever working in the reverse direction, descending toward the rear. As this second lever's front end rises, it carries with it a small upright wooden kind of movable jack, sometimes called a "hopper." Maffei calls it "movable tongue." The hopper is independent; it can be lifted off the rear lever by the key stroke, but is brought back to its original position by a pair of little springs. Furthermore, the far end of the rear lever holds an upright rod capped by a felt damper that is normally in contact with the string from below. Thus, the finger striking the key—that is, the front lever—raises the front of the rear lever and the hopper with it, whereupon the hopper strikes the protrusion on the base of the hammer shank and swings the hammer up against the string with just the amount of force originally applied by the finger. But as the hopper strikes, its springs cause it to jump back into place; moreover, enough space is allowed so that the hammer, having delivered its blow, can fall back to its original position without the finger having to release the key. Meanwhile, the far end of the rear lever, in descending, carries with it the damper off the string, so that the string's full resonance is not impaired. When the key is released, the rear end of the front lever drops; so does the front of the rear lever, hopper and all; while the far end of the rear lever rises, padding the damper once more against the string. The original rest position is re-established, and the sound is erased. The description makes the mechanism sound rather complicated, and later improvements—both by Cristofori and other makers—have tended to simplify it in some respects.

Let us see what this system of levers accomplishes. Merely to send a rigid knob at the end of a stick up against a string, in the manner of a clavichord tangent, is a very simple matter; but if the string were to be allowed to vibrate freely, the key could then only be struck and immediately released, in a sort of staccato. Indeed, Marius' crude "hammer harpsichord" was of this design. If such a simple device were not provided with a damper, a succession of staccato attacks would produce a muddle of different sounds; but if there were dampers, each tone would be intolerably short and dry. The basic problem of the keyed hammer-instrument, then, is to allow free string vibration (that is, immediate rebound of the hammer) while the key is still depressed, as well as instant erasure of the sound by a damper the moment the key is released. In other words, the mechanism must permit immediate finger control of wanted or unwanted resonance.

Fundamentally, the full rebound of the hammer could only be provided for by allowing space for it between the hammer's rest position and the extreme upward position of the rear of the key at the climax of its stroke. Indeed, this space was, and is, essential in all pianoforte actions. It follows, however, from this necessity, that the key with its appurtenances—jack or hopper or pilot—can never get into actual contact with the string. A hammer can never be "pressed" against a string; it must always be *tossed*. At the moment of hammer impact, the player's finger must relinquish his connection with it. It must always be possible on a keyed hammer-instrument to depress the key so slowly and gently, down to the bottom, that no toss is made and no tone is produced. On a harpsichord or clavichord this is impossible.

Tossing a hammer through a certain amount of space does not impair the action's stroke-responsiveness in principle: a sharp blow will always give a louder tone than a gentle one. Still, the closer and the more gradually the key can come to the string before making the final definitive toss, the greater the control and flexibility that the player can exercise. Most of the ingenuity of pianoforte makers, for several generations after Cristofori, was concentrated on this problem, the problem of "escapement." Cristofori's early rear lever and elastic hopper, which we have described, was one solution of it. Apparently he found a better one for the instruments he made later, dated 1720 and thereafter, in which his second lever worked in the same direction as the key and was called an "underhammer."

One further problem was fundamental to a hammer action. If a hammer were sent briskly against a string and allowed to fall back freely, it could often happen that the simple rebound did not exhaust the energy of the stroke and that the hammer made one or more gratuitous additional strokes, or re-rebounds; in other words, that it jiggled up and down a few times before coming to rest. Cristofori, the earliest successful maker of the instrument, also tackled this difficulty. In the Maffei diagram the hammer is represented as being held at rest, after the stroke, by means of two crossed silk threads, but in his later instruments he worked out something better. From the rear of the key he erected another upright, thickened at the top and covered with leather or other similar substance. Upon its rebound, the back of the hammer head came in contact with this surface and its friction prevented the re-rebound. The device became known as the "check" and has become an integral part of most pianoforte actions since that time. Modern American piano mechanics call it the "back catch."

The hammers swinging from their separate rail or rack, the escapement, the synchronous damper, and the idea of the check—all these were in this first instrument "with the *piano e forte*," as they are in those of the present day. Besides describing the instrument's working parts, Maffei evaluated its musical qualities, its purpose, and its function, as follows:

> Certain professors have not given this instrument all the approbation it deserves; first, because they have not understood what ingenuity was required in overcoming its difficulties, nor what wonderful delicacy of hand it took to complete the work with such precision; second, because it has seemed to them that the tone of such an instrument, different from the usual, was too muffled and dull. This, however, is a feeling that is produced only when the hands are first laid on it, through our habituation to the silvery sound of the other harpsichords; in any case, the ear adapts itself to it in a short time, becomes so fond of it that it cannot detach itself therefrom and takes no more pleasure in the ordinary harpsichord. We must also call attention to the fact that it is heard to more agreeable effect at some distance. The objection has furthermore been raised that this instrument does not have a great volume of tone, that it does not have all the forte of the other harpsichords. To this may be answered, first, that it does indeed have a great deal more tone than many people think, when someone who wishes, and knows how, brings it out by striking the keys with vigor; and second, one must understand how to take things for what they are and not to judge with regard to one purpose something that has been made for another. . . . [For] this is properly a chamber instrument; it is not really suitable for church music or for a large orchestra. . . . This much is certain, that for accompanying a singer, or for seconding one other instrument, or even for an ensemble of a moderate number of pieces, it succeeds perfectly; even though its principal purpose may not be this, but rather that of being played alone, like the lute, the harp, the six-stringed viols, and others of the gentler instruments.
>
> But, in truth, the greatest opposition that this new instrument has suffered consists in the fact that people in general do not know how to play it at the first encounter, since an ability to play the ordinary keyboard instruments will not suffice here. Being a new instrument,

it requires a person who understands its virtues, who to some extent has made a particular study of it, so that he may regulate the measure of the varying impulses that he must impart to the keys in order to achieve graceful gradations at the right time and place, and so also as to select appropriate pieces.

It is interesting to observe how remarkably close this first word about the pianoforte is to the last word that could be said about it!

5. THE ITALIANS SOON LOSE INTEREST IN THE NEW IDEA

IT IS NOT HARD to understand how it came that the first successful attempt to construct a keyboard instrument *"col piano e forte"* should have occurred in Italy. Though not untouched by the rationalism of seventeenth-century thought, the Italians in general could not, like many North Germans, find full musical satisfaction in the segregation of phrases, voices, or sections into rigid, monotonous dynamic levels. For a hundred years before Cristofori, "expression" had been one of the chief concerns of Italian musicians and their hearers. It was the Italians who, late in the sixteenth century, had created the opera, with its preoccupation with solo singing and the surges and droops natural to it. Indeed, opera was practically an Italian proprietary recipe, exported as such over the rest of Europe.

The Italians were also interested in making instruments "sing." The bowed string-instruments were the most likely subjects for that endeavor, and we see that same seventeenth century in Italy witnessing a matchless development in the making of violins of all sizes. Let us recall that Cristofori's early pianofortes coincided with Stradivari's "golden period." It was a near-lying idea, then, for an Italian to wish to build a capacity for "expression" even into a keyboard instrument.

For a time the *"nuova invenzione"* aroused a moderate interest among Cristofori's countrymen. As we have seen, he himself improved his designs and made probably about twenty instruments between 1709 and 1726. Two of his later examples, from 1720 and from 1726, are still in existence, one of them in the United States, we are happy to say. One of the objections to the new instrument was, as Cristofori himself understood, that it seemed difficult to play. Organists and cembalists had theretofore never tried to produce effects by the varying force of their strokes, and their first attempts to do so must have been rather awkward. Nevertheless, at least one composer made a point of writing for the new mechanism. In 1732 there was published in Florence, the very city in which Cristofori had worked, a set of twelve sonatas specified as being for the *"Cimbalo di piano e forte, detto volgarmente di martelletti"*—the "piano and forte keyboard, commonly called hammer [keyboard]"—by one Ludovico Giustini of Pistoia. Judged as music, these sonatas have little that sets them apart from the average keyboard style of their day; yet they have the distinction of being the first published compositions that were specifically designated as being for the instrument destined to become the most widespread in Christendom. As one might expect, the indications *"piano"* and *"forte"* are constantly to be found in them, and sometimes, even more significantly, the marking *"più piano."*

The Italians were melody-loving and expression-loving, and it was natural for one of their number to think up a pianoforte; yet, by the same token, it was just as natural for them to consider it unsatisfactory once its feasibility had been demonstrated. Although a modicum of expression could be had from a pianoforte of the Cristofori type, its quality was a dull thing compared with the warmth and vibrancy of the human voice or of the bowed instruments. Thus, the Italians continued to put their best efforts into their singing and their violin making and playing. Cristofori had a few disciples who made pianofortes during a couple of decades, at the most, after his death. In fact, five Florentine pianofortes were delivered to the court of Spain—probably during the 1730's—giving Domenico Scarlatti ample opportunity to play them there. Yet interest in this new keyboard instrument proved to be a mere temporary flurry: presently the thing all but died out in Italy, and some of the Spanish court pianofortes suffered the ultimate indignity of being rebuilt as harpsichords!

Cristofori made the first properly functioning pianoforte of which we have any positive knowledge, and for that he deserves the fullest recognition. It is permissible to call him the "inventor" of the instrument, as people usually do, if only a realistic understanding of that word be maintained. There exists a vague impression of an inventor in some minds, as of a fellow who, singlehanded, has made something new under the sun, something hitherto unheard-of and magically useful, which an unsuspecting world presently embraces while showering an exclusive gratitude upon the maker. In point of fact, a man who makes or finds something that no one else has ever dreamed of, or tried for, is normally dismissed as a trifler or an eccentric. It is when something is finally made or discovered that has long been sought for—that corresponds with an active craving of the times, something that many ingenious persons have already worked on—that a rather superstitious glory is focused on some one individual connected with the new thing, one whose contribution to its fulfillment may even have been small or belated.

Thus, it is relevant to point out that Cristofori had forerunners and that the idea of a keyed hammer-instrument had been in the air, if not too pungently, for some time. A drawing of a keyed dulcimer, from the fifteenth century, exists—so says Rosamond Harding in her important *History of the Pianoforte*—and now reposes in the *Bibliothèque nationale* in Paris. But a keyed dulcimer is practically a pianoforte. Furthermore, Father Mersenne in his *Harmonie universelle,* published in 1637, describes and illustrates a keyed xylophone—hammer-operated, of course. Finally, there exists a little pianoforte dated 1610, possibly of Dutch make, which now stands in the Belle Skinner Collection in Holyoke, Massachusetts. However, competent authorities have cast some doubt on the authenticity of this date.

On the other hand, the decline of interest in the pianoforte in Italy for a long time all but obliterated Cristofori's credit for priority. It was in Germany that most of the pianoforte making and experimenting took place during the middle half of the eighteenth century, and the Germans assumed uncritically that one of their number had first devised the instrument. The French agreed with them, for the *Encyclopédie des Metiers,* from an edition of 1778, definitely states so; and when Beethoven in 1816 wrote that the pianoforte was certainly a German invention, he was merely voicing a generally held view. Not until after the middle of the nineteenth century was Cristofori's achievement again properly evaluated.

No one in Germany preceded Cristofori in the constructing of a workable pianoforte; in fact, the first complete German-made one was almost certainly directly inspired by the Italian craftsman. Yet there is a certain truth in the idea that the instrument is a "German invention." Germany was certainly its spiritual nursery;

it was Germans who had enough interest in its peculiar capabilities to keep working on it, trying out new shapes, new gadgets, and new materials; it was from Germany that the instrument was first introduced into England and probably into France; while throughout a century and a half in France, in the United States, and in Russia, German names among piano makers have outnumbered all others. Let us return to Germany.

6. THE NEW "SOFT-LOUD" MAKES MODEST BUT STEADY PROGRESS IN GERMANY

THE TITLE PAGE of the *Giornale de' Letterati* carried the name of a Prince of Tuscany, as well as the printer's proud claim of the license granted him by His Holiness Pope Clement XI. All this august frontage lent an air of worth to the contents of the publication; thus, we are not astonished that the treatise on the "*gravicembalo col piano e forte*" was translated into German some years after its appearance by one Johann Ulrich von Koenig, master of ceremonies, court poet, and official flatterer to the King of Saxony, resident at Dresden, his capital. The translation, with Maffei's diagram, was incorporated into a collection of musical essays edited by Johann Mattheson and published under the name of *Critica Musica* in the year 1725.

There is reason to think that this translation was known to Gottfried Silbermann, organ builder of Freiberg, twenty-five miles from Dresden. Silbermann was a true manual craftsman, of outstanding skill, not a mere musician, thinker, or expositor like Schröter. No fewer than forty-seven fine Saxon church organs, besides many excellent clavichords, were ultimately to be the work of his hands. According to some persistent old yarns, he had been an unruly youth, a player of rather crude, Eulenspiegel-like practical jokes. Finally he fooled some guileless fellow-villagers of his tiny native Klein-Bobritzsch into digging for mythical treasure in a neighborhood ruin, and there he let those nocturnal Argonauts trip over a shrewdly stretched rope that set off concealed guns. On the basis of that exploit he became for a short while the nucleus of a jail cell. When he escaped, his family enabled him to get to Strassburg, hundreds of miles away in French terrain, where he had an elder brother well established as an organ builder. It was from him, Andreas Silbermann, that young Gottfried learned his trade.

His old imp was still poking. While working on the organ in a Strassburg convent, they say, he embarked on a precarious affair with a young novice. An elopement was carefully prepared, with a horse and buggy in waiting and a ladder against the convent wall at night. The girl was poised on the parapet—but the alarm had been given and she was pulled away, whereupon Gottfried busied himself dodging the sheriff for a few days before squirming his way back to his native Saxony.

Gottfried Silbermann had been born in 1683; at forty years of age he had settled into a respected citizen of Freiberg and a master craftsman whose high reputation for fine workmanship was spread over a considerable region. He appears to have been a lively, spiny, tactless old bachelor, and the tales of his eccentricities probably did much to advertise his work. How once while working on an organ he smashed several church windows trying to locate an offensive rattle, how he demolished his own unsatisfactory claviers with an ax, how he skirted *lèse-majesté* when he expressed his forthright disapproval of royal mistresses and the royal conversion to Catholicism—the stories all tended to show his zealous perfectionism and his aggressive integrity.

Pantaleon Hebenstreit was living in Dresden in those days, enjoying the warm afternoon of his fame, as well as his title of Royal Chamber Musician and the adulation of the court groups for whose pleasure he occasionally let loose the reverberating sonorities of his peculiar instrument. His bulky dulcimer was difficult and expensive to keep in repair, and it was to Gottfried Silbermann in Freiberg that he entrusted this important job of maintenance. In fact, he even had the esteemed organ- and clavier-builder make him a new pantalon when he needed one.

Silbermann's integrity was proverbial; still, he might have differed legitimately with others on ethical points. Apparently he had no inhibition against building unauthorized new pantalons on his own hook, instruments which might have reached the hands of some promising Hebenstreit rival. Hebenstreit objected vigorously, petitioned his master the King, and was rewarded with an edict, dated November 20, 1727, which confirmed his monopoly and prohibited anyone else, under penalty of a fine of fifty Rhenish gold florins, from constructing, or causing to be constructed, pantalon counterfeits.

Silbermann's little enterprise was struck down; but tinkering with dulcimers had put ideas into his head or, rather, had activated certain ideas that were already in his head because they were in many other people's heads. By then he must have read the Maffei article—he was on friendly terms with Koenig, the translator. About 1730 he made two pianofortes, the first—so far as we know—ever to have been built in Germany. He showed them to Johann Sebastian Bach, possibly on the occasion of the composer's visit to Dresden in 1736. We know of this on the evidence of one of Bach's pupils, who claimed to have seen the instruments. The great musician was a conservative genius, little impressed with things merely because they were new. He remarked on the difficulty of playing the new pianofortes and said they were weak in the treble. (A defect, alas, that has not been completely remedied up to the present day.) Silbermann's feelings were hurt. He sulked and destroyed his pianofortes, yet he persisted in trying to improve them.

To a degree he succeeded: toward the end of the 1730's he made a pianoforte for the Prince of Schwarzburg-Rudolstadt which was so much admired that a Rudolstadt maker named Lenker executed a couple of copies of it. All the time Silbermann was continuing to make clavichords of superior quality. Carl Philipp Emanuel Bach, the great Sebastian's second son, had bought one of them, which he cherished until near the end of his days.

Since 1740 this junior Bach had been a clavier player in the service of the new King of Prussia, Frederick II, later called "the Great." The King was an eager musician, a fluent if self-willed executant on the flute, and the name of Silbermann was easily broached to him. By 1746 Silbermann could make so bold as to offer His Majesty one of his newfangled pianofortes. Frederick took a fancy to it and ordered several more. An old story says he took six of them, and another version has it that he acquired as many as fifteen. Certain it is that, when an interested investigator had the old Potsdam and Berlin palaces searched in 1881, no more than three Silbermann pianofortes were to be found, one in each of the palaces associated with Frederick.

The old account says that the King paid Silbermann 700 thalers apiece for these instruments. This is an exorbitant figure, difficult to accept in view of Frederick's known frugality and the craftsman's equally well-known honesty. A pianoforte of the simple mid-eighteenth-century type had no such multiplicity of delicately moving little parts as did a large-sized harpsichord of several registers. It was correspondingly less troublesome to make, and therefore, could normally be sold at a somewhat lower price. At Sebastian Bach's death in 1750, his large veneered two-manualed harpsichord was appraised at 80 thalers. If we can assume, without extravagance, that an instrument of that kind had cost 150 thalers when new, we may arrive at a figure of about 125 thalers as a fair price for a fine new pianoforte. Yet the sum of 700 thalers is distinctive enough to suggest that it may be authentic; in that case, the plausible conjecture is that Frederick paid that amount of money for the whole lot of instruments. If, then, there were only three pianofortes, the individual price would still come out quite high, though perhaps not out of the question. It may have been an offense in those days to overcharge a king too recklessly, yet it may have been equally insulting to offer him too brash a bargain. A glance at a picture of one of those royal Silbermann pianofortes dispels the notion that fancy carving, inlay work, or painting could have brought the cost up abnormally high.

The pianofortes were probably delivered to Frederick during 1746. The story has often been told of how, the following year, the old master Sebastian Bach accepted Frederick's invitation to visit him at Potsdam. Most of the accounts are repetitions of a tale told at third hand, forty years after the event. Here is how the incident appeared to Berlin citizens when it was "spot news." We quote *Spener's Gazette,* a Berlin newspaper, from the issue of Thursday, May 11, 1747:

> We learn from Potsdam that Mr. Bach, the famous music director of Leipzig, arrived there last Sunday with the intention of enjoying the pleasure of hearing the excellent Royal music. Toward evening, at about the time that the customary chamber music in the Royal apartments usually commences, His Majesty was notified that Music Director Bach had reached Potsdam. His Highness straightway gave the command to have him come in; upon his entrance [His Majesty] went to the so-called Forte and Piano and without any preparation deigned, in His own exalted Person, to play a theme for Music Director Bach, which the latter was to work out into a fugue. This was accomplished so successfully by the aforesaid Music Director that not only was His Majesty pleased to express His own gracious approval, but all those present were moved to astonishment. Mr. Bach found the proposed theme so outstandingly beautiful that he

> wishes to commit it to paper as a formal fugue and later to have it engraved in copper. On Monday the famous man gave a performance on the organ in the Church of the Holy Ghost in Potsdam, and earned the universal approbation of crowds of listeners. In the evening His Majesty again requested him to execute a fugue of six voices; [a feat] which he achieved to the Royal satisfaction, and by common consent as skillfully as he had on the previous occasion.

This time, it was said, Bach praised "the so-called Forte and Piano"; but we need not make too much of his approbation. Kings aside, it would always be rude for a guest to make derogatory remarks about a host's new toy. Old Bach, in any case, showed no further interest in pianofortes: at sixty-two he was not learning new tricks.

Fortunately, it was a professional piano-maker who examined the extant Silbermann pianofortes in Potsdam in the late nineteenth century. He had accurate drawings made of the actions; and these revealed the fact conclusively that Silbermann made his instruments on the Cristofori principle, with hammers swinging on a separate rail and jacks with special escapement.

The constellation of the Silbermann repute, the musical King's interest, and the impressive, familiar name of Bach combined to give the new instrument a certain prestige. Presently it had a "good press." Johann Joachim Quantz was Frederick's guide in his flute-playing endeavors, as C. P. E. Bach was his accompanist. In 1752 Quantz brought out his monumental *Essay of a Guide to Playing the Transverse Flute.* This treatise goes far beyond mere flute playing and, in fact, constitutes a sort of compendium of musical practice of the day. It contains a detailed discussion of the art of accompanying, and the sixth section of Chapter XVIII treats "of the clavierists in particular." On page 231 the author speaks of the devices whereby the illusion of some kind of shading may be tricked from the harpsichord. "However," he continues, "upon a pianoforte everything may be achieved in the most convenient manner: for this instrument has more of those virtues necessary to a good accompaniment than any that is called by the name of clavier: here everything depends only upon the player and his judgment. The same quality can be predicated of a good clavichord, so far as playing is concerned, not however in point of the effect, since the fortissimo is lacking."

In 1753, the year after Quantz's work came out, C. P. E. Bach himself first published his great *Essay on the Right Way to Play the Clavier,* a weighty book which went through many editions and remained the standard disquisition upon the subject for more than forty years. Philipp Emanuel also praised "the newer pianofortes," somewhat more cautiously than did Quantz, and said they were useful and expressive "if durable and well constructed"—though he concluded that, on the whole, they were not superior to good clavichords.

In all the slow, gradual spread of awareness of the pianoforte the name of Silbermann was prominent, and it was believed for many decades that he had been the instrument's inventor. In the afore-mentioned *Encyclopédie,* the continuation of the famous one begun by Diderot and D'Alembert, we may read—under the heading *"Forté-piano ou Clavecin à marteau"—"Ce clavecin a été inventé il y a environ 25 ans à Freyberg en Saxe, par M. Silbermann."*

Meanwhile others had been working on the making of pianofortes. Christian Ernst Friederici, said to have been a pupil of Silbermann, set up as an organ and clavier builder in the city of Gera, in the western part of Saxony, some time in the 1730's. He was noteworthy for having been one of the first to construct an upright pianoforte. He accomplished this by the simple plan of turning the wing-shaped instrument up vertically on end, its narrow terminus pointing to the ceiling, the keyboard of course remaining supine to the player's hands in the usual position. Perhaps one had better call this an "upright flügel-shaped pianoforte." As a basic idea, this procedure was certainly not new, for harpsichords had long before been thus uprighted and provided with a correspondingly suitable modification of their actions. Those towering affairs had been given the fancy name of *"clavicytherium."* In the case, however, of the uprighted pianoforte, the alteration of the action was considerable. From the earliest years of the pianoforte, mechanics had experimented with hammers that struck the strings from above—on the analogy of the pantalon sticks—rather than from below. One of Marius' stillborn *clavecins à maillets* had such an action, and we may remember that in one key of Schröter's early model the hammer likewise struck down upon the string, according to his claim. The down-striking action impinging upon horizontal strings involves certain special difficulties in obtaining a quick rebound, and few makers of the earlier days cared to do much with it; however, the problems are eased somewhat where the hammer is made to strike from the front upon a vertical string. Friederici was able to find a provisional solution through a modification of Cristofori's action principle.

In a still existing example of Friederici's uprights, dated 1745, the case is not permitted to retain its natural wing shape, with its longest—that is, highest—dimension on the extreme left, curving gracefully down toward the right. Instead, an infantile conception of symmetry seems to have possessed the maker—or, more likely, the customer—and the case's highest point is made to come in the exact middle, its lines curving down equilaterally on both sides. Friederici was able to stow away his strings in their normal order into this pretty but tortured shape by stretching them diagonally.

In 1933 there was still in existence, however, another old upright pianoforte, perhaps unjustly attributed to Friederici, which displayed a rather significantly awkward construction. Its case, too, had the afore-mentioned isosceles, symmetrical form; but its strings were strung perpendicularly, so that the longest, lowest-pitched bass strings were in the middle and the shortest, highest-pitched treble strings on *both* ends. The keys, however, were built in their usual order. Thus, the leftmost bass keys had to play the middle strings, while some of the rightmost treble keys had to play the strings on the extreme left! This could be accomplished only by providing almost every key with its own metal rod pivoted into it, directing its motion sometimes as much as two feet away to its proper hammer. A whole network of these trackers evidently cumbered the poor, crazy instrument. But this outside-inside, wrong-side-to, expensive arrangement of parts made for no economy of space, nor for any increase of resonating surface. Its only purpose could have been to grant a minimum of musical usefulness to a piece of furniture whose chief aim was to "look nice."

The structure of this instrument reveals an important attitude of mind, one peculiar to the keyboards and to the pianoforte in particular. No other kinds of instruments have ever been made in which a designer would dream of obstructing the efficiency of musical function for the sake of mere appearance. It is interesting thus to observe the demands of the pianoforte as a decorative house furnishing invading its rights as a musical tool, as early as the 1740's—and that, too, in a country that was still poor and backward and not yet jiggled by the recurrent tantrums of fashion. Later in the century, in England, we will encounter imaginative interior-decorating geniuses who designed pianos so "handsome" that they could hardly be played at all. It would be unfair to say that such contrafunctional essays were anything but eccentric rarities; yet they show up, in the extreme of their absurdity, the trend of a widespread feeling that the pianoforte lived not by music alone.

Friederici is sometimes also spoken of as the one who first made square pianofortes. It might be questioned, however, whether any of his make antedated one known to have been built in 1742 by an obscure maker in faraway upper Bavaria. We shall hear of this instrument again later on.

Boxing the natural wing shape of a pianoforte or harpsichord into an oblong case was not done primarily for the sake of looks: a real saving of space and material was effected by this procedure, and the "square" or "table-form" instrument, as the Germans called it, was economical and eminently convenient for placing in a small room. We may say that the square harpsichord—called "spinet"—and the square pianoforte were at least situationally functional, if not musically so.

Gottfried Silbermann died in 1753; whereupon, for several decades after that, C. E. Friederici maintained a reputation over wide portions of the Germanies as the foremost builder of keyboard instruments. These were not all pianofortes by any means. For example, Imperial Councilor Johann Caspar Goethe of Frankfurt am Main purchased a Friederici *"Flügel,"* that is to say, a harpsichord. He was a well-to-do, high-minded person, accustomed to the best of things, and his choice of instrument reflected the esteem in which its maker was held. The small town of Gera was perhaps a week's journey from the large "free" commercial city of Frankfurt, and one might imagine that *Herr Rat* Goethe could have obtained a serviceable clavier instrument of less distinction right at home had he wished. He noted the *"Flügel"* in his account book in an entry dated January 25, 1769, where its cost is set down at 300 florins, in addition to an outlay of 12 florins 16 kreutzers for its transport. The sum was equivalent to about 180 thalers in Saxon currency—a substantial price, as we can see, for a clavier. Fräulein Cornelia Goethe, the councilor's daughter, was the chief user and beneficiary of this fine Friederici *Flügel;* and a few years later it appears to have been sent, together with much other household furniture, to her new home in Carlsruhe, shortly after her marriage. The *Herr Rat*'s son Johann Wolfgang, the great writer-and-poet-to-be, was a young man of nineteen at the time of the purchase, at home after his Leipzig university days. He had already outlived by some years his early unsuccessful bouts with the keyboard.

The fact that C. E. Friederici, at the head of his trade at the time, devoted so much of his energy to the devising and making of the new-fashioned pianofortes must have done its share toward establishing their acceptance. After the middle of the century many Germans took to inverting the components of the new instrument's name and most often called it "fortepiano," and the habit persisted well into the nineteenth century. Germans evidently brought this appellation, along with the instrument, to Russia ere then; and the Russians call it "fortepiano" to this very day. In the accent of some Germans, notably Saxons, the word often sounded "forte*b*iano"; and by a clumsy and pointless pun, Friederici's special-shaped instruments came for a time to be called *"Fortbien."*

During the 1750's then, wing-shaped, upright, and square pianofortes were being made and played in Germany, and probably nowhere else. Saxony was evidently the center from which they spread, at least as far as North Germany is concerned. Undoubtedly craftsmen other than Silbermann and Friederici, now all but forgotten, were busying themselves with hammer-struck keyboard instruments from the 1740's on. Still, we must not suppose from the emphasis of the foregoing account that there was any great bustle of interest as yet in pianofortes during the sixth decade of the eighteenth century, or that such claviers were as yet known and in demand everywhere. We must rather think of them as being looked upon in some quarters as promising experiments, but the older instruments retained their hold for quite a while. We may, for example, consider Friedrich Wilhelm Marpurg, a noted Berlin musical scholar, critic, and writer, whose high social standing as a former secretary to a general and a later director of the Prussian state lottery gave all his utterances a ready *a priori* prestige. Among many others, he published three books entitled *Guide to Clavier Playing* or some variation thereof, in 1751, 1754, and 1762; but in none of these does he mention the pianoforte by so much as a syllable.

The main reason for the pianoforte's slow diffusion was that it was as yet deficient in fulfilling its fundamental purpose, that of aiding musical expression. True, it could play louder and softer, relatively speaking, at the immediate discretion of the player's fingers; yet the subtler gradations of tone eluded the capabilities of its mechanism and could mostly not be realized upon it. It was an imperfect temptation to customers to whom the cheaper clavichords were readily available.

It would, indeed, be a grave mistake to picture a modern grand when thinking about these eighteenth-century pianofortes. They were frail little affairs, and the image-patterns of the harpsichord and clavichord still hovered in them. They had thin wire strings, not much stouter than those of the harpsichord, those in the bass sometimes made of brass. The tension on them was necessarily slight, one that wooden parts could easily sustain. The massive complex of iron bars and plates that modern pianos carry in their insides was nonexistent and undreamt-of; indeed, there was a positive prejudice against the use of metal for purposes of resonance. If wires were thin and not highly tense, it followed that they could withstand no heavy blows and that hammers could only be small and light. Their heads were small knobs, sometimes almost pointed. Felt had not yet been thought of as a covering for them: mostly deer leather was used, as in Cristofori's first instrument; sometimes layers of parchment; sometimes the naked wood was made to impinge upon the strings, and at times the hammer head had a narrowed edge suggestive of a clavichord tangent. Choice of the acoustically most favorable striking place along the length of the string constituted a problem that had not yet been approached with any scientific calculation, though experience of course had taught some rudimentary facts. Thus, no rich, sustained quality, no fuzzy sea of tone could be achieved upon these early pianofortes. Because of the small impact-surface afforded by their little hammers, their tone was brisk and slight—a little like that of a harpsichord, but duller. Moreover, even the actual volume of tone possible to them was less than that of a large-sized harpsichord. It is quite likely that until the 1770's they were most successful as accompanying instruments.

The idea of obtaining tonal variety by "stops," as in the harpsichord, persisted in the plans of the pianoforte makers. A number of devices were applied for softening or drying the tone, such as strips of leather or cloth to be inserted as desired between the hammers and the strings. They were variously called "lute," "harp," or "piano" stops. One simple mechanism was sometimes used in the case of pianofortes that were double-strung: it was a lever shifting the entire action slightly to the side so that the hammers would hit only one of the two strings—an *"una corda,"* as it was called later. Furthermore, it was inevitable that some mid-century instrument makers should try to combine the harpsichord and the pianoforte, that is, both quilled jacks and hammers, into a single instrument, with levers to throw either of them in or out. None of those attempts, however, was even remotely successful.

It was the memory of Pantaleon Hebenstreit that encouraged the application of the most important of all the pianoforte stops. We recall how the famous dulcimer player enchanted his hearers by making his sticks roll great chords over the strings and letting their resonances mingle and reverberate, to spread a great wash of harmony over the air. In the effort to permit something of a similar effect on the pianoforte, a contrivance was designed whereby the entire set of dampers could be raised off the strings independently of the hammers or keys at the player's discretion, by a single lever. In mid-eighteenth-century German instruments, all stops were at first worked by hand levers. The usefulness of the damper release, however, was much impaired by requiring the continued immobilization of one hand; thus, makers presently built it to be operated by a knee lever. The use of foot levers, or pedals, for pianoforte stops was not customary in Germany until it was introduced there late in the century from England. The damper-release lever together with the action-shift or cloth-interposition levers are, of course, the equivalent of what later came to be called the "loud" and the "soft" pedal.

Pantaleon's ghost indeed hung for a long time around German pianofortes. For at least a generation the word "pantalon" was used to designate a pianoforte, more especially, we are told, one of those which attempted to utilize a down-striking action upon the strings. One writer of 1758 called a keyboard instrument "hammer-pantalon," rather redundantly. On October 15, 1784, the most powerful of Friedrich Schiller's prose dramas, *Kabale und Liebe,* was given its first performance at the theater in Mannheim, in the Palatinate. In Act V, Scene 7, the author lets the heroine, herself the daughter of a musician, address her estranged lover, and adds the following stage direction, thus:

> *Luise.* If you will accompany me, Mr. von Walter, I'll play a strain on the fortepiano. (*She opens the pantalon.*)

More than thirty years after his death, and hundreds of miles from his living haunts, the celebrated *Hackbrett*-player's name and that of the newish keyboard instrument were still synonymous in the mind of a young writer.

7. TOWNSPEOPLE BECOME RICHER AND MORE ASSERTIVE

As the decades mounted after 1700, a slowly growing moderate prosperity seeped through the German towns. Hungarian gentlemen learned to smoke tobacco, while Polish ladies learned to drink tea and to sweeten it with sugar: these overseas products often came to them through the efforts of German traders. A new kind of merchant called a "*Verleger,*" a putter-out, began to overshadow the tradition-bound guild craftsmen. He lent expensive tools to little people in cottages in the country, paid them a flat wage, and marketed their product to his own profit. Production, and therefore wealth, was vastly increased in that way. So linen was woven in Silesia, so watches were made in the Black Forest, so toys were produced in Thuringia.

The Prussian kings set themselves the problem of supporting a large army in a poor country. They rigorously forbade the importation of certain finished articles such as cloth, compelled the population to buy the home factories' products, and then slapped a brisk tax on the profits. It all helped to make and distribute wealth. On the other hand, German-made products were exported to a modest extent. German knife blades from Solingen were peddled as far as the Seine and the Thames, while Aachen cloth. woven with Spanish wool, was sold back to Spain.

An outrageous form of revenue-producing export was especially favored by half-pint princes: they sold some of their own population, mostly young male rustics, to foreign armies for cash. The most famous of these deals occurred later in the century, when George III, King of England, bought a load of Hessians for the purpose of annoying George Washington. He paid the Landgrave of Hesse-Cassel, and some others, £500,000 for these droves of human livestock; and with the money the Landgrave added to his already exquisite collection of paintings and helped to finance his pleasure in sitting down to dinner every day with sixty parasites. Still, alas, many an innocent German tradesman got his legitimate share of the £500,000. It all made for prosperity, at least so far as the towns were concerned.

Certain cities became the special centers of this heightened commercial activity and developed cultural reflections of its benefits. Hamburg, the best North Sea harbor, was the place where foreign ships crowded. Many of its wealthier burghers had dealings with foreign parts, and foreigners could be seen there any day. A certain broad-mindedness, a certain cosmopolitanism, could flourish there more readily than in a mere provincial capital.

Berlin became the center of the new Prussian government-inspired commercial growth. Its citizens were conscious of belonging to an increasingly powerful state, and their intelligence and political acumen were well known to strangers. The construction of the Oder-Spree canal was a great help to their trade. In 1721 Berlin had 60,000 inhabitants, but by 1760 the number had grown to 120,000.

The rise of Leipzig was in many ways the most interesting of all. The junction of two east-west trade routes, it was a natural market place. Three times a year its great fairs were held, attracting sometimes as many as 7000 visiting traders. Englishmen and Hollanders could be found there then, and also Polish Jews, Russians, and Greeks. Moreover, Leipzig was also the center of the powerful, growing implement of culture: the printing trade.

For the most part the cities that were thus improving their fortunes were not the capitals of kingdoms or principalities, not court towns. Their richest and best-educated citizens could all the better indulge in a feeling of pride and independence when they were not too crassly or continually reminded of the existence of a superior caste of beings to whom they were expected to show deference, if not servility.

Handling more money and goods, and dealing with remote strangers, gave a greater sense of their own dignity to more members of the middle class: merchants and their families could aspire to a more abundant humanity. For one thing, they could treat themselves to purchases that their fathers might have shyly considered luxuries: more and shinier kitchen implements, costlier suits of apparel, and less starkly utilitarian furniture. A sharpened appetite for mental goods also came with the growing self-importance of these people: a demand for books, the theater, music, and education. An increasing number of people grew up who wanted to read and write the German language unlarded with French or Latin caste marks. That in itself was a kind of declaration of independence from courtly and academic influence. Not long after 1750 it was the German books that outnumbered the Latin by four to one. This, in turn, made a difference to the printing trade; for Latin books might be imported from anywhere, while German books could be made only in Germany.

The most powerful intellectual ferment of the age was affecting German minds, along with those of all Western Europe: Protestant orthodoxy, as well as Pietism, was corroding under the growing pervasion of a mechanistic conception of the universe. The import of Kepler's, Galilei's, and Newton's tremendous mathematically implemented generalizations had sunk into many persons' consciousness, and it was difficult for them any longer to picture the world as ruled by the wanton proddings of a super-Human residing a few miles above the highest hill. Instead, they dimly imagined the world as an inconceivably complex machine, every smallest part of which ran by an inexorable, inscrutable law. An awful vision, indeed, but mightily stimulating. For if men troubled to find out what all these "natural" laws were, in detail, what could they not hope to accomplish to better their condition, their circumstances of life. They could seem to invade what had always been thought God's province, and steer their own destiny. "Enlightenment" was what this view was called by its devotees, and one's own "enlightenment" was instantly paired with a zeal to enlighten others. The spread of "useful" knowledge, of knowledge of nature, among great numbers of people, was a postulate of this scientific attitude of mind, as we now call it. In the earlier decades of the eighteenth century, numbers of periodicals known as "Moral Weeklies" circulated widely in northern Germany, aiming to enlighten extensive sections of the middle class by the dissemination of presumably scientific information. Even the lowest classes were to be given some education and literacy in order to make them better workers.

The "enlighteners" still believed in God, so they said—in fact, they sometimes called themselves Deists—but they kicked Him far, far upstairs. Let the moveless Mover stay in His ethereal attic, they said, and meditate upon new worlds to create, or give an occasional slow nudge to this one in favor of general righteousness—so long as He leaves us alone to count the moons of Saturn, to build balloons and barrel organs, and to teach long division to farm hands.

Knowledge and control of nature is an endless vista, and any little success could be thought of as a progress toward a glittering horizon. In fact, the word "progress" was ceasing to be used as theretofore—to denote a mere dimension of motion—but became as if spelled with a capital P, an abstract beneficent principle, vaguely allied to the ghostly Deity itself. "Enlightenment" and "progress" were two of the most impellent words ever to possess human beings; and in Germany, as elsewhere, it was the literate middle class that derived the greatest moral support from them.

Still another circumstance helped to swell the German burghers' collective ego. Often their enthusiasm for education was mingled with a consideration other than a pure striving after light or the desire to achieve wealth and comfort. For some time the German princes had needed extensive, elaborately organized skilled help in the administration of their domains. There were several hundred sovereign territories in Germany, not to speak of countless semi-independent baronies. Each ruler fancied he required battalions of officials—revenue collectors, privy councilors, building inspectors, and what not—to keep his establishment running, as well as to make himself feel important. A soggy blanket of bureaucracy weighed on all public affairs. There simply were not enough members of the noble ranks available for all these positions. Recourse was had to the sons of burghers, who had to prove their ability and eligibility by a successful course of study at a university.

Despite the growing sense of their own importance, many of the burghers felt that they were not yet "the best people," even in their own estimation. Buying and selling were still somehow more ignoble than government. A young man might feel that—though it would be fine enough to go into his father's wholesale paper business and make some money—it would be more glamorous, and therefore more satisfactory, to become a ducal archivist or secretary in Reuss-Gera. To prepare himself for this high career, he would have to study at a university, preferably *"iura."* During his student days, he might have plenty of time and opportunity for a leisurely and disinterested cultivation of other intellectual interests.

The infiltration of German officialdom by people of middle-class background was a social phenomenon of considerable importance. For one thing, it gave middle-class ideals, attitudes, and ways of life a kind of sanction from above. Although some of these officials were given to adopting certain manners and habits of the aristocracy, in general it was the middle-class frame of mind that thus became more dominant and that tended to sound the keynote for the rest of society.

8. SINGING WARMS A HOME, AND A KEYBOARD HELPS THE SINGING

MIDDLE-CLASS family life covered a distinct octave of personal relationships. It involved continuous, comfortable intimacy between persons of differing age and sex; yet middle-class houses had enough room, and middle-class circumstances allowed enough leisure, for the single members of a family to follow their own bents and pursuits and to cultivate the peculiarities of their own personalities. A middle-class family was a perpetually affectionate, sensitive community of characters who still had plenty of opportunity to affirm the principles of their separate natures.

A middle-class husband and wife did not each have a separate apartment in a palace: they habitually shared a bedroom and a bed. Their children were not, most often, herded in a nursery by servants, even for their meals; but grandparents and parents, adolescents and infants dined together at the same table. Only among the very wealthy were the children sent away to a boarding school far from home; usually they attended a day school within the town in which they lived. After school hours they were again free to partake of family life. When they were taught by tutors at home, the interruption of home life was even less. Moreover, middle-class people could afford to protract the education of their children through the end of adolescence, and the developing mental life of the youngsters could waft a stimulating breeze into the domestic atmosphere.

Many were the occasions that involved the family as a body: family prayers, reading aloud—and also picnics, calls on friends, visits to the theater. A thousand little contacts and associations, objects of sentimental recollections and attachments, were made within this close but not constrained society. Middle-class family life was "warm"; but its participants tended to think of the ceremonies, the formalities, the studied grace of manner, the punctilio of rank discriminations among the aristocracy as "cold." True, among peasants and others of the lower classes, family life could be even closer. Yet it could only be a communion on a cruder physical level. Chill penury, the early requisition of children for productive labor, the absence of leisure and literacy would prevent that association from developing its finer vibrations.

It was an object of particular pride to a middle-class household that its women did not engage in "gainful" pursuits; this seems to have been a means by which the burghers could distance themselves from peasants and menials. The more money a family had, the less physical work its women were expected to perform, even in the home itself; and this was a point by which the richer burghers could mark their height above the poorer, the wholesale merchant above the storekeeper, the *Verleger* above the simple handicraftsman. Nor were females expected to exert themselves beyond the simpler intellectual pursuits. Learning was not supposed to be their province, and that they study at universities was a preposterous notion—all the more since no careers were open to them for which such an undertaking could be a preparation.

Well-to-do wives and mothers had the executive responsibility of their households and the more anxious care of the younger children, but their unmarried daughters could lead what looked like an easy life. They could do their school lessons without goading by the stings of ambition, and from the end of their school years until marriage they could enjoy an existence of decorative idleness, their articulate worries confined to personal appearance or the management of decorum. And already in the eighteenth century middle-class women were given to drugging their minds with fiction.

A moderately well-to-do, comfortable, somewhat educated German burgher family needed music through which to pour the overflow of its affections; it wanted to participate in music actively at home, even more than listen to it in passive admiration in church or elsewhere. Rarely, however, did a family harbor the special talent or provide the opportunity for the practice necessary to realize concertos of the kind that ducal orchestras performed. Most polite music was much too difficult for middle-class home use. Members of a household and their friends enjoyed singing together, but German burghers were too artless for the complex precisions of madrigals. Inevitably, simple single-line vocal melodies or jingly dance tunes were best suited to the mediocre capacities of most people.

Single-line melodies need instrumental support: they need harmony to give them meaning, as well as to provide a rail for preventing insecure singers from falling off the pitch. A keyboard instrument, stationed in a common room of the home, fulfilled this requirement. Other instruments, it is true, might have been able to perform the same function. Still, only a clavier could be so inalterably associated with a family dwelling. A lute, guitar, or fiddle is easily carried in the hand; and a son might readily conscript it for tavern conviviality, window serenading, or student meetings, or even let it be thrown in careless desuetude into a strange closet. But a clavier, especially one of the larger sizes, was relatively a fixture. It could be moved by the simultaneous efforts of several people, but hardly carried around with comfort: it anchored the music firmly within the family circle. Its inertia, if nothing else, made it the focus of the domestic musical life.

Printed collections of songs for home use began to make more frequent appearance after the first third of the eighteenth century had passed. They came out shyly and self-consciously at first. In a strictly stratified society, in which the ruling classes imitated the French and the intellectuals lived by Latin, the common German word *"Lied"*—"Song"—carried a derogatory plebeian suggestion. It called up pictures of beggars' cries or of lewd ditties in low haunts. To people wealthy enough to buy volumes of music, and literate enough to read them, it might have seemed a perverse sort of trifling to waste the engraver's careful art—ordinarily dedicated to works of lofty pretensions—on commonplace vernacular products. Thus, the earlier song collections consciously avoided the low-class word *"Lieder."* In 1733 Valentin Rathgeber of Augsburg compiled a volume of tuneful singing material which he called, circuitously, *Ear-pleasing, Spirit-delighting Table Confectionery* (*Ohren-vergnügendes und Gemüth-ergötzendes Tafel-Confekt*). It had a good success, going through four editions during the following fifteen years.

A much greater impression was made by a collection issued three years later, in 1736, in the livelier "modern" city of Leipzig. It was called *The Singing Muse on the Pleisse* (*Die Singende Muse an der Pleisse*), the Pleisse being the little river which flows through Leipzig. Its compiler and author, Johann Sigismund Scholze, at first discreetly covered his identity with the pseudonym *Sperontes*. Again the disparaging word *"Lieder"* was evaded, and the ditties were called "odes." The songs were calculated to appeal to a variety of tastes. Many of them celebrated love and wine in age-honored fashion; some also praised country life, or the city of Leipzig, or friendship, or the middle-class virtue of contentment; while others sang of hunting and fishing, or cards and billiards. Scholze had been a *iura* student, and his short, obscure life was occupied with the practice of jurisprudence; thus, we can understand why his texts—though mostly in good colloquial German—occasionally contain the allusions and the literary syntax generally in use among the educated.

The tunes mostly have an attractive dance lilt, and many were of foreign origin, being parodies based on French minuets and Italian canzonas. In the first edition, about one quarter of the items are in polonaise rhythm. This dance appears to have enjoyed a considerable vogue in Saxony at the time, probably because the Saxon king of that period was doubling in the role of King of Poland. We may recall that Sebastian Bach composed a number of polonaises.

The title page of the *Singende Muse* contains an inscription, "At the expense of the jolly company"; moreover, it shows a view of some buildings and streets of Leipzig as seen from a broad terrace, while an imprint in small type at the bottom mentions the name of Richter. The name was that of the proprietor of a well-known coffeehouse; it has been plausibly conjectured that the terrace is an idealized picture of a portion of his premises, while the "jolly company" was a group of men who met there regularly around the same table—a *"Stammtisch,"* as the Germans call it. Thus, the book would appear to be a souvenir of a long series of convivial gatherings.

A volume of this sort, apparently, was what many people had been seeking for some time. University students had indeed made collections something like this before, privately, and had copied them by hand; but those were mostly too bawdy for family use. The *Singende Muse,* on the other hand, had a wide and rapid distribution. Three editions came out within five years of the original. Three sequels were issued within ten years. There were numerous later reprints, some from cities far distant from Leipzig. The songs spread over all the Germanies, were copied on broadsheets, and found their way into the homes of music lovers through wide sections of the population.

The *Singende Muse* was soon followed by other similar collections. The idea caught on vigorously and the song books multiplied rapidly, especially after 1750. As time went on, however, the trend of the songs was away from the parodying of French and Italian melodies, while the language of their texts avoided rococo artificialities, grew less and less literary and polite, both words and music becoming more and more German and "folksy." Presently the word *"Lied"* lost its depreciatory flavor and became respectable. The titles of the later books reveal their middle-class flavor:

Songs for the family circle, Little songs for little girls, Songs for innocent pastime, Joyful songs for German men, Melodious songs for the fair sex, Little songs for children for the encouragement of virtue, and even *Lullabies for German wet nurses;* finally, in 1793, there appeared Wiesinger's *Songs sacred to burgherly and domestic happiness, to amiable morality, and to guiltless pleasure.*

The important thing about these collections, for the purpose of our study, is that the songs were to an overwhelming extent published with accompaniment intended for a clavier instrument. It was assumed that the homes in which people would enjoy singing them would also possess a clavier of some sort. In fact, in many cases a preface directs that the songs may be played without being sung, as simple clavier pieces. The title page of the *Singende Muse* already declares that the "odes" are meant for "Clavier-exercise as desired," besides showing two female figures, possibly allegorical, each fingering a small clavier placed on a table. The pretty minuets and polonaises, then, were often tinkled off for the sake of the tunes alone—without the bother of the text, with its many verses. The song-composer Hertel said, similarly, in 1760: "Such songs are not always sung, they are occasionally played on the keyboards." Other titles are quite specific, such as: *The playing and singing clavier-player* or *Clavier music for serious and comical songs.*

Almost always, in those days, the songs were printed on two staves: the upper carrying the melody, to be played with the right hand; the lower the scanty accompaniment, assigned to the left. The words mostly appeared between the staves, with their later verses at the bottom of the page. Thus, when the song was both sung and played together, the player doubled the tune in unison with the voice at all times. Until the 1780's there were hardly any exceptions to this rule of two-staff publication. Only toward the end of the century do songs begin to appear printed on three staves, with a two-handed accompaniment that does not merely duplicate the voice part.

9. CLAVICHORDS MAKE WEEPING EASIER

By the middle of the century, then, considerable numbers of modest, middle-class families—none of their members tainted with the slightest stirring toward making music a profession—were acquiring claviers for such purpose as we have just recounted. We can follow the widening spread of the instruments by observing the work of Barthold Fritz, a clavier maker of Braunschweig, who has left us a detailed catalogue of his customers. It begins from the year 1721, when at the age of twenty-four he completed his first clavier, and ends with 1757, the year he published his list. During each of his first six working years Fritz made but a single instrument; from 1732 to 1740, however, he advanced to about five or six a year. By 1745 his annual output had gone up further, to ten; after that, to seventeen; and from 1752 to 1756 he turned out a yearly average of no less than twenty-three claviers. We can tell that his patrons were preponderantly middle-class persons from their occupations, which he preposed to their names like titles, after the quaint German pigeonhole-loving manner. During the 1750's we find him delivering claviers to "Mr. Pastor Niemeyer in Königslutter," "Mr. Postal Secretary Thielke in Braunschweig," "Mr. Overseer of Mines Habich in Clausthal," "Mr. Alderman Stisser in Braunschweig," "Mr. Kitchenmaster Wilke in Braunschweig," "Mr. Theological Candidate Ottmer in Riddagshausen," "Mr. Bookkeeper Knust in Braunschweig," "Mr. Council Auditor Scharlach in Klausthal," "Mr. Merchant Graefe in Hamburg for resale," "Mr. Doctor Kortum in Wolfenbüttel." Professional musicians were in the decided minority on the list, and during many years not one is mentioned; while in other years, here and there, we see a few Mr. Organist's or Mr. Cantor's. On the whole, the clavier-buying citizens seem to have been those whose positions suggest that they had had the benefit of some kind of academic education. The great majority of the Fritz instruments appear to have been clavichords, at least two thirds of them of the smaller size and "bound" or "fretted" (that is, with some of the strings having to do duty for more than one note).

Fritz did not have the background of an organ builder, nor did he start by being a cabinetmaker: on the contrary, he had learned the miller's trade from his father and it was his bent toward music and mechanics that had led him to the making of claviers. It is important to realize that the interest in claviers was by then so widespread that he could make an exclusive occupation of producing them. Clavier making in Germany had, by the middle of the century, become an independent trade.

We have already suggested that Pietism, considered purely as a religious movement, began to fade from 1740 on. Many of the mental habits and attitudes that it encouraged, however, persisted with increased strength and found new objects for their exercise. In particular, the cult of "feeling," the propensity to indulge in emotional excesses for their own sake, raged far and wide throughout the German population. To be moved, if possible to tears, was thought to be among the most valuable of achievements. A high capacity for going on these emotional jags was somehow regarded as the proof of a humane disposition, of a deep fineness of sensibility, even by those who could no longer believe that these outbursts were the direct personal caresses of the Almighty. All manner of human events, as well as the contemplation of "nature" and of works of art, were thought to be most favorably emphasized when they aroused tears. Heart-rending family "scenes" were deliberately provoked and enjoyed, just as nowadays, for the most part, they are carefully avoided. Solemn-sounding vows and promises were uttered between parents and children, dramatic reconciliations celebrated between brothers and spouses. Family prayers were an opportunity for the father to balloon himself into an improvisation of edifying sentiments; poetry was read aloud and declaimed with a violent pathos that might seem ridiculous and repulsive today.

Johann Salomo Semler, a pioneer of historical Bible criticism, later professor of theology at the University of Halle, has told us how in 1749, when he had completed his studies at that institution, he delivered to its faculty and to its dean an extempore Latin speech of thanks so fiery that not only he himself but several others present broke into tears. But young Semler had a personal problem: he had fallen in love with that same dean's daughter, while he still had an understanding with another girl back in his home town. So, he went back to his lodgings and wept some more over his hard fate, and his faithful room-servant wept with him. He wept again when he said good-by, and at a way station several days' journey distant he was still weeping. Moreover, when he arrived home and showed the dean's laudatory letter to his father, the old man also burst into tears.

Friedrich Heinrich Jacobi related how, when he traveled with his brother through a sunny Rhine landscape full of fruit trees, he grasped his companion's hand, by this gentle pressure conveying to him his thanks for the many joys he had experienced in the other's company. The brothers gazed upon one another with a tender emotion, a happy tear welled up in the eyes of each, and they fell upon each other's necks and "blessed the region with the holy kiss of friendship."

For several generations after the mid-century, German literature, correspondence, and conversation was full of the rank flavor of this sentimental debauchery—"*Gefühlsduselei*" it was sometimes rather keenly called. The decade 1770–80 marked its climax. Goethe's *Werther* appeared during that time and induced a vogue of suicide, while an absurd, ranting drama by Maximilian Klinger called *Sturm und Drang* appeared in 1776 and was permitted to lend its title to the whole epoch. With a highly articulate mushiness of sentiment widely admired as a virtue, it was only natural that many persons would pretend to it with more or less hypocrisy. Some of the German pathos of those years was fake, for it was better to risk seeming a fraudulent weeper than to evidence a heart of stone. On the whole, the sentimentalists were not to be found so frequently among the nobility, for loud-voiced soul-roiling tended to strike them as bad manners. Again it was the educated middle class that found satisfaction in attitudinizing from that platform.

From all this we can understand how it came that the clavichord was the favorite domestic instrument in northern Germany for more than thirty years after 1750. Its delicate stroke-responsiveness made it a perfect mirror for the finer shades of feeling. It was an instrument "poor in intensity of tone, yet so supple in its poverty," as J. N. Forkel said of it. But its weakness of tone could be a virtue in its way, for because of it the clavichord was best played alone and thus became a useful implement for enabling a "beautiful soul" to make love to itself most privately. One writer called the clavichord "the thrilling confidant of solitude."

I have thus far refrained from mentioning one of the clavichord's most characteristic and attractive capabilities. We will recall that the pressed-down key kept the tangent firmly in contact with the string. If the finger, without releasing the key, then rocked up and down upon it, alternatingly easing and renewing the pressure, it could produce a pulsating prolongation of the tone. This *vibrato,* not unlike that made by string-instrument players on their finger boards, was called *"Bebung"* by the Germans—literally, "quaking." What a potent engine of "feeling" this little movement could be! The throbbing heart, the panting breast, the trembling lip, the quivering voice—all this physiognomy of emotion could seem to be in the *Bebung.* Amateurs overdid it ecstatically, to judge from the warnings issued in the instruction books of the period.

Moreover, all the expressive delights of the clavichord could be had for as little as 30 thalers. An ordinary spinet, bright-toned but monotonous, might cost 60, while a full-sized harpsichord with variable stops might easily come to 150. For a good half-century the clavichord became *the clavier* par excellence, and from 1750 until well into the nineteenth century the word *"Clavier"* in German was substantially synonymous with "clavichord." Numerous treatises of the period confirm this statement, and so do the dictionaries. The harpsichord, progressively obsolescent for the remainder of the century, was now usually called *"Flügel."*

In 1743 Just Friedrich Wilhelm Zachariae, still in his teens, came from his native Schwarzburg-Sondershausen to enter the University of Leipzig and study *iura.* He also appears to have become a follower of Professor Gottsched, the reigning literary pope. Handy with words, the young man attracted a good deal of attention with a poem called *Der Renommiste,* a satire on the vagaries of student life, done in the manner of Pope's *Rape of the Lock.* But Zachariae soon settled down: he was himself to become a professor at an academy in Braunschweig and to set himself the solemn task of translating Milton's *Paradise Lost* into German. In 1754 Zachariae published the following verses:

AN MEIN CLAVIER

Du Echo meiner Klagen
Mein treues Saitenspiel,
Nun kommt nach trüben Tagen
Die Nacht, der Sorgen Ziel.

Gehorcht mir, sanfte Saiten
Und helft mein Leid bestreiten—
Doch nein, lasst mir mein Leid,
Und meine Zärtlichkeit.

Wenn ich untröstbar scheine
Lieb' ich doch meinen Schmerz;
Und wenn ich einsam weine,
Weint doch ein liebend Herz.

TO MY CLAVIER

Thou faithful stringed array,
Echo my sighing soul!
Now fades the clouded day
To night, all sorrow's goal.

Fond strings, obey my hand,
Help me my pain withstand–
But, no, leave me my pain,
My feelings' tender skein.

Disconsolate though I seem,
I love the sufferer's part;
When lonely tears outstream,
Still weeps a loving heart.

There follows a rather irrelevant, though doubtless autobiographical, stanza:

Die Zeit nur ist verloren
Die ich mit gold'nen Thoren
Bey Spiel und Wein und Pracht
So fühllos durchgebracht.

Those hours are only lost
That callously I tossed
In folly's gilded sink
To gaming, show, and drink.

It is not very good poetry by present-day standards, yet it struck a greatly sympathetic note in its day. The researches of Professor Max Friedländer brought to light no fewer than nine different composers who set it to music in the course of a few decades following its publication. Better than that, a crew of other versifiers considered the lines good enough to imitate. For example, Philippine Gatterer, a Göttingen academician's soulful young daughter, decided to throw her thitherto secret poetizings upon a crass world in 1776. Among them were stanzas likewise addressed *An das Clavier,* beginning thus:

Mit stillem Kummer in der Brust
Schleich ich mich hin zu dir;
Bring Harmonie in mich und Lust,
Du liebliches Clavier!

Unspoken grief within my breast,
I slip away to thee;
Sweet clavier, solve my quest,
Bring harmony and joy to me!

Four different composers were presently inspired to deck out these words in tones.

Johann Thimotheus Hermes, an East Prussian preacher who earned much of his living as a private tutor, had a glib literary talent that prompted him to become an imitator of England's Samuel Richardson. His interminable, diffuse serial story *Sophie's Trip from Memel to Saxony,* published in 1769, was greatly successful and became one of the earliest of the adventure-mongering, moralizing "family novels" much to be relished by lower middle-class Germans. One of *Sophie's* characters also addresses herself *An das Clavier*:

Sei mir gegrüsst mein schmeichelndes Clavier!
Was keine Sprache richtig nennt,
Die Krankheit tief in mir
Die nie mein Mund bekennt
Die klag ich dir.

Hail, ingratiating clavier!
What no language can express,
The illness deep in me
Which my mouth dares not confess,
This I cry to thee.

But Hermes was already chewing a cud. Three years earlier he had brought out another novel: *Die Geschichte der Miss Fanny Wilkes.* Fanny too, it appears, was made to extend her courtesies *An das Clavier:*

Bereite mich zum Schlummer
Sanft klagendes Clavier,
Ermüdet durch den Kummer
Komm ich betrübt zu dir.
Dir sing ich meine Klagen,
Vermindre du die Plagen!
Und du gebeugtes Herz
Vergiss nun deinen Schmerz.

Prepare me for my rest,
My plaintive, sweet clavier;
With care I come oppressed—
My trouble thou must hear.
To thee I sing my grief,
'Tis thou must bring relief;
And thou, O heart bowed low,
Forget thy pain and woe.

And so on, for two more stanzas.

Johann Adam Hiller, a leader of musical enterprise in Leipzig during the sixties and seventies, put some unusually charming music to these verses, which came out in 1769. It was his second attempt, for he had already set them in a different version two years previously. The poem must have appealed greatly to him—as well as to six other composers during the following twenty-five years.

Songs "To the Clavier" were indeed a constant feature of eighteenth-century German songbooks. Friedländer has listed no fewer than nineteen of such poems in fifty-six different settings. Almost invariably they draw the same picture: in the evening's quiet, when the noise of the wagons has died down, the shops are closed, and the children put to bed, the sick soul soothes itself in solitude with some soft, soft strains on the keys. Moreover, all this talk about "quiet grief," "gentle plaints," and "gentle strings" makes it clear that it was always the clavichord that was thus apostrophized.

10. THE CLAVIERS ARE FEMININE

WHO PLAYED these middle-class keyboards? Women mostly, and especially girls. They were the ones who had the most time and the most opportunity. The instrument was a house furnishing, and they were mostly at home. Their leisure also allowed the more imaginative among them plenty of encouragement for the tender instrospection, for the emotional autointoxication of which home singing and clavier playing were convenient expressions.

There was another point: the keyboard instrument enabled females to preserve a maximum of decorum in the exercise of their musical efforts. Chastity, especially for women, is of course a universal virtue, yet it was the middle classes to whom it became an especially emphasized object of pride. It was one of their best-fortified perches from which they could strike their poses toward the other classes. Their girls were not tempted to laxity through want, like those of the peasantry; and their mature women did not lead the diffuse lives that would have let them acquire the technique of sophisticated wantonness, or of using their sex in the furtherance of political and social influence, as did those of the aristocracy. At least, that is what the burghers liked to think: it was an ideal to which they aspired and pretended. Later eighteenth-century plays, aimed at a middle-class public, abounded in burgher maidens whose virtue was sharply set off against the lascivious goings-on among the nobility.

Chastity, however, as well as a lapse therefrom, is difficult to prove. Judgments in particular cases are likely to be guesses based on relatively insignificant elements of the suspect's behavior. Rarely did a mean-spirited person shadow a girl and become an eyewitness to her derelictions; but if her dress were too revealing, her ornaments too provocative, her speech and gestures too bold and too charged with abandon, why, it was possible that some people would presume her to be leaning perilously toward sin. In such a case, where great stress is laid on a virtuousness that must, almost always, remain a matter of conjecture, its appearance is almost more important than its reality. It was absolutely essential to her family's good repute that a middle-class girl seem to look and behave with a respectable "modesty."

Moreover, as we have noted before, it was a matter of almost equal pride that the wealthier middle-class women be relieved of heavier physical labor. To make all this unmistakably evident in public, their appearance was expected to exhibit a meticulous personal daintiness, their gestures an absence of violent muscularity, and their clothes and hairdress an unfunctional fragility and extravagance.

When a woman plays the flute, she must purse her lips; and she must do so likewise when she blows a horn, besides also giving evidences of visceral support for her tone. What encouragement might that not give the lewd-minded among her beholders? When she plays a cello, she must spread her legs: perish the thought! "In thousands of people it calls up pictures that it ought not to call up," primly said the anonymous *Musikalischer Almanach für 1784*. When she plays the violin, she must twist her upper torso and strain her neck in an unnatural way; and if she practices much, she may develop an unsightly scar under her jaw. For centuries the violin was generally regarded as a quite unwomanly instrument. Moreover, eighteenth-century clothes fashions could seem especially inappropriate to certain instruments in contemporary eyes. "It strikes us as ridiculous when we look at a female . . . in a hoop skirt at a double bass; ridiculous when we see her playing the violin with great sleeves flying to and fro; ridiculous when we observe her in a high *fontange* blowing a horn," affirms our *Almanach* guide. "Fontange," a lofty headdress made of knots of ribbons, was named for a duchess friend of Louis XIV.

All these negative suggestions were avoided in the case of a keyboard instrument. A girl could finger a harpsichord, a clavichord, or a pianoforte with her feet demurely together, her face arranged into a polite smile or a pleasantly earnest concentration. There she could sit, her well-groomed hands striking the light keys with no unseemly vehemence: and if it were a clavichord she was touching, a flow of ever so delicate shadings would infuse her tones with a tender expression. There she could sit, gentle and genteel, and be an outward symbol of her family's ability to pay for her education and her decorativeness, of its striving for culture and the graces of life, of its pride in the fact that she did not have to work and that she did not "run after" men.

Indeed, the harmonious association of the keyboard instruments —other than the organ—with the feminine portion of middle-class humanity is not an accident or a passing fashion: it is an affinity which springs from the essence of each. Truly, they were made for one another. This affinity was well understood long before the eighteenth century, and it endured unremittingly nearly until the present day.

A number of eighteenth-century German littérateurs were charmed by the spectacle of a clavier-playing lady. The youthful Schiller, fresh out of military medical school, developed a callow "crush" on a thirty-year-old captain's widow Frau Luise Vischer. He called her "Laura," and his verses *Laura am Clavier* are a well-known example of his early poetical skunk-cabbage. The date is 1781. He begins modestly:

Wenn dein Finger durch die Saiten meistert
Laura, itzt zur Statue entgeistert,
Itzt entkörpert steh' ich da.

When the strings are mastered by thy hand
A lifeless statue now I stand,
A soul, now, ravished of its clay.

Presently he continues:

Ehrerbietig leiser rauschen
Dann die Lüfte, dir zu lauschen.

Now softer wafts the awe-struck air
To hearken to thee with more care.

He describes her music in extravagant imagery, and speaks of "thunder," "foaming freshets," and "sweet rustling . . . of aspen woods." The violent contrasts suggest that it may have been a pianoforte with which "Laura" was weaving her enchantment. Finally:

Mädchen, sprich! Ich frage, gib mir Kunde
Stehst mit höhern Geistern du im Bunde?
Ist's die Sprache, lüg' mir nicht,
Die man in Elysen spricht?

O maiden, speak, inform this waiting ear,
Art thou in league with spirits from another sphere?
Dissemble not, I pray, but tell me straight, is this
The language spoken in Elysium's fields of bliss?

Goethe lets his impressionable hero Werther tell of his fateful Lotte: "She has a melody which she plays on the clavier with the power of an angel, so simple and so soulfully! It is her favorite song and it just lifts me away from all pain, confusion, and caprice merely when she strikes the first note of it. . . . Not a word of the ancient magical power of music seems improbable to me. How the simple song touches me!" (This is from the Letter of the sixteenth of June.) Of course, Werther was already desperately smitten, and anything Lotte did was likely to throw him into delirium. Still, it is noteworthy that the author allowed her to aggravate his ailment with a clavier rather than with an oboe or fiddle.

11. IMPROVED MUSIC PRINTING FAVORS THE KEYBOARDS

We have already indicated that among German cities during the eighteenth century Leipzig was in the forefront of progress. It was not a capital, not a court town or *Residenzstadt*, as they said; on the contrary, its prominence was commercial. Its leading people were less concerned with passive administrative routines and courtly precedents than with the needs of a growing trade and the potentialities of new enterprise. The town harbored few privileged aristocrats or court functionaries who could perpetually remind the citizen of his social inferiority. Within the limits set by a small absolute monarchy such as the Kingdom of Saxony was, the Leipzig burghers yet could develop a considerable measure of independence and self-reliance. Nor was intellectual stimulation lacking in the town. The university, founded early in the fifteenth century, had long enjoyed an excellent reputation; and Herr Councilor Goethe of Frankfurt thought so well of it that he sent his gifted young son Johann Wolfgang there for his higher studies late in the 1760's.

Commercial and cultural development went hand in hand and encouraged each other. More people made more money and came into a position to demand more cultural goods; whereupon this demand spurred businessmen to new enterprise toward supplying it, and toward better methods of distributing the supply.

Leipzig had for some time been the center of the book trade; so it need not astonish us to learn that one of the town's best-established printers and book publishers, Immanuel Breitkopf, perfected a process about the year 1755 that gave a strong impetus to the spread of music: he made a significant improvement in the technique of printing notes from movable type. Its fundamental principle was indeed not new, for movable note-type containing pieces of staff had been used as long before as the earlier part of the sixteenth century. What Breitkopf did was to break down each note into tiny component sections: head ∘ stem | staff lines ≣ flag ♪ ♬ beams —— ═══, so that any musically feasible combination of these elements could be set into a tight little mosaic. Thus, any playable number of notes could be cleanly printed under, or over, one another on the same staff. In a way, this was a cumbersome procedure, and ultimately it became obsolete with the development of lithography fifty years or more later. Yet in its time it solved the problem of printing chords, which tended to be of great importance, particularly for keyboard music. The fact that Breitkopf's method was imitated and adapted after not too long a time in Paris, Brussels, Haarlem, and London seems to show that it coincided with a need of the times. His "invention," like so many others, did not create a trend; it merely reinforced one that was already in movement. Indeed, his process would have had little meaning otherwise. Clearly, the number of those who could read music, who had a little extra money to spend, who became interested in acquiring printed notes for home singing and playing, had multiplied to a point where it could arouse the enterprise of merchants.

Music publishing was still in its primary stages in the Germany of 1750. Before then professional musicians and students, who were almost the only persons capable of playing anything of the least difficulty, copied out by hand any compositions they wished to possess. The luxury of printing was indulged in usually only when some fine-appearing presentation was in order—such, for instance, as when J. S. Bach sent his *Musical Offering* to the Prussian king. By the middle of the century a cautious kind of music publication began, with advance subscriptions carefully secured before issue. A decade or two later, however, the number of potential customers was growing large enough for publishers to take a chance on printing the music first and trying to sell it afterward. In the early 1760's Breitkopf was putting out catalogues of music in stock, and music publishing in Germany began to be a business in the modern sense. Progress must have been encouraging, though perhaps not too rapid. It must have been retarded by the Seven Years' War between Prussia and Austria (1756–63), which made battlefields out of a number of Saxon localities. We find Breitkopf complaining as late as 1770 that many people were still sticking to their old habit of having music copied by hand.

Many years later, when the firm came to be Breitkopf & Härtel, one of its spokesmen explained the economy of music printing. This was early in the nineteenth century, before stereotypy and lithography had become developed. Printing from type, he wrote, was profitable if the type did not have to be tied up for too long a period and if the entire edition of the piece of music could be printed at once, so that the type could then be taken apart and used for other publications. That, however, could be done only in the case of music that the publisher could expect to sell out quickly. For uncertain or slower-selling items, which had better be struck off a few copies at a time as needed, it was more economical to use engraved copper or pewter plates.

We can arrange these principles into a vaguely syllogistic succession, with the following result:

1. Type printing was especially useful for printing keyboard music.
2. Type printing was especially economical for printing quick-selling music.

Therefore:

3. Publishers tended to devote much attention to putting out quick-selling keyboard music.

Keyboard music, then, or keyboard-vocal music formed the greatest portion of the publishers' output, already in those mid-eighteenth-century days. Presently they began to put together collections which included songs and clavier pieces in the same volume. A *Musikalisches Mancherlei*, a *Musikalisches Vielerlei*, and a *Musikalisches Allerlei* of that description appeared in rapid succession in different parts of Germany, evidently in competition with each other. The titles all mean "Musical Miscellany" or "Musical Assortment."

Publishing means offering something to a public, and the rapid formation of a public for literature and music was one of the outstanding phenomena of eighteenth-century Germany. In its most general sense, the noun "public" denotes an entire community or population; usually, however, it is taken in a narrower meaning. It is essentially a commercial conception, a disregard of human beings as individuals, but rather a viewing of them purely as a body of purchasers. "Public" means an uncounted, unnamed, unspecified, unselected heap of human beings, to any one of whom a given article or service is available at his choice, on the same terms as to any other. You have a public when an identical dozen spoons, or yard of cloth, or ride in an omnibus, or admission to a theater—or copy of a book or song—can be bought at the identical price by anyone who wishes to pay for it.

A public is essentially anonymous: it consists of people who are not persons. An old-fashioned craftsman carefully considered the peculiar individual needs, tastes, and whims of his customer; but a merchant supplying a public has to make a shrewd guess as to what it might be that could catch the fancy of the greatest number of faceless strangers. The same impersonality can be seen in the merchant's attitude toward the objects in which he deals. The craftsman makes saddles or etchings, watches or sonatas—articles of use or beauty—and his own bodily skill, his personality, and his affections go into every one of them. The merchant, on the other hand, is interested primarily in sales; and the intrinsic nature of the things he sells is a side issue. He even calls them by an utterly characterless, empty word such as "goods" or "stock"; and a merchant too much in love with his own "goods" is generally adjudged insufficiently hardheaded or "businesslike."

Ample quantity of sales is important to all merchants, and to printer-publishers in particular, since that is what enables them to pay off their expensive tools and keep them in good repair. Large sales, too, permit merchants to keep the prices of their goods down to where they can be marketed at all. A publisher with good sense realizes that cultivated intellect, fine perceptions, or great special skill—such as that required for playing an instrument well—are qualities to be found in but few people. If he wants to sell his goods to a great number of buyers, it is clear that he cannot issue things that need those qualities for their proper understanding and enjoyment. Thus, with small but significant exceptions, published literature and music must tend to be cheaply accessible to commonplace minds, to put no strain on ordinary brains, to run in well-worn grooves and formulas, to be trifling. There is no special demon of corruption at work in this process: it is a necessary consequence of the commercial way of thought, a simple piece of elementary arithmetic.

The idea of a "public" is clearly repugnant to all traditional notions of nobility. A true nobleman is always conscious of his personal distinction, of his uniqueness as a soul. Moreover, it is in his relation to the creations of the mind and the spirit, such as works of art, that this uniqueness may be particularly well displayed. A nobleman's artistic possessions are intended to be reflections of his most personal sensibilities, of the fineness of his taste, and of his acumen in the patronage of craftsmen. It impairs his individuality to buy one of a thousand copies of a piece of jewelry or cabinetwork of which any random mob of moneyed boors might buy the other 999. It humiliates him to have his cultivated discriminations huddled amongst the superstitions of a herd of outsiders and degraded into a single lowly factor in a common denominator of mere crude purchasing power. Modern Americans cannot easily sympathize with this frame of mind, or even readily understand it. They may get an inkling of it by considering the well-dressed, fashionable woman who dreads nothing so much as seeing another woman wearing a replica of her expensive gown.

Yet the burghers, being merchants primarily, could hardly be expected to show much interest in any such proud attitude of reclusiveness. They could hardly be expected to despise the very process which gave them their own excuse for living. For them to sell identical books of poems or sheets of music to as many unassorted people as would pay for them was as proper and as honorable as to sell identical broom handles or lumps of cheese on the same basis. Publishers could claim that they were distributing art just as grocers were distributing food and cleanliness. And who will blame them, if, according to their lights, the art merchants tended more and more to promote those articles that they could sell the most of and the quickest? Sales and profits are the only possible mercantile evaluation. On the other hand, and conversely, a member of the "public" must be willing, and even eager, to identify his taste and thought with that of a multitude of others. He must enjoy reading and hearing and seeing what "everybody" else does. It must give him a feeling of security and justification to be one of a large group.

Cognate with music publishing is the institution of musical journalism. Active music lovers of the more intelligent kind became interested in musical goings-on in other cities and countries, and publishers became desirous of having an organ whereby they could have attention called to their new issues. Johann Adam Hiller was Leipzig's most prominent musical character during the 1760's. The son of a schoolmaster, he grew up into a talented, thoughtful, and industrious musician and became an organizer of choruses, a director of concerts, and in general the leading promoter of the whole new middle-class musical movement in

Leipzig. As a composer, he had already published a book of *Songs with Melodies for the Clavier;* and he was also to have an unusual significance in his writing for the stage. By 1766 the general interest in music was sufficiently widespread for him to feel impelled to get out his *Wöchentliche Nachrichten und Anmerkungen die Musik betreffend* (*Weekly News and Comment concerning Music*). It was one of the first true music-news periodicals ever issued, for previous vaguely comparable publications such as those of Mattheson and Scheibe had more of the character of learned pamphlets. In his manly, nonerudite, non-Frenchified German, Hiller discussed the newer musical manifestations from all parts of Germany and even from abroad. Almost every issue heralded, described, and criticized newly published compositions. In an issue of September 1768 he said:

> The most acceptable and best-known instrument among music lovers seems to be the clavier; therefore the quantity of things that has been written, printed, and engraved for it exceeds everything that music can show for itself in its other fields.
>
> . . . We may say here, without boasting or vanity, that the true spirit of clavier playing is properly to be found among the Germans and that consequently their works for this instrument deserve preference above any that have ever been written by foreigners.

He was right, substantially, though the word "ever" is a little strong.

Hiller could be irritated by the deliberate feminization of keyboard music that was going on. In his issue of June 13, 1768, he discussed a set of *Clavier Pieces for Ladies* by one J. F. W. Wenkel:

> It is an artifice that does not rightly appeal to us, when various authors say in the titles of their little works that they are written for females. Much poor stuff has been sold under such a heading, and the ladies will hardly admit to these authors that what is written for them must necessarily be poor. Then why did he etc. Perhaps because he found them easy, because they consisted of trifles such as minuets, polonaises, songs, and the like. Alas, there are plenty of male creatures whose taste is restricted to such frivolities.

12. CLAVIER PLAYING BECOMES LIGHTER, AND OFTEN MORE TRIVIAL

EVIDENTLY Hiller recognized an important trend: that as the practice of music expanded, it also became shallower. More and more people played, but with a flimsier, scantier musicianship. The thousands of girls who sang and fingered ditties at home were not expected to "bother their pretty little heads" with counterpoint and harmony. Signs of ambition or of intellectual strain were not supposed to render them attractive. It was enough that they could execute a few easy melodies with rudimentary accompaniments; and anyway, their fathers often had little use for anything else.

The spread of claviers was in itself, actually, a phase of this shallowing trend. The keyboard instruments are indeed the easiest on which to achieve a small plausible musical result. They do not present the perpetually acute problem of the stringed or wind instruments—namely, that of making the true pitch. A key marks it ready-made, and any infant can press down a light lever. It is true that a clavier must be tuned in advance, but the spread of the instrument among the minimally musical led to the curious consequence that the tuner and the player were more and more rarely the same person. It is hard to imagine the most primitive player of a fiddle or guitar who did not know how to pull up his own strings to their proper pitch, but among clavier tinklers this incompetence became the rule. The complication of the tempered tuning may have added to the difficulty.

For example, Herr Johann Caspar Goethe required outside help for tuning the small harpsichord which he had kept for his children before acquiring his big Friederici *Flügel*. As a learned doctor from the University of Giessen, as well as an Imperial Councilor and the possessor of a fortune of more than 100,000 florins, he considered it proper to keep his household account book in Latin. On January 28, 1755, he entered in it: "*pro cimbalo accommodando,* 24 kreuzer"; and again on April 11, 1764:

"*p. clavicimbalo temperando* 30 kr." His famous son Wolfgang, in his late memoirs—*Aus Meinem Leben* (*From My Life*)—recounted how, as a young man studying at Strassburg, he paid a visit to the home of an Alsatian clergyman in the village of Sesenheim and how the daughter of the house, at the request of her father, waited upon him with music. "She played a few things with a certain fluency, in the manner in which one usually hears it in the country, upon a clavier which the schoolmaster ought to have tuned long before if he had had the time." That was in 1771.

The problem of tuning became more acute as more and more tyros acquired claviers; and Barthold Fritz's book afore-mentioned, in which he listed his customers, was actually a volume of "Instructions [on] how to tune Claviers, Clavecins, and Organs according to a mechanical method, in all twelve keys equally cleanly . . ." "For there are persons," he said in his preface, "who live in the country and cannot always get hold of a tuning master. There are music lovers in cities who would like to undertake this exercise partly in order to save expense, and partly for their own satisfaction and for the confirmation of the science of music they have themselves acquired. Yes, there are a lot of teachers in cities who are no real organists, and who have never had instruction in proper tuning, but who ought to be able to tune their pupils' instruments before, during, and after their lessons." The remarks are dated 1756.

The art of tuning never did catch up with the sale of instruments, especially not after the pianoforte developed its tensions and complications. Normally, tuning became a special skill after the middle of the eighteenth century and a separate occupation in the nineteenth.

There were other ways in which the increased distribution of keyboards encouraged a slovenly musicality. For one thing, string and wind instruments were rarely played alone, but almost always together in some sort of ensemble. Now, the first prerequisite of ensemble playing is sharp rhythmic precision, and the keenest feeling of responsibility toward the prescribed note-values, since laxity in this respect will crack up any ensemble right in the first measure. But lone keyboard players, or those who merely accompany their own singing, can be as easygoing as they please about rhythm. They can plaster themselves at length, shamelessly, over notes that they fancy, and nonchalantly gulp away notes that are too hard for them; yet the injury to the music may not necessarily be fatal. They can make a freak out of a composition without actually cutting off its respiration. Solitary keyboard playing, if it is not aimed at a higher artistic achievement, is a cheap picnic for people unwilling or unable to acquire the firmer musical discipline.

Moreover, during the seventeenth and earlier eighteenth centuries a boy with the expectations of becoming a professional musician would, if he played an organ or harpsichord, begin early to learn to read a "figured bass." This meant that the keyboard part of most ensembles, when it represented an accompaniment, was written out merely as a single bass line. Under these bass notes were marked certain Arabic numerals indicating the exact nature of the harmony—without, however, specifying its disposition or its density. The figures gave the chords, but the player's own taste would have to tell him whether to make them thick or thin, open or close, broken or straight. Only a good musician could play a proper "thorough-bass" accompaniment. Furthermore, the art of embellishment had also formed an important part of a musician's education. In all the music of the period many tones were provided with ornamental modifying notes sometimes called "graces." These little notes were of varying grouping and rhythmical import, and each type of combination had its special designation and symbol—such as trill, mordent, or appoggiatura. The music of the day could hardly have been imagined without their livening effect. Some properties of the "graces" were unalterable, others were left to the discretion of the player; and here again, only a well-trained, good musician could execute them satisfactorily.

Female amateurs of mediocre talents could hardly be expected to master these complicated games. As more and more music came to be written and printed for them, the figured bass quickly became obsolete. It began to die out, except for professional training purposes, not long after 1760. The girls could not bother to figure out the figures: it was better to spoon-feed them all the actual notes they were supposed to play. Similarly, the "graces" began to lose their rigorous meaning: some of the symbols went out of use entirely, others came to be very loosely interpreted. The whole subject became less and less important. Karl Philipp Emanuel Bach in his *Essay on the Right Way to Play the Clavier,* published in 1753, devoted forty-five pages to the subject of embellishments; while fifty years later an instruction book would have been likely to dispose of the matter in a few paragraphs.

Musical style became lightened and simplified in other ways. The massive polyphonic weaves of the earlier years of the century were rapidly dying of discouragement. Serious musicians, of course, deplored this. F. W. Marpurg, a conservative musical scholar, in his treatise on the fugue, published in 1753–54, said: "The number of Protestant churches in which one can still hear fugues is not too great. How many church composers are there not who seem to have borrowed their taste from the Nicolini theater." (The reference is to a successful traveling Italian opera troupe of the time.) Hiller, too, in 1768, speaking of J. S. Bach, said: "It is to be regretted that the spirit of levity, which is so easily satisfied with a glittering exterior, does not permit the clavier players of the present day to devote themselves any more to his work as much as they ought." And later, speaking of Bach's and Handel's clavier works: "Of these compositions we have just mentioned we often hear amateurs say: 'They are too difficult, I don't like them.' " He quoted in a spirit of regret, of course.

We will say, in passing, that the mid-eighteenth-century shift of style need not necessarily impress us now as an absolute deterioration. We must be careful not to compare incomparables. The inane but occasionally pretty tunes that pleased average purchasers of "Musical Miscellanies" cannot fairly be set up, to their disadvantage, against superlative masterpieces such as the fugues of Bach or the choruses of Handel. We must think of them rather as bringing relief from the wooden, uninspired, polyphonic claptrap practiced by second- and third-rate German organists and cantors.

As the century wore on, the publishers controlled the composers and a loose horde of musical duffers controlled the publishers —a state of affairs much admired in many quarters under the name of "democracy." The cry went up increasingly for music that was "easy," and even musicians of attainments and ideals could not help but heed it. Johann Friedrich Reichardt, generous-minded enthusiast, a director and composer at the Royal Prussian Opera, the author of well-turned books on music, had written many collections of songs with clavier accompaniment. In Berlin in 1775 there appeared his *Songs for the Fair Sex,* and to its preface he added the following note:

> Because of the delicate eyes and small hands of the fair ones, I have written an occasional middle part in small notes, in order that they may all the more easily distinguish the notes to be sung from those that are intended only for the clavier; and again, in order that, if the pretty little hand cannot reach far enough, they may play only the voice part, and thus recognize much more easily which notes they may leave out . . .

A glance at these songs could lead one to think that even with the "small notes" they are already wading in the most transparent shoals of simplicity.

Some time later there came out Johann Wilhelm Hässler's clavier sonatas. Hässler was no genius, but a competent musician with his heart in the right place and anything but a commercialist. In fact, he struggled for many years to get rid of a profitable plush-cap factory that he had inherited, in order that he might devote his entire life to the fascinating art of tone. Hässler's title reads *Easy Sonatas for Clavier or Pianoforte,* and his preface to one series tells the affecting tale of his conversion. Up until then, he confessed, the greater part of his clavier compositions were usable by but a few people. True, before sending any manuscript to Breitkopf's, he had made a point of playing it to a few music lovers and connoisseurs, begging them "to indicate to me frankly any difficulties or other unpleasantness, so that they could still be altered for the benefit of my interessees"; and he was always told that everything was "right, good, and useful for everybody [*gemeinnützig*]." Therefore, it was really not his fault if his works contained difficulties for amateurs. From then on, however, he would make more sure: thenceforth one could "count on the true common usefulness of my future compositions. They are to be easy and pleasant, so that the beginner as well as the expert . . . may bring them forth without trouble and will certainly play them many times for pleasure."

Even in clavier compositions of greater pretensions than the minuets, polonaises, and ditties that were being so readily proliferated, the composers showed a strong tendency to drop into easy formulas of figuration. After 1750 all music rapidly took on a predominatingly homophonic character; that is, it consisted of one principal line, usually in the treble, supported by a purely harmonic accompaniment in the bass. This accompanying harmony often needed rhythmic animation, and that is where certain obvious little figures proved all too convenient. One that was especially favored was a device of spreading a three-tone chord over a four-note rhythm, by letting each of the two lower notes alternate successively with the upper, thus:

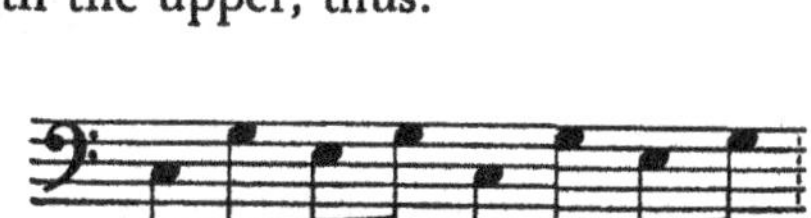

The composer Alberti is said to have made much of this simple pattern, and it was often called an "Alberti bass."

A still more primitive bass-figure was much indulged in, possibly by fingers that were even too clumsy for an Alberti bass. It consisted of a simple alternation of a note with its upper octave, thus:

Apparently, many lighter-minded amateurs who could achieve a tune with the right hand liked to keep drumming in that manner with the left hand on the same note for a good many measures before continuing the drone on another bass note. The Germans made up a slang word for this repetitious wiggling: they called it "*Murky*" (pronounced "moorky"). It had certainly been in vogue before the middle of the century, for the *Singende Muse* of 1736 contained several "*Murkys*" expressly so labeled. The word has no derivation; it is a couple of nonsense syllables that may have originated at some convivial occasion or in the mouth of a child. That silly-sounding name given to a barbarously reiterated bass might remind us modern Americans of something quite close to home: perhaps "*Murky*" could be regarded as a former incarnation of "boogiewoogie."

Indeed, the whole technique of keyboard playing underwent a profound change during the middle years of the century. The most evident feature of this development was a standardization of the use of the thumb. In earlier days the normal position of the hands did not include a place for the thumb upon the keys, that member being ordinarily supposed to hang loosely below. The thumb was not actually banned from use, but was regarded as an occasional convenient help in managing strained digital situations. The more resourceful and intricately polyphonic the music, the more such situations naturally occurred. The few fingerings left us by J. S. Bach and by François Couperin give us an inkling of those masters' free manipulation of the thumb. Ordinarily, continued progression along a scale line was effected by allowing the longer fingers to cross over the shorter: the fourth finger over the fifth, and the middle finger over either of its neighbors to the right or left.

Clearly, no great speed can be attained when the fingers have thus to step over one another. The new technique demanded a hand position further in from the edge of the natural—nowadays, white—keys, allowing the thumb to rest upon them. Continuity of scale progression was secured by passing the thumb under one or another of the middle fingers, or by passing one of the middle fingers over the thumb when proceeding in the opposite direction. Not only is this a smooth method of playing a shorter stretch of scale, but in this way the scheme of fingering can readily be arranged so that every scale note is played by the same finger in every successive octave. Thus is facilitated a rapid sweep of scale through several octaves, by one hand. The successive order of black and white keys is different for every one of the twelve major and twelve minor scales, and the most convenient fingering for each one was worked out and made into a norm. The same principle of thumb-underpassing was also applied to chords broken in a continuous line, the so-called "arpeggios."

Scales and arpeggios sweeping over larger areas of the keyboard are effective and pleasant, but they belong to a showier, lighter, and more exclusively homophonic style of music than the older German composers favored. J. S. Bach, for example, undoubtedly understood the value of the thumb, yet he set down few trans-octave scale or arpeggio passages in his works; and most of those that do occur—such, for instance, as those in the B-flat major and D major Preludes of Book I of the *Well-Tempered Clavier*—are written so as to be best executed with two hands.

It is not exactly known when the new fingering came in, nor what persons deserve the most credit for thinking it up. My guess is that those ingenious Italians, despite their relatively lesser interest in the keyboard, were here again the pioneers. The pieces of Domenico Scarlatti abound in single-hand scale and arpeggio passages covering ranges of considerably more than an octave—figures that could hardly be executed at anything approaching a suitable speed except by the passing under of the thumb.

A plausible period in which to look for the beginnings of the innovation would be the second quarter of the eighteenth century. So far as Germany is concerned, there appeared as early as 1749 a treatise entitled *The Theoretico-Practical Musician, "Part II containing a Methodical Guide to the Clavier that expounds a convenient, speedy, artful, and artful-appearing application of the fingers . . ."* The author was a Swabian clergyman who called himself P. C. Humanus, the name seemingly being a Latinistic false-face for *Hartung*. The book was printed in Nürnberg, in Bavaria, not at the time a music center of any great significance. Humanus favored the passing under of the thumb, gave the modern fingering for the C major scale, and called the thumb "1," the first finger, as Germans have always done subsequently, and not "o" or "x" as the English did. Not long afterward F. W. Marpurg in his *The Art of Playing the Clavier,* first published in Berlin in 1751, gives the modern thumb-under scale fingerings as a fundamental rule. On a later page he also notes the old step-over fingerings, but generally repudiates them except for practicing. Carl Philipp Emanuel Bach in his well-known *Essay on the Right Way to Play the Clavier,* appearing two years later, also gives the modern fingerings and notes the old. Let us reflect that by the time a precept gets into an instruction book, it has probably been practiced for some time.

The important thing for us to consider is not the invention of the new fingering, but the fact of its having been erected into a standard. After a while scales and arpeggios became the basic shapes of all clavier study—not only with reference to their tonal meaning, but even more for the sake of their kinesthetic satisfaction: that is, the speed and smoothness to which they could be cultivated. The new fingerings made for fleetness: a talented, limber-fingered student—aiming to be a professional musician—can soon learn to produce a succession of sparkling "runs" that give much pleasure, if of a superficial kind, to many listeners. A player, however, who concentrates his efforts upon the fluency of pre-fingered scales and arpeggios and their many variants and derivatives, including the above-mentioned Alberti-bass-like figures, will inevitably tend to neglect the much more taxing art of playing polyphonically. Keeping four, three, or even two independent voices distinct and coherent, even though at a slower speed than that at which one can play "runs," requires a high mental grasp of music, as well as many resources of unstandardized finger-squirming and shifting. It is a much more difficult task than dashing off scale and broken-chord figures, and much less cheaply rewarding in approval on the part of average hearers.

Soon it was not merely the girl tyros, but the professional clavier players, who found Bach's and Handel's compositions "too hard." Many new music publishers sprang up in the Germanies during the 1770's and 1780's; business looked good, but practically none of them attempted to print as much as a single item of the vast quantities of Sebastian Bach's works that had been rotting in manuscript form for half a century. Not until 1800 did publishers excavate the *Well-Tempered Clavier* in its entirety. When brought to light, it fell upon an uncomprehending world; and even for most trained professionals it was an archaeological restoration rather than a resurrection. Meanwhile, musicians and music lovers of the more cultivated sort beguiled themselves with sonatas, rondos, and variations whose light charms consisted of symmetrical tunes swathed in facile, stylized figuration.

There remains for us to remark a change in the customary notation of keyboard music. Until well after the middle of the century, in Germany, the treble portion of keyboard compositions was generally written in the so-called soprano clef, namely the C clef upon the first line. After 1750, however, clavier composers increasingly tended to use the G clef for this purpose. It was a practical innovation in some ways, since it assimilated the clavier notation to that of the violin, the flute, and the oboe. In any case, it became the rule by the last decade of the century and has remained so ever since. As late as 1786 Hässler announced that the first series of his *Easy Sonatas* would be "printed in both clefs" so as to increase their "common usefulness," as he loved to call it.

The exalting wine of music was now being served to increasingly large quantities of people, but that could be accomplished only at the price of a heavy dilution of its strength and a deterioration of its flavor. Music teaching, clavier teaching in particular, as it was widely practiced in the later eighteenth century, partook of the prevailing paltriness. Most of those bungling burgher daughters had little capacity for musical discipline, and their most successful teachers were those who could share the mediocrity of their pupils' talents and aims.

We have had previous occasion to refer to Friedrich Wilhelm Marpurg, the noted Berlin critical and didactic writer about music. In 1750 he published a collection of little essays, whimsical and otherwise, which he entitled *Der Critische Musicus an der Spree* (*The Critical Musician on the Spree*)—the Spree being the stream that flows through Berlin. In piece No. 2 he gives an ironical picture of music lessons of the day by presenting a letter purporting to come from a young lady. Under a date of March 11, 1749, "she" begins by explaining that "not only do I think very highly of music, but am having myself instructed in it with vehement ardor." She proceeds to give a startling, colorful description of her singing lessons at the hands of "our" sexton, thus:

> But I am not letting things rest with mere singing; I go in for the clavier with great pleasure and mighty good progress. My dear papa got me quite a fine one at a certain auction for 15 groschen and 6 pfennigs. A rather clever suburban organist from a nearby town is teaching me how to play it. We have him come over to us by accommodation post every couple of weeks, and he gives me a half-hour lesson

every trip. He isn't at all expensive, and it is only about every month that we have to pay him 2 or 3 ducats. Every year my dear mama presents him with a few pecks of oatmeal. Even if I had no inclination for music, this man would be able to arouse one in me. He is very modest and for a man of middle-class ancestry he knows very well how to behave toward people. He always sits at my left side when I play and never forgets, after the lesson, to make me a reverence from a certain English dance. He marks all the notes with letters so as not to trouble my head needlessly, even though I am now beginning to recognize the first and the second line on the C clef. But the G clef in the treble is something he cannot abide at all. He says the thing is beginning to be introduced these evil days by a few musical free-thinkers, and that the grandfather of his former teacher was a sworn enemy of it. The choice of fingering he leaves, as a trifle, to my discretion, though he would like to see the two thumbs banned from the positions and he often gets worked up talking against the present-day clavierists because of their frequent use of these. Since he is very unselfish and has no desire to hold me back for two or three years, he discards all ornaments and at the same time maintains that they hinder speed in playing. Moreover, he gives me hope that I will be able very soon to begin the latest arias; meanwhile I have at least a half a dozen chorales in my fingers in addition to the *Blacksmith's Courante,* the *Alley-Ballad* [*Gassenhauer*], and two Polish dances, and consequently am prepared for difficult pieces. I must not forget to tell you that my cheerful master usually carries a mouth organ with him, with which he often accompanies my tones, so as to give me some idea of concertos, as he says. This brief sketch of my musical efforts, my dear Mr. Critic, can convince you sufficiently that the minds of our women are not all so insensitive and that they are not busied all the time in the smokehouse with bacons and hams. We are just as well able as your duskiest foreign ladies to use our hands to animate an instrument or to beat time. . . .

Of course, this is a caricature, but a good caricature is also a good likeness. Perhaps all the above absurdities did not actually coexist in any one course of lessons; yet the battered instrument, the incompetent, obsequious old fogy of a teacher, and the fatuous dullard of a pupil all have a vivid ring of truth.

Goethe as an elderly man, writing his memoirs, recalled the clavier lessons of his childhood. In Part I, Book 4 of *Aus Meinem Leben* he first speaks of some rather unimaginative drawing lessons to which he and his sister had been subjected. He continues:

The project of having us instructed in music had long been deliberated, and it too was carried out at about this time: the final impulse to it might deserve some mention. It had already been agreed that we were to learn the clavier; there was, however, still some dispute concerning the choice of a teacher. Finally I came one day by chance into the room of one of my young friends just as he was taking a clavier lesson, and found the teacher to be a most charming man. For each finger of the right and the left hand he had a nickname with which he designated it, in the jolliest fashion, whenever it was to be used. The black and the white keys were likewise pictorially named; the very tones themselves appeared under figurative names. The members of this colorful company were then worked into a gay interplay. Fingering and meter seemed to become quite easy and clear, and while the pupil was roused to the best of humors, everything proceeded as famously as could be.

As soon as I came home, I appealed to my parents please to take this thing seriously and to give us that incomparable man as a clavier master. They still hesitated somewhat, they made inquiries; nothing derogatory was heard of this teacher, nor indeed anything especially favorable. I had meanwhile told my sister about all these merry appellations, and we could hardly wait for our lessons; we carried our point, and the man was engaged.

We started with note-reading; and as no fun seemed to be forthcoming from this, we consoled ourselves with the hope that when we got to the clavier, when we should come to work with our fingers, the playful atmosphere would begin to take its sway. Neither keyboard nor fingering, however, seemed to provide occasion for any metaphors. The black and white keys remained as dry as the notes with their marks upon, and between, the five lines, and not a syllable was more to be heard of a "thumbling" or "pointerling" or "goldfinger"; the man kept as straight a face with his dry instruction as he had previously with his dry joking. My sister reproached me bitterly, saying that I had deceived her; and she really thought the whole thing was a mere invention of mine. I myself was dazed and learned but little, even though the man went to work systematically enough; for I was still expecting the former jests to make their appearance, and tried to put my sister off from one day to the next. Yet they failed to come, and I would never have been able to explain the puzzle to myself if an accident had not solved it for me.

One of my playmates entered during the middle of the lesson, and all at once all the pipes from the well of humor were opened: the thumblings and pointerlings, the crawlers and wigglers, as he used to call the fingers, the little *faxies* and *gaxies,* as for instance he called the notes F and G, and the *feexies* and *geexies* as he called F-sharp and G-sharp, were suddenly at hand again and cut the most amusing capers. My young friend could not stop laughing and was delighted that one could learn so much in so merry a way. He swore he would give his parents no peace until they gave him such an excellent man as a teacher.

And so, early enough, the way to two arts was opened to me according to the principles of a newer theory of education—at random, without any conviction that a native talent could advance me in them further. Everyone must know how to draw, maintained my father . . . Moreover, he urged it upon me more seriously than he did music, which, on the other hand, he recommended preferably to my sister. Indeed, he kept her at the keyboard for a considerable portion of the day apart from her lesson time.

Young Goethe was probably nine or ten at the time of this episode, we may plausibly assume, thus dating the "newer theory of education" from the decade after 1750. The teacher's way of bribing the dull or the uninterested with foolery seems to be approved nowadays by a still newer theory of education. The man's identity has been ascertained: he was Johann Andreas Bismann, choir director of St. Peter's Church in Frankfurt.

In many families there were special qualms about letting girls take lessons from male teachers: female pedagogues were called in, but the chances of finding competent musicians among them were even less. Music lessons, however well adapted to their frail aptitudes, were often a trial to pupils. Clearly, many girls, despite their sentimental propensities, approached the clavier from no irresistible inner impulse. All too often it was their aspiring, ambitious parents who held them to it. Ladies in their later days sometimes voiced complaints about the irksome lessons and practicing, and the unpleasant personalities of the music teachers of their youth. We will only recount the pitiful prayer which Frau v. Ebner-Eschenbach remembered having said as a child: "Dear God, make it so that Frau Krämer won't come today." Frau Krämer was the clavier instructor.

13. THE CLAVIER FAVORS THE MUSIC OF "HUMANITY"

Serious older musicians such as Hiller and Marpurg regretted the neglect into which the older style of polyphonic music had fallen; but in general, of course, the current situation was satisfactory to the people for whose benefit it had developed, namely the rising, multiplying class of merchants, professional men, and lower officials. Far from deploring the simplification and shallowness into which music was moving, they regarded it as a beneficent process.

The development coincided with the burghers' growing resentment against the privileges of the nobility. Once upon a time, noble ranks and privileges had represented social duties and responsibilities; but now so many administrative functions were assumed by people of middle-class background, and so much of the countries' liquid wealth was in their hands, that patented rank seemed more and more like a meaningless fiat, an affirmation of a superiority that had become mythical.

It was natural, then, for burghers to emphasize their intrinsic worth as human beings against the arbitrary, purely traditional arrogance. "The rank is but the guinea's stamp, the man's the gold for all that," they would have said enthusiastically could they have anticipated the Scottish poet. "Humanity" became a heartening slogan; by mouthing it, a wealthy, educated, public-spirited cotton manufacturer could rightfully tell himself that he was a better man than the gracefully mannered ne'er-do-well son of an impoverished baron. "Humanity" may have been a mere stilt on which an able but slighted class of people could strut; yet at its best it meant a striving for the general enhancement of all mental, moral, and emotional capacities. It meant the urge toward skill and knowledge, toward betterment of social relations, toward the most sympathetic awareness of all human feelings: the "fullness of the heart."

The word "humanity" connotes that which brings men together rather than that which separates them; the adjective "common" is readily paired with it. The melody and harmony that could be readily shared by many people could be considered the music of humanity, the right music. It was a persuasive thought—especially for those who were gifted with but an average ear and had not bothered to cultivate it very intensively. The idea of "commonness" did not everywhere strike people as a moral gravitation toward a lowest level, as a mean cry of "give me the cheapest": it could be an ideal of brotherhood for generous minds. We have seen how the good ex-plush-cap-manufacturer Hässler recommended the "common usefulness" of his own sonatas; and fine, well-connected musicians such as J. A. P. Schulz and the aforementioned Reichardt could, on the strength of a feeling for "humanity," take an especial pride in having devoted much of their talent to composing the thinly accompanied popular songs for which they became best known.

"Liberty" was another slogan that powerfully elevated the German burghers' dispositions. Perhaps, in practice, "liberty" often meant no more than a desire to pursue commercial schemes without bureaucratic hindrances, or a longing of little tradesmen's wives to wear finery resembling that of a well-born lady; but in its highest ethical aspects "liberty" meant an unfettering of all creative impulses, an infinite soaring of thought, a hatred of slavery and bigotry. "Expression" was the musical correlative of "liberty." The incalculable interplay of loud and soft in endless gradations, of excitation and depression, of severity and gentleness, was a picture of the soul unchained from a sterile logic or a lifeless convention. "Feeling," "humanity," "liberty"—all these sweet words of the time had their faithful musical reflections.

Many German burghers enjoyed the writings of Jean Jacques Rousseau: his trend of thought fortified their own. Rousseau was a professional musician of sorts, and his views on music had prestige if not authority. He was, indeed, an outspoken champion of simplicity: the single line of vocal melody, scantily accompanied, was the most natural, and therefore the best, of music, according to him. For the majestic structures, as well as the intricate devices, of a preceding generation he had nothing but hard words. In his *Dictionnaire de musique,* published in 1764, under the article *"Accompagnement,"* he denounced what he deemed the inconsistencies of conventional figured-bass; but as early as 1753, in his *Lettre sur la Musique Française,* he had already thrown down the glove to all polyphony, all "fugues, imitations, double designs, and other arbitrary, purely conventional beauties which have hardly any merit save that of a difficulty overcome." But when the contrapuntal structures became truly complex, he angrily called them "difficult sillinesses [*sottises difficiles*] that the ear cannot endure and reason cannot justify; they are evidently the remains of barbarism and bad taste that only persist, like the portals of our Gothic churches, to the shame of those who have had the patience to construct them."

Rousseau's famous paradigm of education, *Emile,* first appeared in 1762. The author condescended to include in it a section on the education of "woman," who, he says, "exists only by reference to man; she is made to please him and to obey him, so nature has willed it." With so many who have had God in their pockets, we have to have a little indulgence for one who has "Nature" in his. Rousseau built a little model whom he called "Sophie" and proceeded to limn her verbal portrait:

> Sophie has natural talents; she feels them and she has not neglected them, but not having been in a position to put much art into their cultivation, she has contented herself with using her pretty voice to sing in tune and with taste, her feet to walk lightly, easily, and with grace, to make a reverence in all sorts of situations without embarrassment or awkwardness. Otherwise, she has had no singing master save her father, no dancing mistress save her mother; an organist of the neighborhood has given her a few lessons on the harpsichord in accompanying, which she has since cultivated by herself. At first she only thought to have her hand appear to advantage upon the lower keys; thereupon she found that the sharp, dry sound of the harpsichord made the sound of the voice sweeter. Little by little she became aware of harmony; finally, in growing up, she began to feel the charms of expression and to love music for itself. But it is a taste rather than a talent; she is completely unable to decipher a tune from the notes.

This pretty but somewhat insipid picture seemed very attractive to many middle-class people, males in particular. It is true, the illiteracy that enchanted Rousseau was a little hard for the education-loving Germans to swallow; yet on the whole the paragraph made encouraging reading. A German burgomaster, fiscal agent, physician, or wholesale coffee merchant now had a famous French philosopher's and musician's assurance that his daughter, suiting a few fragile chords to a ditty from *Songs for the Family Circle,* or playing a slight minuet from a "Musical Miscellany," was the rightest of the right, an arrow point of progress, aimed at the target of the time-spirit.

14. CONNOISSEURS AND AMATEURS ARE INFLUENTIAL. CONCERTS MAY BE MEETINGS OR SHOWS

IT WOULD BE UNFAIR to say that ten thousand young females playing rudimentary accompaniments to easy ditties on ten thousand clavichords, harpsichords, and pianofortes constituted the whole of German middle-class musical life. There did, indeed, exist a small minority of persons who, without being professional musicians, were possessed of a much keener-than-average musical skill, knowledge, and cultivation, and whose proficiency on an instrument allowed them to tackle compositions of more than elementary pretensions. Some were men in government service, or members of the learned professions, whose musical talents may have helped them through their university careers; some were the more gifted women whose intrinsic devotion to music drove them to continue playing and singing even after marriage.

These people formed a well-defined little group, and they were given the stock name of "*Kenner und Liebhaber*," meaning "connoisseurs and amateurs." During the third quarter of the century many composers, through their publishers, began to address themselves consciously to this group: in particular, C. P. E. Bach wrote several sets of sonatas thus superscribed. The *Kenner und Liebhaber* were not numerous, yet they exerted influence; and in a way, their judgments were a guide to the aspirations of the less cultivated.

Their sway had an even deeper significance. Despite their business initiative, their keenness of intellect, and their superabundance of humane sentiment, the German burghers were somehow deficient in political sense. Their sons could sometimes rise to high official administrative positions in advisory capacities; yet they seem never to have entertained the ambition to wrest from the decadent princes, to whom they were mostly subject, the right to make the laws under which they had to live. Perhaps their disunity discouraged them: it would have required half a dozen revolutions organized simultaneously—in Saxony, Prussia, the Palatinate, and elsewhere—to achieve any lasting result. The inhabitants of the smaller principalities, too, were paralyzed by the consciousness of their obscurity and provincialism, and their remoteness from the large European centers of power. After the Bastille fell, most of the German *bourgeoisie* felt a mighty thrill of sympathy for the French revolutionists in their early years' struggle against the *ancien régime*—yet ultimately they did little about it, save to spout some brave talk. Some one said later: "The Germans prefer lectures on the Kingdom of Heaven to the Kingdom itself."

Delight in emotional orgies, in sentimental ecstasies for their own sakes, diverted many a good head from the plotting of practical political gains. At the end of the century many Germans were beginning to be proud of constituting "the land of poets and thinkers." Much revolutionary ardor and enterprise in Germany vaporized itself in lofty poetry, precarious idealist metaphysics, scientific speculation, humanitarian sentiment, freemasonry—and music.

Music formed, for many fine spirits, an especially good moral equivalent for action. For them it was, indeed, no mere entertainment: rather, it was a high adventure that could not be dulled by a partner's defection; it was a world that could be conquered without the infliction of suffering and without compromise with rivals; a Heaven that could be built right here and now without thought to the sinfulness of men. Poetry, drama, fiction, and philosophy, too, were beams to a better world; but they had to use language, the tool of reason, and thus give reason the opportunity of repudiating them as unreal or untrue. What language, however, could assail the truth of music?

The *Kenner und Liebhaber* played a leading role in the establishment of an atmosphere favorable to music—an atmosphere in which it was treated with profound respect, sometimes even with a sort of religious reverence. These people were mostly well-to-do, learned, or the holders of government positions, and their bents could seem exemplary to countless other members of the middle class, even to some who had no great ear for tones. In Germany of the later eighteenth century, and for three or four generations thereafter, music, especially wordless instrumental music, was a more serious concern to more people than it has ever been anywhere before or since. The great German composers from Bach to Brahms merely are the tallest, stoutest timbers towering over a thick forest and a rank undergrowth that grew with them, all out of the same nutrient soil.

Any single *Kenner* or *Liebhaber* might have tended to feel lonely with his pursuit. Clearly, he felt the urge to associate with others of his kind, to make music together and talk about it, to "musicize"—as the Germans call it—for mutual pleasure and edification. Such regularly meeting groups of music lovers, which may have included a few professionals for stiffening, had already been formed during the seventeenth century. At the time, any mental activity worthy of the slightest respect seemed most properly dressed in a Latin name, and the meetings were mostly called *"collegia musica."* Sometimes they were called "musical academies." At first they were strictly private affairs, but in the more progressive German towns early in the eighteenth century *collegia musica* began to be held in larger rooms and projected to less carefully assorted listeners. For instance, numbers of Leipzig university students—variously proficient as fiddlers, pipers, or clavierists—used to convene regularly to play together at certain taverns. One such group met at Enoch Richter's coffeehouse, another at Zimmermann's hostelry, the ordinary customers sipping beer and puffing their long pipes while they listened. Usually the performers came together twice a week, from four to six in the afternoon. The young men played for fun and for the good of their souls, but apparently also for emolument or the hope thereof. The *collegia* were an advantage to the taverns, for during the times of the fairs many strangers as well as residents were attracted by them. Undoubtedly, Richter and Zimmermann assured the permanence of their interesting house-feature by giving the young men free meals and, possibly, a small honorarium. Then, as now, students "worked their way" through their education. Many interesting new concertos and suites were played on these occasions, and sometimes singers joined the instrumentalists for festival cantatas. The music must have been quite good, for we find that the fastidious Johann Sebastian Bach condescended, for nine years, beginning 1729, to be the regular leader of one of these *collegia,* the one at Zimmermann's. Incidentally, these *collegia* were invariably stag: "nice" women did not enter taverns in those days.

Hamburg also supported a *collegium musicum,* from 1721 on. It may have been somewhat more solemnly conducted than those in Leipzig, for it was under the direction of Georg Philipp Telemann, the city's director of church music. Regular performances of elaborate vocal and instrumental works were undertaken; however, sanctimonious voices were raised against the appearance of church personnel in a tavern, and so Telemann's music makers moved their activities into the building used by the city militia for its exercises, the *Drillhaus*. Admission was charged, and soon Telemann offered his patrons the purchasable luxury of printed programs and cantata texts.

In 1743 thirty-two musical Leipzigers, half of them players and half listeners, came together at a private home to organize a new musical group. There were students among them—but by then Latinizing pretensions were beginning to seem somewhat old-fashioned, and they called their enterprise "Great Concert." Businessmen ran the little institution, and it was occasionally called "Merchants' Concert." The bookseller Gleditsch was the first moving spirit, while later on Gottfried Benedict Zehmisch, a tobacconist, took the executive lead. The merchants contributed twenty thalers a year to the association, paid off the musicians, invited their own guests, and solicited suitable new members. Presently the thing grew and the meetings had to move to the Three Swans—again, an inn—where there was more room. Sometimes as many as two hundred persons came to attend the performances there. The "Great Concert" had a rather different atmosphere from the older *collegia,* since its meetings were less like collegiate stag parties and more like polite family parties: women were welcomed; and when they came with the men of their households, admission was free to them. The "Great Concert" suffered vicissitudes, interruptions, and reorganizations; but eventually it moved to a suitable hall in the Clothiers' House—the *Gewandhaus*—where it became Leipzig's most important regular social-and-musical event, and one of the most celebrated, persistent musical institutions in the world.

Berlin's burgherly musical association started in 1749; it was called "Music Exercising Society" and consisted of both amateurs and professionals. Among the latter, the organist Saks was the directing force. The group met at his house in the Brüderstrasse on Saturday afternoons at five or six, with the aim of performing "the latest and most select overtures, symphonies, and trios." Guests were brought to listen and guest musicians also performed; after a few years the meetings became so crowded that they were moved to the City of Paris Hotel and admission tickets had to be printed.

Wealthy, long-established citizens of Frankfurt had likewise organized a private *collegium musicum,* with Georg Philipp Telemann at its head, as early as 1716. But soon there was another, less exclusive one; inevitably, it moved to the hall of the "Great Emporium" and then to the premises of Mr. Johannes Scharff, the caterer.

Other types of musical performance flourished, not based on the association of *Kenner und Liebhaber* with professionals. Cities like Frankfurt and Leipzig, which had regular fairs—or like Hamburg, which harbored a perpetual floating commercial population —were regularly visited in time-honored fashion by itinerant jongleurs of various sorts: puppet shows, medicine shows, rope walkers, and exhibitors of strange animals and strange machines. Some of these shows consisted partly of music; at any rate, musical performances more or less allied to this traffic were increasingly given as the eighteenth century wore on. Certain ones probably had genuine musical merit, but frequently they were on a stunt basis. Often they were spoken of as "virtuoso concerts." Older twentieth-century Americans, former frequenters of vaudeville houses, would be readily familiar with their physiognomy: musical sister-acts, family acts, exploitation of foreignness or of physical defects such as blindness, presentation of unusual or tricky specialties—all added to a core of music that was easy to take. For example, we read in a Hamburg paper dated April 19, 1727, of a concert to be given by a "celebrated" horn player, at the *Drillhaus*. "He will perform, solo, artfully, on two horns simultaneously, in a manner hitherto unknown and surpassing all human understanding." By June 20 of the same year this nameless marvel was barking his act in similar verbiage in a Frankfurt journal. On May 14, 1755, the Hamburg *Drillhaus* was expected to witness two Italians singing "the latest arias and duets," with the added inducement that "for the greater pleasure of those present, six beautiful painted landscapes will be raffled off among them. Should attendance be very numerous, there will be eight such items." On November 18, 1777, Frankfurt citizens could read in their public prints that "Mlle. Perisse, born in Corsica, 17 years old, 7 feet 1 inch tall, for which reason she may rightfully be called a giantess, and who is even more to be admired for her high, exceptional voice, will have the honor today for the first time of offering the august public a number of great vocal and instrumental concerts." Later in the century we hear about Jakob Scheller, a fiddler who amused many audiences by imitating chickens, cats, and cranky old women on his instrument. Modestly, he advertised himself: "One God, one Scheller!"

Instruments alleged to be new were rated as a special attraction. On September 13, 1739, Frankfurters were summoned to a great concert of vocal and instrumental music in which, among other things, there would be performed "a concerto for a peculiar kind of mouth organ, with other instruments, composed by Mr. Telemann." In the middle of the century there were public exhibitions of a "Gamba-clavier," a "new" keyboard instrument in which the strings are activated by mechanically induced bowstrokes. (It had been known for a hundred and fifty years before.) Furthermore, we hear of demonstrations of a *"Verrillon"*—a set of musical glasses that were not to be rubbed, but struck by cork hammers—and of other "new" instruments now difficult to identify, such as *"Hand-bassetel," "Cälisoncini,"* and *"Salterio."* It was all a phase of the burgeoning interest in mechanisms, a manifestation of "enlightenment" and "progress."

It had been known since the dawn of time that musically talented persons normally manifest their gifts early in childhood, yet it was in the eighteenth century that considerable numbers of naïve burghers could be found able and willing to pay money to see the evidences of this fundamental fact. A Hamburg newspaper of September 17, 1736, announced the final concert of "three excellent musical boys," the Kröner brothers, again at the *Drillhaus;* they played violin and pleased so well that they played again the following year. A Frankfurt paper, on April 17, 1742, reported that a "ten-year-old virtuosus on the violin" was being requested to give another concert; and on April 22, 1756, that "a child of six years, of the female sex . . . will perform publicly on the violin." On November 20, 1764, still in Frankfurt, we have an early, if not the earliest, encounter with a species of name-calling that has survived with obnoxious persistence until the present day, to wit: "Production of a musical child prodigy [*Wunderkind*] of ten years and two months, who will offer nine different feats [*Kunststücke.*]" The sentimentalism of the age encouraged drooling over children.

It was in the year 1763 that Leopold Mozart, "high-princely Salzburg chapelmaster," took his two gifted children, Maria Anna, aged twelve, and Wolfgang, aged seven, on a grand European tour, to show them off for profit. Kings and dukes were his main targets, but he was not indisposed also to let the infants earn him a few worthy bourgeois dollars between courts. The Mozarts came to commercial Frankfurt late in August. They were a success and made a number of appearances; their "positively the last concert" was announced for August 30. Among his various remarkable harpsichord feats, little Wolfgang was billed "to completely cover the keyboard, or manual, with a cloth and play upon the cloth as well as if he had the keyboard before his eyes." It is a most revealing claim. Anyone with even a rudimentary experience of musical practice knows that a person who needs to guide his hands upon an instrument by means of his eyes cannot really be said to know how to play it at all. Else how could he play while looking at his notes? Yet father Leopold was right in assuming that there were plenty of aspiring middle-class simpletons to be gulled by that stunt.

It must not, however, be supposed that the virtuosos advertised as the center of interest in this type of concert were ever expected to entertain their audiences for the entire evening. Always, an ensemble of some kind, often an orchestra, was planned as a background to the soloist: to take up the slack of initial inattention by starting the proceedings off with an overture or symphony movement and to play the focal attraction's accompaniments. Subsidiary soloists were also common. Moreover, traveling virtuosos sometimes arranged to perform within the frame of the regular concert societies in such cities as had them. A little-known performer could launch himself thus with a certain prestige, if not much profit; if he pleased his audience, he might then arrange another concert on his own account and risk—which might in that case be all the better attended.

In general, virtuoso concerts were considered to be on a lower plane than the events staged by locally well-sponsored, permanent musical organizations. They were understood to deal in cheaper effects and to make less appeal to *Kenner und Liebhaber*. Moreover, their franker money-gaining purpose constituted a strong ethical detriment in the minds of the more learned, more "idealistic" citizens.

Thus, during the latter half of the eighteenth century, middle-class townspeople became thoroughly familiar with the habit of attending public musical performances in return for an admission fee. The older words *"collegium musicum"* and "academy" went out of use, and such events were generally called "concerts," as they have been ever since.

Concerts were clearly a middle-class institution. In former days a burgher might possibly have been able to hear skilled execution of complex music either in church or—if he were so exceptionally lucky—as a nobleman's invited guest. Now he was free to buy himself entrance to a more or less professional concert for a moderate sum of money, just as he could buy a bolt of ribbon at a dry-goods store. Despite the "idealists," music became, to a considerable extent, an article of commerce. Here again we see the formation of an anonymous "public."

The very admission prices to concerts exposed their middle-class nature. Earlier in the century, in Frankfurt, 15 kreutzers was charged as a basic admission fee to a regular subscription concert; but by the late 1770's the average rate was 1 florin 12 kreutzers—that is, 72 kreutzers. Heavily touted or specially recommended virtuosos often charged higher prices. The directors of the Leipzig *Gewandhaus* concerts, in 1781, fixed the tariff for single concerts at 12 groschen—that is, ½ reichsthaler, equivalent to about 54 kreutzers. Now, in the earlier days of the century Christian Ludwig, Margrave of Brandenburg, had spent as much as 48,945 thalers on his music in a single year. Leopold of Anhalt-Cöthen was a rather minor prince, yet the group of eighteen musicians over whom he set Sebastian Bach cost him about 2000 thalers annually; while Count Kayserling, the Russian envoy at Dresden, thoroughly appreciative of the same Bach's superlative abilities, was happy to pay him 100 louis d'or—about 600 thalers—for a single set of harpsichord variations. It would be difficult to think of those lords dribbling away their expenditures for music a thaler or two at a time, or to imagine them habitually visiting a tavern hall to sit next to a random haberdasher at a potluck performance.

At the same time, a thaler ticket to a concert would have been a crazy extravagance for vast multitudes of the population. Drovers and servant girls, porters, coachmen, and laundresses would hardly care to squander a week's wages to be present at a performance which, neither in form nor in content, was calculated to appeal "to the likes of them." Concerts were for one-thaler citizens, not for one-hundred-louis-d'or gentry or three-pfennig folk.

However, in the latter half of the century, in a few localities, "enlightenment" and "humanity" had begun to round off a few of the sharpest edges of orthodox class segregation; for in commercial Leipzig, at least, noble individuals did occasionally come to the public meetings of the citizenry. A man named Riemer, the secretary and minute chronicler of the doings of the "Great Concert" or "Merchants' Concert," set down with painstaking snobbery every occasion on which Count von Brühl or some other noble personage condescended to grace the performances with his august presence.

15. "HERE THEY HAVE PIANO-FORTES EVERYWHERE"

IN THE AUTUMN of 1777 the twenty-one-year-old Wolfgang Mozart set out to seek a better fortune than the irksome conditions of his native Salzburg afforded him. His solicitous father could not come with him this time, being tied down by duties at home, so it was his mother who had to accompany the young man to watch over his health and morals. Paris was the goal of this journey, but several important intermediate stations were to be taken in. On December 28, Frau Mozart wrote to her husband from Mannheim:

> Wolfgang is highly regarded everywhere; but he plays very differently than he does at Salzburg, because here they have pianofortes everywhere and he knows how to handle these so incomparably that nobody has ever heard the like; in one word, everybody who hears him says that his equal is not to be found . . .

We have thus far insisted on identifying the progress of the keyboard instruments with that of the middle classes, but Mannheim was certainly the last place in which to look for a burgherly atmosphere. It was the capital and residence of the ruler of a domain known as the Palatinate (*Pfalz*); and since this prince was one of those to whom was vouchsafed the exalted, but slightly decayed, privilege of casting a vote for a Holy Roman Emperor whenever a new one should be required, he was called the "Elector Palatine" (*"Kurfürst von der Pfalz"*). The reigning Elector's name was Karl Theodor. His last predecessor but one had been so statesmanlike as to marry a Tuscan princess who had brought with her a large pile of inherited Medici wealth; in fact, she was a sister of Prince Ferdinand, Cristofori's patron. At her own death, in 1743, she had left behind great quantities of cash, jewelry, and real estate aggregating 15,000,000 florins, now Karl Theodor's property. The lady had already earmarked a substantial portion of her fortune for musical and dramatic purposes; and she seems to have secured it by some kind of "spendthrift clause," so that apparently not even an Elector Palatine could succeed in diverting it to palaces, armies, stables, or mistresses. Perhaps the string to it was held at the other end by the Vatican.

Karl Theodor kept a magnificent court, all correctly imitation-French in language and ceremony. In 1745–46 the *Pfalz* numbered about 300,000 inhabitants, and during that year the ruler's "state" cost him 389,839 florins. Of this sum, 80,000 florins were said to have been devoted to his opera. Every last court stipendiary, from the Lord High Chamberlain down to the sauerkraut stewardess, was dependent on the Elector's grace and bounty, while the rest of Mannheim lived on what the court people spent.

We could imagine Karl Theodor aggressively conservative, if not archaic, in his ideas and tastes. No doubt he was so, on the main issues; yet we find him carried away by the strong intellectual and cultural currents of his time, most of which were of middle-class origin, and fundamentally hostile to his pretensions. For example, he took a great fancy to Voltaire, invited him to spend weeks at Mannheim, had him read *Candide* aloud, and kept on corresponding with him for years. The Elector, brought up by Jesuits, was notably intolerant in religious matters; nevertheless, he had the portrait of the famous anticlerical deist who had said *"Ecrasez l'infame!"* hung as an ornament over the entrance to his library. Like the princely cooks, Voltaire was a Frenchman; perhaps that was what gave him his invincible prestige.

On the other hand, pressure was piling up for the movement favoring the use of a purified German language as a vehicle for fine literature and drama. Until the 1760's, German in Mannheim had been the vulgarest of jargons, suitable only for menials and petty shopkeepers. But now we find Karl Theodor collecting German writers, decreeing the organization of a "German Association," dismissing his long-established French comedy, and sponsoring the uncertain experiment of a serious opera in German. He was morally incapable of not climbing on these middle-class band wagons: in one chamber of his heart the Elector, like other "benevolent" despots of his time, could no longer believe in himself, if only because so many others no longer believed in him.

In the redoubtable Mannheim musical establishment, the orchestra shone with an outstanding brilliance. It was judged the finest in Europe in its time; certainly it was one of the largest, sometimes numbering sixty pieces or more, with twenty-two violins, four permanent horns, and a choir of the newfangled clarinets. The orchestra made prodigal sacrifices to the new goddess Expression; a perpetual throb of progressions from softer to louder, and back again, delighted its hearers. "Its *forte* is a thunder, its *crescendo* a cataract, its *diminuendo* a crystal stream rippling away in the distance, its *piano* a breath of spring . . ." said C. F. D. Schubart, who had ample opportunity of hearing it.

In this citadel of the *piano* and *forte*, small wonder that the pianoforte would be at home!

16. THE "GERMAN-ACTION" PIANOFORTE AND ITS MASTER MAKER. A LESSON FROM MOZART

MOZART had already been converted to the pianoforte prior to the date of his mother's letter. During October 1777, the month before he arrived at Mannheim, he had spent some time in the Bavarian city of Augsburg; there he saw a good deal of the esteemed clavier-maker Johann Andreas Stein. He was deeply impressed with Stein's extraordinarily fine pianofortes, and portions of his letter about them to his father have often been quoted. Before, however, we can properly understand the full meaning of Stein's work, we will have to take a little time to explain some of its evolution.

Hitherto we have been concerned with what might be termed the Saxon school of pianoforte making. Most of the fundamental ideas of that group of craftsmen go back to old Gottfried Silbermann, who, in turn, probably got them largely from Cristofori. Meanwhile, however, another group of pianoforte makers appears to have clustered in Bavaria. A pianoforte has been found (it was still in existence in 1933) inscribed with the maker's name of Johann Socher together with his location in Ober-Sonthofen, Allgäu. Sonthofen is a small community in the mountains of Upper Bavaria, very close to the Tirolese border. The instrument bears the date 1742, which makes it the oldest example of a square pianoforte of which we have any knowledge. By the 1760's and '70's we find pianofortes being made in the Bavarian towns of Regensburg, Ulm, and Augsburg, with Erlangen soon to follow.

Many of these instruments, however, show a significant difference in construction from those originating in Saxony. I submit the guess that it was some nameless and forgotten South German who first devised a kind of pianoforte action fundamentally different from that of Cristofori and Silbermann, one which—in a modified form—later came to be normally thought of as specifically "German." In it, the hammers were not fastened so as to swing on a specially constructed rail, with their heads pointing to the rear of the instrument: instead, each hammer was swung on a hinge fixed into the key itself, with its head pointing to the front of the instrument. In other words, the key did not raise a separated hammer shank by hitting it with a jack or hopper, but the hammer shank was attached only to the key and rose with it. In order to function properly, the hammer hinge of this "German" action was fixed into a forklike upright sheath, and the hammer's butt, or tail end, was prolonged into a kind of beak projecting toward the rear. Now, into the rear of the instrument, over the remote end of the key lever, was built a wooden ledge known as the *"Prell-leiste"*—literally, "bouncing rail." As the finger pressed down the key, its rear portion rose carrying with it the hammer sheath and hinge, together with the hammer; the hammer's beak-like prolongation then impinged upon the lower surface of the "bouncing rail," shooting the hammer head up against the string. In the simplest form of these German actions, the hammer's return was effected by the easy device of leaving enough room for the hammer head to drop back off the string after the impact.

It is clear that this rather primitive mechanism could not be very responsive to the more delicate and cautious finger impulses, for the hammer had to be shot against the string through too great a distance. Nor did it provide against the hammers' annoying re-rebound, the so-called "blocking." Stein's great merit was that he succeeded in constructing, perhaps inventing, an escapement for this type of action. He accomplished this by slicing through the continuity of the "bouncing rail" and giving each key its own little segment of it. But this rail segment, instead of being rigid, was now pivoted at the bottom of the case and made elastic by a wire spring at its rear. When the key was then pressed down, the hammer-"beak" engaged the under surface of the bouncing rail—which, however, now gradually gave way rearward; and not until the beak had slid past it and "escaped" could the hammer be given its final little toss against the string. Thus, the player's finger could remain in contact with the hammer, and control it, almost up to the final tiny bit of free space it had to traverse before delivering its blow. Furthermore, Stein also provided his action with padded "check pieces" to keep the hammers from bobbling up and down superfluously, that is "blocking."

The greater responsiveness of the Stein action, plus the craftsman's fine workmanship, aroused a ready approval. Let us now listen to Mozart, as he writes home to his father:

Augsburg, October 17, 1777

Now I must start right away with the Stein pianofortes. Before I ever saw any of Stein's work, I liked the Spath claviers the best; but now I have to give Stein's the preference, for they are much better than the Regensburg instruments. When I play vigorously, whether I leave the finger down or lift it up, the tone is finished the moment I sound it. I can attack the keys any way I want, the tone will always be even, it will not block, will not come out too loud or too soft or perhaps even fail to sound; in one word, everything is even. True, he will not let such a pianoforte go under 300 fl., but the trouble he takes and the diligence he applies are not to be paid for. His instruments have this distinguishing feature: they are made with an escapement. Not a man in a hundred bothers with this; but without an escapement it is impossible for a pianoforte not to block or leave an aftersound. When you strike the keys, his hammers fall back again the instant they jump against the strings whether you leave the keys down or up. When he has finished such a clavier (as he tells me), he first sits down and tries over all kinds of passages, runs and jumps, and whittles and works away so long until the clavier does everything; for he works only for the benefit of the music and not just for his own benefit alone, otherwise he would be finished right away. He says often: "If I weren't myself such a passionate lover of music and weren't able to do a litle bit myself on the clavier, I would certainly have lost patience with my work long ago; however, I am a lover of instruments that do not deceive the player, and which are durable." His claviers are really durable. He guarantees that the sounding board will not break or crack. When he has a sounding board ready for a clavier, he sets it out in the air, rain, snow, heat of the sun, and all hell, so that it cracks open; then he inserts wedges and glues them in, so that it becomes really strong and firm. He is quite glad when it cracks; you can be sure then that nothing more is going to happen to it. Quite often he even cuts into it himself and glues it together again and fixes it right. He has three such pianofortes ready. I played on them again today.

Later:

I have played all my six sonatas by heart quite often, here as well as in Munich; . . . the last one in D comes out incomparably on

> Stein's pianofortes. The machine which you press with the knee is likewise better made on his instruments than on the others; I need scarcely touch it and it works, and as soon as I take away the knee the least bit, you don't hear the slightest aftersound.

The "machine which you press with the knee" was a lever on the underside of the front of the case; it raised the dampers from the strings independently of the action of the fingers. As we have said previously some years were still to elapse before German pianoforte makers learned from the English how to render this mechanism operable by the foot. It was, of course, what we now call the "pedal."

Stein's early career was that of an organ builder; he had learned that craft in Strassburg from Johann Andreas Silbermann—a nephew of the famous Gottfried—and when he settled in Augsburg in 1750, it was in that capacity that he first worked there. Stein, a Protestant, was naturally drawn into the society of the relatively small Protestant minority among the town's 30,000 people. It was that minority, however, whose wealth was large in proportion to its numbers and which included most of Augsburg's musical connoisseurs and amateurs. Soon Stein was engaged to make claviers for some of these people. What with the general increase and spread of middle-class prosperity and culture, the clavier trade soon became large enough to take up all of his time. After his especially fine pianofortes had made him a wider reputation, we find him filling orders from an extensive section of southern Germany; and his instruments went as far as Salzburg and Vienna on the one side, Zürich and Freiburg on the other.

Stein left a notebook, probably pertaining to his earlier Augsburg years, in which he jotted down the names of a few of his customers, as well as the amounts of money he received from them. For one or two of his pianofortes he noted the small sums of sixty or seventy-five florins: perhaps those were early instruments without the all-important escapement. There is one, however, listed for the Archbishop of Salzburg, the Mozarts' difficult master, which is put down for two hundred florins. As we learned from Wolfgang, Stein's minimum price for a fine pianoforte in 1777 was three hundred florins; but a week after writing his letter, Mozart had word from father Leopold saying that the Countess Schönborn, the Archbishop's sister, had paid Stein seven hundred florins for one. This was an exceptionally steep price in its day—though possibly it may have included the value of some unusual woodwork or ornamental painting.

Stein was an unusually sensitive, intelligent workman, more of an artist than an artisan. He was a good musician, a member of one of Augsburg's "music loving and exercising" societies, in whose concerts he occasionally performed. It was true, as Mozart said, that musical considerations were always foremost in his designs for instruments. He was a high type of practical idealist, and his great aim apparently was to make a keyboard instrument that would combine delicate stroke-responsiveness with a considerable variety of tone colors. Thus, as early as 1769 he constructed a *"Politoniclavichordium,"* a combined harpsichord and pianoforte, and later he made a so-called *"Vis-à-vis Flügel,"* which was a union of a three-manualed harpsichord faced by a one-manualed pianoforte, to be played by two persons. Wind tone continued to interest the former organ builder, though only if he could render it expressive. He made a pressure-responsive reed-organ which he combined with a pianoforte and to which he gave the name of *"Melodika."* None of these experiments, however, had a future, apart from his regular pianofortes. In the quarter of a century since his settlement in Augsburg, the sentimentalizing sweep of the times had carried Stein some distance away from his original bent toward organ building. Mozart wrote:

> When I said to Mr. Stein that I would like to play his organ because the organ is my passion, he was much amazed and said "What? A man like you, such a great clavierist, wants to play an instrument on which no tenderness, no expression, no piano and forte can take place, but which always goes the same?"—"All that means nothing; in my eyes and ears the organ is still the king of instruments." "Well, it's all right with me!"

Stein's daughter Nanette acquired some of her father's talents, and she was later to play an important role in the pianoforte-making trade. At the time of Mozart's visit, she was a child of eight and had already played the pianoforte publicly. However, she evidently had a number of bad habits, which the well-disciplined Mozart took the trouble to criticize:

> Apropos, about his little girl. Anybody who watches her play and does not burst out laughing must be made of *stone* [Stein] like her father. She sits way up toward the treble, never by any means in the middle, so that she has more chance to move around and make faces. She twists her eyes around, she smirks: when something comes twice, she plays it slower the second time; if it comes three times, again

slower. The arm has to go way up high when she plays a passage; and as the passage is articulated, that's how the arm must do it, not the fingers—and that on purpose in a heavy, clumsy way. But to cap the climax, when there is a passage that is supposed to flow away like oil and where fingers must necessarily be changed, she doesn't pay much attention to that; but when the time comes, she leaves something out, lifts her hand, and begins again very comfortably. In that way she might rather hope to catch a wrong note, and it often makes a curious effect. I am only writing this to give Papa an idea of the state of clavier playing and teaching [here], in order that Papa might derive some advantage from it some time. Mr. Stein is completely silly about his daughter. She is eight years old and learns everything only from memory. She might amount to something, she has genius; but in this way she will get nowhere, she will never get much speed, because she makes a special effort to make her hand heavy. She will never get what is the most needful and the hardest, and the principal thing in music, Tempo, because from infancy on she has made it a point not to play in time. Mr. Stein and I talked with each other about this point for certainly two hours. But I have pretty well converted him, and he now asks my advice about everything.

What a vivid likeness Mozart draws of this little situation! The child's poor stance, the facial contortions, the stiff wrist, the inept use of the arm, the anarchic fingering, and the rhythmic sloppiness—anyone who has ever taught piano must smile with recognition at the recounting of these familiar foibles.

Little Nanette's failure to play in time involved more than her own childish indiscipline. An age given to sentimental excesses was likely to develop a dull conscience with regard to rhythmic precision. Distorting note values was a cheap way of seeming to play "with feeling." Furthermore, once a teacher or audience was willing to approve an emotionally specious metrical trespass, a flood of freakish antirhythmical sins based on sheer digital incompetence would presently be overlooked. Mozart wrote:

> The fact that I always stay accurately in time—at that they are all amazed. The *tempo rubato* in an adagio, the fact that the left hand takes no notice of it, that is something they cannot conceive at all. With them the left hand also gives way.

We need not take this statement absolutely literally in order to understand that Mozart was able to achieve the expression of spontaneous emotion by a very subtle easing of rhythmical stress that was never allowed to dislocate the music's fundamental metrical beats. This very twentieth-century day, that is still regarded as the truly satisfying way of playing lyrical music.

Stein had apparently been much impressed by one Ignatz von Beecke, music director to the Lilliputian prince of Oettingen-Wallerstein. He was a shallow but plausible clavierist who had dazzled the Augsburg burghers before Mozart's arrival.

> He was quite crazy about Beecke; now he sees and hears that I play more than Beecke, that I don't make any grimaces and still play so expressively that no one, by his own admission, has yet known how to handle his pianofortes so well.

Other discriminating Augsburgers evidently thought so too:

> Count Wolfeck and several others who are very enthusiastic for Beecke said recently at the concert that I can play Beecke into a bag.

Mozart's mention of grimaces is also interesting. Making faces while playing a keyboard was already an old vice before Mozart's time. François Couperin in his treatise, *The Art of Playing the Harpsichord,* published in 1717, speaks of it disapprovingly. C. F. D. Schubart, an elder contemporary of Mozart, refers to it also: he praises the pianoforte because on it "one can alter the strength of the tones without grimacing." But since when could facial disorders affect tonal volume? What they actually do is to give a player the illusion of expressing a "feeling" that his fingers and the instrument are incapable of bringing forth. No wonder they were—and are—so common.

17. THE CLAVIERS ARE NECK AND NECK, BUT THE PIANOFORTE WINS OUT

A KEYBOARD INSTRUMENT was essential at all concerts: since the seventeenth century a harpsichord had been regarded as furnishing the indispensable harmonic background and filling to all instrumental ensembles. The leader of the group was customarily seated at it, signaling his directions in collaboration with his first officer, the first violinist. The following diagram will show the seating arrangement customary at the Leipzig "Great Concert":

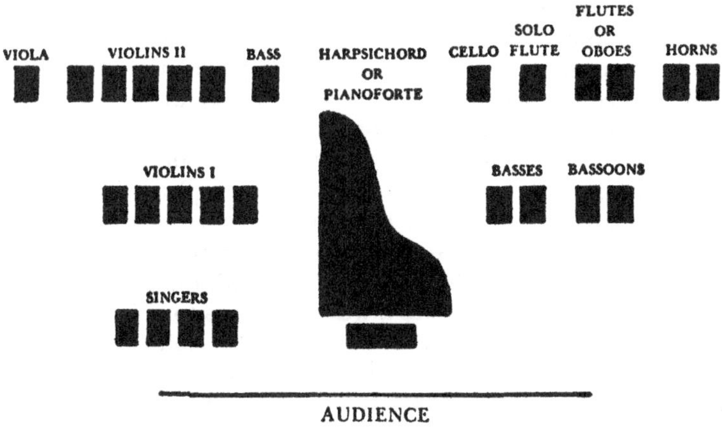

From Arnold Schering's *Musikgeschichte Leipzigs*, Vol. III.

The practice of conducting an orchestra from the keyboard persisted well into the nineteenth century; late in the eighteenth, however, in Leipzig at least, a change was made in its placement: it was set in front of the orchestra, its position reversed, the player-conductor facing his colleagues but turning his back upon the audience.

The keyboard was equally indispensable for accompaniments to the human voice. Accompaniments to arias and recitatives were generally scored more thinly than overtures or symphonic movements, and the keyboard had an even larger share in their fulfillment. Small-ensemble compositions involving a keyboard—such, for instance, as trios—were also common on eighteenth-century programs. Every once in a while the harpsichord was also heard in a featured solo performance: for example, at one of the very first meetings of Leipzig's "Great Concert," on September 16, 1743, it was recorded that "a twelve-year-old boy was heard to advantage in a concerto upon the *cembalo* [harpsichord]." Until late in the century, however, the keyboards were favored far less than the violin, or even certain wind instruments, as a focus of public attention. Accompanying remained their primary function until the 1780's.

It was especially as a concert instrument that the pianoforte could win out over its rivals. This was the instrument that had not only expression, but also enough volume to fill a larger room. After 1760 the bright, inflexible sound of the harpsichord gave less and less satisfaction to the sentimental Germans. The "changes" built into it in the form of octave doublings and muted "stops" failed to make up for a lack of the living warmth that only a completely smooth, completely supple crescendo and diminuendo could express. In the hands of a clever player the larger, more complicated harpsichords could achieve a tasteful variety of color, yet all their alternations of tonal quality or volume had to be accomplished with an angular suddenness that but poorly mirrored the stirrings of the heart. The *Flügel* could "please" (*"ergötzen,"* the Germans called it), but it failed to "move" (*"rühren"*); and being "moved" meant everything in those days.

On the other hand, the beloved clavichord, for a generation the "clavier" par excellence, was a weak thing: its tone began to peter out at a distance of ten feet, a single healthy violin could crush it into a confused murmur, and in an ensemble it would be totally inaudible. The "sufferer's solace," as it was once called, was a fine aid to a lovesick miss trying to have a good cry in a corner; it might offer a puny support to the shy half-voice in which they tell us home singing was mostly done; and an imaginative artist like C. P. E. Bach could enjoy using it to improvise unusual delicate, cloudy harmonic speculations, especially when an appreciative colleague such as J. F. Reichardt or Charles Burney visited him and sat by his side. But in a large room it was of no use at all.

Inevitably when it came to concerts, minds turned to the new-fashioned pianoforte. By the 1770's it had practically as much volume as a large harpsichord, though its timbre seemed dull compared with the crisp pluckings of the older instrument; and although it lacked the finer subtleties of which the clavichord was capable, its general dynamic flexibility was satisfactory. However flat its tone quality and however imperfectly sensitive its touch, the pianoforte still represented the best practical alliance of expression with viable volume of sound that the craftsmen of the age were able to build into a keyboard instrument.

The critics in general seemed to feel at first that the pianoforte was difficult to play. We can readily understand this: its proper touch required something more than the simple, unconcerned little stroke that sufficed to pluck all harpsichord strings with the same degree of loudness. Yet, unlike the clavichord, the pianoforte key and hammer lost all contact with the string—and, therefore, all control of the tone—from the moment of impact on. The stroke had to be properly gauged for loudness, once and for all.

To this many musicians were unaccustomed, and they found it troublesome.

In any event, the prestige that was gathering around the pianoforte from its use in public performances tended gradually to influence customers into buying it, and thus to urge makers to improve it. Slowly but steadily after 1760 it made its way toward universal acceptance. There was, naturally, a normal inertia resisting its spread. Private persons and concert societies were not always inclined to throw away their adequately functioning clavichords and harpsichords merely because something new and different and possibly better was available. Yet, newly prosperous families, new households, new musical organizations, unencumbered by established possessions, might well be more readily attracted to the new object. We will recall that Councilor Goethe had, conservatively, bought an expensive harpsichord for his family in 1769 and had later donated it to his daughter Cornelia after her marriage; but when the Councilor died in 1782 and his widow wished to console herself with clavier playing, it was a pianoforte that she purchased.

Christoph Gottlieb Schröter, who claimed he had made the first model of a pianoforte action back in 1721, had since settled down as an organist in the small Saxon town of Nordhausen, and there he also took time to indite wordy, learned treatises on thorough bass and intonation. "He was a little bit of a man, but gave himself a very important air"—so the lexicographer Ernst Ludwig Gerber described him. As an elderly person Schröter could witness the growing vogue of the pianoforte; thus, he felt encouraged to continue trying to convince people that he had "invented" the instrument. In 1763 he wrote an elaborate letter, outlining his claims in detail, to Friedrich W. Marpurg, the Berlin musical thinker and disquisitor. He begins:

> More than twenty towns and villages are known to me in which, since 1721, in place of the customary harpsichords, there have been made keyboard instruments with hammers . . . which their makers and purchasers call "*pantalons*" when the stroke upon the strings comes from above; but when such an instrument with hammers is so designed that the hammers strike from below, they call it *pianoforte*.

He continues testily, grinding his ax:

> If one finally asks each maker of such an instrument, who it was that really invented it, almost every one claims himself to have been the inventor.

Twenty towns is a goodly number, though it does not blanket the map. The figure may be a pretty good indication of the extent to which the pianoforte had come into use early in the 1760's.

By the latter part of the decade, smaller communities were beginning to follow the lead of the larger cities in organizing "music-exercising societies" or "concerts." We read of one such group in the little town of Weida, in western Saxony, "to which His Excellency *Herr Amtshauptmann* [bureau-chief?] von Watzdorf, himself a skillful musician, has contributed a pianoforte." That was in August 1767. Weida is not far from Gera, claviermaker Friederici's headquarters. In November of the same year we hear of a similar "concert" group in Nordhausen, C. G. Schröter's residence, somewhat further distant. Every Wednesday evening at seven, sixteen active younger burghers met "in one of the handsomest houses of the town" to perform symphonies, concertos, cantatas, arias, and solos; and, says the account in the *Weekly News and Comment concerning Music,* "we are proud to state here that Mr. Christian Vopel, an esteemed citizen of the town, has had the goodness to dedicate an excellent brand-new fortepiano to the concert for its permanent use."

We left Carl Philipp Emanuel Bach, the great Sebastian's second son, as Frederick the Great's accompanist at Potsdam and Berlin. After more than twenty years at this job, he had begun to be bored with the task of playing retriever on the King's flute-playing chases, of putting salt on the royal tail whenever the monarch indulged in some of his absolute and sovereign ideas of rhythm and meter. Anyway, after 1756 Frederick's interest in shooting Austrians all but eclipsed his interest in music. Philipp Emanuel was happy when, in 1767, Hamburg offered him the position, succeeding Telemann, of city church-music director. As a great clavierist, he soon found himself participating in many Hamburg concerts. A correspondent of the *Weekly Music News* described such a one of February 1770, at the Commercial Academy:

> On this occasion various male and female amateurs were heard, besides our Mr. Bach, whose playing compelled the admiration of all, especially when he allowed us to observe his dexterity upon his magnificent-sounding pianoforte.

Thus, the great exponent of the clavichord transferred to the newer instrument when he had to launch his sounds before a larger audience. We know, too, that he had a pianoforte in his home at about this time.

The sonatas that Giustini composed and published in Florence in 1732 expressly for the pianoforte had been an isolated phenomenon, without sequel, and they had long been forgotten—if, indeed, they were ever known—in Germany. It was a few years after the middle of the century that German composers began to mention the pianoforte on the title pages of their printed works. Johann Christoph Friedrich Bach, still another son of the great master's, in ducal service in Bückeburg, near Hanover, is said to have composed a sonata which he labeled, as early as 1757, as playable also on the pianoforte. Johann Gottfried Eckard, a German musician living in Paris, published a set of six sonatas there, probably in May 1763. As a frontispiece, he offered an "*Announcement.* I have sought to render this work equally suitable to the harpsichord, the clavichord, and the forte & piano. It is for this reason that I considered myself obliged to mark the louds and softs so frequently, which would have been useless if I had only the harpsichord in view." There were practically no clavichords or pianofortes in Paris at that date, and Eckard must have been thinking of his German friends back home. In 1771 announcement was made by Johann Gottfried Müthel of Riga, a pupil of Sebastian Bach's, of *duettos* "for two clavichords, two harpsichords, or two fortepianos." After that, in northern Germany, during the next two decades, keyboard music was published mostly as "for clavier or pianoforte," clavier in this case meaning clavichord. In the 1790's the publications, for the most part, read simply "for the pianoforte."

By 1770 the ultimate prevalence of the pianoforte might well have been foreseen, but in the course of the next fifteen years the three domestic keyboard-instruments coexisted actively on terms of a sort of hypothetical equality. A number of German writers of that period pleased themselves with penning more or less gracefully worded evaluations of their respective merits. One of the best was set down by Christian Friedrich Daniel Schubart. This man, the son of a Protestant minister, was a good musician, a fluent littérateur, a liberal, a libertarian, and a libertine—a generous, gifted vagabond and an attractive if unreliable character. He tossed about various South German towns, editing little newspapers, playing the organ, carousing with male and female companions, and writing poetry. One of his poems is *Die Forelle* (*The Trout*), to which Franz Schubert later fashioned his famous lilting tune. A few of Schubart's mildly subversive utterances had aroused some high-ranking displeasure; thus, finally Duke Karl Eugen of Württemberg lured the hapless writer into his jurisdiction and had him seized and tossed into prison. In the Germanies of those days this high-sovereign kidnaping could be perfectly legal, coming under the head of what was respectably called "cabinet justice." Schubart had to spend ten years in the Hohenasperg fortress; but after a year or two the conditions of his detention relaxed some of their grimmest features, and it was in this wretched situation that he penned his book *Ideas on the Aesthetics of Music.* The jail provided him with no reference books, and his contacts with the outside world were very few. Schubart's rambling treatise, set down out of his own recollections and fantasies, is full of factual inaccuracies; yet it is valuable as a reflection of the aesthetic climate of his time. His incarceration began on January 24, 1777, and we may date his remarks as approximately of that time. He discusses the keyboard instruments:

> Of all the instruments of our day, the clavier has fared the best. In the last century and in the first half of the present one there were entire provinces in which one could scarcely find a clavier player; [but] now everybody plays, thumps, drums, and doodles: the noble, the commoner, the bungler, and the expert; woman, man, boy, girl. Indeed, the clavier has become a most important article of fashionable education. The instrument, moreover, has this general enthusiasm to thank for the great improvements it has presently undergone. In order to formulate exactly the principles of the clavier, the claviers themselves must be accurately distinguished from each other.
>
> I. *The Harpsichord,* which scratches and vibrates the strings either by means of crows' quills—or, much more expensively, with little golden picks—provides mere simple contour, but one as clearly marked and as sharply drawn as one of Chodowiecki's unshaded figures. It is on this instrument that one must first learn clean execution, or, what amounts to the same, one must exercise the hand in correct musical delineation. One needs but to let the hand swerve, and the outlines of a piece will be distorted upon this instrument. For that important reason, the beginner ought to practice on the harpsichord first, so as to acquire a fleet, well-developed hand and to secure himself in the most accurate, most measured performance of a piece of music, before he goes over to the other kinds of claviers.
>
> He who has learned to execute a piece roundly upon a Friederici, Silbermann, or Stein harpsichord (for these are by far the best

among those hitherto known), will progress all the more readily on other claviers. Only he must not tarry too long with the harpsichord; for this instrument is more suitable for allegro- than for adagio-playing, consequently more for show of dexterity than for the performance of pieces full of sentiment.

II. *Fortepiano.* This excellent instrument is—bless us!—again an invention of the Germans. Silbermann felt so deeply the deficiency of the harpsichord—which could bring out shading either not at all, or bring it out by means of stops in all too violent contrasts—that he thought about means for bringing colors into the harpsichord. He and his followers thus came upon the great invention of eliciting the forte and piano without stops—because stops only take up time—entirely through the pressure of the hand and with the utmost quickness. If one could only carry the *mezzo-tinto* into the fortepiano, there would be nothing a great player could wish for further. . . .

III. *Clavichord,* this solitary, melancholy, ineffably sweet instrument, when constructed by a master, has advantages over the harpsichord and the fortepiano. Through the pressure of the fingers, through the vibrating and trembling of the strings, through the stronger or gentler touch of the hand, may not only the musical colors of whole sections [*musikalische Lokalfarben*] be fixed, but also the half-tints, the swelling and dying of the tones, the trill which melts and expires under the fingers, the portamento . . . in one word, all the features of which emotion is compounded. He who does not like to rumble, to rage, and to storm, whose heart prefers often to pour itself into tender feelings, will pass by the harpsichord and the fortepiano and will choose a clavichord by Fritz, Spath, or Stein . . .

The clavichords have nowadays all but reached their peak: they are of five or six octaves, are fretted and unfretted, with and without lute stops, and there seems scarcely to be an improvement that the sensitive player could still wish to have imparted to this instrument.

The above paragraphs contain errors and ambiguities, yet they give a vivid impression of a later-eighteenth-century German state of mind.

By the mid-eighties the victory of the pianoforte was pretty well decided, even though many specimens of the older keyboards remained in functional existence for a time thereafter. Some North Germans, with good reason, still preferred the sensitive clavichord, despite its weakness; but now the success of the pianoforte in Austria, France, and England—where there were hardly any clavichords—had its inevitable reaction upon them. It was indeed from

Germany, directly or indirectly, that the pianoforte had been introduced into its neighboring countries; but their example, in turn, helped to sweep along the Germans themselves into making the pianoforte triumphant in their own homes and concert rooms.

Indeed, before 1785 the Germans had lost their leadership in the making of pianofortes. Austria, England, and France were much wealthier, much more powerful empires than the fragmented German lands, and they offered far greater resources and opportunities for the production and sale of a complicated, expensive article. The development of the piano now shifts in their direction; and we will take them up, each in its turn.

SECTION

TWO

Austria

1. SOCIETY AND MUSIC

VIENNA, the heart of a German-speaking region, was the capital of the Holy Roman Empire in its decline. The Empire, that magnificent medieval conception and structure, had indeed given way before the modern idea of the sovereign nation-state; yet an efficient remnant of its ancient sway lingered on. The Imperial crown had long been hereditary in the Hapsburg family; in its heyday, its scions had ruled Spain and Flanders along with the Germanies and the Italies. By the eighteenth century they had long lost effective political authority over the Protestant North German realms, they had relinquished the Spanish throne, and their hold on Flanders was precarious. Still, Voltaire's famous gibe was forced: the Holy Roman Empire may not have been holy, but it was Roman from all the clerical influence it underwent—and it was certainly an empire. It was really an Austrian empire, a coherent community of multilingual Austrian hereditary crownlands. Princes, church princes, dukes, and counts of Tirol, Salzburg, Upper and Lower Austria, Bohemia, Moravia, Hungary, and many Italian regions all owed allegiance to the Emperor at Vienna. The nobles extracted wealth from their lands and their peasants, but they liked to live near their sovereign—their font of honor, prestige, and big jobs; in the winter months, at least, they inhabited their Vienna palaces.

Vienna, then, was full of noble, lavish money-spenders. Tradesmen and craftsmen could easily get rich there: purveyors of shoe buckles and leather goods, armchairs, teacups and emerald brooches—caterers, hairdressers, and coach builders—could find a perpetual array of well-paying customers. Let us remember that the purveyors, too, had to have their meat and potatoes, their shoes and stockings, their pots and pans, all giving an incentive to enterprise. Moreover, the broad, yellow Danube was a natural thoroughfare, flowing from well inside southern Germany down through the Turkish lands into the Black Sea, the obvious avenue of a far-reaching trade. It was a favorable situation for the formation of liquid capital: besides being the seat of a large, complex government, Vienna became also a great center of commerce and money-lending. Before the end of the eighteenth century its population came to exceed 225,000, making it the greatest of all German-speaking cities.

The Imperial court had been medieval in its outlook and conservative in its habits: it carefully nurtured all the characteristics of a "regime of status"; rank and precedence were matters of primary importance in all official life. An exquisite etiquette of ceremonial and speech was cultivated, some of it seemingly derived from Spain, from the days when the Hapsburgs had also ruled that country. Every one of the thousands of official personages "knew his place" most sensitively and was also alertly aware of everyone else's "place."

In time, however, this stiff, delicate structure could be elasticized. Early in the eighteenth century Austrian ruling groups began to be impressed with the advantages of large-scale foreign trade, steered and protected by government. Emperor Charles VI, for instance, had supported the formation of an Oriental Trading Company; it was badly managed, went through some perilous vicissitudes, and by 1725 it was breaking up. In 1752, under Charles's daughter, the Empress Maria Theresa, there was formed a "Court Commercial Council" (*"Hof-Commerzien-Rat"*)—we might call it "Imperial Board of Trade" nowadays; it aimed to promote and control a number of grandiose schemes: a Fiume Company for sugar importing, a Temesvár Company for exporting grain and potash, a Bohemian Linen Company for export to America, an Egyptian Company, and a Black Sea Company. Nobles of high official rank staffed the Commercial Council; other noble, landed magnates put money into these enterprises. But the grandees had little understanding of trade; they had to form partnerships with more competent merchants and bankers. Somehow, the screen between the nobility and the *bourgeoisie* had to be tastefully perforated if these arrangements were to be successful. The simplest and most practical way to accomplish this was to confer patents of nobility upon the wealthier and more plausibly mannered among the financiers—upon their payment of a substantial fee. Maria Theresa's remarkable son Joseph became coregent with her in 1765. He was rather impetuous in his devotion to "enlightenment" and "progress"; under his influence, money-men came to be ennobled by the dozens. We will also note, incidentally, that the enzymes of the newer thought had long been dissolving the more rigid fibers of the braces that held Vienna to Rome.

After the mid-century we hear of success stories of an almost American flavor. J. Thomas Trattner at fifteen had lost his parents and became a printer's apprentice in a provincial town. At thirty he came to Vienna; he propelled his career by diligence, intelligence, and his capacity for making influential friends. One of the latter staked him to the capital for setting up a shop of his own; soon he was a printer to the university, then a patented court printer. Soon he built a "Typographical Palace," with sixteen presses, a bindery, a type foundry, and a copper-engraving shop. Literary activity burgeoned in Germany in the sixties and seventies: Trattner's plant was able to do a vast, if not truly ethical, reprint business. The poor orphan boy ended by owning eight bookshops, eighteen warehouses, countless presses, two paper factories, the largest apartment house in Vienna, and a great country estate. Somewhere on the way up he was made a noble knight of the Holy Roman Empire, with a legitimate *"von"* before his name.

Johann Fries, native of Switzerland, merchant and financier, came to Vienna bringing some capital, before 1750. Mines and textile factories were among his profitable interests. He lent money to Maria Theresa during her Seven Years' War against Prussia, and she let him have a contract for supplying one of her armies. Later he engaged in far-flung enterprises—minting trade dollars for Turkey, selling Hungarian copper to Holland. He was made a knight and then a baron; and when he paid his twenty thousand florins, his incorrect Protestant religion did not prevent Emperor Joseph, on April 5, 1783, from making him a count.

Karl Abraham Wetzlar's beginnings were so obscure as to be indiscernible. Probably he was a little peddler or broker. By the late 1750's he had enough means to make it warrantable that he too be given contracts for supplying the wartime army. The profits gave his fortune a good push; it swung up as high as five million florins, they said. He, too, was made a baron, on November 23, 1777, after he and his family had exchanged their still more acutely incorrect Jewish religion for the prevailing Catholic one.

On the other hand, banker Nathan Adam Arnstein succeeded in getting himself baronized while remaining Jewish—a triumph of "enlightenment," or of corruption, as some may have thought.

Wealth was not the only gateway to aristocracy; talents, too, were rewarded with ennobling recognition: botanists, librarians, physicians, and archaeologists acquired the beneficent *"von"* when their achievements were sufficiently noted.

All in all, the last third of the eighteenth century was a time of comparative social fluidity for Vienna. Shrewd financial schemers, careful sycophants, and farsighted matrimonialists—as well as bright men of science and learning—could coddle the ambition of someday being given an official, Imperial certificate of class superiority. Yet this fluidity did not signify a wiping out of class distinctions: in an age of rapid moral and social change, a liberal dispersal of patents of nobility was helpful in preserving the principle of aristocracy at the cost of a certain devaluation. Vienna bootblacks and cab drivers called every well-dressed man "Mr. Baron" as a piece of plausible flattery; but even true noblemen sometimes addressed important commoners as *"von,"* pretending not to hear themselves conversing with "inferiors" on equal terms.

In all this social ferment music played a role that was far from negligible. To begin with, the Hapsburgs had always been musical. Charles V, the fabulous King of Spain, felt he had to have a clavichord made for him when he retired to Lierre to escape the plague. Leopold I, who reigned from Vienna during all the later seventeenth century, was a musician of considerable attainment, an interesting composer. His expenditure of 60,000 florins on the single opera *Il Pomo d'Oro* might have been set down as mere ostentation, but not so the fact that he had a harpsichord in every room of his palace, convenient for trying out any musical idea that might suddenly occur to him. When his teacher and orchestra leader, Johann Schmelzer, once tried to flatter him by telling him that he ought to have been a professional musician, the Emperor answered ironically: "Well, it doesn't matter, I'm better off as I am." Leopold, too, was one of the few privileged persons to whom the Pope could not refuse a copy of the famous Allegri *Miserere,* sacred and peculiar to the Sistine Chapel. Charles VI was likewise benevolently disposed toward music; and his daughter, the future Maria Theresa, had sung in opera performances as a young girl. Later her son Joseph, in turn, became a good cellist.

Other exalted houses of the Empire, encouraged by their sovereign, set great store by music and cultivated it in a lordly manner. Many of them kept private orchestras, some of which were excellent ensembles of professional musicians working full time in that capacity. The Esterházys were the most famous of those music-patronizing families, but there were many others—the houses of Kinsky, Schwarzenberg, Thun, Grassalkowitz, Lobkowitz, and a dozen more; their musical establishments were the subject of prideful rivalry. There may have been an element of ostentation in all this, yet that was surely subordinate to the keen intrinsic personal interest which the members of these houses took in music. Just as horse-loving English lords might keep large stables and hire jockeys for important races, yet throw themselves and their families with zest into riding to hounds and into gymkhanas, so these Austrian magnates—in addition to trotting out their liveried orchestras at formal functions—themselves became ardent participants as skilled amateurs (gentlemen riders, so to speak) in string quartets and other chamber music. Some of the less affluent gentlemen sometimes formed their house orchestras by using domestic servants to double as musicians; in fact, lackeys were often hired with a view to their instrumental qualifications. Butler-cellists and oboe-playing valets were common in mid-eighteenth-century Vienna; as late as 1789 we could read in the *Vienna Gazette* (*Wiener Zeitung*) the following type of advertisement:

> Wanted, for a house of the gentry, a manservant who knows how to play the violin well and to accompany difficult clavier sonatas.

It may have happened, once in a great while, that a Vienna burgher was invited to a ducal palace and there could catch some strain of music; but generally speaking, Vienna citizens, tradesmen, laborers, and menials had little or no experience of the tonal magnificence that went on inside the noble residences. Nevertheless, they gossiped about it respectfully and were proud of it. You may call that servility, or "loyalty," or sublimated envy, or self-extrapolation, or whatever you wish; it is a familiar human attitude, as those can testify who remember the intense empathic concern with which a million newspaper-reading New Yorkers of about 1900 used to absorb the daily details of Vanderbilt and Astor recreations.

Music, especially instrumental music, then, was a highly honorific indoor sport in Vienna; any Viennese understood that it was something the best people cultivated in a big way. A small number of public concerts began to take place during the 1770's, but most of the important music—professional and amateur—was made in private mansions.

If music was eminently socially correct, if it was so positively associated with social altitude, it would not fail to be impressive to the bevies of newly rich and newly noble. They could think to better themselves cheaply by aping their betters, so they too assiduously cultivated their musical talents and interests. Music could be a good lubricant of advancement, an efficacious social balm. A freshly turned-out, twenty-thousand-florin count—much less a three-thousand-florin baron—could hardly expect to receive a dinner invitation from the Esterházys by the next mail; but if his son were known to be an unusually good amateur on the viola, the young man might be asked some fine evening to make a fourth in a string quartet at a house a few degrees closer to the Esterházys than his own. What might not result from that?

Concerts increased after 1780; some of them were for charitable purposes and wealthy people supported them readily. It was easy for the "full nobility" and the "half nobility"—Mozart's phrases—to meet without embarrassment on the same subscription list and make courteous encounters in the lobby and the aisles of the hall. In the list for a series of Mozart's own concerts during March 1784, we find the afore-mentioned upstart money-names of Wetzlar, Trattner, and Fries cozily cushioned against those of the ancient, lofty, feudal princely throne-supports of Auersperg, Schwarzenberg, Waldstein, and, indeed, Esterházy. Music was a good social alpenstock; if some on the higher trails of the ascent seized it, many, many times that number sought to employ its pleasant help up the lower slopes. After a time, music lost much of its fashionable potency; but during the fifty years of which 1800 marked the mid-point, the cultivation of instrumental home-music—that is, chamber music—in Vienna reached an extent and an intensiveness unparalleled in history. It was that atmosphere of wide, eager approval that encouraged the genius of Haydn, Mozart, Beethoven, and Schubert, as well as the talents of untold lesser composers.

2. "CLAVIERLAND"

THE KEYBOARD INSTRUMENTS played their necessary part in the phenomenon we have just described. Harpsichords, of course, belonged in all the chamber orchestras kept by old-established grandees; the *novi homines* then faithfully placed them in their own homes. There were clavichords in Vienna too, but the extroverted Catholic Austrians had little taste for the masturbatory reclusiveness with which North Germans liked to weep into those boxes—nor was their cheapness much of an attraction to the luxury-admiring Viennese. When in the later seventies pianofortes began to be made with a good capacity for accurately controllable shading, the Viennese went after them rapidly.

Georg Christoph Wagenseil was Maria Theresa's harpsichord teacher; he lived long enough to inscribe some of his last works "for harpsichord or pianoforte." After he became old and gouty, his good-humored disciple Josef Anton Stefann, a native of Bohemia, took over the keyboard education of the Hapsburg children; it was he who taught young Marie Antoinette, the unlucky French queen-to-be—as well as many another, lesser girl. Many clavier masters came to Vienna after the Seven Years' War, lured by reports of the lively circulation of wealth there. Many came from Bohemia, that active cradle of musicians. J. B. Wanhal was first brought from there by his patrons as early as 1760; despite intervals of mental disturbance, he succeeded in establishing a Viennese clientele and composing much glib keyboard music in addition to many symphonies. Leopold Koželuch, another Bohemian, descended upon Vienna in 1778 and soon was made clavier master to the Archduchess Elizabeth and other court personages. He made a highly respectable career as a composer and pianist, though many of his colleagues belittled him.

W. A. Mozart arrived there in 1781, in the entourage of his mean master, the Archbishop of Salzburg. He was much aroused by the lively interest in clavier music among the circles into which he was thrown. "This is the best place in the world for my line of work . . . This is clavierland," he wrote home. "If I only had two pupils, I could do better than I do in Salzburg," he said. With their regular payments, plus the fees he might get playing in wealthy houses, he felt he could make himself free of his hated Archbishop, "who can annoy me every day for the sake of his lousy 400 florins"—Wolfgang's annual stipend. He did not say so in words, but in that way he could also hope to make himself independent of his loving but oppressive father.

After a time Wolfgang realized these manly aims, in addition to the related one of getting married. He achieved a few regular pupils: one was the Countess Rumbeck, of old aristocratic lineage and a vice-chancellor's cousin; another was Frau von Trattner, the printing mogul's talented wife. He charged a good, swanky price for his instruction: six ducats for twelve lessons (a ducat equaled 4⅓ florins, or about $2.00 in our money). His father, working away in the sticks of Salzburg, must have been quite impressed with a fee of this kind. The good Leopold was then giving lessons at the rate of twelve kreutzers (*i.e.*, ⅕ of a florin) apiece—in other words, for less than a tenth of what his son was getting. Wolfgang was not too invincibly shy with rich music-lovers. Countess Rumbeck had a way of going away for intervals to her country place and missing lessons, for which Wolfgang did not charge her. Soon he took a firmer line: he charged the six ducats by the month—insisting on his full fee whether she took her lessons or not. The Countess accepted the arrangement, but the more arithmetically minded bourgeois Frau von Trattner did not let him get away with it at first. With four pupils, he was now saying, at six ducats each, he could support a wife decently, provided he and she lived quietly. That was at the rate of 104 florins monthly, not counting uncertain receipts from performances.

There were other sources of revenue for musicians: when Dr. Burney visited Vienna in 1772, he stated that there were no music shops there at the time; but in 1780 art dealer Carlo Artaria started to print and sell music as a side line. It was a profitable business; competition soon developed. Mozart and other composers could also make a few ducats selling compositions to publishers.

Mozart's repute grew steadily higher: presently he was in great demand at private concerts. Between February 26 and April 3, 1784, he played fourteen different times at the homes of the Esterházy and Galitzin families, not to mention three concerts of his own enterprise and two, for charity, at the theater, during the same period. The following year, 1785, when his father visited him during the Lenten season, he was putting on a series of six subscription concerts at the *Mehlgrube,* an old flour warehouse converted into a hotel. Let us avoid setting up twentieth-century mass-production standards for these events and rejoice with father Leopold that the hall was crowded with a large audience of 150 subscribers, and their families, who had each paid 3 ducats for the series. The receipts from one concert alone amounted to 559 florins. At that moment Wolfgang was paying an annual rent of 460 florins for his apartment. Yet how can we explain the fact that the hall-rent at the *Mehlgrube* cost him only 1½ ducats for each concert, half the price of a single subscription? Perhaps the proprietor felt himself sufficiently compensated by the intoxicating presence of all those coronets upon his premises.

Viennese musical "gentlemen-riders" generally liked to exercise themselves upon violins, cellos, or flutes; but the ladies' favorite mount was the keyboard. In Vienna, as everywhere always, the overwhelming majority of clavier players were females. Many of them are known to us. There was Franziska von Auenbrugger, daughter of the famous physician who had gotten the idea for his great invention of chest percussion and auscultation by tapping his innkeeping-father's wine barrels. A prominent visiting listener called Franziska's clavier playing "masterly." There was Karoline von Greiner, daughter of the union of one of Maria Theresa's former body-servants with a court councilor; she later became well known as a novelist, under the name of Karoline Pichler; in her youth she was an accomplished amateur on the clavier. There was Barbara Ployer, whose father was the Salzburg principality's fiscal agent in the capital: she was proficient enough to have played Mozart's two-piano sonata with the composer before an audience. Frau von Trattner, too, must have had no mean ability on the keys: Mozart wrote for her his great *Sonata in C minor* as well as the *Fantaisie* that is usually bracketed with it. There was Maria Wilhelmina Countess Thun, who had married into one of the oldest of noble families: the Emperor himself sometimes deigned to attend gatherings at the Thun palace. The Count gave himself to mind-healing, Rosicrucianism, and other mystical absorptions; the Countess raised her children and cultivated music. She was a person of extraordinary charm, intelligence, amiability, and hospitality—so visiting foreigners were pleased to describe her. Dr. Burney had been presented to her by the British ambassador during his visit in 1772; he calls her "a most agreeable and accomplished lady of high rank, who, among many other talents, possesses as great skill in music as any person of distinction I ever knew; she plays the harpsichord with that grace, ease and delicacy which nothing but female fingers can arrive at." The list of competent clavier-playing ladies could be extended *ad taedium.*

We even begin to meet, in the ninth decade of the century, with well-born girls who projected well-shaped designs for becoming professional clavierists, at least on a part-time basis. We will admit that they were persons whose physical assets did not suggest a ready marriage. Josephine Aurnhammer was described as a "fright" to look at, very fat, given to excessive perspiration, and somewhat aggressive. Yet Mozart, never lenient in judgments, said "she plays delightfully." She confided to him her plan: to study seriously for two or three more years, then to go to Paris and make a profession of her playing. "I'm not pretty," she said, "on the contrary, I'm ugly; I don't care to marry some office hero with a salary of three or four hundred gulden, and I won't get anybody different. So, I'll stay as I am and live by my talent." We do not know whether she ever got to Paris, but she was able to live in Vienna, at least partially, by her talent. She seems to have achieved some kind of influence that assured her the use of the Imperial theater for an annual concert, a privilege that many envied her. She even became a respectable composer, putting forth a number of sets of merchantable variations. We are gratified, also, to report, finally, that she succeeded in acquiring a husband.

A physical handicap also proved decisive in the case of Therese von Paradis, the daughter of a well-placed bureaucrat. She had been blind since her third year; in 1777, when she was eighteen, she was brought to the celebrated Dr. Mesmer—then at the height of his Vienna fame—with the idea that he could "mesmerize" her with "animal magnetism" into regaining her sight. She underwent his treatments; he claimed stoutly that he had made her see and put her through certain performances that might seem to prove it. There were many skeptics, however, whose opinions impressed her parents. After a painful scene between the latter and the doctor, Therese's treatments were stopped; Mesmer left Vienna and the girl stubbornly remained blind. Marriage could hardly come into question; she continued to develop her considerable musical, clavier-playing abilities. Koželuch, the court teacher, was her guide; they said she could ultimately play no fewer than fifty of his concertos. Her professional career began in 1784 when, escorted by her mother, she embarked on a concert tour of Germany and Switzerland. The following year her professional travels took her as far as London and Paris. Later she settled in Vienna, where she composed and taught.

Pianofortes were played in Vienna early in the seventies, but they did not gain favor very quickly at first. It was about 1780 that Countess Thun acquired a fine pianoforte made by Stein. The instrument made quite a stir in Vienna society, it was in great demand, and she generously lent it for many musical affairs at other people's houses. Toward the end of December 1781 there arrived in Vienna, in the course of a long tour, an accomplished, youngish keyboard virtuoso—an Italian-born, adopted Englishman whose name was Muzio Clementi. The Emperor invited him to play at court, also requesting that Mozart, the rising star of the clavier, appear at the same occasion. Mozart proved wise in prevailing upon Countess Thun to lend her Stein for the event, for the only other pianoforte available at the Imperial palace was found to be out of tune and to have three keys that stuck. Mozart admired Clementi but slightly; he did not, however, scruple later to purloin one of the sonata themes he had heard him play that day.

Countess Schönborn, the Salzburg Archbishop's sister, we remember, had had a Stein pianoforte made for her in 1777. Soon thereafter Johann Rudolph Count Czernin, another old-line aristocrat, ordered a pianoforte from Stein for his wife. Stein instruments, we can see, were by way of becoming a vogue among the Vienna elite; presently the near-elite—the financial Wetzlars, Henikstein, and Puthons—would be pressing close behind. Ordering instruments all the way from Augsburg was troublesome; furthermore, there were natural limits to Stein's capacity to finish them. Thus, the cue was given for resident Vienna craftsmen to build pianofortes on the Stein model—in any case, incorporating their most significant features, in particular the escapement. Patent protection was unknown in those young days of invention, especially not across a boundary line such as Bavaria-Austria.

There may well have been quite a number of Stein-type pianoforte makers in Vienna during the 1780's; we definitely know of two: Anton Walter and J. Wenzel Schanz. Mozart preferred Walter, who made him a pianoforte some time before 1784. That was the instrument he had had hoisted about to the Esterházys and Galitzins for his many private engagements during the Lenten season of that and the following year. One might wonder why those opulent houses did not already contain instruments that Mozart would have been satisfied to play. We can suggest one explanation: about this time Mozart had an attachment built on to his Walter, whereby the damper action could be raised and lowered by the foot—a pedal, in other words. This mechanism had been invented in England, had only recently been applied to pianofortes there, and was probably little known in Vienna. We can imagine that he did not want to do without this highly useful gadget. On the other hand, he may have remembered, painfully, those keys that stuck on the Imperial palace instrument and decided to take no chances at the homes of mere princes. Schanz's pianofortes were said to have had a gentler tone and a lighter action than Walter's. Joseph Haydn, who was often in Vienna during the eighties, preferred them; he bought one in 1788.

For his subscription concerts, Mozart felt that he had to offer his patrons a new program each time—in fact, to a large extent a newly composed one. He could not appear to assume that an exquisite group of rajas and nabobs would pay golden ducats for any great quantity of "slightly used" music. He hired his little orchestra, plus one or two solo singers, and gave the customers his symphonies and arias; but the main dish was usually a new pianoforte concerto. No less than seventeen such concertos, many of them masterpieces, were the fruits of his concert activities during the 1780's.

They were among the earliest true pianoforte concertos ever to be composed, and their general style and layout became a norm for a couple of generations thereafter. No longer was the concerto soloist a regular orchestra member to whom an intermittent prominence was granted; now he was a hero, a "star," for whose significant utterances the entire orchestra was to supply a mere discreet background or accompaniment. The display of his prowess and his personality was the aim of the performance. Mozart's piano concertos, as well as those of his Viennese colleagues, were set in the fluid homophonic style of the time: with plenty of Alberti basses, and rippling runs in scale and broken-chord shapes that often passed over two or more octaves in a single sweep. Melody was mostly of the symmetrical tuneful type. Three movements was the standard, each one formed in a pattern involving conventionalized repetitions and recapitulations.

One rather curious convention is worth talking about. Let us first say that it would have been considered ineffective, if not rude, to have the soloist, the "hero," barge right in at the opening of the composition; his "entrance" could seem to gain its proper importance only if projected against a tension of expectancy built up by his supporting cast. This principle, however, confronted concerto composers with the following problem, a tri-lemma, if we may be permitted the expression:

1. As befitted the soloist's pre-eminence, he had to play all the concerto's most important themes and melodies.
2. According to the straightforward logic of the time, the composition's essential themes and melodies had to be exposed at the beginning.
3. The soloist might not play at the beginning.

The concerto tailors solved the paradox by having the work's exposition played twice over. The orchestra would begin by announcing all the material of the movement: first theme, episode, second theme, coda—whereupon the soloist would play the whole thing over again, usually with ornamental modifications. Listeners of those days were simple-minded enough not to object to this systematic redundancy; they rather enjoyed watching the soloist squirm in his seat, wiggle his fingers, tap his toes on the floor, and throw his head in the air while waiting for the long thematic preaudition to take its course. Not until the middle of the nineteenth century did this type of concerto design fall into disuse.

Another concerto feature we must speak of is the cadenza. The word is Italian for "cadence," meaning a short progression of tones leading directly and inevitably to the close of a musical section—a "dying fall," Shakespeare once called it. Eighteenth-century opera singers had been forming the habit of spicing this penultimate point of their arias with all manner of extracurricular runs, trills, and jumps, thus imparting a pleasant little delay to an otherwise foregone finish. Presently the word cadenza came to mean the twiddly bits themselves, rather than the point at which they were introduced. Cadenzas in pianoforte and violin concertos took on a rather rank vigor. Somewhere near the end of the movement the orchestra would stop on a loud, inconclusive chord; thereupon, the soloist would emit geysers of difficult-sounding passage work, roam away into strange keys, and toy with altered reminiscences of former themes. He might continue on this joy ride for whole minutes, with the audience wondering whether he could ever find his way home; but eventually he always did, and at his signal the orchestra would re-enter and help bring the piece forthwith to a well-deserved end. In theory, the cadenza was improvised at the moment, and probably this was sometimes true in practice. Yet it was important merely for it to give that impression, and it was nobody's business whether or not a pianist wrote the cadenza all out beforehand.

Concertos such as we have described became the normal fare for all public solo performance on the pianoforte. From about 1780 until about 1840 any pianist offering himself for public hearing as a soloist was expected to play a concerto that had this standard equipment: a pale orchestra accompaniment, an abundance of fleet runs, a lengthy orchestral preamble, and cadenzas in the first and third movements.

Competent new pianoforte practitioners continued to appear in Vienna during the eighties. Young Anton Eberl, a native Austrian, began to make a name for himself. His agreeable compositions found ready acceptance in "clavierland"; some of them were later issued fraudulently, though evidently not implausibly, under Mozart's name. Josef Gelinek, still another Bohemian, had taken holy orders, but devoted himself entirely to music. Upon Mozart's recommendation, Prince Kinsky appointed him private tutor to his children. From that point of vantage Gelinek began to turn open a faucet of variations, on all manner of momentary tunes, all neatly made, easy to digest as well as to eliminate.

Shortly before November 10, 1792, the twenty-two-year-old Ludwig van Beethoven plunged into the Viennese welter of officialdom, luxury, social climbing, and music. One of his first acts there was to follow up an announcement in a newspaper offering a piano for rent; he got it for six florins and forty kreutzers a month. He had come to the city under the auspices of Count Waldstein, and soon he found himself going about in the most exalted society. It was playing the piano in a number of aristocratic houses that gained him his first successes; his high capacity for emotional tension and the reckless originality of his musical ideas gave his improvisations, especially, a compelling—sometimes repelling—power. Beethoven was not pretty to look at: he was short, swarthy, pock-marked, flat-nosed, and buck-toothed; nevertheless, he fascinated many a female, as well as male, music lover.

Presently Beethoven had a pianistic competitor. Josef Wölfl, a native of Salzburg, pupil of Leopold Mozart, came to Vienna about 1795. He was tall, wavy-haired, with large hands and a gentle, dreamy look in his eyes, good-humored, and a good mixer; probably he was a smoother, more accurate pianist than Beethoven. His particular patron was Baron Raimund von Wetzlar, son of the nobilitized old profiteer of whom we have already spoken. Beethoven and Wölfl were often invited together to Freiherr von Wetzlar's delightful suburban villa, where they entertained the other guests by playing the pianoforte with, for, and against each other in ostensibly friendly rivalry. Listeners took sides, and the play of arguments supporting the partisans' choice was part of the residual fun of these events. A contemporary writer stated that the Wölfl "rooters" seemed to be in the majority. Evidently the Salzburger's style was close to the norm of taste for the time: he gave easy satisfaction to almost everybody, whereas Beethoven's rough technique and hazardous harmonic sallies affected some people unpleasantly.

3. AN OLD "NEW DEAL"

THE SOCIAL CHANGES that had been brewing since before the middle of the century went on at a much accelerated rate after 1780. By that time the numbers and wealth of the commercial classes had grown greatly; their improved education, their infiltration into the learned professions and into all but the highest reaches of government had proceeded so far that it could be foreseen that their habitual attitudes might ultimately pervade, and even dominate, society as a whole. The wholesale ennobling of bankers and professors was in itself a symbol of that process. In its course, some of the richer bourgeois imitated a few of the superficial habits of the aristocracy; but this was a small counter-eddy in the progressive burgherization of society. The educated, well-to-do middle class, likewise, was the chief vehicle of the newer thought-trends; of the interest in science, invention, and historical research; of the loss of confidence in the dogmas and the authority of the church; of the zeal for liberty of thought, speech, and publication.

After Emperor Joseph II became sole regent in that year, 1780, his celebrated "New Deal" merely confirmed the results of tendencies that had been working for some time. He did, indeed, abolish the remnants of peonage, dissolve a superfluity of religious orders, affirm his right—against Rome—to review ecclesiastical appointments, and set up an equable basis for taxation; furthermore, he established religious toleration, allowed an unprecedented liberty of the press (including some rather mean attacks on his own person), and broke down much of the burdensome, complex delicacy of court etiquette.

Indeed, some of his reforms were too extreme for ordinary people to stomach. For instance, he felt that it was senseless and wasteful to spend money for funerals and the disposal of the dead; so, on September 15, 1784, he ordered that all corpses were to be put into gunny sacks and buried in quicklime. The general outcry was so pained that he rescinded the order five months later because, as he said sarcastically, "my subjects wish to remain carrion for a longer time." Had this sumptuary legislation been attempted ten years later, it would have been denounced as "Jacobin," just as certainly as in 1920 it would have been called "Bolshevik." Another drastic, sweeping Josephine ordinance, dated July 15, 1782, was typically Jacobin-Bolshevik in its animus: on the principle of "evenhanded justice," noblemen and privy councilors were compelled, equally with menials and vagrants, to sweep streets as punishment for minor infractions of the penal code. The inequality of the mental suffering involved was soon made clear to the overeager, perhaps well-meaning ruler, and this law too was abrogated.

It was an absolute monarch of ancient, legitimate lineage—a Holy Roman Emperor—who attempted to destroy these persistent, venerable values. No revolution, no rapid transfer of political authority, took place in Austria; Joseph himself died in 1790, and many of his innovations were then modified or erased. Yet, it is clear, from what we have just recounted, that the social climate had altered irrevocably and that even conservative old nostalgiacs were beginning to understand that they were never going to go back to the old country again.

In 1789 many aristocrats were disturbed by the news from France; by 1793 they were mortally shocked. It was true, then, that a large section of Western Europe—"the world," as they naïvely called it—no longer believed in them as a class, in fact considered them expendable. Perhaps they could hang on to some remnants of their ancient privileges if they kept quiet and behaved themselves discreetly. They discarded their powdered wigs and acquiesced in the general class-indiscrimination of clothes styles; they stopped dancing the polite minuet and took up the plebeian waltz. They relinquished their leadership as art patrons: only a few music-foolish stragglers such as Prince Lobkowitz, or that fabulous spendthrift Prince Nikolas Esterházy, failed to disband their excellent private orchestras. These few still commissioned musicians to compose works for their own private use and performance; but in Beethoven's case, six months or a year was considered the limit of their prerogative: they gave their silent permission when the composer resold them to a publisher after that period.

The devaluation of nobility did not come as a tide of mere abstract opinion or sentiment; it was the expression of a change of balance in the very foundations of power. European nobility was, in itself, originally a mere certification of the ownership of land together with the accompanying rights of its administration and defense. Land had been for many centuries almost the only source of wealth; thus, wealth, power, and rank mutually supported and justified each other. What happened in Northern Europe in the eighteenth century was that wealth in the form of money was becoming as great and important as wealth in the form of land, and much more widely distributed. This new money was derived from trade and industry, from newly invented mechanical techniques, from a more productive organization of labor, from the improvement and spread of communications, from cities rather than from the country.

Land is a fixed thing—it is unchangeable in total amount—it is difficult to transfer, to convert, to conceal or camouflage for diplomatic reasons, and impossible to transport. Social organization based on it tends to assume a corresponding fixity, a quality of sanctified status. On the other hand, the essence of money is circulation—a quick, incessant, elusive flow from hand to hand, a perpetual transformation into a thousand different commodities—no one can conceive, much less follow, the sum of its movements. An unalloyed money-society can have no fixities, since money cannot stay still: in the face of its incalculable flux, all persons are reduced to a basic hypothetical equality of opportunity.

The principles of social imitation reflect the contrast between solid land and liquid money. In a feudal community anyone may properly have only that to which his rank entitles him: ranks are recognized boundaries, and it would be supremely incorrect—in fact, subversive—for someone to attempt to ape his betters across a fence (a wholesale grocer trying to wear a sword appears ridiculous). But money has a very limited tolerance for boundaries; it may seep through partitions, pour into unexpected basements and sewers, and evaporate from the best-protected reservoirs. Under a money rule, anyone may correctly have anything he can pay for; any object that a millionaire can acquire for a hundred dollars may be bought with perfect propriety by one whose fortune is a mere hundred thousand or ten thousand.

The old high nobility had taken up the pianoforte in the earlier 1780's. When the money-barons followed suit, a sort of chain reaction was set up, by which the financially less and less potent began to ape their richers. As the 1790's progressed, moderately wealthy families—merchants and manufacturers, doctors, lawyers, professors, and middling government officials—felt impelled to own pianos. The majority seem to have been those who had enjoyed some sort of higher education and who could point to the instrument as a symbol of that proud condition.

The pianoforte was the thing: it was the instrument of the "New Deal," of the bourgeois, the money culture. The harpsichord, once the collector's object of princes, was passé, was hardly being made any more: the new class of customers all wanted the new-fashioned article. It is true, we occasionally find music still published "for pianoforte or harpsichord" for some years after 1785; that inscription does not mean, however, that composers ever gave the older instrument much of a thought when setting down their notes. Some people, indeed, still possessed harpsichords that had not yet been completely eaten by worms, thrown out for firewood, or broken up for the sake of an ornamental painting; and the "or harpsichord" phrase was merely the publishers' way of not discouraging the owners of such orphans from buying copies.

We can get an idea of the spread of piano playing in Vienna at the turn of the eighteenth century from the remarks of an anonymous resident who acted as correspondent for the newly founded *Allgemeine Musikalische Zeitung* (*General Music News*), a Leipzig publication destined to be the most important witness of German musical events for fifty years to come. In his article of May 15, 1799, the writer states that Vienna harbors more than three hundred piano teachers. The autumn of the following year the correspondent (probably the same man) gives his estimate, in a letter, of the opportunities for musicians in the Austrian capital. Pianists, he says, can make a living without having a permanent engagement, but "they must have sufficient abnegation to endure subservience in many ways to the houses that support them, and to give lessons from morning till evening."

If we take a heavy discount off the "morning till evening" statement and conservatively allot, say, ten pupils to each of the three hundred teachers, we find three thousand pupils—mostly girls, of course—actively taking piano lessons. To this number let us add, arbitrarily, an equal number of persons who have at one time taken lessons but have discontinued them—perhaps after marriage; we then arrive at a figure of six thousand piano players in a city whose female population (assuming it to be half the total) was about 110,000. This works out at about five per cent and would, therefore, include a large fraction of all the more well-to-do people of Vienna. This "calculation" is, of course, a mere toy balloon, blown up by a number of unsupported guesses; nevertheless, it may prove suggestive, especially to people who feel more confident of knowledge when it is in the shape of numerals.

4. PIANOS BECOME A BUSINESS

More people now actively wanted pianos than had ever before tried to buy any keyboard instrument; certain changes had to be made in the circumstances of piano production if the demand were to be adequately supplied. Johann Andreas Stein, the esteemed pianoforte maker of Augsburg, became afflicted with dropsy and died of it in 1792, aged sixty-four. We will remember his daughter Nanette, whose playing as a little girl Mozart had criticized. She had inherited much of her father's genius and had grown up to be a person of great practical intelligence, thoroughly conversant with the mechanics of piano building. After the old man's death, she and her brothers decided to continue making pianos, but to do so in the place where the most people wished to buy them—that is, in Vienna. They moved to the capital, but Nanette soon separated from her brothers; she had already married a worthy, mediocre musician named Johann Andreas Streicher, and a firm of which she was guiding director was set up under the name of "Nanette Streicher, *née* Stein."

Father Stein, during the forty years of his Augsburg instrument making, had—aided by a small number of assistants—turned out about seven hundred claviers, an annual average of seventeen to eighteen; his rate of production was about normal for craftsmen of the period. Nanette set up her enterprise in 1794. By 1809 her output had progressed as far as pianoforte No. 804; by 1816 she had reached No. 1152—indicating a yearly rate of about forty-nine to fifty-three. Clearly, this could be accomplished only by a considerable enlargement of plant facilities, an increase of working personnel, a fairly rigorous division of labor, and a steady purchase of certain ready treated materials. It could only be done by an organization approximating what we would call a factory.

Factory production involves problems that do not affect individual craftsmen-makers. A factory must pay a considerable number of regular wages and salaries, it must pay high ground-rent or taxes, and it necessarily has money tied up in large amounts of materials. It can only meet these expenses by assuring itself a rapid, uninterrupted sale of its products. Inevitably, the head of a factory tends to regard sales as more important than production. Unfilled orders give him less of a stomach-ache than excess inventory. A piano maker who expands into a factory ceases to be a craftsman; he becomes a businessman.

If continuous sales are what keep a factory afloat, it is clear that these cannot be left to the inertia or the unguided whims of potential customers. The factory owner must make a purposeful effort to stimulate the buying impulse of as many likely persons as he can reach. He must artificially prod, lure, or bully the possible purchaser into bestowing his pay-dirty attention and approval upon the factory's product—in other words, he must advertise.

Apparently, piano makers were doing so before 1790, even outside of Vienna. Johann David Schiedmayer, a Stein disciple, had set up his business in Erlangen, near Nürnberg. In the *Erlangen Occasional Notices*, probably during March 1789, there appeared an offering of his instruments, which were described thus:

> A construction whose accuracy and care gives the case the smoothness of seamless marble, a keyboard that is a delight to look upon and whose unsurpassed mechanism is receptive to the gentlest finger-play, a tone which rivals the bassoon in the bass and the sweetest fluting in the treble, one that can be raised from the softest breath of a pianissimo to a smashing fortissimo. These are, very shortly, the

qualities of the Schiedmayer fortepianos, which may be purchased, though hardly paid for, with 40 louis d'or.

The affected arrogance of this verbiage, with its curious undertone of cajolery, is characteristic of a mind that is nervous about sales. Bourgeois people, especially Americans, who have been pressed into feeling that the limitless piling up of profits is the worthiest of all human efforts, will look upon advertising of this kind with a rather sympathetic amusement. Its ethical falsity, however, afflicted many Europeans, especially old-fashioned Germans, with a cold distaste. They had a good name for this sort of talk: they called it "market screaming."

Advertising in Vienna was often more subtle. Competition had developed among piano makers: in addition to the names of Schanz, Walter, and Streicher, already mentioned—and that of Nanette's brother, Andreas Stein—we also come across those of Jackesch, Joseph Moser, Z. Pohak, Matthias Müller, Brodmann, and Conrad Graf, all making pianos in Vienna before and during the earliest years of the nineteenth century. Most of them tried to entice Vienna's many, many piano teachers into helping them dispose of their wares: they offered a commission to any musician who steered a piano sale onto their books, rather than onto those of the opposition. Beethoven had many opportunities of garnering an unchallenged florin in this way, but he never did so; he disapproved the practice, at least for himself, and did not fancy himself as a household-goods broker. Nevertheless, he was sometimes willing to use his influence with piano makers to have the price of an instrument reduced for the benefit of his friends. If the maker were ready to pay a commission, figuring it as "selling expense," he could not object to having the sum turned back to the customer. Thus, we see Beethoven writing to a friend in 1807 that he was hoping to select a piano at Schanz's for a certain Frau M.—probably Frau Malfatti, the wife of a friendly physician. "It is not to cost more than 500 fl., but will be worth a great deal more," he said, and proceeded to explain the principle of the commission. Some years later we find him arranging with Schanz for the purchase of an instrument for a Mr. Varena, attorney for the Imperial Exchequer, living in the provincial city of Graz. "It cost 400 fl. with packing," wrote Beethoven to Herr Varena; "any other person would have had to pay 600 fl." If Beethoven's statement is to be taken literally, it means that a well-established maker such as Schanz was willing to pay a commission of 33⅓%, indicating a high selling expense and markup. That seems to be the prevalent principle in the case of luxury goods or those having snob appeal. The practice of paying a commission to musicians for their assistance in piano sales became well-nigh universal and has continued to the present day.

The piano makers had other forms of advertising: they liked, if they could, to borrow the prestige of a famous or well-connected musician—presenting him with an instrument, if necessary, in order to be able to boast that he was using it. Beethoven writes, in November 1802, ". . . ever since one has been under the impression that I am at loggerheads with Walter, the whole swarm of pianoforte makers is impatient to serve me—and in vain. Each of them wants to make me a pianoforte to my liking . . ." He says he can get one gratis anywhere.

He began to get them gratis from some distance. At about this time the up-and-coming firm of Erard Frères was making pianofortes in faraway Paris; it could already claim that it had supplied one to the august First Consul, named Napoleon Bonaparte. In Vienna, Josef Haydn's great oratorio *The Creation* had recently been performed with unparalleled acclaim; the composer's sun was setting in a blaze more glorious than it had ever put forth in the previous seventy years of his life. The Erards hoped to catch and reflect a bit of its quickening warmth, so they sent the grand old man one of their instruments. Leopold Koželuch was considered an arrogant ass by many; yet he was a much respected court music director and court composer as well as a generally esteemed pianist. They sent him a piano likewise. Beethoven was among the younger Viennese musical stars; the canny Erards gave him also a free sample of their product, with the expectation that his expanding repute would impregnate their brand with some of its potent radiations.

5. ASPIRATION AND PRETENSE

IT IS CLEAR that by the beginning of the nineteenth century pianos were being bought by all manner of people who had little understanding of their points, who had to grope among the vaguest associations to form any judgments about them. The opinion of a dubious "expert" in the form of a teacher might decide the purchase. Relatively few persons had any keen appreciation of Beethoven's greater works, but everybody had heard of him, in more or less fabulous terms. Any make of pianos he was known to play would have to be fine: was he not famous, were not his compositions sprinkled with dedications to princes and countesses, and was he not reported to hobnob with his pupil His Royal Highness the Archduke Rudolph? Such excellence would have to be contagious.

Having a piano in one's home, then, was fashionable in the 1790's and thereafter. By fashion, we do not necessarily mean a quickly passing craze; the instrument was too expensive and too substantial for such trifling. We mean that it was a luxury in which many people indulged because others whom they felt urged to imitate did so. Fundamentally, for middle-class people to own a piano was an aspiration: to practice literate, artful music within the family circle was a gesture toward living a more abundant life, toward the fulfillment of one's finer capabilities. Alas! It is difficult to penetrate the deeper insights, the subtler craft, of exceptional minds, to follow the flights of genius; it requires much time and devoted effort over and above a gift of talent and intelligence. How much easier it is to spend money, learn a few glib formulas, and take an unconcerned little pleasure in a shallow aesthetic routine—in having one's few mental grooves mildly caressed—and thereby to earn a thoughtless credit for cultivation among one's inferiors. The piano did represent an aspiration, but almost instantly it became a pretense. No one could draw a line between the two—trying to be, making believe to be—no one can tell where the one stops and the other begins: they merge insensibly. In middle-class circles, the gesture—aspiring or pretentious—soon became current as a substitute for the inner reality from which it was supposed to spring, a bill of moral-inflation currency passing as legal tender. For a family to own a piano, to make its daughters play the instrument whether or not they wanted to or had any aptitude therefor, became an accepted badge of the house's prosperity and refinement. Excellent music could indeed be made at home with no equipment whatsoever, as madrigal singers know; but the costliness and complexity of the piano was an object in itself, rendered it a convenient implement of ostentation, was part of the pretense involved.

The afore-mentioned correspondent of the *Allgemeine Musikalische Zeitung* describes the music culture of well-to-do Viennese rather vividly. We quote from his letter of October 22, 1800:

There are probably few cities where musical amateurism is as general as it is here. Everybody plays, everybody learns music. Quite naturally, there are some very able dilettantes amongst this great crowd; but they are not so frequently met with as they used to be. Music is being looked upon as something easy, as if it were something that could be learned in passing. as it were: one thinks one knows everything right away, excuses one's self finally with the word "amateur," and regards the whole thing more as a matter of *galanterie* and good form. Yet the city contains a larger number of solid connoisseurs and lovers of music *as an art* than outsiders seem to believe . . . Countless so-called "private academies" (music in upper-class houses) take place here throughout the winter. There is not a saint's day, not a birthday, on which music is not made. Not much can be said about these performances, nothing at all if one does not want to give a humorous impression. Most of them resemble each other pretty closely; they look like this: First a quartet or symphony, which at bottom is looked upon as a necessary evil (you have to begin with something) which the company chatters away. Then, however, there appears one young lady after another, lays open her piano sonata—possibly not without a certain demureness and grace—and plays it off as best it will go. Then come others who sing some arias from the latest operas, in the same way. The thing gives pleasure—well, why not? And who has any business saying anything against it if it is regarded merely as a family entertainment? But one must not think of it as a promotion of art. On the contrary, this widespread all-too-easy amateurism has spoiled taste and allowed the sense for greater things to fall asleep. That accounts for the otherwise remarkable belittling of musicians on the part of upper-class people, even when these are themselves amateurs; but to this the coarseness and immorality of many musicians contributes.

Our correspondent writes at the moment when Haydn was an elderly man, at the height of his fame; when Mozart had died, prematurely, not quite ten years before; when Beethoven was thirty and Schubert still a baby. It would be wrong to speak of a musical decadence at this period. But if music in upper-class houses was as tainted with triviality as he says, what must it have been in more modest circles? The writer continues describing an interesting social phenomenon:

. . . a few words about speculation through musical amateurism . . . every well-bred girl, whether she has talent or not, must learn to play the piano or to sing: first of all, it's fashionable; secondly (here the spirit of speculation comes in), it's the most convenient way for her to put herself forward attractively in society and thereby, if she is lucky, make an advantageous matrimonial alliance, particularly a moneyed one. The sons likewise must learn music: first, also, because it is the thing to do and is fashionable; secondly, because it serves them too as a recommendation in good society; and experience teaches that many a fellow (at least amongst us) has musicked himself to the side of a rich wife, or into a highly lucrative position. Students without means support themselves by music . . . if somebody wants to be a lawyer, he acquires a lot of acquaintances and clients through music by playing everywhere; the same is true of the aspiring physician.

. . . it proves that one may not reason from the favorable condition of music here in point of amateurism to its favorable condition as an art.

6. WHAT DID VIENNA PIANOS LOOK LIKE?

LET US TRY to get a more vivid physical image of the Viennese pianos of the 1790's. They were made almost entirely of wood: of the essential parts, only the strings and the tuning pins were metal, unless we want to include the pedals and their rods. Five octaves was the normal range, from contra-F to f'''

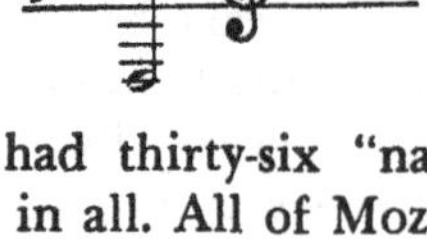

In other words, they had thirty-six "natural" and twenty-five "sharp" keys: sixty-one in all. All of Mozart's and practically all of Haydn's pianoforte works are contained within this limited compass, as well as all of Beethoven's until his Third Concerto, published in 1804. That includes some of his most impassioned and grand-sounding compositions, such as the Sonata *Pathétique* and the *Kreutzer* Sonata. It was in the very first years of the nineteenth century that Vienna piano makers began to follow the lead of the English and expand the range by several notes high in the treble. Indeed, there is extant an advertisement of a German-made piano (not from Vienna) of a six-octave range, F to f'''' —that is, a full octave higher than Beethoven's—dating from October 1799. Pedals, likewise an English invention, had been introduced into Vienna instruments during the eighties, as we have seen; knee-action levers, however, were still in use in 1800.

Somebody in the Streicher firm made a number of refinements upon J. Andreas Stein's escapement, and the improved Stein "*Prellmechanik*" ("bouncing action") became the standard for Vienna-made pianos and was thenceforth gradually called the "Vienna action." The Vienna action had a shallow key-fall: it had small hammers covered with leather. Its extreme lightness was due also to certain other mechanical reasons, which we shall discuss elsewhere in connection with English pianos. In the higher registers there were two or three strings, tuned in unison, for each note. Heavy, overspun bass strings such as we have on modern pianos were not yet in use; the wooden framework could not have supported the tension they require. Instead, long, thin bass strings were used, sometimes made of brass; they may have given forth a good quality of tone, but they sounded much weaker in proportion to the treble than is the case in today's instruments. That may be why Beethoven occasionally specifies "*ben marcato il basso*" in passages that seem to us to require little emphasis, but merely distinctness—as, for instance, the piano part of Variation No. VII in the last movement of the Trio Opus 11. Yet the overspun bass strings—cores of steel wire wound with copper—did make their appearance gradually in the earlier part of the nineteenth century.

The horizontal wing-shaped instrument was naturally the type generally used for concert performances. Yet square pianos were evidently much in use in private dwellings; their simpler shape was economical of space and also lent itself more readily to the endless whims of housewives possessed by a lust for rearranging furniture.

The notion of owning a piano was pervading a further and further reach of atmosphere, so that many families with small living rooms could also begin to sniff it. It was in the cards that some day some one would think up a still greater economy of space in designing the instrument. In 1800 Matthias Müller, Vienna piano maker, announced something new in the world: a true upright pianoforte. We have already encountered attempts, far back in the 1740's, to set a wing-shaped piano up on end upon a stand. Müller thought up the ingenious scheme of setting up the piano on its tail—not on a stand, but on the floor. Complete stability was achieved by supporting the entire works within a rectangular case. A convenient, compact shape was thus realized, as well as a considerable saving of floor area. The instrument stood about five feet two inches in height. Furthermore, it avoided the mechanical weakness of having to make a gap in the sounding board to allow the hammers to strike the strings from behind: a clever, practicable down-striking action was devised.

Müller's idea was quite sound; but he was about twenty-five years ahead of the time when it could have been more readily successful, and we do not hear of him making conspicuous headway with it. Perhaps the production methods available to him made it impossible to fix his price low enough for the kind of people who could have been most interested in his creation. Furthermore, he compromised the success of his invention by tying it up with a design for combining two of these uprights back to back, a sort of double piano. Finally, he saddled his instrument with a rather unsalable name. True, he fell in with the current brand of artiness by giving it a synthetic Greek label; but it was one that no one could understand, one that did not contain "lyro-," "harmono-," "melodo-," "Apollo-," "Orpheo-," or "-chord"—he called it *"Ditanaklassis,"* or, alternatively, *"Ditalleloclangé."* The former word's meaning is hard to take apart—apparently it is something like "double-stretch-bend"; the latter word means "double-mutual-sound." Müller was clearly a better mechanic than sloganeer. Later in life he took out patents on railroad tracks and propellers.

Vienna was built dense, especially its inner area, the city proper, constrained within its ancestral battlemented walls. By 1800 a considerable section of the population was living in apartment houses. Some of these were huge complexes—such, for instance, as the so-called *"Bürgerspital,"* whose three stories and garret occupied a whole block, one front facing the Kärntnerstrasse, right near the heart of the city. Its thousands of tenants and their visitors had ample opportunity to get lost in its maze of courtyards, passages, entrances, stairways, and corridors. People of some means and social position lived in this building. For example, Zmeskal von Domanovecz, Hungarian court secretary and exquisite musical amateur, had bachelor quarters there; that was where he staged his select weekly Sunday-noon chamber-music gatherings, with himself sometimes taking a cello part and with his friend Ludwig van Beethoven occasionally trying over new creations on the good Streicher piano. Living quarters near the Imperial palace, the theaters, and the good restaurants were desirable, but scarce; early in the nineteenth century we begin to hear of apartment buildings erected in the suburbs, speculatively, against the ever-increasing number of well-to-do people desirous of occupying them.

J. F. Reichardt, the Prussian composer whom we have already briefly met, spent the winter of 1808–9 in Vienna, making endless acquaintances. We can sympathize with him, then fifty-six years old, when he complained several times of the unusually steep flights of stairs he often had to climb, only to find his visitee out. His discomfort, however, allows us to understand that if Vienna builders tucked in tenants fairly tightly side by side, they were a little more lenient in caking them over each other's heads.

Limited floor space—high ceilings—well-to-do people: a Viennese piano maker, whose name has eluded us, fitted his thoughts into this constellation of notions and devised a piano shape more appropriate than Müller's to the facts and to the yearnings of the time. He too uprighted the instrument upon the floor, but on its broad end, with the narrow tail sticking way up into the air on the left side. The case followed the general curve of the shortening strings down on the right. Often the tail top was rounded off into a scroll and the entire structure, for obvious reasons, was usually called a "giraffe." It was a true upright piano with the hammers striking down upon the strings; the action was, however, placed below the level of the keys. "Giraffes" certainly took up relatively little floor space; on the other hand, their height was slightly monstrous, being on the order of seven and a half to eight feet. They were eminently successful and continued to be made in Vienna and elsewhere on the continent almost until the middle of the nineteenth century. They satisfied a need for showiness that developed in many newly enriched citizens. In addition to its spectacular outline, the structure afforded a number of purely ornamental opportunities: the nether (*i.e.*, right-hand) terminus of the great curve was often leveled into a small shelf onto which a built-on brass urn or an arrangement of lyre-shaped metal could be fastened, or possibly even a full-length wooden statue of Apollo carrying his lyre in his very own hand. The long, straight left-hand side underneath the scroll might be costumed into a Corinthian-capitaled column standing on the ground; however, even the elegance of the scroll was sometimes sacrificed for the sake of another flattened surface on the pinnacle, which could then be crowned with a carved-oak garland, or again with an urn. The keyboard was often held up by a pair of bronze caryatids, and many little bronze plaques and medallions were pasted on other parts of the façade, above and below the keys. The main front of the instrument, immediately covering the strings, was silk or other luxurious cloth stretched between or behind various patterns of wood paneling.

"Giraffes" could be expensive, and there is a record of one in maplewood—with ivory keys, complete with oak garland and lyre-holding statuette—that was offered for sale in 1817 for eighty carolins, which is about nine hundred florins. The long curve of the "giraffe's" back, the brass and the ivory, were all congruous with a style of furniture much esteemed at the time and since generally known as "Empire," after the reign of Napoleon I.

We can readily understand that the family of a prosperous kitchen-utensil manufacturer, or a successful pawnbroker, or a resourceful supplier of fodder for army horses, might feel that placing an eight-foot "giraffe" against a wall of its drawing room was a chic way of affirming its new-found importance. We notice that all the "giraffes" of the period were furnished with a large number of pedals, anywhere from four to six. Their use is a further indication of the musical taste of their purchasers; we will discuss them in due course.

7. WHO COULD AFFORD PIANOS?

WE HAVE some evidence of the price of pianos at the time; it is contained in a curious book called *Yearbook of Music* (*Jahrbuch der Tonkunst*) put out in 1796. It was a venture on the part of a large and prosperous publisher by the name of Schönfeld. The volume is a sort of "social register," listing prominent Viennese; against each name are written remarks, mostly flattering, describing his or her qualifications as a musical amateur. Other musical information is also included. We learn that Schanz asked 40–100 ducats for his pianos, Walter 50–120, and that the Streicher firm would not let the cheapest go under a price of 66 ducats. That gives us a range from about 175 to 650 florins for an instrument, depending, of course, upon its size and the finish of the case.

Let us try to set these prices against the information we have about Vienna incomes. Toward the turn of the century we hear that certain Austrian high-titled landed grandees, from counts up to princes, enjoyed annual receipts of anywhere from 100,000 to 1,000,000 florins. Some of the great new money-magnates also dwelt in that same exalted financial ether. Count Moritz von Fries, for instance, inheritor of an 80% interest in his father's banking house, often credited himself with a semiannual profit of 300,000–400,000 florins. From that level we can trace a steady descent through a prosperous region of less overbearingly opulent businessmen; in 1781, however, a license to operate as a wholesale merchant was granted only to one who could prove that he had a fortune of at least 30,000 florins. At that period—it is reported to us—certain busy fashionable tailors, employing as many as twelve to twenty assistants, often had accounts receivable up to 30,000 florins. A *Hofrat* (court councilor) was the third in the hierarchy of government service, outranked by the *Staatsrat* (state councilor) and the *Geheimerat* (privy councilor). We know that such a *Hofrat,* as early as 1773, drew a salary of 4000 florins. Mozart had written that with a little more than 1200 florins he might be able to support a wife very modestly. A private tutor in a rich family was considered well compensated by 300–700 florins annually, plus his board and lodging. We may remember Miss Aurnhammer's references to a mediocre "office hero" with 300–400 florins. At that rate counts, financiers, wholesale merchants, and fashionable tradesmen could well afford pianos; a *Hofrat* would likewise be a plausible customer for one, especially if he also enjoyed an income from his wife's dowry; a budding young professional man might have to make sacrifices in order to pay for any except a very cheap one; while an ordinary white-collar employee was out of the market, in all likelihood.

What was the numerical distribution of the members of the various social classes? Accounts differ somewhat, but the average estimate seems to show that in about the year 1800 Vienna harbored less than 20 families of princes, about 50 families of barons, and anywhere from 30 to 70 families of counts. At the most generous calculation, then, the aristocracy numbered less than 1000 persons. True citizens—that is, owners of city property—were said to number about 4000–5000 individuals; unpropertied educated people—such as clergymen, army officers, physicians, university professors, and higher officials—swelled this amount by a considerable percentage. Thus, we can figure the putatively "well-bred" at 1/25 of all the inhabitants and consider this equivalent to the potential piano-owning fraction of the population.

On the other side, we hear that 40,000 Vienna persons were

engaged in domestic service. That would leave about 200,000 people who were factory workers, independent mechanics, tradesmen, little shopkeepers, cab drivers, petty officials, office workers, and shop assistants—mostly without pianos.

After the signing of the Treaty of Campoformio in 1797, the expenses for hostilities against Napoleon began to burden the national economy and Vienna was squeezed by a steady rise in the cost of living. The French occupied the city in 1805, and again more thoroughly in 1809: 100,000 Gallic stomachs had to be filled with free Austrian victuals that year. By that time inflation had puffed out wildly. On February 20, 1811, the government's bankruptcy was made official; the currency was reorganized, with five old paper florins redeemable for one new one.

As always in such cases, many people suffered but some people profited—especially speculators, bankers, merchants, and others who were in a position to make financial deals. In general, the situation favored the influence of the money-handling classes, the *bourgeoisie,* as against the landed gentry and those living on fixed incomes. The piano business, like all other businesses, reflected these dislocations; still, it must have adjusted itself fairly soon to the new conditions. After all, the new profiteers felt impelled to put on the same airs as had the old ones, and were sure to demand their instruments. We have a report that the Streicher firm, in 1816, asked 250 florins for a large *Flügel*—we would call it a "grand"—in walnut. This shows that the florin must have been rather severely dehydrated, since that sum is less than what the Streichers had asked for their lowest product in 1796. True, the same 1816 instrument, in mahogany, was quoted at 500 florins. In any case, the great main trend—that of broadening prosperity and demand for luxury—was not reversed, in Vienna or elsewhere in the Western world.

8. BEETHOVENIANA PIANISTICA

THE VIENNA PIANOS had a light action and a relatively poor resonance; thus, they were well adapted to a graceful, elegant style of playing—full of fleet, pearly runs and figures, and not too greatly encumbered with successions of heavy chords. This was precisely the style and the music most enjoyed by the Viennese. Johann

Nepomuk Hummel, a pupil of Mozart's, was a pianist whose concerts were especially well liked by the Vienna public during the first decades of the nineteenth century; his neat, fluent sonatas, concertos, rondos, and fantasies give us a good illustration of the politer taste of the period.

After 1809 Ignaz Moscheles, then still a teen-ager, began to make himself similarly attractive to Vienna music lovers. His touch may have been crisper than Hummel's and his phrasing more ostentatiously precise. In 1814–15 the Great European Powers, in their own august monarchial persons, gathered in Vienna to hold the famous congress that aimed to clean up the mess Napoleon had made; of the visiting royalties it was Alexander, Czar of the Russias, who aroused the most interest, what with his magnificence and the fits of benevolence that relieved his despotism. When a certain ballet tune in rudimentary 4/4 jingle was published as his "favorite march," that glittering association pushed it into a wide popularity. Young Moscheles hopped onto the balloon as it rose: he composed a set of showy, agile variations on the *Alexander* March and played them at a concert at one of the Imperial theaters. The costumed melody carried his name far, if at no great height. What could be more irresistible than the tune of the moment garnished with the streamers of the day?

Then there was Carl Czerny. When he was a boy, Beethoven had given him lessons; the master even wrote him a fine letter of recommendation. He saw and heard much of his teacher and also ran important professional errands for him. His talent was extraordinary: within the limits of a narrow harmonic scheme, he developed a prodigious understanding of the motion-shapes feasible to keyboard-traveling fingers. Czerny was a sweet-natured person, too unaggressive to be a good public player; he was all the more esteemed and sought as a teacher, from his early days on. Presently he began to compose, with an incredible diligence; he fed the publishers great rivers of salable merchandise. Rapid, feathery, well-articulated pianistic passage-work, chiefly for the right hand, was his best product—just what the light, bouncing, leather-covered little hammer-heads of the Vienna pianos could deliver best. It was a music without depth, intensity, or wit, but always smooth and pretty and rather ear-tickling when played fast: it displayed tonal ruffles and ribbons, ruching and rickrack, in endless variety of patterns and endless monotony of import. Its low specific gravity made it easy to take, and the Viennese as well as other Europeans took it in vast quantities.

On the other hand, Beethoven's greater pianoforte works were rather sharply set apart from the currently prevailing musical manner. His unexpected dissonances, his explosive accents, his terrifying crescendos, his outbursts of heavy chords—such as those in the first movement of his *Appassionata*—seemed wonderful but fearful to most of those upon whose ears they first so brusquely impinged. A relatively small group of accomplished amateurs, connoisseurs, snobs, and romantically minded devotees of "the grandiose," as they liked to say, were the carriers of his repute; they were an influential lot that could not readily be opposed. For most people, Beethoven's fame was an article of superstition; for the most part they much preferred the works of his less assertive, less inspired contemporaries. One critic advised him not to be so self-willed and extravagant and to take the well-behaved Anton Eberl for his model.

There were two women, both unusually capable pianists, who helped bring many of Beethoven's pianoforte works to life. Neither was a musician by profession; one of them played in public, though rarely. Marie Bigot de Morogues, *née* Kiéné, Alsatian born, was the wife of the curator of the library of Count Andreas Rasumovsky, the lavish music-patronizing Russian envoy in Vienna. It was she who first played for Beethoven his great Sonata *Appassionata* from his difficult, rain-soaked manuscript. There is a record of at least one concert that she gave, on her own account, in December 1808, at the smaller *Redoutensaal* of the Imperial palace. The program consisted almost entirely of Beethoven's compositions; Reichardt, who was in the audience, has informed us that "for the larger public, the choice of pieces was not very fortunate, since she picked out one of the most difficult concertos, as well as one of the most difficult, most bizarre variations of Beethoven on a queer theme of eight measures . . ." The *Thirty-two Variations in C minor,* to which he was undoubtedly referring, are somewhat in the style and pattern of the chaconnes that were so much enjoyed in the earlier eighteenth century and of which Bach and Handel furnished notable examples. That they should seem "queer" and "bizarre" to a mature musician of 1808 is another sure indication of the great shift of taste and values that had taken place during the middle of the eighteenth century.

The other remarkable feminine pianistic exponent of Beethoven's works was Dorothea von Ertmann, *née* Graumann; her husband was a professional army officer, stationed near Vienna for many years. Beethoven used to go and sprawl on her sofa: she played him his compositions and accepted his corrections. Affectionately he called her his "Dorothea-Cecilia." It was to her that he dedicated his *Sonata in A major*, Opus 101, one of his most artful, esoteric, and difficult works. All accounts agree that Frau von Ertmann's playing was worthy of the honor. She was tall, brunette, and fine-featured; her performance radiated a marked spiritual power. Clementi, first hearing her during his second visit to Vienna, exclaimed enthusiastically: "She plays like a great master." Praise indeed, considering the source. Clementi was himself a great master of music; on the other hand, Dr. Carl Bursy, a physician from a small Baltic town, was but a fairly accomplished pianist and was consequently willing to be a little captious in his judgments of a fellow-dilettante. He called on Frau von Ertmann when he visited Vienna; she played for him. He could not refrain from criticizing the way she occasionally rolled chords that were written to be struck together. "Even though she does it economically, I don't like it." Still, he did not fail to join in the unanimous approbation, saying she "plays gloriously" and "otherwise she plays the music just as it is indicated, and therefore so well."

There is reason to think that Beethoven was somewhat restless under the limitations of the Vienna pianos. He seems to have worked them to the extremes of their capacity, certainly as regards the forte. He was known at times to have hit them so hard that strings and hammers broke. About 1817 we find him asking Frau Streicher for an instrument with an especially loud tone, because of the infirmity of his hearing, as he said. Even before his deafness became severe, we can be sure that he craved an extreme intensity of tone (*i.e.*, loudness) to express the extreme intensity of his feelings.

He ultimately got a piano that more nearly matched his musical ideas when John Broadwood & Sons, the oldest and foremost firm of English piano makers, sent him an instrument, a so-called "grand," from London. It had a range of six and a half octaves, more even than the enlarged Vienna pianos and going down lower in the bass. Its action was a development of the Cristofori-Silbermann principle, a *"Stossmechanik,"* or "pushing action," quite different from the Vienna "bouncing action"—much heavier and harder to play, but productive of greater volume of sound.

The Broadwood piano had a troublesome journey before it was established in Beethoven's rooms. We will remember there were no railroads as yet: the instrument was shipped by sea from the London docks through the Strait of Gibraltar as far as Trieste on the Adriatic; from there it was carried over unpaved mountain highways, bumped uphill and down by the horse-drawn trucks of the period, 360 miles to the capital. Meanwhile, Beethoven took advantage of some influential connections: he got one of his high and mighty aristocratic friends to pull the right wires so that he did not have to pay the legal import duty on the instrument. Vienna piano movers and tuners had no experience with a strange, large English instrument of this type and they might well have committed some unwitting atrocity upon it. Fortunately, Cipriani Potter, an English pianist, was in Vienna at the time; he was familiar with the Broadwood make and was of great help in having Beethoven's present uncrated, hoisted about, set up, tuned, and put in order.

The whole affair might have seemed a rather expensive advertisement for the Broadwoods at the moment, yet it certainly paid off in associative prestige over a long time. Broadwoods are still in business, and the sentence "Broadwoods made a piano for Beethoven" is repeated by any number of English music lovers to this very day. Not that Broadwoods in their best period really needed to borrow their excellence from anyone. Beethoven wrote a letter of thanks to Thomas Broadwood, in miserable French, which we translate as follows:

> My very dear friend Broadwood! Never did I experience a greater pleasure than was caused me by the announcement of the forthcoming arrival of this piano with which you honor me by making me a present: I shall regard it as an altar upon which I will place the choicest offerings of my mind to the divine Apollo. As soon as I shall have received your excellent instrument, I will send you the fruits of the inspiration of the first moments I shall spend with it, as a remembrance from me to you, my dear B., and I only wish that they be worthy of your instrument.
>
> Vienna, Feb. 3, 1818

Beethoven received his Broadwood toward March 1818. By that time his hearing was pretty well gone and he had not played publicly for some time; yet he felt in some way that this piano was appropriate to his mature tonal dreams. He was tremendously proud of it and very jealous of having it touched by others, even for tuning purposes. His last three marvelous sonatas were composed after it was available to him, and the majestic final low C of the first movement of his last sonata, Opus 111, might be looked upon as a kind of tribute to the English manufacturer.

In 1813–14 diverse German states were at last able to co-operate politically, to beat to pieces the pawns of that unpleasant foreign tyrant Napoleon, and to throw them and him out of their realms. A gust of ethnic, cultural self-assertion blew up among the various Germans, coalescing the sparks of those slogans "liberty" and "nationalism." It had its effect on the language; and the puristic re-Germanizing of the vocabulary, which had been going on steadily for generations, received a quick temporary inflammation. Thus, we find Beethoven suddenly trying to find an equivalent for that Italian word *pianoforte*. In 1816 he sent his publishers, Steiner & Co., a title page for a new sonata—the one in A major, Opus 101—which he proceeded to designate "for the Pianoforte or *Hammerclavier*." He seems not to have been sure whether the word was correctly formed or whether it had not better have been "*Hämmerclavier*." "*The title must first be shown to an expert linguist*," he wrote; "*Hammerclavier* is certainly German, moreover the invention also is German"—everybody thought so in those days—"honor to whom honor is due." On January 23, 1817, he informed Steiner that "henceforth all our works that have German titles are to have *Hammerclavier* instead of pianoforte . . ." and indeed the following sonata, Opus 106, was so published and has been so nicknamed ever since. Four years later Beethoven again indited a new sonata—the one in E Major, Opus 109—"*für das Hammerclavier*." This time the publisher was Schlesinger of Berlin, who apparently had no enthusiasm for this sort of priggishness, especially as his customers showed little disposition to change their speech habits; so, the sonata was called "for the pianoforte" on the printed page. We hear little of "*Hammerclavier*" after that.

But the word stuck to Opus 106, as we have said, and has caused some confusion among a naïve posterity. Some persons have vaguely guessed that the word referred to some kind of newly invented instrument with a new name; others have imagined that Opus 106 was Beethoven's first work to be expressly designated as not for the harpsichord—a much more absurd notion.

Beethoven is said to have toyed with other, intentionally humorous, Germanizations of musical terms at about that time, especially in his correspondence with his friend Carl Holz. Along with "*Tonsatzwerker*" (literally, "tone-setting worker") for "composer," and "*Klangmachwerkzeug*" ("sound-making tool") for "instrument," we hear of "*Schwach-stark-tasten-kasten*" (soft-loud key-box) for "pianoforte."

9. WHAT DID THEY PLAY ON VIENNA PIANOS?

(a) OPERAS AND VARIATIONS

In speaking of the music actually performed on these Vienna pianos, we have thus far discussed concertos and briefly referred to sonatas and to airs with variations. The concerto was the one type of composition that a pianist was bound to offer a paying concert-audience for a solo performance. That was generally the case everywhere in Europe until near the middle of the nineteenth century. It is true that Mozart as well as other pianists, having played the expected concerto in the earlier half of the program, sometimes lightened the fare by playing a set of variations, or a fantasy, in the latter half.

Solo sonatas, nowadays such an important element in all piano programs, were not regarded as suitable for concert presentation until toward the end of the 1830's; they were looked upon as chamber music, to be enjoyed, if possible, at one of the "private academies" of which we have quoted a description. It may sound strange, but only one of Beethoven's piano sonatas was ever played in a Vienna concert during his lifetime. What that means is that in Vienna music in private homes still far overshadowed public concerts in importance and extent until the nineteenth century was fully one third gone. Those high Austrian aristocrats, with their skilled amateurism and their fine house orchestras, had made their mark on the musical habits of the city; they abdicated the more expensive forms of cultural leadership during the 1790's, but a long, vigorous resonance of their noble example lingered on well into the commercial age.

Concertos, sonatas, rondos, and fantasies formed the cream of pianistic fare; but there was much else, of smaller pretension, that a majority of people preferred to hear. To show it more clearly, we will take another expository detour.

It will be readily understood that long before the end of the century the German theater, along with literature and music, had come to derive its support primarily from a middle-class paying public: it had, too, become "burgherized." Let us leave Vienna for a moment. From 1720 on, the city of Leipzig had licensed a succession of theatrical companies to play in specified houses during the periods of the fairs. More or less educated middle-class people were the patrons of these performances. Comedies and tragedies were given, but the burghers tended to prefer comedy: it was comedy that showed characters close to the audience's own experience; the loftiness of tragedy was associated with the grandeur supposed to belong to remote kings and heroes. By 1755 Gotthold Ephraim Lessing, later known as the father of modern German literature, had presented his play *Miss Sara Sampson,* which later critics called "a bourgeois tragedy." It is a difficult designation for modern Americans to understand. In its day it meant that for the first time middle-class people were to be represented on the stage as serious characters; that their actions and feelings were to be regarded as having enough ethical content to be considered tragic; that for the first time stage-burghers (not just distant potentates) were allowed to seem heroic—to an audience of burghers. As it was, even the good Lessing was timid: he set his piece in England, so as still to flavor it with a little pathos of distance; and even so, one of his burghers has the title "Sir." Let us note here that many of these plays, comic and tragic, contained a certain amount of incidental music: overtures, entr'actes, and dances.

We approach the story of the burgherization of opera, but we can only point out a few of its relevant episodes. Attempts on the part of German commercial cities such as Hamburg and Leipzig to establish permanent opera houses similar to the court operas of Dresden or Mannheim broke down and disappeared, probably for financial reasons, before 1740. After that time, well-to-do Germans who were interested in the athletics of Italian vocalism had opportunities to attend the performances of one or another traveling Italian operatic troupe: Mingotti's, Locatelli's, and others. The traveling Italian troupes afforded many Germans the unfamiliar titillation of witnessing female singers on the stage, besides the pleasure of becoming directly acquainted with much ingratiating florid melody. After the mid-century point a good many prosperous German burghers were getting their share of opera—enjoying much of its music and its virtuoso singing, as well as flattering themselves with the thought that they, like the dukes, were now partaking of a fancy foreign luxury. Serious opera—that is, a musical magniloquizing of Nero, Andromeda, or Mithridates—was still the standard in court opera houses; but it appears that an unselected paying audience of burghers preferred the newer *"intermezzi"* and *"opere buffe,"* the short comic pieces that were playing such an important part in newer Italian productions. Pergolesi's famous *La Serva Padrona,* for instance, was a notable success in Germany, as it was everywhere else. Theater directors were far from anxious to discourage this trend, since these "light" shows were economical to put on.

Opera was seeping into the middle class from the top down, but a somewhat different kind of musical theater was bubbling into it from the bottom up. A man named Heinrich Gottfried Koch, director of a theatrical company, had obtained a Leipzig license. He had a hard time making ends meet, but for his sixty-eighth show he had an exceptionally bright idea: he produced a comedy translated from an English piece by Charles Coffey called *The Devil to Pay, or the Exchanged Wives.* Koch's chief fiddler, J. G. Standfuss, composed new melodies to its incidental verses, and it opened on October 6, 1752. The show was a rather low-brow farce, with plenty of swearing and scolding, full of roughhousing and ridiculous situations. The tunes and "lyrics," as we now say, were easy to remember, and the production was a smash hit. With this performance begins the significant history of the German *"Singspiel"* (literally, "song-play"), sometimes also called *"Operette";* we would call it "musical comedy."

Here was a new form of entertainment, with music as one of its most important ingredients. Clearly, it was something to appeal to large numbers of people, to all sorts of little citizens who would be abashed, estranged, or bored by opera. It was theater about real people with whom it was easy to feel identified, not about unapproachably remote demigods or Roman emperors; it was in the native language, not in incomprehensible Italian; its conversations were spoken—every least syllable was not steeped in artificial exaltation by being chanted; on the other hand, the introduction of musical "numbers" came as a welcome relief to spoken dialogue; finally, the music consisted of folksy German tunes—it was not decked out in artful Italian vocal brocades.

We say it was new, but only its respectable presentation and its comparative literacy could have been entirely new; in principle, that sort of mixture of mimicry, fiddling, singing, and dancing must have gone on at fairs and festivals all over Europe since the Dark Ages.

The Leipzig *Singspiel* was struck dumb—together with all other music and theater—during the Seven Years' War between Austria and Prussia (1756–63), which made Saxony into an innocent bystanding battlefield. After the peace treaty was signed, music soon started up again; Koch brought his troupe back almost immediately. Soon he made connection with J. Adam Hiller, whom we have met before as a fine musician and supporter of various kinds of new musical enterprises. *The Devil to Pay* was revived, this time with new tunes by Hiller, and it again became such a hit that Koch felt encouraged to produce a new Hiller musical comedy every following year, except one, for eight years. The names of these offerings give some indication of their flavor: *Lottie at Court, Love in the Country, The Hunt,* and *The Village Barber.* Some of them contained as many as thirty musical numbers. Their plots were decidedly "class-angled," which was one reason for their success among the humbler citizens. Among their characters, members of the nobility and the upper social ranks were shown off at a disadvantage against members of "the people": noble skirt-chasers, lascivious squires, and hardhearted landlords were ultimately foiled and held up to ridicule by simple country girls, forthright rustics, and sly farmers. The somewhat pretentious notion of "art" was minimized in the production of these shows: the tunes slid easily into the established hearing habits of multitudes of people; no trained vocalists or exceptionally endowed performers were required to sing them—any actor with a moderately agreeable natural voice and a basic sense of rhythm was judged qualified to send them out to an audience which, in turn, was soon able to repeat them unaffectedly.

A fine new playhouse was opened in Leipzig on October 10, 1766, in which these musical shows were given. A glance at its capacity will make clear the level of public to which they could appeal. It held 1186 persons and no doubt was often sold out. Let us remember that the Leipzig "Great Concert" was considered well attended when the audience numbered 200–300. At that time the city's population probably did not exceed 40,000. Yet we must not suppose—because admission to the house was available to large numbers of little shopkeepers, tradesmen, and employees—that the wealthier and more educated burghers disdained to patronize it. The rich and the learned too, in their frequent unbuttoned moods, enjoyed Hiller's tunes as much as anyone.

The Hiller tunes were whistled in the streets, we are told, sung on picnics, and played on, and sung to the accompaniment of, countless domestic claviers. The Leipzig publishers, Breitkopf's at their head, did a good business with clavier-vocal reductions of the *Singspiel* scores. *Lottie at Court* and *Love in the Country* went through four editions—2750 copies altogether—within fifteen years;

The Hunt was issued immediately in an edition of 2000 and twice again in editions of 1000 each. Hiller understood very well the limited capacities of his public: in his keyboard arrangements of his *Singspiel* scores he reduced the music to its lowest recognizable terms—without exception, the right hand plays the melody along with the voice, the left hand rumbles or pokes a scanty bass (perhaps "because of the delicate eyes and small hands of the fair ones," as Reichardt said).

Companies of players eagerly took up the quickly appealing, and therefore profitable, Hiller musical comedies; they spread far and wide. It may be that Vienna had an opportunity of hearing *Singspiele* even before a version of *The Devil to Pay* was first given there in 1767. French musical shows on the same order had been played there since the early 1750's, and translating them into German was an obvious step to take. Mozart's early little piece *Bastien and Bastienne,* composed in 1768, adapted from a French model, is a proper *Singspiel*—and is "class-angled" too. In any event, it was in Vienna that musical comedy found its most warmly favorable climate; within a few generations the city was to become a world center in this respect, and Vienna *Operettes,* translated into all languages, were to become a part of the folklore of all Western civilization. There were composers and authors, indeed, who were inclined to treat the *Singspiel* more "seriously"; that is, they put more blood and thunder into it, and plenty of supernatural characters such as fairies, demons, and ghosts: that tendency finally led to the creation of a distinctively German opera.

Thus, by the end of the century a large proportion of the Vienna population was enjoying the theater, much, perhaps most, of it musical. Together with the dance halls, which were even more essentially musical, it formed the chief resource of public entertainment for all classes of citizens. During the nineties Vienna had five playhouses. It was hard to get a seat in any of them; they were all filled every evening. It would not be a wide guess to say that every night in the week five to six thousand people went to a show, most of them bringing home some kind of tune in their heads. Italian opera, spoken tragedy, and imported French pieces were largely confined to the two court theaters, leased to a private entrepreneur since 1794; elaborate romantic German operas—with all kinds of supernatural hocus-pocus—were best given at the great Theater an der Wien, in which ample tricky stage apparatus was available. Two smaller theaters were located in plebeian suburbs, the Leopoldstadt and the Josefstadt Theaters; they dealt mostly in easy musical comedy, burlesque, and melodrama. Those productions, too, were liberally spiked with fairies and demons. We need not suppose that the rich and the well-born boycotted those places on any principle; the swells were often glad to enjoy less polite diversions. Nor did the high-class theaters disdain to put on *Operettes.*

For many years, the musical director and chief composer for the Leopoldstadt Theater was Wenzel Müller, born in Moravia, an artless, fertile, uninhibited tunester who in the course of half a century—beginning 1786—turned out more than two hundred shows for his house. Some of their racy, inelegant titles give a clue to their nature: *The Live Bag, The Bride in a Jam, Love Is Round as a Ball, The Snake Festival in Sangora, Vienna in Another Continent, The Shadow of Faust's Wife, The Swindle in Fool Alley, The Orangutan, Nina, Nanette, and Nancy, Felix Mouse, Fido Savant the Wonder-Dog,* and *Sixty Minutes Past Twelve.* Müller's melodies spread so far so easily that, like much other truly popular music, they often failed to earn their author due credit.

On the other end of the scale, Antonio Salieri had been, until 1790, the respected musical boss and composer-in-chief of Italian opera at the court theaters. It was, however, his most important conductor-underling and successor who became the Vienna public's favorite composer, the one who struck the truest average of taste among the generality of music lovers. His name was Josef Weigl; he was a native Austrian, personally well liked by the Empress, a middle-brow musician ambidextrous toward light Italian productions and sentimental German *Operettes*—such, for instance, as his once famous *The Orphan Asylum,* and *The Swiss Family.*

A steady spray of melody, then, was passing nightly—by cab and on foot—from five playhouses into thousands of homes, mostly middle-class. There it echoed and re-echoed—best aided and protected by the family pianos. Single airs, duets, and ensembles from operas and musical comedies, most readily accompanied at the keyboard, formed the chief fare at Vienna's endless private music meetings: so we are told by persons who were there. Informal, mixed opera singing—hanging close all the while to the piano life-line—was an invincibly satisfying pastime for thousands of Viennese.

Tunes from current stage productions formed a most convenient, plausible basis for the manufacture of pianoforte variations. Johann Peter Milchmayer, court musician to His Transparency the Elector-Prince of Bavaria, published his *The Right Way to Play the Pianoforte* in 1797; in it he says: "Pieces with variations ought always to be on such ariettas [little tunes] as are known to the listeners and are generally liked. With such pieces one must not grudge the public the pleasure of being able to sing along with them gently." Milchmayer recommends no more than six variations, possibly twelve if the tune is very short. The air with variations certainly provided an effective fusion of satisfactions: the easy pleasure of recognition could be joined to the kinesthetic tingle of pianistic runs, arpeggios, and trills. The great composers of the period, as well as the lesser, tossed off many specimens of this well-going type of composition. Mozart wrote sets of pianoforte variations on current hit tunes such as *"Unser Dummer Pöbel meint,"* from Gluck's *Pilgrims of Mecca,* as well as on old popular tunes such as the nursery rhyme *"Ah, vous dirai-je maman,"* mostly known as "A,B,C,D,E,F,G" in German and English. He often played them, as we have said, in the second part of his concerts. Beethoven, too, was a diligent confectioner of variations on slight tunes from both the Italian and the German theater—as well as on "Rule, Britannia" and "God Save the King." Even late in his career, long after he had any good reason for issuing potboilers, he amused himself by fashioning some highly ingenious variations—for piano, violin, and cello—on a petty ditty called "I Am the Tailor Cockatoo"; it was taken from the light opera *The Sisters from Prague,* by that genial vulgarian Wenzel Müller. Müller's show had had its brief day in 1796; if, as is quite possible, Beethoven composed his trio variations shortly before they were published in 1823, we must assume that the great composer had kept the trite little jingle in his head lovingly for twenty-five years.

If a tune succeeded in catching the public fancy, it was only reasonable for publishers to want to cash in on it: a variety of composers were encouraged to cut out their own particular sets of pianistic dresses to fit the little paper doll. The musicians probably needed little urging anyway, since they were going to share in the cash. Thus, J. Weigl, in 1797, produced a successful *opera buffa* called *Love the Sailor* (*L'Amor Marinaro*); it contained a rakish little melody whose words begin *"Pria ch'io l'impegno."* Joseph Eybler, capable church and chamber musician who had nursed Mozart in his last illness, came to find himself unequal to the task, imposed by the widow, of completing the deceased master's famous unfinished Requiem. However, he proved himself fully equal to the simpler chore of writing piano variations on Weigl's hit number. Perhaps Antonie von Lilien—talented, penniless daughter of an Austrian army officer—made a little pin money when her variations on the catchy *"Pria ch'io l'impegno"* were published. An obscure pianist named Knafel also hoisted a tassel of variations in the same prevailing breeze. Josef Wölfl, Beethoven's rival, also paid his tribute of nine piano variations to the popularity of the same tune; and yes, so did the prestigious Beethoven himself, as the last movement of his Trio Opus 11. Incidentally, Wölfl was one of the numerous crew who wrote variations on *"Ach, du lieber Augustin,"* and there is no good intrinsic reason why Beethoven should have refrained from similarly honoring that famous, ancient little waltz. We are glad to insist that, even in his shallower puddlings, Beethoven's superior resource and craft are readily noticeable; still, many of his productions differ only in quality, not in aesthetic intent, from those of his long-forgotten colleagues.

Vienna's premier one-man wholesale piano-variation factory was Josef Gelinek. We left him a while back, in his clerical garb, teaching ABC's to noble young Kinskys. Having established reliable sales-outlets for his variations, he concentrated on them almost exclusively and is hardly known ever to have composed any other species of music. Carl Maria von Weber later penned a good verse about him:

Kein Thema auf der Welt verschonte dein Genie;
Das simpelste allein—Dich selbst—variirst Du nie!

Your genius spares no theme that comes within your thrall;
Yourself you never vary—the simplest theme of all!

Gelinek could afford to be teased, what with his large turnover and his considerable export business. A back-page advertisement from a London publishing house, appearing about 1810, illustrates 36 of his items. We notice *"Pria ch'io l'impegno"* among them, also *"Ach, du lieber Augustin,"* as well as at least three different airs from Mozart operas and at least one more of Weigl's. About 145 of Gelinek's "varied airs" were known to have been printed, but no less than 1000 of them remained unpublished; undoubtedly, he carefully refrained from drugging his own market. It takes a good businessman to lose money on a grand scale, and thus we hear that Gelinek's fortune melted away later in his life. Despite that calamity, he survived long enough to be able when he died—two years ahead of Beethoven—to leave an estate of 42,000 florins, a pile that variations built.

(b) DANCE MUSIC

DANCE MUSIC was a copious material on which home pianists could use up their energies. The older court dances such as the allemande, the courante, and the sarabande, were obsolete by 1750; only the minuet remained. The polonaise had a local vogue in Saxony, as we have seen. A little before that time we begin to hear of a dance imported indirectly from England: the "country dance," a lively set of steps in halved 2/4 meter. Originally it had been a "round" dance, with people holding hands in a line or circle; any number could join in, and often there seems to have been little discrimination as to the participants. This "democratic" character may have been the reason why it was first attractive to the lower classes on the continent. In Paris the "country dance" became manicured and hairdressed, regularized into neat figures, and its name garbled into *"contredanse"* before it broke into polite society: it was as a *"contredanse"* that the Germans practiced it throughout the later eighteenth century; but some of its original informal flavor seemed somehow still to hover about it.

The Germans were soon to develop their own "New Deal" step from their own "grass roots." A dance of moderate speed, in gently revolving motion, in triple meter, had been danced by country people of the Alpine regions since no one knows when. The mental climate of the 1760's and '70's encouraged young intellectuals—such, for instance, as Goethe—to find this rustic expression of joy interesting and alluring. It was mostly called *"Deutscher Tanz"* ("German dance"); under the circumstances, that word "German" was almost synonymous with "popular." Sometimes it was also called *"Dreher"* ("that which turns") or *"Ländler"* ("the thing from the country"). Early it had made its way into Vienna, the big city nearest its rural home; a coarse clown known as Bernardon, singing from a vulgar neighborhood stage, first referred to its movement as *"walzen"* ("waltzing": literally, "revolving"). That was in 1754. After a while the dance attained some respectability in the capital.

Here again it was Emperor Joseph's influence that was decisive. His Imperial Apostolic Majesty, crowned in 1765, presently promoted the fancy-dress balls given during the pre-Lenten season in the so-called *Redoute*-rooms at the Imperial palace. By way of deliberately softening the partitions of caste and rank, he encouraged people of all stations in life, including the humblest, to mingle with each other and enjoy themselves at these affairs. He set his more reticent aristocrats an example by attending them himself; they would not hesitate then to make a habit of following him, especially once they had had pleasant adventures there. Waltzes were certainly danced at the *Redouten* after a time—as well as minuets and *contredanses*—for we know that Mozart, in his capacity as court composer, wrote some for these occasions, especially after 1788. By then, apparently, well-born, respectable Viennese were dancing the waltz at more or less informal gatherings in their homes, and even in public places. Friedrich Nicolai, inquisitive Berlin traveler, described Vienna life in detail as of 1781. He reported with astonishment that it was quite proper among the youth of middle-class families to frequent public dance halls; his fundamental distaste for the city did not prevent him from acknowledging that the Vienna manner of dancing the waltz was less extravagant, slower, and more decorous than its corrupt version had already become in North Germany.

Elsewhere than in Vienna, certainly, there were strong doubts of the waltz's decency. The idea of a couple of opposite sex remaining joined in what looked like a close embrace for the entire duration of a dance was shocking, if not repulsive, to many sensitive ladies and gentlemen who had been brought up to enjoy the stylized mummery of polite bows, curtsies, and reverences that constituted the minuet. Public "hugging set to music" struck them as a form of low-class lewdness. The waltz had other subversive features: it seemed utterly disorderly—it had no fixed number of steps, no prescribed direction of movement, no general pattern. It was for no settled number of couples: each pair danced without caring about any of the others—any couple could enter the dance or leave it at any second, as the whim might strike them. Truly, the waltz was an illustration of the two most intoxicating virtue-words of the age: the "people" and "liberty."

Reputable composers were writing waltzes in the 1780's. Mozart composed several sets of them, as we have seen, and also of *contredanses*. In the minuet movements of a number of his later chamber-music works he allows the middle section, the so-called "trio," to break into waltz rhythm. During the 1790's the Vienna Society of Artists used to give elaborate annual balls that were patronized by many of the highest-ranking personages, from the Emperor down. A prominent musical luminary was always asked to compose the music for the dances. Haydn, Koželuch, Wölfl, and Beethoven all felt it an honor to write waltzes and *contredanses* for these occasions.

As the century waned, dancing—especially waltzing—burgeoned from a craze into a frenzy. Dance halls multiplied, both within the city and in the suburbs; we still know some of their names: The Buck, The Pheasant, Moonlight, The New World, and Sperl. In 1808 there was played out the ace of trumps of all the commercial entertainment mansions: a man by the likely name of Siegmund Wolfsohn, having made money in trusses and bandages, put up a super-dance-palace in one of the suburbs later known as the seventh ward. It was called the Apollo Rooms and had six large dance floors and thirty-five smaller rooms for private parties, besides opportunities for other diversions. Probably some capital from the banking firm of Arnstein and Eskeles was invested in the enterprise. Its capacity was planned for at least six thousand simultaneous customers; five florins was the price of a single admission ticket, and five florins was the minimum charge for a supper without wine.

J. F. Reichardt, our observant Prussian visitor, went to the Apollo Rooms on the opening night of its second season, January 8, 1809. He tells us how impressed he was with its enormous candelabras and wall lights, its handsome decorations of cedars and balsams, its grottos and fountains, its billiard rooms and pastry shops, its great dining tables, its ninety-four waiters and its 200,000 florins worth of new silverware—as well as with the beautiful waltzes that the large band, from an elevated position, threw out over the dancers' heads. He went again later in the month; this time he estimated an attendance of seven to eight thousand, "of which probably not five hundred were people of 'good society.' " Many of them apparently were prosperous farmers from the nearby countryside, who arrived with their wives, children, and hired help. On that same night four thousand people went to the public dance at the Imperial ballrooms; what with known comparable attendance at other halls, it was calculated that forty to fifty thousand people went dancing publicly that night in Vienna. The city's population was then about 250,000.

How many were dancing at home? And to what? Needless to say, mostly to music from pianos.

Lady Fanny Arnstein, wife of the banker-baron Nathan Adam von Arnstein, was a much-admired person: from every side we hear praises of her talent, her charm, her wit, and her capacity for attracting and stimulating all manner of distinguished men. She was often compared to her Parisian contemporary Madame Julie Recamier, and the comparison even included the criticism that her parties, like Madame Recamier's, were sometimes too crowded for thorough enjoyment. On an occasion in the middle of December 1808, the Baron and Baroness invited a large assembly: that night there milled through the Arnstein rooms a swarm of three to four hundred guests. One of their number has reported to us that before the jam had become too close, the hostess' married daughter, the Baroness von Pereira, and a Miss Kurzbeck, one of Vienna's best amateurs, played together on the piano a brilliant four-hand sonata by Steibelt "and then with incredible patience and kindness many pretty waltzes, to which the fair young world turned itself round and round within the ever thickening throng."

On about February 1, 1809, our reporter attended "a large party, really a ball," at the Henikstein. That was their fancy title-name. The original man of distinction had been born simply Adam Albert Hönig, and his profits from farming the salt and tobacco excises in Galicia were large enough to warrant the Emperor's endowing him with an official preposition; thereupon, he had re-enforced a version of his name by an extra syllable, the better to bear the weight of that tremendous trifle. His son Baron Joseph von Henikstein, the present head of the house, was notable equally for his financial strength and for his enthusiasm for music: he imparted this latter interest to his sons and daughters. At the party of which we speak there were many dance-lusty young people: "The excellent sons . . . of the house, who all live in music, though they are fathers of families and have many fine children, themselves formed the band for the ball, which lasted until late in the night, and with much variety they made such entertaining dance-music as ten hired musicians could hardly have brought forth." A most warmly personal kind of hospitality, indeed, for the grown children of a director of the Austrian National Bank to play waltzes for his guests to dance to; it would be hard to imagine such a situation, however, in a comparable English home of the period.

The Arnsteins and the Heniksteins were fairly high-society: if their pianos were thus used for domestic dancing, we can be sure that the instruments of more numerous, less glittering citizens were resounding as frequently, as happily, and as informally with the lilts and jingles of waltzes, *contredanses,* and *écossaises.* The very freedom of the waltz made it an ever timely recreation in which to indulge; no special assortments of people were required —any impromptu mixed gathering, at any home, any afternoon or evening, might drop into waltzing at the first encouraging measures struck from the keys.

Inevitably, a steady demand was growing for new waltz tunes

for home use, and the activities of the music publishers show this up clearly. The composing and arranging of the music for the splendiferous Apollo Rooms was first entrusted to that fleet, neat pianist J. N. Hummel. No doubt he had supplied the band with some kind of score and individual parts; but when it came to printed copies for the public, it was *Dances for the Apollo Rooms for the Pianoforte* that were brought out under his name—many sets of them: Opus 27, 28, 31, 32, 39, and 45. All composers of the day wrote waltzes for the pianoforte: Wölfl, Eberl, Gyrowetz, Eybler, and others even more thoroughly forgotten. So did Anton Diabelli, another amiable Salzburger and a bland musician; presently he also became a publisher and had no trouble seducing himself into harvesting manufacturers' profits from his own tunes. He even succeeded in flaking off for one of his waltzes a crumb of parasitical posthumous persistence—sometimes quaintly called "immortality"—by giving Beethoven the opportunity of contriving a set of profound variations upon it.

Waltzes were among the publishers' safest aids to staying in business, and they disliked to be short of them. Under the Vienna circumstances of the early 1800's, any average young lady with a reasonable allowance of money might gaze at the display in any music-shop window and feel impelled to enter and to buy a copy of any pianistic thought, however insipid, that was shaped in 3/4 or 3/8 time. At that rate, the most platitudinous musical thinkers could find their way into print, and even profit, so long as they stuck to waltzes. Even composers made of sterner stuff could be tempted to turn some of their less than choicest ideas into cash. For instance, Muzio Clementi, in faraway London, had acquired a high distant repute, mostly justified, for musical seriousness and pianistic craft. When Artaria & Co. of Vienna issued a set of *Twelve Waltzes for Pianoforte* with Clementi's name on the title page, a Leipzig reviewer, on May 15, 1799, was so outraged by the flimsiness of those little pieces that he refused to believe they were genuine. He spoke of the "tremendous impudence" on the part of the publisher "thus to misuse the name of an artist still living. . . . Clementi would laugh himself sick over such a bear dance . . ." Alas, the critic did not understand that under Great Britain's glorious rays Clementi had gone commercial—in a dignified way, of course, but with an unguarded moment or two.

After a time Franz Schubert, Josef Lanner, and the two Johann Strausses showed that it was possible to put real genius into waltz composing.

In 1819 the waltz, for pianoforte, invaded the concert room. In that year Carl Maria von Weber, summer-vacationing near his Dresden opera job, composed and had published an elaborate, brilliant piano composition, mostly in waltz rhythm, which he called *Invitation to the Dance*. In its day, it was a very suitable piece for a virtuoso to play in the second half of his program—or as an encore—after he had demonstrated his prowess in his concerto. But the *Invitation* hardly could stay confined to concerts: thousands and hundreds of thousands of girls seized upon it (or had it thrust upon them by the connivance of their parents with their teachers); and it continued to resound—however stumbled, lumbered, or wounded—from numberless living-room pianos, throughout the nineteenth century and beyond, over much of "the world." Endless editions of it were published, in various arrangements, facilitations, and mutilations; after a time, versions were devised to make it more difficult—more appropriate to the extended acrobatics of later virtuosos. *Invitation,* too, afforded the invincible combination of easy tunefulness and rapid movement, besides another attraction of which we shall speak shortly.

(c) "PROGRAM" MUSIC

STILL ANOTHER KIND of music issued from pianofortes, in Vienna and elsewhere, during the decades just before and after the 1800 point. Again we will endeavor to fill in some of its background.

The musical imitation or suggestion of sounds in nature, or in nonmusical human life, can be traced back in Western music for several centuries. Operas, beginning in 1600, gave obvious opportunities for such devices; but even before then we know of pieces of music built up, for example, on the notes of the cuckoo's call. Late in the seventeenth century Johann Kuhnau composed *Biblical* Sonatas in which certain events, such as the fight between David and Goliath, are given musical illustrations. Sebastian Bach's similar appositions are well known, as are the onomatopoetic pleasantries in French harpsichord pieces such as Rameau's *The Hen* and Couperin's *The Knitters.* In all those cases, the suggestive sounds are secondary to the general musical design: they are a foreign element, a condiment, to the musical essence; their very extrinsic quality is often the cause of the amusement they arouse.

These tonal toys had an ever wider-spreading vogue as the eighteenth century waned and the nineteenth waxed. The cruder they were, the more readily they were enjoyed: we have already mentioned the fiddler who made a career out of imitating chickens and cranky women. It reached a point where the onomatopoeia—that is, the nonmusical suggestion—became the important thing and the music itself secondary. To some extent, this vogue was yet one more symptom of the increased general participation in the more cultivated manifestations of music. Thousands of well-to-do middle-class simpletons, many with no particular acuteness of hearing, were now ambitious to own instruments and to attend concerts and operas; they found it much easier and much more entertaining to recognize something that was supposed to sound like a croaking frog than to savor the delights of a well-woven three-voice counterpoint. On the other hand, nonmusical tonal suggestions had some high intellectual support. There always are deep thinkers and exquisite verbalists whose ears are dull, perhaps just because they have never trusted them. Baffled and exasperated, they ask: "But what does the music *mean*?" Jealously they observe the potent effect that sounds without concepts, without associations, without ulterior purpose, have on persons blessed with the capacity of being moved by them. Many a poet or philosopher may have been glad to rescue a rippling brook or a galloping horse from his own chaos of musical insensitivity.

Georg Joseph Vogler was another correctly ordained priest who went about the world devoting his entire life to music, including the composition of comic operas, and whose precise ecclesiastical status consequently is a little difficult for some of us to understand nowadays. He was usually referred to as Abt (Abbot) Vogler; he was an excellent musician, an accomplished organist and clavierist —though given to queer ostentations of vanity, if we may believe contemporary gossip about him. Several generations after Vogler's time, Robert Browning made him the mouthpiece for his most inspired lines concerning music.

Vogler was in Düsseldorf, they say, in 1785 and visited an art gallery; there he had a clavier moved around in front of various Italian and Dutch masterpieces and proceeded to impress an audience with his improvised musical "interpretations" of the pictures. This sort of thing is sometimes called "tone painting" these days, though in that case one might have said "paint toning." When in place of a static "painting" the music is supposed to "represent" a whole series of events, the result is called "program music"; that designation, however, was not used until the middle of the nineteenth century.

Toward the end of the eighteenth century and later, one of the favorite subjects for "program music" was a storm. Thunder, the patter of raindrops, the surge of waves, and the chromatic howl of the wind are easy noises to suggest tonally. Human interest could be inserted into this nature-worship, in the form of a shepherd playing his pipe or a flock of peasants scampering for cover. Daniel Steibelt was a piano virtuoso who had known considerable success in Paris and London and who, when he aimed to impress his name on Vienna in 1800, was so foolhardy as to try to compete with Beethoven. During the late 1790's he had composed a concerto, the last movement of which was spoken of as the "Storm" Rondo; it was one of his most effective compositions.

The piano was a most convenient instrument for making storms: it could readily be induced to churn up great billows in the shape of arpeggios, and it had a decided gift for giving forth thunder; you needed merely to make a rumbling tremolo on a couple of notes close together in the left hand, far down in the bass. Steibelt made quite a name for himself as a tremolist. Note, however, that the crescendo and the diminuendo, the pianoforte's very essence, were also essential to both waves and thunder, to say nothing of wind. Josef Wölfl gave a concert in Berlin in December 1800 at which he delighted his hearers with a "musical badinage" that was recounted thus: "The quiet sea—the rise of a squall—lightning, thunder, a heavy storm which however subsides after some time—former condition of the sea—transition into a well-known song on which the player makes variations and improvisations."

Abt Vogler was an esteemed master of harmony and counterpoint, as we have stated; he lived in Vienna for about two years after 1802 and there became the teacher of young Carl Maria von Weber. Later, elsewhere, young Giacomo Meyerbeer also placed himself under his tutelage. In between the exercising of his august pedagogical influence upon these illustrious composers-to-be, Vogler gave an organ concert in Frankfurt, in September 1807, which consisted of the following program.

Part I

1. Chorale: How Brightly Shines the Morning Star
2. Song of the Hottentots, which consists of three measures and two words: Magema, Magema, Huh, Huh, Huh!
3. Flute Concerto: Allegro, Polonaise, Gigue

Part II

1. The Siege of Jericho
   a) Israel's Prayer to Jehovah

   b) Sound of Trumpets
   c) Crash of the Walls
   d) Entrance of the Victors
2. Terrace Chant of the Africans, when they seal their flat roofs with lime, during which one chorus alternately sings and the other one stamps
3. The Pleasure Ride on the Rhine, Interrupted by a Thunderstorm
4. Handel's Hallelujah, treated as a fugue with two subjects and counterpointed with a third subject

We are convinced that with this program Vogler thrice riveted his reputation as a man of God, a solid musician, and a purveyor of innocent pastimes.

Weber's *Invitation to the Dance* also had its "programmatic" appeal. The composer did not bully the player's understanding with verbal captions; nevertheless, a plausible tradition developed to the effect that the sections of this composition were intended to call to mind the elements of a scene. Many a nineteenth-century piano teacher explained to his fair pupil how the opening rising single notes in the bass are intended to make one think of a cavalier's approach to a seated lady and his request for her companionship in the dance; how the following little trebly phrase indicates her decorous acceptance; how the next little two-part melody suggests some polite, pretty conversation between the pair while waiting for the dance to begin; how, after an anticipatory pause, the band strikes up a loud fanfare; how a professional solo dancer, customarily hired for the entertainment of ball guests, then makes his amusing leaps; how the couple next rock together in the suave undulations of a real waltz, and how a tender, glowing sentiment develops at the close of that lilting strain; how the dance becomes more crowded and noisy; how it ends in a whirl of joy—and, finally, how the gentleman escorts the lady back to her chair and receives her courteous, exhausted thanks. No wonder this composition was perennially enjoyed by unnumbered well-bred burgher daughters, even though very few of them could ever learn to play it properly.

Let us affirm, nevertheless, that the "programmatic" aspect of the *Invitation* is a side issue and that its true charm lies in its intrinsic tonal and rhythmical values. It is, indeed, a happy musical thought: its course unfolds with undrooped interest, its episodes are well interlocked, it reaches a successful climax, and its end justifies its beginning. *Invitation to the Dance* is still popular, though no longer primarily as a piano piece: its original imagery has now been disturbed because of association with a well-known ballet, *Le Spectre de la Rose,* that has been composed to it.

(d) BATTLES

AMONG THE FAVORITE TYPES of program music of the period were pieces that "depicted" battles. Such compositions were not at all new in the 1790's; in fact, they go back, sporadically, for some centuries. There is a piece called *The Battell* to be found in *My Lady Nevell's Booke,* an English collection of keyboard pieces dated 1591 and attributed to no less a master than William Byrd. *The Battell* has a number of headings that are more or less happily illustrated in the music: "the souldiers' sommons, the marche of footemen, the marche of horsmen, the trumpetts, the Irishe marche, the bagpipe and the drone, the flute and the droome, the marche to the fighte"—including "tantara, tantara" and "the battels be joined"—"the retreat, the buriing of the dead, the morris, Ye souldiers dance" followed by "the Galliarde for the Victorie."

In 1724, in the high tide of the *ancien régime,* François Dandrieu, organist of the chapel of His Majesty Louis XV, published a set of harpsichord pieces one of which is called *Les Caractères de la Guerre.* It too has its running subtitles: *"la bouteselle, la marche, première fanfare, seconde fanfare, la charge, la mêlée* (with *'les cris'*), *les plaintes, la victoire, le triomphe,"* and *"double du triomphe."* One historian says it was composed for a puppet theater with a popular audience; that would seem plausible if not for the magniloquent royal dedication with which it is prefaced. We would say, at this remove, that the inflexible harpsichord does not seem a very effective instrument for making this sort of representation vivid.

It is certainly true that toward the end of the eighteenth century pianistic battle pieces came into great general favor and were dished up in large quantity, if not variety, by publishers, composers, virtuosos, and of course young ladies—the ultimate retailers. These compositions were, indeed, extraordinarily conventional in conception; they all show a remarkable family resemblance, not always short of actual plagiarism: all are rigorously provided with approach marches, bugle calls, cannon shots, cavalry charges, fog of battle, cries of the wounded, national anthems, and victory balls. These items were always carefully ticketed in the printed notes, and we wonder whether players generally announced the captions orally to their hearers in the course of the performances.

The names of the battles, however—and therefore the titles—did vary considerably, on the sound commercial principle that you can always sell the same hokum over again under a different label. Naturally, no battles could be profitably marketed that might hurt the customers' patriotic feelings; on the other hand, battles close to home could be presumed to arouse a higher degree of empathy than those remote in time or space. We quote a successful title-page of the day:

THE BATTLE OF WÜRZBURG

on the 3rd of Sept. 1796.

between the royal Imperial army under the command of His Royal Highness the Archduke Karl of Austria, Imperial Field Marshal, and the enemy French troops under the command of Gen. Jourdan.

A MILITARY HEROIC PIECE OF MUSIC
for
CLAVIER or PIANOFORTE

reverently dedicated to
His Royal Highness

KARL OF AUSTRIA,
IMPERIAL FIELD MARSHAL

on the occasion of his glorious birthday
by the undersigned firm, and composed according to
the official Vienna communiqué of 8 Sept. 1796 by

MR. JOHANN WANHAL

Vienna, from the Art & Music Publishing House of
Jos. Eder & Co., on the Graben.
1 fl. 20 kr.

"Mr. Johann Wanhal" was getting to be an old-timer; we met him in the early 1770's, as one of the first to take advantage of Vienna's expanding music market. Recovered from his former mental illness, he had developed the tremendous fecundity of a low-grade organism and was ultimately known to have laid sixty sonatas, fifty trios, nine concertos, and one hundred symphonies. The "Würzburg" opus must have done pretty well, for soon we hear of him announcing *The Threatening or the Liberation of Vienna, a military, heroic composition, a companion piece to The Battle of Würzburg.* The Austrian armies were evidently understood to have behaved well in face of the forces of the *Directoire,* in which young General Bonaparte had much influence.

Beethoven also composed a politically correct battle piece; it was called *Wellington's Victory, or the Battle of Vittoria,* commemorating an important success of the English over the French in Spain. He wrote it to be reeled off on a contemporary equivalent of a juke box, a musical automaton put together by J. N. Mälzel, the famous metronome improver. The idea was a business speculation, hence the pro-British slant; for the entire apparatus—music, machine, and all—was to have been taken to England for the purpose of attracting notoriety and money there, and possibly even a favor from the Prince Regent. The voyage was never accomplished; but an orchestral version of *Wellington's Victory,* played at a Vienna concert with all its brash sound effects, earned Beethoven more immediate acclaim than he had ever enjoyed in his life before. A piano arrangement was duly published: its title page was dressed up with a picture showing a heroic-looking mounted officer brandishing his sword while seeming to urge his associates to plunge into a cavalry charge; the foreground is decorated with a broken wagon wheel and a couple of interlocked uniform corpses.

That was in 1813; some years before, however, an individual in Edinburgh had wished to order from Beethoven a vocal battle-piece celebrating the bombardment of Copenhagen by the British fleet. Beethoven had answered this correspondent as follows:

> For the cantata about the battle in the Baltic Sea I ask 50 ducats, but on condition that the original text contain no invective against the Danes; otherwise I will not be able to undertake it.

In interpreting the outbreak of this infection of battle pieces, writers usually state that it was encouraged by the wars that roiled Europe almost continuously from Valmy (1792) until Waterloo (1815). There is truth in this notion, but there is also evidence that these pieces had been coming into wide favor for some time before 1790. A more general cause for their flourishing is the one we have already adduced for related phenomena: by the last decade of the century there had grown up large numbers of crude people with money to spend; the childish imagery of these compositions was suitable to the limitations of their understanding;

the noisiness and length of the pieces, added to the great pith and moment of the events with which they pretended to deal, gave the good Philistines the feeling that they were getting a lot for their money. So far as they were concerned, clamor rhymed with glamour.

There was another reason: again, it lay in the rising vogue of the pianoforte. "Battles" were sometimes set for orchestra and often they were issued for a keyboard abetted by violins and drum, but in the main they were most satisfactorily executed by single belaborers of unaccompanied pianos. The percussive impact of the hammers was favorable for marches and also for the rhythm of hoofs; fog of battle was remarkably easy to suggest upon an instrument that required two separate hands and ten different sound-producing fingers, co-ordinable with difficulty, for its proper handling. Indeed, a good deal of pianistic young-lady battle-fog was probably quite unintentional. In any case, the favorite flash of wit remained the cannon shots. These were usually accomplished with an ingenious simplicity: already Dandrieu in the preface to his old *divertissement* explains:

> In that section of the *Caractères de la Guerre* that I call "The Charge" there are several places named "cannon shots" that are indicated only by four notes forming a complete chord. But in order better to express the noise of the cannon one may, each time, in place of these four notes, strike the lowest notes on the keyboard with the entire length of the flat of the hand.

Directions from a German battle piece of the early nineteenth century read thus:

> The cannon shots are to be expressed by the flat of the left hand upon the lowest portion of the bass, all at once, *loud;* all the notes are to be struck without distinction and to be held till the dying away of the sound.

A French piece from about 1800, called *La Bataille de Maringo* (that is the nearest the French ear came to "Marengo"), offers a similar firing mechanism, but suggests "the flat of *both* hands on the three lowest octaves." It was probably a large-bore siege gun. The clever artillery composer also used a special symbol—or had we better say command signal—for his bursts, thus: $\otimes$.

This striking idea, as it were, was soon to endure amplification and refinement. In the piano version of Beethoven's *Wellington's*

Victory, at the climax of the engagement, we find the afore-mentioned symbol ⊗, but it is especially labeled "English cannon." A second symbol—⦶—also occurs, almost simultaneously, and is designated "French cannon." Just how many palms of how many hands were to be employed in the bombardment, and on what tone-clusters, the great composer does not say; nor does he suggest what parts of the body are to be used for playing the rest of the music. It is possible that the *Vittoria* guns were to be foot-operated: we will explain this notion later.

What fun to make these detonations—in one easy lesson; you did not even have to be a pianist. The young enjoyed it especially; and to this very day many a seven-year-old warrior, innocent of all other music, has to be estopped from making unseasonable cannon shots on the home keyboard according to the old approved method

In Vienna at least, battle pieces, however noisy and pretentious, were not necessarily treated with an extreme of seriousness, even by those who enjoyed them. Far from always aiming to compel spasms of romantic solemnity, their composers sometimes linked them lightheartedly with dance music. Mozart, for example, wrote a set of *contredanses* each of whose five movements "represents" the conventional elements of a battle; he calls it, in fact, *La Bataille*. Hummel's Opus 91 is entitled *Waltzes with Trios and a Battle-Coda for the Apollo Rooms*. This coda has been described as undanceable; thus, we might arrive at a picture of the Apollo Rooms customers suddenly poising on tiptoe in mid-waltz to enjoy the musical fracas. More likely that is what happened in the drawing rooms of the citizens who purchased copies of Opus 91 for the pianoforte.

Related to the taste for battle pieces was the fashion for "Turkish" or "Janizary" music. In the course of the many contacts—hostile and otherwise—that central European nations had had with the Turks ever since the Middle Ages, they became much impressed with the Turkish military bands. Apparently, these were made up of a number of high, shrill pipes and a variety of percussion instruments not too common in the West at that time—such as the cymbals, the tambourine, the triangle, and the bass drum. In the eighteenth century, after the actual Turks had stopped being much of a menace, some of their ways began to seem amusing to toy with. Kings, dukes, and field marshals then kept "Turkish" bands, partly authentic and partly fake. If real Turks were not available as players, Negroes were employed and dressed in fantastic garb to make an effect of outlandishness. Loud batteries of mixed rhythmic sounds without definite pitch struck eighteenth-century people, quite correctly, as something barbaric and barbarous, to be enjoyed in small doses for what it expressed. "Turkish" music was considered a regular, appropriate way of accompanying heathen hordes on the stage. Gluck used it for the "Chorus of Scythians" in his *Iphigénie en Tauride;* Mozart had it, obviously, in *The Abduction from the Seraglio.* "Turkish" marches, in a sort of quickstep, were a stock style of late eighteenth-century composition; Mozart and Beethoven supplied examples of it.

The pianoforte, in its rise to fashion, inevitably caught some of this flying fancy and became allied to a number of extraneous percussion effects. The piano virtuoso Daniel Steibelt, whom we have just mentioned, had married a good-looking English girl possessed of some musical talent. She was quite an able manipulator of the tambourine, and joint performances with her husband were much enjoyed by a generation of new-formed music customers. Steibelt published a series of the pieces he played with her, giving them the classical-arty title of *Bacchanales.* They are nothing but waltzes with tambourine obbligato.

Battle pieces, "Turkish" music, and similar fads were persistent enough so that they made their mark on the construction of the piano itself, as Rosamond Harding, in her excellent work, has pointed out in great detail. Early in the 1800's continental piano makers began to furnish their instruments with the capacity for making sound effects—that is, "attachments" for making program music more "realistic." The noises could all be brought into play by the use of pedals; some pianos had as many as seven or eight such pedals. "Cymbals," for instance, were achieved by hitting several strips of brass against the lower strings; "triangle" or "bells" consisted of one or more little metal hemispheres struck with little rods; "drum" was a mallet with padded head made to hit the back of the sounding board. Think of Junior making a cannon shot and a drumbeat, both at the same time! But perhaps it is only the boorish Americanism of this writer's imagination that allows such a licentious thought to arise; he ought to remember that European children are always well brought up and have respect for "art" and furniture from their tenderest years.

There were other pedals, not all percussive in purpose. A strip of parchment-covered wood pressed against the lower strings gave the tone a kind of nasal twang; it was called "bassoon," and so people thought it sounded like one. There were several soft pedals. Simplest was the *"una corda"*: by it, the entire keyboard and action were shifted a few millimeters to one side so that the hammers struck on one string instead of on the two or three unison strings with which every note—except the few lowest—was strung. The *una corda,* however, produced a change in tonal quality as well as a lessening of the volume; therefore, an additional "pianissimo" pedal was also devised whereby the hammers were brought closer to the strings before their activation. Their striking distance thus reduced, they acquired less momentum and therefore brought forth less tone. This softening mechanism is still being built into upright pianos at the present day; the *una corda* principle is the one still in general use in grand pianos.

It was the "giraffe"-style pianos that were most often accoutered with all these "attachments" and pedals. The association suggests a congruity of taste: the sort of people who liked to display eight-foot-tall Empire camelopards in their drawing rooms were also the sort who liked their daughters to enhance them by showing off with battles, storms, and "Turkish" marches all harnessed in full-sounding, full-furious finery. Serious masters of the piano—such as J. N. Hummel, in his book of *Instruction in the Art of Playing the Pianoforte*—flatly wrote off these supernumerary pedals as worthless toys; still, they persisted for a whole generation.

The "giraffe" design still preserved the basic, normal shape of the pianoforte; but there were some who felt that such obviousness reflected a careless lack of cultivation, a lowly unsophistication not worthy of a digitiferous bank account. We know American hostesses who feel that they are living up to their station in life by serving Thanksgiving Day ice cream molded into the shape of a turkey: so, in the 1820's we find households acquiring uprighted pianos disguised as enormous lyres. In order to achieve this bilaterally symmetrical façade, the strings had to be strung obliquely—without any functional saving of space; yet in thus making the sign of the lyre, the owner no doubt achieved a reputation for a commendable art-piousness.

Miss Harding has illustrated for us an especially spectacular pianoforte: it is built in the symmetrical form of a right pyramid. (Could that have been a late fluorescence of Napoleon's Egyptian campaign?) Its height is given as nine feet (274 centimeters), a figure probably including the garlanded urn that crowns the apex. The holy lyre is given its due prominence: it appears high on the front face as part of the silk-backed latticework. The keyboard is again held aloft by faithful twin caryatids. A small shelf space is left on each side of the pyramid's base and is taken up by two little Negroid figures, one carrying a set of bells, the other a sort of drum. The piano has six pedals, including a "pianissimo" and a "bassoon"; the last pedal is for "Janizary" music. When pedal No. 6 is pressed, not only do the "Turkish" drum and bells sound —but lo! the Negritos turn out to be automata, making the motions of banging their little gimcracks!

10. THE PIANO IN PUBLIC

CONCERTS involving a solo pianist increased gradually after 1790, in other German towns as well as in Vienna. We have indicated in a previous section that an ethical distinction was felt to exist between the meetings of a local music-exercising society and the rarer concerts that aimed to exploit the showier skills of an exceptional visiting performer. The former were thought worthy attempts to promote art; the latter, exciting but superficial diversions—often far from edifying. Let us try to describe the flavor of these events, while dispelling any anachronistic images of them that may have arisen in our minds.

The Germanies of the early nineteenth century were a very slow-moving world, a world without railways, telegraphs, photographs, or news services, with few daily newspapers and few truly good wagon roads. A piano virtuoso who hoped to subsist by exhibiting himself in various places could make no quick tours, could fill no distant engagements. Rarely could a performing musician build a fabulous reputation, sight unseen, outside of his own community. There were no managers or civic organizations who could, or would, send for virtuosos from afar. A proficient pianist, finding the home-town air a little stale, often felt he would like to snatch some distinction and attention by becoming a stranger. His first need was to develop a set of antennae in the shape of a pack of letters of introduction, written by his well-wishing friends to their music-loving acquaintances in other places; in fact, he would probably confine his early invasions to such towns as were named on the envelopes of these missives. If our musician were, or had been, court pianist to the Duke of Pumpernickel, he would be sure to wear that noble necklace of a designation around his name at all public occasions, knowing that any German would tend to respect it highly.

Upon arriving at a town, he would establish himself at a hostelry and prepare to spend the next few weeks making acquaintances. The houses that received him often expected him to hand out free samples of his music; he was usually glad to do so, tacitly assuming that his hosts would presently feel obliged to reciprocate by helping him when he came to pull off his concert coup, both by taking blocks of tickets and by peddling them to others. Influential music-patronizing citizens, however, ordinarily had little wish to by-pass the local concert society—of which they were probably supporters. It was deemed proper that the visiting virtuoso make his first appearance within the frame of one of the society's regular performances. After that, its directors could feel justified in offering him the services of the society's orchestra as an accompaniment and background, as well as the use of its hall, gratis, for a later concert for his own benefit. No small favors, these. In cities that maintained a permanent theater or opera, a visiting virtuoso could sometimes introduce himself to a larger audience by playing during an entr'acte.

At that rate it might take a little time before our pianist—or violinist or singer or other performer—could dip his hands into any box-office honey; meanwhile his innkeeper would keep track of him quite accurately. It sometimes happened that the hotel man's arithmetic of the past outran the virtuoso's arithmetic of the future; in that case the musician usually made a concertless exit. On the other hand, a successful concert might tempt a performer to try a second one shortly thereafter. There were dangers in such an enterprise: the longer he remained in town, the more his personality would become invested with a contemptible familiarity—the more opportunities he would also have to bet on the wrong cards and to ogle the wrong women. That, in turn, would lessen his chances of getting good letters of introduction to the next place.

We can begin to understand the importance of the orchestral background in the concert circumstances we have described. Concertos were positively obligatory; so were assistant soloists, often singers. Not until the late 1830's did a pianist venture to offer an audience nothing but his own unassisted playing. A concert featuring a piano virtuoso—like most other concerts—usually consisted of two parts, separated by an intermission. The program usually opened with an orchestral overture or symphonic movement; there followed an operatic aria, probably with piano accompaniment. Then came the virtuoso and his concerto; this sometimes was a work by another composer, but more often was the performer's own composition, abounding in self-made openings for the kind of tricks at which he was best. Another orchestral piece, or possibly a smaller ensemble, completed the first half of the proceedings. The second half followed the same general pattern: the virtuoso sometimes played a second concerto; if he were a pianist, he often also played a set of variations or a fantasy—such, for instance, as Wölfl's *Musical Badinage*—at his later appearance.

Audiences especially enjoyed hearing a pianist improvise on given themes. The piano has an endless capacity for figuration: on a keyboard, any chord can be broken, rolled, zigzagged, looped, or overlapped in countless alternations and rhythmic groupings; so can any scale line, including the chromatic. A quick-fingered musician, well trained in the fundamental formulas, can easily learn to combine fragments of them into new permutations on the spur of the moment. The concentration of keyboard technique on scales and broken chords (arpeggios)—a process that we saw consummated by 1770—had encouraged a readily acquired glibness among clavier practitioners. Audiences of the early 1800's were quite naïve: the assured execution of any rapid musical passages that fell into well-understood patterns seemed admirable and delightful to them; so did obvious motions such as wide skips, crossing of hands, and rapid repetition of notes. It was all new and wonderful to the simpler minds of the day. When—in the midst of this mobile interplay—portions of a well-known melody bobbed up recognizably, a seductive combination of pleasures was afforded. They were the same joined pleasures, substantially, that could be gleaned from an air with variations, plus the heady feeling of watching the man make it all up as he went along. The cadenzas we have described previously were, of course, a special case of this kind of fantasy.

It is obviously impossible now to know exactly what those early-nineteenth-century piano improvisations were like, but an expert guess might not be far amiss. One could well imagine, for instance, that Beethoven's *Fantasie* Opus 77 is a transcribed remembrance of something extemporized at the keyboard shortly before. The first half of this work shows no evidence of any plan or cohesion whatsoever: it consists of tentative fragments separated by holds (fermatas). The beginning contains a lot of descending scales, all breaking off abruptly and alternating with mutually unrelated incomplete melodic phrases. A proper tune emerges, but it wanders away. Suddenly we hear a flourish of rapid arpeggio sequences, seemingly irrelevant. Then come some more willfully dissociated passages mostly based on keyboard formulas. Finally we reach a complete eight-measure original tune;

it is treated to eight variations, some of them ingenious, some claptrap. The tune might as well have been a well-known operatic air or popular song. It is all fairly feeble for a master of superlative ability to offer in cold print, yet it might have been impressive to hear him dream it up at the piano, with much pathos of delivery and a rapt look on his queer face. In any case, Beethoven's poorest was likely to be better than most others' best.

For some forty years people kept on liking this sort of thing; finally Carl Czerny, Beethoven's diligent acolyte—who always aimed to please while he instructed—published *The Art of Improvisation* as his Opus 200. It contained sage words of advice and many tasty practical recipes in notes. Alas, the good Czerny's ear was a little off the ground when he did this deed about the year 1829, for right thereafter—with the advent of a newer pianistic style-fashion—the taste for public improvisations began to wane; it became all but extinct after 1840.

There is good evidence that many virtuosos of the early 1800's played publicly without using their notes, though there are also reliable accounts that others did need the services of a page turner. Of Liszt, who functioned mostly after 1834, it was often said—generations later—that he was the first to make a general practice of playing by heart; the persistence of this myth is another example of the superstitious nature of fame.

It is unlikely that concertos, even new ones, were ever prepared with the care that we associate with professional performances nowadays. One rehearsal was usually considered sufficient; a particularly self-intoxicated virtuoso might not even care to spill his peculiar and proprietary parcel of stunts to his fellow musicians in advance of the concert, and would confine the rehearsal exclusively to the orchestral parts. Mozart gave a concert in Leipzig on May 12, 1789, which included two concertos, without rehearsing at all. "The parts are written out correctly; you play right and so do I," he told his collaborators in just the right shade of flattery.

The years 1780 to 1830 were the age of Mozart and Haydn, of Beethoven and Schubert and Weber. We would be quite wrong if we inferred from that fact, however, that any large number of people expended their musical desires in contemplating the unique excellences of those distinguished masters' works. On the contrary, almost everybody was willing to live on the average musical productions of the day, and to be nudged and tripped by any least fad of the moment. It might be worth while to listen to Václav Jaroslav Tomašek (Wenzel Johann Tomaschek was his

Germanized name), learned Bohemian musician and noted scholar and teacher; early in March 1800 he was an eye and ear witness of a concert given in Prague by Daniel Steibelt. We have mentioned that pianist before: born in Berlin, he had deserted from the Prussian army and gradually made his way to Paris; there the good-looking young man's talents seemed plausible to the women of some of the new big-shots thrown up by the Revolution and the *Directoire*. After a few years some of his finances, as well as his love-making, became sufficiently incorrect to make his departure seem prudent; he proceeded to settle in London, where his compositions and his playing had a considerable appeal. In 1800 we find Steibelt making exploratory operations in the interior of the Continent: he might well have hoped that his repute, since it emanated from Paris and London, would prove irresistible to Central European upper-class yokels, at least for a first hearing.

Tomašek writes in his memoirs:

> Steibelt was pretty well known already then to all musical amateurs through his fresh-sounding compositions, which were provided with the most fanciful titles. His was a welcome appearance to all those who love the superficialities of the art. . . . Steibelt came to Prague to try his luck, hoping to gain money and laurels. In the springtime, while the nobility is still in town, it was not hard for him—what with a recommendation he had brought from the then Duchess of Kurland—to dispose of more than 300 tickets, at a gold ducat a ticket.

Tomašek went to the rehearsal, which he describes thus:

> Steibelt, wrapped in his cloak, only had the orchestral interludes and *ritornellos* tried over, without himself touching the pianoforte. The quartet that he played at the concert he rehearsed in his lodgings, and that behind locked doors. The actual performance, like all concerts at that time, was to have taken place at 7 o'clock; yet the artist, befogged by a rare conceit, was pleased not to meet the hour. After the nobility, which has a better understanding of the active than of the passive side of waiting, had exhausted itself in French in all kinds of indignation and the orchestra was ready to go home with its job undone, the long yearned-for virtuoso finally came, one hour after the appointed time. He arrived nearly out of breath, distributed the parts and gave the signal for the overture. Then began the Concerto in E Flat, with the "storm."
>
> At the end of the concert he improvised on the well-known theme . . . *"Pace caro mio sposo,"* in a manner degrading to the artist;

for he did nothing but repeat the theme in C major a number of times *"vibrando,"* [this probably means *tremolando*] into the midst of which he squeezed a few little runs with his right hand, and after a few minutes he concluded the entire *fantasie.* The "fantasie," as he called this cling-clang, and certain of his moral blemishes startled the nobility; indeed, they even doubted his identity and later took him for an impostor who was passing himself off as Steibelt. . . .

There is also a critique of Steibelt's music:

In his compositions there is no echo of German music; everything makes one think of French *odeurs;* so also the titles that he has introduced resemble the frequently ridiculous labels on French products. . . . As a pianist he had a neat and yet rather firm touch. His right hand was excellent in its cultivation; . . . on the other hand, the development of his left hand stood in no harmonious relationship whatsoever to his right; clumsy, almost imbecile, it hobbled along.

Perhaps that is why he took refuge in so much tremolo, yet:

Although Steibelt's artistic performance was not adequate for the Prague nobility, he was still able to make good with it in another way. For he had with him an Englishwoman whom he introduced as his wife and who played the tambourine, accompanying him with it, with him at the piano; for this ensemble he had written several little rondos.

These were the *Bacchanales* we have spoken of before, of which Tomašek says:

The new combination of such diverse instruments so electrified the gentlefolk that they could hardly see their fill of the Englishwoman's pretty arm. The wish likewise to manipulate this instrument stirred in all the ladies, and so it came that Steibelt's girl friend was gladly persuaded to give instruction in it (Note: the same in Dresden). The course was completed in 12 lessons, for which the teacher was paid 12 gold ducats; she received the same price for a tambourine. Thus it happened that Steibelt remained in Prague for several weeks and gradually sold a large wagonload of tambourines.

We must not imagine that, during the golden age of music, citizens at concerts behaved with the pious decorum, or even the elementary consideration for others that they learned to affect in later generations; on the contrary, complaints of restlessness and inattention were incessant. J. F. Reichardt, visiting the Leipzig "Great Concert" as early as 1776, said of this organization that:

> [It] has the pretty gift of chattering and noise-making in common with all other concert societies. True, a businessman in charge of the concert arrangements stands guard against this and, when someone talks all too loud, beats with a large . . . key against the harpsichord, which he thereby puts out of tune; with that he commands silence to the culprits, which they nevertheless fail to keep. This heroic behavior, however, he confines toward males; toward females he reserves the Paris-learned politeness of joining their company and adding to the discourse.

A music lover writes, in the year 1793, about the subscription concert in the small university town of Göttingen:

> The noise of the sweet gentlemen and cackle of the ladies, everywhere beleaguered by dandies, often drowned out the music completely and went on pell-mell just as when the spawn for a new generation of frogs is coming to the light of day.

The simile is quite nasty.

The ladies seem always to have been regarded as the virus of disturbance; evidently, burgher men were not yet able to take strange women for granted. After the concert had begun, no gentleman was expected to endure himself seated while a late-coming lady was standing; up he jumped, in spite of the music, and gave her his chair or made way for her through the row. A correspondent from Copenhagen, writing in 1783 to *C. F. Cramer's Magazine of Music,* deplored the babbling and flirting during the performance. "That is a complaint," said Cramer, "that touches all concerts at which ladies are present." He suggested a placard like the one sometimes found on art cabinets: *oculis non manibus.* His would read: *auribus non linguis.*

Some wise words were written about virtuoso concerts of this period by an observer who signed the pseudonym "Triest." They appear in a series of articles called "Concerning Traveling Virtuosos" published in the *Allgemeine Musikalische Zeitung.*

> Unfortunately, improvement of the fine arts (notably the arts of music and of the theater) is held back almost everywhere by the fact that the artist—the true one as well as the false one—cannot do without the great mass and its money contributions. Thus a *free* art

has been changed into a *servile* one, whereby it is of no great consequence whether the patron consists of a single high-placed gentleman or of a mixed public. In the latter case, taste *for* music spreads more rapidly, but taste *in* it all the more slowly. The best of artists sees himself compelled to waste his time in the practice of showy artifices and charlatanries because the little cluster of connoisseurs is unable to pay for his *real* art. Yet these distortions and excrescences that the vulgar tend to consider something sublime are not the only evil consequence of the dependence of the virtuoso upon the public. All compliments and polite speeches that may be heaped upon him will not secure him and his art against disparagement, as soon as his value as a citizen is called into question. The eternal query about practical benefit cannot be answered favorably for a musician. His contribution to the culture of the spirit is not understood by those who see in him merely a person who uses sensual means for sensual ends. The two most numerous sections of the concert public, namely the higher official and the businessman, who have accustomed themselves to consider important only the written and the—not musically—resounding products of human effort [he means legal documents and money], regard the musical artist as a kind of idler who lures money out of people's pockets, in return for letting tones die away in the air; and they would conceal this judgment even less if the more inflammable female sex did not here and there befriend the poor virtuoso. They count a subscription to such a concert merely as a refined form of begging, to which they will lend an ear, either because a letter of recommendation obliges them thereto, or because the dear family wants to be amused, or a musical friend persuades them, or the artist's great repute arouses their curiosity.

Dear, dear! Did we overhear anyone suspecting to himself that the point of view expressed at the end of this quotation was something modern, and specifically American? The article is dated August 18, 1802, and was published in the great music city of Leipzig, once the home of the sainted Johann Sebastian Bach.

In Vienna, as we have stated several times, concerts formed a comparatively less important element of musical life than did music in homes; still, their number increased gradually and those of pianists multiplied in relatively greater proportion. On the whole, we may safely say that the piano was the latest of the instruments to be exploited for public performance on a large scale.

In general, the public concerts staged by individuals—though open to any purchasers of tickets—tended to be performers' private parties, with audiences made up of friendly paying guests. One of the obstacles to concerts in Vienna was the unavailability of good halls. An Imperial theater could only be had on the rare days when no other show was going on, mostly during Lent. But even if an unoccupied hall were found, what would the concert-giver do for an orchestral accompaniment when most of the good musicians were busy at the theater and the opera? Permission to use the ballrooms of the Imperial palace was usually granted only for charity concerts. Sometimes recourse was had to a hall on the premises of Jahn the caterer; it held about four hundred persons, which made it too small for many events. Very often concerts had to be given in the early afternoon, not an inspiring time for music, as many complained. There was other chicanery connected with concerts: licenses, taxes, and censorship of the texts of vocal numbers. Despite all this, there were more and more of them: a Vienna newspaper of 1819 reported that one hundred great and small concerts had taken place during the preceding season.

In the years after 1815 there was a great rise in concerts by resident Vienna pianists. Most of them were women and children. The latter, of course, had no say in the matter, but were bullied into the business by ambitious teachers and vain parents. The names of some of those innocents have been preserved: Leopoldine Blahetka, aged seven; Julius Szalay, aged nine; Antonie Pechwell, eleven; Fanny Sallomon, eleven; Anna von Belleville, eleven; Friederich Wörlitzer, thirteen; and many others. Some of them did indeed succeed in making modest musical careers for themselves.

One very gifted, handsome, blond eleven-year-old boy had been sent by his wealthy noble Hungarian patrons to study in Vienna; for a year he was under Czerny's guidance, and on December 1, 1822, he was brought out in a concert at which he played a concerto by Hummel. He was enthusiastically received and gave another concert the following year. An effort was made to interest Beethoven in this young person. The composer, however, had an understandable distaste for child virtuosos; moreover, the master did not feel flattered by the fact that the boy, at his concert, for his scheduled improvisation, had chosen to miscegenate a theme from a Beethoven symphony with a tune from a new opera by the lighthearted Rossini, Vienna's latest "crush." Nevertheless, after some demur, the great composer consented to hear the lad, was impressed despite himself, and kissed him, they say. The young fellow was heard from later; his name was Franz Liszt.

SECTION THREE

England

1. GENTILITY AND MONEY, MUSIC AND VIRGINALS (I)

A COMMERCIAL SENSE of values began to grow upon England for many generations before a comparable stirring was felt in Germany. Before the end of the fifteenth century the great English feudal lords had ruined themselves by warring with each other, and with their decline also declined the way of life of which they were the guiding representatives. The Tudor sovereigns then gave England a strong centralized rule, and the trade that they encouraged and protected became the basis of England's wealth and power. Their era was that of the great English maritime adventures, of the exploration and commerce in Africa, Asia, and America that became the foundation of England's later greatness.

Socially, the arms-bearing knight had given way to the civilian gentleman as the basic unit of nobility. Who was a gentleman?—all members of the landed and titled ranks, of course, and certain others. We will refer to the words of Sir Thomas Smyth, Cambridge professor, churchman, clerk of the privy council, Secretary of State, and finally Queen Elizabeth's ambassador to France. His treatise on the English commonwealth, *De Republica Anglorum,* was completed March 28, 1565, and the often quoted statement from its Book I, Chapter 20, may be taken as of that date:

> Ordinarily the king doth only make knights and create barons or higher degrees; for as for gentlemen, they be made good cheape in England. For whosoever studieth the lawes of the realme, who studieth in the universities, who professeth liberall sciences, and to be shorte, who can live idly and without manuall labour, and will beare the port, charge and countenance of a gentleman, he shall be called master, for that is the title which men give to esquires and other gentlemen, and shall be taken for a gentleman.

Sir Thomas begins his next chapter by admitting that "A man may make doubt and question whether this manner of making gentlemen is to be allowed or no, . . ." But for his part, he is "of that opinion that it is not amisse." It was, indeed, generally maintained thereafter, in practice.

It soon raised the precarious question: may a gentleman properly engage in commerce? By traditional medieval standards, the answer would certainly be negative. Buying cheap and selling dear—fawning and telling little lies to gain possession of a few dirty coins—was a contemptible way of life, in the estimation of those prepared to risk their lives for loyalty or personal prestige. By the days of Elizabeth, however, commerce could take on certain heroic aspects. Various overseas trades could be associated with the hardships of strange, fierce climates, with the hazards of catastrophic storms, and with desperate fights against Spaniards and savages. Leaders of large commercial enterprises—themselves engaged in no physical labor—could begin to be esteemed as members of a superior class, especially when by speech, deportment, and habits of life they distinguished themselves from those who executed the menial details of business.

Thus, a trader could pass as a gentleman if his business brought him enough money and if he, personally, were removed from proximity with its physical evidences and could thus vaguely pretend that it did not exist. A shopkeeper standing behind his counter was not thought a gentleman; a wholesale merchant living within sight of his own warehouses was doubtful; but a director of the Hudson's Bay Company was acceptable.

A certain social potential energy was now laid up in the concept of the gentleman by the fact that one could not, in a great many cases, say precisely whether someone was a gentleman or not, especially among the commercial classes. Some people were unquestionably gentle, others unquestionably not; but always a large fragment of the English population consisted of borderline, transitional, or inconclusive cases. The king could not create a true gentleman, even though he could make knights and peers; you were a gentleman, it seems, if everybody accepted you as such—a certain appearance, a special effect produced on others, was the deciding point.

The potential energy of this social uncertainty was rendered kinetic by the corollary that one who was not a gentleman to begin with, might under especially favorable circumstances become one. If he made the right gestures, said the right things with the right accent, and made the appropriate expenditures—if he tried and pretended thus aptly and persistently for a long enough time, some of his acting might become second nature; he would eventually give the unfailing impression of a gentleman and so actually be one—if not himself, then his sons, he might hope.

There was Thomas Kytson, native of Lancashire, who came to

London to be apprenticed to a dealer in textile fabrics ("mercer," they called it) early in the sixteenth century. By 1507 he was in business for himself: he began to have a large trade in satins, velvets, cloth of gold, tapestry, and furs—also in pepper, cloves, and madder. He belonged to the Merchant Adventurers Company and traded at the cloth fairs in Antwerp and elsewhere overseas. "Citizen and mercer, otherwise called Kytson the merchant": so an act of Parliament of 1524 refers to him. Profits were great; he began to have extensive financial dealings with the Crown. In addition to enjoying his London dwelling, with its staff of servants, he bought the manor of Hengrave, in Suffolk, from the Duke of Buckingham, for many thousands of pounds. After getting permission from Henry VIII, he improved this property by building upon it a pretentious embattled manor house, thus dressing himself up like a twelfth-century armored baron—almost as if he had been a Pittsburgh millionaire of 1895. The castle, or "hall," was laid out on a magnificent scale and took thirteen years to complete; its owner stocked it with furnishings of the highest elegance, including a portrait of himself by Holbein. Kytson was knighted somewhere up the slope, and we can well understand that the translated drygoodsman's daughter Frances had no difficulty in marrying an earl.

To achieve and maintain gentility, we may say without much exaggeration, was the most anxious ambition, the very aim of life, of most English middle-class people from that day almost to this. It was an endless quest—for gentility, it seems, was relative and competitive: it was not enough merely to have attained it; one could always get more of it, at least more than someone else. In order to fulfill gentility's primary requirement—that is, to "live idly without manuall labour"—one had to have money. In good times, money came readily from trade, from manufacturing, and from usury. Once the money was at hand, further progress was unpredictable. To achieve the lordly facial expression, the confident bearing, the proper accent, the "bold grace" of manner —as Middleton called it—was difficult and tedious. How much easier it was to make the gentlemanly expenditures, to acquire the gentlemanly and ladylike possessions. They had their importance, no doubt, but upstarts who concentrated on these exclusively could not fail to be ridiculed for missing the point. Ben Jonson wanted his audience to laugh at his Signor Sogliardo, who thought he could become a gentleman by diligently playing *primero* and *passage* (gambling games); the authors of *Eastward Hoe* want us to be amused at Gertrude, the tradesman's daughter who insists on marrying a dubious knight named Sir Petronel Flash. "I must be a Lady and I will be a Lady," she says, proceeding then to dream of cherries at 10s a pound and "smocks of 3 pounde a smocke."

To acquire a lot of money, to hush up its commercial origin, to buy the right articles, and to play the right games: that was the curriculum. Many people, however, got no further than the money. The notion that correct and sufficient spending would of itself produce gentility was too persistently comforting for a handful of Elizabethan playwrights to laugh out of existence; if enough people harbored the idea, that made it true, at least to the extent of those people's influence. "Your father's only a merchant, Osborne," said one schoolboy to another, characters in *Vanity Fair,* a famous mid-nineteenth-century novel. To which the other replied haughtily: "My father's a gentleman and keeps his carriage"—whereupon the first boy, a retail grocer's son, retired in silence.

In retrospect, the sixteenth-century tempo of commerce and industry seems slow and its scope narrow; its opportunities appear small and its techniques inefficient. Money making hastened and widened, sharpened, grew, and spread in fabulous multiple proportions as the ages went on, rolling up a prodigious tide of wealth and population by the end of the nineteenth century. There rolled up corresponding waves of aspiration and pretense to gentility, with all its paraphernalia and insignia. Among the latter, one of the most persistent was a domestic keyboard instrument, as we shall recount.

2. GENTILITY AND MONEY, MUSIC AND VIRGINALS (II)

Music had its relationship to gentility, though the terms of the connection became somewhat altered from one century to another. During the days of the Tudors and of the earlier Stuarts, musical joy was eagerly and constantly invoked by all classes of English people. Ayres, ballads, and singable dance tunes were in everybody's mouths and ears. We quote W. Chappell, a historian of the music of the period:

> Tinkers sang catches, milkmaids sang ballads, carters whistled; each trade, and even the beggars, had their special songs; the bass-viol hung in the drawing-room for the amusement of waiting visitors . . . They had music at dinner; music at supper; music at weddings; music at funerals; music at night, music at dawn; music at work, and music at play.

The unamiable moralist Stephen Gosson complained in 1579 that "London is so full of unprofitable pipers and fiddlers that a man can no sooner enter a tavern than two or three cast [company] of them hang at his heels to give him a dance before breakfast."

An exquisite, artful music was enjoyed by some of the higher gentry; the intricate madrigals, the polyphonic fantasies for string instruments, and the ingenious variations—"divisions," they called them—in which they delighted were rather sharply set off from the lewd catches and ballads that common people liked to mouth. Music was well regarded among the leaders of society, from the Crown on down. A few rich nobles—notably Sir Thomas Kytson, kept musicians as part of their households, for the pleasure of hearing them perform and for the instruction of their families. In other gentle families, servants were engaged with a view to their musical abilities. Still more often musicians were hired for special occasions.

Often upper-class love of music was genuine; as often, perhaps, music was held in a conventional good esteem. But even that pretense implied respect. The etiquette books of that time—such as Castiglione's *The Courtier*—mostly indicated that some skill in music, providing it was not too showy, was a suitable ornament to a gentleman. He might with perfect propriety, if he were so inclined, carry his part in a madrigal or read his part in a consort of viols. Henry Peacham in his *The Compleat Gentleman,* in speaking of the unmusical, even goes so far as to say he is "verily perswaded that they are by nature very ill disposed and of such a brutish stupidity that scarce anything that is good and savoureth of virtue is to be found in them." Shakespeare says it better, in his famous lines from *The Merchant of Venice,* Act V, Scene 1:

Lorenzo.

> The man that hath no music in himself,
> Nor is not mov'd with concord of sweet sounds,
> Is fit for treasons, stratagems, and spoils;
> The motions of his spirit are dull as night,
> And his affections dark as Erebus
> Let no such man be trusted. . . .

Even here we seem to feel a tinge of conventionality in the expression of this point of view, which nevertheless involved an authentic tribute.

The charms of music were considered even more becoming to ladies than to gentlemen; the literature of the period rarely praises a lady but that her skill in music is held up as one of her attractions. Here is a verse from the earlier seventeenth century:

> This is all that women do,
> Sit and answer them that woo;
> Deck themselves in new attire,
> To entangle fresh desire;
> After dinner sing and play,
> Or dancing, pass the time away.

This only slightly overdrawn picture of unmarried feminine gentility remained a good likeness for three more centuries. We will add one more familiar feature to it, as described during the same epoch. Says Robert Burton in his *Anatomy of Melancholy*, published in 1621:

> A thing nevertheless frequently used, and part of a gentlewoman's bringing up, to sing, dance, and play on the lute, or some such instrument, before she can say her paternoster, or ten commandments. 'Tis the next way their parents think to get them husbands, they are compelled to learn . . . 'tis a great allurement as it is often used, and many are undone by it.

But once the man has been got, alas!; then:

> We see this daily verified in our young women and wives, they that being maids took so much pains to sing, play, and dance, with such cost and charge to their parents, to get those graceful qualities, now being married will scarce touch an instrument, they care not for it.

After dinner sing and play—play what? The lute very likely, for it made a good accompaniment for an air; the viol less likely, for "there be a thousand close dames that will call the viol an unmannerly instrument for a woman"—especially a viol da gamba—as one of Thomas Middleton's characters tells us. As often as not, the young ladies played the instrument especially dedicated to them and named for them: the virginal. It was a keyboard instrument: its keys lifted upright jacks; crows' quills on the ends of the jacks plucked sets of stretched strings from below. It was, of course, identical with the Italian *clavicembalo,* the French *clavecin*—of which we have often spoken before—the very same that the English themselves later were to call "harpsichord." Virginals were built into cases usually oblong, but sometimes five-angled; their length was on the order of five feet, their width about sixteen inches, and their depth perhaps seven inches. We have heard of simple ones weighing as little as twenty-four pounds; thus, they could be lifted and set on a convenient surface by a single person, though that person was more likely to be a servant than a lady. Four octaves was the normal range of keys. By a curious quirk of the English language, the word "virginal" was most frequently used in the plural, but to denote a single instrument, and with the auxiliary numeral "pair": a "pair" of virginals, or a "pair" of organs, meant one virginal, one organ. Perhaps the row of keys suggested a flight, or "pair," of stairs. The rarer instruments with two keyboards were called double virginals.

We first hear of the virginal in the earlier sixteenth century, during the reign of Henry VIII. Persons who knew that talented monarch testified that he was a competent performer upon it, as well as upon other instruments, besides being a creditable composer. The inventory of his possessions taken after his death reveals no less than thirty-four "pairs" of virginals scattered over his residences at Westminster, Greenwich, Hampton Court, and elsewhere. This was enough to assure the instrument the most solid social approval; soon Sir Thomas Kytson, the glorified drygoodsman, included single and double virginals among the many instruments with which he furnished his newly built Hengrave Hall.

The keyboard skill of Henry's daughters Queen Mary and Queen Elizabeth emphasized, though hardly established, the prevailing femininity of the instrument. Indeed, in Elizabeth's time the virginality of virginals, while preponderant, was by no means exclusive: we hear of young men casually fingering them in taverns; moreover, they were sometimes stationed in barber shops, to let a man amuse himself till he was "next."

By the early seventeenth century the little keyboards had spread to the homes of the wealthier retail tradesmen. In his play of 1607, *Michaelmas Term,* Thomas Middleton finds it plausible to let his crafty woolen draper, Ephestian Quomodo, shoo his daughter Susan out of the shop by telling her to "get you up to your virginals." In the same author's *A Chaste Maid in Cheapside,* first performed about 1613, the play opens with Mistress Maudlin Yellowhammer, a goldsmith's wife, nagging her daughter Moll thus: "Have you played over all your old lessons o' the virginals?" The woolen draper is made to commit usurious rascalities for the sake of becoming a rural landed proprietor—that is, a truer-seeming gentleman. The goldsmith's wife is anxious to brighten up her daughter's behavior with music and dancing so as to make her the more fit to marry a noble knight by the all too apt name of Sir Walter Whorehound. Middleton was a much-enjoyed playwright, a man of the world, and a great connoisseur of London; it is significant that he considered virginals appropriate to the households of socially ambitious burgesses.

It was evident by that time that in the array of appurtenances for achieving gentility, a "pair" of virginals was among the more easily acquired. For one thing, it was an article not expensive enough to be restricted to "the great." We have little direct information about the precise prices of virginals in the early 1600's, but we know that an expense account of Henry VIII as far back as 1530 listed two "payer of virginalls in one coffer with iiii stoppes"—that is, double virginals—at £3, or £1 10s apiece. A larger item from February 13, 1531, records five "pair" of virginals for £8 6s 8d, or £1 13s 4d each. Prices rose mightily through the sixteenth century. We are not astonished to hear that in 1638 Charles I's resident agent in Brussels offered the King a Ruckers *clavecin* (that is, a virginal) at £15. That, however, we must understand, was a fancy imported object by a widely famous maker. Thirty years later Mr. Pepys was still able to buy a small London-made virginal for £5. We may reasonably guess that a well-made unadorned virginal could be had in 1600 for £5 or less.

The sum of £5 was, of course, worth many times as much in 1600 as it is now; yet compared with the living costs of the more prosperous middle classes—or with the luxuries of the aggressively fashionable—it was a relatively modest amount of money. In a schedule of living expenses submitted in 1618 to the Lord Mayor and the aldermen, the bakers of London calculated their average individual rent at £30 per annum. Bakers were less likely than woolen drapers or goldsmiths to come into frequent contact with people of "quality" and thus become smitten with their ways, yet at that rate an imaginative baker in whose mind had flowered the ambition of buying a virginal for his daughter might have had one for one sixth the price of his year's living and working quarters. It is as if an American shopkeeper who pays $1800 a year for store and dwelling rent could buy a piano for $300.

On the other side, the famous ruff—that great maze of eye-assaulting white stuff that surrounded the necks of all gentlemen and ladies of importance in those days—cost as much as £4, we are told, in 1620, by which time it had grown to be a foot thick. Back in 1564 Mistress Ann Dinghen, the daughter of a Dutch gentleman, had taught flocks of London citizens' wives how to starch the ruff, charging £5 for her course of instructions. A Puritan moralist of 1586 found it "horrible to heare" of shirts at £10 apiece, but he could have shredded his soul even more effectually by contemplating the embroidered waistcoats being sold at £20 or £40. The lucky group of persons who in 1600 invested in the first voyage of the East India Company pocketed the easy swag of an 87½% dividend; they—as well as the thousand privy councilors, titled ladies, judges, clergymen, widows, merchants, and tradesmen who rushed to subscribe more than £1,500,000 to the second venture—might well have thought that £5 for a virginal was pretty small potatoes.

Of course, one could spend a lot more money on virginals if one chose. During 1595–96 the Queen paid for "fourteen yards of carnation velvet and eight yards of wrought velvet black and ash colour, employed and spent in covering of our virginals, and for twelve yards of grene velvet to cover a greate instrument, all being garnished with lace of gold and silver and silke riben and sowing silke to them." Thirteen years previously she had ordered gold and silver lacquer for ornamenting some of her virginals, also Levant leather and ironwork. Crimson velvet seems to have been a favorite virginal covering; we hear of it in connection with other than royal instruments. The same letter that offered Charles I a virginal for £15 also offered him another one, a double one, at second hand:

> an excellent peece . . . The Virginal was made for the latte Infante, hath a faire picture on the inne side of the Covering, representing the Infantas parke, and on the opening, att the part where played, a picture of Rubens, representing Cupid and Psiche, the partie asks £30. starling.

The bulk of the English population, however, as of all populations, belonged to the classes of people who worked with their hands. In 1588 the earnings of the most skillful London journeymen craftsmen were estimated, for tax purposes, to be 10d to 14d a day; at that time farm laborers made about 7d a day. Clearly, such people could hardly dream of owning virginals.

3. VIRGINAL MUSIC

Judging by the specimens of their music that have come down to us, the leading English composers of the Elizabethan and Jacobean reigns were Europe's most skilled practitioners of their time in the learned art of polyphony, as it had been developed during the preceding centuries; and they put their craft solidly into the compositions they wrote for the virginal. Orlando Gibbons' *Fantazie of Foure Parts,* for example, is a masterly structure, of a well-controlled complexity, leading to an inexorable conclusion. The *Fantasie on "Ut, Re, Mi, Fa, Sol, La"* by Oxford professor Dr. John Bull is a remarkable manipulation of the six notes of the medieval scales, full of bold harmonic—even enharmonic—enterprise and ingenuity.

Still, the learned musicians were sometimes glad to salute the common humanity of the masses and the classes. For instance, William Byrd, once organist of Lincoln Cathedral, setter of much liturgical Latin, most admired and revered of composers, seemed less severe than Dr. Bull in his aloofness toward vulgar musical products. He did not disdain to use his artifices for the enhancement of plebeian tunes such as "The Carman's Whistle," or "John Come Kiss Me Now," or "The Woods So Wild." His and other masters' variations on melodies such as these contain much nimble figuration—of an interesting, often disconcerting, irregularity. Our admiration goes out to those ladies, and occasional gentlemen, who could twine themselves sure-fingeredly in and out of those difficult notes. However, we can safely guess that most of the dilettantes put their keyboard efforts into the simple accompaniments of the genial airs and into the simpler dance tunes, courtly and common—the pavans, gailliards, and almans, the jigs, brawles, and dompes—that rang brightly in all ears of the time.

On February 14, 1613, the sixteen-year-old Elizabeth, daughter of James I, was married with much pomp and ceremony to Frederick, Elector Palatine, *Pfalzgraf*—or "Palgrave," as the title was transliterated. We may suspect some musical talent in the young princess, unless we wish to imagine a vexatious frustration on the part of her master, who was no less than the celebrated Dr. Bull.

A lady named Dorothy Evans has been conjectured to have been one of Elizabeth's companions or teachers. Mistress Evans seems to have thought up a particularly graceful wedding present: she had William Hole, Esq., the engraver, print a collection of twenty-one excellent pieces for the virginal and dedicate the volume to the young couple, more especially to the bride. The printing of any music was a luxury in those days and not at all common. In fact, virginal music had never before been printed at all. Moreover, this collection was probably the first music ever to have been impressed from engraved plates. A handsome title page adorned the book; it read: "Parthenia, or the Maydenhead of the first musicke that ever was printed for the Virginalls, Composed by three famous masters William Byrde, Dr. John Bull & Orlando Gibbons, gentlemen of his majesties most illustrious Chappell." Below this is a picture of a young lady playing the instrument, and at the bottom is the legend: "Lond: print. for M. Dor. Evans."

The word "Parthenia" is a nominalized adjective derived from the Greek πάρθενος—meaning a virgin, or young female. "Parthenia," "maidenhead," "virginals," "Dorothy Evans," and the picture—there we have it: a five-barreled charge of girlishness fired off at the domestic keyboard instrument's first sortie into print.

4. VIRGINALS AT HOME

THE GROWING WEALTH and ambition that impelled families to put virginals in their homes also made them acquire all manner of other new, improved household furnishings. Teen-age daughters of the citizens and knights who attended the *premières* of *Twelfth Night* or *Hamlet* had grandmothers who may well have spoken sarcastically of the newfangled, effeminate foreign fashion of using forks at meals; the old ladies may have gone on to reminisce about the brave days when nobody drank from glasses and when, in fact, glass was not even used for windows. People were becoming more fastidious: stone floors had been ordinarily strewn with rushes—that is to say, straw—that were not removed even for purposes of dancing (in fact, the flooring was allowed to lie unchanged till it reeked); but presently plaited mats came in, still made of rushes, costing about fivepence a yard. All houses now had solid "court" cupboards in the dining hall; many had fine oaken buffets in the parlor; some also had delicate inlaid cabinets in the drawing room for displaying porcelain and other curios. Everywhere there was an abundance of paneled chests of varying heights; often they were carved and painted.

Seating facilities were relatively deficient in Elizabethan days: chairs were scarce and were reserved for the aged and the worshipful. The young ladies pressed their dainty behinds upon stools while fingering their keyboard lessons, or on benches or settles; cushions often eased the impact. Virginals that did not rest on their own stands may have been set on tables. We are tempted to think that the tops of some of the numerous chests may have served as virginal platforms; still, the chests' straight fronts left no room for the fair seated players' legs. On the other hand, it appears that the girls often played standing up, to judge by a number of seventeenth-century paintings showing them in this position and act. It is true the pictures are by Dutch, rather than English, artists.

After the second decade of the seventeenth century, chairs became much more numerous. Women liked to tie a bone hoop around their middles, standing off a few inches from the body; it gave their skirts a graceful bump and droop. They called it "farthingale"; the new-type chairs, built without arms so as to give the expanded clothes ample room, were called "farthingale" chairs. We may picture our young lady virginalists draped upon them as they played.

5. THE VIRGINAL BECOMES A HARPSICHORD; THE INSTRUMENT ACCORDING TO MR. PEPYS

The seventeenth century was a troubled period for England. It saw violent fights between people of differing religious principles, conflicting political ideals, and divergent ways of life; it witnessed significant shifts in many ethical values. Those dry political abstractions—Civil War, Protectorate, Restoration, and Revolution—fail to suggest a vivid appreciation of the complex drama of thought and feeling that they cover. Musical habits naturally shifted along with the others. Madrigals went out in the 1630's; the Puritans struck down music in churches during the 1640's and 50's, but meanwhile they permitted opera to make its shy debut; lutes and viols declined, and the unfretted, more brilliant, more difficult plebeian violins rose into vogue. In all these vicissitudes one thing remained constant: the custom of keeping a virginal in the house for one's daughters.

The word "virginal," however, went out of use gradually during the latter half of the seventeenth century; it is not altogether certain why this should have occurred. By 1652 the publisher John Playford was isuing a volume of *Select Ayres* to be accompanied by the "harpsicon." The word was later to become "harpsichord" and was occasionally corrupted to "harpsical." It is likely that the name was invented to designate the larger-size, wing-shaped instruments whose strings stretched directly away from the player—so as to distinguish them from the smaller, oblong or pentangular ones whose strings crossed the axes of the keys (the latter retaining the old name for a time). Thus, in the volume called *Musick's Handmaid* published by the same Playford in 1678, the contents are averred to be "for the Virginals or Harpsychord," meaning for both small and large instruments. Charles II, before his restoration in 1660, had spent much of his life in France; after his accession, he encouraged French fashions in many things—including music. Thus, the small keyboards began to take on their French name of *"espinette"* (or "spinet"), while the old word "virginal" —which had once been used for all the species of the genus—became obsolete by 1700.

Samuel Pepys tells of the prevalence of virginals and harpsicons during his time. He was Clerk of the Acts in the Navy Office, surveyor of victualing—we would say quartermaster—during the Dutch War of 1665–67, a diligent public servant; but all this would have earned him no "immortality" if it had not been for his famous diary. Its nine years of daily entries form a unique document: a candid, detailed record of the daily living of its time; a treasure pile for the historian with an eye to the important things of life, that is, the so-called small things.

Pepys was a devoted music lover, an amateur on several instruments, with ambition to become a composer and musical theorist; his references to music are persistent, copious, and fairly expert. On December 8, 1660, he tells us:

> [I] went to dinner with my wife . . . to Mr. Pierce the Purser . . . who does live very plentifully and finely. We had a lovely chine of beef and other good things very complete and drank a great deal of wine, and her daughter played after dinner upon the virginals, and at night by lanthorn home again. . . .

On May 22, 1661, he paid another visit:

> . . . by water to the Wardrobe, where my Lord and all the officers of the Wardrobe dined, and several other friends of my Lord, at a venison pasty. Before dinner, my Lady Wright and my Lady Jem. sang songs to the harpsicon. Very pleasant and merry at dinner . . .

"My Lord" was Sir Edward Montagu, first Earl of Sandwich, "general-at-sea," a high ranking Navy officer, and a kinsman of Pepys, to whom the latter owed his appointment. "My Lady Jem." was his daughter, Lady Jemimah Montagu; "my Lady Wright" was her relative.

Pepys was discriminating in his taste; he did not always find the music good. For instance, on May 1, 1663, he wrote:

> I took leave and went to hear Mrs. Turner's daughter, at whose house Sir J. Minnes lies, play on the harpsicon; but Lord! it was enough to make any man sick to hear her; yet I was forced to commend her highly.

Sir John Minnes was a vice-admiral; Mrs. Thomas Turner was the wife of one of Pepys's colleagues in the Navy Office. Apple polishing was clearly in order at the moment, despite the bad music. The same was true when he came to the house of Mr. Bland, a merchant who had lived in Spain and who was doing business in Tangier, on Sunday, June 21, 1663. Mr. Pepys had been "invited to dinner, which we had finely and great plenty"; however:

> . . . they had a kinswoman, they call daughter, in the house, a short, ugly, red-haired slut, that plays upon the virginalls, and sings, but after such a country manner I was weary of it, but yet could not but commend it.

Pepys's own instruments included a flageolet and a viol (he spells it "vyall"); on June 14, 1661, he rounded out his collection as follows: "I sent to my house by my Lord's order his shipp ['s glass] and tryangle virginall." The instrument was apparently either a gift or a loan from Lord Sandwich, on the occasion of the Earl's departure on a mission to North Africa. We do not know exactly what a tryangle virginal was; we might suspect a small harpsicon, but more likely it was a small crosswise-strung virginal with the case worked into a triangular shape. Pepys still had it three years later, for he says on July 1, 1664:

> Up and within all the morning, first bringing down my tryangle to my chamber below, having a new frame made proper for it to stand on.

It was evidently not very heavy. That same evening he reports:

> . . . by agreement came Mr. Hill and Andrews and one Cheswicke, a maister who plays very well upon the Spinette, and we sat singing Psalms till 9 at night, and so broke up with great pleasure, and very good company it is. . . .

For his time, Pepys was conservative—if not to say old-fashioned—in his musical ideas. A "good English tune" was more to his liking than the florid Italian music that latterly was beginning to be steadily imported. When he heard something by Carissimi well sung, and "the best piece of musique counted of all hands in the world," he said: "Fine it was, indeed, and too fine for me to judge of." Time-honored, too, was his practice of hiring domestic servants with a view also to their musical qualifications. We find him, for instance, engaging a master to teach the lute to his boy Tom Edwards; later the same master was called upon also to instruct the boy in playing the theorbo, "which he will do and that in a little time, I believe."

We were not surprised to learn from Mr. Pepys that lords, overseas merchants, pursers who lived "very plentifully and finely," and other Navy officials kept virginals for their daughters; however, he makes it clear that females of much lowlier rank also had opportunity to acquire skill upon the keyboard. It was characteristic, likewise, that whereas Tom Edwards played the lute, it was the maidservants who took to the spinet. There was, for example, Mary Ashwell, who entered his service as his wife's woman on about March 12, 1663. Four days later he "heard Ashwell play first upon the harpsicon, and I find she do play pretty well, which pleaseth me very well"; and on the eighteenth: "This day my tryangle, which was put in tune yesterday, did please me very well, Ashwell playing upon it pretty well." She played for him a number of times during the following weeks. He apparently seemed at first to think she merely played by ear; however, by April 3 he "found that above my expectation Ashwell has very good principles of musique and can take out a lesson herself with very little pains, at which I am very glad." On Sunday May 3, after church, he went "up to teach Ashwell the grounds of time and other things on the tryangle, and made her take out a Psalm very well, she having a good ear and hand."

The pleasant-fingered maidservant apparently made Pepys more attentive to the keyboard instrument than he had been before. Less than three weeks after she came into his house he was:

> . . . calling on the virginall maker, buying a rest for myself to tune my tryangle, and taking one of his people along with me to put it in tune once more, by which I learned how to go about it myself for the time to come.

"Rest" means "wrest," a tuning wrench. Pepys does not seem to have played the virginal very much himself until then; but perhaps Ashwell inspired him, for on June 21, after dinner, he:

> . . . went up and tried a little upon my tryangle, which I understand fully, and with a little use I believe I could bring myself to do something.

Mary Ashwell evidently appealed to him personally as well. At first he finds her a little rude "for want of being abroad," but soon considers her "such good company that I think we shall be very lucky in her." Soon he is "home again merry with our Ashwell, who is a merry jade." Presently Mr. and Mrs. Pepys and the girl are spending "all the afternoon talking and laughing." Two days later, Mrs. Pepys having been lazily in bed all morning, "Ashwell and I dined below together, and a pretty girl she is and I hope will give my wife and myself good content." All the attention Pepys paid to this girl inevitably began to annoy Mrs. Pepys, whose only recourse was to take out her feelings on the girl. She accused her of stealing yards of ribbon; soon Ashwell called her mistress a liar; after that the lady began to beat her. Finally, on August 25, after serving a scant five and a half months, the merry Mary was fired. Pepys said he was glad.

Nevertheless, the sprightly Clerk of the Acts found it hard to forgo the fun of having a musical Mary in the house: Mary Mercer, a new woman-servant, started working for Mrs. Pepys on September 8, 1664. The very next day Pepys rejoices:

> . . . and so back again home, and there my wife and Mercer and Tom and I sat till eleven at night, singing and fiddling, and a great joy it is to see me master of so much pleasure in my house, that it is, and will be still, I hope, a constant pleasure to me to be at home. The girle plays pretty well upon the harpsicon, but only ordinary tunes, but hath a good hand; sings a little, but hath a good voyce and eare . . .

Mercer also played the viol, he found a few weeks later; he joined her in it and sang.

She had a good hand, said Pepys; but he had a good hand himself. He must have kept it under pretty good control for a while, for it was nearly two years later, on June 19, 1666, that he reflected on:

> . . . Mercer, whom I feel myself beginning to love too much by handling of her breasts in a morning when she dresses me, they being the finest that I ever saw in my life, that is the truth of it. . . .

Mercer's musical and mammary charms produced their unfailing effect on Mrs. Pepys, for six weeks later the comment is:

> . . . I find my wife plainly dissatisfied with me, that I can spend so much time with Mercer, teaching her to sing, and could never take the pains with her. Which I acknowledge; but it is because that the girle do take musique mighty readily, and she do not, and musique is the thing of the world that I love most, and all the pleasure almost that I can now take. So to bed in some little discontent, but no words from me.

Thus Mr. Pepys claimed, as many a devoted music lover sincerely might, that for him the proposition, Love Is the Food of Music, was just as true as its more familiar reverse.

Pepys gives us further evidence concerning the widespread ownership of keyboard instruments. On September 2, 1666, he was trudging through London, alert and anxious, while the great fire was sweeping much of it away. Many people were trying to save their possessions by water. He reported:

> River full of lighters and boats taking in goods, and good goods swimming in the water; and only I observed that hardly one lighter or boat in three that had the goods of a house in, but there was a pair of Virginalls in it.

One out of three is a large number. We are reluctant to surmise that this estimate was due to his happening to be in a particular, prosperous neighborhood at the moment; for there is reason to think that he himself was in a boat when he made the observation.

In any event, what with the fire and the confusion, not many people succeeded in saving their instruments, for few genuine pre-fire English virginals have been preserved. Pepys's own house was not burned; nevertheless, he had evacuated his possessions. He noted later with great satisfaction that he had lost nothing save a few mislaid books. He did not, however, at that time any longer mention his "tryangle"; we might guess that it had been returned to its original owner, "my Lord" Sandwich.

About eighteen months after the fire he again felt the need of a keyboard instrument, for the purpose of making "a few more experiments of my notions in musique . . ." He found that the harpsicon maker he used to know in Bishopsgate Street, before the fire, was now gone; but in Aldgate Street he came across one Charles Hayward:

> . . . that makes virginalls, and there did like of a little espinette, and will have him finish it for me; for I had a mind to a small harpsicon, but this takes up less room, and will do my business as to finding out of chords, and I am well pleased that I have found it.

Pepys often uses "virginal," "harpsicon," "spinet," and "triangle" interchangeably, which is proper, since they are all fundamentally the same instrument, differing only in size and shape. The above entry proves that the harpsicons were the larger type, even when they were small specimens.

After changing his mind once, he decided on a purchase; and on July 15, 1668, he writes:

> At noon home to dinner, where is brought home the espinette I bought the other day of Haward; costs me £5.

We have mentioned this transaction before, but must hasten to insist that the price paid was a low one, suitable for small, possibly for secondhand, instruments. Pepys himself was witness to a higher price for a larger article. Already on February 26, 1661, Shrove Tuesday, he had gone to dinner to his family connections, the John Turners. Turner was a sergeant-at-law and Recorder of York; and his only daughter, Theophila, was usually referred to by Pepys as "Mrs. The."

Very merry and the best fritters that I ever eat in my life. After that looked out at window; saw the flinging at cocks. Then Mrs. The. and I, and a gentleman that dined there and his daughter . . . and Mr. Thatcher the Virginall Maister to Bishopsgate Street, and there saw the new Harpsicon made for Mrs. The. We offered £12, they demanded £14. The Master not being at home, we could make no bargain, so parted for to-night.

We can only regret that Mr. Pepys's eyes went back on him in 1669, thus depriving us of the intimate account of a further thirty-four years' worth of fascinating private life—in the course of which much musical information would undoubtedly have been vouch-safed us.

6. THE HARPSICHORD GROWS FEET

THE RISING VOGUE of the larger wing-shaped instruments inspired a far-reaching thought in the mind of a harpsichord maker named John Hayward. We know very little about that person and cannot say how, or even whether, he was related to the craftsman on Aldgate Street whom Mr. Pepys had patronized.

Be that as it may, the larger harpsichords—especially those with two keyboards—were now mostly made with several sets of superposed strings tuned in unisons or octaves; each key was then correspondingly equipped with several quilled jacks that could be moved from side to side so as to pluck—or not pluck—any set of strings, as the player chose, for the sake of variety: they were stops, or registers, as in an organ. The shifting of the jacks in and out of play was accomplished by levers worked by a number of knobs protruding from a rail right above the keys. The hand that pulled them out or pushed them in, then, had to cease playing for the moment, even if it had to steal time from the music to do so.

If the stops, reflected Hayward, could be devised so as to be operated by the feet, the hands could confine themselves to the keys alone and thus avoid making unpleasant gaps in the tonal continuity. Hayward executed such a plan and built a structure of rods and springs under the instrument, to be worked by a couple of pedal levers. It involved much delicate labor and could only be applied to an instrument that rested on its own, built-in stand. We know about it from a charmingly written book called *Musick's Monument,* by Thomas Mace, an elderly clerk of Trinity College, Cambridge, and a devoted musician. Writing just before 1676, Master Mace tells us that the "pedal" is "an instrument of late invention," that it is "a most excellent kind of instrument for a Consort, and far beyond all Harpsicons or Organs, that I have yet heard of . . ." Still, he continues, "It is not very commonly used, or known; because few make them Well, and Fewer will go to the price of them: Twenty Pounds being the Ordinary Price of One; but the Great Patron of Musick in his Time, Sir Robert Bolles . . . had two of them, the one I remember at 30£ and the other at 50£ very admirable instruments." We will remember that a scant eight years before this was published, Mr. Pepys bought his little "espinette" for £5.

The Revolution of 1688 gave the commercial classes a go-ahead signal for an unprecedented expansion of activity and influence. The Bank of England was founded in 1694; investors in overseas companies, stockbrokers, promoters, and money lenders began to swagger conspicuously. Soon there gathered a storm of financial riotousness of which the South Sea "bubble" was a part. Many people now sprang up who would go to the price of £20 or £30 or more for a harpsichord; by the middle of the eighteenth century the large pedal instrument was well established. Let us emphasize the fact that a pedal apparatus for modifying the tone of a keyboard instrument was an English invention and for some time a predominantly English practice. Moreover, it was an English maker, as we shall see, who later first adapted the pedal idea to the pianoforte.

7. MUSIC BECOMES AN ARTICLE OF COMMERCE

IT WAS in the nature of events for music to become an article of commerce in England long before it did so in Germany. The year 1672 is the date usually accepted as witnessing the first true public concerts; that was when John Banister, once Charles II's chief violinist, disgruntled at having had his leading position handed over to a Frenchman, collected some good musicians and offered regular performances at his own house. He built a platform for the players, and to the audience his message was "a shilling a head and call for what you please." That was nearly fifty years before any similar enterprise was heard of in Germany. Soon Banister had followers; some of them held forth in taverns, and during the first half of the eighteenth century such places became favorite locations for musical performances—open to all and sundry who handed over the admission fee.

The influx of Italian opera early in the eighteenth century further confirmed the habit of paying money for the privilege of sitting for a few hours in a public place to listen to music. Opera in England often enjoyed royal patronage; but the people who had chopped off one king's head and booted another king overseas were not likely to feel uplifted by a true "Royal Opera" in the Continental sense, as an outward and visible sign of the sovereign's superhuman magnificence. Nevertheless, a few decoy-dukes on an Italian-opera enterprise's board of directors might influence ambitious Bank of England shareholders or South Sea Company promoters and their sycophants to attend performances. "My Wife is a great Pretender to Musick, and very ignorant of it; but far gone in the *Italian* Taste"—so Addison makes believe to quote from a correspondent in No. 212 of his *Spectator.*

"Many concerts are given in England for money," wrote the learned German critic Johann Mattheson as late as 1740, with an air of astonishment. By that time his old Hamburg chum George Frideric Handel, now a British subject, was sharply distinguished from all his colleagues in Germany by the fact that he was not in the service of a prince or a church consistory or a municipality, but was his own entrepreneur—producing his own operas and oratorios in his own hired theaters for his own account and risk, for the enjoyment of anyone at all who would pay half a guinea or half a crown to get in: insolent nobles and showy citizens, with true music lovers sprinkled among them all.

Many English—patient, but unconvinced by the tortured contrivances of the foreign opera, and indifferent to the fate of Arsinoe, or of Pyrrhus and Demetrius—found a joyful relief for their strained feelings in the celebrated *Beggar's Opera* when it was first given in 1728. They could open their hearts easily to Polly Peachum and Captain Macheath; moreover, its delightful tunes, already long familiar by the time of the *première,* were quickened into a new life by the epoch-making production. The sixty-three performances of its first run made it seem worth imitating; a string of similar "ballad operas" battened for another five to ten years: *The Quaker's Opera, The Village Opera, The Cobler's Opera, The Lover's Opera, The Grub Street Opera.* There also appeared *The Beggar's Wedding, The Mock Doctor, The Sham Captain, The Intriguing Chambermaid, Trick for Trick, The Rival Milliners,* and *The Female Parson or Beau in the Sudds.* When these palled, comparable pieces were produced with newly composed easy tunes and catchy English words. The musical theaters became and remained a bubbling spring of commercial melody.

Eighteenth-century Londoners could not easily spend a day in the country and get back home before dark. Instead, they nursed their need for greenery in numbers of pleasure gardens in various parts of the city. Vauxhall, first called Spring Gardens, on the south bank of the Thames, was the most frequented, most famous, and most enduring of these. Its twelve acres of tree-lined walks, leafy nooks, and open parks—as well as its refreshment booths and spectacles—formed a pleasant locale for various kinds of dalliance during the spring and summer months. One lowly shilling was the admission charge; all ranks of people, servants in livery excepted, flocked there by the tens of thousands. One would not, however, call it "democratic"; on the contrary, it gave an outstanding opportunity for enjoying discriminations of rank and fortune at close range.

Light music is a good lubricant of all such contacts as well as a good associate of other easy pleasures; and about 1738 the manager decided to make more of it. Soon he built a kiosk—we would call it a bandstand—in the open part of the gardens and hired a group of good musicians to play and sing every evening, at first from six to nine. On rainy days the music was given inside an adjoining building; presently an organ was installed. Concertos and other instrumental solos were heard; but the favorites were the singers and the songs, the latter mostly sentimental, but occasionally humorous or arch. James Boswell spoke of Vauxhall as:

> that excellent place of public amusement which must ever be an estate to its proprietor, as it is peculiarly adapted to the taste of the English nation; there being a mixture of curious show, gay exhibition, musick, vocal and instrumental, not too refined for the general ear; for all which only a shilling is paid; and though last, not least, good eating and drinking for those who choose to purchase that regale.

Tavern concerts, Italian opera, English light opera, pleasure gardens—all this music in public warmed a desire to relive it at home, often with the aid of a harpsichord. That was the basis of the rapidly growing music-publishing business. Already by the middle of the seventeeth century London seems to have had a fair-sized musically literate public: John Playford, the most persistently successful music publisher of his time, issued his first print in 1651, fully seventy-five years before anything of the kind was attempted in Germany. He brought out collections of dance tunes for a single violin and books of music for the cithren, the viol, and the harpsichord, as well as sonatas by Purcell. Toward the end of the seventeenth century the business broadened and cheapened; we hear of half-sheet "single songs" put out in great numbers. The financial and operatic flurries of the days of Queen Anne and George I gave further aid and hope to the makers and distributers of printed notes: John Walsh made plenty of money publishing salable portions of Handel's and others' works. The *Beggars' Opera,* of course, was a fountain of cash, its printed songs going through numerous editions in quick succession. The third edition, of 1729, had basses with the tunes, making them more readily playable on the harpsichord. The tendency thenceforth was to print most of the tunes with basses, so that almost any young lady could elicit a minimum of harmony from the keys—while the brightest ones might even supply an occasional complete chord according to the subscribed figures. After the enlargement of the musical establishments at Vauxhall, Marylebone, and other similar places, the songs heard there were in great demand for home reproduction: annual sets of "Vauxhall Songs" were published by various firms for a century or more.

Dance music came to be more and more desired for home enjoyment: country dances began to appear in print early in the eighteenth century and multiplied vigorously thereafter. They usually came out in sets of twenty-four. After a time various publishers put them out in annual series, and by 1718 there appeared a *Great Dance Book* containing 364 of these tunes. Minuets were well liked and usually appeared annually in sets of twelve. Hornpipes also had their partisans: a book of thirty came out in 1759, and *Thompson's Compleat Collection of 120 Favorite Hornpipes* was issued a few years later.

So-called "Scotch" songs found increasing favor after the first third of the eighteenth century. Just what made a song Scotch is a little hard to say. Often an English song became especially popular in Scotland; sometimes an old tune had had words composed to it in the ancient English dialect known as "Scots." Possibly the activities of the Stuart pretenders to the English throne aroused a sympathetic bent toward Scotland among some Londoners of the 1740's; probably, however, the songs were nurtured by a budding sentimental fancy for the quaint, the primitive, and the distant that somehow came to coalesce with the notion of Scotland in many minds at about this time: it was a place that could seem interestingly exotic without being inconveniently foreign. Scotch songs in London had approximately the flavor value acquired much later by "Dixie" songs in New York. In any case, the fancy grew and Scotch songs became a favorite musical tipple by the end of the century and well beyond, as well as a staple article of trade—as also, to a lesser extent, did "Irish" songs. Scotch dances were also played on London harpsichords: reels, in particular, and also a rhythm known as "strathspey."

Regular harpsichord music of greater scope and elaboration, such as sonatas and suites, was also published and no doubt occasionally played at home, though rather infrequently. Any compositions of a more serious nature—like those of Handel, D. Scarlatti, Mattheson, or others—were ordinarily called "lessons"; they continued to bear this label for a century more. The term is invidious: it seems to suggest that this sort of music was imposed on the girls as a kind of edifying penance, but was not to be touched for pleasure, like the prevailing airs and country dances. One publisher did indeed try to sweeten the pedagogic medicine. He announced *The Lady's Banquet, being a choice collection of the newest and most airy lessons for the Harpsichord, continued annually, for the year 1702.*

We get a good picture of a live harpsichord in its natural habitat from a passage in Fielding's *Tom Jones.* The episode takes place in the house of that hearty squire Mr. Western (Book IV, Chapter 5):

> It was Mr. Western's custom every afternoon, as soon as he was drunk, to hear his daughter play on the harpsichord; for he was a great lover of music, and perhaps, had he lived in town, might have passed for a connoisseur; for he always excepted against the finest compositions of Mr. Handel. He never relished any music but what was light and airy; and indeed, his most favorite tunes were *Old Sir Simon the King, Saint George he was for England, Bobbing Joan,* and some others.

His daughter, though she was a perfect mistress of music, and would never willingly have ever played any but Handel's, was so devoted to her father's pleasure, that she learned all those things to oblige him. However, she would now and then endeavor to lead him into her own taste; and when he required the repetition of his ballads, would answer with a "Nay dear sir"; she would often beg him to suffer her to play something else.

The squire's favorite *Old Sir Simon,* which he preferred to Handel, is an old tune in a swinging 9/8 time. The first verse contains the following lines:

My hostess was sick of the mumps,
The maid was ill at her ease,
The tapster was drunk in his dumps,
They were all of one disease.
Said old Sir Simon the king,
Says old Sir Simon the king,
With his ale-dropt hose and his Malmsey nose,
Sing hey ding a ding ding.

8. BUT MUSIC'S STOCK GOES DOWN

ONE COULD call this commercialization of music "progress," as indeed it was—progress in a direction. But it coincided with, perhaps was related to, a heavy social devaluation of music that became much accelerated in the early decades of the eighteenth century. By the end of the Restoration, English gentlemen had pretty well given up the practice of music themselves. Peacham's "compleat gentleman" of 1622 was required to sing and play the viol adequately at sight—though perhaps no inordinately difficult parts—and was considered ill-disposed and "brutish" if he had no music in him. Now in 1693 we have John Locke, foremost political and social thinker of his time, spokesman for the dominant ideals of a long era, spiritual ancestor of the United States of America, setting down *Some Thoughts on Education.* He means education of a gentleman, of course:

> ". . . a good hand upon some instruments, is by many people mightily valued. But it wastes so much of a young man's time, to gain but a moderate skill in it; and engages often in such odd company, that many think it much better spared: and I have among men of parts and business, so seldom heard any one commended or esteemed for having an excellency in music that among all those things that ever come into the list of accomplishments I think I may give it the last place. Our short lives will not serve us for the attainment of all things; nor can our minds be always intent on something to be learned. . . .

Locke does not exactly condemn music, but he values it the least, puts it in last place. The disesteem grew rapidly stronger; the belittling of music on the part of influential social leaders tended to make budding musicians ashamed of their talent, rather than eager to improve it. After the death of Henry Purcell, in 1695, the cultivated creation and performance of music by native Englishmen dried up into a few feeble trickles. England, lush garden of artful music in Elizabeth's day, soon became, for two centuries to come, a sterile arena for the exhibition of foreign potted plants.

The phenomenon has often been observed, but never satisfactorily explained. For a long time it was glibly said: "The Puritans killed English music"; cruel and sanctimonious, these sectaries were accused of having stepped on all the joys, including music. Did they not abolish organs in churches, and did they not shut down the theaters? But here is a peculiar thing: when one of Cromwell's gangs of pious roughnecks smashed up the two organs of the Peterborough cathedral, some of the fellows then played jigs on the amputated pipes while others danced. Evidently, Puritans approved of some forms of musical pleasure.

Mr. Percy Scholes, eminent present-day musicologist and lexicographer, has written an elaborate book of 428 pages called *The Puritans and Music* in which he brings up vast amounts of evidence to show that the Puritans were not to blame for the withering of English music. Nothing in their theology opposed music, he proves, except in church; otherwise, they considered it a harmless gratification. In fact, leading Puritans such as Cromwell, and especially John Milton, were eager music lovers. Old New England laws alleged to have forbidden musical instruments were the fabrications of an ignorant faker, he shows. With Mr. Scholes as counsel for the defense, the Puritans have won a brilliant acquittal of the charge of willful murder. Still, Scholes is pretty vague on who the real culprits were; and it may develop that in a subtler relation the righteous Puritans were, after all, unconcerned accessories before the fact. We may still have to find an indictment of third-degree manslaughter against them.

I would say, the enemy of music was what might loosely be called the spirit of business. One had better use the word in its pristine sense of busy-ness. It does not mean primarily the direct desire for gaining money, which is a feeling that animates the most dissolute of gamblers. Rather, it means a persistent, hour-to-hour, devoted, rational application to a progressive task, a self-denying, calculating dedication to a perpetually growing achievement—not necessarily a lofty one—a suffusion by the feeling that "we are here in life for a purpose." The life of purpose can readily be directed toward handicraft or commerce; its fruit then would be money. But the money that came from this steady, alert industry would not be a mere gratification of greed or opportunity for indulgence; it would rather be interpreted ethically, as the just and visible reward of good behavior. A man, for instance, who got rich and richer by making felt hats relentlessly and intelligently for eighteen hours a day for forty years could then fix a self-satisfied gaze upon his wealth as the sign of God's approval of his intelligent relentlessness. It is clear that, to a mind of this set, music or any other fine art must be a thing of doubtful worth. The time spent in acquiring skill on an instrument is a "waste of golden hours." Music in itself may do no harm, but overfondness for it might lead a young man to spend too much time in taverns where he might overdrink, or in theaters where he might associate with loose women: all that would distract him from his busyness.

Perhaps there is nothing in the fundamental religious doctrines accepted by Puritans, Presbyterians, Huguenots, members of the "Dutch Reformed" Church, or more extreme Protestants, that specifically teaches this ethic; nevertheless, countless minds have developed an affinity between it and the more or less Calvinist cosmic scheme in which they believe. The important point for us to mark is that it was a view of life that became generally prevalent. God's gold was persuasive: money was the palpable justification of those sterling virtues of diligence and frugality; and by a slight contamination of notions, it could become an exhilarating comfort to money-men—even if their riches were acquired by bribing government officials or taking graft on war contracts—to think of their wealth as a proof of their righteousness. The commercial classes, including money lenders and stock jobbers, had won their victory in the Revolution of 1688. Their influence in the government was now all but dominant: nothing succeeds like success. Presently, docile, conforming Anglicans, not themselves merchants or manufacturers or money lenders, veered unresistingly to the assumption that for a young man the practice of music was a waste of time and an instigation to the keeping of bad company. The attitude became conventionalized, correct—and remained so for a couple of centuries.

Let us not distort the picture: Englishmen did not quickly lose their ears, their muscles, or their guts; they continued to enjoy music in a lively fashion, but they tended to think of it as a lower, sensual form of gratification, a somewhat infantile form of pleasure. Richard Steele quotes approvingly from a correspondent in the *Spectator* for December 26, 1711:

> . . . meer musical Sounds are in our Art no other than nonsense Verses are in Poetry. Musick therefore is to aggravate what is intended by Poetry; it must always have some Passion or Sentiment to express, or else Violins, Voices or any other Organs of Sound, afford an Entertainment very little above the Rattles of Children . . .

Oh, the wounded ghosts of Orlando Gibbons and Dr. Bull!

Under the circumstances, it was the artful, elaborate, attention-requiring music that suffered the most; for it was in an unpretentious, uncultivated, relaxed, and commonplace environment that this low form of activity might still flourish appropriately. Formalized popular songs and dances, in and out of the theaters, remained the only viable native English musical productions for a long time. By the same logic, if music was an unworthy pursuit for a lord of creation, it therefore came to seem an eminently suitable occupation for inferior segments of the human race—such as, primarily, females and foreigners. An equation of cultivated music with femaleness and foreignness came to be generally assumed. To have the females of the family learn to sing and play a little, to pay a high price to attend a public musical performance by a foreigner temporarily fashionable, this was a prevailing pattern of musical experience among the English gentry.

The English were now rich, by European standards; the alluring aroma of the fat crumbs that fell from their tables penetrated the remoter parts of the Continent. German and Italian musicians had a well-warranted feeling that some of these morsels were especially intended for them; they flocked to England in steady bevies, to fill the places the English musicians had abdicated. For a couple of centuries from the days of Queen Anne the foreigners did their stuff in England: playing, teaching, and composing, becoming prosperous if not always happy.

On April 19, 1749, the same year that saw the first publication of *Tom Jones,* Philip Dormer Stanhope, fourth Earl of Chesterfield, wrote to his illegitimate son, then visiting Venice, as follows:

> As you are now in the musical country, where singing, fiddling and piping are not only the common topic of conversation, but almost the principal objects of attention; I cannot help cautioning you against giving in to those (I will call them illiberal) pleasures (though music is commonly reckoned one of the liberal arts), to the degree that most of your countrymen do when they travel in Italy. If you love music, hear it; go to operas, concerts, and pay fiddlers to play to you; but I insist upon your neither piping nor fiddling yourself. It puts a gentleman in a very frivolous, contemptible light; brings him into a great deal of bad company; and takes up a great deal of time, which might be much better employed. Few things would mortify me more, than to see you bearing a part in a concert, with a fiddle under your chin, or a pipe in your mouth.

As we see, the Italians' interest in music is the very badge of their inferiority, so the noble lord implies. We can now trace the descending slope of English music by these three outcrops: Peacham in 1622 says a proper gentleman must be able to play his part in a "consort" and that the unmusical are brutish and stupid; Locke in 1693, while admitting that some persons still regard music highly, says he values it the least of all gentlemanly accomplishments and thinks it better spared; Chesterfield in 1749 says playing an instrument makes a gentleman look frivolous and contemptible and that he would be mortified to imagine his son handling a fiddle or a pipe.

Again, let us evaluate this testimony fairly. Lord Chesterfield seems to have considered his admonition necessary: in other words, there did exist some young gentlemen who swung fiddles under their chins and held pipes to their mouths. Every prevailing ideology, of course, has its dissidents. The German flute, so-called —it was the eighteenth-century name for the modern transverse flute—was an instrument that these nonconformists especially favored, to judge by the amount of literature published for it. We take no risk in guessing that it was the men of the high aristocracy who could best get away with this disregard of current standards.

Willoughby Bertie, for example, the fourth Earl of Abingdon, was an eager amateur on the flute. This piece of wrongheadedness might well have been judged congruous with his outrageous support of John Wilkes—the fiery, irreverent champion of Parliamentary rights—or his repulsive willingness to let his daughter marry a beastly foreign dancing master. But even after Lord Abingdon went to jail for an irregularity in connection with a newspaper, he still remained an exalted peer of the realm; nor could he ever cease for one second to be the scion of an ancient noble family. No amount of eccentric behavior could possibly have lowered him in the deferential estimation of butlers and tradesmen. On the other hand, woe to the son of an aspiring city businessman who would have dared to compromise his respectable standing or his hopeful future by letting plebeians hoot at him for carrying a violin case in the street.

Some few unusually talented musical English youths were strong enough to withstand the social pressure against them—for instance, Thomas Arne, whose ambitious upholsterer father had gotten him through Eton and then placed him in a solicitor's office. Thomas practiced his muffled harpsichord undetected in the dead of night, took secret lessons on the violin, and disguised himself in servants' livery to hear opera from the gallery. Such determined strategy finally defeated the father, who then allowed the son to lose caste as gracefully as he could. Arne was an able melodist, tried hard to improve English theater music, wrote reams of songs for Vauxhall, and was even made a doctor by Oxford.

In 1740 he composed "Rule, Britannia," a fine song that helped British men through many a heavy naval and convivial encounter; however, his patriotic countrymen never have seemed to consider this deed of much consequence.

A needle's eye was left through which promising polite young musicians might squirm into the heaven of British respectability: that was the service of the Established Church. Godly, ungodly, and godless Englishmen somehow felt the invincible propriety and safety of that institution; by becoming an organist and choirmaster, a musician could automatically exonerate himself from the suspicion of being—or keeping—"bad" company, or that of smelling like a foreigner. A majority of musically gifted well-bred Englishmen took this narrow road for many generations to come. Young Charles Burney took it in the 1740's: he had talent, charm, and a lively mind; he kept very "good" company, such as the dandy Fulke Greville, and later Samuel Johnson and Edmund Burke. Besides composing and teaching music competently, he became one of its best commentators and historians. It is as a littérateur upon music that he achieved his greatest distinction: in the accounts of his travels, in his *History of Music,* and in his articles for Rees's *Cyclopaedia.* We will draw upon him freely.

Even the making of instruments reflected the general derogation of music in England. The names of seventeenth-century virginal and harpsichord makers that have come down to us are all English: Stephen Keene, John Loosemore, Thomas and John Hitchcock, Charles and John Hayward, Thomas and James White, Adam Leveridge, Gabriel Townsend, and Philip Jones. However, in the second quarter of the eighteenth century this craft, too, became relinquished to foreigners. Hermann Tabel, a Fleming, set up shop in London before 1721; he had been trained in the celebrated house of Ruckers, of Antwerp, whose sweet-toned *clavecins* were the most highly regarded in all Europe. After Tabel's death, his widow married Jacob Kirchmann, a canny German who had been a foreman in the shop and who thereupon carried on as its chief with great success. Burkhart Tschudi, a young Swiss immigrant journeyman joiner, arrived in London in 1718; he later also became one of Tabel's assistants. He too set up his own shop about 1740 and soon achieved considerable repute. By 1742, when he moved to Great Pulteney Street, Golden Square, he was already "Harpsichord maker to His Royal Highness the Prince of Wales."

Both Kirchmann and Burkhart Tschudi felt they would sell more harpsichords if they put no baffling strain on the slender linguistic talents of the English—so they called themselves Kirkman and Burkat Shudi, respectively. The two shops soon dominated the harpsichord trade: they built instruments larger and louder and of better over-all workmanship than almost any that were made on the Continent. These often reached a length of nine feet (Continental instruments rarely exceeded seven feet) and their range was five to five and a half octaves; those with double keyboards mostly had five, six, or seven stops, to be worked by a couple of pedals. On the other hand, they dispensed with the pretty lid paintings and lettered mottoes so much admired by French and Flemish customers.

9. THE HARPSICHORD BEGINS TO PALL

DURING the middle decades of the eighteenth century we notice a vague growing dissatisfaction with the harpsichord. A new religious movement, of which John Wesley was an important leader, sprang up. It had a certain resemblance to the Pietism that had previously diffused over Germany in that it too was a cult of direct religious enthusiasm as against the lifeless routines of the established church; furthermore, it too appealed to the lower classes. A wave of sentimentalism swept over England, reflected in the viscous novels of Richardson and later in the works of Sterne; but the English stopped short of the heights of exhibitionistic self-roiling upon which the Germans preened themselves. We notice, however, that English talk about music became increasingly concerned with "expression." In fact, Charles Avison, organist of St. Nicholas' Church in Newcastle, published in 1749 a whole *Essay on Musical Expression.* In it he speaks of harpsichord concertos, advising that the violin parts be few and purely accompanying, "by which Means they may assist greatly in striking out some Kind of Expression, wherein the Harpsichord is remarkably deficient." Eight years previously, an instrument maker curiously named Rutgerus Plenius (could his right name by any chance have been Roger Fuller?) announced a keyboard instrument of his invention which he called a "lyrichord"; it was a complex new adaptation of an old idea—of which the hurdy-gurdy is the prototype—that of keeping strings in vibration by the application of revolving wheels. In 1741 Plenius found it a good talking point to claim that "it admits of playing Forte and Piano; as also of swelling any Single Note (or many Notes ad libitum) in ye same key, by ye simple Pressure of ye Fingers." Varying the loudness of a tone by the simple stroke of a finger is, of course, the very basis of "expression" on the keyboard.

Musical glasses were the next move in the direction of a more expressive instrument. It had long been known that rubbing the edge of a glass with a moist finger will produce a sweet kind of sustained tone, also that the tone's pitch will differ according to the level of the water inside the glass. A number of glasses of differing pitch can provide a kind of instrument from which a clever player can extract good music. Several such pleasing performances were given in London taverns and theaters during the 1740's and 50's—until the great American Benjamin Franklin, with his keen practical sense, showed how the glass instrument could be immeasurably improved. Instead of differing levels of water in each glass, he explained in writing to the Abbé Beccaria in 1762, let us have a sort of sink with a constant level of water; variety of pitch can be obtained by using circular glass cups of graduated size, fitted one into the other without touching, all revolving in the water together. Fix the cups by a single iron bar through all their centers, and revolve the whole machine by a foot treadle. The player then need merely apply his fingers to the wet edges of the cups as they spin around. The Franklin instrument, then called the harmonica, had some following in England, especially when it was played by a Miss Marianne Davies. Brought to Germany, the glass harmonica's celestial tone quality—together with its capacity for shading—became much relished there for about thirty or forty years. It was improved by the addition of a keyboard and even succeeded in enlisting the creative attention of Mozart and Beethoven. But for the English it was not the answer.

Nor was there any permanence to a craze that broke out, toward the end of the 1750's, for the guitar. A queer, gloomy, insolent character, the Rev. Dr. John Brown, let loose a lurid blast against the sloth and effeminacy of the English—at just about the moment when the English were achieving their greatest military and political triumphs in Canada and India. It was called *An Estimate of the Manners and Principles of the Times;* the English loved it and bought up seven editions within a year. Dr. Brown added a second volume in 1758; in it he said:

> The Harpsichord, an instrument of power and compass, is now going out of use. The guitar, a trifling instrument in itself, and generally now taught in the most ignorant and trifling manner, is adopted in its place; while the theorbo and lute, the noblest because most expressive and pathetic of all accompaniments, are altogether laid aside. What is the reason of this? Because the guitar is a plaything for a child, the harpsichord and lute require application.

Dr. Burney later related the sequel to the guitar fad. His account can be found in the article "Guitar," which he wrote long afterward for Rees's *Cyclopaedia,* published early in the nineteenth century. He speaks of the guitar's "fits of favor" in England:

About fifty years ago its vogue was so great among all ranks of people, as nearly to break all the harpsichord and spinet makers, and indeed the harpsichord masters themselves. All the ladies disposed of their harpsichords at auction for one third of their price, or exchanged them for guitars; till old Kirkman, the harpsichord maker, after almost ruining himself with buying in his instruments, for better times, purchased likewise some cheap guitars and made a present of several to girls in milliners' shops, and to ballad singers, in the streets, whom he had taught to accompany themselves, with a few chords and triplets, which soon made the ladies ashamed of their frivolous and vulgar taste, and return to the harpsichord.

We need not believe this story literally and in every particular in order to appreciate its essential truth. Whatever the ladies' whims might have been, they could hardly hope to stay in the fashionable vanguard for long with an object that cost only two or three pounds.

10. THE PIANOFORTE ARRIVES AND STAYS: ITS EARLY PROMOTERS

THE LYRICHORD, the musical glasses, and the guitar earned but short rides on the wheel of time; the pianoforte was the object that fulfilled the needs of a longer day. It had expression; playing it required only a slight adaptation of an existing skill; and it was expensive enough to be socially desirable. Furthermore, for a couple of decades it kept a proper flavor of foreignness.

We first hear of it in England during the 1750's. Samuel Crisp, gentleman and author, is said to have claimed that he bought one in Rome about the year 1752; the instrument is supposed to have been built there by an English monk named Father Wood, as early as 1711! On Mr. Crisp's return to England, he sold the instrument —as a curiosity—to his friend Fulke Greville, at one time in the British Embassy in Bavaria, for the large sum of one hundred guineas. The object aroused considerable interest, and an unsuccessful attempt to imitate it was made by Plenius, the lyrichord man. Fulke Greville had been a patron of Charles Burney, and we have the whole tale purely on Burney's say-so—which, we will admit, is pretty reliable for anything he claims to have observed himself. No traces, however, of this fabulous first English piano have ever come to light; nothing else that Mr. Crisp said about it has ever been reported; no one has picked up the trail of an English Father Wood in Rome. It remains an interesting story.

Let us take a moment to consider Thomas Gray, gentle antiquarian scholar and Cambridge professor. He was a good amateur on the harpsichord and enjoyed singing arias by Pergolesi and Marcello to his own accompaniment on the little instrument in his rooms. This outrageous eccentricity, added to a number of his other effeminate mannerisms, so irked several chivalrous young gentlemen students as to induce them one night to set up a false alarm of fire and trick Gray, unclothed, into scrambling down a thirty-six-foot rope plump into a specially prepared tub of water. It must have been great sport to watch the illustrious poet of the famous *Elegy* shiver thus ignominiously in the February night. On the other hand, Gray's musical propensities were among the many things that drew to him the friendship of the Rev. Dr. William Mason, later canon of York Minster, who also was no mean musician.

Mason, recently ordained, was traveling in Germany. He wrote from Hanover on June 27, 1755: "Oh, Mr. Gray! I bought at Hamburg such a pianoforte and so cheap!" He does not explain the word, but seems to be sure that Gray knew what it was. He proceeds to describe his instrument as a combined pianoforte and harpsichord, united "by the cleverest mechanism imaginable . . ." Then, in a burst of enthusiasm, he adds: "Won't you buy my Kirkman?" It is likely that Dr. Mason brought the instrument back with him when he returned the following year.

Pianofortes, then, were known and spoken of in England during the middle fifties. The first direct evidence of their presence, however, is found in Mortimer's directory for 1763, listing musical instrument makers: here we come across a Frederic Neubaur who, after the familiar harpsichords, advertises the rarer "pianofortes, lyrichords, and claffichords."

It was a Saxon immigrant, a refugee from the Seven Years' War, who made the right move at the right time. His name was Johannes Zumpe, and there is some talk of his once having been a disciple of Gottfried Silbermann of Freiberg. Upon his arrival in London toward 1760, he is said to have worked in Shudi's shop; soon he set up one of his own.

He began to make small, compact square pianofortes with a

very simple action. A jack fixed rigidly into the key, and provided with a rounded terminal knob, was made, upon rising, to impinge on a so-called "underhammer"—which, in turn, tossed the true hammer up against the string. The hammers and underhammers were swung upon a rail of their own. There was no escapement: the highest reach of the raised jack left a sufficient space for the hammer to rebound fully.

Zumpe's neat little boxes had a moderate success at the very start. The hammer-made tone seemed dull compared to the brisk, pointed twang of a quilled instrument; yet the capacity for shading, for "expression," was one of its decisively desirable properties. Early amateurs found it a bit hard to handle, but soon it was tried out before a large audience. A playbill tells us that in an entr'acte of the perennial *Beggar's Opera* a Miss Brickler sang a song, "accompanied by Mr. Dibdin on a new instrument called the Piano Forte." This was on May 15, 1767, and the occasion is generally regarded as the instrument's public debut. Though widely known in Germany by that time, there is no record of its use in a concert there until some months after that date—by which time Thomas Gray was already playing one of Zumpe's products in his Cambridge rooms.

Presently the "hammer-harpsichord" received more influential support. The sainted Johann Sebastian Bach's youngest son, Johann Christian, was far from a chip off the old block: had his father lived to see him depart for Italy, turn Catholic, and later compose operas, he might, in fact, have thought him rather a black sheep. John Christian arrived in England late in 1762 and joined the large bevy of foreigners who provided the nobility and the gentry with facile, refined music. His first operas, Italian, were so successful that George III's German-born Queen Charlotte could in good conscience appoint him her official private teacher. He composed much keyboard music, "such as ladies can execute with little trouble," as Charles Burney reported. After two or three years "the nobility and the gentry," to whom all such solicitations were invariably formally addressed, were asked to attend a regular series of concerts to be given by Bach and a fellow German, Carl Friedrich Abel, an excellent viola-da-gamba player. The pair asked five guineas for a series of six events, an alluringly snobbish high price. Still another German, Johann Christian Fischer, an oboe player, arrived in London a few years later, hoping also to be hit by some of the loose gold that those strange English were throwing around so lightly. His compatriots Bach and Abel gave him their aid, lending the prestige of their participation to his first public appearance, at the Thatched House, St. James Street. On that occasion Bach played the first pianoforte solo ever heard in an English concert, on June 2, 1768. There were other signs of Bach's interest in the new instrument: his previous keyboard works were designated "for the harpsichord" or left unspecified; from then on, they were all "for the harpsichord or pianoforte."

The new instrument was now associated with the Queen's own music master, who at the same time was the director of London's most expensive nontheatrical musical events. That was enough to give it a fashionable potency: a hesitant social climber, or swimmer, could now be pretty sure that pianofortes were correct. Zumpe's price was likewise persuasive; Bach's checkbook seems to indicate that he paid him £50 for an instrument. The Zumpe creations were small and rectangular, not much more than four feet long, let us remember; purchasers would tend to compare them with the rectangular-shaped, cheaper spinets rather than with the great harpsichords. At the moment of Bach's pioneer performance, Shudi's standard price for a single harpsichord, without stops, was £35; for one with an octave stop, 40 guineas. At that rate, Zumpe's £50 pianofortes would have been thought of as smart, expensive little new-fashioned spinets, whose smartness justified their expense. The price may have been well adapted to the immediate fashion situation; however, a simple hammer-instrument, not much more elaborate than a clavichord, was easier to make than one with delicately tongued jacks and quills. Thus Zumpe's profit must have been large. In any event, his pianofortes became all the high-class rage and he could not supply the demand; a maker named Pohlmann, again a German, made a fine living out of the customers Zumpe had to pass by for lack of time. Half a dozen more Germans edged into the trade during the next decade or two.

The little Zumpes were rather crude; in the absence of a check piece, we can readily imagine that their hammers tended to rebound—that is, to block. Thomas Gray said something about the higher notes being "somewhat dry and sticky" on the one he was playing.

The harpsichord makers felt confidence on the whole, but they were determined to defend themselves against the competition of the new article. The pianoforte's capacity for shading was the real menace: so Shudi, after 1769, equipped his dearer instruments with a so-called "Venetian swell," a set of foot-operated shutters by which the sound could be confined or released at will, and gradually, whereas Kirkman, now competing with both Zumpe and Shudi, retaliated with a pedal-operated mechanism for raising and lowering the instrument's lid, for the same purpose. These improvements held good for a while, but they were fundamentally not congruous with the nature of the harpsichord and were a sign of decadence. Shudi was asking eighty guineas for his largest double-keyboard instruments with the "swell" contrivance.

The modish little pianoforte received further encouragement, once again through a German immigrant. Young Johann Samuel Schroeter (no kin of C. G. Schroeter the piano-action "inventor") had grown up in Leipzig, where pianofortes were no longer exactly new. Again Bach and Abel acted as godfathers—when Schroeter made his concert debut in London on May 2, 1772. His playing was neat and slick, well adapted to the new stroke-responsive instrument; he knew how to make it compensate for its relative dullness of quality. His performance charmed many ladies, and he became much in demand as a teacher in the higher circles of society.

Schroeter's behavior seems to have been as slick as his playing: an acquaintance described him as "fascinating, fawning, and suave." He was a lady-killer, but the last lady he killed proceeded to kill him—as a musician. She was of "good family" and her people were rich. She was determined to marry the unreluctant pianist, thus threatening unspeakable disgrace upon her parents. Schroeter finally magnanimously accepted a compromise: the marriage was arranged, and the lady's father—anxious to assure himself an ostensible gentleman for a son-in-law—settled an independent income on him for life, on condition that he cease thenceforth from engaging in any professional musical work. So we may say that Schroeter played so well that he was finally paid to stop; it is the sort of thing that sometimes happens to organ grinders.

Bach and Schroeter helped to propel the vogue of the pianoforte. A third artist, abler than either of them, now became its champion—this one a native of Italy. Peter Beckford, an intellectual, polyglot, Dorsetshire fox hunter, descendant of a fabulously rich family of Jamaica planters, was on a tour in Italy during the 1760's. While in Rome, he became much impressed with the prodigious musical talents of a fourteen-year-old boy: Muzio, the son of a poor silversmith named Clementi. Mr. Beckford induced the father to accept a sizable sum to let him take Muzio to England, there to educate him further and to launch him into the great world. "The celebrated Clementi, whom I bought from his father for seven years," was how Mr. Beckford later referred to the transaction, with a touch of Jamaica in his wording.

In 1766 Muzio was installed in Mr. Beckford's Dorsetshire estate, to remain for the term of the contract. As he was already an accomplished player and composer, it is hard to think who could have taught him anything in music. But in the English country house he had plenty of time to peruse the ample Beckford library as well as to develop his own style and technique. Mr. Beckford became a member of Parliament during the Clementi years; we could be easily tempted to imagine that during one of his London sojourns he ordered one of the new pianofortes to be sent up for the use of his protégé. For as soon as Clementi, at age of twenty-one, came out of his Dorset cocoon into the London of 1773, he immediately published a set of sonatas "for the harpsichord or pianoforte" that show a complete understanding of the new instrument's peculiar capabilities. In fact, later critics have considered these sonatas to be a foundation stone of the true pianoforte literature.

Clementi was devoted to the pianoforte, yet he understood that it was in the infancy of its development and still inept for many purposes. We find him still playing the harpsichord, especially in concerts, for quite a while during his earlier London residence.

In any event, his repute as a performer and composer grew steadily: the speed, firmness, and brilliance of his passages were much admired; his smooth, rapid double thirds and sixths were something new and startling in the realm of keyboard kinesthetics. After his return from an extensive tour of the Continent—that was when he had his encounter with Mozart—he was judged the foremost of all practitioners of the keyboard art. In fact, his reputation, like all reputations, became an object of superstition. He was, however, glad to monetize it at the rate of a guinea a lesson, at a time when many a well-established rival had to be content with half that honorarium. Soon he raised himself to the summits of esteem—for a music teacher—by demanding, and getting, the fee for twenty lessons in advance.

11. BETTER AND BIGGER

Meanhile the pianoforte itself was being significantly improved. Some of this mechanical development was accomplished by men of flawless British ancestry; indeed, they soon succeeded in making the pianoforte a naturalized British object. John Broadwood, twenty-nine-year-old cabinet maker from Scotland, entered the employ of harpsichord maker Shudi in 1761. He was a fine worker in wood and a thorough but less fast worker upon Shudi's daughter Barbara, for he did not marry her until eight years later. That achievement made it logical for him to become his aging father-in-law's partner until the old man died in 1773; for a time after that, the Shudi of Shudi & Broadwood was Burkat Jr.; later Broadwood became the sole proprietor. He sensed accurately the trend of the instrument trade—that the pianoforte was to be no fleeting fad; he concentrated his efforts upon it with outstanding success, and the name of Broadwood became the most long-lived in the entire history of the pianoforte trade throughout the world, persisting to this very day.

He proceeded to work on the Zumpe-type squares, finding a better way of stowing their internal workings so as to leave more space for resonant surface. He provided his pianofortes with improved brass-wire dampers, and in that connection devised a mechanism for raising and lowering them by means of a pedal. It was Broadwood, then, in 1783, who first launched the sustaining —miscalled "loud"—pedal, for six generations of artists to use and duffers to abuse. He also added a "soft" pedal to muffle the tone by applying a piece of cloth to a portion of the strings.

Broadwood's name is linked with an even more important improvement. His young apprentice and tuner, Robert Stodart, together with a friendly instrument maker named Backers, worked on the problem of an action suitable to a large wing-shaped pianoforte. They found a very satisfactory solution and invented a mechanism logically in line with the devices of Cristofori, Silbermann, and Zumpe, but simpler and more ingenious. The secondary lever was abolished; the jack was made to fit into a notch in the butt of the hammer in such a way as to escape after the stroke; a check piece caught the rebounding hammer to prevent it from oscillating; and a special screw regulated the precise point of escapement.

The pianoforte was the coming instrument, it was now understood; yet the harpsichord was still going strong. The idea of combining the two by a system of "stops" could not fail to seem practical for a while. It was on a centaur of this kind that young Stodart got a patent in 1777, and it was here that the principle and execution of the new action was first described. Incidentally, the patent application for this instrument included the first use of the word "grand" in connection with a pianoforte. The new action was a distinct success: it prevented blocking and made possible a powerful stroke upon the strings, if perhaps at the cost of a certain loss of speed. Soon it was referred to as the "English grand action"; Germans simply called it the "English action." Later it became amplified and refined, but its basic principle remained standard for a long time. Its devising was the work of several minds, but it was John Broadwood who first applied it systematically and on a large scale.

Science, or "natural philosophy," as it was called, became a growing preoccupation of later-eighteenth-century minds. Europeans, and especially the English, were deriving a profound satisfaction from their increasing grasp of the processes of nature, especially the simpler ones of physics: a palpable proof of that grasp was the constructing of successfully working machines. Englishmen enjoyed machines; they enjoyed making wood, metal, and water move in neat, ingenious, planned ways—just to show that it could be done and that they could do it. Mechanisms became self-justifying works of art; it is invidious to call them toys.

There was James Cox, clever jeweler and watchmaker. He had hoped to sell his precious contrivances to Indian rajas; but failing in this, he arranged his entire collection—valued at nearly £200,000—in a museum of its own at Vauxhall. There thousands of people paid 10s 6d—the price of a good seat at the opera—to gaze on a jeweled bull rolling his eyes, or a mechanical pineapple that opened to reveal a nest of mechanical singing birds.

About 1760 John Joseph Merlin, a sharp, imaginative mechanician, came to London from his native Belgium. For a time he was associated with Cox's Museum and later went into a variety of enterprises for himself. Principally, he made and sold startling little machines: self-propelling, pedaled wheel chairs; mechanical tea tables that poured a dozen cups at once; wood-turning engines; and similar devices. He advertised them by his spectacular behavior and his queer use of the English language. It became quite chic in London to visit his shop in Princes Street—his "cave," as they called it—and buy some of his tricky constructions. Merlin was on good terms with certain literary and artistic people, such as the Burneys, who enjoyed, admired, and liked him while finding him personally rather ridiculous. It was logical for Merlin to turn his attention to musical instruments. He made a number of harpsichords and even preceded Stodart in his effort to combine one with a pianoforte. We may regard him as a minor pianoforte pioneer. Mrs. Thrale, Dr. Johnson's friend and protectress, had little ear for music, but hoped always to be in fashion; by 1781 she possessed several pianofortes and was having Charles Burney, by then an Oxonian Doctor, give lessons to her daughter Queeney. She wrote to his daughter Fanny Burney from her Streatham home on January 4 that she had had Merlin come to tune the instruments: "He told Mrs. Davenant [a cousin, also of the "smart set"] and me that he had thoughts of inventing a particular mill to grind old ladies young, as he was so prodigiously fond of their company. I suppose he thought we should bring him *grist"*; she goes on kittenishly: "Was that the way to put people in tune? I asked him."

By the time the Mozarts, father and children, arrived in England in the spring of 1764, Londoners had already heard quite a few musical child "prodigies"—none, it is true, quite so gifted as Wolfgang. After an initial success at court and at a few concerts, public interest in the young artists began to flag. However, the eight-year-old boy was adding cubits to his stature all along and also benefiting from J. Christian Bach's guidance. A year later, on July 9, 1765, father Mozart wrote home to Salzburg: "In London Wolfie composed his first piece for four hands. Until then a four-hand sonata had never been done." It seemed true: at the time no previous record of a piece for two players at one keyboard was known. The idea prospered greatly afterward, as we know; not immediately, however. It was another twelve years before Dr. Burney composed a set of four-hand sonatas, but an interesting problem arose concerning these. Little Wolfgang and little Marianne Mozart had no trouble sitting together at a five-octave English harpsichord; in 1777, however, Burney had to have recourse to Merlin—always eager for a mechanical adventure—to make him an enormous six-octave pianoforte, roomy enough for two hoop skirts, so he claimed. But what about the numerous four-hand compositions that Mozart wrote in the 1780's to be played on five-octave Vienna pianofortes? Were they for men and children only, or had the skirts abated by then? Pictures from those times do not confirm the latter notion. We remain mystified.

Broadwood went on to the problem of tension: the long bass strings gave most of the trouble; furthermore, the relative weakness of the sound they emitted was also related to the matter of the striking place (that is, the precise point along the string at which the hammer hit). Broadwood got good, experimentally confirmed, scientific advice on this and other points and then decided to divide his sounding-board bridge—in other words, to make a separate bridge for the bass strings. That allowed him a greater tension, enabling him to use shorter but stouter strings; this, in turn, enabled him to establish the acoustically best striking place—at about 1/9 the string's vibrating length—in the most spatially economical manner. He made these improvements in 1788; soon afterward he decided to expand the instrument's range and built out the treble for half an octave higher. The extension was usually referred to as "additional keys." In 1794 he also expanded the bass, and a six-octave pianoforte was complete, practical, and on the market—safely beyond the stunt stage to which Merlin had carried it.

By then the term "grand pianoforte" had been in general use for a few years. It was an appropriate expression, for it suited the object intrinsically and gave a sense of elation to the new people who were likely to be its purchasers. In the 1790's Broadwood had a product that was unmatched anywhere in its day for strength, sonority, and range. Harpsichords had gone into a dignified decline throughout the eighties; the grand pianofortes of 1790 nudged them into their final, fatal, illness. After 1793 Shudi & Broadwood made them no more, though they kept a few on hand for special purposes—for instance, to send to St. James's Palace for the performance of the King's birthday ode. The King's band, we hear, was a conservative institution, likely to stick to old ways as long as possible. On June 4, 1795, Shudi & Broadwood sent a harpsichord as usual; but it was used only for rehearsal, and a grand pianoforte was delivered for the performance and was always used thereafter. That was the harpsichord's ignominious public farewell. So says William Dale, who has studied the Broadwood books. That same year the name of Shudi, with its harpsichord associations, was erased from the firm; it became John Broadwood & Son. Kirkman struggled on and gasped forth a final harpsichord as late as 1809.

Other firms came into the growing pianoforte business. One of Robert Stodart's relatives, for instance, had set up for himself successfully. A notable enterprise was that of Longman & Broderip; they began as music publishers and dealers and by 1786 were making harpsichords and pianofortes on a considerable scale. These instruments likewise boasted the improved English action: one of their advertisements of 1789 speaks of its simplicity, saying it "can never fail in the operation . . . Soon as the Hammer strikes the String it immediately falls back; whereas in other Instruments, the Hammer dances on the Jack, and occasions jarring noise in the Tone." They dealt in specialties such as "portable" grand pianos and little pianos that "could be conveyed, and even played on in a coach."

These last items found takers: we hear from the singer Michael

Kelly that the Duke of Queensberry had one such, which he carried with him on his travels. The afore-mentioned lively bluestocking Mrs. Hester Thrale scandalized her circle, after the death of her husband, by marrying the singer Gabriel Piozzi; a long sojourn abroad offered the best escape from the nasty treatment the couple were receiving from her "friends." They had a special traveling carriage built for their trip, designed so that a small portable pianoforte fitted under one of the seats. They spent the spring of 1785 in Italy, and the lady reported that Piozzi played pretty regularly in the coach. At Padua they left their vehicle and floated on a barge down the Brenta to Venice; Piozzi took the little pianoforte with him and played his music, "which never sounded so sweet, I think, as on that Water, which is used to the Freightage of Musick." So wrote the new Mrs. Piozzi to her daughter on April 22.

By 1789 people had been buying pianofortes for more than twenty years. However, family vicissitudes, climbing ambition, changed fortunes, fashionable restlessness, and improved construction—to say nothing of the scars of hard usage—had already induced many persons to get rid of their instruments; for we notice that Longman & Broderip, in the advertisement mentioned previously, offer "a large assortment of second-hand Piano Fortes, of all prices."

12. KEYBOARD MUSIC OF THE LATER EIGHTEENTH CENTURY

FEW VIVID DESCRIPTIONS of music in private circles have been left us from the days of Dr. Johnson and Boswell, of Goldsmith, Sheridan, and Horace Walpole. We know about pleasant musical parties at Dr. Burney's house, but those were largely informal rendezvous of professionals. The fact is that amateur music making in England was considered hardly worth talking about, even if it had quality. The many well-known lady pianists who brightened Vienna society at the time had no London equivalents; there probably were London ladies who played well, but almost nobody of social or literary importance cared much. The witty, cultivated women who formed the bluestocking circle, such as Mrs. Montagu and Mrs. Vesey, seem never to have valued music; perhaps they considered themselves too intellectual to put much mind on such a frivolous, sensual matter as they might have termed music: their interest was in thoughts rather than in sounds, they might have put it. Another of the bluestockings, Elizabeth Carter, a great Greek scholar, did indeed spend some time learning the spinet and the German flute, as her biographer states. Dr. Johnson admired her versatility and praised her because she "could make a pudding as well as translate Epictetus"; but we somehow feel that in the order of her achievements the spinet was generally ranked closer to the pudding than to the philosopher.

We must draw upon our fancy for any attractive tonal images with which to associate the feminine names that Clementi inscribed above some of his sonatas: Miss Meysey, Miss Blake, Mrs. Meyrick; later, Miss Gilding, Mrs. Benn, Miss Newburg, Miss Savery. They must have been rather proficient if they were able to execute his not very easy compositions to his satisfaction. But perhaps his dedications were merely hopeful. One Clementi pupil, Therese Jansen, the daughter of a successful German dancing master, was indeed known to have been an unusually fine pianist; so much so that Haydn, during his London stay, later composed several of his most difficult and interesting sonatas for her, including the great one in E-flat. Miss Jansen was not known ever to have played publicly; nevertheless, she was on the fringe of professionalism, by family and friendly associations.

We have mentioned the firm of Longman & Broderip, who also sold pianofortes. They were, all in all, the foremost English music publishers of their period; their extensive catalogue for the year 1789 gives some indication of what music people were actually making for their own pleasure. It lists a total of 1664 items, and we are struck by the fact that 565 of these are "for harpsichord or pianoforte" alone, including about 30 duets. A total of 333 items offered are for a single voice with the accompaniment of a "harpsichord," while the publications of dance music—minuets, cotillions, country dances—involving the services of a keyboard add up to 90. That makes a total of 988 numbers, almost exactly 60% of all the items for sale, that could appeal only to people who had pianofortes or harpsichords in the house. We are not even considering the violin and cello solos that almost certainly required accompanying keyboard parts.

Of the 535 keyboard solos, 300 come under the heading of "sonatas or lessons." Among them we find works by the most prominent composers of their time, some of the still known English-resident foreigners such as J. C. Bach, Clementi, and Schroeter as well as others now forgotten such as Tommaso Giordani and J. D. Benser. Other famous and well-known Germans and Italians of the time are there: Haydn, in particular, is well represented; Mozart, Pleyel, and Koželuch are somewhat less so; numerous works listed are by a group of Paris-immigrated Germans, highly thought of in their day: Edelmann, Schobert, and Hullmandel. We also note the better-remembered names of Boccherini and Cherubini, as well as the "ancient" ones of Corelli, Scarlatti, and Pergolesi. We wonder about some of the English composers, now barely traceable by their epitaphs in Grove's *Dictionary,* who are represented by one or two sonatas apiece: Butler, Barber, Burton, Bellamy, Clark, Gladwin, and Smethergel. They probably all gave lessons, fancied themselves in print, and were in a position to dispose of copies to their pupils.

The "sonatas or lessons," in sets, were mostly sold at 7s 6d or 10s 6d a volume; in the category of "single sonatas and lessons," we see them offered mostly at 1s or 2s apiece. In this group we come across a few titles that are not quite so lessonlike: *Benser's Storm* and *Burton's Tit for Tat.* This last was probably a rondo on the tune of a familiar song, for a few lines further down we see *Dibdin's Rondeau (Sweet Willy O).* Presently we have *Free-Mason's Anthem, Rondeau, Butler,* also *Scheniman's Entertainment* and *Lunardi's Flight, by Corri.* Lunardi was the man who had made the first successful balloon ascension over London in 1786.

Under the heading of "favorite airs with variations" we meet titles of an alluring *négligé* flavor: *Ally Croaker, Black Joke*—with variations by Clementi, no less—*Jack's Return from Dover, Sow's Tail to Geordie,* and *Twiggle and a Friz.* Many of these, we feel sure, were Vauxhall songs. The Scotch addiction was in full virulence, to judge by other titles: *Allan a Roon, Auld Robin Gray, Highland Laddie, Locheroch Side, Over the Muir among the Heather,* and *Sae Merry as We.* Together with others they all were methodically put through the variation grinder.

The list of overtures arranged for the keyboard reveals the names of some theatrical shows enjoyed at the time. There are a few of the older type of lofty-making Italian operas: Giardini's *Astarte,* Vento's *Artaserse,* and Tenducci's *Athridates;* most of the overtures, however, seem to be from English musical comedies: Charles Dibdin's *Blackmoor, The Institution of the Garter, The Padlock,* and *Poor Vulcan;* Samuel Arnold's *Inkle and Yarico;*

William Shield's *The Choleric Fathers,* and *The Farmer.* These as well as the "favorite airs with variations" were mostly available at 6d or 1s. More or less complete piano-vocal scores of these shows were sold at anywhere from 3s to 10s 6d. Many other amusing titles appear in this group: *The Brick Dust Man, Buxom Joan, Dead Alive, Flora, or Hob in the Well, Peep Behind the Curtain, Pigmy Revels, Theatrical Candidates,* and *The Enraged Musician.* "Single Italian songs" are also rather numerous, mostly from classic-posturing operas: *Iffigenia, Alessandro nel Indie, Virginia, Alceste,* and *Armida;* but we also notice a number of light Italian operas: *La Cosa Rara, Gli Schiavi per Amore,* and *Il Contadino in Corte.*

The 300 keyboard "sonatas or lessons" by estimable composers, that were arrayed in the Longman & Broderip catalogue, might seem to reveal a rather high state of musical cultivation among a goodly section of the British public. One hesitates to draw this conclusion, however. The catalogue gives no indication whatsoever of the relative sales of its various items. Apart from the keyboard music, the list also contains—as its lead offering—no less than 136 symphonies, overtures, and concertos for orchestra, with individual parts: surely there was no great market for these. Longman & Broderip had two large shops, at 26 Cheapside and at 13 Haymarket; they proudly called themselves "Music Sellers to His Royal Highness the Prince of Wales" and they even were allowed to let the prince's feathers shine at the head of their business announcement. Clearly, a show of high-class goods—right at the lead, close to the emblem—seemed necessary to their standing and prestige—even though they may actually have sold many, many more copies of *Platt's Twelve Dances for 1787* (at 1s 6d) than they did of *Pleyel's Six Sonatas, dedicated to the Queen—on imperial paper* (at 15s). Their catalogue looks much overweighted to one side: their lists list to starboard. They seem overinvested and overstocked in the more serious, complex forms of music: the fact is that within a few years of this catalogue's appearance, Longman & Broderip were already on their way to bankruptcy.

13. THE PIANOFORTE AND THE INDUSTRIAL REVOLUTION

MERLIN'S TRICKY self-flicking buggy whip and Cox's woggle-necked silver swan were short-lived little bubbles thrown up by the portentously fermenting mechanical arts. Somebody's chess-playing automaton was no better. A fishing apparatus holding five hundred hooks, and a razorless, soapless shaving compound, might have promised more of a future, but they failed to develop at the time. A mysterious horseless carriage was built and balloons ascended in the 1780's—but these were even more premature. Deep, canny money-seekers, more versed in human realities than were mere mechanicians, were able to harness inventive lust to the substantial demands of the time. The decades from 1760–90 saw the growing use of new and newer machines for the making of cloth, that basic human necessity. Using the carding machine, the "jenny," and the "mule," one man or woman could spin as much as ten, one hundred, or one thousand had done in the past. Machines for making pottery and lumber followed in this line; but behind all these menial demons loomed their terrible black chieftain, the steam engine. From the 1790's, nonhuman power was increasingly guided, as best it would allow, into the making of goods and the rendering of services.

The leaders of manufacturing enterprises ceased to worry much about the production of goods, which was attaining incredibly enormous quantities; their chief concern was to sell and deliver what they had made. Parliament somehow became persuaded to help the expansion of markets, and by the later eighteenth century the island of Great Britain became lacerated with turnpikes and canals.

Later the whole process was given a vague general name: it was called the Industrial Revolution. It was, indeed, the greatest change of habits and attitudes the human race had ever undergone. All manner of human values were shifted; for instance, workers were now organized into what was called "the division of labor." It was seen that a person could go faster if he confined his actions to a set of incessantly repeated small movements: if separate groups of workers each concentrated on mere fractions of a manufacturing process, the entire working force could ultimately turn out much more than if every worker made a complete assembled unit. The tendency was, thus, to have the workers' movements themselves approach the senseless simplicity of those of a machine; presently, factory workers were no longer spoken of as people, but were called "hands."

The Industrial Revolution—together with its companion the rationalization of agriculture—seems to have promoted the general health and vitality, for in some strange way it became associated with an unprecedented increase in the number of the country's native inhabitants. England's population since the days of Elizabeth had wavered lazily between five and six million; after the middle of the eighteenth century it rose dramatically, attaining an unheard-of nine million by 1800 and reaching a dizzy fourteen million by 1831. The country boasted a doubled, tripled population, working with ever improved machinery, exploiting natural resources more radically, produced an amount of wealth that left all previous standards far behind. Naturally, some persons got a larger share of it than others, but those whose fortunes rose were in the overwhelming majority. The owners of the new factories were the new wealth's most spectacular beneficiaries, but their riches necessarily contributed to those of many others: their noble landlords; their business lieutenants and skilled engineers; their allies, the bankers and shippers; their professional protectors, the lawyers and doctors; their purveyors, the butchers and bakers; and their personal enhancers, the dressmakers and music teachers.

Music, as an insignificant activity in Britain, might well have remained little influenced by the Industrial Revolution; instruments of the fiddle or pipe species, by their relative simplicity and rarity, might never have tempted anyone to build them by factory methods. But the pianoforte, with its manifold, intricate structure—and especially with its abundance of serially repeated parts—seemed particularly suited to the new mechanical processes. Any zealot for factory production would have cast a lecherous eye upon the pianoforte's tens of identical wooden keys, its dozens of identical jacks and hammer-shanks, its greater dozens of identical tuning pins and hitch pins, and its yards of identically drawn wire. The pianoforte was the factory's natural prey; purely on the basis of its structure, it was the instrument of the time.

The millions that accrued from the mining of coal, from the import of cotton and the export of cloth and other trade goods, swelled the flood of the older type of millions that had been pouring in for the previous hundred years from West Indian sugar and rum and East Indian tea. It all percolated through the English population, often in sizable individual gobs: the widespread thickening of the money-fluid fertilized a prodigious enlarging potential market for pianofortes. The achievement and maintenance of gentility had been the chief aspiration and pretense of most English men and women for many centuries; possession of money was one of its first prerequisites. Gentlefolk for a long time had been in the habit of owning keyboard instruments; in fact, such an instrument had become a regular trait in the physiognomy of a gentle home. Any of the numerous families recently come into money, and wishing to simulate the gentry, could begin easily by buying a pianoforte and having its daughters go through the gestures of learning to play it.

The figures for the Broadwood output illuminate the situation. Old Burkat Shudi and his son, in their 64 years of harpsichord making, turned out less than 1200 instruments, about 19 per year. That was almost exactly the average maintained by Johann Andreas Stein in his Augsburg workshop and by other shops of the period. It seems to have been a constant maximum quantity, the most that a master craftsman, employing five or six assistants, could conscientiously put out as having been made under his direct personal supervision and as being therefore worthy of bearing his name. Now, John Broadwood, in the 20 years that he directed the altered old Shudi firm (from 1782 to 1802), turned out 7000 square and 1000 grand pianos, an average of 400 a year! This average annual figure includes the earlier experimental years and, therefore, must have been even higher for the final years. Contrast this with the 50 instruments manufactured annually at this time by Frau Streicher, Stein's competent daughter, whose establishment was at the head of the Vienna trade. Shudi and Stein produced in equal quantities and retired at almost the same time; 10 years later successor Broadwood outproduced successor Streicher 9 times over. That illustrates vividly the superior potency of the English manufacturing methods, as well as the superior purchasing power of the English people. Moreover, although Vienna pianos had certain special advantages and although they adsorbed much musical glory from their surroundings, the English instruments were better made and had wider capabilities and potentialities. Apart from the action, Vienna makers systematically copied English developments: the pedal, the extended keyboard, and later the metal bracing. Beethoven's admiration for the Broadwood piano was by no means exceptional among German musicians. North German piano makers, in Berlin and Leipzig, increasingly tended to take English instruments for their models; the word "English" became a talking point, a virtue word, in the mouths of German piano salesmen.

We are, unfortunately, not able to give a detailed description of the Broadwood manufacturing process at the time when it first got into full swing: we cannot say what machines were used, what the division of labor was, or what materials or parts were bought ready-made or ready-treated. It was clearly a plant capable of unstrained enlargement: its 8000 pianos completed by 1802 grew to something like 45,000 by the year 1824, thus achieving an annual average of about 1680 during that twenty-two-year period —more than five instruments completed a day.

The use of steam power for manufacturing was a function of the quantity of production. Steam power was properly efficient only if it kept wheels, pistons, belts, and cams operating as nearly incessantly as possible; every interruption of motion meant a dissipation of the dynamic heat energy. Only when busy could steam power pay off the large expenses of its installation and upkeep. Thus, only firms that could expect to sell in large quantities would have an incentive for employing it. We cannot state exactly when steam power was first applied to the making of pianos, nor whether it was Broadwood's or one of their several effective competitors who first made this move. We are safe in guessing, from the Broadwood output figures, that it must have happened fairly early in the nineteenth century and also that only in England was such a thing economically feasible—even though the requisite technical skill had been available in other lands. Thus England, herself almost sterile in the finer flowers of music, became the undisputed, unapproached leader in the making of a certain kind of musical instrument.

The large-scale production that resulted from factory methods operated to reduce the unit cost, and the profitable sales price, of a pianoforte. This, in turn, broadened the market for the article still further by enabling more people to buy it. We remember that Zumpe's rather imperfect little squares cost £50 in 1768 and that Shudi's simplest, cheapest harpsichords came to £36. According to a Broadwood price list of 1815, the firm was ready to sell a neat square piano provided with the excellent improved action —an instrument incomparably better than anything Zumpe or his imitators had approached—for £18 3s. Even a square that was labeled "elegant" retailed at only £26; while a large, six-octave "ornamented" grand was offered at £46, still below the price of Zumpe's petty object.

This price reduction occurred during a period of rising standards of living; the vast increase in the number of the pianoforte's "marginal purchasers"—as the economists' peculiar lingo used to term it—caused the instrument to lose some of its voltage as a badge of putative gentility. It was still fashionable, in a sense, but no longer acutely so in the higher circles. During the 1770's the wife of a "nabob"—that is, a base-born profiteer returned from India—might have thought to lessen slightly the difference between herself and the Duchess of Richmond by also acquiring a fancy Shudi harpsichord or a smart little new-fangled Zumpe; by 1820 the pianoforte was tending to become a piece of furniture by owning which a lower-middle-class family could appear a shade less lower.

". . . the Daughters of Mechanics, even in humble stations, would fancy themselves extremely ill-treated, were they debarred the indulgence of a pianoforte," said an obscure gentleman named A. Burgh, in 1814, in the preface of a rather serious historical work on music. Mr. Burgh was exaggerating slightly.

Yet the upper classes did not discard the pianoforte because it had slid down the social ramp. For one thing, the more elaborate instruments were still expensive enough to confer a certain distinction. Mainly, however, the possession of a keyboard instrument had become such a habit among those who could afford it that it ceased to be an object of simple ostentation; the habit had become sanctified. The pianoforte became a symbol of respectability, an idol that aroused little fervor, yet which insisted on its tribute. People, musical or not, bought pianos just as people, religious or not, supported churches: they would have felt somehow indecent had they not.

14. THE PIANOFORTE IN LONDON CONCERTS

THE TAVERN concerts of the earlier eighteenth century, such as those at the Castle or the Swan, were relatively small occasions; they could almost have been chamber-music sessions held for their own pleasure by groups of professionals, to which interested outsiders were admitted for a small fee. The Academy of Antient Music at the Crown and Anchor was similar, but somewhat larger and more widely public. Beginning in 1731, the eminent violinist Geminiani ran a series of twenty weekly concerts, with a subscription fee of four guineas for the season, at Hickford's Great Dancing Room. These events seem to have had more of a fashionable atmosphere and they included the appearances of a number of popular singers.

With the elegant events offered by J. C. Bach and C. F. Abel in the 1760's, the fashionable potential of concerts became higher, as did the price of admission: at first, half a guinea each; then five guineas for the series of six. These concerts luxuriated in high-society patronage. The music given was doubtless of fine quality, yet we imagine the audience was largely interested in itself and came to see and be seen. The events must have been regarded as very honorific, for they had to be increased in number to satisfy some of the demand for tickets; but for the season of 1768, Mr. Bach blew up their snob value even further by announcing that the subscriptions would be limited to four hundred. That was the year, we remember, when he played the first public pianoforte solo in London history. In 1774 Bach deposited £3595 in the bank as the season's gross revenue from the undertaking—not a bad intake in any century.

In 1775 Bach and Abel moved their enterprise to a new hall, the Hanover Square Rooms. Evidently its size, location, and acoustical properties were especially favorable, so that it became London's most important concert room and remained so for a long time. Bach died in 1782, and a new organization was soon formed—calling itself first the "Hanover Square Great Concerts" and then the "Professional Concerts." It constituted, substantially, what we would now call a symphony orchestra series. Nobility shone in abundance on the subscription list. The price was relatively moderate—six guineas for twelve concerts—but the number of subscribers was limited to five hundred. Soon John Peter Salomon, the German violinist, set up a rival series that continued for some time with varying prosperity.

The steady invading stream of foreign musicians, which had continued since the early 1700's, swelled to a torrent in about 1790 and for a number of years thereafter. The swell was caused partly by the dangerous ructions that were bursting forth in France at the time. No large proportion of those musicians who fled to England were Frenchmen; they seem mostly to have been

Germans and Italians who had previously been attracted to Paris. The refugees added their music to that of the already resident foreigners and the transient virtuosos: the decade 1790–1800 witnessed an unprecedented number of public performances, many of them certainly excellent. The *Morning Chronicle,* in an issue of January 1791, affected to be alarmed at the consequences of this musical flood, saying that it would be difficult to stop up one's ears if one did not also have to protect one's pockets at the same time.

The harpsichord had at first played a comparatively minor role in concert performances, its function being largely accompanying. During the 1760's, however, there developed a greater taste for it as a solo instrument. By the time the pianoforte was dominantly established during the 1780's, we hear of more and more concertos for it being publicly played; while during the 1790's, pianoforte solos were among the favorite features of concerts.

We will recall Johann Nepomuk Hummel, who had been Mozart's pupil and apprentice. He was a boy of twelve when his prodding father—that customary, familiar spirit of all musical children—brought him to England. During 1791 the boy worked up support by playing in private homes; on May 5, 1792, "Master Hummel from Vienna" presented a concerto by his revered master Mozart at the Hanover Square Rooms in a concert directed by J. P. Salomon. Three or four years earlier there had been produced a comic opera *The Farmer,* with words by O'Keefe and music by William Shield, a well-liked confectioner of popular tunes. Its crashing hit-number was a song called "The Ploughboy," whose verses told of a pretty flaxen-haired rustic who was made into a good-looking footman, then a butler, and presently became a steward—in which post he could amass a lot of graft from the handling of his master's accounts. He then took on airs, rode in a carriage, ran for Parliament, was elected, sold his votes, and finally became a peer.

> In court or city honor
> So great a man I'll be,
> You'll forget the little ploughboy
> That whistled o'er the lea.

The zooming ploughboy was probably not entirely mythical; he was evidently a collateral ancestor of the fellow who later "polished up that handle so care-ful-lee that now he is the ruler of the Queen's Na-vee." Londoners took an unquenchable delight in him for some time, with the aid of Shield's innocuous melody. So we are not astonished to learn that Master Hummel diligently displayed his own pianoforte variations on "The Ploughboy" by way of encouraging the attendance of paying guests at his concert.

Jan Ladislas Dussek was one of the Paris refugees. A native of Bohemia, he had been for a short time a disciple of Philipp Emanuel Bach and had become a player of distinction and a composer of talent. They called him "le beau Dussek" after his first Paris appearance—he seems to have been quite good-looking until he got fat—and his learned countryman Václav Tomašek later credited him with being the first pianist to play with his right side to the audience, so that his hearers could also get the benefit of his attractive profile. Right after the first installment of the French hell broke loose, he hied himself to London; by early March 1790 he was already playing a concerto of his own, again under the auspices of Salomon.

Mrs. Papendieck, the musical wife of one of the Queen's pages, was at the concert and recalled some of it later:

> A pianoforte of Broadwood's was then brought in with as much ease as a chair, and immediately after Dussek followed . . . The applause was loud as a welcome; Dussek, now seated, tried his instrument in prelude, which caused a second burst of applause. This so surprised the stranger, that his friends were obliged to desire him to rise and bow, which he did somewhat reluctantly.

Rather naïve behavior on the part of the English gentry; that sort of unseasonable applause is what we might occasionally expect from high-school adolescents in the modern United States. The lady continues:

> He then, after reseating himself, spread a silk handkerchief over his knees, rubbed his hands in his coat pockets, which were filled with bran, and then began his concerto.

The bran, presumably, was to dry off the sweat from his hands. Our informant describes the concerto and the cadenza and then proceeds:

> . . . Dussek finished his cadence with a long shake and a turn that led in the "Tutti" to finish the movement, and he was rapturously applauded.
>
> His music was full of melody, was elegantly pathetic, and even

sublime. He was a handsome man, good dispositioned, mild and pleasing in his demeanor, courteous and agreeable.

Dussek was much enjoyed by London concertgoers during the next ten years; his *Military* Concerto was especially praised: the title was timely under the circumstances of the day. A successful ploughboy had given rise to a successful song; a successful pianist could not fail to be drawn into that magnetic field: soon Dussek, too, uttered a rondo upon the familiar ditty.

Salomon's chief claim to glory was that he succeeded in bringing Haydn to London, to conduct the orchestra of which he was himself the chief. The great composer's London debut took place on February 25, 1791; Haydn directed the orchestra from the pianoforte, a vestige of an older practice in which the harpsichord was supposed to hold all other instrumental harmony together. Haydn offered one of his newly composed symphonies; the Hanover Square Rooms are said to have held about six hundred, but the hall was not filled, according to our lady reporter.

Haydn was relatively undistinguished as a keyboard player; nevertheless, his pianoforte lessons presently came into some demand, against all his own disclaimers. He was reputed the greatest of all living masters of music: the fact that he was a glamorous foreigner, a high-ranking Esterházy house-officer, and that members of the British royal family were now receiving him—all this seemed to demonstrate his musical eminence. People believe profoundly in the magical contagiousness of qualities, more sincerely than they believe in Almighty God; thus, numbers of ladies were convinced that Haydn could infect them with his excellence through the sorcery of his presence. There was a story that "one of the most exalted personages" requested him to give her pianoforte lessons, only to take up the time in conversation or in letting the artist wait in an anteroom; a magnificent honorarium and a handsome present were vouchsafed him for his expenditure of time. The tale comes at second or third hand and may not be exactly true; however, Haydn did jot down in his diary some of his own impressions of music lessons in England:

> . . . if a singing, pianoforte, or dancing master charges half a guinea a lesson, he demands six guineas entrance fee, payable at the first lesson, because during the course of the winter many Scotch and Irish* people engage the best masters for their children as a

*Haydn unconsciously made an amusing pun in writing of the Irish: he calls them "*Irrländer,*" misspelled with a double r. The word "*irre*" means "erring"; it also means "crazy." Thus Haydn called the Irish "Crazy-landers."

matter of pride, but end up by being unable to pay them. The entrance fee is waived when the master charges a guinea; the guinea, however, must be paid at each lesson.

That the Scottish or Irish parents were unable to pay seems doubtful; more likely, they tended to be careless about settling up before leaving. The sentence seems to indicate that they, as well as the English country gentry, were in the habit of having their children take lessons during the months of their annual stay in London. Haydn himself "made big eyes," as he says, at the guinea he received for each of his own lessons. It made him hark back to his young days in Vienna, around 1750, when his instruction was requited at the rate of two florins a month; or a little later, when his growing reputation justified a monthly fee of five florins. Five florins was then $2.10 in our money; a guinea, $5.10.

The Broadwood firm, from the early days of its big business career, understood very well that its pianos would be known by the company they kept: it tried hard to have every successful and fashionable musician in London use its instruments. We are not astonished to learn that the firm furnished them to Master Hummel and to the handsome Dussek, as well as to the prestigious Haydn. It was in a Dussek concert in 1794 that the six-octave grand was first publicly launched.

Other pianoforte soloists were applauded in concerts during the 1790's. Clementi no longer played much in public by that time, for the most part confining himself to presiding at the keyboard during performances of his symphonies. However, his star pupil—John Baptist Cramer—was becoming a plausible heir to his solid kind of reputation. Cramer was almost a native of England, having been brought there at the age of two by his German violinist father. On March 10, 1784, a budding thirteen, he and his master Clementi had played a *Duetto for two Pianofortes* at one of the "Hanover Square Great Concerts"; their performance took place in the second "act" of the concert, as the part after the intermission used to be called. This was the first public duo-pianoforte performance on record. Cramer's playing, as well as his compositions, had refinement and learning; moreover, he was a devotee of the music of Sebastian Bach, of whom there were few in his time. He traveled abroad, where his work was praised; during his Vienna visit he even made a favorable impression on Beethoven, who was ordinarily rather cranky about other people's music. Cramer's Continental reputation no doubt hoisted him into higher esteem at home.

Another Clementi pupil, first brought to the fore in 1793, was destined to achieve a measure of illustriousness: he was John Field, then a slender, dreamy Irish boy. His delicate tone-blossoms eventually throve better in Russia than they ever could have in England. Toward the end of the decade, the mercurial, impudent Daniel Steibelt began his sojourn in London; not the Revolution, but certain personal affairs were said to have made Paris a little hot for him. He tickled many Londoners cheaply with his "Storm" Rondo; but he never achieved Clementi's soaring guinea a lesson, having to content himself with a pedestrian 10s 6d.

The flurry of concerts had died down somewhat by the very end of the century, yet enough interest remained in 1805 for Josef Wölfl, Beethoven's onetime rival, to come over and to continue making a modest success as a player and teacher for the remainder of his short life.

Clementi, Hummel, Dussek, Cramer, Field, Steibelt, and Wölfl, were the world's leading pianists of their time; their compositions, while falling short of genius, yet for the most part reflected the best average musical thought of their day. Their presence in London through and beyond the last years of the eighteenth century made that city the world's shining citadel of publicly performing pianism. Their concerts were events of interest in certain small sections of polite society, and the attention directed to pianists supported the attention paid to pianofortes. English people were piano-conscious as never before, and it all boosted the business of Broadwood's and of their rising competitors. Not that we need suppose a marked spread of improvement in English musical taste because of this situation. We rather suspect that the presence of an unusual number of cultivated foreigners may have done much to make London concerts of this period a success. The London music world of the 1790's seems to have comprised a disproportionate number of refugees, as did the music world of Paris in 1830's and 40's, or that of New York a hundred years later.

In any event, not all London concerts were of high artistic merit. Often they were mere stunts in the guise of music. For instance, we have a report that in the year 1789 an Italian came to London and gave a concert with eleven cats. The animals were well trained: each one had its own particular timbre and range; each one made correct entrances upon a given signal and also kept pretty good time. So it was said. Or again, some years before that, the current mechano-mania was fed by a performance on the harpsichord by what looked like a young lady. Actually, the performer was a doll with an incredibly complicated jungle of clockwork for entrails. The machinery moved "her" fingers so as to strike the right keys for a number of compositions; it also cunningly simulated other accompanying bodily movements such as breathing, jerking of the head, and the normal sway of the torso. P. J. Droz and his son, famous Swiss mechanicians, were the builders of this work of artifice.

London had a good climate for child "prodigies." After 1750 at least one fresh, unhappy little brat was extruded into a concert every couple of years or so. Esther Burney, Charles's daughter, whose famous sister Fanny took after her father more in the literary than in the musical way, formed one of a whole cluster of such children who performed at a concert at the Little Theatre in the Haymarket on April 23, 1760. Little Esther, then about ten, played a "lesson" on the harpsichord; and the program also offered two violinists, female and male (ages nine and thirteen, respectively), as well as an eleven-year-old cellist—playing solos, duets, and quartets.

That was four years before the Mozarts arrived. On June 29, 1764, the eight-year-old Wolfgang played at Ranelagh, of all places. This was the swankiest of the London pleasure gardens, its chief area of activity being its enormous Rotunda, a circular building five hundred feet in circumference. Little Wolfgang projected the thin tinkle of his harpsichord from a platform not exactly in the center of that great vault; some of his hearers must have been eighty feet away from him. He also played the organ on that occasion, we are relieved to know. He and his sister were shown off successfully a few times to "the nobility and the gentry" at fashionable halls, at 10s 6d a ticket, but curiosity was soon appeased. The following year their managerial father was content to let them play for rank outsiders at the Swan and Hoop Tavern, Cornhill, with the admission marked down to a measly 2s 6d. He even made them do that stale "trick" of playing with the keys covered with a handkerchief.

Francis Kotzwara was a native of Bohemia. After some vicissitudes he arrived in the British Isles around 1788. A middling fiddler, he landed a job in the viola section of the opera at the King's Theater. Some childhood memories or traditions must have hovered in his head when he set down the piece that he called *The Battle of Prague*. There had indeed been such a battle, a very bloody one, which had taken place during the Seven Years' War between Austria and Prussia, some thirty years before Kotzwara began his London residence. The piece was for pianoforte with the dispensable accompaniment of a few other instruments; it had all the proper battle appurtenances: marches, bugle calls, "the word of command," the hail of bullets, cannon shots, an "attack with swords," cries of the wounded, and so forth, all captioned in the text and musically illustrated in a highly flimsy, if noisy, manner. It is noteworthy that the composition came out in 1790, some years before general warfare in Europe might have rendered this sort of thing especially timely.

The Battle of Prague became a phenomenal success and spread like a petty plague that seemed unabatable through the decades. We will not hesitate to state that among the English and their culural dependents, it remained for more than half a century the best known, most played long piece of pianoforte music in existence. It appeared in countless editions on both sides of the Atlantic; there are persistent references to it in nineteenth-century literature, from the novels of Thackeray and Mark Twain down to cartoons in *Punch* and nameless books of etiquette. At any moment, during fifty years, the loud, silly clatter-clutter might have resounded simultaneously in Llandudno and Londonderry, in Philadelphia and Annapolis, in Malta, Madras, and Melbourne—wherever a form of English was the speech of the realm and the London piano factories could ship their products.

The Battle of Prague was put forth with some éclat in London not long after its original publication. A Miss Hoffmann, a pianist, placed it on the program of a concert given for her own benefit at the Assembly Rooms, Turnham Green, in June 1792, while the musical world was still a-chatter with the fine, hearty, witty new symphonies that Haydn had just produced. Miss Hoffmann, age six, had already enjoyed the honor of having her playing graciously received by Their Royal Highnesses in Windsor Castle; thus, her concert's success seemed preassured. She played a concerto on the pianoforte and a sonata on the harp; when it came to *The Battle,* she was accompanied on the kettledrums by her brother, an artist who had attained the discreet age of three and a half.

But Kotzwara was not permitted to enjoy even this early harvest of glory. He had already achieved another perpetration—not a musical deed, but one that later critics might have thought a subtly appropriate companion piece to *The Battle of Prague:* on September 2, 1791, he had gone to Vine Street, St. Martin's, and there hanged himself in a whore house.

15. THE PIANO AS FURNITURE

As we have seen, the English during the eighteenth century had little taste for the delicate ornamentation and the exquisite painting with which Flemish and French makers liked to decorate their harpsichords. About 1760 Kirkman made a few that had profuse marquetry inside the case and inlay inside the lid, but these were exceptional. In general, he and Shudi were paid to turn out plain, smooth-finished walnut or mahogany cases with brass hinges. The great curve of the case, formed by the progressive shortening of the strings on the right side of the instrument, was the harpsichord's chief beauty spot; when the grand piano came in, the change in stringing may have tended to impair somewhat the grace of this line. Despite the early experiments of Hayward, no firm under-keyboard structure for the support of the pedals had yet been perfected during the eighteenth century. The pedals were mostly fastened sideways to the instrument's fore-legs, forming one of the English harpsichord's less eye-appealing features.

When the little Zumpes were first brought out, they seemed very pretty in their rectangular trimness; that was surely one reason for their success. Their day of vogue coincided with the fad for ingeniously joined dual-purpose objects, sometimes known as "harlequin" furniture: a stepladder concealed in a library table, a dressing table with an infolded washstand, a looking glass enclosing a dressing case. Presently Zumpe disciples were beguiled into seducing the neat, new little pianofortes into likewise leading a variety of ladylike double lives—as sewing tables, tea tables, or writing tables. An illustration of one of a pair of "harlequin" side-table pianofortes of about 1785 can be seen in Philip James's book *Early Keyboard Instruments;* it was photographed from a specimen in the Victoria and Albert Museum in London. The object is elliptical in shape, and its surface is watched over by an upright paneled, fanlike mirror.

The later eighteenth century saw the flourishing of a great development in the art of furniture making. It was the time of Thomas Chippendale, of George Hepplewhite, of the Adam brothers, and later of Thomas Sheraton. Their products indeed had a high elegance within the taste ideals of their time, though perhaps they were not worthy of all the idolatrous esteem in which latter-day Americans of the more pretentious sort have held them. At any rate, these craftsmen took rather little interest in keyboard instruments. In fact, the few professional encounters they are known to have had with them reveal a decided lack of sympathy, or even of plain common sense, on their part. Robert Adam, for example, drew designs for a harpsichord as well as a pianoforte ordered for Catherine, Empress of Russia. The former was intended to be a square-shaped instrument; its surface was to be tattooed densely enough with festoons, and its case to be held aloft obsequiously by enough curlicued, satyr-shaped atlantes to allay the most barbaric appetite for magnificence. Unfortunately, the designer placed the keyboard plumb in the middle, practically an impossible spot, structurally, in a square instrument. He probably did not know any better, and did not trouble to find out. Later somebody wrote on his drawing: "This design was much altered when it was executed."

Sheraton did much better when he designed a remarkable pianoforte especially ordered by Don Manuel de Godoy, a Spanish officer high in the favor of his Queen Maria Louisa. Through her influence he could swing himself up to the position of his country's foreign minister. In that capacity he had recently concluded the Treaty of Basel with the new French Republic, a deed that earned him a special title: The Prince of the Peace. On February 8, 1796, the Prince placed an order with Broadwood's for a superb six-octave grand pianoforte, intended as a present to his liege-lady-friend; it was for this commission that Sheraton was called in. The order took four months to execute; the bill for it reveals that the instrument's case was made of Sheraton's favorite satinwood decorated with "different woods," as well as with "water gilt mouldings and Wedgewood's and Tassie's medallions." The Prince's own portrait was contained in an oval in front. It was, indeed, a gallant gift to set before a queen: the price of the instrument alone was £223 13s; the portrait and shipping charges cost the Prince an additional £34.

According to Sheraton's principles as enunciated in his writings, he considered beauty of form to reside in a perfection of functionality—quite a modern idea. However, he balked at pianoforte pedals. He was not enough of an industrial designer to think up a really efficient understructure; he could only imagine the pedals fastened to the legs in the hitherto customary way. Rather than contribute to this lumpish intrusion upon his elegant lines, he left them out altogether in his drawing. Someone, however, had pedals built onto this piano later, either the Spanish Queen or some other brash creature who insisted on playing on the instrument as well as gazing upon it.

Another interesting phenomenon was a pianoforte whose works were made in 1775 by Frederick Beck, one of the coterie of early German immigrant makers of whom Zumpe was the chief. According to Mr. James's description, the object stood three feet four inches high, five feet four inches wide, and two feet eight and a half inches deep. Almost the entire extent of its surface was "extensively inlaid with colored woods and a herring-bone pattern of harewood and wood lines dyed green; in the middle of the front panel there is a medallion framed in a ribbon-banded metal border representing the muse Thalia." Mr. James adds that it "seems to have been executed by a cabinet maker of great skill and taste."

Taste of a sort, perhaps; the fact is, however, that in his zeal for putting together his wooden bouquet the craftsman built the front of the pianoforte straight down to the floor from the fore edge of the keyboard, leaving no recess for a player's legs and thus rendering the instrument playable only with considerable inconvenience, inasmuch as the seventeenth-century practice of playing while in a standing position had long been obsolete. We do not know for whom this piece was confected; we suggest it was for a "nabob." The customer apparently considered the xyloplastic gorgeousness as a work of art for art's sake and permitted something of a pianoforte to be thrown in, condescendingly, almost as if to degrade it.

The frame of mind that prompted this brand of purse-pride became rather conventional during the later nineteenth century. We recall sets of brilliant chased-brass fire irons, much too fragile and precious ever to be soiled by contact with fuel, reposing in burnished dignity before fires that were regularly stirred with simple black iron pokers standing near by. The ideal was a complete room lavishly stocked with imposing satin-covered upholstery, ormolu mantelware, brocaded hangings, and crystal chandeliers—which no human being was ever expected to live in, or even enter. Later piano factories had their closely calculated routines and were reluctant to go to the trouble of constructing unplayable instruments; however, an ostentation chamber such as the above-described was more than likely to contain a purely symbolic grand pianoforte, beautiful but dumb.

Robert Stodart—the pioneer who had assisted John Broadwood

in the development of the "English action" and the perfection of the grand pianoforte—had a younger relative, William, who set up in the piano-making business for himself during the nineties and became one of Broadwood's substantial competitors. Pianofortes were spreading to all manner of town houses, and the space problem began to obtrude itself in London as it had in Vienna: many people who wanted the latest thing in a full-sized grand also had a lot of other furniture they wanted to put into the same room. William Stodart's patent for an "upright grand," taken out in 1795, proved to meet the requirements of the time. It was a regular grand piano set up vertically on a stand, but inserted into a rectangular cupboard. It had the regular up-striking grand action, suitably adapted to its less advantageous striking angle, from behind. The instrument's great curve was, naturally, preserved; but it was now inside the straight box. Between the true frame and the cupboard's right wall an empty space was thus created, which the patentee planned to have divided by two horizontal shelves so as to form a bookcase. The entire structure could be opened or closed from the front by a couple of large doors. These, in turn, gave decorators another chance for playing their expensive games: an upright grand made for the Prince of Wales—later George IV—had doors made of looking glass. Stodart's—and other makers'—upright grands were tall, on the order of eight feet eight inches; the one made for the Prince reached the imposing eminence of nine feet one inch. At that rate, the highest shelf of the bookcase might have been on a level of seven feet, pretty far up for a decorous little lady to reach. We have heard no reports of furniture dealers selling handsome little inlaid sandalwood stepping stools, with fluted Corinthian columns, at ten guineas, whose sole purpose was to facilitate the fetching of volumes from the top shelves of upright grands; yet that might have been the sort of idea by which imaginative tradesmen hoped to separate money from fashionable people.

English customers, we are glad to say, were almost never bullied into demanding the supernumerary pedals: the drums, bells, and cymbals that clanked on Continental pianos of the early nineteenth century. Still, sometimes a lady-of-the-house may have felt impelled to use the shelves of an upright grand for the display of brass or glass bric-a-brac, which in its way may have vibrated an appropriate accompanying din to *The Battle of Prague.* It seems strange to think that the giraffe-style instrument had very little vogue in England during the time of its Continental heyday.

Upright grands remained no monopoly of Stodart's, but were

taken up by Broadwood's and other enterprising manufacturers; according to price lists of the time, they were generally sold for about ten to fifteen per cent more than the horizontal grands. They remained in good demand until about 1830; but for all their combined pomposity and space-economy, they had certain detriments. Notably, they were anxiously top-heavy. A slight unevenness in the floor, a tipsy moving man, a false tug on a rug, and—crash! That, at any rate, was the perpetual apprehension. Broadwood's list for 1840 no longer includes them.

Nevertheless, the "upright" idea seemed fundamentally sound, the question being how to manipulate it to the best advantage. As early as 1798 William Southwell of Dublin had the scheme of setting a square piano upright on a stand. It was not successful, but he later made a more positive contribution to the piano business by inventing a word to describe a different, better kind of upright instrument: the word "cabinet." Many of the improved English designs for upright, and other, pianofortes seem to go back to an interesting instrument made in 1800 by one John Isaac Hawkins, a young man of English parentage living in Philadelphia. Like the *"Ditanaklassis"* invented almost concurrently by Matthias Müller of Vienna, it was a piano stood up on its tail, the long, bass side to the left, the whole enclosed, of course, in a rectangular case. The action was down-striking, thus avoiding the disadvantageous gap between the wrest plank and the soundboard. Its height was strikingly small: four feet seven inches; furthermore, the soundboard was suspended in a metal frame and was braced by metal rods. The wrest-pin block was also covered with metal, and the bass strings seem to have been made of coiled wire. These were very suggestive ideas that were all to be developed further during the next thirty or forty years.

Meanwhile, for a time, a desirable instrument was the so-called "cabinet"—that is to say, a tail-based upright with down-striking hammers, with bass strings parallel to the left wall of the case, reaching down to the ground; the whole box stood about six feet to six feet two inches tall. Its front was usually covered with silk —pleated or waved in loose, small folds. Often the silk was "radiated," that is, shirred together in the middle and fastened with a rosette. The word "cabinet" carries a suggestion of compactness, which was indeed the main purpose of the design; however customers who had retreated from nine-foot upright grands were still glad to impress their guests with an appearance of stateliness. Thus we find the upper sides of the "cabinets" accented with a pair of "carved pillars"—as the early-nineteenth-century sales catalogues called them—or, more pretentiously, "pillars superior." Sometimes pianos were offered decorated with "buhl work." Apparently this was a color effect intended superficially to resemble the beautiful brass and tortoise-shell inlay work once made by André Charles Boulle, Louis XIV's cabinetmaker.

Later, in the 1820's, certain improvements, such as the metal plate, were applied to the "cabinet" pianofortes. Broadwood's called these new-style instruments "Patent Grand Cabinet," thus using that grand word "grand" to promote the rank of a piano that was not really a grand—for an advance in price, naturally.

The piano makers were eager to squeeze their products into more and tighter homes; more and poorer families wanted to contemplate themselves as owners of the most respectable of all instruments: a further reduction in size, or at least in height, and a corresponding reduction in price, was indicated. In the "cabinets" the great curve creates the empty space between itself and the wall on the lower right side of the case, underneath the treble portion of the keyboard. Already Thomas Loud, as early as 1802, had thought of stretching the strings, especially the bass strings, obliquely, from the upper left to the lower right-hand corner—thus either giving greater and more sonorous string length for the same height of case or permitting a lower height of case for the same length of string. Robert Wornum is usually credited with the first successfully accomplished stowing job according to this principle, namely with oblique strings, in a reduced case less than four feet tall. He called it a "cottage piano," and its type became enormously successful. Those terms "grand," "cabinet," and "cottage" are nicknames of pleasant and potent suggestion; they contrast with the clumsy, high-flown names thought up by German makers and show up the superior commercial sense of the English.

16. THE MUSIC BUSINESS GROWS WIDE AND SHALLOW; THE PIANO THRIVES ON IT

THE TOTAL AMOUNT of music bought to be played on pianofortes increased enormously after 1790; as the quantity grew greater, the average quality grew poorer. There is nothing mysterious in this process: the finest music, for the most part, requires skill to perform and cultivation to enjoy; but very few people are skilled or cultivated. No one can reproach a strictly rational publisher or merchant for wishing to sell as many copies of the same article to as many people as he can, for that is the way he can garner the greatest return on his investment and that is the way he must take to pay himself back for the articles he has put out and failed to sell. Now, if he has to have a great many customers in order to stay in business, he must draw them from the vast majority of the unskilled and uncultivated; he must tend to favor them and pass the high-brows by. It is as simple as that.

In June 1805 Josef Wölfl, not long after his arrival in London, wrote to the publisher Härtel in Leipzig:

> Since I have been here, my works have had astonishing sales and I already get sixty guineas for three sonatas; but along with all this I must write in a very easy, and sometimes a very vulgar style. So much for your information, in case it should occur to one of your critics to make fun of me on account of any of my things that have appeared here. You won't believe how backward music still is here, and how one has to hold oneself back in order to bring forth such shallow compositions, which do a terrific business here.

A few rudimentary figures will give an idea of the tremendous growth of the music business in England during the years that covered the Industrial Revolution. There were no more than 12 music shops in London in 1750, we are told by Thomas Busby, Mus. Doc., in his *Concert Room Anecdotes;* a directory of 1794 lists about 30; by 1824 there were 150. The numbers of titles they offered are equally revealing: among the leading publishers, Bremner's catalogue in 1766 contained about 120 items, Welcker's in 1773 about 500, and Longman & Broderip had 1664 items for sale in 1789. By 1824 Boosey's catalogue of 280 pages listed 10,000 foreign publications alone. In 1838 D'Almaine & Co. were said to have accumulated the enormous figure of 200,000 engraved plates!

A modest phase of the Industrial Revolution concerned music printing: it was in 1768 that a rather obscure Henry Fougt, probably a Scandinavian living in London, was granted an English patent for printing music from type. As we know, Immanuel Breitkopf of Leipzig had already perfected this process about fifteen years earlier; however, no one seems to have contested Fougt's claim. He soon was able to offer very well-printed single-sheet ballads—that is, two pages of music—for a penny a page or eighteen for a shilling, at a time when all other music publishers were asking threepence a page for their engraved sheets. The force of the new, cheap process was felt toward the end of the century; it must then have been a factor by which the vast expansion of the music market was compounded still further.

In view of the progressively widening, shallowing musical flood, we could expect that sonatas and "lessons" drooped in the music shops sales accounts. We notice publishers trying to revive them with sugar injections: musicians were urged to compose sonatas with well-known Scotch songs as themes. Beethoven was to receive such a request; Wölfl evidently complied with one, for he did compose three of such Scotch-shot sonatas as his Opus 38. Were those the ones for which he said he had received sixty guineas? Rondos, likewise, were less likely to induce shelf-constipation if they were based on popular tunes: in addition to "The Ploughboy," Dussek also turned them out on "Lord Howe's Hornpipe," "To To Carabo," and others. He also labeled one of his sonatas *The Sufferings of the Queen of France;* that was good merchandizing in 1793. Variations on familiar melodies, of course, required no stimulants; their native essence made them swell upward from their already high level of prosperity.

Battle pieces grew rank by the end of the 1790's and stayed in vogue for about thirty years more; the Revolutionary and Napoleonic campaigns—Jemappes, Neewinden, Marengo, Austerlitz, Jena, Leipzig, and that last trick Waterloo—were all frequently refought by female piano-stool strategists. A lot of this stuff had come from brave new France where now, officially, the worst was like the best, especially the music; but the English lapped it all up with a good appetite. In fact, as befitted the subjects of a wave-ruling Britannia, they thought up a new nuance in the shape of naval battle pieces. The handsome Dussek, for example, composed *The naval battle and total destruction of the Dutch Fleet by Admiral Duncan, Oct. 11, 1797*. This was to celebrate the engagement at Camperdown that frustrated an attempt to invade Ireland. Dussek also wrote a neutrally titled *Le Combat Naval,* handily salable in mutually hostile countries. The highhanded Baltic violence of 1807 was commemorated by a *Battle of Copenhagen* "dedicated to Lord Cathcart . . . price 5 shillings." The clever publisher of this work hid the composer under a safe anonymity, since the piece was a literal transcript of a previously published French *Bataille d'Austerlitz.* Late in the game Stephen Francis Rimbault, godly organist of St. Giles-in-the-Fields, offered a "characteristic Fantasia" for the pianoforte on *The Battle of Navarino,* fought 1827 in the eastern Mediterranean; the price, a paltry three shillings. On page eight we hear "Turkish and Egyptian ships blown up," and later "The Asia looses her Mizzen Mast" by means of a rapidly descending semichromatic scale.

None of these pieces, apart from *The Battle of Prague,* could paste themselves with any adhesiveness into the hearts of the girls who played them or of their elders who had to endure them. No Englishman, so far as is known, had participated in the Prague engagement; few had ever even heard of it. Yet the piece commemorating it outlived all other similar ones by nearly two generations. Fame can be as unreasonably stubborn as it can be unconscionably fickle.

Dance music continued strong: minuets declined, but cotillions, strathspey reels, and—later—quadrilles reported a healthy, natural increase. Country dances kept on coming out vigorously in sets of twenty-four.

In the autumn of 1812 Lord Byron composed an amusing poem entitled *The Waltz: An Apostrophic Hymn;* it was published anonymously the following spring. In a footnote signed "Printer's Devil," the poet gives his testimony as to the beginning of the waltz habit in England:

> . . . the bard means . . . [that the] Waltz was not so much in vogue till the Regent attained the acme of his popularity. Waltz, the comet, whiskers, and the new government, illuminated heaven and earth, in all their glory, much about the same time; of these the comet has disappeared; the other three continue to astonish us still.

The "new government" was undoubtedly the Regency, established 1811; the comet may have been Flaugergue's, which appeared the same year. Waltz music had been published in England as early as the 1790's, and probably waltzes were danced by some people during the early years of the century. Byron's date is that of the fashionable flowering. The poet was much enchanted, as were many other people, with the new dance's lewdness and disorderliness:

> Endearing Waltz!—to thy more melting tune
> Bow Irish jig, and ancient rigadoon;
> Scotch reels, avaunt! and country dance, forego
> Your future claims to each fantastic toe!
> Waltz—Waltz alone both legs and arms demands,
> Liberal of feet, and lavish of her hands;
> Hands which may freely range in public sight
> Where ne'er before—but—pray "put out the light."

He describes the movements in detail, then follows with:

> Thus all and each, in movement swift or slow,
> The genial contact gently undergo;
> Till some might marvel, with the modest Turk,
> If "nothing follows all this palming work?"

It seems that a Persian, after seeing a waltz danced in the European quarter of Istanbul, actually put that last question to an English traveler.

In any event, it is certain that from that time on English pianofortes, like all others, were a-flicker with 3/4 time.

As for a more refined, resourceful music, we see a landmark of a sort set up in pianoforte music when J. B. Cramer, in September 1804, brought out his earliest books of *études*, or studies, the first of their kind ever to be issued. They were rather different from the various kinds of pieces that had been indiscriminately called "lessons." Each of them was based on a short, rather rapid figure in even rhythm, mostly four to six notes in length; the entire composition then consisted of inexact reiterations of the figure in various forms of sequence, of change of key, or with an occasional slight alteration of interval. The *étude* was not rigorously restricted to its basic figure; variant figures were sometimes introduced. The whole piece created the effect of a continuous flow of notes variedly developed upon a single pattern. In general, the *études* emphasized the kinesthetic and harmonic elements of music rather than the melodic or rhythmic. A smoothly, rapidly executed *étude* gave an impression of skilled, controlled brilliance; the word "*étude*" itself suggested that pianists were to play the work in order to develop their finger dexterity and their resources of co-ordination, as well as their muscular endurance. Cramer's *études* were "practice pieces" in a sense; yet their harmonies were rather sensitive, within the musical idiom of their day; their pianistic figuration was very imaginative for their time; and altogether they seemed fresh and charming. Indeed, their charm has not entirely faded up to the very present, 150 years later.

Cramer's book of forty-two *études* was so well, and so immediately, received by connoisseurs that Steibelt became jealous: he proceeded to put out, the very next year, a *Study for the pianoforte, containing 50 exercises.* Steibelt was something of a charlatan; his exercises approached Cramer's style very closely, without once actually stealing a figure from his predecessor—thus proving that it takes a man of ability to be a good counterfeiter. Cramer composed a second set of forty-two in 1810, whereupon Wölfl presently retaliated with a *Practical School for the Pianoforte consisting of 50 Exercises.* Six years later the old master Clementi gave out the first part of his magnum opus, the *Gradus ad Parnassum,* which also contained a number of remarkable studies.

There was an endless sequel: throughout the nineteenth century everybody, it seems, who played or taught the piano professionally sweated forth his drops of *études*—twelve, twenty-four, or fifty at a time. We have spoken of Carl Czerny of Vienna, who probably achieved the world's record for quantity exudation in this field. His exercises became the best known of all their kind; that was a little unfortunate for some of them, for they stimulated the formation of bitter antibodies in the minds of many sullen youngsters to whom they were undiscriminatingly administered. We say it was a pity, for many of them are very pretty when played fast and smoothly enough, not always a simple feat. The value of any work of art, regardless of its form, depends upon the quality of the artist who creates it; thus, we find the pianoforte *étude* later rising to heights of poetry in the thought of Chopin and Liszt, and descending to tedious banality in that of a multitude of piddlers.

The *études* were part of a growing interest in the simple athletics of piano playing; the association of the piano with the showiness of public concerts had helped to propel that trend. It was logical that London, with its emphasis on concerts, should have become the birthplace and nursery of the pianoforte *étude.* Thenceforth, for professional pianists, the difficulty of music became one of its boastable virtues: the greater the obstacle, the greater hero he who overcame it. It was in that sense that Wölfl in 1808 composed a *Grand* Sonata, Opus 41, which he subtitled *"Non Plus Ultra."* Thereupon, Dussek, by that time gone from London, felt honor-stirred to raise this ante by a retorting sonata that he dubbed *"Plus Ultra."* Wölfl failed to reraise.

Nevertheless, if a statistical time-study had been made during the early decades of the nineteenth century, it would probably have shown that only a minority of woman-hours at the piano were taken up with straight piano music. For the most part, the girls' modest abilities were most nearly adequate to playing simple supports to their own singing. Songs for a single voice, with piano accompaniments, were a large fraction of what the publishers and music sellers expected to dispose of to their customers. Some songs may have been hopefully printed without benefit of special advertising; many others enjoyed the advantage of some public emphasis in their launching.

Theaters continued to be a primary spring of song, both in light opera and, more pretentiously, in Italian opera. As individual singers became objects of temporary popular affection, the particular songs or arias they sang were included in the attention bestowed upon their personalities. Among the pleasure gardens, the sedate Ranelagh, with the endless decorous promenade around its Rotunda, began to seem dull in the late 1790's; it was shut down in 1803. Vauxhall, on the other hand, continued to prosper; in addition to providing leafy walks, hedge-bound nooks, and a variety of food and drink, it began to serve a more sophisticated plebeian taste with fireworks, tightrope dancers, and parachute drops from balloons. Those who enjoyed watching the aerialists and the aeronauts were given a music suitable to their tastes. James Hook, the Vauxhall organist and music director from 1774 to 1820, turned out his annual parcels of songs, which had already been delivered to pleased throngs by favorite singers such as Mrs. Billington, Mrs. Bland, and Charles Incledon, to name but a very few. Later on, vaudeville shows and complete operas were given, in which especially esteemed vocal artists such as John Braham and Madame Vestris delighted the multitudes.

It was only natural that hundreds of thousands of girls were glad to relive some of these musical experiences in their own voices, while also addressing themselves to the square, grand, "cabinet," and "cottage" instruments at home.

Scotch songs continued to be almost as habit-forming and intoxicating an indulgence as Scotch whiskey. Both were irresistible; therefore, both were vulnerable to adulteration and to counterfeiting, for it appears that many "Scots songs" were mere imitations. By the end of the eighteenth century, Scotch songs began to blow up into delusions of grandeur. George Thomson, Secretary to the Board of Trustees for the Encouragement of Arts and Manufactures in Scotland, spent a good part of a lifetime making ambitious collections of Scotch, Irish, and Welsh songs. His idea of glorifying these melodies consisted in having famous writers such as Robert Burns, Walter Scott, and others set new words to them and in getting celebrated musicians such as Haydn, Beethoven, Pleyel, Koželuch, and Hummel to compose elaborate accompaniments to them for pianoforte, with violin and cello obbligato—not merely accompaniments, but also enhancing instrumental preludes, interludes, and postludes. The composers were all unalloyed Austrians, culturally speaking; the fact that they might not have been able to utter a plausible Scottish harmonic dialect did not seem to bother Mr. Thomson. He paid Haydn almost £300 for his instrumental decorations and Beethoven altogether more than £500. The collections were finally published; after so much expert manhandling, the songs had little value for folklore research. Their expensive party dresses did nothing to further their popularity: Mr. Thomson's well-meaning volumes did not sell enough copies to pay for more than the cost of their printing. Still, they came out handsomely engraved, the tunes were bedded with some famous names, and those who were fond of them were no doubt plased to admire them in such magnificent surroundings.

The teeming music trade, with its many competing sellers, naturally brought forth some fanciful market screaming. James Harrison, the unsung pioneer who first published *The Battle of Prague,* advertised a scheme in the London *Times* a few years later: he announced the publication of a *Pianoforte Magazine,* containing nothing but pianoforte music. Beginning in 1797, it was to appear in weekly numbers at a price of 2s 6d each; each number was to contain a promissory note signed by Harrison; upon completion of 250 issues, the notes were to be exchanged for "a Brilliant and elegant Pianoforte, far superior to many instruments sold for 25 guineas each." It sounded like a good "come-on"; whether any instruments were actually handed over as premiums, we do not know. On second thought, we wonder how attractive the scheme really was: anyone who did not as yet possess an instrument could have no use for all that music, but anyone who already did own a pianoforte might have no room for a second one. The offer might have appealed to a young girl using the parental instrument, as well as the parental pocket money, who was planning to get married and live in her own home in not less than five years. At any rate, Harrison's *Magazine,* consisting entirely of reprints, went on to thirty volumes.

Another trolling spinner was thought up by George Walker, who set up his music shop in Great Portland Street about 1790. After a while he advertised music at "half price." Frank Kidson, the most extensive student of British music publications, seems to think that this may have been the beginning of a curious practice, widely prevalent throughout the nineteenth century, of marking music up to double the expected price and then giving a fifty per cent discount. One might imagine that hardly any adult would be impressed by such an empty twiddling of figures; yet there seem always to have been people who could be lured by the flimsiest facsimile of a bargain, as well as pusillanimous merchants who would not take the lead in abandoning a competitive trade practice no matter how foolish.

We can readily understand how music for the pianoforte, and vocal music with pianoforte accompaniment, got the lion's share of the music-business boom of those lively times; in fact, the further we advance into the nineteenth century, the more does music involving a piano tend to usurp—almost to monopolize—all publication and performance. Early in the century the pianoforte was already spoken of simply as "instrument," as if there were no other. It is indeed the easiest of all instruments to play a little, the perfect tool for persons of small talent or ambition. Intonation is up to the tuner, the keys are roomy—7/8 inches wide—if you hit the right one, it will give the right sound whether you hear the tone in your head first or not. There is little problem of tone-production, nothing like the hazards of embouchure or bowing attack: any imbecile can press down a light lever. No piano gently stroked can ever inflict the distress caused by a squeaky reed or a scratchy, out-of-tune fiddle. The piano can make both melody and harmony; simple, plausible chord formulas are easy to acquire upon it. It can be played alone, without invoking the problem of co-ordinating with other players; it is a good-looking piece of furniture, expensive enough to be proud of. Moreover, in England, amateur music-making was properly a purely female activity; the stance and movements necessary for pianoforte playing were happily congruous with polite middle-class conceptions of feminine decorum.

All in all, the instrument was ideally suited to the inseparable emulsion of aspiration and pretense that suffused the entire European *bourgeoisie.* To enhance a living room with a carved and shiny pianoforte costing twenty or one hundred guineas, and to play on it an um-ta-ta accompaniment to a tune from a high-priced opera, seemed an easy advance toward leading the more abundant life. Indeed, the gesture was apt; one merely ought not to overrate the abundance.

17. CLEMENTI—AND COMPANY

WE HAVE mentioned a few of Broadwood's competitors: Stodart and Wornum, for example. There were others, and by 1824 the number of piano makers in London was said to have increased to fifty—most of whom, however, must have been fairly small concerns. A special interest attaches to the firm that rivaled Broadwood's the closest and the longest.

We last observed Muzio Clementi as a greatly sought-after teacher, an occasional performer in well-established concerts, and a composer of rather weighty sonatas and symphonies. Being at the head of his particular branch of his profession, he might well have felt content; nevertheless, we begin to sense a certain restlessness, a dissatisfaction, in him as he approached his fortieth year. There were rumors of his preoccupation with scientific studies: a German music journal stated that he was giving up music to devote his life to astronomy. This was surely an exaggeration of a germ of truth; the germ was that the thought of his status of professional musician, however successful, left him with a sour aftertaste. Clementi had lived in England, not counting his travels, since his adolescence; already during his years on the Beckford estate he had had ample opportunity to absorb, however resistantly, the current English sense of social values. By his great native talent, by his early Italian associations, and by his devoted self-cultivation, he had become a musician of the highest attainments: he was one of the greatest masters of the keyboard; his compositions were notable for their seriousness and their craft—indeed, the young Beethoven was conning Clementi sonatas admiringly for his own improvement. He was well read, fluent in several languages, and had a positive scientific bent. For all this the English had insufficient respect, even when they appreciated its achievement and even when they enjoyed it. If Clementi played in public for money, that made him a "fiddler," somebody on a par with a circus tumbler or an animal trainer; if he gave lessons, that made him a hired menial, somebody like a hairdresser. In either case, he was disqualified from ever entering the sunny precincts of gentility.

In 1788, when he was thirty-six, he might have smiled unpleasantly had he come across a passage in *Newberry's Familiar Letter Writer, adapted to the Capacities of Young People,* published that year. It is from a "Letter to a Young Man on his too Strong Attachment to Singing and Music," which reads thus:

> Dear Cousin,
>
> In the first place, my dear cousin, these pleasures of sound may take you off from the more desirable ones of sense, and make your delights stop at the ear, which should go deeper, and be placed in the understanding; for, whenever a good singer is in company, adieu to all conversation of an improving or intellectual nature. In the second place it may expose you to company, and that perhaps not the best or most eligible. Hence your business and your other more useful studies may be greatly, if not wholly neglected, and very possibly your health itself be impaired. In the third place, it may tend, which it naturally does, to enervate the mind and make you haunt musical societies, operas, and concerts; and what glory is it to a gentleman, even were he a fine performer, that he can strike a string, touch a key or sing a song, with the grace and command of an *hired* musician?

The final sentence is particularly exquisite.

Many pointed accounts must have come to Clementi's ears: the rumor that Handel had never married because the mother of a girl he once favored could not bear to have her the wife of a musician; the later story of Thomas Roseingrave, the gifted organist of St. George's, Hanover Square, whose mind became unhinged when, because of his profession, a wealthy father refused him the hand of a daughter he had loved and by whom he was loved devotedly. Clementi must have heard all about J. S. Schroeter and could not have failed to be curiously touched by the report of how the suave pianist rescued his family-in-law from degradation by giving up his profession.

Clementi did not need to learn his lesson vicariously: on one of Muzio's trips to the Continent, he had visited Lyons, and there a mutual affection had sprung up between him and young Mademoiselle Marie-Victoire Imbert-Colomès. Father Imbert-Colomès, a banker, was a music lover; in fact, he was a pillar of the local Philharmonic Society. That did not abate one tittle of his iron disapproval of taking a *jongleur* into his family. A precarious elopement of the girl and the pianist was rigorously pursued and struck down. Musician sons-in-law, it seemed, could be as leprous in France as in England. The very year of Clementi's Lyons misadventure there occurred a sensational scandal that seemed to shake a whole section of London society. That was when Hester Lynch Thrale, then a widow, married the singer Gabriel Piozzi on July 23, 1784. The pained general outcry was extraordinarily vehement. Nasty squibs appeared in public prints; Hester's family all but disowned her, and her old friends deserted her—including the vastly overrated Dr. Johnson, who accused her of betraying her country, her religion, and her family. No shadow of a stain had ever attached to her first husband, Henry Thrale: a rich, neglectful English brewer, who suffered an occasional bout of gonorrhea, seemed an eminently suitable spouse for an English lady of unusual culture—just as certainly as a high-minded, devoted Italian musician made her *déclassée*.

Clementi was a far better Italian musician than Piozzi, if less affectionate. The affair must have made him self-conscious; perhaps it influenced his life. At any rate, since in England business was a pathway to gentility—while the profession of music was a barrier thereto—and since gentility was the greatest of all human goods, he resolved to go into business. He needed some time to acquire capital; meanwhile, during the 1790's, his appearances in concerts became increasingly infrequent. Let us try to guess at his financial vigor. He had been collecting his lesson guineas for some time; there was gossip that he gave as many as sixteen lessons a day. If we discount that figure at fifty per cent and suppose him to have taught two hundred full days a year, that would return him an annual £1680. Adding to this his fees from concerts and the sale of his compositions, we might estimate his total income at £2000 per year. Clementi was unmarried and was generally considered a tight man with a shilling. Meat was fivepence a pound in those days; therefore, even if he had paid the high rent of £30 a year for a house—as J. C. Bach had done—he might well have kept his living expenses within £500: that would have let him salt away £1500 every twelve months. After ten years of this, even without interim investments, he would have had a working potential of £15,000 ($75,000) to put into a business venture. Our speculations seem conservative; he may have been worth much more.

It was probably early in the 1790's that he began investing money in the firm of Longman & Broderip, who had been the chief publishers of his works; in fact, he became a silent partner. Their bankruptcy took place about 1798; upon reorganization, the business was named Longman, Clementi & Co. Upon Longman's departure, a short while later, new members were taken in; the firm was now accoutered with the complex, agglutinative title of Clementi, Banger, Hyde, Collard & Davis. The partners decided to go in heavily for piano manufacture and sales. The notions "Clementi," "pianoforte," and "excellent" had straggled together in loose comfort into many people's minds; thus, it was judged attractive and profitable to shorten the firm's name to a neat Clementi & Co. The musician's contribution to the business was almost certainly not restricted to the use of his name and his money: for a long time he had been thoroughly conversant with the mechanics of piano construction, and many of his suggestions in this connection must have been decisive.

Clementi now stopped playing the piano altogether; he even gave up incidental playing while conducting his symphonies: thenceforth no one would be able to libel him with the name "fiddler." He was becoming a gentleman—that is, someone not a hireling, who could handle money without having to handle goods. In fact, he could now take a patronizing position toward other musicians: he persuaded his greatly gifted disciple John Field, now about eighteen, to act as a salesman and demonstrator in his warerooms. The slender youth had a notably sensitive touch and an elegant style; later he was to become famous as the composer of delicately sentimental nocturnes. He charmed the ears of prospective buyers of Clementi pianos as he fondled their keys; it might be that never again would the customers hear their purchases sound so well.

Soon after the reorganization the firm of Clementi & Co. was operating so smoothly and prosperously that it no longer required the encouraging personal presence of the illustrious partner whose name it bore. In July 1802, Clementi set out for a long trip to the European continent; he was not to return for eight years. He became the firm's foreign minister, as it were, whose aim was to enhance its overseas relationships—in other words, to promote its export and import trade. He took Field with him, as a prestige-conferring protégé and also for useful services. Thirty-six years earlier the Honorable Peter Beckford had "bought" the young Muzio Clementi from his father for a sizable sum; Clementi was almost a gentleman himself now, but he indulged in no such lordly largess when he, in turn, became the senior participant in a somewhat similar transaction. Far from "buying" young Field from his parents, he induced them to pay him, the financial Clementi, the sum of £100 for the young man's maintenance for a time. So the story ran, at any rate: the tales of Clementi's money-lust seem too pointed always to be quite accurate, yet too persistent not to be true in principle.

The pair arrived in St. Petersburg, Russia, late in December 1802. Clementi proceeded to establish his pianoforte warerooms, appointing a resident sales representative and also one for Moscow. His reputation as an artist facilitated his making good social connections: presently, Russian generals, bankers, and musicians were buying Clementi pianos. Field was a diligent, persuasive demonstrator; but his fine playing made him many friends in the artistically dependent, impressionable country. Thus, when Clementi departed the following June, Field stayed on and made the rest of his career as an artist in Russia.

We soon find Clementi in Leipzig, spending several months with Breitkopf & Härtel, the foremost of German music publishers. Undoubtedly, the possibility of mutually advantageous business was discussed. A letter from Breitkopf's to Clementi & Co. dated February 13, 1804, offered their entire catalogue at a fifty per cent discount off the list price: "Since the prices of our stock are extremely moderate, you can raise them considerably without making them too high." Breitkopf's also say they can use numbers of pianofortes "upright, square, and horizontal," but they ask for "rock-bottom dealers' prices." Germans were relatively poor; they were not used to paying for things on the English scale. At the time of this letter, the best *"Flügel"* (*i.e.*, grand) by a North German maker could probably have been bought retail for 200 thalers, about £30, almost the lowest price for which any similar pianoforte was available at retail in England. At that rate, a cheap Clementi instrument delivered in Leipzig at the lowest possible wholesale figure—allowing, of course, for the cost of transportation as well as a reasonable dealer's markup—might have been offered at a price attractive to a certain number of wealthier Germans who liked to feel that they owned one of those fabulous English pianos.

Eventually, North German piano makers made instruments imitating the English construction, especially with regard to the action. To a certain extent, North Germans also bought Vienna pianos. In any case, the situation shows up the relative industrial immaturity of Saxony and Prussia and their dependence on foreign countries for the best in pianofortes. Not until the latter part of the nineteenth century did Berlin and Leipzig occupy a leading position in the piano trade.

The year 1804 found Clementi in Vienna. As a high and mighty businessman, he refrained from seeming too anxious to meet Beethoven—especially since he was interested in making some kind of deal with the great composer. Beethoven, on the other hand, was far from being a self-abaser; though he admired Clementi as a musician, he did not feel it his part to pay the first call. The two saw, recognized, and ignored each other studiously a number of times at the Swan Tavern. Still, money eventually recovered its choked voice, talking both the musical and the gentlemanly dialects: when Clementi again visited Vienna a few years later, a meeting was somehow arranged and Clementi & Co. acquired the English rights for a number of Beethoven's finest works. These included the Fourth Symphony, the *Coriolan* Overture, the great *Rasumovsky* Quartets, and the Violin Concerto, the last also arranged by the composer for pianoforte "with additional keys." Clementi was very gratified at having put through this transaction; yet we wonder whether his less artistically minded London partners did not feel that the name of Beethoven, especially in symphonies and quartets, was worth more to them in glory than in cash.

On the Continent, Clementi's claim to distinction was his great reputation as a musician, and especially as a pianist. Naturally, there was much interest in hearing him perform, and he was requested many times to give concerts or to play at private gatherings. But he refused all such suggestions consistently; not a note did he bring forth that anyone could hear. During his revisit to his native Italy he had excused himself by saying that the available instruments were unsatisfactory. That was true, but the same excuse would not suffice in Vienna—where, in fact, a few pianos from his own factory could have been put at his disposal. Still he would not play. It was the same in Prague. Perhaps he felt that if he gave one concert, he could not avoid giving more and thus falling into the danger of again becoming a mere artist. Or perhaps, realizing he was out of practice, he was afraid that his actual performance might fail to justify his reputation.

While he was in Central Europe, the report came to him from London that the Clementi & Co. premises on Tottenham Court Road had burned down, on March 20, 1807. The damage was pretty thorough; according to a piece in the *Morning Chronicle* the following day, the workshop, storerooms, and finished instruments, to the total value of £40,000, were lost. Toward the end of the month the *Gentleman's Magazine* reported that only £15,000 of the amount had been covered by insurance. It was a major calamity, yet Clementi made no move to hasten to England. At that moment he probably could not have gone, even if he had wanted to. Those were the years of climax of the Napoleonic disturbance: the Emperor's interdiction of trade with England and Britain's blockade of Continental harbors paralyzed all overseas commerce except for dangerous little sneaks. Mail, news correspondence, and money transfers—all were delayed or interrupted. Clementi stayed on the Continent, though he began to have to sell some of his jewelry. Still the Clementi & Co. publishing business continued to flourish; its profits probably helped to rebuild its piano factory, whose prosperity soon climbed to new heights. Clementi finally returned to England in 1810; even then, the passage was not readily achieved.

He never seems to have contemplated the extravagance of a trip to the young United States of America. Perhaps the company business there did not need any special encouragement; for among the makes of instruments imported into that budding nation, Clementi's appear to have been the favorite. Many are still extant: there is a Clementi & Co. piano in the whaling museum in New Bedford, Massachusetts; another reposes in an upper floor of the New England Conservatory of Music in Boston; a third is in Barnard Hall, Barnard College, New York City—to mention but a few.

After Clementi's return, his metamorphosis could be regarded as complete; he married an English lady and also put on the truest diagnostic *insigne* of an English gentleman: a place in the country —namely, in the Vale of Evesham, in Worcestershire. "I am a young Italian, but an old Englishman," he said of himself once, keenly. As a member of the landed gentry he could now feel entitled to his little eccentricities, such, for instance, as that of composing music. He had not played to speak of, or composed anything worthy of mention, for a decade or more; yet leaving his creative mind fallow had enriched it: his finest, strongest works date from this peaceful period well after his sixtieth year. They include some of his best pianoforte sonatas, notably the one in G minor subtitled *"Didone Abbandonata,"* a work still not sufficiently appreciated. They include his celebrated *Gradus ad Parnassum,* by an abbreviated version of which he is chiefly known nowadays. Its first volume was brought out with considerable éclat, appearing in 1817 simultaneously in London, Paris, and Leipzig; two further volumes came out subsequently.

Even before his death, however, which occurred in 1832, his style had lost much of its appeal. His mind had been formed during the middle of the eighteenth century, and the patterns of those times dominated his thought; moreover, in his youth he had absorbed the rigorous polyphonic traditions of a still earlier day. By 1820 his best ideas, for all their ingenuity and cogency, seemed severe, dry, and old-fashioned to a younger generation. The trend was toward reckless fantasy, toward shameless emotionalism, or toward frivolous prettiness; in any event, it was away from Clementi's tight counterpoints and hard, logical sentences. His *Gradus ad Parnassum,* hailed as a sort of pianist's Bible, suffered the worst of all fates: not oblivion, indeed, but the widest of celebrity in an unconscionable disfigurement. The work originally consisted of one hundred pieces of all kinds: sonata movements, rondos, fugues, canons, adagios—a compendium of all phases of musical and pianistic science. Unsympathetic editors, inflated with their own reputations as virtuosos, proceeded to discard all the most interesting numbers—all the fugues, canons, and slow movements—to retain thirty *études* and publish these under the name of *Gradus ad Parnassum* as if that were the entire work: mayhem doubled with slander.

Already, Clementi's funeral and his burial in the cloisters of Westminster Abbey aroused less attention than his friends had anticipated. After his death, his firm immediately erased his name; it made its pianos under the title of Collard & Collard. The business prospered substantially: by the time of the great London industrial World's Fair of 1851, it was second only to Broadwood's in the number of instruments manufactured and the gross amount of money taken in.

Clementi's career was a product of the English moral atmosphere, though it had counterparts in France. In Germany it would have been difficult to imagine. Educated Germans thought—or pretended to think—of music as a form of revelation or prophecy, of something akin to poetry or religion and worthy of a comparable respect. The idea that a distinguished composer and virtuoso could think to better himself in the general estimation by throwing up his art and going into commerce would have struck them as the ethic of a world turned upside down. It would have been as if a gifted, learned, eloquent, and widely admired clergyman had succeeded in getting his fellow men to treat him with greater respect by giving up his pulpit and devoting his attention to manufacturing religious articles and selling prayer books. The Germans, however, apparently forgave Clementi his revolting apostasy—perhaps because he was a foreigner; possibly, many of them never clearly comprehended it.

Clementi was not the only superior, successful musician whom the English climate had bullied into commercial pursuits. The handsome Dussek, at the very time that his concertos were most applauded, formed a business partnership with Domenico Corri, music publisher and seller. The enterprise flourished for a while, then declined and failed; and Dussek ran away to the Continent to escape certain pedantic creditors. Away from England, he never again felt impelled to undertake a similar venture. J. B. Cramer, Clementi's excellent pupil, for many years also succeeded in eliciting a guinea each for his forty-minute lessons; he too then decided to make Plutus his mascot and in 1824 helped to found the music-publishing firm of Cramer, Addison & Beale—later changed to J. B. Cramer & Co. He composed few—if any—sonatas, concertos, or *études* after that, but wrote mostly low-cost potpourris and routine variations.

18. THE PIANO AS A FEMALE "ACCOMPLISHMENT." THE WRITERS' TESTIMONY

THE HISTORY of the pianoforte and the history of the social status of women can be interpreted in terms of one another.

Among the genteel ranks, the lord and master of a house understood that the idleness of his wife and daughters was a necessary feature of his prestige as a gentleman; the more he felt constrained to be preoccupied with his business, the more their function became that of wasting time and money for him vicariously, in the most respectably showy way. Simple idleness, however, is a negative thing that had little ostentative glow; it looked more ladylike to do something uselessly pretty than to do nothing, just as a man carrying a swagger stick gives a brisker proof of his exemption from carrying bundles than does a man who walks merely empty-handed.

In eighteenth- and nineteenth-century England, as well as in the rest of Europe, young feminine genteel idleness was mostly filled with a number of trivial occupations superficially related to the fine arts: they were known as "accomplishments." Fancy needlework and embroidery were among the oldest of these, but the eighteenth century saw the rise and fall of many others: framing pictures in shellwork; embellishing cabinets with a tracery of seaweed, filigree, and varnish work; crapework, chenille work, ribbon work, waferwork, and purse netting; making artificial flowers of wax or fabric; cutting out paper ornaments. The ability to stammer a few selected words in French was a standard "accomplishment"; so was an ability to draw or paint slightly. Music was, indeed, considered one of the most important of the young ladylike "accomplishments"; it was a favorite because it could be shown off best while actually being accomplished. In this sphere, music reduced itself to singing and playing the pianoforte, though the guitar and the harp were the keyboard's occasional temporary rivals.

It is questionable how much these feminine activities were enjoyed, intrinsically, by the families in which they operated; yet they were in great demand. A contemporary writer spoke of a "frenzy for accomplishments." Being "accomplished" generally was judged to render a girl a more valuable prize in the marriage gamble; her little singing and piano playing was not only an amorous lure, as described long ago in *The Anatomy of Melancholy,* it was also a way of confirming her family's gentility. A possible candidate for a young lady's hand was expected to feel pleased to ally himself with a family of such refinement that its daughter had learned how to make a needlework picture of Solomon and the Queen of Sheba, paint roses on china buttons, and sing "Auld Robin Gray" to her own accompaniment.

Jane Austen, the daughter of a provincial clergyman, had cats' eyes for the vanities of the denizens of the petty, well-bred, semirural world in which she lived. The incidents in her novels may well have happened as she tells them, and they may be considered true even when they cannot be shown to be facts. Her first completed work, *Pride and Prejudice,* was written in 1797, when she was a mere twenty-two; it contains a number of scenes reflecting the gentry's current attitudes toward music and toward the pianoforte in particular.

Right at the beginning we meet the ironical Mr. Bennet in his residence at the village of Longbourn, twenty-four miles from London. He enjoys an estate—that is, an unearned income—of £2000 a year, not a lavish revenue on which to support five daughters with any elegance. Mrs. Bennet has a little fortune of £4000, but has certain low connections that are regarded as detrimental to her daughters' chances of advantageous marriages. The Bennets attend a large party at the home of Sir William Lucas, who had made a fortune "in trade" in the small neighboring town of Meryton; he had retired from his business to the country upon being knighted and is now a gentleman by royal decree. His daughter Charlotte speaks to Eliza, the second of the Bennet girls: "I am going to open the instrument, Eliza, and you know what follows." The author uses the word "instrument" as synonymous with pianoforte. Eliza answers:

> "You are a very strange creature by way of a friend!—always wanting me to play and sing before anybody and everybody! If my vanity had taken a musical turn, you would have been invaluable; but as it is, I would really rather not sit down before those who must be in the habit of hearing the very best performers." On Miss Lucas's persevering, however, she added, "Very well; if it must be so, it must."

Eliza is the story's heroine; therefore, her elaborate show of modesty is intended to be something admirable. The story continues:

> Her performance was pleasing, though by no means capital. After a song or two, and before she could reply to the entreaties of several that she would sing again, she was eagerly succeeded at the instrument by her sister Mary, who having, in consequence of being the only plain one in the family, worked hard for knowledge and accomplishments, was always impatient for display.
>
> Mary had neither genius nor taste; and though vanity had given her application, it had given her likewise a pedantic air and conceited manner, which would have injured a higher degree of excellence than she had reached. Elizabeth, easy and unaffected, had been listened to with much more pleasure, though not playing half so well; and Mary, at the end of a long concerto, was glad to purchase praise and gratitude by Scotch and Irish airs, at the request of her younger sisters . . .

Poor Mary! But then, no author of the period could be expected to expend sympathy upon a girl expressly labeled "plain," since no feminine readers—the vast majority—would have cared to identify themselves with such a one. The above passage makes it clear that music, being a trivial thing, could be unpleasantly overwrought by too much cultivation. A performance that was "pleasing but not capital," by a young lady who did not try too hard, was the right thing; Scotch airs were better than concertos. A little singing and piano playing is an ornament to a pretty girl, but an ugly one cannot use the pianoforte to escape her damnation. Later on we are informed, mockingly, that Mary is studying thorough bass.

A Mr. Darcy attended the Lucas gathering; he is the novel's hero, so we may expect his opinions to have the author's approbation. He ". . . stood near them in silent indignation at such a mode of passing the evening, to the exclusion of all conversation. . . ."

Mother Bennet's low connections consist in the fact that her sister is married to a country-town attorney, in nearby Meryton, while her brother is actually "in trade"—"somewhere near Cheapside." Nevertheless, the Bennet girls go to visit their ungenteel small-town uncle and aunt, Mr. and Mrs. Philips; the event allows the author to tell us that though these people of little account had "imitations of china" on their mantelpiece, they had no "instrument."

Early in the book we are introduced to the Reverend Mr. William Collins, who is pictured as a ridiculous toady. He is present at still another party at which Mary Bennet is again too eager to sing and play.

> "If I," said Mr. Collins, "were so fortunate as to be able to sing, I should have great pleasure, I am sure, in obliging the company with an air; for I consider music as a very innocent diversion, and perfectly compatible with the profession of a clergyman—I do not mean, however, to assert that we can be justified in devoting too much of our time to music, for there are certainly other things to be attended to! . . ."

In view of Mr. Collins' character, this must be regarded as an obvious platitude that no one could disagree with. The "innocence" and harmlessness of music as a girlish pastime is frequently extolled in the literature of the period.

The Reverend Mr. Collins has married Charlotte Lucas; on a visit to him and his new wife, the Bennet girls are invited to dinner at "Rosings." That is the name of the gorgeous mansion of Lady Catherine de Bourgh, Mr. Collins' patroness who has "presented" him "to his living," as the queer slang of the Church of England has it. Lady Catherine is something of a magnate, one of the "great": she has "family" and is both rich and rude.

During the course of the gathering Elizabeth Bennet is conversing with a gentleman, when the titled old dragon barges in, demanding to know what they are saying. They admit they are talking of music. The lady proclaims:

> "Of music! Then pray speak aloud. It is of all subjects my delight. I must have my share of the conversation if you are speaking of music. There are few people in England, I suppose, who have more true enjoyment of music than myself, or a better natural taste. If I had ever learnt, I should have been a great proficient. . . . How does Georgiana get on, Darcy?"
>
> Mr. Darcy spoke with affectionate praise of his sister's proficiency. . . .
>
> "I assure you, madam . . . that she . . . practises very constantly."
>
> "So much the better. It cannot be done too much; and when I next write to her, I shall charge her not to neglect it on any account. I often tell young ladies that no excellence in music is to be acquired without constant practice. I have told Miss Bennet several times, that she will never play really well unless she practises more; and though Mrs. Collins has no instrument, she is very welcome, as I have often told her, to come to Rosings every day, and play on the pianoforte in Mrs. Jenkinson's room. She would be in nobody's way, you know, in that part of the house."

Mrs. Jenkinson was the housekeeper. When coffee was over, Eliza complied with a request to play and sat down to the instrument.

> Lady Catherine listened to half a song, and then talked, as before, to her other nephew . . .

The falsity of her pretensions to music loving, as well as her admonitions about practicing, are, naturally, part of the unattractive lines with which the author has aimed to draw Lady Catherine; it seems to show what Jane Austen—and, of course, a multitude of her readers—thought about overdoing music.

Thus, we learn from *Pride and Prejudice* that families "gentrifying" themselves in the country on £2000 or £4000 a year, including those of retired knighted businessmen, all had pianofortes; and that "great" ladies not only had one in the drawing room, but also kept one for the use of the housekeeper; whereas country lawyers and lesser clergymen did without them.

A later novel, *Emma,* written between 1811 and 1816, takes place in "Highbury"; it is the same old Austen village, shifted eight miles closer to London. We find several characteristic little piano-playing episodes in it. In fact, one of the significant elements in such "plot" as the tale affords is a pianoforte, sent up from Broadwood's by a pointedly anonymous donor as a gift to Miss Jane Fairfax. It is a square piano, suitably selected for the small dwelling of Miss Bates—Miss Fairfax' aunt, with whom she is staying. Miss Fairfax is an orphan, a gentlewoman—"accomplished" and of course beautiful, even though she is only an assistant heroine. A group of people are admiring the new instrument, and a young gentleman has been helping to wedge paper under one leg because of an unevenness in the floor. Clearly, it is not heavy, by later standards. With the piano came some music, and the young man is inspecting it:

> "Here is something quite new to me. Do you know it? Cramer. And here are a new set of Irish melodies. . . ."

Very plausible. The fair Fairfax has no fortune: only kind friends are helping her postpone the day when she must enter the bondage of being a governess, as she herself speaks of it; it is her only resource if she remains unmarried. Gentility is sweet, but sometimes difficult. She is evidently a good player; two other young ladies are discussing her:

> "Besides, if she does play so very well, you know, it is no more than she is obliged to do, because she will have to teach. The Coxes were wondering last night whether she would get into any great family. . . ."

The brash Coxes, however, are almost directly labeled "vulgar." "Last night" refers to a dinner party given by Mr. and Mrs. Cole, at which all the novel's major characters were present. The Coles are described:

> [they had been] settled some years in Highbury, and were very good sort of people, friendly, liberal and unpretending; but on the other hand, they were of low origin, in trade, and only moderately genteel.

The Coles' investments, however, have prospered recently; they are now in money, have expansive urges, and even begin to dare to invite some of their less moderately genteel fellow villagers to dinner. The heroine, Emma Woodhouse, one of those so singled out, first determines to put the Coles "in their place" by refusing; but she relents when she hears that all her best friends are accepting. At dinner, Miss Fairfax' mysterious new gift-pianoforte is being discussed. Mrs. Cole says:

> "It always has quite hurt me that Jane Fairfax, who plays so delightfully, should not have an instrument. It seemed quite a shame, especially considering how many houses there are where fine instruments are absolutely thrown away. This is like giving ourselves a slap, to be sure; and it was but yesterday I was telling Mr. Cole I really was ashamed to look at our new grand pianoforte in the drawing room, while I do not know one note from another, and our little girls, who are but just beginning, perhaps may never make anything of it; and there is poor Jane Fairfax, who is a mistress of music, has not anything of the nature of an instrument, not even the pitifullest old spinnet in the world, to amuse herself with."

She explains that she hoped "some of our good neighbors" might someday put it to use.

The Coles' pianoforte is useless but hopeful: very appropriate for people who are mezzo-genteel but crescendo. Dinner being over, tea was served in the drawing room. It soon followed that:

> . . . a little bustle in the room shewed them that tea was over, and the instrument in preparation; and at the same moment, Mr. Cole approaching to entreat Miss Woodhouse would do them the honor of trying it. . . .
>
> She knew the limitations of her own powers too well to attempt more than she could perform with credit; she wanted neither taste nor spirit in the little things which are generally acceptable, and could accompany her own voice well. . . .

Emma sings and plays, but she is agreebly surprised when Mr. Frank Churchill approaches and correctly improvises a second vocal part to her song. Mr. Churchill is young and handsome, a scion "of a great Yorkshire family," a visitor in Highbury. Everyone is excited about him; even Emma is momentarily smitten. But his unsolicited participation in a musical performance proves him something of a coxcomb; the act is too frivolous, in the Austen scheme, to allow him to be a hero—that is, a mate for the heroine. Furthermore, on another occasion, while virtuously disclaiming any skill, he had said that he was "excessively fond of music." Several Austen characters at various times claim to be "passionately fond" of music; they are invariably made out to be frauds. "Excessively" suggests a mitigated fraud. Indeed, it ultimately develops that Mr. Churchill has been guilty of a monstrous deception: all the time he has been making himself agreeable to various Highbury damsels, especially Emma, he has been secretly engaged to Jane Fairfax. In fact, it is he who was the concealed giver of the pianoforte. It is all good poetic justice, thus to have the slightly false and musical Mr. Churchill, for all his great Yorkshire family, marry a Grade B girl.

To return to the Cole party: Jane now plays and sings, and elicits much favorable attention; Frank Churchill sings with her; while Mr. Knightley, the tale's twenty-four-carat gentleman, and therefore its true hero, also looks at her with quiet interest. Emma and Jane have been the only young lady performers; so when the latter stops, there ends the concert part of the evening, which continues thus:

> . . . but soon (within five minutes) the proposal of dancing—originating nobody exactly knew where—was so effectually promoted by Mr. and Mrs. Cole that everything was rapidly clearing away, to give proper space. Mrs. Weston, capital in her country dances, was seated, and beginning an irresistible waltz; and Frank Churchill, coming up with most becoming gallantry to Emma, had secured her hand, and led her up to the top.

Mrs. Weston is one of the guests; in fact, she is a family connection of Frank Churchill. This proves that, in good society, it was customary for informal dancing to be musically sparked at the "instrument" by a member of the party. It seemed fair, too, that it should be an older woman, such as Mrs. Weston was, who performed this service for the benefit of the young and marriageable.

The mention of a waltz is interesting: while *Emma* was being written, Byron published his *The Waltz,* in which so much is made of that dance's supposed impropriety. It is difficult to think that the Highbury group actually indulged in a real hugging waltz; probably they danced country dances to waltz tunes.

On the following day Emma thought over the party:

> She did unfeignedly and unequivocally regret the inferiority of her own playing and singing. She did most heartily grieve over the idleness of her childhood and sat down and practised vigorously an hour and a half.

But this was hardly a matter of artistic ambition; the quantity and quality of masculine attention such as Jane had harvested might well be worth several hours and a half of keyboard exercise.

Jane Austen enjoyed poking fun at her little world, yet her roots were in it, she believed in it. Toward music she seemed to blow hot and cold: she scorned the polite pretense associated with it, yet she herself played the pianoforte apparently with some conviction.

"I practise every day as much as I can," she wrote to her sister Cassandra on September 1, 1796, just before she began *Pride and Prejudice*. However, five years later she wrote to the same sister from Bath concerning a Mrs. and Miss Holder who were not well accepted: "I cannot utterly abhor them, especially as Miss Holder owns that she has no taste for Music." Miss Austen had a rather persistent grudge against the passionately fond. Yet again, at the end of 1808, when she had become an aunt, institutionally speaking, she wrote to Cassandra: "Yes, yes, we will have a pianoforte, as good a one as can be got for thirty guineas, and I will practise country dances, that we may have some amusement for our nephews and nieces, when we have the pleasure of their company."

On November 30, 1814, she wrote her niece Lady Knatchbull about a certain Anne Lefroy: "I was rather sorry to hear that she *is* to have an Instrument; it seems throwing money away. They will wish the twenty-four guineas in the shape of sheets and towels six months hence—and as to her playing, it never can be anything." Miss Austen had all the genteel feminine anxiety for the integrity of furniture surfaces. On October 30, 1815, she admonished her niece Caroline Austen to practice her music and not ill-use "my instrument. Do not allow anything to be put on it, but what is very light. I hope you will try to make out some other tune besides the Hermit."

"The Hermit, a favourite English ballad by Dr. Beattie, set to music . . . by Signor Giordani . . ." was listed as having been published by William Napier about 1780.

William M. Thackeray published *Vanity Fair* during 1846–48; the story's earlier events are made to take place during the year 1815, when its author was an infant. Nevetheless, he must have learned a great deal about that period from his elders, and he has not been found guilty of any serious anachronisms; besides, as he contends in Chapter 51, in the days of George IV "the manners of the polite world were not, I take it, essentially different from those of the present day: and their amusements pretty similar."

Vanity Fair recounts an endless succession of cruelties inflicted upon each other by various English people in their unremitting competitive pursuit of money and gentility, and its imponderable reflection; indeed, Thackeray himself uses the term "cruelly genteel" at the end of Chapter 61. It is a melancholy tale, full of revolting little incidents and bitter comments; the author says as much in a preface, though a few laughworthy spots have deluded some insensitive readers into thinking the novel "amusing."

Throughout the book there are occasional references to music, and to piano playing in particular. The action takes place within the circles of more or less "good" society: the author shows practically all musical experiences in this milieu as being of the most trivial kind. Only late in the story, when the scene shifts to a small German principality, do we encounter the notion of music as a fine art and are we told about performances of *Don Giovanni* and *Fidelio*—this in spite of the fact that Becky Sharp, one of the book's two principal female characters, is represented as being a rather fluent pianist. The author does not endow her with that ability, however, in order to arouse our sympathy; on the contrary, he connects Becky's pianistic talent with her green eyes, her half-French descent, and her disreputable artist parents in order to assure his virtuous English reader that her guile and her "immorality" are thereby all the more plausible. By contrast, her schoolmate Amelia Sedley is calculated to make all true Englishwomen warm with self-identifying affection for her softheartedness, her loyalty, and her stupidity. Amelia too plays the piano, but she could not be permitted to compromise her heroinity by playing it really well—or by any other cleverness, for that matter. The slightness of her powers is soon brought out: in Chapter 4 we learn of "her little store of songs" and of how much poorer a performer she is than the tricky Becky.

Some of the piano situations and attitudes in *Vanity Fair* are not unlike those retailed in the Jane Austen novels. In Chapter 3 we have a pointed comment on the true purpose of the girlish "accomplishments":

> What causes young people to "come *out*," but the noble ambition of matrimony? What sends them trooping to watering places? What keeps them dancing till five o'clock in the morning through a whole mortal season? What causes them to labour at pianoforte sonatas, and to learn four songs from a fashionable master at a guinea a lesson, and to play the harp if they have handsome arms and neat elbows . . . but that they may bring down some "desirable" young man with those killing bows and arrows of theirs?

Thereupon, we soon find Becky Sharp sprouting matrimonial designs and air castles in the direction of Amelia's elder brother Joseph, the nabob. She tries to lure him with music, singing to her own piano accompaniment. Her songs are described as "those simple ballads which were the fashion forty years ago"—thus 1807 —"and in which British tars, our King, poor Susan, blue-eyed Mary, and the like, were the principal themes." But Becky's musical glibness indeed eventually contributes to her ultimate downfall, for much later in the story she will exercise her potent piano-vocal fascination much more hazardously and illicitly upon the great and sinister Lord Steyne.

Among the London people, Amelia's father John Sedley has a kindly nature, on the whole, though he is not very gentlemanly and is described as "a coarse man from the Stock Exchange, where they love all sorts of practical jokes." His house is described as having harbored a "state grand piano"—"state" being a curiously suggestive European word meaning "formalized ostentation." This instrument ". . . was situated, as pianos usually are, in the back drawing room," says Thackeray. It must have been the one upon which Amelia was shown playing while singing for the delectation of her fiancé Captain George Osborne. For Amelia had another piano, which her parents provided for her own private use when she was a child and which she kept in her own room. The latter is the instrument that the author molds into a sentimental embellishment for several points of his tale, from which we can piece together its description. It was a small square, ornamented with brass—buhlwork?—"a natty little instrument"; it had a drawer, supposedly for sheet music, but in which Amelia later kept family mementos.

John Sedley, stockbroker and fatuous speculator, had bad luck and went bankrupt; his possessions, including his wine and his household furniture, had to be sold; the smaller items, including the little piano, were auctioned off. Becky Sharp attended the sale: when the instrument was knocked down for twenty-five guineas, she remarked that the price was "monstrous dear . . . We chose it at Broadwood's for Amelia when she came from school. It only cost five-and-thirty then." Alas, that was in Chapter 17; when the instrument appears again in Amelia's possession—far along in Chapter 58—we are told it is a Stodart, not a Broadwood. Well, the most credible fictioneers may have their lapses, and anyway, maybe Becky was lying, as she often did.

Mr. Osborne, the father of Amelia's fiancé, is drawn as a plebeian of rude speech, who, however—as he admitted—had "by my own talents and genius," plus a little help from friends, acquired "that proud position, which, I may say, I occupy in the tallow trade and the City of London." "City," in the British language, means Wall Street. Osborne is a villainous character, so purple with money lust that he is nearly insensible to any but money values. He is merciless toward his financial inferiors and to those who have been defeated in the money game. By the same token, he is a repulsive bootlicker toward those richer than himself and, more especially, toward the peerage. He is, indeed, a vicious embodied caricature of the mainsprings of English social life. Old Osborne's house was in Russell Square; besides his son George, he had two daughters. They had invited Amelia for dinner one evening. After the repast "all made sail for the drawing room," George remaining behind; but Amelia hoped he would come soon. She occupied herself thus:

> . . . playing some of his favourite waltzes (then newly imported) at the great carved-legged, leather-cased grand piano in the drawing room overhead. The little artifice did not bring him. He was deaf to the waltzes, they grew fainter and fainter; the discomfited performer left the huge instrument presently. . . .

The fact is that old Osborne was beginning to develop a grudge against Amelia because her father was showing signs of financial failure. On the other hand, he began to look with favor upon a Miss Rhoda Swartz, a school acquaintance of his daughters; the girl was a West Indian mulatto, an orphan heiress to £200,000 worth of plantations in St. Kitts. George Osborne was an officer in the British Army; Napoleon had just landed from Elba, war was on, and the young man's regiment was to be ordered overseas any day. But papa Osborne actually suggested he ought to get out of the army and marry Miss Swartz, telling him he was a fool to go abroad when he could make £8000 a year by staying home. In pursuit of this design, the Osborne girls were persuaded to ask the swarthy Miss Swartz to dinner. She was a good-natured soul who had also been sent through the "accomplishment" mill, and she was glad to exhibit her genteel achievements to win George's favor.

> The girls would ask her, with the greatest gravity, for a little music, and she would sing her three songs and play her two little pieces as often as ever they asked, and with an always increasing pleasure to herself. During these delectable entertainments, Miss

Wirt and the chaperon sate by, and conned over the peerage, and talked about the nobility.

But George sulked through all this.

The sisters began to play the Battle of Prague. "Stop that d—— thing," George howled out in a fury from the sofa. "It makes me mad. *You* play us something, Miss Swartz, do. Sing something, anything but the Battle of Prague."

"Shall I sing Blue-Eyed Mary, or the air from the Cabinet?" Miss Swartz asked.

"That sweet thing from the Cabinet," the sisters said.

"We've had that," replied the misanthrope on the sofa.

"I can sing Fluvy du Tajy," Swartz said in a meek voice, "if I had the words." It was the last of the worthy young woman's collection.

"Oh, Fleuve du Tage," Miss Maria cried; "we have the song," and went to fetch the book in which it was.

For the unconcerned young lady of Longbourn to play accompaniments to her own singing of Scotch airs, pleasingly but not capitally; for a well-born, snobbish young lady of Highbury to play the little things that are generally acceptable; for a moderately genteel couple in the same village to have an instrument standing about unused; for the middle-aged Mrs. Weston, or Aunt Jane Austen, to play country dances so that the young people could dance; for well-bred girls to learn a little music and give it up after marriage; for a speculating stockbroker to display a piece of "state" furniture in his back drawing room and present a natty little square to his daughter for her to play waltzes in her room; for a blustering, vulgar tallow-merchant-turned-banker to have a huge article of carved and leather-covered house equipment so that his daughters could bang out *The Battle of Prague* or a bespangled West Indian heiress could show off her two little pieces and accompany herself to "Blue-Eyed Mary"—it was for all this, then—while Napoleon was coddling his carcinoma, while Beethoven was meditating his final sonatas—that the Stodart, the Clementi, and the Broadwood factories were chugging forth their two, their three, their five pianos a day.

19. ANTI-"ACCOMPLISHMENT"

THE AVERAGE docile, young, well-bred female blockhead was content enough to spend her time in indolence frosted over with "accomplishments"; women of superior mentality and enterprise, however, felt such a life to be humiliating. Several of these used their literary abilities to make protests against the prevailing customs.

One was Hannah More, the daughter of a schoolmaster. She had mingled in the literary life of London and had become acquainted with Edmund Burke, Horace Walpole, and Dr. Johnson; after several unsuccessful attempts at writing plays, she retired to the country—from where she gave forth well-phrased reflections on moral and religious themes.

Her parable *Two Wealthy Farmers, or the History of Mr. Bragwell,* appearing about 1800, was a tract aimed at the false conceptions of gentility inculcated in young females by the spirit of the times. Mrs. Bragwell is represented as a stupid, ambitious, rich, low-class woman who aims to set her two daughters above their neighbors by having them put through a fashionable education.

> When the mother found her girls were too polite to be of any use, she would take comfort in observing how her parlor was set out with their filigree and flowers, their embroidery and cut paper. They spent the morning in bed, the noon in dressing, the evening at the harpsichord, and the night in reading in novels.

The preface to Mrs. More's *Strictures on the Modern System of Female Education* is dated March 14, 1799. In this work the author addresses herself more specifically to music.

> The science of music, which used to be communicated in so competent a degree to a young lady by one able instructor, is now distributed among a whole band. She now requires, not a master, but an orchestra. And my country readers would accuse me of exaggeration, were I to hazard enumerating the variety of musical teachers who attend at the same time in the same family; the daughters of which are summoned by at least as many instruments as the subjects of Nebuchadnezzar, to worship the idol which fashion has set up.

We will certainly accuse Mrs. More of some exaggeration, since we can think only of the voice, the piano, the harp, and possibly the guitar. Still, we apprehend her gist.

The difficulty of playing the piano well was much emphasized by teachers, of course, and the new rich seemed to have embraced the stimulating idea that a person of small gifts could nevertheless achieve substantial proficiency by a lot of brute "practice." In a footnote, Mrs. More tells of a "person of great eminence" who calculated the amount of time spent by a girl in piano practice "in one instance." The poor child began at the age of six and practiced four hours daily, omitting Sundays, all the year round (except on thirteen days when she was traveling); thus, by the time she was eighteen she had given no less than 14,400 hours of her life to playing scales. The pith of the story lay in the fact that eventually she married a man who disliked music! But Mrs. More found an even greater absurdity in contemplating this girl as the victim of a system which, regardless of aptitude, "erected the whole sex into artists."

Maria Edgeworth, whose writings were much read and admired during the nineteenth century, published her *Practical Education* as early as 1798; its Chapter 20 in Volume III is entitled: "On Female Accomplishments, Masters, and Governesses." She shares Hannah More's disapprovals, but expresses herself a little more mildly. In an imagined conversation, she addresses herself to a fashionable lady:

> "Would not you, as a good mother, consent to have your daughter turned into an automaton for eight hours in every day for fifteen years, for the promise of hearing her, at the end of that time, pronounced the first private performer at the most fashionable and the most crowded concert in London?"
>
> "For *one* concert," says the hesitating mother, "I think it would be too high a price. Yet I would give anything to have my daughter play better than any one in England. What a distinction! She might get into the first circles in London! She would want neither beauty nor fortune to recommend her! She would be a match for any man who had a taste for music . . ."

Eight hours a day for fifteen years, to be a good pianist!! The masters certainly were successful in cracking up the marvels of their craft. The hypothetical lady of fashion continues: "And music is universally admired, even by those who have the misfortune to have no taste for it . . ." Valuable admiration, in such a case. She goes on:

"Besides, it is such an elegant accomplishment in itself! Such a constant source of innocent amusement! Putting everything else out of the question, I should wish my daughter to have every possible accomplishment; because accomplishments are such charming *resources* for young women, they keep them out of harm's way, they make a vast deal of their idle time pass so pleasantly to themselves and others! This is my *chief* reason for liking them."

Again, the "innocence" and "harmlessness" of music.

"Accomplishments" are a ticket of gentility; but the worry does not stop there, for gentility is relative and competitive. They become a kind of game.

> It is admitted in the cabinet council of mothers, that some share of the value of accomplishments depends upon the demand for them in the fashionable world. "A young lady," they say, "is nobody, and nothing, without accomplishments; they are as necessary to her as a fortune; they are indeed considered as part of her fortune, and sometimes are even found to supply the place of it. Next to beauty, they are the best tickets of admission into society which she can produce; and everybody knows, that on the company she keeps depends the chance of a young woman's settling advantageously in the world."

Miss Edgeworth proceeds to analyze the situation still further, with clear penetration:

> Every young lady (and every young woman is now a lady) has some pretensions to accomplishments. She draws a little; or she plays a little; or she speaks French a little . . .

Any innkeeper's daughter can do all this, she says; but she continues:

> Now it is the practice in high life to undervalue and avoid as much as possible everything which descends to the inferior classes of society. . . . accomplishments have lost much of that value which they acquired from opinion since they have become common. They are now so common, that they cannot be considered as the distinguishing characteristics of even a gentlewoman's education. The higher classes in life, and those individuals who aim at distinction, now establish another species of monopoly, and secure to themselves a certain set of expensive masters in music, drawing, dancing, etc. They endeavor to believe, and to make others believe, that no one

can be well educated without having served an apprenticeship of so many lessons under some of these privileged masters. But it is in vain that they entrench themselves, they are pursued by the intrusive vulgar. In a wealthy mercantile nation there is nothing which can be bought for money, that will long continue to be an envied distinction.

Miss Edgeworth might have been interested to learn that—what with the growth of population and the spread of West European habits over other parts of the world—feminine "accomplishments," especially an ability to play the piano a little, politely, survived well into the twentieth century.

20. LATER LONDON PIANISTS AND THEIR ADVENTURES

THE NUMBER of high-caliber artist-pianists living, playing, teaching, and composing in London during the last years of the eighteenth century diminished after the new century was fairly launched: Clementi retired from the active profession; Field and Dussek left the country; Steibelt left for good, after some goings and returnings. Wölfl's career was short; he died in 1812. Cramer alone remained. He was much liked; they called him "glorious John"; ladies enjoyed his lessons, even though he often spilled snuff over their drawing-room floors and though his long, legato-potent fingers, with their well-shaped nails, were much stained with the filthy stuff.

Interest in concerts had declined since the flurry of the days of Haydn and Salomon. However, the year 1813 marked a return of activity; that was when a group of London's leading musicians formed the Philharmonic Society to replace the former Professional Concerts and Salomon Concerts. The Society was efficiently, co-operatively organized; it was a well-built igloo within which true music lovers, that devoted little band, could comfort themselves with each others' warmth. For a long time it was the focus of all that was best in instrumental music in England.

The formation of the Philharmonic Society nearly coincided with a transfusion of good, fresh pianistic blood when Ferdinand

Ries came to make London his home. He was an old family friend and pupil of Beethoven's, a solid—if not spectacular or inspired—player and composer.

Another, more powerful injection was given when a more elegant pianist followed Ries a year or two later: Friedrich Kalkbrenner. German-born, largely Paris-educated, who evidently had many personal attractions in addition to being an excellent performer. He had been accustomed to "good society" from his early days, his learned father having been on good terms with the Elector of Hesse-Cassel. Young Friedrich was one of the earliest, youngest graduates of the newly founded Paris Conservatoire; he received one of those famous "first prizes" there as early as 1800, when he was a mere twelve. The piano, however, did not have his undivided devotion; on the contrary, he became fired with military ambition. Besides the piano, the youth labored with more gentlemanly implements, such as swords, horses, and lances. In fact, he was all set to become an aide-de-camp to a certain General F. (our unidentified informant of the London *Quarterly Musical Magazine* did not reveal the full name) just before the campaign of 1807–8. He was only nineteen, so that his sedentary-minded father was still able to frustrate this plan. In any case, the young man's exercises undoubtedly had their beneficial effect upon his bearing and manners. Subsequently, after the old man's death, Friedrich was reported to have been captured by a mysterious, discreetly anonymous lady, probably of means, who held him for a time in a country retreat in the attempt to build him into a rural *seigneur*. It was from that Venusberg that Friedrich escaped to England.

There he first turned up in Bath, where he played in a concert. At the time, that place was one of England's few "resorts," as we now call them; during its "season" it was teeming with high gentry and some not quite so high. It is easy to understand how the fashionable Bath bathers, gamblers, *flâneurs,* and intriguers would have liked the young near-army-officer-almost-turned-country-gentleman even if he had not played half so well. "The success was complete; he was rapturously applauded and caressed by all, and returned to London amply supplied with connections to commence his career in the metropolis." So says our eulogy on Kalkbrenner published in the *Quarterly Musical Magazine and Review* a number of years later. The article tells about the pianist's later successes, his tour through Ireland and Scotland. He played in Dublin at the Rotunda, we are told, and "families of the first consequence came thirty or forty miles from the country to be present at the occasion," continues the *Quarterly* with unaffected snobbery. In

Edinburgh, between eight and nine hundred people came to his concert, a notably large attendance in those days (1822).

We last caught sight of young Ignaz Moscheles riding his variations on the *Alexander* March at the Congress of Vienna, with all the Allied princes looking on admiringly. The Countess Hardegg was so delighted with him that she collected for him the basic ingredients of a European tour—namely, a large packet of letters of recommendation to all manner of dukes, diplomats, and high financiers in various places. Moscheles justified these friendly intimations by his pleasant, modest demeanor, as well as by his crisp runs and chords, his tricky skips and startling repeated notes, his *Alexander* March variations, his variations on *"Au clair de la lune,"* and his excellent G minor Concerto. For six or eight years he traveled, playing in concerts and at private gatherings: at the Dresden and Munich courts; at the Leipzig *Gewandhaus;* in Paris at the homes of the Princess Vaudemont, the Marquise de Montgerault, and Monsieur de Chateaubriand; and also with the London Philharmonic.

In December 1823 he was back in Vienna; he must have been lucky enough to catch Beethoven in a relaxed mood, for the great composer gave him permission to use his precious Broadwood in a concert. The deaf master had beaten it up pretty thoroughly in the five years he had had it; still it was put into some kind of usable shape for the performance. The concert had a certain historical significance, for—along with the Broadwood—Moscheles also used a Viennese instrument by Graf, playing both alternately. It was a fine opportunity to contrast the effect of the heavier English pilot, or pushing, action with that of the light Vienna bouncing action. "I tried," said Moscheles, "in my Fantasia to show the value of the broad, full, though somewhat muffled tone of the Broadwood piano, but in vain. My Vienna public remained loyal to their countryman—the clear, ringing tones of the Graf were more pleasing to their ears."

Moscheles was most successful in his English appearances—so much so that in 1826 he decided to make London his home. He had recently married Charlotte van Embden; his bride was related to a certain family of Paris bankers of Jewish origin. He had already played at *soirées* at the home of James Rothschild there; thus, we are not astonished to find him in the house of brother Nathan Rothschild in London.

Nathan was the third eldest, and probably the ablest, of the five fabulous Frankfurters who were to build up Europe's greatest financial power during the nineteenth century. He had come to

England as early as 1798, not knowing a word of English, but bringing a capital of £20,000, which he soon expanded in regular, but bold, ingenious commercial ways. His more distinctive career and more impressive financial rise, however, came by his ability—through his family connections on the Continent—to facilitate the transfer of money subsidies from the British government both to its own armies in Spain and to numerous Continental governments and princes who were helping to fight Napoleon. All this had brought Nathan Rothschild into close touch with powerful persons high in British government circles. The Rothschilds were all made Imperial Austrian barons in 1817. Nathan had long been naturalized, if imperfectly assimilated, in England; certain sections of high society were interested in being on good terms with him and were glad to be guests at his glittering parties.

We hear, for example, of a grand *soirée* given by the Nathan Rothschilds on July 11, 1821, at their country home at Stamford Hill, for all the foreign ministers then present in England on the occasion of the approaching coronation of George IV. Expensive music was clearly a suitable embellishment to this gathering, and we learn that Moscheles, together with a number of opera singers, helped to supply it. By 1829, after Moscheles had established his permanent residence in London, Madame de Rothschild made him the steward of her musical ostentations—she let him select the artists, make the programs, and arrange the fees. He noted down some of the payments he made on her behalf: to Madame Stockhausen, an esteemed singer, £35 for two evenings; to De Beriot, the well-known violinist, a mere £5 for one evening; to Benedetta Pisaroni, leading Italian contralto, £20 for one appearance; to the attractive soprano Claudina de Begnis, £25 for two; and to himself, £40 for two concerts. It is interesting that he paid himself at the highest rate of all. The fees seem low for present-day notions, yet Moscheles remarked on how high they were in comparison to German standards of the time.

Moscheles' high-society associations naturally gave him a correspondingly high standing in the world of musical fashion; for some time, publishers had been glad to pay for the right to print his name on the title pages of easily digestible, salable compositions, such as variations and medleys. He speaks of them as "fugitive pieces"; after establishing his regular Rothschild connection, he records that he has raised his price for composing them to thirty guineas each. He, of course, taught busily, often giving nine lessons a day. In 1833 he put down in his diary that he had given 1457 lessons during the year, of which 129 were gratis. By that time a guinea a lesson had become something of a standard fee for a first-rate fashionable music master; we know that Moscheles got it: it would have been beneath his dignity to take less. Thus, we can calculate his income for that year at more than £1300 from teaching alone. During January 1828, while spending a few weeks in Edinburgh giving concerts, he was besieged by demands for instruction. "Some ladies," he said, "are bent on galloping through my compositions with me at their side, no matter how difficult the music is, or how short the time"; and, in fact, a double fee—that is, two guineas a time—did not hold them back.

Moscheles refers a number of times to his daily stint of nine lessons; but in the London of the 1820's and 30's it appears that guineas or not, the prominent fashionable, high-society piano teacher had no specially equipped professional workroom to which his clients might repair: he taught his pupils in their homes, walking from place to place. Setting up a studio separate from one's living quarters, and making one's pupils come to it, was an air not yet put on by an individual music master of the time, even though he was the reflectedly glorious music steward at the posh Rothschild affairs and was soon to become the official pianist to His Royal Highness Prince Albert. We might try to elucidate this waste of professional time on the supposition that respectable young girls were, in those days, reluctant to go out alone and that it was often inconvenient to have them convoyed. However, this explanation does not seem quite satisfactory; for in that case, the "academies" that we shall describe under a subsequent heading could not have functioned.

In the course of giving his lessons itinerantly, the inevitable slight was eventually to be offered Moscheles. In the house of a certain lord whose daughters he taught—he generously does not mention the name—the servants tried to show him up the back stairs (that is to say, the servants' and tradesmen's way). After several other rudenesses and a failure to pay his bill in full, Moscheles refused to continue. He was asked to call and state his reasons verbally; he did so, whereupon Lord and Lady X "overloaded" him "with civility" and he resumed the lessons. That a music teacher could assume himself a gentleman, and even act like one, was probably a fanciful, novel notion in the mind of the noble peer—though seemingly not an unacceptable one: it is a pleasure to think he was so educable. We feel sure, however, that his butler secretly despised him after his conversion.

As we have intimated, Moscheles was engaged to play a good deal at private parties. The rich and powerful evidently liked to include skilled musical performances by well-known artists at their ostentatious social meetings. It is curious that they should have wanted to do this, since in England only a tiny minority of persons at such gatherings had any interest in—or love for—music and since, therefore, general attention was hard to compel. Nothing would seem more inappropriate, one would think, than to hire strangers to thrust a refined music upon an arrogant crowd of persons who mostly either did not care for it, had no respect for it, or who were in no mood for its proper reception in any event. For the most part, the gesture was one of swank: a flourish to show one's power by ordering up something fine and costly in order to have it thrown away. At best, it might happen that female opera singers could arouse some masculine attention and some feminine interest in consequence. Moscheles played at a party given the day after the Reform Bill was passed, April 14, 1832; he does not say at what house. He was much interested in hearing the timely political discussion:

> . . . but alas! a great musical *soirée* followed, attended by the whole Tory party, the Duke of Wellington at the head. One cannot play one's best in the presence of these great men, who concentrate all their attention upon an Italian prima donna; it doesn't matter whether I or any other artist plays the piano, they don't care about it; their applause on these occasions, I regard as an expression of delight that they have got rid of me. My wife and I sacrifice as short a time as possible in such *soirées*, and hurry home again, as soon as good manners will allow us.

Through his wife's family connections, Moscheles may occasionally have been a bona fide dinner guest at the Rothschild's parties, and so at some others; but in general the performing musicians were in a rather ambiguous position when they came under "great" roofs. It does not appear that they were always expected to walk in the servants' entrance—nevertheless, they were clearly second-class guests, huddled off somewhere by themselves and expected to speak only when spoken to. Wilhelmine Schroeder-Devrient, the most eminent German opera singer of her time, was quoted as saying: "Oh! the horror of a stiff English *soirée*, where the ladies stare at me and quiz my behavior." A passage in *Vanity Fair* describes the life of Becky Sharp, now Mrs. Rawdon Crawley, when—through rather oblique circumstances—she has succeeded in squirming into the glitter of fashionable, exalted London society:

> Becky always made a point of being conspicuously polite to the professional ladies and gentlemen who attended at these aristocratic parties—of following them into the corners where they sate in silence, and shaking hands with them, and smiling in the view of all persons. She was an artist herself, as she said very truly: there was a frankness and humility in the manner in which she acknowledged her origin, which provoked, or disarmed, or amused lookers-on, as the case might be.

Moscheles was fundamentally a serious artist: his core was one of integrity, despite his occasional lenience toward "fugitive pieces"—which stood in amusing contrast to his stony rejection of truly interesting newer musical developments. He was an effective agent of musical idealism in England at a particularly difficult time. He was made a director of the Philharmonic Society; in 1837 he became, probably, the first person ever to play publicly an entire program of pianoforte music, without the collaboration of any other musicians: the first piano "recital," in other words—at least, the first in England.

Ries, Kalkbrenner, and Moscheles were glad to hold open their pockets and let easy excess English money drop into them; but they must often have felt frustrated and humiliated by the lack of sympathy that the English, on the whole, had for their artistic ideals. Each of them steadily contemplated his eventual departure. Ries returned to his native Rhineland after eleven years; by that time he had saved up enough sterling to be independent in a modest German way. Kalkbrenner gave up after ten years; Moscheles, after sticking it out for seventeen years, became deeply touched by the courtship of the newly formed Leipzig Conservatory of Music, which his old friend Felix Mendelssohn had just founded. It was a poor but honest suitor: three years later he left London for good, to become its director. Even "glorious John" Cramer, the all-but-native Englishman, found it more pleasant to spend most of his later years in Paris.

On January 1, 1823, there was brought out in London a new *Monthly Magazine of Music*. In it appeared a review of *Flow on thou shining River*—air with variations, "for 2 performers on the pianoforte," by Ferdinand Ries—which read as follows:

> Mr. Ries has been educated in the school of Beethoven, and like his gifted master, abandoned himself too much to the ambition of being *new;* hence it is that his pianoforte works, with all their accuracy, are sometimes deficient in elegance and grace; while, actu-

ated by this feeling, he forgets that the *ladies,* who constitute a majority of the patrons to whom he must appeal, are won by the most gentle and persuasive means, and turn with repugnance from mere judgment or ungarnished erudition. In studying to be *classical,* Mr. Ries has renounced the attributes of *fashion,* and been frequently mortified by seeing his austere and laborious effusions rejected for works of inferior skill, which came recommended, however, by traits of ease and animation, highly gratifying to the amateur.

Was this sarcasm, thus to reproach Ries for his seriousness? It would seem so, to judge from another review, a page or two later, of an *Austrian Melody with Variations* by Moscheles.

"Sonate, que me veux-tu" exclaimed Fontenelle, and we are tempted to bestow a similar apostrophe upon the fantasias and variations by which the reign of the sonata has been succeeded. Augmenting in number every day, not a theme is suffered to escape which offers the slightest appearance of a melody; it is seized upon with eagerness by composers of every description, and not an air from *"God Save the King"* down to the newest French quadrille can now aspire to be unvaried. We really entertain the agreeable hope of seeing Handel's mighty choruses put into variations by Messrs. K.L.M. etc. etc. nor would it surprise us if all the airs of Haydn's "Creation" were then submitted to a similar treatment. From what has this *furor mutandi* arisen? Or may it not be fairly traced to those musicians of the third and fourth classes in which London abounds? people who find it much easier to produce variations than compose a sonata, and whose efforts are highly acceptable to such amateurs as desire to be *showy,* without much expense of either time or trouble.

We appeal to professors in general, if an importunate mother does not address them, now and then, in something like the subsequent terms: "Sir, I shall have a few friends next week, who are *immensely* fond of music, and as my Anna Maria has now been learning of you for *more than three months,* I hope she will be able to play some showy piece—if only for three minutes—that's full of fine passages, with plenty of taste and expression; that last sweet thing of Kettledrum's, for instance, which has got a favorite air in it, and a waltz, and a march, and"—etc. etc. The unfortunate professor argues in vain against this silly scheme; if Miss is applying to the pianoforte, he proposes the "studies" of Cramer, and the fugues of Bach . . . as proper media for exhibiting his pupils' proficiency;

> but Mamma is obstinate; the *showy* thing of three minutes must be procured; the music seller is applied to for it: nor will he purchase anything different from what is so much desired; and hence we discover the principle on which most of our modern variations are published and encouraged.

The *Monthly Magazine of Music,* we regret to say, perished after this, its first issue.

21. "BRILLIANT BUT NOT DIFFICULT"

EARLY IN THE CENTURY we heard of ambitious parents urging their daughters to practice scales by the hour by the year, in order to become acceptable players. By 1827, however, soon after Moscheles moved to London, we find him complaining of "a certain class of pupils" for whom he has to confect his "fugitive pieces." "They shrink from all serious study," he charges; "occasionally a Mama says: 'Will you give her something with a pretty tune in it, brilliant but not difficult?' "

Brilliant but not difficult—it is fascinating to see how this phrase was repeated endlessly in the advertisements and reviews of printed pianoforte music. From the beginning of the nineteenth century until well into the twentieth, the chant droned on—with occasional inessential modifications—in Germany and France, England and the United States, in all the catalogues and music journals, and on the back of sheet music: "Brilliant but not difficult" was the music publishers' favorite blurb. The idea was expressed with particular grace in one of its earliest occurrences; a brief review of a set of variations on a theme by Pleyel composed by one Joseph D. Bayer appeared in the so-called *"Intelligenz-Blatt"* ("News Bulletin") of the *Allgemeine Musikalische Zeitung* of Leipzig on October 28, 1801:

> These variations will fulfill their purpose most surely in the hands of young pianists who would sometimes like to gleam in the tinsel of the art without having to wipe sweat from their brows.

Brilliant but not difficult—shortly after Moscheles made his notation, François Joseph Fétis, the eminent Belgian musical scholar, brought out in Paris an "educational" book called *Music within the Reach of All—By means of which anyone can be a judge of music and talk about it without having studied it.* About the same time, as we learn from Miss Rosamond Harding, pianos were being treated thus:

> The less costly pianofortes which constituted the bulk of those usually made had often ornaments which were a cheap imitation of those used on the pianofortes for the wealthy clients. Thus cast brass moulding sold by the foot and nailed around the instrument, stamped brass ornaments and sometimes cast lead ornaments painted and gilded to imitate brass, supplied the place of the finely chiselled work after the designs of artists which were used for the better class of instrument.

To seem skilled without work, to talk plausibly without knowledge, to own something precious-looking without expense—these all hang together: their purpose is to produce a showy effect at little cost. That is what people strove for in a money culture. The very rich, indeed, could acquire material objects, at least, that were truly costly; but it was the swarms of their less potent emulators and worshipers—unable to afford the real evidences of wealth and leisure—who liked to express their adoration of Mammon with something shiny and cheap that might seem like riches for an instant in the eyes of those still more naïve. Hordes of inferior people were continually anxious to get rid, quickly, of the more obvious stigmata of their inferiority. Plated silver, patent leather, mercerized cotton, mahogany finish—these were all brilliant but not difficult. Of similar implication were the numberless books of etiquette that the customers of those articles also bought: read the ten easy chapters and then you, too, may pretend more plausibly to be a gentleman or a lady.

Brilliant but not difficult. Winged words—they could be the slogan of the nineteenth century.

22. BOARDING SCHOOL MUSIC; LOGIER AND HIS CHIROPLAST

People who teach music, like other people, tend to behave appropriately to the manner in which they are treated and to what is expected of them. There were always some few, in Regency England as well as in other times and places, whose devotion to music could not be swerved by any adversity or lack of sympathy. However, when what the teachers had to give was undervalued, or ignorantly overvalued, or ill understood, it was inevitable that baser motives should taint their profession and that incompetent or fraudulent persons could thrive in it. We will call back Jane Austen; she wrote to sister Cassandra on December 2, 1815:

> Mr. Meyers gives his three Lessons a week—altering his days and his hours however just as he chuses, never very punctual, & never giving Good Measure. I have not Fanny's fondness for Masters, & Mr. Meyers does not give me any Longing after them. The truth is, I think, that they are all, at least Music Masters, made of too much consequence and allowed to take too many liberties with their Scholar's time.

The masters who lacked conscientiousness were certainly outnumbered by the governesses who lacked competence. Business and the professions were barred to women; to be a domestic teacher, a time-passer or mischief-preventer for other people's children, was the only gainful pursuit in which genteel young females of no fortune could engage without loss of respectability. Young girls who had taken some sort of lessons during their two or three years' passage through a boarding school thereupon shamelessly announced "music" as one of their qualifications when they applied for jobs—"situations," as they liked to prettify it; upon this foundation a great deal of pianoforte teaching was built!

We can imagine that at the boarding schools themselves, the music education was of a highly superficial kind. The prospectuses of some of the school-keepers announced that music instruction would be imparted "by the lady herself," or by her daughter or niece or apprentice. In any event, the cotton millionaires and other upstarts who were paying for this did not know enough about it to be discriminating. Many a school did, indeed, engage the services of a presumably competent music "master"; his maleness and his status as a visiting expert gave him a suggestion of a special importance and value, which was appositely expressed in money. We are told that some schools, later in the nineteenth century, announced: piano instruction—from a master, one guinea; by a lady, five shillings. The custom was that low-paid governesses supervised the pupils' daily practice, while the master came twice a week and heard them all in succession for a fifteen-minute period each. In any case, the music fee was not part of the school tuition: it was an "extra." We have some evidence that, earlier in the century, masters on the average received less than a guinea a lesson from the schools; it was nearer something like ten guineas per annum for two quarter-hour lessons—or one half-hour lesson —per week. Figuring forty weeks in the school year, that would come to twenty hours for ten guineas—or ten shillings sixpence per hour.

Appointments at well-to-do boarding schools apparently were much desired by pianoforte teachers; it was, for them, a convenient way of acquiring a compact block of pupils—an easily filled quantity order. A correspondent to the *Quarterly Musical Magazine and Review,* signing himself "The Father of a Family," wrote on May, 13, 1824, complaining of the commercialization of the boarding schools:

> . . . when a music master is to be engaged, the question with these *tradespeople* is—not his ability to teach the children committed to their care, but his willingness to make them a *handsome allowance* from the sum paid by the parents of those children. Accordingly five and twenty, thirty, and even fifty per cent. deduction is occasionally claimed and allowed—but by whom? Certainly not by the man who is conscious of his talent, but by the driveller who is conscious of possessing no talent at all, and who is glad to *purchase* employment which he cannot hope to obtain or to secure by any other means.

So the boarding school positions were worth a substantial "kickback," as we vulgar Americans say, to the musicians.

By 1815 the domination of business interests and the Industrial Revolution, with its inherent large-scale production of goods, were in full swing. Quantity business is a principle not readily adapted to pianoforte teaching, yet it was inevitable in those years that someone would develop such an idea as far as it might go. There were now tens and hundreds of thousands of aspiring, pretending, ignorant, well-to-do English families, begetting multitudes of female fry—all potential pianoforte pupils. Most teachers, hoping to live off them, went after them with a hook and line, one by one, in time-honored fashion; but inevitably a clever fellow came along who felt that the abundance of the run warranted his securing a more profitable haul by using a net, as well as some special, shiny bait.

His name was John Bernard Logier; a native of Alsace, he had come to Ireland as a wind-instrument player in a military band and seems to have lived in Dublin for a good many years. Logier was a musician of sorts, and we are pretty sure that he could play the piano to some extent. In 1813 he came in with his thunder—a few beats ahead of Beethoven—when he put out a piece on *The Battle of Vittoria,* which was played as early as July 23 of that year at the Dublin Rotunda, in full orchestral panoply, by "upwards of 150 performers." So says the first title page. The second title page, which indicates that the piece is published for the pianoforte, informs us that Mr. Logier had a "Music Saloon" at 27 Lower Sackville Street in the same city.

Logier reflected that an ordinary piano teacher, giving his girls two weekly hour lessons, could finish off about twenty-four pupils a week if he worked eight hours every day. At a guinea a lesson, that might gross him a substantial income—but very, very few teachers could get such a fee, especially outside of London. Most of them would be unlikely to get half that sum; and few, even at that rate, could acquire a sufficiently large clientele to keep them so perpetually busy. But what if a way could be found to teach whole groups of pupils: six, eight, ten, or more, at one and the same time? A teacher might then handle hundreds in a week and could take in a greatly increased amount of money even if he reduced his fee. Teaching young piano pupils in simultaneously meeting groups might strike some parents as a rather chaotic, insulting idea: the problem was, then, to dress up the scheme so that it appeared remarkable, new, keen, fascinating, and desirable.

He accomplished this by a combination of features. It was true that, for generations, ordinary music teaching had degenerated into little else than the inculcation of a number of manual coordinations; the average young lady learning the piano was rarely harassed with such fundamental principles as those of scale formation, harmony, counterpoint, or composition. Logier now proposed to teach some of these basic notions of musical grammar and syntax—long learned by every serious music student as a matter of elementary decency—to his young girl charges as if they were a new revelation. His prospectus implied that he had some secret, whereby he had "removed the *tremendous* barriers which have hitherto stood in the way of *general* pupils procuring a scientific knowledge of music"; that he "alone has succeeded in rendering the *complete possession* of a skill in music an advantage to which almost anyone may aspire"; and—now comes the joker—"that pupils of *ordinary capacity* and *ordinary industry*" can be rendered "capable of emulating Corelli, Handel, Haydn, and Mozart!"

Logier's "academies" taught his pupils in groups of twenty, in two-hour sessions. Each class was divided in half, ten pupils devoting an hour to harmony while the other ten were receiving "individual lessons"—as he called them—on the pianoforte; for the second hour, the pupils changed places, exchanging their harmony for the pianoforte and vice versa. Just what these "individual lessons" amounted to is hard to imagine; it seems that assistant instructors were engaged and that one pupil might possibly have been fortunate enough to snatch as much as eighteen minutes of such an assistant's undivided attention. Otherwise, the children were taught "in concert"—that is, by playing on four, six, or ten pianos at a time. For that purpose, Logier composed certain exercises containing very easy parts together with more difficult ones; apparently they consisted of simple themes with numbers of simultaneous variations. Obtaining suitable multiple-piano material later became one of Logier's problems.

Logier charged his pupils five guineas a quarter, or twenty guineas a year, for their two-hour sessions twice a week. With four such sessions a day, he could work in twelve such groups every six days—in other words, 240 different pupils a week. This would give him a greatest possible revenue of 4800 guineas—or £5040—a year, to which he could add the 1½ guineas "entrance fee" that he exacted from each applicant—that is, £378 more. This theoretical yield would amount to more than $26,000 in our money, quite a neat take, by early-nineteenth-century standards; it would enable him to pay five assistants a generous annual £200, take care of his rent and the amortization of his instruments, as well as provide for a secretary—and still leave him a very satisfactory profit. On the other hand, the pupils received fifty-two hours of some kind of instruction per quarter at the rate of a mere two shillings an hour, a very low fee indeed.

As we see, Logier built his kite pretty firmly; all it needed was some snake oil to make it fly. This he supplied in the shape of the "Chiroplast." It was a gadget of his invention that boasted its status as a magniloquent Royal Patent and was made up of three or four elements; it consisted, in Logier's own words, of:

> [the] *Gamut Board* . . . an oblong board, which on the one side has, drawn upon it, two staves of five lines each, one for the treble, the other for the bass, containing all the notes used in music, so written that when placed over the keys of a Piano Forte, fronting the performer, each note, with its name, will be exactly over its corresponding key.

So the little imbeciles, instead of being encouraged to learn their keyboard, were to rely on having it perpetually labeled. Then came another element:

> [the] *Position Frame,* which consists of two parallel rails, extending from one extremity of the keys to the other; to the ends of these are fixed two cheek pieces, which, by means of a brass rod and extending screw, are attached firmly to the instrument. . . . The rails must be adjusted by means of the screws . . . in the cheek pieces . . . so as to admit the hands of the pupil passing between them nearly as far as the wrists; being so regulated as to prevent any perpendicular motion of the hands, though sufficiently wide to allow a free horizontal movement when required.

The unoffending pupil, after thus having her young forearms clamped between two sticks of wood, was then subjected to:

> [the] *Finger Guides* . . . two moveable brass plates with five divisions through which the thumb and four fingers are introduced. These divisions correspond perpendicularly with the keys of the instrument, and may be moved to any situation by means of the brass rod, on which they are made to slide . . .

It makes one think of brass knuckles, somehow. As if this rack were not sufficiently confining, the invention was further provided with:

> [the] *Wrist Guide* . . . a brass wire, with a regulator attached to each finger guide, to prevent the wrists from being inclined outwards.

Good hand and finger position is, of course, important in developing efficient piano playing; perhaps some teachers sincerely thought it worth while to compel it, even by means of a metallic instrument of torture. Furthermore, many people's sin-consciousness convinced them that anything unpleasant must be "good for you." However it may be, Logier extracted some impressive testimonials for his infernal machine; for example:

> I have examined your new invention, called the Patent Chiroplast . . . and am so well persuaded of its great utility, that I cannot but give it the warmest approbation and recommendation. I am etc.
>
> MUZIO CLEMENTI.
>
> Aug. 19, 1814.

A curious clue to the relevance of this recommendation might be seen in the final statement of the descriptive brochure from which we have quoted:

> The apparatus is manufactured by Messrs. Clementi & Co., Cheapside, London; and may be had of all the principal Music Sellers in the United Kingdom. Price, with the Instruction Book, 5 Guineas.

It is possible, however, that Clementi's approval was partly disinterested; for we find "glorious John" Cramer, who can have had no ulterior motives, also appending his signed tribute to the chiroplast.

Logier put on public demonstrations—"examinations," he called them—of his methods; simple-minded mammas were much impressed by hearing their darlings answer questions about abstruse, myterious words such as "chromatic," "diatonic," or "enharmonic." They were likewise impressed with that blessed word "Chiroplast" and with the magic of its machinery. One can hardly blame them: only a short while before, "Animal Magnetism" had had its high-class adherents and someone had sold the exalted George Washington a pair of metallic "electric tractors" for the cure of all the diseases.

Logier claimed that with the aid of his machine "a pupil may play *without knowing a note of music* by merely observing the finger marks." Surely, brilliant but not difficult. His pianoforte demonstrations were made "in concert," at six or eight or ten instruments simultaneously, and he showed the "rapid advancement" of those who had taken lessons for from three weeks to four months by having the tender beginners—their fingers fastened in the Chiroplast—play a few selected notes while the more advanced players carried on the composition's essential melody and harmony. If fond relatives cared to imagine an exaggerated contribution to this ensemble on the part of their own pianistic toddlers, so much the better.

We must not get a false picture of Mr. Logier. As an inspired individual, he would not waste much of his time actually teaching pupils himself. He was the prophet of a new "system," and his chief aim was to secure adherents and apostles among other teachers. His "system," as we have so unfeelingly dissected it, was mostly elementary arithmetic; nevertheless, he insisted on claiming it to be an arcane secret—a secret that, however, he was willing to communicate to other, interested, teachers, for the sum of one hundred guineas, on condition that they, too, keep the "secret" to themselves. We are rather astonished, under the circumstances, to find no evidence that the adherent teachers were required to pay the prophet an annual rake-off; perhaps the royalties from the sale and rental of Chiroplasts made this superfluous. As one of the "system's" critics said: "those who reject such a system of musical education must be influenced by some other motive than that of self-interest."

Logier furthered his cause by certain kinds of assault upon the defenseless mind that many Europeans, in their ignorant malice, like to stigmatize as "American." For instance, he had stationery printed calling his Dublin place of business "Chiroplast Hall." He also organized a "Chiroplast Club" there, whose members are said to have worn a distinctive costume; its coat seems to have been fastened by buttons bearing an emblematic embossing: it was a crown, probably symbolizing the Royal Patent, and under it were the figure 3 5 8, no doubt indicating the intervals of the tonic triad, and also a scroll with two scales. At this point, however, Mr. Logier exposed the hole in his stocking, for he made the bass clef of the emblem curve around the third line instead of the fourth. Later events proved that he did not know any better.

The Chiroplast was ready by 1814, and Logier probably spent the next two or three years multiplying his "academies" in Dublin. By April 1817 he had invaded Edinburgh with some success. His goal, naturally, was London—with its vast shoals of succulent suckers. He arrived there later the same year, but the leading London music professors were laying for him, as the saying goes. They appeared in a considerable body at the "examination" of the pupils of his exponent Mr. Samuel Webbe on November 17 and proceeded to ask some sharp questions. The group included a number of redoubtable musicians, members of the Philharmonic Society, not all of them pianists: Henry Bishop, Dr. Crotch,

Charles Neate, Ferdinand Ries, Sir George Smart, J. B. Cramer, and many others. Most of them were unfavorably impressed, and a committee of them published a pamphlet expressing their disapproval and practically calling Logier a faker. Logier then put forth a retaliating pamphlet: a minuscule war was on. It is to the literate debris of the encounter that we owe most of our present information about it.

Despite opposition, the "system" gained ground. The dapper Kalkbrenner decided to climb on the Logier wagon and opened an "academy" jointly with Webbe at Bedford Place, Russell Square, even though he was aware of one of the Chiroplast's most absurd shortcomings: namely that since it imprisoned all the fingers, it rendered it impossible to pass under the thumb—thus making it useless for playing the simplest scale. Still, Kalkbrenner's conversion probably had certain remote consequences, which we shall point out later.

In 1818 Logier boasted twenty-eight "academies" operating under his "system" in various parts of Great Britain and Ireland. By the middle of the following year they had increased to eighty-two; indeed, by then the "system" and the Chiroplast had crossed two oceans: there was one Logier exponent each in New York and Philadelphia, as well as one in Calcutta. That meant a minimum revenue of 8200 guineas, more than $41,000, for the prophet, not counting the royalties from nearly a thousand Chiroplasts.

Still, at the height of success, the concealed worm in the bud had already been active. The novelty of the "system" began to wear off, and certain difficulties appeared, such as the shortness of the fashionable London "season" in comparison with the expense of keeping an "academy" open all year round. Logier's good angel, however, was still looking out for him: he was "called" by Baron Altenstein, Minister of Public Education in Prussia, to promulgate his wisdom in that country. He started his trial run in Berlin with sixteen pupils in September 1822; five months later he held a satisfactory "examination" before a number of dignitaries. The spectacle of sixteen youngsters all playing pianos together in time, almost like an infantry formation, was evidently so intoxicatingly delightful to a Prussian official that he could not fail to consider it the rightest of things. Logier received a contract for two and a half years; he was to begin by indoctrinating eighteen German teachers with his "system," at 150 thalers a man. This was pretty poor emolument for a man accustomed to golden guineas, yet perhaps he thought it had prestige value.

The speculation did not pan out: the British "academies" faded perceptibly after the hypnotic Logier's departure for Germany. Among others, Kalkbrenner deserted the "system"; in fact, he deserted London, returning to inhale the more genial, congenial air of Paris. No brilliant future awaited the Prussian experiment. Piano teaching everywhere soon slid back into its old ruts. The Chiroplast, however, continued to fascinate some people: fifty years after its highest rise, rusty old machines could occasionally still be seen in secondhand shops—so Sir George Grove said. Furthermore, it had derivatives. Logier lived on until 1846.

23. IRON ENTERS THE PIANOFORTE

THE GRAND PIANO that Broadwood & Sons sent to Beethoven in December 1817 as yet had no metal in its frame; but three or four years later we note that the English pianoforte, as a species, began to grow an iron skeleton around its wooden entrails.

There were several reasons why metal began to seem a desirable and necessary element of pianoforte construction. For one thing, it seemed to offer a solution to the problem of keeping an instrument in tune throughout the caprices of temperature change. Two men in Stodart's factory thought up a scheme whereby a set of metal tubes was made to bear on metal plates resting on the rear surface of the soundboard, brass tubes over brass strings, steel over steel. The tubes and plates expanded and contracted with the temperature as did the strings, and it was expected that they would carry the soundboard with them in their movement—thus compensating for the accompanying changes of tension.

Keeping the piano in firmer tune, however, proved to be one of the lesser considerations. The instrument's "additional keys" in the treble had added greatly to the strain on both the case and the soundboard. Furthermore, it appears that musicians felt impelled, during the earlier years of the nineteenth century, to raise the basic pitch of all music. Mozart's A is said to have been equated to 421 vibrations per second; but by 1828 the London Philharmonic Society was setting A at 435. The reed-instrument players of the time, so it is said, preferred the higher, more brilliant tuning and thus influenced the orchestras; the pianoforte had, perforce, to trail along with this trend, at least in public concerts. In any case, the higher tuning put additional strain on the instrument's frame.

There was another cause—the most important of all—which, from the 1820's on, made for the necessity of putting greater tension on pianoforte strings: that was the craving for a greater range of expression in the instrument, one more appropriate to the projection of its music into larger rooms and to more numerous and more distant groups of people. The expression could only come, fundamentally, from the musculature of a player; the problem consisted in strengthening the instrument so that its parts would respond to more forceful muscular impacts by emitting a greater volume of sound, without crumpling or breaking. More tone required heavier hammer heads hitting harder on the strings; strings then had to be thicker and heavier to take the blows; but these then, in turn, required tighter stretching. The entire system of higher tuned, harder hit, heavier, thicker, tighter strings had to have greater ultimate support to withstand all this stress and strain; the ordinary wooden soundboard and case could not take it without cracking or buckling: that was where the iron came in.

During the earlier 1800's several attempts were made to provide grand pianos with solid iron resistance bars, parallel and superior to the strings, screwed into the wrest plank (tuning pin block) in front, their ends extending to the rear of the soundboard. By 1821 the Broadwood firm were using three to five such bars on their grands. The following year Broadwood fixed a solid metal plate over the further end of the soundboard, right against the wall of the case; the plate contained the hitch pins—that is, the distal attachments for the strings—and it also formed the support for the resistance bars. All this increased tension, which was now supported by the bars and the plate, tended to loosen the wrest (tuning) pins in their sockets; metal strengthening of the wrest plank became the next obvious demand. Solid metal wrest planks were devised, but they had disadvantages. The final solution was a pin block made of wood with a metal covering. There was one further important stress to which piano strings were subjected: that was the tendency of the upstriking hammers to bend the strings upward and away from the bridges on which they are supposed to rest. This problem of rigidity, which was suitably dealt with later, we shall discuss in due course.

On May 9, 1822, Moscheles participated in "glorious John"

Cramer's annual London concert; for the occasion he composed a two-piano piece later to become well known under the name of *Hommage à Handel.* Both artists played on Broadwood instruments—Cramer, as usual; but Moscheles, only for this evening. Moscheles, in describing the event, stated:

> The strong metal plates used by Broadwood in building his instruments, give a heaviness to the touch, but a fullness and vocal resonance to the tone, which are well adapted to Cramer's legato, and those fingers softly gliding from key to key. I, however, use Clementi's more supple mechanism for my repeating notes, skips and full chords.

The remark helps us to date the effective employment of the metal plate in pianofortes, shows us that its use was not as yet general, and gives us an idea of the kind of tone quality it aided in producing.

Making the pianoforte responsive to the full strength of the human arms and fingers was a long process; its complete realization took nearly half a century. Meanwhile, the larger-sized instruments were becoming more and more massive; from now on we hear less of polite young men tilting them in order to put leveling wads of paper under their legs.

The English makers were the first to adopt metal bars and plates, but the French and Austrian factories were not far behind. The Americans, new at the game, nevertheless began to show especial inventive enterprise in this phase of piano construction, as we shall see.

Iron in the piano rhymed with its time. There had long been a prejudice against the use of metal in indoor musical instruments; people may have said it spoiled the tone—but probably they imagined that, without ever having tried it out. Metal, especially iron, was thought of as something inhuman, black, and dead—in fact, deadly—something from which to fashion swords and cannon, something ghostly cold or hellish hot, useful for certain severe purposes but incompatible with the gentle, generous feelings associated with music. Trumpets were brass, it is true. But those too were linked with harsh military behavior; their tone was intended to be rough and loud and to be heard outdoors; besides, they were at least pretty when shined up. In the days of the steam engine, however, the idea of iron, in itself, could begin to seem attractive. It became associated with wealth-producing machinery, with the thrill of rapid transportation and of scientific discovery. In 1750 "iron" was a word of terror, having to do with unpleasant violence far removed from music; by 1820 "iron" had something to do with the agreeable notions of money making and of "progress." People now could look on it with some kindness, even in drawing rooms.

SECTION

FOUR

France

1. THE GREAT MONARCH, MUSIC, AND THE MYTH OF PARIS

IN REGARD to its valuation of music, France may be placed midway between Germany and post-seventeenth-century England. The businesslike point of view according to which the practice of music is a waste of golden time and a lure toward low company was widely held in France; nevertheless, it never became dominant there, never became the unassailably correct notion that it did in England. Among many groups of French social leaders, music remained a respectable form of activity whose sensuality did not necessarily render it trivial. On the other hand, music in France never called forth the mystical devotion, the idealism, that it aroused in influential German circles: participation in the finest music could be admired by the French as an Epicurean achievement, as a feat of taste; but it could never become there, as it did in Germany, the service of an ineffable divinity.

Earlier in the seventeenth century France had become continental Europe's largest, strongest, and richest unencumbered monarchy; and it was Louis XIV who riveted its centralization ever more firmly in the region of Paris and who caused its unrivaled power to be decorated with an unprecedented glitter. Provincial lords were made to spend much of their time in the capital so as to revolve about him more closely, and the most exquisite artists and artisans, writers and thinkers were summoned or attracted there to magnify him. The reflection of his glory exalted them; but they, in their turn, transmitted their eminence magically to Paris, his residence. In the Western world's mind, Paris became thenceforth the font of all that was excellent in the arts and the crafts: when centuries later people flocked there from Seattle and Saloniki to buy fine clothes, perfumes, upholstery, or liqueurs, they were—in their way—still chasing the luminous tail of the Sun King's ghost. On such a principle, the myth of Paris could be stretched to cover music: the musical habits of the glamorous place could also seem proper to imitate. Paris often proved, indeed, to be very hospitable to foreign music; and this very acceptance, during many centuries, was then seen as a supreme mark of worth by the fond eyes of an abject world.

Louis XIV was actively interested in music; he kept a large, choice musical establishment: he had his opera, his chamber music, and his special platoon of twenty-four violins. He knew how, judiciously, to order a talented youngster to take up an instrument of his royal choice and how to make a composer alter the plan of a work to its advantage. His taste was so good that there is no record of any attempt on his part to play or to command performances of his compositions. Nor did he spare expense: it is recorded that one concert in his St. Germain palace cost 2766 livres (a livre was very little more than a franc); that sum included the musicians' overtime, their board, their twenty-two miles of round trip from Paris, as well as transportation of "the King's great harpsichord."

In Europe, papa is always right; by doing as he does—at a respectful distance—one can be sure of being right oneself. French grandees less than royal also kept musicians; still lesser gentry hired them more modestly, for fixed regular occasions, to perform at their residences. In those days music was a sort of compulsory luxury for people of quality. By the third quarter of the seventeenth century, it appears that rich burghers also became swelled with the desire of aping the gentry. Molière's celebrated *Le Bourgeois Gentilhomme* dates from 1670. (An English version called *The Citizen turn'd Gentleman* appeared in London two years later.) Its rich, ridiculous Monsieur Jourdain is the son of a dry-goods merchant; he engages a dancing master, a fencing master, and a master of philosophy—all to help make a gentleman out of him in his mature years; likewise, a music master. This last instructor tells him:

> "A person like you, who is magnificent and who has an inclination for beautiful things, must have a musical concert at his home every Wednesday or every Thursday."
>
> "Do the people of quality have them?" asks Monsieur Jourdain.
>
> "Yes, sir."
>
> "Then I'll have one. Will it be beautiful?"
>
> "Undoubtedly. You will need three voices: a soprano, a contralto, and a bass, which will be accompanied by a bass viol, a theorbo, and a harpsichord for the *basso continuo,* with two high violins to play the *ritornellos.*"

Titled amateurs often deigned to mingle their noble performance with that of the hired minstrels at these private gatherings;

and as the devotees of this fashionable indoor sport required steady professional guidance, teaching music was a good livelihood if one could get pupils of substance. Musicians drummed up this phase of their trade by giving regular little concerts at their own homes.

The harpsichord was generally esteemed in good society and was an element in most musical combinations; it was primarily an accompanying instrument, having gradually replaced the lute for this purpose during the latter half of the seventeenth century—just about the period in which the violins succeeded in superseding the viols. However, it was also played by itself; and a number of capable composers, including one or two distinguished masters, supplied it with suitable literature—among them, Jacques Champion de Chambonnières, Jean Henri d'Anglebert, and above all François Couperin "le grand." This music consisted chiefly of little pieces. Stiff, dainty, speckled with brisk little ornaments—largely in variation or *rondeau* form, or in the rhythms of court dances—they were often labeled with picturesque or associative titles such as *Cythera's Chimes, The Knitters,* and *Gentle Nanette.* They made admirable "recreations" for polite ladies, and their charm is still viable today.

What with all this upper-class patronage and practice of music, its social value in the Paris of the early 1700's was high. The situation there had a resemblance to that of Vienna a few generations thence, as we have described it in a previous chapter. A German visitor, in a book called *Paris Sojourn,* published in 1727, advised travelers staying in Paris to practice their music, since "that gives the *entrée* to high society, and one may then attend the best concerts, available every day, with complete freedom and thus spend many hours that would otherwise be disagreeable."

Perhaps it was a jealous littérateur who inveighed as follows against ambitious gentleman and lady amateurs:

> Formerly people of quality left the job of accompanying to those who were musicians by birth or by profession; nowadays they make a supreme honor out of it for themselves. To play pieces to amuse oneself pleasantly, or to entertain one's friend or sweetheart, is beneath them. But to nail oneself to a harpsichord for three or four years in order eventually to attain the glory of being a participant in a concert, of being seated between two violins and a bass viol from the Opera, and to brush off, well or ill, a few chords that will be heard by no one—that is their noble ambition.

2. BEFORE "THE DELUGE"

Louis XIV reigned so long, and survived so many descendants, that it required an infant great-grandson to succeed him on the throne. As Louis XV grew up, it became clear that he had no interest in music. His queen, Maria Leszczinska, likewise, preferred cards to fiddles. Under his reign, patronage of music became diffused: individuals of means cultivated and promoted it without depending on the royal initiative.

Money, that pungent enzyme, began to effect its fermentations ever more noticeably during the earlier eighteenth century. We find financiers becoming personages of increasing importance; for example, Antoine Crozat—who was said to have started his career as a simple shop assistant, or perhaps even a lackey—had by 1712 built himself up financially to the point at which the King felt justified in granting him a monopoly on trade with that wild and distant land Louisiana. He was called Crozat "the Rich," to distinguish him from his slightly less opulent brother—the treasurer of France—who was ironically nicknamed "the Poor." Presently, Crozat began to show off with regular elaborate monthly musical parties at his mansion in the rue Richelieu; the royal prince Philippe d'Orléans, regent during the new King's minority, was a frequent guest at these events. Other high-society amateurs participated in the performances: the papal legate occasionally played the bass viol; while Mademoiselle Guyot, the daughter of a barrister of the Supreme Court, "combined delicacy and brilliance of touch with perfect science of composition at the harpsichord" and "performed all the most difficult music on the spur of the moment," as a polite journal of the day reported it.

Among the most important money-men of the time were the so-called "farmers-general." Back in 1681 Colbert, Louis XIV's minister of finance, had devised a scheme—very convenient for the monarch and his staff—of farming out certain of the nation's taxes and duties. Forty selected financiers, upon depositing a total security of from 60 to 140 million livres, were given the privilege of collecting certain tributes from the population—especially excises, such as those on salt and tobacco—for a fee. The crown benefited from this devolution of sovereignty; so, of course, did the farmers-general, what with the splendid opportunities for graft that naturally rained on them. It is true that the taxpayers often did not consider themselves benefited. "There are in Persepolis forty plebeian kings who hold a lease on the empire of Persia, and who give some of it back to the monarch," was Voltaire's acetic view.

Many of the farmers-general began to splurge in Paris and became acceptable *bourgeois gentilhommes.* Some did so plausibly with music. There was, for example, a Monsieur Ferrand whose parties around 1730 included numbers of distinguished musicians, among whom Joseph-Hyacinthe Ferrand—the host's own son, a pupil of Couperin's—proudly functioned as harpsichordist.

We may take it as a sign of the times that a farmer-general, Alexandre Jean-Joseph le Riche de la Popelinière, became France's greatest patron of music during the 1730's, 40's, and 50's. He was not the richest of his class, but apparently the most lavish in expenditure on the arts. At his great house in Passy he lodged, fed, and entertained streams of musicians, native and foreign. Young composers had their concerted works tried over by his excellent permanent orchestra; others had an opportunity to see their operas realized on his capacious stage, performed by some of the best members of the Royal Opera. Symphonies and operas were rehearsed during the day and presented with great éclat in the evening. The La Popelinière mansion was, indeed, a gateway to success for musicians. Jean-Philippe Rameau, for instance, who became the learned dean of French composers, had lived at this house for some time, composed some of his best works there, and played the organ for the services in the Maecenas' private chapel, as well as the accompanying harpsichord in ensemble performances. All sorts of persons were greatly eager to be invited to Monsieur la Popelinière's musical gatherings: after the program, the affable host frequently served a sumptuous supper to his large, mixed company of guests—which included artists, noblemen, savants, ambassadors, adventurers, and other "interesting people."

Meanwhile, music itself had begun to become a retail business enterprise. Musical commercialism, in a respectable upper-class sphere, set itself a starting landmark in Paris with the establishment of the *Concert spirituel,* which presented its first program on Passion Sunday, on March 18, 1725. This organization is generally considered the earliest Paris undertaking, for private profit, to provide public musical performances for unselected payers of admission fees. Yet it was not a "free" enterprise in the nineteenth-century sense: rather, it took the predominantly mercantilist-monopolist shape of its time. Against an annual payment of ten thousand livres, Anne-Dancan Philidor, a mediocre musician, received from the royal *surintendant* of music a short-term renewable concession to hold musical performances, and to sell admissions to them for his own benefit, at a small hall in one of the royal palaces famously known as the Tuileries. They were to be sacred concerts primarily and could take place only on the official church holy days on which opera performances were prohibited. Those included three weeks at Easter time; Christmas Eve and night; the feasts of the Assumption, of the Annunciation, of Pentecost, and others—amounting to thirty-five days in all. Only Latin words were permitted to be sung, but no restrictions were placed on instrumental music.

The *Concert spirituel's* use of the royal building, together with the collaboration of some Royal Opera personnel, gave the events a high social prestige; nevertheless, the prices charged for admission were relatively moderate: four livres for the best seats, two for the "pit"—later they were scaled at six, four, and three livres. Thus, it was inevitable that people of middle-class background would constitute an important part of the audience and that the music offered would tend to reffect their taste. Indeed, after some time the music at the *Concert spirituel* developed some inevitable flimsy aspects. The solemnly elegant motets of De la Lande, which were much enjoyed during its earlier years, gave way here and there to cantatas embodying strings of Christmas carols—and, still later, to ostensibly sacred compositions theatricalized by sound effects illustrating the earthquake at the Crucifixion or the destruction of the world on the Day of Judgment. By virtue of its semiofficial character, the *Concert spirituel* remained a primary focus of music in Paris and continued to function with varying success until the Revolution. The religious fig leaf was never removed from its performances, yet it grew more and more transparent as time went on. The center of interest tended to shift to the instrumental portions of the programs. After some years we hear of a growing appetite for adulterated music also in this field: a "descriptive" symphony called *The Calm After the Storm* was a permanent success after 1757; and the child "prodigy," perched on a table and dressed in a sailor suit, or playing two flutes at once, likewise found his doting admirers.

On the whole, however, the instrumental music was of good quality and involved no outstanding extravagances. For the most part, it consisted of sonatas or of concertos with prominent solo parts, almost invariably played by their composers. Foreign virtuosos became increasingly frequent after 1730. The violin was the favorite solo instrument; we also read of concertos for the cello, the flute, the oboe, and the harp. The harpsichord was, of course, always the indispensable orchestral filler and accompaniment; yet interestingly enough, we rarely find it as a concerto instrument in Paris during the middle years of the century. Its function in being played by itself seems to have been very largely restricted to the domestic circle.

As for musical affairs in Paris private homes, and the use of the harpsichord on such occasions, we will quote a description given in 1757 by an obscure person, possibly himself a musician, by the name of Ancelet:

> [They are] assemblages made up of large numbers of idle people, and of a small number of connoisseurs; the ladies constitute their ornament, and give a sense of rivalry to the performers. A few among these ladies are in a position to form, and even to pronounce, judgments upon talent; but the greatest number only come to be amused, to chat, and to show themselves. A large number of thoughtless young people, who have only the assembly in mind, come to be seen there and by their manner find fault with the [very] things they ought to applaud.
>
> Fathers and mothers bring their children, to procure for them a certain courage and self-confidence, so necessary for playing or singing in public; moreover, they also wish to get the benefit of the expense they have gone to for their education. One is bored to death by these budding talents, by sonatas and vocal pieces that one is forced to applaud so as to please the parents. A timid young lady allows herself to be coaxed for a long time to sing: she is induced to proceed to the harpsichord. After many curtsies, she proclaims that she has a cold, and finally sings by heart the lesson composed by her teacher. By dint of hastening the tempo, the little song comes to an end and the curtsies begin again. Scarcely do the people with real talent have time to make themselves heard.
>
> Every house has its favorite musician; they are the ones that give the tone; their pupils are infatuated with their productions, and all the music racks are decorated with them. The master of the house is busy praising their works, and procuring copies of them for persons complaisant enough to buy them. The concert closes with a well-worn harpsichord piece: the audience suffers, boredom takes hold, there is yawning, then bowing, and people leave.

It was during the 1750's that the fervent and frustrated Jean-Jacques Rousseau, still an unassimilated associate of the *Encyclopédiste* intellectuals, published his *Discourse upon the Arts and*

Sciences, following it even more startlingly with his *Discourse on Inequality.* These writings greatly moved many persons who, though themselves of the higher ranks of society, had begun to lose their faith in the principles on which that society was built. Rousseau's doctrine—that "natural man" was good, but had become spoiled by the artifices and falsities of civilization—seemed an agreeable thought to many of the spoiled. All sorts of remote "natural men," such as Huron Indians or Tahiti Polynesians, now became invested with a glamorous haze. "Natural men" more close to home, digging on French farms and milking French cows, likewise became pleasant objects of imaginary contemplation. While continuing to go through all their old accustomed motions, some upper-class persons now took up peasant-fancying as an intellectual fad—at a safe distance, to be sure, without themselves doing much actual manure pitching.

An affectation of rusticity became quite a smart gesture in mid-eighteenth-century good society: a generation before the day of Marie Antoinette, royal princesses enjoyed dressing up as shepherdesses and playing the hurdy-gurdy (*vielle*) and the bagpipes (*musette*). This play-acting became a musical movement of some extent: ladies anxious to do the proper thing, especially if it were easy, had their fine old lutes broken up to be converted into hurdy-gurdies, and it was said at the time that the teachers of that boorish instrument made more money than the best organists. The hurdy-gurdy and bagpipe vogue in Paris overlapped the guitar vogue in London, of which we have spoken previously. Both fads were trifling, though significant; neither had any great musical sequel in itself; yet they proved that the reign of the complex, delicate harpsichord as a domestic and accompanying instrument was no longer absolute, that a less troublesome, more flexibly expressive keyboard mechanism could soon be likely to have a future.

3. "CET INSTRUMENT BOURGEOIS"

On September 20, 1759, the semiweekly *Annonces, Affiches et Avis divers*—a sort of "Public Advertiser"—carried an item offering for sale:

a harpsichord of new invention called *piano e forte,* having a round, pithy harmony, imitating the harp or the lute in the bass, the flute in the treble as well as the quality of bells. . . . When the full sound is let out, it is louder and more pleasing than an ordinary harpsichord. All changes are made instantly, without being observed, upon a single keyboard. . . . This instrument is very easy to play and to maintain. There are no quills as in other harpsichords. Address: Quai des Orfèvres, at the Duke of Burgundy." ["The Duke" probably means a hotel.]

It is likely that pianofortes were known in Paris even before this. The previous year, 1758, the esteemed Johann Andreas Stein, later to be Mozart's favorite clavier maker, had taken a trip from his Augsburg home to the French metropolis and in all likelihood had exhibited some of his newly designed hammer-operated instruments there. He had brought with him J. G. Eckhard, a skilled keyboard player. Eckhard settled in Paris; his sonatas published there five years later specified their availability for the *"forte e piano."* We hear of a few other cases during the sixties in which composers recognized the new instrument in print. As yet, its acceptance was tentative; it needed socially potent support for its furtherance. Presently it received this support.

The pianoforte made its public Paris debut at the *Concert spirituel* on September 8, 1768; it was played on that occasion by a Mademoiselle Lechantre, a lady known on other occasions as an organist. From that minute, the pianoforte was "in"—as the fashion news writers now say in their unpleasant jargon. For the *Concert* derived its prestige from the King, at several removes, as we have seen; and we may also well wonder whether the pianoforte's first public solo appearance in London a few months previously, under the fingers of Her Majesty's very own master, did not influence the *Concert*'s directors' decision to try it in Paris. England stood high in the opinion of advanced thinkers on the Continent in those days: it was the remarkable country whose sovereign elected Parliament had dressed down two kings—and was by way of establishing freedom of the press—building up the world's greatest overseas empire all the while. Anything English had an attractive *avant-garde* flavor during the 1760's, '70's and '80's. Before the middle sixties, any pianos in Paris could only have come from Germany, so they were not entirely convincing. Now, at the end of the decade, when they began to trickle in from Zumpe's shop in London, they were irresistible.

Advertisements of music "for harpsichord or *pianoforte*" begin to multiply; the outlandish word is always italicized at first, but after a few years it becomes common and appears in ordinary type. The *Avant-Coureur* for February 25, 1771, announces the publication of a song: "The Arrival of the *Pianoforte,* ariette dedicated to the Count d'Affry, by Mr. Albanèse; price 3 livres, 12 sous." His verses begin:

Oui, cher ami, tu me viens d'Angleterre,
Hélas, comment lui peut-on déclarer la guerre!

Then they continue:

Il est donc vrai qu'enfin je te possède,
Mon cher ami, mon pianoforté.
Au plaisir de te voir tout autre cède.
Ah, que tu vas être fêté!
Ah, comme tu seras goûté!

Roughly rendered,

What, dear friend! from England dost thou come to me,
Alas, how can I then declare war upon thee!

It is true that I possess thee, oh bless the happy day,
My cherished friend, my dear *pianoforté*!
To the joy of seeing thee all other joys give way.
Ah, how thou shalt be favored!
Ah, how thou wilt be savored!

Albanèse was a singer, once a member of the Royal Chapel. A few years after perpetrating the above lines, he explained less giddily: "I prefer the fortepiano to the harpsichord for accompanying the voice. I find that the former has more fullness of sound and consequently more analogy with the voice, while the latter, though quite agreeable in show pieces, becomes a bunch of keys in an accompaniment."

By 1772 the famous Gluck, hero of the Paris *Opéra,* was using a little pianoforte made for him by Pohlmann of London.

The bright, inflexible, complicated, pretty harpsichord now seemed a feature of the visibly decaying old regime; the pianoforte, English, stroke-responsive, and therefore more "natural"—and cheaper as well—seemed to a Rousseauist generation to be the more plausible domestic musical instrument of a new order to come.

Nevertheless, not every one went after it recklessly at first. On November 24, 1774, the old Marquise du Deffand, lively correspondent of several outstanding literary figures, wrote a letter to her friend Voltaire, who was then lording it in his magnificent Swiss border-retreat. She explained that she was planning a little Christmas Eve party for some old acquaintances:

> I want to give them a pleasant reception that will make for entertainment and good spirits; I have already made sure of Balbastre, who will play a long suite of carols on his fortépiano. I would like some pretty verselets for those same tunes for Grandpa and Grandma and Mlle. de Grammont . . .

Voltaire complied, sending some impertinent rhymes, the tone of which the lady did not consider appropriate. He wrote again, offering a second batch of verses: "These are not as good as the former," he noted; "they sound like a *fête de Vaux,* but they are good enough for a fortépiano, which is a kettle-makers' instrument in comparison with the harpsichord." It is interesting that the old mocker meant to convey an image of something crude and plebeian with these words. Once again, he was being more witty than wise.

In any event, the harpsichord partisans fought a few rear-guard actions. Even before the invasion of the pianoforte, numerous owners of harpsichords were having them *"mis à ravalement"*—that is to say, rebuilt, usually with additional keys and stops. Often it was the older, more valuable instruments whose serviceability seemed worth preserving by this surgery. About 1768 Pascal Taskin made a bid to support the staggering harpsichord by using stronger, more durable little cowhide wedges in place of crows' quills for making his plectra. Even with good propaganda, including an unfounded claim that it was a new invention, this device made little headway. Taskin himself shifted over to the pianoforte and later attempted to construct what was probably the first "grand" in France for the Princess Victoire.

Claude Balbastre, Madame du Deffand's afore-mentioned Christmas carol entertainer, was the esteemed organist of the church of St. Roch. Although one of the earliest French musicians to play a pianoforte, he appears not to have believed in it very firmly. Watching Taskin labor over a pianoforte for the royal family, he is supposed to have said: "You are wasting your time; never will this newcomer, this bourgeois instrument, dethrone the majestic harpsichord." Alas for prophecy!

The public advertisements echo their side of the tale: during the seventies and, especially, the early eighties, *Annonces, Affiches et Avis divers* carried frequent offers of harpsichords for sale at low prices. On October 7, 1776, we read: "Will trade harpsichord for pianoforte." Six years later: "Harpsichord by Waters, 2 keyboards, rebuilt, . . . lute stop, green veneer with lacework tracery in gold, will trade for a fortépiano. It cost 600 livres undecorated." A good little piano could be had in those days for 240.

Here is an offer from March 2, 1782: "Will trade harpsichord of a good make for a light one-horse carriage, in the fashion." After 1786 the conflict was decided: the flurry of harpsichord sacrifice sales subsided and most of the offers thenceforth concerned pianofortes and harps.

Not until the 1780's do we hear much of keyboard concertos at the *Concert spirituel,* by which time the piano was crowding the older instrument out. In 1783 Julie Candeille, the daughter of an incredibly unsuccessful composer, played a piano concerto; the following year so did Marie Therese von Paradis, the blind girl from Vienna. The big break came in 1786, when eleven different pianists played solo within the frame of the *Concert,* finally overcoming the objections of those who did not consider it a suitable public solo instrument.

Abt Vogler, that curious musical holy man, was in Paris in 1783 and on March 8, together with a flutist, he performed a duo of his own composition with himself at the piano. That year he reported on Paris to a German music magazine:

> Of feminine amateurs who play the keyboard exceedingly well there is an untold number in Paris. There are not a few ladies who can compete with any keyboard professor in playing off a difficult sonata, perhaps even a sonata of his own composition. Scarcely a city in Europe could count so many fair dilettantes who know how to shade their tones so beautifully, so sensitively (they have the temperament for this), with such tender appeal, breathing pleasure, and with such naïve deportment.

All this talk of shading, and this use of sentimental adjectives, suggests that it was pianofortes by that time, for the most part, that the girls were caressing.

In 1784 Dr. Mesmer and his ideas, discredited in Vienna, became quite a fad in Paris. We hear that music from a pianoforte was used to promote the flow of healing "animal magnetism" at a test demonstration held in the house of a Mesmer disciple during the spring of that year: a modern implement for modern methods.

4. FRANCE PRODUCES HER OWN PIANO MAKER

WITH IMPORTED PIANOFORTES selling briskly, it was inevitable that some people would think of making them right at home. So it happened. However, few Frenchmen had any experience in building them. According to one historian's reasonable guess, Johann Kilian Mercken (the name was probably German or Bohemian) may have been the first to make pianos regularly in Paris; an example of his work is dated 1770. A few pianoforte makers were established in Paris later in the seventies, and their number increased substantially during the eighties. Again to judge by their names, most of them were Germans: Klein, Schwerr, Hillebrand, several Zimmermanns, Bosch, Daickviller, Eberhard, Lange, Schmidt, Stirnemann, and Korwer. The Germans had had a whole generation of experience in making the new instrument before western Europeans showed any interest in it. We remember that most of the English makers at this time were also natives of Germany.

In 1768, the very year that the pianoforte made its concert debut, sixteen-year-old Sébastien Erhard arrived in the metropolis from his native Strasbourg. Presently he dropped his unfunctional, gangling *h* and became a dapper, flawlessly French-appearing Erard. The son of a cabinetmaker, he had been a kind of boy wonder, showing an unusual aptitude for architecture, drawing, geometry, and mechanics. In Paris he became apprenticed to one or another harpsichord maker, but offended his masters by his precocity. Soon he attracted attention by designing and making a "*clavecin mécanique,*" a harpsichord with several registers using cowhide plectra as well as quills, all to be readily shifted and combined by means of an ingenious pedal mechanism. It is interesting to observe the significant trend toward flexible shading. Machinery of this simple sort had an intrinsic, self-justifying aesthetic value in the vogue of those days. The Duchess de Villeroi—lively, eccentric dabbler in the theater and literature—could look upon the young mechanician as a plausibly interesting protégé, one of a new nuance. She gave him a room in her house to work in; that was where he made his first pianoforte. It was heard by many of her guests, mostly lords, ladies, and dilettantes. They began to order pianofortes from the young man, and from then on, Sébastien Erard could ride "in" on the wave of the new fashion. He opened a shop of his own in the rue Bourbon, in the Faubourg St. Germain, and presently his brother Jean Baptiste came to share his work and his fortunes.

The undertaking prospered but aroused the jealousy of certain dealers whose trade consisted in importing English pianos. They tried to raid the Erards' shop, invoking an ancient regulation and claiming he did not belong to the right guild—he was not a union member, as we might now say. But by this time Erard had influential friends; and his appeal reached the King—Louis XVI by now—who responded with a complete vindication, giving him a full *"brevet,"* or license, to continue his work. "The King," says the proclamation:

> informed that Master Erard, by a new method of his own invention, has succeeded in improving the construction of the instrument named the fortépiano, that he has even obtained preference over those manufactured in England, in which there is quite a traffic in Paris . . . and wishing to honor him for contributing to the useful and the agreeable arts, has permitted him to manufacture, have manufactured, and to sell fortépianos in Paris, its suburbs, or anywhere he pleases . . .

And he was permitted to take all measures necessary for that purpose without the interference of any craft associations.

Actually, Erard's early instruments—like those of his competitors—while their workmanship may have been exceptionally fine, were copies or variants of Zumpe's squares, with single, later double, pilot action without escapement. Five octaves was the usual range. In any event, the name of Erard thenceforth became the most illustrious in the history of French piano making.

We must state, in passing, that Sébastien Erard began to take a great interest—as early as the 1780's—in the improvement of the harp, an instrument that became a serious domestic rival of the pianoforte as a ladies' music tool during the next thirty or forty years. The ingenious mechanism devised by Erard—applied to the so-called double-action harp, which admits of playing the instrument in all keys—is the basis of all modern harp construction.

5. AN INVENTORY UNDER THE TERROR

THE REVOLUTION blasted and dissolved all established French patterns of polite music making. Long accumulated and overdue, the movement began to precipitate in 1789. We could date it logically from June 17, when the Third Estate proclaimed itself the National Assembly and swore to give France a constitution. However, there is nothing so fascinating as bloodshed, and it is the storming of the Bastille on July 14, in itself an event of minor relevance, that came to be celebrated as the momentous Day. Still, the violence carried its threat, impelling some persons to take French leave and leave France. Among them were a number of foreign musicians, as we have seen.

Sébastien Erard was fortunate; he had departed a few years earlier to reconnoiter London, where the piano trade was livelier than at home. He had left his prospering shop in the safest hands he knew, those of his brother; and when he heard how hot Paris was becoming, he decided not to return for some time. He started a London shop, for both harps and pianos. It was located in Great Marlborough Street, and in due time it rivaled the best and largest English establishments of its kind. Undoubtedly, Erard learned much from English piano makers at close hand.

French events proceeded in their explosive course. Soon many nobles left the country—some merely out of fear for their personal safety, others to plot with foreign magnates to help crush the Revolution at home. This was surely treason, by any popular or nationalist standards: after the Republic was proclaimed, on September 21, 1792, that was primarily the ground on which the King was put to death. The armies of foreign monarchs continued to invade France, and the situation became critical the following year. The Committee of Public Safety had to make quick decisions in tackling treason at home, and its famous Reign of Terror probably saved the country, even though many of the 2600 death sentences it imposed were no doubt unfair individually. The Convention, the celebrated parliament that proclaimed the Republic, was swollen with public-spirited enterprise. Many excellent institutions owe their foundation to its decrees—the elementary school system; the *Ecole polytechnique;* the metric system; and also the National Institute of Music, soon to be widely known as the *Conservatoire.*

Those who had been condemned, as well as those who had been declared emigrated, were logically considered "enemies of the people"; their goods were forfeit and declared property of the state. Goods included works of art, and a Temporary Commission of Arts was set up to protect such objects from vandalism. On May 3, 1794, this commission announced that the Committee of Public Safety "authorizes the professors of the National Institute of Music to betake themselves, together with the commissioners, into the houses of the emigrated and the condemned, there to choose the best musical instruments for the use of the Institute." The instruments were to be brought to a specially designated depot, namely the old offices of the *Menus-Plaisirs du Roi*—equivalent to The King's Revels—in the rue Bergère. The operation was entrusted to the leadership of one Antonio Bartolomeo Bruni, an otherwise undistinguished violinist at the *Comédie Italienne.* He began his seizures on the date of the decree and did not finish until August 18, 1795, more than fifteen months later. Bruni made an inventory of the instruments taken, which was published late in the nineteenth century.

Some of the names on this list call forth historical echoes and overtones—for instance, that of Count Archambaud Joseph de Talleyrand, younger brother of the wily diplomat and statesman. The Count got away safe after having been warned of an order for his arrest, leaving an anonymous pianoforte, in oak, as well as a less fortunate wife, who perished on the scaffold.

There was Louis Philippe-Joseph, the Duke of Orléans, of royal blood. His liberalism may have been sincere; it may also have been aggravated by a feeling of spite toward his family. In any event, it seemed so eager that it earned him the nickname "Philip Equality." With forty other nobles he had ostentatiously joined the Third Estate and later voted for the death of the King, but the Terror would not let him live down his relatives. He was operated on by guillotine on November 6, 1793, and Bruni took over his English piano, by Beck.

There was the sad case of the elderly Simon Charles Boutin, who had been treasurer of the Navy under Louis XVI. Lamed on his right side, he followed his doctor's orders and went off to Bath, England, to take the waters, armed with an absolutely regular passport. During his absence the harsh law was passed banishing all emigrated Frenchmen forever on pain of death. When Boutin returned confidently, to regularize his position, he was kept under arrest for six months and then tried. He may have rightfully claimed *ex post facto* immunity from the law; but it was too good an opportunity for showing the former royal official who was boss now, and so the seventy-four-year-old paralytic was triumphantly erased. His piano was English, a Schoene of 1787.

German-born Baron Melchior Grimm—a resident of Paris for thirty-seven years, noted corresponding diarist of its doings for the Duke of Saxe-Gotha, and unsuccessful promoter of Mozart during the young composer's stay in the city—left with the diplomatic corps in 1790. He seems vaguely to have had hopes of returning, for he left his precious furnishings behind in good order. They were duly plundered in October 1793, the Commission of Arts rescuing a harpsichord with a black background and gilt molding, as well as a Pohlmann piano.

Being a foreigner carried small advantage in those times: Antoine Doria, a rich Portuguese with an Irish wife, had spent a year or two in Paris looking after an inheritance. No members of his family were French, and the Dorias' somewhat prolonged trip to London could hardly be called an emigration. Nevertheless, his house and belongings were sold during his absence. We wonder what there was remarkable about his Erard piano that made Bruni appraise it at eight thousand francs.

The farmers-general made flashy targets for revolutionary ardor. Twenty-eight of them were detained, herded together at the Hôtel des Fermes, ostensibly to let them prepare their accounts more conveniently. They made delicate calculations and offered to buy themselves off for two million francs. But the authorities thought up a cheaper way to handle them. After circulating a spicy story to the effect that the financiers had watered the people's tobacco, their captors had them passed quickly through a space called a courtroom; the ax was then allowed to fall through each of their twenty-eight well-fed necks on that selfsame May 8, 1794, with complete equality and fraternity. The Republic became richer by several times two million francs worth of property, including a rather thin dividend of four pianofortes and two harpsichords.

One of the twenty-eight is worthy of special notice. Antoine Laurent Lavoisier, one of the great pioneer scientists of all time, often called "the father of modern chemistry," was the son of a rich man. He had been persuaded to become a farmer-general while quite young, so as to give him more means for his researches.

He earned his country's gratitude by successfully applying the new chemistry to agriculture and by improving the army's gunpowder. Later he became a member of the Constituent Assembly and was of great help in organizing the new system of weights and measures. At his so-called trial his services to the country were mentioned as a possible extenuation. However, a most democratically minded member of the Revolutionary tribunal settled the question by saying: "The Republic has no more need of learned men." For the greater glory of the common man, Lavoisier's head was carried off in a sack, while his pianoforte was carried off to the rue Bergère. It was French-made, by Zimmermann, and was appraised at four hundred francs.

All in all, Bruni visited 111 houses and mansions of the emigrated and the condemned, removing 367 items, of which 127 were keyboard instruments. Had he started sooner, he might have made a bigger haul: surely some of the earlier birds had flown with more of their possessions. Nevertheless, the inventory gives us some picture of the instrumental preferences of upper-class Parisians of the time.

Of the 127 keyboards, 63 were harpsichords and 64 were pianofortes. This, however, need not mean that preference for them was as evenly divided. For one thing, 11 of the harpsichords were by the highly valued Ruckers of Antwerp; that meant they were about 150 years old and were antiques, or collectors' items, as much as functioning instruments. A further 11 harpsichords—of those whose dates were recorded—were from 40 to 170 years old. Of 78 houses that contained keyboards, only 32 had harpsichords alone; the others all had pianos as well. When considering the pianofortes, it is easy to see the dominance of Erard: out of 20 French-made instruments, 12 were by him—half again as many as all other French makes put together. The other 44 were mostly English: of 29 whose makers' names were listed, Zumpe and his successor Schoene account for 16, while Pohlmann, Beck, Adam Berger, and Longman & Broderip make up the sum of almost all the others. It may be significant that only 78 out of 111 well-to-do houses had harbored keyboards of any kind, for it seems to show that these instruments had not yet achieved the absolute musical predominance that was to be the piano's in the century to come.

In any event, the harpsichord was far on its way out by the time of the Terror; it became extinct shortly thereafter. It is true that the articles setting up the organization of the *Conservatoire*, dated July 30, 1795 (12 Thermidor, III), provide for six professors of the harpsichord and say nothing about pianoforte; but that can be written off as the working of an old speech habit. For a while, pianofortes had been called "hammer-harpsichords," we recall. An early *Conservatoire* class, that of 1800, records the awarding of prizes for pianoforte, nothing else. Constant Pierre, historian of French musical instruments, has counted twenty-one Paris makers of harpsichords in 1789, five in 1791, four in 1799, and not one after the turn of the century. No doubt, numbers of orphan harpsichords were still in use for some time. Let no one be misled, for example, by J. A. D. Ingres's portrait drawing, dated 1804, of his fiancée Julie Forestier, the daughter of a judge, in which the girl's hand is shown resting on one of the keyboards of what must be a harpsichord. That same year the *Conservatoire* published its own elaborate *Méthode de pianoforte,* edited by Louis Adam, one of its leading professors. The preface states:

> The fortepiano is the most widely cultivated of all instruments. It has obtained preference over the harpsichord because it gives forth its sounds with whatever degree of force or gentleness one wishes, . . . something for which one could look in vain in the one it has replaced.

6. SEQUEL TO THE INVENTORY

ALL THROUGH the Revolution's most tense days some of the opera houses had kept going. Parisians liked their shows: after a thrilling day spent watching the little jugular fountains spurt red in the Place de la Guillotine, a person could relax to well-sung tunes at the Théâtre-Français. For example, on September 16, 1793, with Marie Antoinette in prison awaiting her final disposal, he could go to hear the new comedy *Bathilde,* composed and sung by the beauteous Julie Candeille—in the course of which the composer prima donna managed to show off her piano playing. Six evenings earlier he might have gone to the Théâtre Feydeau to hear the *première* of Daniel Steibelt's opera *Roméo et Juliette,* with words by the Vicomte (!) de Ségur. Steibelt already had had some success with his piano compositions, his left-hand tremolo, and his impudent manner. Now this stage acceptance nailed his repute fast, for opera was ever the Frenchmen's favorite musical situation.

After the historic ninth Thermidor (July 27, 1794), when Robes-pierre came to an end, the Terror became revulsed at itself. There was a temporary lull in the foreign war; the spasm of bloody idealism could relax into a "normalcy" of calm corruption. A new kind of government was formed, consisting of a popular legislative assembly of five hundred and a "Council of Ancients" presided over by a committee of five known as the Executive Directory. Finances were in terrible shape—the paper *assignats* rushed down a steep place to bankruptcy, but some persons got fat selling them short. So did other well-placed people, who got more than their share of lands and estates confiscated from the nobles and the clergy.

Incidentally, what happened to those musical instruments taken from the emigrated and the condemned? The *Conservatoire* needed time to get going efficiently and seemed in no hurry to acquire them. Probably, only a small number of the pianos and harpsichords gathering dust in the rue Bergère would have been of any practical use to the new school anyway. Little by little, refugee Frenchmen began to drift back from abroad, often successful in having their names stricken from the official list of *émigrés*. In certain cases, they or their heirs recovered some of their possessions; and it seems that a number of the sequestrated instruments were returned to their owners. Not all, however. The Revolutionary decree had declared them "property of the nation," and the high executives of the Directory—as well as other highly placed officials—seem to have taken the word quite personally. (Some of these subtler ancient royalist habits of thinking were hard to break.) One of the Directors, for instance, Jean-François Rewbell by name, had a Taskin harpsichord and a Schoene pianoforte, quite impartially, sent home for the use of his wife. Lazare Carnot, another exalted Director, must have been quite a music lover, for he helped himself to three pianofortes. The high-talking political moralist Larevellière-Lepeaux, another of the nation's chief executives, took four instruments. Benezech, Minister of the Interior, inspired by the example of his superiors, also took a grab from the bag, but contented himself with a single organ—as did citizen Cochon, a mere modest Minister of Police. However, citizen Angibault, Comptroller of Buildings, seems to have been quite drunk with musical enthusiasm, for he pilfered no fewer than seven instruments, some of them among the most valuable, such as both an Amati violin and a Stainer. It appears that years later, when the *Conservatoire* aimed to form a museum, not one of the enthusiastically "socialized" instruments was at hand for inclusion.

This might be a nice theological problem: does the Devil prefer to inspire truly good intentions for the sake of thwarting them thereafter, or does he like better to promote wickedness by letting it become bold under a mask of good will?

7. ASPASIA STRUMS A CITHARA; CAESAR SMITES A LYRE

WITH THE GUILLOTINE taking a rest, numbers of prominent people began to show a zest for what is often called pleasure. Racketeers and politicians chose public luxury, while certain ladies gave spectacular parties. Madame Thérèse Cabarrus-Tallien seems to have been among the most conspicuous of the latter group. As the daughter of a Spanish banker and the wife of a highly placed politician, she could well afford it. Josephine de Beauharnais, a guillotine widow, soon to become Madame Bonaparte, was her friend and moral support. Madame Tallien was the one who started the fashion of wearing straight-lined robes and sandals, a style that broke sharply with the immediate past. It suited the imaginative demands of the moment, and the "tubular" feminine silhouette, long to flourish, replaced the frilly "back fullness" that had dominated much of the eighteenth century.

The garb had its associative significance. European higher education, for centuries, had consisted largely in the inculcation of an obsessive awe before the details of old Greek and Roman history. A need was now felt in France for repudiating the rococo coquetry of the regime just overthrown: for a leading woman to dress like an ancient Greek was a way of affirming a lofty "republican simplicity" or even "republican severity," as the fraudulent cant went, against the frivolous finesses of the late aristocrats. Romanish, Greekish antiquishness became an affectation in many phases of life, and the works of the painter Louis David, a Jacobin and a member of the Convention, confirmed the vogue.

Under the Terror, France had been filled with implacable hostility toward Britain—the reaction against that country's opposition to the Revolution. Gone suddenly was the old liberalist admiration of the land across the channel. A statute was enacted on October 9, 1793, the title of which was: "Law that prohibits from the soil of the Republic all merchandise fabricated or manufactured in the countries under the domination of the Britannic government." All possessors of British goods were supposed to declare them and surrender them to the public authorities. The antagonism remained unabated during the *Directoire,* for the tariff law of October 31, 1796, was even severer, absolutely forbidding all imports from Britain and prohibiting a list of goods always to be presumed to be of British origin. It was clear that the day of the imported English piano was over; a French family with a hankering for an instrument would now have to gratify it with one of domestic make. It was that same year, 1796, that Sébastien Erard chose as propitious for his return to Paris.

There he began to construct large-sized grands, equipped with the escapement-armed "grand action" that he had learned to make in London. They were the first large wing-shaped pianofortes to become more generally known in France, and their stronger tone no doubt made them readily acceptable. However, they had another quality that must have given them a happy affinity with the style of the time. Harpsichords, we remember, were passé and were reminders of the old regime—therefore, well done away with. Most pianos until then had been squares; but these new grands had the unadorned great curve, a long flowing line, which might now be interpreted as yet another symbol of a heroic Greek simplicity. So, for that matter, might the outline of the harps that the Erards were also steadily supplying. The wife or daughter, then, of an important *Directoire* figure—approximating the long, flowing line of her high-waisted dress more or less functionally to the great, flowing curve of a grand piano or harp—could fancy cloudily that she was thereby rhyming herself with, say, Aspasia with a cithara.

Ruling *Directoire* ladies took piano lessons from Steibelt. Josephine de Beauharnais entrusted her daughter Hortense, barely in her teens, to this practitioner's pedagogy. The daughter of General Barthélemy Schérer, the *Directoire's* War Minister, also became a Steibelt pupil; so did Madame de la Rue, whose somewhat royalistically tinged husband was soon to be thrown out of the Assembly of Five Hundred. Steibelt taught them his garnished medleys of current opera tunes, his variations and rondos, as well as his storm and battle pieces. *Directoire* society was corrupt and trifling, its ways scarcely worthy of imitation—but ah! it was Paris. It was his irresistible Paris aroma that gave Steibelt a head start when he set himself up in London, that later enabled him to attract a quality audience to the Prague concert we have spoken of previously, and that even let him dare the throw of challenging

Beethoven. Undoubtedly it helped him to spend his still later years living off the fat of Russia.

The *Directoire* was letting France run into an ever more hopeless internal swamp; but, by contrast, its armies were doing very well against the Austrians and the Italians. A fateful gravitation was accumulating: the people who a few years back had kindled generously for "liberty" and "the rights of man" were now preparing to hand over their liberty and their rights, their lives and their deaths, with ecstatic servility, to one single peculiarly repulsive barbarian who had proved to be an excellent artillery tactician. A group of upstart capitalists supported him in his *coup d'état* in the fatuous expectation that he would run the country for their benefit. He got rather out of hand, as it turned out. Sure enough—when he first became boss, he was given a title that had the proper antique flavor of "republican simplicity": he was called "Consul."

Napoleon probably, like most people, enjoyed music a little, especially when it did not require his complete attention. Enjoy it or not, music was one more thing, its professors one more set of people, that he insisted on subjecting to the jerks and quirks of his megalomaniac will. It was to the Erard brothers that he naturally turned when he wanted to have a pianoforte made. The instrument is dated 1801. It is interesting for several reasons: it had the movable-hammer-bouncing-rail Vienna action, showing that the Erards were broad-minded enough to give all action-principles a try; it also had the row of condimentary pedals customary in Vienna instruments, five of them—an *una corda* soft pedal, an ordinary sustaining pedal, a "bassoon," a "celeste" pianissimo made by a cloth damper, and a "Janizary music" (that is to say, drums and triangle). The last suggests that Napoleon may have been treated occasionally to faint, symbolical re-percussions, we might say, of his own battles.

One story told about the "Little Corporal" tends to illustrate his peculiar musicality. The incident is said to have occurred in the year 1808. To seem like a proper European ruler, the new self-made Emperor had also to play at being an art patron: France's most prominent singers and instrumentalists were frequently summoned to the Tuileries to perform for him. On this occasion he was worried about some affair of state and was much out of sorts. He stopped Kreutzer, the great violinist, right in the middle of an andante, uttered an offensive criticism to Madame Branchu the singer, and then left the room. The singers hung about for a short while and were dismayed to see the Emperor come back.

"I want you to sing the chorus from *Nina,*" he said. A bold musician stuttered that they did not know that chorus.

"You must know it, everyone knows it."

"But, sire, we have not the music here."

"Then sing it from memory."

"But, sire, the orchestra players are gone, we have no accompaniment."

"Here is a pianoforte."

"Sire, no one here can play it."

"Very well, then I will accompany you myself."

And with that, to everybody's amazement, he sat down to the instrument and struck out some ear-rending sounds.

"Now begin," shouted the Emperor, "and keep good time." The voices arose somehow, discordantly; the piano groaned a cacophonous mess beneath the imperial fists; and thus "the chorus from *Nina*" was performed.

"I am satisfied," said the superman. "See, everything succeeds when one but wills it."

Some of us would like to believe this tale, it seems so true in spirit.

One pianist, named Louis Jadin, appears to have played often for Napoleon without displeasing him. But Jadin evidently aimed to please everybody: he had been a music page at the court of Louis XVI; came the Revolution, we find him a member of the National Guard band, composing cantatas for Revolutionary festivals on such words as "Enemy of Tyrants" or "Citizens, Arise"; during the Bonaparte episode he obligingly brought forth *La Grande Bataille d'Austerlitz* and *Hommage à Marie Louise;* and then, with perfect elasticity, bounced all the way back to compose *The King's Festival* for the restored Bourbon Louis XVIII. After that, who would have grudged him either his Legion of Honor or the government pension he finally received? Meanwhile, Jadin was professor of piano at the *Conservatoire,* an accompanist in much demand, and an industrious manufacturer of new piano pieces for insatiable girls: rondos and variations, assorted arrangements of current opera hits—the tunes fastened onto each other end to end by the most artless harmonic thumbtacks.

8. THE ERARDS GROW; THE PIANO ASPIRES AND PRETENDS TO SING

In 1802 Napoleon reduced the government appropriation for the *Conservatoire* by nearly three fifths. It had operated on an annual budget of 240,000 livres, he let it vegetate on 100,000, saying it ought to confine itself to the teaching of military music. Somehow, this decree has the ring of sincerity: it seems to have sprung more directly from the Napoleonic heart than the concerts he ordered up at the Tuileries or the operas he attended in state. In any event, the deprivation hardly daunted the general progress of the pianoforte.

Johann Friedrich Reichardt, the intelligent, articulate Prussian musician who informed us in such detail about Vienna's social and musical life, had spent the winter of 1802–3 in Paris, leaving us his "confidential letters" about the visit. His letter of November 22, 1802, tells how impressed he was with the size and activity of the Erard shop as he observed it. It occupied two substantial houses, he says, "in one of the best neighborhoods of Paris." The firm made squares and grands, "and in what incredible quantities!"—everything on a much larger scale than any shop in Germany. He speaks of its division of labor: joiners, turners, metal workers, all working at their specialties in well-equipped workshops, as well as "the painter, the lacquerer, the enameler, the gilder, the wire drawer, and who knows who else . . ." The final assembly, he says, is accomplished under the direct surveillance of the master himself.

> Great anterooms and halls stand full of finished mahogany cases . . . several laborers may be seen day in day out busy with the packing of instruments. The courtyards are surrounded by sheds full of costly woods of all kinds.
>
> A complete office with its bookkeeper and clerk keeps the accounts and the correspondence; a cashier's office takes care of payments and calculates outgo and income.

The Erards, reported Reichardt, sold their small squares for 40 louis (1000 francs) and their "most tastefully ornamented wing-shaped fortepianos at from 100 to 200 louis" (2500–5000 francs), a price that even exceeds that of the English makers. He does not, however, explain that the lower English prices may have been the result of a larger output and a wider market. The Erards exported many of their pianofortes, tells Reichardt, "to all countries of Europe, wherever water transport favors it." Railroads were hardly as yet a gleam in a crazy brain.

As a member of a poor and "backward" nation, Reichardt may well have been astonished by the Erard establishment. Its division of labor, as well as its businesslike organization, undoubtedly made it a factory rather than a craft shop; but this talk of "good neighborhood" (meaning socially good), the fact that the boss actually supervised the finishing of every instrument in person, and also the fact that he and his family lived on the premises—all these things show that much of the feeling and habit of old-fashioned handicraft still clung to the place. We might guess that the "incredible quantities" of which Reichardt speaks may have amounted to two instruments per week, or one hundred a year. That would have been twice the production of Nanette Streicher's Vienna shop, the largest in the Germanies, but still less than one quarter the output of Broadwood's at the time.

Our informer also speaks of the new-style Erard harps, at sixty to a hundred or more louis each. Who got the most and the handsomest of these? "Russians and English," he says, "who appreciate finished workmanship the most, and always have enough money and good will to pay better for better work. . . . Yet one also sees them"—the harps, and the pianos as well?—"frequently in the hands of the new rich, who acquire such things as fine, fashionable furniture, even though they are not musical, and encourage their children less eagerly toward music than once used to be the case, when all that was rich and great lived and had its being in the arts and especially in music." The new rich, it seems, consisted largely of those who supplied the fabulous armies with boots, uniforms, horses, harness, wagons, rifles, gunpowder, and a thousand other things. Napoleon, we hear, did not object to their pocketing a certain amount of excess profit provided they delivered good merchandise. The pianos and the harps were pretty symbols of their graft.

There was plenty of piano playing in French homes during the later Revolutionary and Napoleonic periods, yet one could hardly contend that this activity was anything but highly superficial in quality. Nothing in the Parisian social life of this time, or even somewhat later, could have encouraged the creation of such piano music as Beethoven, Schubert, or even Hummel were putting forth in Vienna. France had, indeed, some fairly distinguished composers: the lighthearted Grétry was still alive, and one of his operas had been given 508 times; the severe Cherubini, whom Beethoven admired, had been eminently successful with his *Lodoïska* and *Anacréon;* Méhul had made a long-standing mark with *Joseph;* later on Boieldieu and Hérold upheld the honor of French creative musicianship with *La Dama blanche* and *Zampa.* The prevailing musical predilection, however, determined the course their talents took. All these people, except Cherubini, were able pianists; yet they worked little in that field, since it offered but trifling rewards of glory by comparison with what they could reap as successful fashioners of operas. Hérold, for example, regarded his fifty-odd piano pieces as pure potboilers, insignificant bread-and-butter productions. Compare these estimable musicians with their German colleague and contemporary Carl Maria von Weber, who was equally successful in opera but who felt encouraged by his surroundings to find the time and inclination to set down quite a few valuable pianistic thoughts—and to perform them in public as well.

French people of the time valued piano music even less, if possible, than did the British. The rare concert that involved a piano soloist received bare mention in the public prints as compared with the columns of comment devoted to musical stage productions, the Parisians' true love. A few exceptional concert pianists, foreigners, did function as such, briefly, during the Consulate and the first Empire. Wölfl, for example, spent a few years of the early century in Paris but made little stir; we know that when he offered some quartets to a publisher, the merchant advised him rather to compose waltzes.

J. L. Dussek had not done badly since clearing out of England; presently he became a companion-in-pleasure to the music-loving Louis Ferdinand of Prussia. When the musician-prince was killed on the battlefield, the gay times came to an end; Dussek composed his best and most expressive sonata in memory of his patron and reappeared in Paris some time after 1806. He was no longer handsome; in fact, he was quite obese, besides being heavily alcoholic in his habits. His playing, however, was substantially unimpaired, especially in the evening; and that tricky survivor Talleyrand, now a Napoleonic "Prince de Benevento," still rich and old-fashioned, appreciated him sufficiently to make him his chief chamber musician.

Dussek played at least once publicly during this final stage of his career. It was at a large concert put on jointly, strangely enough, by two rival violinists, Pierre Rode and Pierre Baillot. It took place in 1808 at the Odéon Theater, Dussek playing on a new Erard grand. His performance on this occasion was much admired; we hear a characteristic comment about him: that he understood, like no other artist, "to sing upon his instrument."

The words are significant, not so much as a description of Dussek's work but rather as an expression of a tonal ideal toward which pianists and piano makers were striving. The instrument had long since proven its fitness for rippling passage work, for polyphony, for rhythmic incisiveness; now its practioners were aiming to give it greater melodic, lyrical expressiveness, to let it produce the illusion of singing.

An illusion it surely is. Singing means an uninterrupted, continuous application of force to a vibrating medium: bowed or blown instruments can "sing"—not, however, those whose sound-producing elements are struck or plucked. A quick impact, instantly released, can induce an immediately dying resonance, but it cannot produce sustained live vibration. A pianoforte cannot "sing" any more than can a xylophone, a gong, a harp, or a pair of cymbals. Careful, ingenious pianoforte construction can, however, prolong the life-expectancy of a struck string's tone; more accurately said, it can lower the rate of a tone's resonant fading. Moreover, a clever pianist, in playing a melody, can shelter this slowly decaying resonance by subduing accompanying chords and figures to a minimum; he can also simulate a legato by overlapping the resonances of two successive tones, either by fingers or by pedal. Thus, he can create an impression of melodic continuity —make a series of shaded dots seem to fuse into a line—a procedure that some persons might enthusiastically call "singing."

The Erards, with what they had learned from their English rivals, were making larger, more impact-resistant pianofortes than had previously been known. As yet, these had no overspun bass strings, no metal bracing bars or plate, no felt covering their hammers. To our twentieth-century ears, they might have sounded dry and puny; yet they could "sing" in the wishful ears of their contemporaries.

One impact-resistant, and therefore tone-encouraging, device may at this time be credited to Sébastien Erard: the agraffe. This was a short upright metal blade or stud, one to a note, each one perforated with as many holes as the note had unison strings. The agraffes were screwed into the rear edge of the wrest plank, behind the tuning pins, each string passing through its apposite perforation. The agraffes formed an upward bearing for the wires and prevented the hammer blows from bending or buckling them. Other makers soon adopted the agraffes, and they have remained a standard part of all pianofortes to this day.

Young Hortense de Beauharnais, like her mother Josephine, married a Bonaparte—whereupon her oppressive in-law artillerist-emperor was then able to set her up as a brief synthetic queen of Holland. From that privileged perch she could make effective her musical talents, such as they were. Apparently, her lessons from Steibelt had done her a little good; as a new first lady she managed, with the help of a professional instrumentalist, to have set down the music and words to a song of her invention. It was of military association and began: *"Partant pour la Syrie."* The ditty caught on readily and became especially popular much later in the century, after Hortense's son had had himself proclaimed Emperor Napoleon III; in fact, for a while it took on the status of an auxiliary *"Marseillaise."* The no longer handsome Dussek, some time during his final Paris years, composed a set of moderately brilliant variations on Hortense's new tune. Did he play them at the Odéon concert? It would have been timely and appropriate. Generations later, deep in the Third Republic, Camille Saint-Saëns quoted *"Partant pour la Syrie"* in his *Carnival of the Animals.* Alas, he placed it under the heading of "Fossils"!

Dussek's performance at the Odéon may have aroused some fresh interest in the piano as an instrument capable of realizing higher artistic values; but in general the instrument was looked upon as a means of harmless, shallow domestic diversion—widely used but of no great import. On April 1, 1822, Luigi Cherubini became "Inspector General," that is to say Director, of the *Conservatoire.* He had been brought up in the strict tradition of Italian church music; his masses, requiems, and other choral works were distinguished for their purity of style; and after his removal to Paris, his serious operas were much admired. On entering upon his executive duties at the *Conservatoire,* Cherubini found forty-one women as well as thirty-two men enrolled there as piano students. Less than two months later he issued an order calling this abundance of would-be professional pianists *"abusive et pernicieuse"* ("excessive and harmful") and therewith reduced the acceptable number to thirty—fifteen men and fifteen women. We can understand his feelings, but still must rate him rash. He seems not to have been aware of the more imaginative recent developments of piano music. It was not until fifteen years later, when young Carl Halle played him some of Beethoven's piano sonatas, that he heard those masterpieces for the first time.

However "excessive and harmful," the crowd of piano aspirants might have suggested that a new trend was forming.

9. ANOTHER GREAT PIANO NAME

THE ERARDS, meanwhile, were being treated to the stimulation of some domestic competition worthy of their eminence. Ignaz Pleyel, born in Austria, had studied for a while with Haydn and become a composer of talent and fluency whose quartets and symphonies were widely and readily enjoyed. Emigrated to France, he achieved a good position at the Strasbourg Cathedral. When the Revolution made things desperately uncomfortable, he hopped over to England—just in time to have the manager of the "Professional Concerts" make a "star" out of him, setting him up rather gracelessly as a rival to his old master Haydn.

Pleyel's English stay seems to have infected him with certain ideas: we do not know how closely he became acquainted with Clementi at the time, but when within a few years he returned to a less fevered Paris, he began to follow the Clementi life pattern. Again, the English atmosphere helped to lure an esteemed, gifted musician and composer into forsaking his art, and to push him into the arms of that bustling bitch commerce: in 1797 Pleyel became a Paris music publisher and dealer. Presently we find him corresponding with Clementi & Co. regarding the exchange of publications. On October 20, 1801, Clementi & Co. wrote to him in another connection: they asked him to act as agent in selling "a variety of grand and small pianos" of their manufacture, "calculated to answer the purpose of all ranks of people." In view of the rigorous import restrictions officially in force, this probably would have had to be a black-market operation—one of many at the time.

By the following year Pleyel was still being thought of as a practicing musician, for the Clementis then asked him to compose and send them six sonatas using Scotch songs as themes. That Scotch habit again! A year or two later Steibelt, now in London, wrote:

Dear Pleyel,

You did not send the title for your sonatas which I arranged. I beg you urgently to send it. I would like to print on it that the sonatas are arranged by me at your express wish, and I think it is necessary to dedicate them to someone. If you haven't anybody, I believe it will be good to dedicate them to the Empress of Russia.

So these two skilled, commercialized musicians conspired—in the line of business—to use the name of a distant innocent lady potentate for parsley on a dish of their merchandise.

By 1807 Pleyel, now fifty, considering the piano business promising, and piano importing difficult and dangerous, decided to go into piano manufacturing himself. He seems to have made pretty fair early progress in his own estimation, though we might now consider his operations to have been on a rather small scale. On July 15, 1813, he wrote to his son Camille: "We have manufactured thirty-one pianos since January 1, almost all large ones; you see that I am not falling asleep and that I will easily reach fifty pianos this year, and maybe even beyond that." At that moment Broadwood's annual output was a thousand or more. The Pleyel firm, in any case, became second only to the Erard, the leading piano maker of France during most of the later century.

10. THE MODERN PIANO EVOLVES

THESE WERE THE YEARS during which Sébastien Erard was meditating his most momentous invention, the one that fastened his name most securely and famously to the progress of pianoforte construction. We have seen that Erard learned to make pilot-action grands in England; we know that he also understood how to make Vienna-type bouncing-actions on the Stein-Streicher principle. His thought seems to have been to combine the valuable qualities of both: the solid, accurate blow of the former with the light response and fluency of the latter. He accomplished this by retaining the basic mechanism of the English grand action and providing it with an additional complex device known as the "double escapement." This consisted of a number of smaller levers and springs, the effect of which was to let the hammer rebound from the string, not to the original point of rest, but to an intermediate point much closer to the string, to remain thus as long as the finger was still holding the key down. Only upon complete release of the key did the hammer eventually return to its zero position. It is clear that this action greatly facilitated the repeating of single notes; the hammer had now to traverse less than half the distance for each reiteration that it traveled for the initial stroke. Figures involving rapid repeated notes were beginning to become an attractive feature of piano music, and the new Erard action was sometimes called "repetition action."

A certain amount of justifiable skepticism was at first aroused by the Erard action. It was thought, for example, that such a complication of small moving parts might easily go out of order. The grand that Dussek played so impressively at the Odéon in 1808 had an early form of repetition action, but we are told that its parts became loose after a while and began to rattle. Not until 1821 did Erard consider his double-escapement action sufficiently improved to warrant his taking out a new patent on it in England.

The facilitation of repeated notes was only one advantage of this action. Its more general virtue lay in its lightness, rapidity, and responsiveness, which were all achieved without loss of firmness or strength, thus uniting the good points of both the English and the Vienna mechanisms. It was this Erard action that made possible the smaller, quicker shadings on the piano, the breathless ultra-pianissimos, the delicious swoon of a high note suddenly whispered, and the plastic relief of prominent and subordinate voices in closely woven tone-textures. Thirty years after Erard had taken out his basic patent and the firm had learned how to apply it most advantageously, Sigismond Thalberg, a leading pianist of the time, wrote about it:

> By its ingenuity the mechanism surpasses anything of its kind that has been made or tried. It permits the performer to communicate to the strings everything that the most skillful and most delicate hand can express.

At first the Erards furnished only their grand pianos with the double-escapement action; by the 1830's they were building it into all their instruments. Early hesitation was overcome, pianists began to accept it eagerly, and it was understood as a decisive advance in piano construction. Within a period of twenty years all other piano makers adopted it, sometimes with modifications and even with further improvements. It is still a standard piano equipment.

The double-escapement action, as well as the metal bracing and frame, were both being developed gradually during the 1820's; and another problem, that of the covering for the hammer heads, began to be solved during the same decade. It had long been felt that the tanned deer-leather thitherto used for this purpose was not entirely satisfactory. It became brittle and hard with age and tended to produce a dry, sharp, poor quality of tone. A pliable, durable material was needed, one light enough to be applied in some thickness without unduly increasing the hammer's weight. For it was found that impact by a larger, softer-striking surface at the hammer's end allowed the string to develop its vibration more slowly along its entire length, thus encouraging the formation of stronger lower harmonics—on which a richer quality of sound depends. We can readily understand this principle by listening to a kettledrum struck alternately by a side-drum stick and by a tympani stick. Cloth, sponge, and tinder were all tried, with indifferent results. At last the definitive answer was found when in 1826 a patent was taken out on the covering of piano hammer heads with felt. The advantages of felt were soon appreciated; sooner or later it was adopted by all piano makers and has remained the standard material for its purpose to this day.

The holder of this patent on hammer felt was a remarkable man by the name of Pape. A native of Germany, like so many piano makers, he had come to work in Pleyel's establishment during the 1810's and had soon Frenchified his given names, Johann Heinrich, to Jean-Henri. By 1818 he had set up his own shop in Paris, and in time became the most original and most ingenious of all devisers of piano mechanisms. We shall hear more of him.

The metal frame permitting a stronger blow and therefore greater volume, the rapid double-escapement action making for more delicate stroke-responsiveness combined with speed, the thickly felt-covered hammers giving a "rounder" tone than those formerly used—all these developments converged into one trend: the making of an instrument suitable for use by a person who could project piano music commandingly, fascinatingly, in a large room, a concert virtuoso in other words; a piano that could be played louder and faster, with more sensitive shading, more violent contrast, and a richer, more "singing" quality than had been possible previously. It was about 1830 that this newer ideal of piano making and piano playing was taking definite shape; it was fully realized a few years later. By then the last echoes of the eighteenth century were being stilled: the conception of what was desirable in a tone quality had completed its long period of change, and the fading ghost of the harpsichord was finally laid. A sharp, bright sound—a clear, well-defined, unambiguous statement of individual tone—such as the earlier eighteenth century had liked, was no longer wanted. The yearning was for a vague, mellow tone-cloud, full of ineffable promise and foreboding, carrying intimations of infinity.

A gulf lies between these two ideals of sound. The former belongs to a philosophy that values logic, that wants to control the world by dividing it into neat, tight, inviolable categories, orders, and ranks. The latter is characteristic of a fluid, pietist, libertarian cast of thought, which has little respect for what it regards as contrived boundaries or limits—a frame of mind harboring the mystical suspicion that anything might merge into everything. The former was gratified more by the distinctness—that is, the separateness—of tones; the latter, more by their fusion and their blend. Taken literally, the above dichotomy may be an oversimplification: it is intended as a mere hint of the truth. Still, its obvious social and political allusions seem to have their significance.

The shift of tone-ideal was gradual; it had taken about eighty years to accomplish. It seemed to have been completed, as we have suggested, by about 1830, the time that also marked the final political triumph of the money-wielding classes over the older landed aristocrats, and the general acceptance of their habits of mind as social ideals.

Few, if any, significant fundamental developments of the pianoforte can be said to have taken place after the first third of the nineteenth century. During the following thirty years, its range was increased from six and a half to seven octaves, still later to seven and a third; and a very important improvement in stringing and tension bracing was achieved by American makers shortly before 1860. Otherwise, the piano of the 1830's was substantially that of today.

11. THE RESTORATION RICH MAKE LIKELY PIANO CUSTOMERS

WHEN NAPOLEON was finally put away, stocks on the Paris exchange went up, not down. People gave an *ouf* of relief, just as Napoleon had predicted they would, and the businessmen, his original backers, were among those who emitted it the loudest. The arts and machines of peace could now move more securely, and capital began to feel more free for investment and expansion. France had had a nervous, bloody time for a generation; after twenty-five years many old aristocrats were ruined; peasants and laborers may hardly have been better off than they had been before all the turmoil started; but the money-manipulating classes: merchants, manufacturers, shippers, bankers—the city dwellers or *city*zens, the burghers or *bourgeois*—grew steadily in wealth and influence, despite all political zigzags.

The restored Bourbon, Louis XVIII, was a man of compromise. He called himself king by the grace of God, yet he swore to rule by a Constitutional Charter and to share his law-making function with a Chamber of Deputies. This body was indeed assembled by election, but only those paying a direct annual tax of three hundred francs were given the right to vote—a mere 88,000 persons out of a population of 30,000,000. The deputies were not even remunerated as such. They were only eligible if they paid one thousand francs in taxes and were therefore presumed to be independently wealthy. Among these governing rich, landed gentry were still predominant, but they now shared their power with those whose moneys came from trade, industry, or banking.

It was in the trend of the times that the latter group would enlarge their prestige. At the beginning of the Restoration, France was still predominantly an agricultural country: it was barely begun on the road of industrial and mechanical development along which Britain had already traveled some distance. Progress, however, was fairly rapid: in 1814 there were in all France only fifteen plants using steam engines; by 1820 there were sixty-five such; by 1830 they had increased to six hundred and twenty, all churning and burning themselves into gold for the pockets of businessmen. Napoleon's various wartime blockades and trade restrictions had accustomed people to conceiving of the economy in nationalist terms: all parties of the Restoration parliament seemed agreed in imposing an extreme protective tariff against foreign goods, especially manufactured articles.

It was Napoleon, already during his consulate, who had tried to encourage manufactures by holding regular industrial expositions; and even at an early one, in 1801, two of the exhibitors had been piano manufacturers. The next year the number had increased to five, and by 1806 there were twelve. But as his pudgy fist bore down more heavily, the luxury trades throve less, and at the exposition of 1819—four years after his removal—the pianoforte exhibitors still numbered only thirteen. Now, however, under the orderly, peaceful Restoration, the improved mechanical arts, and the beneficent tariff, the piano business was destined to shoot up.

Paris society became increasingly relaxed and buoyant after the Restoration. Napoleon had had little sympathy with the feminine mind, having discouraged intellectual, artistic, or political stirrings in women; but now the ladies felt freer, and their peculiar stimulative and mediative talents were released. Some of the more prominent ones invited men of distinction and wit to mingle regularly in their living rooms, their *salons*. The hostess' personality pervaded these meetings, determined the nature of the people who frequented them, and gave them their individual character—literary, religious, or political. A kind of aristocratic pure-minded intellectuality prevailed at the *salons:* many of the hostesses were not poor, but luxuriousness was at a minimum among them; plain refreshments and high thoughts were mostly handed about.

Social cleavages reflected the divergences of economic and political interest. The hereditary territorial nobles, what was left of them, had now mostly returned from exile, their property largely returned to them. They were the natural leaders of the restored monarchical society and they lived mostly in a suburb called the Faubourg St. Germain. The elderly Princess de Tremoille, recognized as one of their chiefs, collected at her *salon* groups of ultraroyalist conservatives who enjoyed expressing resentment at the government's compromises with the current century. "And what foolishness have you been planning for us today?" she used to say in greeting to the Count de Villèle, the minister who executed some of the King's concessive measures.

The Faubourg St. Germain denizens may have looked with

uneasy condescension upon the moneyed set, the bankers and businessmen, whose pretensions to leadership were becoming increasingly cogent. The outlook of the latter was almost unanimously "liberal"; that is, they were anticlerical and imagined sincerely that they believed in the liberty of the press. At their gay parties, given in residences that clustered about the street called the Chaussée d'Antin, they acted out proverbs and sang the songs of Béranger. There one could find the amiable Jacques Laffitte, financier, at one time governor of the Bank of France, custodian of Napoleon's St. Helena funds; or Benjamin Delessert, "self-made" cotton and sugar manufacturer, founder of savings banks and admirer of Benjamin Franklin.

James Rothschild was also proceeding to make his mark on Paris. The youngest of the famous brothers, he had arrived during the latter part of Napoleon's reign. His financial operations were quiet at first, but always in close harmony with his family in London, Vienna, and Frankfurt. After the Restoration, James began to assume importance as "the King's lender"; soon he received an Austrian patent of nobility and was made Austrian consul general in Paris. Some of the reserve toward him as a Jew and a foreigner began to break down; he took a large house—the palace that had once belonged to Fouché, Napoleon's fearsome chief of police—and in it he gave a large, brilliant party during the winter of 1821. Ten or fifteen years later he was a power in the land, an undisputed leader of society. The Rothschilds were money people and so, theoretically, bourgeois; but the government finances in which they were involved threw them in with high officials, a group still largely confined to members of the landed aristocracy. Thus, the social atmosphere surrounding the Rothschilds was rather different from that in which ordinary businessmen moved.

The musical life of the Faubourg St. Germain was rather colorless. Normally, one might have expected these people to convene in state at the old *Opéra*—now again named the *Académie royale de musique*—and to build up its pristine artistic distinction, if only for ostentative purposes. That venerable institution, however, had fallen on shabby days, vocally and scenically, and the aristocrats, its logical supporters, permitted it to languish. Instead, they preferred to sip the glib tunes held forth at the Italian opera, the Théâtre-Italien, an establishment that warbled even more brilliantly after 1824, when the great Rossini became its director.

In their dwellings the Restoration nobles patronized music in a distant sort of way. Gone were the genial days of their ancestors, who took pleasure in mingling their amateur efforts with the playing of professional musicians in their own living rooms. We will let the Countess Marie d'Agoult describe music in the Faubourg St. Germain as she experienced it. Her testimony ought to be authentic, for she belonged to this social group both by birth and by marriage; yet her associations with her mother's family, who were descendants of Frankfurt bankers, gave her judgments a broader viewpoint. She says:

> Composers and singers still had their place apart; in spite of the eagerness to have them, they appeared in the *salons* only on the footing of inferiors. If someone wanted to give a fine concert, he sent to Rossini, who, for a recognized fee—it was small enough, only 1500 francs if I recollect rightly—undertook to arrange the program and to see to its carrying out, thus relieving the master of the house of all embarrassments in the way of choice of artists, of rehearsals, and so on. The great maestro himself sat at the piano all evening accompanying the singers. Generally he added an instrumental virtuoso—Herz or Moscheles, Lafont or Bériot, Nadermann (the leading Paris harpist), Tulou (the king's first flute), or the wonder of the musical world, the little Liszt. At the appointed hour they arrived in a body, entering by a side door; in a body they sat near the piano; and in a body they departed, after having received the compliments of the master of the house and of a few professed dilettantes. The next day the master sent Rossini his fee and believed he had discharged his obligations toward them and him.

The scene the Countess describes must have been as of 1824, or 1826 at the latest. Rossini did not move permanently to Paris until the summer of the former year, while Liszt was fifteen in the autumn of the latter year and could not well have been called "little" for long thereafter. Indeed, after a time the Countess achieved a wide, unending publicity by becoming the "great" Liszt's mistress. Marie admits also that "in certain of the more modest homes, in families where music was cultivated by reason of inclination rather than simply as a matter of conventionality, relations between artists and society people were established with greater affability."

The dominance of the Restoration nobles was precarious and short-lived. Nothing could stop the progress of the businessmen—in view of the increasing accumulation of private capital, the development of productive machinery, and the growth of larger and larger circles of persons directly dependent upon the prosperity of the commercial interests. Regardless of the framework of government, the financiers, or higher *bourgeoisie,* were destined to become the ruling influence in society. Well-to-do people felt increasingly impelled to imitate those richer than themselves, to aspire and pretend to gentility by laying upon themselves its purchasable trappings. More and more people wanted to afford pianos and to have their daughters try or make believe to play them.

The year 1824 is a kind of landmark in the history of the French piano trade: both the Erard and the Pleyel firms underwent reorganization. Sébastien Erard was now old and ill; he had been more an inventor and art collector than a businessman; he had neglected his Paris shop to its financial detriment. It was up to his nephew and heir, Pierre Erard, to build up greater and more profitable sales. Apparently the junior began by selling some of his uncle's valuable paintings in order to acquire fresh capital. Then he took a candid look at the square pianos that had thitherto formed a large fraction of the firm's output. In the words of an advertising pamphlet published by the company some thirty years later, he judged that "the great dimensions" of these models "were to become an obstacle to their sale, as a consequence of the growing narrowness of apartments." He immediately set about designing a practical six-octave true upright piano—not an "upright grand"—which gradually was to replace the horizontal type.

"The growing narrowness of apartments"—let us try to dispel the metonymic fog of this phrase. What is meant, surely, is that more and more of the less wealthy people, who therefore had to live in narrower quarters, now also were stung into acquiring musical furniture. The upright shape represented a way in which they, too, might own something they could call a piano, something that would fit their smaller rooms and their smaller purses. In modern terms, Erard was entering a lower-price market with a new model, more practical and compact than his older ones, and with certain modern improvements. A proper upright piano, its tail on the floor, its action striking from the front, had been devised, as we have seen, in both Vienna and Philadelphia nearly twenty-five years before; but neither the market nor the most practical designing was available for its promotion at the time. Although "cabinet" uprights had indeed been on English makers' lists since 1815, they appear to have been put forward as something new and fancy and were actually priced higher than the squares. It was toward the end of the 1820's that the rectangular upright began to become the standard cheaper form of instrument. Other Paris piano makers soon followed Erard's lead: as early as 1827 the firm of Roller & Blanchet put out an upright one meter high and one meter thirty centimeters long; J. H. Pape advertised a one-meter upright in 1828.

The Pleyel reorganization likewise involved a change of personnel. In 1824 the founder Ignaz, who was getting old, handed over the business to his son Camille. By that time the elder's fame as a composer may have declined; the younger felt the need of again associating the firm with a name of musical prominence. At about this opportune moment there returned to Paris Friedrich Kalkbrenner, his pockets well upholstered with the takings from his London concerts, his compositions, his private lessons, and his percentage from a Logier "academy"—besides the residue of an inherited fortune and the availability of a rich new wife's funds. The eminent pianist became a partner in the Pleyel enterprise. Probably he invested money in it; certainly he became its artistic front. He opened a Paris studio, played Pleyel pianos in public concerts, and recommended them to both his fashionable and his talented pupils and their friends. Again we see a famous pianist and musician go into the selling of instruments—and he was not to be the last. In any event, the fortunes of Pleyel & Cie. began to soar, and soon the firm shared with Erard the leadership of the French piano trade.

Presently the Pleyels took on an auxiliary line: they built a hall in connection with their premises at No. 9 rue Cadet, with the aim of hiring it out to concert givers. The idea was related to that of tying up with the esteemed Kalkbrenner: by attracting numbers of reputable or celebrated artists to its rooms—in which, of course, its pianos were used exclusively—the firm could associate its product, or at least its name, with their fame. In the arts, borrowed glory may be as workable as borrowed capital. Pleyel Hall was opened with a concert on January 1, 1830, with much acclaim from some of the newspapers. The program was of the piebald kind everywhere customary at the time. Various leading singers from the somewhat rejuvenated *Opéra* made their contributions: Messrs. Nourrit and Dabadie sang the duet from the current great hit *William Tell,* in which they had starred so conspicuously: Mesdames Cinti-Damoreau and Dabadie sang a different Rossini duet; another singer sang vocal variations on an air by Mozart; Tulou, the *Opéra* flutist, played his variations on yet another opera tune; Vogt, a well-known oboist, played *"une fantaisie de sa composition"*—on an opera air, or perhaps on *"airs populaires allemands."* In the midst of these salads, the meat was served: Kalkbrenner himself, then at the height of his considerable digital powers, showed off a Pleyel grand by playing on it his new Concerto No. 3, a work of fair substance for its day. The papers raved, calling him "majestic," "elegant," "brilliant," "graceful"—any kind of admiring adjective. The learned musicologist F. J. Fétis, often a discriminating critic, duly got on the band wagon for this concert: "Never did a musical matinee," he wrote in his journal, "more completely satisfy a select audience than did this one." Note the flattering of the customers. He continues to say what was expected of him:

> The instrument on which Mr. Kalkbrenner was heard is one of the excellent pianos manufactured by Messrs. Pleyel, whose reputation is now assured in the world and among the artists. With regard to tone quality, these pianos leave nothing to be desired. They seem to me even to have the advantage over the English pianos which have been the standard of manufacture for a long time; Messrs. Pleyel have improved their product by changing the system of their keyboards [he means actions] and by giving them a lightness that they did not use to have.

The Pleyels must have made a good profit on their hall, for they felt encouraged to open another one, in 1839, at their new location in the rue Rochechouart. By 1844 we hear that the two Pleyel halls accounted for more than two hundred concerts in the course of a single season. Long before then, the Erards had also been touched with the idea and had expanded their rooms likewise to accommodate an auditorium.

We may try to understand these variegated concerts sympathetically. They were a form of pretentiousness that, nevertheless, involved deference to an audience. In bourgeois circles, it would have seemed slighting in those days—and for long thereafter—to invite guests formally for dinner, to expect them to go to the trouble of putting on evening clothes and of calling a carriage, in order then to serve them anything less than a seven-course meal with suitable wines. Just so, a concert entrepreneur, whether himself a performer or not, would not wish to belittle an audience's sense of its own importance, or that of the occasion, by offering less than a substantial array of varied musical viands. Moreover, a mixed audience seemed to require a variety of program that was likely to please many people at least part of the time.

Nevertheless, as the 1830's progressed, the conventional type of concert, with an orchestra as a background, began to obsolesce. As more and more performers wanted to make themselves heard in Paris, it became increasingly difficult to assemble a group of orchestra musicians as a support and to rehearse them adequately.

A concert without singers was not yet thinkable by 1830, even if a violinist or harpist was staging an event for his own benefit; but the trend then developed of having all accompaniments played on a piano, possibly with the reinforcement of a string quartet. This meant increased opportunity for, and interest in, public piano playing.

12. THE PIANO BECOMES A PURPOSE IN ITSELF

For subtler reasons, the aesthetic climate of the later 1820's favored the growing interest in piano virtuosity. The instrument was now being made in factories and sold by businesslike methods; its producers were businessmen, the rising class, the people to whom tomorrow the world was to belong. Furthermore, the instrument contained hundreds, perhaps thousands, of moving parts: it was full of "machinery." Machinery was the brightly shining morning star of that day; it was, in its way, a symbol of liberty, of man's freedom of thought and enterprise, of his overthrow of ancient inhibitions and prohibitions in his quest for mastery over nature. Moreover, machinery, purposefully constructed, was creating much of the nation's new wealth, making many favored persons rich beyond the dizziest dreams. Machinery, liberty, mastery, riches—all these stirring notions, fused together, seemed to be symbolized by the piano. The instrument was already vastly improved mechanically, but the desire it aroused made it seem still imperfect: it still appeared to offer a field for adventurous undertaking, a happy playground for ambitious putterers with wire and wood, with levers and springs. In that sense too it was the instrument of the hour, a live issue. To the generations maturing during the mid-1820's, the 1830's, and the 40's, the piano was fascinating intrinsically, and for many it became what the Germans call a *Selbstzweck,* an end in itself.

Without insisting on the parallel too rigorously, we may compare the piano in Paris in the decades after 1825 to the automobile in the United States in the 1900's and 1910's. It was a rapidly improving mechanism put forward and adopted by the ascendant group of leading people; to own one, especially one of the latest models, was honorific: it was a badge of successful modernity. Not that too many persons were able fully to appreciate the ingenuities of its construction, or paid much tribute to its designers. The function of an automobile is rapid locomotion; that of a piano the performance of a certain kind of music. In either case, the individual who could triumphantly force the mechanism's full capacity became a special object of thrilled admiration. As racing drivers—Barney Oldfield or Ralph de Palma—became heroes in the American earlier twentieth century, so piano virtuosos—those who could play fast and loud, make complicated turns and twists and leaps, and execute breath-taking successions of double notes —were made into heroes by Paris and then, obediently, by the rest of the European continent during the 1830's and 40's. Virtuosity on the piano became a heady sport, an auditor and spectator sport: the pianists were reckless-seeming acrobats on an improved implement; their every particular stunt—playing thundering runs of octaves, playing a melody in the middle broken over on either side by waves of arpeggios, playing whole compositions with the left hand alone—was hailed with detailed joy and even fainted over.

The climax of the piano-virtuoso orgy came between 1836 and 1846, after the full force of the new improvements had made itself felt; but a number of pianists began to blossom in Paris earlier than that. We have mentioned Kalkbrenner, as well as Liszt, who made some stir as a boy "wonder" after 1823. Pierre Erard seized upon him immediately as a profitable advertisement and converted the young innocent forthwith to a near lifetime of loyalty to the Erard instruments. It was Monsieur Erard who took him, that very first season, to London and showed him off there in a concert. Here is the announcement in the *Morning Post:*

NEW ARGYLL ROOMS

Master Liszt, aged twelve years, a native of Hungary . . . respectfully informs the Nobility, the Gentry and the Public in general, that his benefit concert will take place this evening, June 21, 1824, to commence at half-past-eight precisely, when he will perform on Sébastien Erard's new patent Grand Pianoforte a Concerto by Hummel, New Variations by Winkhler, and play extempore on a written Thema, which Master Liszt will request any person of the company to give him . . .

Leader, Mr. Mori, Conductor, Sir George Smart. Tickets half-a-guinea each, to be had of Master Liszt, 18, Great Marlborough Street.

No. 18 Great Marlborough Street, be it remembered, was the address of the Erard London warerooms. In addition to the program mentioned, young Liszt also took part in *Di Tanti Palpiti* performed "as a concertante with Signor Vimercati on his little mandolin." Variety was the spice of life. At Liszt's concerts at the Theater Royal in Manchester that August there was mention also of "Erard's new patent grand pianoforte of seven octaves."

Another important successful piano virtuoso was Henri Herz. Born in Vienna and brought to Paris as a child, he was talented enough to be entered in the *Conservatoire* at the age of ten. That was in 1816, before Cherubini cracked down on pianists. During the 1820's Herz developed into a lively, agreeable manipulator of keyboard figuration. His playing was greatly enjoyed by the Parisians and so were his compositions. These made no pretense at depth or intensity, but contained many a graceful loop of arpeggio, many a thrum of titillating repeated notes, many a provocative octave leap. The modest aim of this music, along with its cheerful mobility, was one element of its quick acceptance. Furthermore, the things he offered for publication were well adapted to the capacities of the young ladies who were expected to buy them: his pieces were plausibly brilliant but not discouragingly difficult. For a dozen years, until the later thirties, Herz's compositions sold more than those of any other composer whatsoever and publishers reputedly paid him four times as much per page as they did almost anyone else. He was applauded in Paris and on his tours in Germany and other lands; as a teacher, too, he was in great demand. One of his pupils recalled much later that he sometimes had to edge in his lesson with the sought-after master at five in the morning!

While more of an extrovert than his somewhat older contemporary Carl Czerny of Vienna, Herz resembled Czerny in his untroubled facility for pleasant pianistic motion-shapes and in his diligence in putting them down in black and white—in the very flavor of his musical idiom.

Herz profited from the current bull market in piano pieces, piano concerts, and piano lessons; but inevitably the amiable commercial musician's mind was attracted to the kernel of the whole business: at some time in the 1830's he decided to enter piano manufacturing. Clementi, Pleyel, Kalkbrenner, and now Herz: the eminent musicians turned piano makers were forming quite a procession. Despite the fact that an important improvement of the Erard repetition action was patented in Herz's name, his factory does not seem to have been entirely successful at first;

however, it was doing well by 1844, and after the exposition of 1855, when Herz won a prize, it sailed on briskly.

Let us give our picture the right shade: these piano virtuosos were not primarily "interpreters," they were not aiming to realize the music of someone greater than themselves. Their public was interested in them personally, in watching them do their own particular tricks. The showy pianist, unless he were a child, was always expected to offer some music of his own composition or concoction; if it was based on tunes already familiar, so much the better. Herz composed concertos and *"morceaux brilliants,"* but one of his most pervasive productions was *La Violette,* a variated medley on melodies from an ephemeral opera by one Carafa. The Herz opus survived its still-born operatic source by decades, going through thirty editions.

Other able pianists appeared in the twenties. Johann Peter Pixis, a native of Bohemia, arrived in 1825 and promptly found admirers. Ferdinand Hiller, serious-minded Frankfurter, came in 1828. There were still others. It is interesting to observe that none of these Paris-thriving virtuosos were native Frenchmen. Parisians were now eager to pay money to pianists, but something in the atmosphere of French family life seems to have prevented this type of *artiste* from developing at home at this time. Later, in the thirties, we hear of one or two actual French pianists, but they were minor phenomena and could not compete with the immigrants from Germany, Bohemia, Poland, and Hungary.

We must mention one more personage, not a pianist, important in this connection. Moritz Schlesinger, son of a Berlin businessman, arrived in Paris as early as 1819. His attempts to establish himself as a book publisher were struck down by the severities of Louis XVIII's censorship, but in 1823 he went over completely into the publishing of music. It was a sagacious move: the music market rose and spread mightily, especially after the Revolution of July 1830. Maurice (as he was now known) Schlesinger made money and became widely influential in the world of music. In 1834 he purchased the *Revue Musicale,* thitherto run by F. J. Fétis, enlarging the title to *Revue et Gazette Musicale.* It became France's most important organ of music news and opinion over a long period. Some notable musicians and writers worked for Schlesinger as contributing editors including Berlioz, Fétis, and the Countess d'Agoult, who was encouraged to publish her articles over the signature of Franz Liszt.

A general air of seriousness and competence permeated the principal pieces in the *Gazette,* yet Schlesinger was careful to let the journal further the prosperity of his music publishing house and of those individuals on whom, in turn, that prosperity depended. Like all editors, he was a politician; his paper had its "sacred-cow list" as well as its "son-of-a-bitch list." On the latter, Henri Herz figured prominently. At some time or other those two lively music promoters, Schlesinger and Herz, seem to have been unable to settle which one was the hand and which one the glove; it is quite likely that the irresistible Herz asked for more money per page than the immovable Schlesinger was willing to pay. In any case, it is amusing to see how the pages of the *Revue et Gazette* never refer to Herz in any except the most slighting terms —and that went for his playing, his compositions, and his inventions. The feud began to give pleasure for its own sake and was carried on with heavier weapons. Schlesinger was finally sentenced to a fine of fifty francs for *"diffamation,"* but not before he had inflicted a bruise, in a duel, upon a fiery Herz loyalist. By 1844 we notice Herz taking an advertisement in the *Gazette:* apparently the hatchet was eventually buried, as it often is, in bank notes.

13. THE FINANCIERS WIN

THE EUROPEAN *bourgeoisie,* then, headed by the Chaussée d'Antin, escorted its favorite and peculiar instrument, the pianoforte, up to a glittering heyday during the second quarter of the nineteenth century.

The break came in July 1830. Old Charles X, the last of the true Bourbons, attempting once too often to exercise an ancient royal prerogative, aroused an angry mob of Parisians who set up barricades in the streets, clamored for a second republic, and drove the King out of the city. The insurgents seemed to want old Lafayette for president, but the businessmen got ahead of them. At a meeting in the house of Jacques Laffitte a group of financiers and political thinkers, including the young Adolphe Thiers, decided they needed a monarchy as a symbol of stability and continuity; but, of course, it had to be a monarchy they could control. They fixed on the Duke of Orléans, a Bourbon cousin and the son of the unlucky "Philip Equality," to be its titular head. Somehow, the businessmen persuaded Lafayette of the wisdom of their ideas: he and the Orléans, both wrapped in great tricolor flags, appeared together on the balcony of the Hôtel de Ville before an enormous crowd; the old gentleman kissed the younger and proclaimed that as a citizen king, he would be found to be "the best of republics."

So it was: Orléans became King Louis-Philippe, and Laffitte the first prime minister. The new monarch seems to have inherited some of the ambiguous leanings of his father. He made a great show of his commonness—his "democratic" behavior, as we now miscall it: he made a point of going about carrying a prosaic, middle-class umbrella; threw his first residence, the Palais-Royal, open to everyone; and erased the old Bourbon fleur-de-lis from his carriage. Yet he too somewhere cherished dynastic ambitions that ultimately were to prove his downfall. The story went that he wore coarse, thick gloves when he went out to shake hands with grocers and truck drivers but replaced them with fine kid gloves when he returned to the noblemen and bankers with whom he habitually associated.

The real bosses were the financiers. Their political aim was a *juste milieu,* an exact middle: they were against both tyranny and democracy, against both clericalism and irreligion. Soon their banker-minister Casimir Perier abolished new titles and suppressed republican riots with equal conviction. Legislation was by a parliament, with a ministry responsible to it, and the property tax qualification for the suffrage was reduced from three hundred francs to two hundred. Yet that still gave only 240,000 well-to-do Frenchmen out of a population of 32,000,000 the right to vote. Government was by property for property interests. No American chamber of commerce or association of manufacturers could have asked for more.

The shift of political influence had its inevitable reflection in what is called "society." After the accession of the not-really-legitimate Louis-Philippe, the ultraroyalist traditionalists of the Faubourg St. Germain went into a kind of ostentatious mourning and refused to give parties or go to them. When it became evident that the new regime was there to stay a good while, they relaxed from their more extreme sulking and were at least willing to meet the money people at the necessarily neutral home, for example, of the Count d'Apponyi, the Austrian Imperial ambassador. It was clear, however, that the habits and predilections of the Chausée d'Antin were the ones to seem worthy of being respected, and therefore imitated, by lesser people. The tone of society changed, not too gradually: *parvenu* splurge began to dominate over the aristocratic decorum of the previous regime; the show of visible luxury became more important than the unpurchasable brilliance of intellectual conversation. The cigar habit began to separate the sexes, to the disadvantage of each, as did the establishment of the Jockey Club, which preoccupied the less mental masculine interests.

Political Europe from 1815 to 1848 might be described as a conflict between the so-called Holy Alliance and "liberalism." The former, we will remember, was the understanding between the rulers of Russia, Prussia, and Austria to use their power and influence to support the principle of legitimist monarchy and established religion everywhere on the Continent. The French Revolution of 1830 was generally looked upon as a defeat for this constellation of might; it was correspondingly hailed as a triumph of right by all supporters of free thought and representative government. Paris immediately became the beacon, the citadel of the liberal view of life, a refuge for those guilty of "dangerous thoughts" in countries to the east. All manner of nonconformist writers and thinkers went there now to breathe more freely and dream more hopefully. From Germany came Heinrich Heine, tender poet, piercing critic of manners and morals, scurrilous lampooner and defamer of his opponents. He made a living writing his pungent pieces for journals in Germany. So also came Ludwig Boerne, Christian democrat idealist who elated himself by preaching to laborers on the Montmartre. Karl Marx came, a two-hundred-proof high-brow, a philosopher of history who had thought up a potent deviation from the system of his respectable master Hegel. But when the trend of Marx's writings and doings seemed directly to undermine the roots of the money tree, he became an easy man to expel. Richard Wagner, frustrated showman, unorthodox musician, and conceited windbag as well as potential genius, also tried to mingle his sounds with those of Paris in those days. He had good introductions to important people, but somehow no one learned to care much for him or such works as he could then produce and he left, defeated, after thirty months.

By no means all of the escapists were poor foot-loose German littérateurs. For example, the Princess Christina Belgiojoso-Trivulzio could never agree with Prince Metternich that her native Milan ought to remain forever under the ancient legitimate rule of the house of Hapsburg. After some detrimental encounters with the Austrian prime minister, she and her playboy husband fled to France; in Paris she used her $40,000 annual income to keep a fine residence in the Faubourg St. Honoré, to finance plots for an Italian republic, and to patronize musicians and writers.

Then there were the Poles, mostly innocently proper Catholics and royalists. However, the powers that made up the Holy Alliance were the very ones that had carved up and swallowed their precious country a generation or two before. Many of them, not the poorest or lowliest ones by any means, preferred the pleasures of retreat in Paris to the irritations of demotion at home, and the miscarried uprising of 1831 added to their numbers. They collected in the *plaine Monceau* and the Ile St. Louis; they wept for their old home, kissed each other on the nostalgia, and treated their Prince Czartoryski as a sort of king in exile. Their gifted young countryman Frédéric Chopin arrived in September of that same year, and they formed the main body of the audience before which he gave his first public performance in the city some months later. On that and on other occasions another countryman and lesser pianist, Adalbert Sowinski, also could beguile them with his playing and give lessons to their daughters.

Many other migrants to Paris were hardly to be classed as refugees. Wealthy English, Russian, and German aristocrats, even a few Americans, with no work on their hands, enjoyed life in the French metropolis. No city in the world could match the variety of its entertainments and the charm of its social intercourse for those who could afford to keep sizable houses and suitable servants. The ancient repute of Paris as the home of everything supreme in the arts and crafts, as the source of the finest clothes and the finest wines, attracted the presence of those who had little further to do than to buy these things. The exiles often had more means and more imagination in using them than had the natives. General de Castellane, head of the Civil Guard, said sourly: "In Paris, in order to have the best company at one's home, two qualifications are sufficient: that of being a foreigner, and that of having money."

Lastly, all manner of adventurous people flocked to Paris who had something to sell that the rich might be induced to buy, who aimed to milk the city's pressing udder: inventors and schemers, artists and musicians. The last-named might not all do too much cash business, but the advertisement of their activity in the fabulous place could impregnate all their future activity elsewhere with golden glamour rays.

14. MAMMON ON PARADE

After the successful Revolution of July 1830, the French bourgeoisie emphasized its triumph musically by a complete overhauling of the old *Académie royale de musique,* or *Opéra.* The story of the procedure has been particularly well told by William L. Crosten in his book *French Grand Opera, An Art and a Business,* and my own remarks about it are derived largely from that excellent treatise.

As we have seen, the *Opéra* had languished during the earlier period of the Restoration, though some vocal improvement had been achieved in the late twenties. It had always been, like most European opera houses, a royal luxury, an expense to the government. But now, under the new regime, the merchants and manufacturers of the Chamber of Deputies, many of them from provincial regions, became as unwilling as if they had been Americans to vote public funds for underwriting the deficit of a badly run entertainment in which they themselves had little interest. They were not yet ready to toss the whole thing out, for—rightly handled—it could be made into a brilliant advertisement for the new regime. They decided on a policy whereby the government kept the *Opéra* as a property—and even continued its subsidies on a reducing scale—but turned its management over to a private entrepreneur who would run it at his risk and for his possible profit. The entrepreneur whose bid was accepted proved to be a Dr. Louis Véron. He was a man of no previous active theatrical or musical experience; in fact, his capital had been amassed through the sale of a patent medicine, a chest ointment alleged to have been helpful in the cure of colds. He was, however, an excellent businessman and a true French bourgeois; his inestimable advantage was that he needed only to consult his own instinctive tastes and predilections to know what the mass of his probable customers would like.

Véron understood that the bulk of middle-class Frenchmen did not care enough for music in itself to permit it alone to carry the success of any show. His public liked spectacle, pageantry, startling action, and dancing. Now that the ambitious stockbrokers, real estate speculators, cotton manufacturers, and their lawyers and doctors were preparing to take over the *Opéra*'s boxes and best seats, he would see to it that they got something they could wholeheartedly enjoy. Even before the July Revolution, a trend toward scenic magnificence could have been seen in such operas as *La Muette de Portici* and *William Tell.* Now Véron prepared a richer dish for his own entrée: he induced the collaboration of the canny playwright Scribe, whose success as a fashioner of spoken drama based on the incidents of bourgeois life had been outstanding; Duponchel, whose imaginative notions of scenic design were derived from the popular theaters; and composer Jacob Meyerbeer, skillful adventurer in tone colors. They say 200,000 francs were spent when together they produced *Robert le Diable,* which opened on November 21, 1831, with a success unparalleled on the French stage.

The piece is a staging of a bloody-thunderous medieval legend, which includes a pageant of knighthood in the first act, the disappearance of a diabolical villain in a cloud of brimstone at the end, and—most startling and Parisian of all—a third-act scene in the cemetery of a ruined cloister in which suddenly a flock of dead nuns arise from their graves, throw off their religious garb, and do a wild dance. Massed movements and dramatic climaxes closely harmonize with the stage setting throughout. But if Véron understood the kind of show his people liked, he likewise understood that they suffered from *nouveau-riche* insecurity and would easily shy away from the indignity of patronizing anything that might seem to show the blotches of failure. So he took good care to insure the complexion of success by hiring an effective claque and also by providing ample slush funds for the press, recently grown insolent with its freedom.

From being the least regarded, the *Opéra* under Véron's management became the most successful, the most talked of, the best attended of all Paris theaters. It began to show a profit for the first time in 160 years. *Robert le Diable* was followed by other "epics," as they used to say in Hollywood: these included *La Juive,* with music by Halévy, and *Les Huguenots,* with music again by Meyerbeer. All were lavish, glittering presentations, stirring productions involving an ingeniously showy fusion of the visual and the lively arts: rich-looking, rich-sounding, rich-feeling events for a rich audience, an audience of caparisoned stock-exchange heroes, their rivals and emulators, their dependents and their worshipers, as well as the remnant of old-regime nobles who helped to decorate their triumph.

In those days the *Opéra,* especially its lobby, became Paris'—and so Europe's—primary focus of "high society." When *Les Huguenots* was first presented on February 29, 1836, Baron James de Rothschild, the world's greatest lord of finance, chose to stress that occasion with a celebration of his own: he gave a great ball, to commence after the performance, inaugurating the new rue Laffitte palace that he had built during the previous two years. Sure enough, Duponchel, the *Opéra*'s star stage designer, devised the decorations for the event. Heinrich Heine staggered home from this party at 4 A.M. or so. Reporting the next day on the utter magnificence of everything, he said that the guests consisted of "a strict selection of aristocratic figures who could be impressive by their great names or high rank, the women, however, more by their beauty and their finery." He called the new mansion "the Versailles of the absolute monarchy of money." Elsewhere he said, penetratingly, of James Rothschild: "One must have respect for this man, if only on account of the respect that he inspires in most people."

Paris "grand opera," as it was called, became the resplendent, adored, dominant art of a new and gilded age. For a generation or more, opera houses in Holland and Belgium, Prussia and Saxony, Austria and Russia could find no undertaking more worthy than that of putting on the posh Paris productions as best they could—thus painting an afterglow of Paris splendor upon themselves and their patrons.

15. THE PIANO CATCHES GLORY FROM THE *OPÉRA*

THE GAUDY FLOWERING of the Paris *Opéra* coincided with the very period during which piano virtuosity broke out in its most exuberant foliage. Those were the years, we recall, when pianos began to be built with metal plates and bars, double-escapement action, and felt-covered hammers as standard equipment. The purpose of these improvements was, ultimately, to permit the instrument to make use of the human body's more extreme capacities: to let the player profitably use more of the force of his arms, and greater quickness and delicacy in the co-ordination of the smaller hand muscles. Even the reach of the arms was exploited further by the lengthening of the keyboard to seven octaves.

To a significant extent, the piano virtuosos were able to apply some of the *Opéra*'s glory to themselves by composing and playing brilliant fantasies, medleys, and variations on salient musical phrases of current grand-opera successes. The currency, luckily for them, was often of considerable duration. Not long after Chopin arrived in Paris, he played publicly with a cellist named Franchomme; and this being 1832, he composed for the occasion a fantasy for both instruments on snippets from *Robert le Diable.* Franz Liszt, early in the adult phase of his career, intoxicated the Parisians with his own steaming pianistic fricassee of the same opera. With an operatic hit-title on its program, a concert might even achieve a fraction of the *Opéra*'s social prestige. Few pianists had the athletic energy and speed of Liszt; however, many amateurs and teachers also wanted to creep a little closer to the marvelous *Opéra* right at home and with less finger strain. At the end of 1834 the one hundred nineteenth performance of *Robert le Diable* was reported—with a box-office take of 9600 francs; some months previously, Maurice Schlesinger had announced the publication of a *Fantaisie sur des motifs favoris de ROBERT-LE-DIABLE,* for piano, by Carl Czerny of Vienna, for non-Liszts and non-Chopins to fumble with.

Things moved faster with *Les Huguenots.* The most fabulous pianist of the time, next to Liszt, was Sigismond Thalberg. He had been in Paris since November 1835 and had spent the winter making himself and his playing mightily admired in private circles and in smaller public ones. It is quite likely that he attended the opening of *Les Huguenots* on February 29. He now planned a great concert of his own in a hall of unheard-of dimensions for such a purpose—the Théâtre-Italien, seating about fifteen hundred. After some postponements, the event was scheduled for April 16. Announcing it, the *Revue et Gazette Musicale* added: ". . . it has been decided in any case that he [Monsieur Thalberg] will play a fantasy of his own composition, upon motives from *Les Huguenots.*" So the pianist would ride the wave of the moment. But the insistence of the announcement had another point: the *Gazette Musicale,* we remember, was a Schlesinger house organ. Two weeks before the Thalberg concert announcement the *Gazette* had informed the public that Schlesinger was the official, accredited publisher of the *Les Huguenots* music and that the score and separate numbers would appear simultaneously in Paris, London, and Leipzig on May 1.

The statement, alas, also incorporated a complaint. During the weeks following February 29 the words *"Les Huguenots"* became an eminently erethic merchandise-label, likely to provoke little hemorrhages of money from almost anyone. Now, this grand opera deals with the historic sixteenth-century war between the Catholics and the Protestants; and to symbolize the latter, Meyerbeer incorporated into his score the tune of the famous hymn *"Ein' feste Burg ist unser Gott."* Through this chink the smooth Henri Herz thought he could squirm himself into a little fresh, if forbidden, sugar. Since he was on the outs with Schlesinger, he could not negotiate for the manufacture and sale of his own *"Fantaisies sur des motifs* . . . etc." of a Schlesinger-owned work. So he tried to jump the gun on the publisher: weeks before the announced publication date, he had printed a *Fantasy on the Protestant Chorale Sung in Meyerbeer's Huguenots,* providing it with a homemade introduction and a gratuitous *air de ballet* as an epilogue. After all, he did not appropriate a single note of Meyerbeer's and Schlesinger's music, for *"Ein' feste Burg"* had been in the public domain for centuries; nor did he, in words, make any unwarranted claims: he merely stated a fact with intent to deceive. Slick trick. The furious *Gazette* called it a "falsification."

Let us look a little more closely at this piano music. Variations on opera tunes were nothing new in 1830, for they had been common since the days of Mozart. Potpourris of operatic melodies were widely enjoyed since the days of Steibelt and Louis Jadin, early in the century. But these newer Parisian artifacts had greater elegance and pretentiousness than their predecessors. Beethoven, Weber, and dozens of lesser composers had been naïvely willing to start their sets of variations with a plain statement of the subject tune. By 1830 this procedure seemed too artless, too pedestrian for the demands of an assertive moneyed crowd. Variations now were made to open with a magniloquent introductory section containing a number of attention-raping chords and flourishes ranging over a good section of the keyboard. A clever composer might also incorporate into these a sly anticipatory allusion to a measure or two of the tune to come. The bustle would subside, and a hold would be arranged upon a leading tone or chord—whereupon the simply attired melody would come forth, effectively set off against the suspense just accumulated. In other words, the tune was made to "make an entrance" in the best theatrical or operatic manner. Moreover, the last variation usually was worked up into a long climactic finale. The medleys, likewise, were begun with a provocative, tendentious preamble;

and the different melodies were now chained together more plausibly with graceful connective tissue, also involving elements of anticipation and suspense. Some of the favorite tunes were repeated, decked out in glossy tonal ribbons, and—as in the variations—the loudest and fastest evolutions were saved for the finish.

We must not suppose that the *Opéra*'s ascendancy necessarily was gained to the detriment of the other Paris theaters. The Italian opera continued to flourish at any rate, and the heady success of grand opera may, through sheer propinquity, actually have boosted the success of the others. The fact was, the music of Meyerbeer's grand operas, while dramatically potent, contained relatively few symmetrical phrases suitable for excerption; it was the operas of Bellini, Donizetti, and Auber, as well as the older ones of Rossini, that gave the most scope and opportunity to the piano medley and variation confectioners.

It is safe to say that, to a considerable extent, the piano music of the years 1825–75 was a dependency of the opera. Together with the dance music of the period, operatic transcriptions, fantasies, potpourris, and variations formed the largest fraction of all music published for the instrument. We must note that these operatic "gems," or "pearls," or "echoes," as they were sometimes called later, were manufactured for all degrees of digital proficiency. Those involving real feats of skill and endurance—that is, those suitable for playing by outstanding virtuosos—were of course in the minority. Mostly they were adapted, for ready sale, to the abilities of a large group of middling players and their pupils: they were, notably, "brilliant but not difficult."

The opera houses, and their patrons, of the Germanies, of the Low Countries, and of England staggered worshipfully behind the Paris productions, months or years later. Local piano transcribers, medleyers, and variators followed in their train. German and English music shops were stocked with sheet-piles of locally contrived Paris-operatic derivations. In many cases—even where the authors', dealers', and purchasers' native tongue was German, or Dutch, or Swedish, or English—it was judged commercially more attractive to print the titles of these works in the French language. Shelves and windows bristled with *"composées et dediées."* Well, prosperous American and German diners-out have long been plagued with bills of fare offering *"potage parmentier," "crêpes suzette,"* and dishes *"au jus," "au gratin,"* and *"du jour"* —all with an odor of musty swank.

Some of the second-rate non-French pianistic processors of operatic pay dirt are names still vaguely remembered by a few old musicians, if only through the invectives aimed at them by Robert Schumann. For example, there was Franz Hünten, like Herz a German immigrated to Paris as well as a graduate of the *Conservatoire*. He gauged the average taste and capacity so accurately that publishers eventually paid him two hundred francs for a printed page. Twenty or thirty such pages, and a fair year's income could be taken in. But Hünten worked much harder than that at his easy stuff: by 1837 he could retire to his native Coblenz and enjoy life on his own acquired acres.

Most industrious of all was Vienna's famous Czerny, aforementioned. In 1848 his English publisher, Robert Cocks & Co., put out a complete list of his works, to date, reaching as far as Opus 798. The composer, however, survived for another nine years and was said to have increased his output still further, to reach Opus 1000. From this list we learn that Czerny had published at least 304 pieces built on melodies from 87 different operas, and, let us add, a few Parisian ballets as well. The enumeration reads like an encyclopedia of contemporary stage productions.

In 1845 John Ella, a London concert manager, called at Czerny's house in Vienna and got a picture of how the composer operated. There were four music desks set up in Czerny's studio; upon each reposed a composition or arrangement in progress. Czerny was apparently in the habit of working on one down to the end of a page, then turning to work on another while the ink was drying on the previous one; by the time he had completed the fourth, the first was ready to be turned over. He claimed to have set down more notes than any copyist. There was something sweet-natured and pure-minded about him; he never married, but lived for music as he saw it. At his death, he left money to have one or another of his masses regularly performed in his memory in church and assigned a portion of his considerable fortune to an asylum for deaf-mutes.

By mid-century all respectable, upkeeping, well-off families in northern Europe and northern America harbored living-room pianos. Daughters and wives, by belaboring them with shavings from *William Tell, La Juive, Norma,* and *Lucia di Lammermoor,* were exhaling faint dilutions of the glorious vapor of Paris and thus were offering and taking holy communion with Louis XIV and James Rothschild.

16. THE MORE PIANOS THE MERRIER

MUSIC FOR TWO PIANOS had been recognized for nearly half a century as an interesting resource of tone combination, capable of many special artistic effects. Mozart, for example, composed a number of excellent works in this medium. Long before that, Sebastian Bach had written or arranged concertos for two harpsichords, one even for three, and one possibly for four harpsichords. That, however, was an extravagance that had no imitators for a hundred years. Now, in the middle 1820's, there broke out a vogue for public performances by three, four, six, or more pianos played together, sometimes by two players at each keyboard. We strongly suspect, though we cannot prove it, that this craze was started when Kalkbrenner returned to Paris from London in 1823. His mind must have been full of the multiple simultaneous piano lessons given to children in the Logier "academies" with which he had been associated. Perhaps he calculated that a more flashy use of this procedure could be made if the participants were all competent professional performers.

We recall that in 1831 young Chopin came to Paris, after some detours, from his native Warsaw. Full of genius, but a little uncertain of how his powers would rate in the big city, he decided he would go to Kalkbrenner—the big man of the piano world of the moment—and ask him for instruction. Kalkbrenner, flattered, could not resist pretending to accept the superior young pianist as a disciple. He could teach Chopin little in the way of music; however, he seems to have converted him fairly consistently to the use of Pleyel pianos, in which he had more than a platonic interest. Kalkbrenner also was able briefly to wear the young composer in his buttonhole by making him a sort of protégé on the occasion of his first Paris concert appearance. The central offering indeed was Chopin, playing his own famous-to-be *Concerto in F minor* as well as his brilliant variations on a tune from *Don Giovanni;* but the program also afforded a Kalkbrenner presentation, a *Grande Polonaise* of his own construction, for no fewer than six pianos. The instruments were not very evenly matched, we hear: Kalkbrenner—as the eldest by twenty years, the very important person, and the august sponsor of the event as well as the composer of the piece—reserved the one available large concert grand for himself; Chopin, acting the acolyte, contented himself with a smaller one; while the other players used a varied assortment of pianos. The pianists were—apart from Kalkbrenner and Chopin—Chopin's fellow Pole Adalbert Sowinski, G. A. Osborne (a British Kalkbrenner pupil and assistant), Ferdinand Hiller, and Carl Stamaty. Felix Mendelssohn-Bartholdy, then twenty-three, on an early visit to Paris, had been announced on the program as one of the six coryphees. For some reason he did not play, but restricted himself to cheering Chopin from the front row. His place was taken by Carl Stamaty. The concert took place on February 26, 1832, in Pleyel Hall, needless to say.

Two pianos, it was generally realized by connoisseurs, could in many ways make more music than a single one; three, however, could add very little to what two could do; and four or more were a superfluity, if not a nuisance. Nevertheless, a flock of rich simpletons might readily be impressed by a lot of apparatus and pay good money to be in a room with it. After all, to people who live for money, quantity *is* quality. Given a public fashionably crazy about pianos and pianists, a multiple piano performance can make a fine opportunity to offer it a lavishness of goodness, a shower of excellence, an expensive all-star stunt. Italy had shown little interest in the piano for a long time. Still, large-city Italians —like other European urbanites—were glad to string along after Paris, and so Milan was willing to rave about an occasion in 1838 at which six pianists—Liszt, Hiller, Pixis, Mortier la Fontaine, Franz Schoberlechner, and Orrigi—played the overture to *The Magic Flute* together in an arrangement for three pianos. Enthusiastically, the newspaper report called it "the concert of sixty fingers."

These many-barreled piano events occasionally could develop internal crises. A story was told about one in London in 1840, in which Herz, Thalberg, Moscheles, and Liszt were the four rockets scheduled to be exploded together. The house was packed, the time had come, but Liszt had not yet arrived. It grew later and later, and the audience began to murmur. As the other three were about to start Lisztlessly, the self-willed Franz appeared. The four pianists forthwith took their places at the keyboards, where they observed that they had the wrong parts before them. Not daring to take any more time for adjustments, Herz cried to his partners: *"Courage! Allons toujours!"* They began as they were, went through the piece to the finish, each one playing one of the other's parts, and reaped great applause.

The multipiano vogue lasted for twenty-five years or so, spanning the whole climax of the piano-virtuoso delirium. It extended over all Europe and into the United States before subsiding for a time.

17. THE GREAT RAVE

HERE WE MUST CONSIDER the relationship of our subject to the phenomenon known as romanticism. The term is properly a vague one, since it covers a large, vague complex of literary and artistic trends, interests, predilections, and pretenses during the later eighteenth and earlier nineteenth centuries. The word had some mockers at first, but by 1830 it was highly virtuous and respectable.

Romanticism could mean a preference for the reckless—the drunken—statement over one that was neatly arranged and innerly coherent; it could mean a mystical yearning for infinity, as well as a fondness for the undisciplined connection of incompatibles. Romanticism emphasized a misunderstanding infatuation with the Middle Ages; it could develop a fancy for old wives' spook stories, including a preoccupation with cobolds, undines, willis, and Norse gods. It involved a feeling for the grandeur of suicide pacts, the allurements of tuberculosis, and the ineffable charms of hashish-taking; it delighted in exaggerating the strangeness of non-European places such as Mississippi, Bagdad, or St. Helena, and in distorting luridly the facts of military and rural life, or those of love between the sexes. Romantic playwrights liked to invent characters who dropped dead in the last act upon no physical provocation; and romantic poets worked themselves into a dull fixation on nightingales and swans, roses, violets, and lilies, and a dozen other plants and animals the total of which they grandiloquently called "Nature."

Here we are concerned with a phase of romanticism that could be called Satanism. For a generation or two, bold people had been playing dangerous games with new forces: their fumbling with steam engines, with hot-air balloons, with portentous little flashes of electricity, all seemed like the impious theft of a divine fire, like Prometheus' snatching the flame from the god's chariot.

Moreover, the challenge to the king of heaven was somehow in harmony with the overthrow of the kings of earth that had just been accomplished in America and France. Apprehension was vaguely felt: would all this end well? It is understandable that men of those times should have enjoyed identifying themselves with a superior being, an angel who bravely defied God and suffered. They liked, through their fictioneers, to dream of tarnished heroes who resembled Milton's Lucifer, with his "baleful eyes," his "faded cheek," and his "brows of dauntless courage." They loved high-minded bandits such as Schiller's *Karl Moor* or Nodier's *Jean Sbogar,* musician, painter, and robber. A real person such as Lord Byron—nobleman, poet, and scoundrel—was idolized in the same sense, especially in lands other than his own, far beyond the merits of his literary productions. The subject is treated with great discernment in the classic volume by Mario Praz entitled *The Romantic Agony*.

It was fitting that the period's "fatal man" of music, the age's Satanic tone-artist, be one who played the fiddle—that well-known gimmick which the Middle Ages liked to thrust into the hands of sinister figures such as Death, the Devil, skeletons, and cats. Paganini had a fierce-looking nose and a lofty brow; his faded cheek was surely the symptom of a chronic spinal ailment. In the poetics of the time, this physiognomy—together with the curious stance he assumed—rhymed darkly with his unheard-of effects on his instrument, his queer methods of tuning, his amazing gyrations on a single string, and his sleight-of-left-hand pizzicatos. A romanticist public needed only the excuse of seeing that sick face and hearing that startling fiddle-trickery attached to the same man in order to pack him off ecstatically into all manner of awful supernatural associations and wonderful secret crimes. The yarns about his diabolical entanglements were widely retold, since they gave the tellers pleasure; Paganini himself, with one of his baleful eyes firmly cocked on his teeming box office, did not dream of denying them.

The Paganini of the piano was Franz Liszt. The statement is more than a mere metaphor: Liszt, at twenty, heard the legendary violinist in his first Paris appearance, on March 9, 1831. Inflamed by his unimaginable feats, his personality, and the frenzy he inspired in the audience, the young pianist vowed he would achieve the same heights with his own instrument. He retired for some years and worked to develop thitherto unexplored possibilities on the keyboard as well as unexplored extremes of emotional resource in his own nature. When he emerged to play again for people, it was clear that he had expanded the limits of piano playing as it had been previously known. Soon he published his *Twelve Etudes of Transcendent Execution,* which did indeed transcend any demands of strength and agility that had yet been made of two hands at a single keyboard. They represent a peak of pianistic prowess that few have scaled since his time. Liszt's playing was now gripping, almost terrifying in its intensity; nevertheless, it never quite threw his hearers' minds so inevitably upon the devilish imagery that Paganini had inspired. Liszt's face and figure were healthily good-looking; yet in the rash vehemence of his impact upon the keys, in the storm of his leaps and sweeps, in the way in which the shake of his long hair seemed to impart a "dauntless courage" to his brow, there was something heaven-defying, something Promethean and Luciferous, that rejoiced the romantic hearts of his time.

In Liszt, the human ideal of the age—the romantic hero—was married to the musical instrument, newly perfected, that best mirrored the age's mechanical and commercial aspirations. In worshiping Liszt, his public also worshiped the piano, and in either case it really worshiped itself. Never before his time did the instrument soar to such blinding heights of social value, and never since. The time was about 1835 to 1848.

Liszt's bounding virility attracted many women, notably the Countess Marie d'Agoult. She abandoned her family and her husband in order to join the pianist on an illicit honeymoon protracted over several years in Switzerland and Italy. The irregular relationship made some practical difficulties for him in soberer bourgeois situations, but its repute added, if anything, to his romantic glamour as a performing artist. Other women felt a mental kinship with him, without tangling with him in a love affair. The Princess Christina Belgiojoso, aristocratic Italian republican conspiratrix, was especially well disposed toward him. She was a pale, sensitive, large-eyed, morbid brunette beauty, a *poseuse* who decorated some of her rooms with black velvet punctuated by silver stars, a little like a catafalque. She displayed herself in her box at the Italian opera dressed in a nun's garb, but with pond lilies in her hair, and sometimes she evinced such overpowering music-inspired emotion that she was to be observed being carried out into her carriage. She did seem to care truly for music and she collected and stimulated prominent musicians and other artists at her Saturday parties. Occasionally they called her the "Romantic Muse."

In a letter to her, Liszt reported an achievement that became a landmark in the history of public piano playing: that of giving an entire concert all by himself, without the background of an orchestra or of assisting singers. Under the date of June 4, 1839, he wrote her, with affected self-depreciation:

> . . . these tiresome *musical soliloquies* (I do not know what other name to give these inventions of mine) with which I contrive to gratify the Romans, and which I am quite capable of importing to Paris, so unbounded does my impudence become! Imagine that, wearied with warfare, not being able to put together a program that would have common sense, I have ventured to give a series of concerts all by myself, affecting the Louis XIV style, and saying cavalierly to the public, *"le concert, c'est moi."* For the curiosity of the thing, I copy a program of one of the soliloquies for you:
>
> 1. Overture to *William Tell,* performed by M. Liszt.
> 2. Fantasy on reminiscences of *I Puritani,* composed and performed by the above-named.
> 3. Studies and Fragments, composed and performed by same.
> 4. Improvisation on a given theme—still by the same.
>
> That is all.

Liszt may not have known that Moscheles had given a public "musical soliloquy," of a sedate historically expository kind, in London two years before. In any event, it is Liszt's overwhelmingly successful example that has been followed by all other pianists since. Small wonder: even for artists poorly qualified to interest an audience for an entire evening alone, it was always agreeably cheaper not to hire a supporting cast.

The idolization of Liszt began in Paris, but the cities to the east whipped it up many degrees higher. In Vienna, said Eduard Hanslick, "the ladies lost their hearts and the critics their heads." One of the latter, Moritz Gottlieb Saphir, only pretended to lose his; a witty verbalist and an unscrupulous character, he enjoyed a considerable and scandalous local fame for a while. He wrote:

> What shall I say now about Liszt as a pianist, about this *Jupiter fulminans* of piano playing? Woe is us! There I see us reviewers . . . sitting downcast, embarrassed, in despair! We have exhausted ourselves! We have handed out all the medals of praise, have flung away all the counterfeit coins of enthusiasm. Just as children who do not know the value of money throw money away, so we, not knowing

the value of words, have squandered praise salve, flattery vapor, poems, wreaths and what not, and now, alas, we have no small and no large praise left. Poor Liszt!! [One of Liszt's concerts had been for the benefit of Danube flood victims.] Come, let us give a concert for the benefit of all reviewers, critics and literary hacks made victims of a flood of praise-sirup, who have lost all their praise and their property, who are now expected to praise a colossal, gigantic artist and have nothing, absolutely nothing, left in their brief cases.

Saphir seems to have broken open a piggy bank, for he managed to bring out a little shiny small change, thus: "Liszt is the Chimborazo of difficulties, on whose slopes there bloom the violets of tenderness . . ." But he must have mortgaged a hoarded sunburst when he wrote as follows:

Liszt . . . is an amiable fiend who treats his mistress—the piano—now tenderly, now tyrannically, devours her with kisses, lacerates her with lustful bites, embraces her, caresses her, sulks with her, scolds her, rebukes her, grabs her by the hair, clasps her then all the more delicately, more affectionately, more passionately, more flamingly, more meltingly; exults with her to the heavens, soars with her through all the skies and finally settles down with her in a vale of flowers covered by a canopy of stars. . . . After the concert Liszt stands there like a victor on the battlefield, like a hero at a tournament. Daunted pianos lie around him; torn strings wave like flags of truce; frightened instruments flee into distant corners; the listeners look at each other as after a cataclysm of nature that has just passed by, as after a storm out of a clear sky, as after thunder and lightning, mingled with a rain of flowers and a snow of petals and a shimmering rainbow; and he stands there leaning melancholically on his chair, smiling strangely, like an exclamation point after the outbreak of general admiration. Thus is Franz Liszt.

The Hungarians remembered that Liszt had been born within their borders; their hearts swelled to think that one of their boys had made it—right up there in the big city, where all that money and all those fancy people were. Liszt had left Hungary at the age of nine, and he never could speak a word of Hungarian. Yet at his Budapest concert of January 4, 1840, after the applause and cheers had subsided, a number of Hungarian dukes came upon the stage and presented him in the name of the nation with a richly jeweled sword, the symbol of service or nobility. Following this, a troop of twenty thousand people formed a torchlight procession to accompany him back to his dwelling and hung about in the cold waiting to see him once more at his window. The next day a deputation handed him the honorary citizenship of the city of Pest, while another deputation appealed to the Emperor to grant him a patent of nobility.

In Berlin, during the first ten weeks of 1842, he gave twenty-one public concerts. The Prussian King Frederick William IV was a frequent attendant and so, of course, was all Berlin's high society. Presently the King decorated him with the order *Pour le Mérite,* a war-service honor to which a "peace class" for artists and savants had been added *ad hoc.* Women became especially hysterical. One woman was seen to kneel before him, begging to kiss his finger tips; another retrieved the dregs of his tea and poured them into her private vial as a sacred relic; another salvaged the butt of his cigar and wore it in her bosom. When he left town, a grand escort procession was arranged to see him past the gates.

> A carriage drawn by six white horses waited for him at his hotel. As Liszt appeared he was hailed by a thousand-headed cheering multitude. He took his place next to the elders of the University. Thirty carriages-and-four followed his, escorted by fifty-one horsemen in academic gala array, representatives of various student fraternities. Hundreds of private coaches attached themselves to this official suite, to accompany him in festive procession through the city. All streets were densely crowded, thundering cheers announced the proximity of the celebrity. Even the court had ridden into town to have a look at the joy. Not *like* a king, but *as* a king did he depart, surrounded by the shouting crowd, as a king in the deathless realm of the spirit.

The biographer Julius Kapp gleaned these gaudy details from the newspapers of the time.

All this for a piano arrangement of the *William Tell* Overture, or a medley from *Lucia di Lammermoor*? To a certain extent, yes; but chiefly, Liszt became an instigation, a detonating cap, for a romantic orgy into which people were trembling at any moment to explode. They were impatient to idealize themselves in the projected image of a pale young firebrand who tossed his tresses and did battle with the gods alone, with his two bare hands, leaving an echo of octave thunder and a debris of smashed pianos in his wake.

In England, Liszt's spell was less potent; his tours there during 1840–41 were, relatively, failures. They had one historic result, however, the coining of a term thenceforth to become inseparable from the concert world. It was said to have been Frederick Beale, an English musician, who first referred to Liszt's unassisted evening's performance as his "recitals on the pianoforte"—in the plural so as to suggest the various compositions played. The word first appeared in print in the announcement of Liszt's concert at the Hanover Square Rooms, June 9, 1840. It was ridiculed at the time: "How can one recite on the piano?" Still it stuck, the plural form curtailed, and has remained in active use until this day.

18. MORE RAVE

DURING HIS BRILLIANT DAYS Liszt had a competitor. Sigismond Thalberg likewise had the makings of a romantic hero, but one so interestingly different from his rival that he could never be belittled as a mere "second Liszt." Thalberg's adorers did not need to be quickened by the image of a noble mistress, for their champion embodied the romantic charms of both illicitude and aristocracy even more fundamentally: he was known to be the illegitimate son of Count Moritz von Dietrichstein and the Baroness von Wetzlar. When he was a baby, there had come up the ticklish question of a name for him; his mother proved quite a romanticist in thinking one up. She wrote to his father:

> May this child be the peaceful Valley [*Thal* in German] in which from now on I will confine all my quiet, secret happiness; but may he also some day become a Mountain [*Berg* in German] upon which my pride and my greatest love will be enthroned on high, and who in his own greatness will tower over everything that, in vain prejudice and caste feeling, now inflates itself and piles itself up between us; and so the child shall be called Thal-Berg.

He had been sent to a fine school in Vienna, and there had been brought up with the young Duke of Reichstadt, the so-called "King of Rome," Napoleon's son by the Empress Marie Louise. People enjoyed believing that Thalberg, disconsolate over the beloved young Duke's premature death, slept for days in the deceased's bed. The story carries just the right romantic flavor of emotional extravagance tinged with obnoxiousness.

It was Thalberg's public manner, however, that was his chief attraction, apart from his very able playing. His behavior seemed almost in pointed contrast to that of Liszt. Instead of the latter's fiery, unruly gestures, Thalberg, perfectly dressed, groomed, and barbered, cultivated an air of perfect poise, an abstention from every superfluous movement, however emotionally apposite, during his most hazardous fingerwork. He appeared to realize the Zen ideal of central peace with peripheral combat. Toward his audience, too, he maintained his attitude of graceful reserve; whether his hearers rioted or applauded politely, he acknowledged them only with a cool, short, condescending bow. A public pianist who was truly a gentleman!—it was something new in the world, something that also had to wait for the days of Louis Philippe. Rich plebeians might now claim the right to look up at him and to him, in a hall, for ten francs. Meanwhile, as they did so, all sorts of swift and sweet sounds issued from his piano as he was operating its keys.

He developed a specialty: in his fantasies and transcriptions he had a way of playing a melody in the middle of the keyboard and drawing scarves of quick arpeggios around it, above and below, in such fashion that to simple ears it might sound as if three rather than two hands were doing it. Apart from his agility, it was his clever shading that helped to make this device convincing; since the accompanying arpeggios were kept very soft, the resonance of the well brought out melody tones could seem to fuse into a continuity—in other words, could seem to "sing." By now the word "singing" as applied to a piano tone had become something of a cliché among the instrument's devotees; perhaps they felt impelled to emphasize it, romantically, just because of its fundamental impossibility.

In due time, Thalberg, like other well-known pianists, published his "Method" of piano playing: he called it, autointoxicatedly, *The Art of Singing Applied to the Piano*. Another famous metaphorical cliché may have had its very first application to Thalberg. It was a reviewer, Henri Blanchard, writing a blurb on him for the *Gazette Musicale* for May 8, 1836, who said that "from under his fingers there escaped handfuls of pearls." It was a good-looking lady, admitted the writer, from whom he had just heard this line: pretties from the pretty.

Thalberg, like Liszt, played Erard's pianos; yet apparently he did not finally make up his mind about them at once. Other makers seem to have had their influence upon him, for at his concert of March 1837 we hear that he played his first and third number on an Erard, but shifted to a Pleyel for his second—rather curious business in our present-day eyes. The Erards, however, had some convincing arguments: in the report of Thalberg's tour of England, Scotland, and Ireland early in 1840, we hear that an Erard grand was shipped with him everywhere he played, at a total expense of six thousand francs.

In March 1838 the *Gazette* reviewer reported that Thalberg's recent concert had been "the most expensive of the year; no one since Paganini had dared to put the exhibition of his talent at so high an assessment . . ." Far from reproaching the artist, says the writer, he finds the fact honorable and significant; paying a high price, he maintains, is of all formulas of praise the least banal, the least ambiguous, "and we will say that, although one paid twenty francs to hear the great pianist, the crowd pushed and piled itself into the Erard rooms: you will understand what kind of a crowd, the fine flower, the prime choice, the aristocracy of art fanciers! It is really a pleasure to raise the art-tax on people who settle it so easily and with such good grace!"

For some years Liszt and Thalberg each had his eager partisans. The antagonism was profitable for both: it got each of them talked about doubly. Enthusiasts bracketed them like certain heavenly twins of the past: there were comparisons with Dante and Petrarch, Michelangelo and Raphael, Goethe and Schiller. All this gave a cue to the Princess Belgiojoso for another of her expensive effects: she persuaded both the rivals to play at her home on the same evening, March 31, 1837. The affair was a charity performance, for the benefit of the lady's pet Italian refugees. The house was crowded, at forty francs (eight dollars) a ticket. Each pianist played an opera fantasy of his own: Thalberg, one on Rossini's *Moses;* Liszt, one on Pacini's *Niobe.* Fortunately, the encounter was a draw—there was no knockout, not even a decision on points. Much encouraged, the Romantic Muse planned a bigger, more complicated operation, again for the relief of her lucky Italian refugees. She induced six leading pianists of the moment to participate in the same concert; they were, besides Liszt and Thalberg, Chopin, Henri Herz, J. P. Pixis (the weak sister of the bunch), and Carl Czerny, who happened to be in Paris on a trip at the time. Six instruments were on the stage at once, and each pianist in turn played his own variation on a tune from *I Puritani*, a successful opera by Bellini produced three years earlier. In addition to his own variation, Liszt, as the shaggiest mane among this little herd of lions, was privileged to compose and play an introduction and finale to this game. The whole thing was published later, and Liszt played it frequently under the name of *Hexameron.*

More piano virtuosos came forth—for instance, Theodore Doehler, whom the Duke of Lucca had retained as his private delectator. Heinrich Heine, writing on April 20, 1841, waxed ironical, as so often, in quoting a puff for him in the *Gazette* to the effect that the pianist had enchanted all hearts at his recent Marseille concert, especially because of his interesting pallor, the result of a recently vanquished illness. Doehler has since given concerts in Paris, says Heine, "indeed his playing is neat, cute, and pretty; his performance is charming, reveals an astonishing finger-fluency, but neither strength nor spirit. Graceful weakness, elegant impotence, interesting pallor."

There was Alexander Dreyschock of Prague, who showed himself off at the Erard rooms early in 1843. He played his own difficult *études* and caprices—no opera fantasies, strange to say—for three hours, with great violence and many gestures. The obliging reviewer spoke of a newly constituted trinity "of which Liszt is the father, Thalberg the son, and Dreyschock the holy ghost." Said Heine: "He made a hell of a racket." In any case, his powerful left hand seemed worth gaping at; servile publics in Vienna and Hamburg raved about it, and his *Fantasy on God Save the King, for the left hand alone* was practically worth a livelihood to him.

Still other kinds of pianists swelled the Paris coagulation. In 1838 Stephen Heller arrived from Hungary via Vienna. A sober, studious musician, not without wit, he played relatively little in concerts but became well noted as a composer and teacher. He turned out plenty of operatic medleys of moderate brilliance and difficulty, but also many original pieces of charm and refinement. His *études* are still played with pleasure by young people.

A young German, Carl Halle, came to Paris to study, remained to play and to teach, and made a small but good impression on a fragment of the public. More aspiring, less vain, and less of a gypsy temperament than some of the other pianists, he found himself drawn to Heller, with whom he formed a lifelong friendship. Much later he was to become the highly respected Sir Charles Hallé, the founder and conductor of Manchester symphony concerts.

Leopold von Meyer, or de Meyer (the particle may be of dubious authenticity anyway), came to Paris briefly in the early 1840's. He seems to have been a lively, muscular player of a shallow kind, and his self-advertisements—such as calling himself the "Lion Pianist"—undoubtedly attracted business to him as well as laughter. A piece of his called *Marche Marocaine* had a considerable vogue for a while.

One evening in April 1845 Chopin betook himself to Pleyel Hall to hear his *Concerto in E minor* played by a sixteen-year-old pianist named Louis Moreau Gottschalk, a native of New Orleans. Much impressed with the performance, he complimented and kissed the youth in proper Polish-French fashion. Gottschalk's well-to-do family had brought him up like a gentleman, fully equipped with Greek and fencing, and for years many elegant Paris families were glad to see and hear him in their *salons*. Soon he began to present his own compositions, many of which were elaborations of popular Creole melodies he had heard in his Louisiana childhood. The romanticist world was charmed with their exotic flavor, especially that of their titles. "An American composer, good God!" exclaimed one critic with typical European rudeness, but then went on to say that Gottschalk was a player "of the highest order" and to rave over his *Bamboula*. Presently his *The Banana Tree, The Manzanilla,* and *The Savanna* proved irresistible as notions and syllables, as well as tunes. The pieces were persuasively short, and audiences never hesitated to encore them.

Gottschalk had the correct looks: pale, frail, and melancholy; correct romantic verbiage invariably gushed upon his performances. "There is a scale like a string of pearls leading you back to the minor key! Oh, listen to that scale which flows so sweetly; it is not the hand of a man that touches the keys, it is the wing of a sylph that caresses them . . ." "Gottschalk afterward played '*Bananier*,' one of the most delicious pieces of imagination; it might have been said that a shower of pearls escaped melodiously from the keyboard." Those busy pearls. ". . . and the artist? Behold how his look becomes animated and how his pale tint becomes colored little by little! how his features express the suffering of his soul; how noble his head is and how all his body seems to grow larger; it is an attraction without example . . ." Too bad he was not consumptive; he would have seemed complete.

Gottschalk toured in Switzerland and in Spain, and some of the response he got sounds as if there had been a regurgitation of Lisztian ichor. In Geneva, we hear at second hand:

> A young, pretty, and robust Genevese girl waited for him at the coming out of the concert where the pianist had been covered with flowers and, enveloping him all at once in a large mantle, took him in her arms and carried him off, which the frail and delicate nature of the victim permitted her to do easily, to the general consternation. We do not know if this be true; we tell it as it was told. What is certain is, that the young pianist precipitately left Geneva after having been the delight of the elegant society there . . .

It was Oscar Comettant, the well known Paris critic, who relayed this tale in the *Feuilleton du Siècle* for November 1, 1850.

In Spain, after Gottschalk had played for the Queen, a noble colonel had the garrison of Valladolid pass in review before him; moreover, a famous bullfighter sent him his precious sword as a souvenir. In Madrid, Gottschalk and his cohorts performed a piece that he composed especially for the occasion, called *The Siege of Saragossa,* for ten pianos. A Madrid newspaper was quoted as reporting on June 14, 1852:

> Applause ran through the room after each phrase, each variation. There is a passage in which Gottschalk in a most ingenious manner imitates a military parade, accompanied by the beating of the drum; it produced such a sensation that all people rose to their feet, men and women, and he was compelled to repeat the entire passage. The Minister of Agriculture was unable to restrain his emotion and shouted forth *"Viva la Reina,"* which was the climax of the mad enthusiasm.

Regarding pianists in general, we cannot refrain from again quoting the incomparable Heine:

> The piano virtuosos come to Paris every winter like swarms of locusts, less to gain money than to make a name for themselves here, which will help them all the more to a rich pecuniary harvest in other countries. Paris serves them as a kind of billboard on which their fame may be read in enormous letters. I say their fame may be read here, for it is the Paris press that proclaims it to the world, and those virtuosos have the greatest virtuosity in exploiting newspapers and newspapermen. They can get to the deafest of people, since human beings are always human, are receptive to flattery, also enjoy playing the role of protector; and one hand washes the other. The uncleaner of the two, however, is rarely that of the journalist, and even the purchasable flattery-smearer is at the same time a

> poor sap who takes half his pay in sweet words. They talk of the venality of the press; it is a great mistake. On the contrary, the press is usually duped, and this holds true particularly for the celebrated virtuosos. They are all celebrated, really, that is, in the advertisements that they promote into print either in their own august persons, or through a brother or through their Madame mother. It is hardly believable how abasingly they beg in the newspaper offices for the tiniest handout of praise, how they bend and squirm. While I was still in favor with the director of the *Gazette Musicale* . . . I could truly see with my own eyes how these famed creatures lay like subjects at his feet and crawled and wagged before him so as to be given a little favorable mention in his paper; and of our high-feted virtuosos, who deign to receive homage in all capitals like victorious princes, we could well say, in Béranger's manner, that on their laurel crowns one may still see the dust of Moritz Schlesinger's boots.

Even after making a suitable discount for the author's own vanity and meanness, we can read the truth in his words.

The bourgeois public that came to piano concerts such as Liszt's was as arrogant—but much more rude, crude, and cheaply snobbish—as the old aristocrats it replaced. In Milan, Liszt had placed one of his *études* on the program, whereupon a man in the audience exclaimed resentfully: "I came to the theater to be entertained, not to hear somebody practice!" The person was expressing the sentiments of the frightening majority, thought Liszt; so to liven things up at his next appearances, he made a point of asking members of the audience to suggest themes upon which he might improvise, and an exquisitely worked silver chalice, attributed to a Cellini pupil, was placed in the lobby to receive the slips of paper that recorded their ideas. When Liszt unfolded them on the stage, they mostly turned out to be tunes from Rossini or Bellini operas; but some "themes" also read "The Milan Cathedral," or "The Railroad," or "Is it better to be married or to remain a bachelor?"

A very small coterie of persons in Paris during the thirties did indeed develop a better, profounder taste for music and began to enjoy the performances of Beethoven's works put on by the orchestra at the *Conservatoire*. In fact, the name of Beethoven was by way of becoming a fashionable superstition. At a chamber-music concert that Liszt arranged early in 1837, two trios were on the program, one by Beethoven and one by J. P. Pixis; for some reason they were played in reverse order, but the audience was not informed. With unerring snobbery, the hearers enjoyed, applauded, and raved over Pixis' composition when it was labeled Beethoven and proclaimed it a work of genius, but were bored by Beethoven labeled Pixis, which they took pains to belittle.

Sometimes their behavior was nastier. Liszt, be it understood, was a musician of high ideals and fine discrimination in addition to being a success-greedy virtuoso. On April 3, 1841, he arranged a concert at the *Conservatoire,* the program devoted entirely to Beethoven's music, for the purpose of raising a monument to the great composer at Bonn. Liszt himself played the *Kreutzer* Sonata with the worthy violinist Lambert Massart; but after the first movement the audience, which had come attracted by the name of Liszt, began to be fed up with Beethoven. "Play *Robert le Diable,*" somebody shouted at him; the word was taken up, and presently the whole auditorium was loudly demanding his flashy fantasy on the well-known opera. Liszt tried to hedge. "Shall I play the *Robert* fantasy after the sonata?" he asked. "Play it now!" was the cry. He played it then and there, as an interruption of the Beethoven sonata, while his collaborator meekly stood aside and waited till he was finished. European intellectuals, brought up to be impudent without realizing it, are of course certain that the foregoing incidents are typical American occurrences and could not possibly happen in exquisite old lands such as France or Italy.

Piano virtuoso concerts were all the rage among a certain class of people, yet they could not in any true sense of the word have been called "popular." The number of auditors at a concert seems triflingly small by modern standards. Pleyel Hall held about three hundred persons comfortably, and possibly another fifty could have been squeezed in; the Erard rooms were crowded with an attendance of four hundred. Herz's hall was of approximately the same size. The Hanover Square Rooms, one of London's principal concert halls, in which Haydn and other celebrities had made their debuts, held about six hundred. When as many as eight hundred people attended one of Liszt's Berlin concerts early in 1842, the fact was worthy of special notice. Concerts at the Paris Italian Opera, seating about fifteen hundred, were rare; still much rarer were such events as Liszt's first appearance in St. Petersburg, at the Peers' Hall, at which something like three thousand people were present. Nevertheless, a "small" Paris concert could make an international reputation, since in the European scheme of values four hundred countesses and financiers were worth more than the rest of the population put together.

19. PIANO TEACHING COULD BE LUCRATIVE

THE GOLDEN GLOW that Liszt, Thalberg, and others exhaled about themselves naturally fired many young people to emulate them. Any youth of above-average musical aptitude might easily be persuaded to dream of fame and money as the reward of assiduous labor at the piano. It was in those days that there became stereotyped the picture of the ordeal of years of slavery upon scales, arpeggios, double notes, and octaves as a prelude to mastery and acclaim. Cherubini, director of the *Conservatoire* until his death in 1842, had not altered his low opinion of the value of the pianoforte, despite the fashion of the times; he kept the number of admissions to that branch of study restricted. But now, for every vacant place there were thirty or forty aspirants. Being a graduate of the *Conservatoire* in itself carried an intrinsic prestige: it was a government school, and Europeans have an exaggerated respect for governments. At that, though the training the *Conservatoire* offered in piano playing was excellent on the technical side, it was far less so in the forming of style and taste. So said an anonymous but apparently competent writer in the *Gazette* of August 14, 1836.

Inevitably, there was quite a demand in Paris for artist teachers. Carl Halle, seventeen years of age, arrived in the metropolis and shopped about for a professor whose price he could afford. He had to live within a budget of two hundred francs a month; his board and lodging cost a hundred francs, and he could not rent a decent piano for less than twenty. At that rate, Liszt or Chopin, at twenty francs a lesson, were higher than he could pay; but that was the sum that all the well-known first-class pianists charged. Kalkbrenner, indeed, only asked ten or twelve francs, rather little for a man of his conceit—probably because he was rich and troubled himself little with teaching. In a letter to his parents dated October 1836, Carl wrote:

> There remains one hope for me, that of giving lessons. Here in Paris the most second-rate lessons are paid 5 francs an hour and good

> teachers easily get from 8 to 12 francs a lesson. Should I succeed in finding a few pupils, I could manage very well . . . Supposing I should succeed in a month or two, to give one lesson a day even at 6 francs, it would make 150 francs a month, that would already be a great help . . . If later on I should get four pupils a day at 10 francs each, we get a monthly income of 1040 francs . . . the result is grand, but not at all impossible. You can calculate what a man like Chopin must earn who gives eight or nine lessons a day at 20 francs . . . tell me any town in Germany, or anywhere else, where it would be possible to earn so much and at the same time have such opportunities of perfecting oneself in musical, and almost all other respects, as in Paris.

Halle eventually tied up with George A. Osborne, a Kalkbrenner disciple, paying him ten francs for a weekly lesson, which, he says, pleased him very much.

We can get a clearer picture of what these fees mean by referring them to incomes. When in 1848 a new French government got around to remunerating the members of the Chamber of Deputies, it fixed their salaries at twenty-five francs a day, a sum supposedly sufficient to maintain a bourgeois—that is, upper-middle class—standard of living. Under the circumstances, twenty francs for a piano lesson would be four-fifths of a day's income. If we roughly equate the annual nine thousand francs of a French deputy with the $12,500 a year of a United States congressman, we can readily understand that such a man might feel rather strained at paying $20 a week, or perhaps twice a week, to his daughter's music teacher. It is clear that twenty-franc lessons were intended to appeal to a restricted and exalted clientele.

Chopin did, indeed, make a good living from teaching; it was truly derived from the kind of pupils—that is, "society" ladies—who not only appreciated his artistic precept and example, but who felt that paying a high price was consonant with their own importance. A glance at the dedications of some Chopin compositions will show the people he went with. Several of them, for instance, are inscribed to various members of the Rothschild family. It was at the mansion of the great Baron James that his career got its decisive start, as he often liked to recall. He was led thither by his Polish acquaintance Prince Radziwill, almost on the spur of the moment, as he was walking the Paris streets in a state of depression, meditating on leaving the world—that is to say emigrating to the United States. A great party was in progress at the Rothschild residence, and young Chopin charmed everybody with his remarkable playing, reaping bouquets of feminine smiles and requests for lessons. From then on, he was "in."

He dedicated his famous *Polonaise in A-flat,* Opus 53, to August Leo, another banker of German-Jewish origin who—with his wife Sophie—was an especial fancier of music and musicians. Other dedicatees were the Countess d'Apponyi, wife of the Austrian ambassador, Baron Stockhausen, the Netherlands' ambassador, and Mademoiselle de Noailles, a descendant of one of France's oldest, noblest families; the Countess de Perthuis, whose husband was an aide-de-camp to King Louis Philippe, likewise has her name written memorably on a Chopin work, the great *Sonata in B minor.* A large portion of Chopin's friends, associates, and pupils were his compatriot Polish aristocrats and a few were well-born Germans. In general, his society was drawn from a rich refugee group, a part of the diplomatic corps, the Jewish financial coterie, and a relative minority of actual French gentry. It was a smart set in any event; he was a most acceptable protégé for its members, and they flocked to his rare concerts. Here is Liszt's description of the audience of April 26, 1841:

> At eight o'clock in the evening Monsieur Pleyel's rooms were splendidly lighted; numerous carriages in turn brought to the foot of a stairway covered with rugs and perfumed with flowers the most elegant ladies, the most fashionable young men, the most celebrated artists, the richest financiers, the most illustrious great lords, an entire elite of society, an entire aristocracy of birth, fortune, and beauty.

Chopin was the incomparable poet of the piano, the explorer of its most secret, delicious places; it is pleasant to think that his fashionable clients kept him in white gloves, in a manservant and a carriage, in flowers for his apartment, and in trips for and against his health, for the remainder of his short life.

Books on how to play the piano, so-called "methods," now came out plentifully, every prominent teacher naturally promoting his own. In 1840 F. J. Fétis, music educator, got Moscheles to join him in putting out a *Method of Methods,* one allegedly based on a distillation of a dozen of the best previous ones from C. P. E. Bach down. As a supplement, eighteen of Europe's best-known pianists were each asked to contribute one or more "*Études* of Perfection." The super-Method died young, but the three short *études* supplied by Chopin are still played frequently and with pleasure.

In August 1843 Henri Blanchard, minor composer and littérateur of some grace, published a slight ironical essay on piano teachers. He begins by mentioning the professions that have been most esteemed under the various regimes of the past: under Napoleon it was military science and mathematics, since the Emperor was supposed to have owed his success to those studies; later, professors of constitutional law, romantic literature, and political economy had their day. Blanchard continues:

> Among the professions most in fashion, we must cite in the front rank that of professor of the piano. The professor of the piano belongs to all classes of society in France; he is officer of the Legion of Honor, battalion chief of the National Guard, industrialist, elector, and eligible for office . . .

This was certainly true of the prosperous Herz and Kalkbrenner.

> If he has no government position, it is because he devotes all of his time to his pupils; that is, however, strictly speaking, not a reason, since he could very well occupy himself exclusively with his art and still hold a job: the thing has been observed, is still being observed, and will always be observed.

So boondoggling is not really an invention of the Roosevelt administration, as some would have us believe.

> The piano professor of the other sex—for there are many ladies who teach the playing of this instrument of such incontestable social utility—the feminine professor could not be better placed in the world for obtaining jobs for her relatives, friends, or acquaintances, and often there is no lack of them.

So it was not what you know, but whom you know, even in those ancient days.

> Since it is recognized that the professor of the piano has a high public usefulness, we must be permitted to inquire what are the qualities most suitable for properly fulfilling this important mission. Since he often has to do with young girls, it is necessary, so far as this is possible, that he be married, in the interests both of morals and of the security of parents. He must speak to his pupils with dignity mingled with grace and friendliness, without nevertheless showing himself too friendly, and he must set forth his principles

with as much clarity as ease. The professor of the piano ought to be an acclaimed, sought-after composer and performer . . . above all, a stereotyped smile on his face ought to conceal the boredom that the incapacity, the unintelligence, often even the stupidity of his pupils cause him to feel. This last part of his functions is easier for the lady professors . . .

It appears that after 1830, under the hegemony of the bankers, musicians were invited to many *salons* on terms of putative equality and that the burgeoning vogue of the piano may have contributed to the spread of this liberality. The piano was a house fixture; a lady possessing such a piece of potentially musical furniture might invite a pianist as if to a friendly gathering, pretending to assume that he was fit for polite society or at least giving him the benefit of what was sometimes a very reasonable doubt in this respect. A few feminine flatteries would suffice to overcome his coyness, and soon he would be fingering the house's keyboard. From a hostess' point of view, a pianist would be—*prima facie*—a more plausible-looking invitee than some other kind of instrumentalist, who would have to carry with him the telltale tool of his trade as well as an assistant, just as any plumber might. A hostess attempting to chisel some free music for her party might tremble lest an accosted fiddler launch the well-known counterattack: "But madame, my violin does not take dinner." In the case of a pianist, an unqualified invitation, tactfully silent on the subject of music, would suffice. He could coddle his ego for days with the fatuous notion that he was being asked for the pleasure of his company, almost as if he were a real estate speculator. Once at the *soirée,* he would usually play, from a natural desire to show off—or in the hope of eliciting requests for expensive lessons or of being able some day to sell blocks of tickets to a concert.

Machinery was wonderful and piano playing was wonderful: what could seem happier than a marriage of these two wonderfuls? So thought a number of promoters who brought out machines to help one learn to play the piano. Kalkbrenner started the thing in Paris. He was fresh from London, where he had been handling Logier's "Chiroplast"; but he appreciated its rather severe limitations, since it did not even permit the passing under of the thumb. He simplified it—abolishing the finger holes but keeping the two rigid rails between which the wrists were to be thrust—and labeled the whole object a "*guide-mains*" ("hand guide"). It had some vogue, though Liszt contemptuously called it a "jackass guide." Actually, it was too unpretentious—not complicated or tricky enough to seem interesting; another fatal defect was that its name was not Greek.

Soon the alert Henri Herz thought he smelled money in that quarter; he came out with a contraption to which he prudently gave the label "Dactylion." It consisted of a set of ten vertical springs, one to a finger, to be hung upright over the keyboard. A wire dangling from each carried a ring at its end, and the player was expected to put each finger through one of these rings, stretching the spring as he did so. The strain of the spring was supposed to encourage the quick lift of the finger when released and thus make for a clear articulation, one of the most important elements of piano technique. Herz was careful not to incubate his egg cell without a supply of food yolk: he also issued a book of one thousand exercises so that the purchasers of his little hunks of tin might have something to use them on. Maurice Schlesinger, always happy to take a crack at Herz, said in his issue of May 15, 1836, that the idea had been somebody else's ten years earlier, that Herz had appropriated it and snatched the patent, and that anyway the most important features of piano playing—such as scales, octaves, and double notes—could not be practiced with this device. "Frankly, the Dactylion is a machine for catching fools, and Mr. Herz has counted on his reputation for levying a tax on them."

On the other hand, some years later, somebody took a paid advertisement on the back page of the *Gazette Musicale* to present another piano-practicing aid called the "Chirogymnaste," allegedly invented by a piano dealer named Casimir Martin. Dutifully, the *Gazette* extolled it without reserves two issues later:

> If one had the patience to study with the *Chirogymnaste* for three or four years, one could be a great pianist without ever having placed one's fingers on the piano. The *Chirogymnaste* has another immense advantage, that of being silent, of educating the hand and the fingers without tiring the ear. The *Chirogymnaste* . . . could only be rejected by those people who find that pianists are already too numerous and who consequently must condemn an apparatus that will multiply them still further, since it cuts down by at least two thirds the study time that the piano requires today.

Well, there are various ways of catching various kinds of fools.

20. THE BUSINESS

Pleyel & Co. in 1827, not long after their reorganization, employed about 30 workmen and probably turned out no more than about 100 instruments per year. By 1834 a piece in the *Gazette* said they had 250 employees and made 1000 pianos annually, an increase of 900% over the previous estimate. The figure seems high, especially when we consider that the firm itself, in its own advertising pamphlet published twenty-one years later, claimed no more than 400 employees and 1500 annual instruments as of 1855. Nevertheless, making due allowances for the puffiness of a friendly journal, the growth of the Pleyel business in the early thirties must have been remarkable.

The Erards seem to have been pretty low during old Sébastien's last days, but the jury at the exposition of 1834, which awarded them as well as the Pleyels a gold medal, stated that they were now hiring 150 men to make 400 pianos a year. Their growth appears to have been more substantial from then on, for by 1855 they too were claiming an annual score of 425 men and 1500 instruments, showing a 375% increase of output in little more than twenty years. Meanwhile, the population of Paris went from about 774,000 in 1831 to 1,053,000 in 1846, less than a 30% gain. Erard prices, however, remained relatively steady. According to figures said to have been furnished by a member of the firm many years later, they asked 1600 francs for a trichord square after 1824; 1800 francs in 1843; and 1800–2400 francs in 1852, after which the manufacture of squares was abandoned. Trichord oblique-strung uprights, the best and most convenient of their kind, were 1200–1800 francs in 1834 and went up to 1400–2000 francs after 1852. Grands actually went down from 3000 francs in 1824 to 2500–2800 francs in 1834, but went up again to 3000–3500 francs between 1843 and 1852, when the seven-octave models became more common.

Other piano firms competed successfully, if not at the same level of prestige, with Pleyel and Erard. Henri Herz's factory did not operate too auspiciously at first, despite his valuable improvement on the Erard double-escapement. He also built a fine concert hall on his premises in the rue de la Victoire, and in the beginning some performers tried to rent it on condition that they did not have to use the Herz piano. By 1844, however, the business was doing well, producing 400 instruments a year. Among many other makers Jean-Henri Pape was especially respected for his inventiveness. Smaller firms were too numerous for us to mention here; in the absence of any associations with artistic celebrities, they tended to emphasize price competition, to make and sell their instruments less expensively. In 1821 there were approximately 30 piano makers in all France; by 1837 the number had grown to 75. In 1847 the Chamber of Commerce reported the extraordinary number of 180 in Paris alone. The making of pianos, and other musical instruments, was taking on increasing importance in the manufacturing activity of the country. In the succession of Paris industrial expositions we notice a sharp rise in the number of exhibitors of all kinds of objects connected with music. From a mere 13 in 1819, they went up to 57 in 1827; at the fair of 1834, out of a total of 2443 exhibitors, 105 were of musical instruments and articles. By 1844 there were 84 exhibitors of pianofortes alone.

From an article in the *Gazette* for November 10, 1845, signed Martin d'Angers, we learn that a careful survey had established that there were 60,000 pianos in Paris, with about 100,000 persons who could play them. The city's million people might have been, roughly, divided into 300,000 families—which would mean that one family out of five, or twenty per cent, possessed a piano and that one person in ten of the entire population could play it or at it. If more specifically one figured only the female population, it would mean that one out of every five young ladies, women, great-grandmothers, and girl babies—in and out of hospitals, jails, and madhouses—could make some minimum of sense on a keyboard. We may recall our rough estimate, in a previous chapter, of the spread of pianos in the Vienna of 1800, where we concluded that five per cent of the population were piano buyers and users. This rise of piano incidence from five to twenty per cent during the first half of the century might be considered a measure of the expansion—in numbers and prosperity—of the middle classes, as well as of the acceptance of their habits and pretensions. Edouard Fétis, the son of J. F., in an article called "Music Then and Now," said, on January 17, 1847: "There is not a home, even of the smallest bourgeois, where one does not find a piano. The instrument forms, in all necessity, a part of the furniture of every family; you will find it as far as the janitors' lodges." Our percentage estimate does not, of course, pretend to a close arithmetical accuracy; for one thing, Vienna and Paris are not necessarily commensurable. On the other hand, we cannot dispute the fact that the general movement of the rise of the *bourgeoisie* was Europe-wide, if at differing pecuniary standards. In 1845 Vienna counted no fewer than 108 piano makers—of which, however, the largest turned out no more than 200 instruments per year. Vienna prices were much lower than those of Paris; an ordinary domestic upright sold for 200 florins (that is, a little more than 400 francs), while a Paris-built one cost 1800. The Viennese construction and tone were correspondingly poorer. In any case, the general economic and social trend pertaining to the instrument was the same in Austria as in France.

During the middle years of the century, French pianos of the foremost firms led the world in artistic prestige; yet France's total annual piano production was only about a third of England's. No Paris factory of 1850 could touch Broadwood's annual 2300; runner-up Collard's 1500 equaled the greatest single Paris output. The total English production for 1850 was calculated at 23,000 units, or 450 per week. "In no country is the acquisition of a piano as a necessary furnishing, even without momentary need, so widespread as in England." So reported Joseph Fischhof, professor of piano at the Vienna Conservatory, honorary member of the St. Cecilia Society in Rome, etc., after his visit to the great Industrial World's Fair at the Crystal Palace in London, 1851. He spent three or four hours a day for five weeks inspecting the piano exhibits; occasionally Pierre Erard piloted him around. He also paid two visits to the Broadwood factory, the biggest in the world, and made big eyes at all the bigness he saw and heard of: the big three-hundred-foot-long three-story factory building, its three hundred workbenches, the separate steam-engine house, the £1000 weekly payroll, the six hundred pianos permanently out on rental at from 12s to £2 12s 6d per month, the ten delivery trucks, and a big piece of veneer fifteen feet long and thirty-eight inches wide, made from a single log of Honduras mahogany. He was also impressed with the fact that much of the business was on credit and consignment—resulting sometimes in an annual write-off of £10,000 for bad bills—and the fact that a hundred and fifty different Smiths were represented on the firm's books.

The great industrial fact in the years before the mid-century point was the development of railroads. They began in the thirties and were widely extended in the forties; that was when their effects began to be fully felt. Quick, dependable, large-scale transportation over long distances made for easy procurement of large amounts of materials and easy delivery of product; it favored large turnover and large central factories. After 1847 the number of piano makers in France declined as the quantity of made pianos increased; it was the factories in the *départements* especially that folded up, since local customers could now be more efficiently supplied from Paris.

By an extension of this process, the railroads, with their adjutants the telegraphs and the trucking facilities, helped to speed up the economic domination of the so-called industrial countries—those that could work the coal and iron found within their borders—over the countries that either did not possess these treasures or did not yet know how to organize their use. The principal large coal and iron countries during the 1840's were England and France; both had long been overseas exporters, especially to their own colonies and possessions; France could now ship economically over the European continent by rail. Thus, we find the Erards in particular selling their pianos briskly in Belgium, Germany, Switzerland, Spain, and Italy. After 1850 both England and France still exported pianos, but in decreasing numbers, to the United States. Germany was the traditional piano-loving and piano-playing land par excellence; its demand could hardly be supplied by imports of expensive Erards alone. Nevertheless, its industrial immaturity prevented it from making instruments whose tone could compete with the French. Most German makers of the forties contented themselves with cheaply imitating the Erard models, just as thirty or forty years earlier they had copied English instruments. Not until the 1860's did German pianos begin to rival those of other countries in quality.

The Broadwood factory of 1851 must have been most impressive. Here are some of the different kinds of woods it used for hammer shanks, hammer heads, smaller action parts, keys, soundboards, bridges, and cases: beech, beefwood (from Brazil), birch, cedar, deal, ebony, fir, lime tree, mahogany, maple, pear, pine, rosewood, satinwood, sycamore, wainscot, white holly, zebrawood, Amboina wood, and walnut. The metal parts of Broadwood pianos included brass studs, pins, hinges, locks, and pedal rods; copper-covered wire; iron bracing bars, screws, and hitch pins; steel arches, bars, wire, and spun strings. The woolen cloths used included baize and felt. Miscellaneous materials included beeswax, emery paper, French polish, glue, ivory, linseed oil, putty powder, spirits of wine, and black lead.

The divisions of labor made an extraordinary list. The workmen were specialized according to the parts they made: bent side, case, bottom, block, sounding-board top, check, beam, damper, hammer, lifter, key, notch, lyre, leg block, leg, brass stud, brass bridge, harmonic bar, iron brace, metal plate, steel arch, wrest pin, and spun strings. There were also sawyers, bracers, markers-off, plinthers, hammer leatherers, stringers, finishers, roughers-up, tuners, turners, scrapers, polishers, carvers, gilders, and action regulators. This variety of activity took up a lot of room, and the variety of procurement involved much executive attention; only a firm disposing of large capital resources could afford it.

Inevitably, as more persons went into the expanding piano business, a further division of labor—or rather a division of enterprise—took place: before the middle of the century we see the rise of the piano-parts manufacturing business. The element of a piano first to become the object of a specialized business was undoubtedly the action—that is, the whole complex of hammers, jacks, and keys with their multifarious little components. We are told that there was a British firm which made nothing but pianoforte actions as early as 1810; we hear of one in the United States in the early 1850's. The piano boom of the 1840's was bound to bring on an expansion of the parts business. An action factory was started by L. Isermann in Hamburg in 1842; shortly thereafter, Schwander established one in Paris, to be followed there by Ferdinand de Rohden. Soon there were factories that made nothing but cases, sounding boards, or metal plates. Tuning pins became a specialty of a small number of plants in western Germany. Under these circumstances, any piano-making firm could give up an inconvenient operation in the process of manufacture and buy the part ready-made. Many businesses, indeed, could practically give up manufacturing altogether, shop around for separate parts, and confine their labor to that of mere assembly and to the stenciling of the firm's name upon the finished instruments.

The piano-parts manufacturing business seems to have suffered from a little self-conscious shyness in its earlier days in France. At the Paris industrial exposition of 1844, silver medals were awarded to the Rohden firm for its actions and to that of F. Giesler for its keyboards. However, a Monsieur G. E. Anders, who reported the musical side of the fair, was perturbed over the fact that—though prizes were given these two companies—their actual products were not publicly exhibited. He seemed to think, rightfully, that this was unfair and a dangerous precedent. We might guess that the piano trade was agreed on the whole in trying to keep the parts manufacturing business out of the eyes of the general public. If it were widely understood that many different firms bought their parts from the same manufacturer, why that would make it all the harder to create a myth of distinctiveness about a particular name of make; all brands except the most famous would tend to lose some of their prestige. Instead of appearing as carefully, personally contrived works of art created for an artistic purpose, they would be seen nakedly as the slapped-together, minimally functional mechanisms they mostly actually were.

Yet the specialization of parts-making in different factories was certainly economical: it made it possible to retail finished pianos much more cheaply. A factory that did nothing but make five thousand cases, or sounding boards, or actions in the course of a year could operate with more efficient "labor-saving" machinery —and consequently at a lower cost of production—than a concern that made only five hundred and had to turn out all kinds of other things besides. It was the necessary trend—for the factories, rapacious for markets, could find them near at hand, expandingly, among the people who had less money to spend. Conversely, as the piano became a more and more thoughtlessly conventional symbol of middle-class aspiration and respectability, and as population and national wealth increased, more and more little people felt the compulsion to blow themselves up a trifle by setting up the musical icon in their parlors—and were content with anything that could properly go by the name of piano. It was fitting that an object of such widespread social desirability—I refrain from saying utility—be produced at low cost and sold at a low price. The only thing that suffered from this easy multiplication was the quality, especially that of the tone. For a fine tone quality is a grace that is only conferred upon an instrument as a reward for long, painstaking devotion to every detail and every essence of its construction, as the distillate of a steady fusion of diverse excellences. Yet if the vast majority of the customers aimed at did not care about fine tone quality, or would not have recognized it if they had heard it, it became an unprofitable virtue, commercially speaking.

Of all types of pianoforte, the upright—while spatially the most convenient—is the poorest in volume, quality, and variability of tone. In 1851, the year of the great London World's Fair, uprights comprised eighty to ninety per cent of the output of the English factories. From five to ten per cent were grands; squares were almost obsolete, about 1500 still being made annually, chiefly for export to India. At the exposition, Collard's exhibited a small upright with a case of simple pinewood, at thirty guineas, half the price of a comparable Erard. Characteristically, it was touted as the "piano for the people." Dr. Fischhof said, with faint praise, that it looked better than one would have expected.

We will risk another reflection. In the eighteenth century, as we have determined elsewhere, a reputable busy pianoforte or harpsichord maker such as J. A. Stein or Burkat Shudi could turn out about 18 instruments per year. If, as we have some right to assume, he accomplished this with the aid of about 4 or 5 assistants, we can calculate a unit output of about 3 to 3½ instruments per man. Now, in 1855 the Erards with 425 employees produced 1500 pianos, or about 3½ per man. At about the same time the Broadwoods with 575 hirelings turned out 2300 pianos, about 4 per man. So, after three quarters of a century of building up working capital, elaborate machinery, and buildings in great amounts—and of degrading craftsmen into dependent laborers—the ultimate productivity was scarcely increased. How could this be, when the machines and the specialization of labor did actually enable a man to work faster? For one thing, a large business becomes cluttered with the by-products of its own size and complexity. It requires all kinds of personnel not needed by a small craft shop: maintenance men, supervisors, shipping handlers, truck drivers, sales persons, bookkeepers, filing clerks, night watchmen, and junior executives, all of whom help to reduce the company's unit output. What, then, was the over-all advantage of making pianos by the factory system? Perhaps it was the metal parts of the instrument, the plates and bracing bars, which could not well have been produced in small individual shops.

The pianoforte, then, in its day of fullest bloom, was a product straight from the loins of nineteenth-century industry and business, a direct issue of the technology, the transportation, and the finance of its time. It was more than their mere image; it was in itself a small unit of the age-substance, a very cell of the dominant life that made it. Placed in a home, it represented the family's participation in that life's benefits. It was an ideal, and so—by the relentless force of spiritual gravity—it became an idol.

The history of the piano does not coincide with the development of musical genius; it follows the development of industry and commerce. The movements of the piano cult reflect the shifts of the Western world's industrial vigor. In the earlier half of the nineteenth century, England was the world's leader in manufacturers, including that of pianos, with France as an important growing rival at a considerable remove. During the latter half of the century, as the United States and the new German Empire exploited their coal and iron and gradually ousted England and

France from their dominant position, they in their turn became the world's leading makers, buyers, sellers, exporters, and improvers of pianofortes.

21. PIANO FODDER

WE HAVE MENTIONED the opera-tune arrangements and elaborations, in all ranges of difficulty, ingenuity, and price, that formed so large a part of what the girls played on their instruments at home. Yet these did not suffice them for all their musical wants, nor did it suffice the publishers for the liquidation of their overhead. All sorts of other piano music was printed and sold, in great and increasing quantities, keeping pace with the ever-growing number of instruments. "A rain of albums, an avalanche of romances, a torrent of airs with variations, a spout of concertos, cavatinas, dramatic scenes, comic duos, soporific adagios, diabolic evocations, classic sônatas, and rondos romantic, fantastic, frenetic, fanatic, and fluoric," so wrote Hector Berlioz in his extravagant manner on January 7, 1838.

There was, of course, a natural demand for new music when the charm of the old wore out, just as there was a demand for new ladies' hats and new sofa pillows. Slow-fingered, slow-minded piano pupils—the vast majority—often grew tired of a composition long before they had properly learned it and were pleased and relieved when their teachers "gave them a new piece." The publishers' problem was to stay in business; it was to no one's advantage if they did not. They had to keep on selling, so as to pay their rent, their help, their banks, and the maintenance of their presses. Public taste in art goods is hardly calculable in any detail, for no one knows specifically what any number of people will buy, will not buy, or will stop buying at any moment. The publishers' solution was a deliberate overproduction of issues, together with a high markup for retail sales of individual sheets. A large list increased the chance of any one number's becoming a hit, but the profit on any copy sold had to be great enough to help pay for all that necessarily lay around on the shelves unsold. Often it was better to get rid of the space-consumers at a loss than to let them rot. An anonymous sarcastic complaint against the publishers came out in 1834: they used to sell at the list price, it went, then they gave a one-third discount, then a one-half; now the beautiful pages of Weber, Mozart, Hummel, and Moscheles will be sold for a penny; soon it will be music for nothing; and when you do not want any more, someone will stop you on the street and shove it down your pocket. It sounds like Berlioz talking again.

Thus, new music was always hopefully being put out, but the publisher could speculate on a quick, wide acceptance only if it conformed to the customers' established habits. Music that traversed familiar formulas, and whose novelty resided in its inessentials, might sell best. The elation of newness could be heightened by what had best be called "the title racket." The same old essence could be masked with an illusion of change by giving it a new name. It is a very ancient failing of the human mind, thus to yield to this deception. A hateful king could be imposed on the Romans by calling him "emperor"; pagan divinities, long ago, could be orthodoxly prayed to by calling them Christian saints; ignoble revenge could be made righteous by calling it "punishment." The same lump of cheese, in varied mold, might be sold three times over as a new delicacy under the name of *"Fetida," "Bockmist,"* or *"Egout de Paris."* On that basis, the same three-part song-form—with the same succession of harmonies, the same modulations, the same syntax, and the same cadences, but with certain varieties of movement and figuration—could be sold over and over again as "The Mameluke's Lament," or "The Enchanted Pelican," or under a thousand other labels, as imaginative as those of brands of cigars.

Before about 1830 the titlers of pianoforte pieces were content to give a vague hint of a basic rhythmical movement, or of a mood, such as "Barcarolle" or "Nocturne." Soon it was felt that rapid chromatic oscillations could readily call up the image of a buzzing wheel, and tunes with such accompaniments were now sometimes called "spinning songs." The suggestion was becoming delightful at a time when women had just about stopped spinning. The dear creatures, however, continued loyally to prepare suppers and mend socks, thus no romantic, nostalgic impulsions could arise to the fashioning of "frying songs" or "darning songs," despite the musical potentialities of sizzling lard or of a thimble tapping upon a wooden egg. On the other hand, "hunting songs," with lots of breezy hoofbeats and horn calls, were much enjoyed by the city-bound daughters of millinery shopkeepers and attorneys.

Presently the headings began to multiply more fancifully. On

February 9, 1834, we find a piece advertised under the alluring title *The Aeronauts, an aerial barcarolle, two francs.* Nothing heavier-than-air as yet, of course. In the January 19 issue of the *Gazette Musicale* for the same year we have a review of a *Fairies' Dance,* dedicated to the famous ballerina Mademoiselle Taglioni, by Ferdinand Hiller, Opus 9. The piece is nothing much, says the fishy-eyed critic, except an assembly of the words "dance," "fairy," "Taglioni," and the author's reputation. We will risk the guess that this was not a Schlesinger publication. All the stale romanticist rubber-stamps began to appear as music labels. After *Fairies' Dance,* we now get lots of *Elfin Dances* and their brunet and red-headed counterparts: *Gnomes' Dance, Dance of the Demons,* and *Dance of the Dwarfs. Witches' Dance* was a great favorite; it became as much of a convention as did an *Annunciation* among fifteenth-century painters. One composer strained at a gigantic toy rattle: in 1843 there was announced a *Grand Characteristic Fantasy for the piano, on the principal personages of the novel "Mysteries of Paris"* "dedicated to Mr. Eugene Sue, by T. Latour, formerly pianist and composer to His late Britannic Majesty George IV." Sue was the author of this eight-volume romance; most of its characters and incidents were ticketed on the piece as it proceeded. The reviewer felt that the composer's musical imagination was unequal to his literary enthusiasm: according to him the various murders, frauds, seductions, flights, and suicides of the guinea-dreadful were mostly illustrated by waltzes—twenty-two pages of them.

The title racket was useful for making package deals, always profitable for the seller. On that same January 19, 1834, we hear of a set of six pieces composed by the harpist Labarre, arranged for piano by F. Hünten. They are called *Les Chasses* (*i.e., The Hunts*) and include *The Wolf Hunt, The Fox Hunt, The Deer Hunt,* and *The Woodcock Hunt.* "Mr. Hünten has arranged the pieces with much taste and skill," says the review polisher this time; "they will find many purchasers among pianists of second- or third-rate skill."

Dance music continued strong as piano fodder, reflecting the fashions as they went by. The waltz had been the rage in Paris early in the century, but a conservative reaction seems to have ensued. Restoration mammas were still worried at the notion of having their maiden daughters seen in public embrace. About 1830 the galop came in, a fast 2/4 hop; in one of its steps the partners held hands and skipped the length of the floor together. The friendly manual contact of the galop eased the closer clasp of the waltz into complete respectability. Galops proceeded to decorate thousands of pianofortes: *Galop brillant, Galop de concert,* and so on. Henri Herz was a generous supplier of them. Liszt often threw crackling dust in the ears of his auditors under the name of a *Grand Galop chromatique* of his own composition.

The polka had long been enjoyed by the Czech people, innocently and obscurely. After 1843, when—with the help of the famous dancer Carlotta Grisi—Parisians got a crush on it, this dance suddenly became important and worth imitating by all Europe's best people. Pianos thenceforth crawled with polkas, their titles garnished with all the sauces: *Grande Polka de concert, Polka de salon, Polka de la Reine, Polka poétique, Polka de Bohême.* Several polka packages came out in Paris during 1844, one being an assortment assembled from the productions of certain German bandmasters—Strauss, Lanner, Labitzki, and others. The titles mostly have a socialite sound irresistible to tradesmen's families: *Polka favorite des princes, Polka favorite de la cour, Le Bal de la Reine, La Duchesse, Le Faubourg St. Germain, The Waters of Ems* (a fashionable resort). Later that year the tireless Herz brought out his own neat set of six home-sliced polkas, tied up in a bright and shiny string. The bundle, announced as *Les Belles du nord,* contained *La Belle Bohémienne, La Belle Polonaise, La Belle Hongroise, La Belle Allemande, La Belle Suédoise,* and *La Belle Muscovite,* a regular international beauty chorus. The adverisement proclaimed that each polka was "decorated with a magnificent picture"—probably what we would call a "cover girl."

As for the waltzes, those intended for actual dancing were usually set into a pattern of six separate successive melodies, plus a finale that recollected the earliest one. Later in the century an elaborate introduction was also added. The formula was established as early as Mozart, and it lasted late, persisting through Johann Strauss II and even to Oscar Straus. On this account a single waltz composition was often referred to in the plural as "waltzes." Waltz labels burgeoned bright, so desperately, in fact, that their fantasy even dared to transcend the stencils of the romanticist world of notions. They were, on the whole, less numerous and varied than the names of race horses, but they made almost as much sense.

When it came to the works of Chopin, the publishers' blurbs sometimes tried to work both sides of the street—to appeal both to those who were frightened by, and to those who were attracted to, his repute as a high-society high-brow and virtuoso. Here is the "line" on his *"Grande Valse brillante,"* Opus 18:

> We recently announced a production of Mr. Chopin, his four latest mazurkas, a work which, despite all the richness of its ideas, and all the freshness and novelty that we admire in it, is nevertheless distinguished by great simplicity and contains few or no difficulties. [Mustn't scare off the paying duffers.]
>
> We must again praise the same qualities, so rare nowadays, in the waltz we recommend to our readers. We think it sufficiently proven that when this artist writes difficult passages he is not driven to it by a vain wantonness, but rather by the sense and the character of the piece, such as it always ought to be in an art creation. [Anyway, if it's hard it's high-class.]
>
> This waltz is among the most brilliant, even though it is particularly suitable for dancing. [Play up the dual purpose.]
>
> It deserves to be found soon upon the pianos whose racks have not the habit of bearing vulgar music. [Snob appeal.]
>
> Even the amateurs who prefer a beautiful sonata by Beethoven to the variations and fantasies of certain fashionable authors . . . even these amateurs, we say, will play with pleasure and satisfaction Mr. Chopin's waltz. [Could be highbrow, but doesn't need to be—just as you choose.]

So a girl buying this piece could get something that was easy to listen to, whose difficulties were reasonable, and which let her keep company with swells—all for six francs.

Far and away the largest single portion of all music published in Europe around 1840 was for the piano. Most of it was for piano solo, but the proportion increases all the more if we add the songs for solo voice, to which a piano accompaniment had long seemed indispensable. We take some figures published in the *Allgemeine Musikalische Zeitung,* the paper put out by Breitkopf & Härtel, the great Leipzig music publishers. The firm probably made its count after receiving examples of the publications of practically all other important Continental houses; hence, the statistics probably are valid for Europe as a whole. For the year 1838 the *Zeitung* reported the receipt of a total of 2633 new issues, of which more than 49% were for piano alone, including four-hand compositions. In 1839 the percentage rose to over 50, but in 1840 it declined to about 45.5. If we add the publications for solo voice with piano accompaniment to those for piano alone, we get a percentage of more than 70.5 for 1838, 66 for 1839, and 64.7 for 1840. It might not be unreasonable to lump together all the music published that could not be played without the aid of a piano, including compositions for the accompanied violin, cello, or flute. If we do this for 1838, we get a sum of 2111 pieces of music out of a total of 2633 issues—or almost exactly 80%—that could be sold practically only to people who had pianos in their homes. Moreover, the piano's predominance may have been even more pronounced than these figures indicate; they merely represent offerings for sale, not sales themselves. Copies of certain piano pieces undoubtedly were distributed in much greater numbers than those for any other musical medium. If a statistic of specific sales quantities could be set up, it might well show an even much greater preponderance of piano music.

On January 10, 1847, Monsieur Blanchard reflects:

> Cultivating the piano is something that has become as essential to social harmony as the cultivation of the potato is to the existence of the people; . . . although the piano is to the violin what the potato is to grain, it is no less the obligatory dish of every musical banquet, since, after the most spicy hors d'oeuvres, the most succulent meats, the most fragrant game, the potato offers itself in all its primitive and nutritive simplicity, or else disguised as a tidbit under the collective name of sweetened *entremets,* and is even occasionally made to figure in the dessert. [He must mean the sweet potato.] Therefore, to banish the piano from the musical world would be as impossible as to cut off the potato from the gastronomic and culinary art. The piano provokes meetings between people, hospitality, gentle contacts, associations of all kinds, even matrimonial ones; it serves as a palliative to the brutality of our customs; and if our young men so full of assurance tell their friends that they have married twelve or fifteen thousand francs of income, they at least add as a corrective: "Sir, my wife plays piano like an angel."

22. HOPEFUL GADGETS

IN THE SECOND QUARTER of the century the piano was the rising thing, the thing everybody wanted because everybody else wanted it. Its recent improvements had been prodigiously successful; its foremost makers and sellers had become rich and admired as leaders of men. What gain and glory could not be had in improving the instrument still further? Hundreds of men felt the blood rise at the thought of adding some permanently useful feature to this most valuable object. According to Rosamond Harding's painstaking research, no fewer than 1098 patents relating to the pianoforte were granted during the period from 1825 to 1851, chiefly in England and France, but also in Austria, Bavaria, Belgium, and the United States. The figure compares with 264 such patents issued throughout the eighteenth century and up to 1825. In other words, the rate of piano inventions increased 833% during the quarter century.

A very few of these devices did become permanently established in piano manufacture; the great majority were vain bubbles. Not all were finally disposed of by their immediate failure; some kept rising to the surface in slightly altered forms again and again, only to burst as futilely as before. Some of the gadgets were mechanically logical, though ultimately unprofitable, experiments; some were wanton eccentricities; but the most interesting inventions, humanly speaking, were those that were plausible in purpose, practical and economical in execution, yet still were unable to compel public acceptance. One cannot, however, feel very sorry for inventors; they are the most unconscionable bullies in the world, for they insist on doing their stuff and ramming it down the throats of others, regardless of what that does to people's habits, affections, or peace of mind.

We may classify the inventions relating to the piano as follows:

1. Those aiming at simple mechanical efficiency of the instrument: its facility of manufacture, its resistance to disrepair, its convenience of maintenance.
2. Those aiming at the nature of the tone, at better sonority or greater resonance.
3. Those aiming at a greater convenience of the instrument's overall shape and size apart from its musical function, or at some visual aesthetic effect.
4. Those aiming at enlarging the instrument's musical scope and capabilities.

1. In the first category we may mention the improved method of fastening the strings. Originally every single wire—especially each of the two, or three, unison strings of a single treble note—was hitched separately, by an eye twisted at its end, over its own hitch

pin. In 1827, we are told, James Stewart of London devised the method of making one wire length serve as two strings by looping it *around* a hitch pin, both proximal ends then fastened to two different wrest pins. When the string is drawn beyond a certain degree of tension, the friction on the hitch pin prevents any alteration of the tension on the one side from affecting that of the other. Where there are three unisons to a note, the wire forming the third must be used to serve also as the first unison of the next note. It is a little difficult to understand the benefit of this system; pianists for several generations have been annoyed to find that breaking a string necessarily means destroying two of them, and often impairing two different notes; yet the method must have its advantages, for manufacturers have adopted it almost universally.

The tuning, or wrest, pins were also improved: from being embedded nakedly into the wood of the pin block, they were made "mechanical"—that is, they were fastened as screws into nuts, making possible a slower, more accurate turning for tuning purposes.

Changes were made in the strings themselves: there was a trend from wires of iron to those of tempered steel. At some indeterminable time the simple old brass bass strings were replaced by those consisting of a steel or brass core spun over more or less tightly with copper. Bass strings tended, too, to become relatively thicker. Moreover, attempts were made to protect strings against rust by coating or plating them with German silver, silver, gold, or even platinum.

The problem, in grand and square pianos, of preventing strings from being bent upward away from the bridges by the hammer blows from below was partially solved, as we have seen, by Sébastien Erard's agraffes. More support was needed, however, as playing got rougher. In the forties there was perfected the "harmonic" bar as well as the "*Capo tasto*" bar (sometimes called "*Capo d'astro*"); they were transverse metal bars, joining the longitudinal or diagonal bracing bars of the frame and lying across the middle and higher treble strings, respectively, right behind the wrest plank. They served as additional bearings against the hammer strokes—acting, in fact, as wrest plank bridges. These bars made the sonorous portions of the instrument even more rigid and so, in turn, made possible a greater capacity for volume of sound.

The pretreatment of wood for the making of sounding boards became much more efficient and rapid early in the nineteenth century. We remember Mozart's letter of 1777 telling how J. A.

Stein used to let his wood season outdoors for months, in all kinds of weather. Between 1808 and 1830 several Austrians and South Germans developed processes for removing resinous substances from the wood by a steam treatment lasting only two or three days.

2. Inventions aiming to improve or prolong the tone—to make it "sing," as people fondly said—were much concerned with the sounding board. It is true that the board is what actually makes most of the strings' vibration audible; anyone can show this by striking a tuning fork in the air and then standing it on its base on a wooden surface. Despite their knowledge of the generally vital function of this part, piano designers nevertheless had only an uncertain empirical understanding of the principles affecting its behavior; most of their "inventions" connected with it seem to have been well-meant guesses. Sounding boards are made of strips of wood glued together; but no one could be sure how the direction of the graining affected the tone, some believing that the "ribs" supporting the structure interfered with the tone, others realizing that they might aid it. The thickness of the sounding board undoubtedly affects the tone; but not one found out conclusively all the relationships between this factor and those of wood chemistry, graining, surface area, over-all shape, support, pressure, pitch, and intensity. All manner of schemes were tried, and of course each was put forward as a new revelation of truth. One maker hopefully built two circular sounding boards at either side of his square piano; another got £15 each time for attaching his clamp-and-screw mechanism altering the pressure on the board. Some other makers stretched a sounding board over the top of a copper resonating bowl, on the analogy of a kettledrum. The image of the violin naturally rose up: some builders made double sounding boards, connected by side pieces all around the edges as well as by sound posts in the middle, and with F-holes cut to make the likeness complete. Some left a lot of space between the two surfaces, others very little, and still others felt the space ought to be somehow graduated. There was a widespread notion that the gap in a grand piano between the wrest plank and the edge of the sounding board—that is, the opening through which the hammers must strike—took away something from the potential resonating surface; so somebody thought up an instrument with the sounding board *on top* of the strings. It played all right; but if somebody broke a string, the whole piano had to be taken apart to repair it.

Some of the efforts at inducing a more prolonged resonance were focused on the strings. Some piano makers thought up plans for greater numbers of unison strings—four, five, or six—together with mechanisms for bringing them in and out of play. One Vienna maker made a piano with four treble strings to a note for Beethoven, at his request, because of his deafness. It does not seem to have had much success as a hearing aid.

In some cases, double sets of strings were drawn up to be hit simultaneously by two hammers, or by one hammer forked with two heads.

The old principle of sympathetic vibrations was invoked. supernumerary strings or rods were stretched or set up, not to be struck, but tuned to the same frequency as those that were, and to vibrate with them. The idea seems to have had but little following in the middle of the century; but a generation or more later, at least one large modern German manufacturer, Julius Blüthner, made a fourth sympathetic treble string standard equipment for his instruments well into the twentieth century.

Already in the later eighteenth century an instrument maker tried to utilize the ancient idea of the aeolian harp—that is, of inducing or prolonging the vibrations of a set of strings by the action of a gust of air passed over them. He tried it with some success on an instrument in which the strings were first agitated by means of little mechanical bows. However, after the discomfiture of his patroness Queen Marie Antoinette, the propaganda for his "*Anemochord*"—Greek for"breeze string"—died down, and the object with it. During the 1820's, '30's, and '40's the idea was revived several times in connection with pianos, sometimes by the attachment of little boxes of compressed air. At least one of these windy instruments also had a fresh-cooked mutilated-Greek name assigned to it, namely "*Aeolodikon.*" Some of them were quite ingenious, and all of them died even more quickly and painlessly than the "*Anemochord.*"

There was at least one other avenue of attempt at varying the piano's tone: an English maker achieved a device for tightening or loosening the leather covering over the hammer heads; in that way the tone could be made brighter or duller. The idea was a little like that of tightening or loosening the hairs on a violin bow.

3. The devices pertaining to the piano's total shape and visual aspect were mostly concerned with making the instrument smaller and more compact. We have spoken of the progress of the upright piano, how its height when strung vertically was much reduced by stringing it obliquely. About 1828 Jean-Henri Pape was able to pack away the instrument's intestines still more neatly by allowing the longest bass strings to cross over the shorter treble and middle strings at an angle, over a higher bridge, and to be fastened to

their hitch pins on a separate piece of plate. At that rate, he was able eventually to get the instrument's height down to 2 feet 9 inches. These little uprights, bearing a certain resemblance to chiffoniers, were called "console-pianos." Another maker built one 3½ feet by 3¼ feet by 7 inches, with a keyboard that folded up, the whole weighing one hundred pounds. The idea was that it could be carted on a trip as easily as a trunk. When all closed up, its painted front and back looked straight and pretty, so it was called a "screen-piano." These little instruments—or *pianinos,* as they were sometimes called on the Continent—took second place, however, to the taller uprights for the duration of the nineteenth century and beyond; not until the second quarter of the twentieth century did the miniatures become the dominant type.

Square pianos, though tending to obsolesce, were likewise given fancy shapes and styles during the 1830's. We find round, oval, and hexagonal table-topped instruments—one cannot accurately say "squares" in such cases. In some instances, the keyboard could be pushed in and out like a drawer. One type was called "writing-desk piano." We can imagine a young lady penning a tender missive upon it with her right hand, while her left doodled "If I Were a Bird."

Desk-pianos, bureau-pianos, and screen-pianos are all quite ladylike; but as we approach the era of the "piano for the people," we occasionally meet with a more racy quirk of style. At that same great London exhibition in 1851, Dr. Fischhof reported the display of "a bed with a pianoforte which starts to play by itself when one lies in it." The exhibitor shyly withheld his name. However, in 1866, after the piano had had fifteen more years in which to seep through to the almost common man—that is to say, the lower middle classes—someone identifying himself as Millward was granted a patent on the following construction:

> The piano, in place of being supported by legs in the ordinary manner, is supported by a frame which again rests upon a hollow base; inside such hollow base is placed a couch, which is mounted upon rollers and can be drawn out in front of the piano; the front surface of the couch when slid inside the base forming the front side thereof . . . A hollow space is formed in the middle of the frame for rendering the pedals accessible to the performer's feet, and on one side of such space is formed a closet, having doors opening in front of the piano, and which is designed to contain the bed clothes. On the side of the space so formed, firstly, a bureau with drawers, and secondly, another closet containing a wash-hand basin,

jug, towels, and other articles of toilet. The bureau and second closet are made to open at the end of the frame, the front surface of that part of the latter being formed with false drawers to correspond in appearance with the doors of the before-mentioned closet on the other side of the space. . . .

Another part of the invention consists in constructing a music stool which is so arranged that in addition it contains a work-box, a looking glass, a writing desk or table, and a small set of drawers.

The present writer can remember, early in this century, hearing the "folding-bed piano" mentioned as a joke; clearly, it was conceived in dead earnest.

4. Efforts to enlarge the piano's musical scope or playing capacity went in several directions. We may first mention an attempt to modify the general shape of the keyboard. Two Austrians, Staufer and Haidinger, took out a patent in 1824 for a concavely curved arrangement of piano keys. The idea seems to have been that the normal sideway movement of the arms is in a curved line, not a straight one, and that a keyboard yielding to this natural bodily direction would make for greater agility and ease of playing. Furthermore, a slight amount of space is saved in this way: the same widths of keys will not extend quite so far around a bend as they will in a straight line; thus, a slight increase of reach is achieved for the hands. Children and small-handed women who have to strain at octaves or tenths might stretch them readily on this keyboard. The Staufer and Haidinger invention dropped away in silence; and about 1840 two new patents were issued for a similar contrivance, which also sank without a splash. However, the idea was revived in the twentieth century with somewhat more success. It became associated with a man named Clutsam; and in the Germany of the 1910's, Clutsam concave keyboards were built into the pianos of several leading manufacturers, were played in concerts by prominent artists, and were even in use in the *Königliche Hochschule für Musik* in Berlin. They too vanished after their brief hour.

Several attempts were made, between 1825 and 1850, to provide the piano with a pedal keyboard on the analogy of the organ, the Erards being among those who tried it. The apparatus consisted of a set of pedal levers connecting with the rears of the same keys that were worked by the fingers and applied to the lowest twenty or thirty notes of the instrument. The only viable result of this contrivance was that Robert Schumann wrote his lovely *Etudes in form of canons* for one of these pedal-pianos. The pieces, still much enjoyed, are usually played in an arrangement for two pianos.

To play a note together with its upper or lower octave by one stroke upon a single key has always been a commonplace capability of the organ, and had also been so in the larger harpsichords. A number of octave-coupling mechanisms were therefore inevitably devised for pianos. They consisted either of supplementary strings tuned to the octave, or of trackers connecting hammers with their octave counterparts, together with attaching and detaching levers. All were complicated, heavy, and unprofitable; none ever succeeded.

One uninhibited putterer even designed an apparatus for producing harmonics on the piano—"harmonic sounds," he called them. It was a bar that was made, by the action of several levers, to touch the strings lightly at their mid-points and thus produce a faraway upper octave echo sound after the notes had been struck.

Double pianos were made—that is, two pianos mercilessly built together as one. We may remember that Matthias Müller's "*Ditanaklassis*" of 1800, the first true upright, was actually built double. The Erards built a double square, back to back, in 1821; in 1850 a double grand interlocked in a single case was made in the United States. The idea is quite absurd and must be set down to the irresponsible foolery characteristic of inventors' mentalities; for it ought to be obvious that duo-piano playing is accomplished most conveniently when the two instruments have the individual freedom of a husband and wife, not when they are riveted in the fateful fixity of a pair of Siamese twins.

A persistently reoccurring contrivance for pianos was one enabling the instrument to play music in transposition—in other words, to make it possible for the keys to sound, not their proper notes, but those a half tone, a whole tone, or any desired interval higher or lower. The idea is an old one, having been used on harpsichords as far back as the sixteenth century. It can be accomplished in several mechanical ways: the simplest is to leave room to allow the entire keyboard and action to be shifted to the right or left and so strike a different set of strings; it can also be done by shifting the strings instead of the keys; and most sophisticatedly of all, by making the keys divided front and back, and allowing the back portion to shift so as to engage different sets of hammers. One would think that playing and reading fluently in all tonalities is a fundamental requirement of musicianship. It is certainly so regarded in the case of string-instrument players. Yet the domestic keyboards, and especially the piano, have always largely been fingered by the musically incompetent; and we are not astonished that there should have been a steady effort to permit them to play in "hard" keys, such as six flats or five sharps, brilliantly but with less difficulty. Under the circumstances, we wonder that transposing pianos never became standard despite their seeming utility. They must certainly have come in handy for coping with the inconsiderate transpository urges of singers.

After the perfection of the fast double-escapement action, people developed a fondness for the titillation of rapid repeated notes, a taste that composers and virtuosos were quite ready to flatter. Here was yet another brilliance clamoring to be executed without difficulty. The piano makers obliged with mechanisms for sending a hail of hammer blows upon strings at the mere depression of a single key. They were all on one principle, that of a toothed cylinder, revolved either by the player by means of a special treadle, or by a second person; the cylinder's projections, constantly re-engaging the hammer shank, made the reiterations. Dr. Fischhof mentions one such instrument, which had been christened *"Trémolophone"* and was exhibited in Paris in 1844, as the work of a Chevalier de Girard, the inventor of a well-known spinning machine. The doctor said that it produced "such a flood of repeated notes in all regions of the keyboard that this stutter-figure shortly becomes unbearable." He added a note: "Mr. Wlczek gave a concert here [Vienna] six years ago on this instrument, without success." Actually this gadget had been thought up early in the century, before the fad of jitternotes had come up. It seems to have been first intended as a substitute for sustaining the tone, as on a mandolin, or as a sort of vibrato. This too passed; yet "mandolin attachments" were still to be found on American pianos as late as 1900.

The line-up of many pedals, of which we have spoken several times before, flourished fairly extensively on Paris pianos during the first quarter of the century. We notice a French maker in 1806 putting out a fairly tall upright with a "bassoon" and a "harp" stop; he lip-sticked it with the name of *"Harmomelo."* But aren't upper-class Europeans supposed to be too cultured to endure such barbarisms, let alone pay money for them? After 1830, when the modern piano began to be perfected, the pedal array was generally retrenched to two, the sustaining pedal and the *una corda.* In the forties, it is true, the "attachments" tried to go on an autumnal binge; during that time both a French and an American mechano-musical exuberator thought up a whole scale of chromatically tuned drums or tambourines, to be thrown in with a pedal and to be played with the finger keys. Nothing happened with these chimeras, of course; like almost all the contraptions we have recounted, they were mere inventors' "fancy work" and blew out at the moment of consummation.

We must mention one foot-operated contrivance, however, that did prove musically valuable to a limited extent. At the Paris exposition of 1844 the firm of Boisselot & Sons of Marseille exhibited an instrument in which it was possible to keep any selected group of dampers—or one single damper—off their respective strings while the rest remained in contact with theirs. In this way it was possible on such a piano, for instance, to strike a bass note or octave, sustain it with the new pedal, and then play a variety of different chords or passages freely with both hands in another register of the keyboard without muddling the harmony. European makers did not, as a whole, eventually adopt this "*sostenuto*" pedal, as we now call it; the Americans, however, began to apply it consistently later in the nineteenth century, and it remains a standard feature of good American grands to this day.

Mechanical enterprise extended to accessories not integrally part of the piano. An item appeared in the *Gazette Musicale* for April 3, 1836, as follows:

> Meyerhofer, piano maker and mechanic in Utrecht, has just invented a music rack the mechanism of which, by means of a simple pressure of the foot upon a spring, turns each of the pages that the performer has played. The author of this ingenious contrivance has obtained a patent from the government.

He was not the first on this path: two patents for a similar device had been issued in England twenty-five and thirty-five years before. Charles Hallé, now become the esteemed director of the Manchester orchestral concerts, was observed using a foot-operated page-turning mechanism in a concert he gave some time during the 1860's. But apart from his notable advocacy, it is remarkable that so seemingly useful an object should never have found more general acceptance.

Another problem that interested the mechanics was the one of making it possible to set on paper, instantly, music as it was being improvised at a keyboard, so as to preserve valuable musical thoughts before they evanesced—in other words, the constructing of an automatic mechanical musical stenographer. At least a dozen recorded attempts were made at such an apparatus—using various dispositions of paper rolls, pencil points, and prickers—in England, Germany, and France before 1850. The earliest seems to have been that of the Reverend Mr. Creed, of London, in 1747; whereas Jean-Henri Pape exhibited his *Piano-Sténographe,* and Edouard Guérin his *Pianographe,* at the Paris exposition in 1844. None was completely successful, and various individuals worried at the idea until far into the twentieth century.

23. THE CHAMPION GADGETEER

In all the welter of inventive effort in behalf of the piano a central figure is that of Jean-Henri Pape. He was the most prolific, the most versatile, the most ingenious piano-inventor that ever lived. Miss Harding lists 109 patents taken out by him, in both England and France; but she stops count in 1851, whereas he lived on until 1875, active much of the time. According to another source, his total patent score reached 137. His truly solid achievements were the use of felt for hammer covering and the device of cross-stringing; but most of the other contrivances mentioned in the preceding chapter have the name of Pape associated with them in some patent—the aeolian harp effect, the hammer *tremolando,* the kettle resonator, the specially ribbed sounding board, the double sounding board, the supernumerary unisons, the two hammers for every note, the improved tuning pins, the protective metal-plating for strings. It was he who designed the "console-piano," the round, the elliptical, and the hexagonal pianos.

Pape had his shop in Paris and, later on, his stores in Brussels and London. He must have sold his instruments pretty steadily, yet we hear little of his business progress. Moscheles played his instruments in his early days, around 1820, but it does not appear that Pape ever persuaded any well-known later virtuoso to use his instruments regularly in public. A suggestion to this end was indeed made in connection with the occasion on which Thalberg played both an Erard and a Pleyel at the same concert, but nothing came of it. Pape seems to have regarded his business largely as a grubstake, a necessary nuisance enabling him to spend his time and thought on inventing. He appears to have been a type of pure artist, living only for his ideas, one to whom the meaning of life was the joy of putting together cleverly movable arrangements of levers, springs, pivots, hinges, pads, wires, and screws, with relatively little regard for their ulterior value to human beings. He makes one think of a young cat, full of vigor and pounce. It lives to pounce on its natural prey and food such as mice and grasshoppers, on catnip balls, bits of paper, dangling ribbons, its master's finger and its own tail. It stalks and seizes a useless piece of string with wonderful craftiness and accuracy.

Pape was one of those irritated by the grand piano's gap between the wrest plank and the sounding board, as well as by the unseating effect of the hammer stroke upon the strings from below. He devised a beautiful down-striking action, allowing for more and continuous sounding-board surface and hitting the strings beneficently toward the bridge rather than away from it. The whole thing was highly efficient mechanically, finely executed, light and economical; connoisseurs praised it. He thereupon worked out a piano without strings, substituting coiled metal springs in their stead. Then he made an instrument using both strings and springs. When he had made his double sounding board on the violin principle and learned to appreciate the importance of the air above the resonating surface, he thought up hinged planks regulating the column of air above a single sounding board. Pianos had begun to go to seven octaves fairly regularly after 1840; by 1844 Pape had designed one of eight octaves. The extreme end tones of eight pianoforte octaves can hardly be distinguished and are very poor in quality; but why bring up such an irrelevance to an inspired inventor?

Yet this was one of Pape's designs that managed to achieve a few concert demonstrations. We have a report from March 1844 of "a very good piece for eight hands for two eight-octave pianos, composed by Mr. Pixis and performed by him, Messrs. Osborne, Rosenhain, and Wolff on two of the new pianos of Mr. Pape. . . ." We hear of this again three years later, at Pape's own warerooms, the piece now being specified as "made up on *Les Huguenots*, and played by Messrs. Hallé, Goldschmidt, Cavallo, and Osborne." The eight-octave piano retired presently, in silence, paying only one or two shy, unprofitable calls on the public within the next seventy-five years.

Pape presently also designed an artful square with the keyboard in the middle. There was nothing wrong with the keyboard in its normal place, nearer to the left, but think of the fun it must have been to overcome the difficulties of making the change! Felt on the hammer heads became worn after some use; Pape invented a device for turning the felt covering around so as to present a fresh surface.

He invented a gauge with a visual tension indicator, so that strings could be drawn up correctly by sight without listening to them: piano tuning, as well as playing, could now be brilliant but not difficult, especially for those with poor ears. Pape even invented a saw for cutting veneer of all kinds, succeeded in making thin sheets of ivory ten or twelve feet long, and once covered a whole instrument with it.

In general, as we survey Pape's inventions, we find him not altogether in sympathy with the newer trends of piano construction, those toward high tension, thick metal, and heaviness. That may be why he had little to do with concert performers. His idea of a piano seems to have been that of a light, small to moderate-sized drawing room instrument, of flawless mechanical workmanship, with a charming but not overbearingly powerful tone, its outer aspect elegant but not showy. Too bad he did not flourish in the eighteenth century, when fine pieces of machinery were often thought of as self-justifying works of art, with little consideration of their social utility; when people of quality paid half a guinea, as they did at Cox's museum, just to admire them as they moved.

The truth is, in Pape's heyday, in the 1840's, the piano was, with one very important exception, already a finished thing. Its development had all but run the course predetermined by the nature of its essence and that of the world in which it grew, and there was no further room for deviations or neoplasms. If one wanted to calculate the piano's maturity from the dates of the significant patents rather than from their general exploitation, one could maintain that the modern piano had practically completed its growth before 1830. The agraffe goes back to 1808, the practical double escapement action to 1821, the metal plates and bracing bars to 1822 or 1823, the felt hammer-covering to 1826, the use of tempered steel wire to 1826, the low oblique-strung upright to 1827, the round-the-pin method of continuous stringing likewise to 1827. A seven-octave grand was played in a concert as early as 1824.

What was the important exception referred to above? It was this: despite the metal frame in use at the middle of the century, the piano was still not rigid enough to withstand the full expressive ardor of an expert adult male pianist. Strings of the best instruments still gave way before the more impassioned impacts. This had been going on for quite a while. Anton Reicha, Czech-born musician who later taught at the Paris *Conservatoire,* tells a story of his acquaintance with Beethoven, probably at some time between 1803 and 1808:

> One evening when Beethoven was playing a Mozart piano concerto . . . he asked me to turn the pages for him. But I was mostly occupied in wrenching out the strings of the piano which snapped, while the hammers stuck among the broken strings. Beethoven insisted upon finishing the concerto, so back and forth I leaped, jerking out a string, disentangling a hammer, turning a page, and I worked harder than did Beethoven.

F. A. Gebhard, an actor engaged at the German theater in St. Petersburg, tells how he attended a concert there, probably in 1811, at which the pianists Field and Steibelt both played. Steibelt, jealously irritated at the beginning of his second solo, "struck at the keys so vehemently and wildly that a string jumped up almost to the ceiling of the hall."

Carl Maria von Weber left the fragment of a novel entitled *Musician's Life, an Arabesque.* In it he creates a scene in which the hero hits a low C on the piano in a fit of temper:

> And the hammer flew out of its fork [clearly a Vienna-action instrument] and a number of strings gave up their lives crunchingly—thus did the anger that so violently overwhelmed me dash my hand upon the keys, the blank music paper on the floor, throw over the chair, and snatch me upright, so that I traversed my narrow room in long strides.

Fiction, of course, but necessarily verisimilar.

According to these anecdotes, the fractures mostly occurred when the pianist was in an uncontrolled rage. When, however, we come to Franz Liszt, we find him exceeding the piano's capacity out of sheer intensity of musical feeling, out of exuberant desire for expression. He smashed pianos everywhere and frequently had one in reserve at his concerts. A review of his concert in Dresden, March 16, 1840, reads thus: ". . . his playing had such strength, clarity, and smoothness that it borders on the marvelous. Rarely does an instrument stay in tune; generally a few strings break." During his fabulous Berlin stay in the winter of 1841–42, he gave his first concerts playing numbers alternately on an Erard and a piano by a maker named Eck, of Cologne. Right at the opening recital, we learn from a reporter, "the Finale from *Lucia di Lammermoor* was ended sooner, owing to the acci dental snapping of a bass string." At the third concert, on Jan uary 5, Liszt presented the well-known Septet by Hummel. "Unfortunately, the Cologne piano was insufficient for the eagle flights of the inspired player. Two hammers were injured; still Liszt accomplished the last two movements." The English took a more sour view of Liszt's muscularity. A short-lived paper called the *Musical Journal* reported on Liszt's London performance with orchestra, May 11, 1840: "Liszt has been presented by the Philharmonic Society with an elegant silver breakfast service, for doing that which would cause every young student to receive a severe reprimand—viz., thumping and partially destroying two very fine pianofortes."

A French-made five-and-a-half-octave square of 1803, containing no metal bracing, was calculated to be under a total tension of two to three tons, depending on whether the treble had two or three strings to a note. A competent writer in the London *Quarterly Musical Review* stated in 1821 that the total tension on a large-sized six-octave grand was six and a half tons. By 1844 French-made grands were built to take ten and a half tons; it was still not enough.

The problem was finally solved, but not in Europe.

24. THESIS AND ANTITHESIS: PIANO BEGETS ANTIPIANO

To A CERTAIN DEGREE, the acute stage of the piano fever stimulated the formation of its own antitoxin. The hysteria that throbbed around the virtuosos aroused resistance and distaste in some quarters. The giddy tributes offered to Liszt in Berlin during the winter of 1842 provoked some prompt sarcasm. A pamphlet appeared, called *Das Lisztige Berlin,* lampooning some of the excesses committed under the influence of the famous musician's vapor. The title, which involves an untranslatable pun, means something like "sly Berlin." A first issue was snapped up so eagerly that the anonymous author brought out a second, with new jokes, and even a third. The booklets contained such tales as that of the lady who devoutly cut out and cherished a piece of couch cover from the very spot on which Liszt had sat; or a low-brow discussion of the current Lisztitis in Berlin dialect in a beer hall; and another in Yiddish dialect in a pawn shop. Liszt's peculiar brand of foreignness, as well as the pretensions to nobility that were thrust upon him, came in for some digs: "The high-noble-born Franz Liszt," a barker at a fair was made to say, "from lower Hungary where they talk French."

The final piece was in verse. It culminated in a description of a wild scene in which flocks of women rushed to a public square to try to climb a pole on top of which a clever demon had hung Liszt souvenirs such as his handkerchief, his nightcap, and a handful of his hair. After a furious scuffle, four half-naked Amazons carried off the trophies while the battlefield remained strewn with female corpses, as well as with torn shawls, mantles, and boas.

Was music's spell the thing that fanned this crazy passion?
Not that alone, we're sure: it was the work of fashion;
For it became the fashion to be in love with Liszt:
On being fashion's slave all ladies will insist.

Hat Zauberei der Töne dies' Leiden angefacht?
Das war's wohl nicht allein, die Mode hat's gebracht.
Denn Mode war's geworden in Liszt verliebt zu sein,
Und Unterthan der Mode will jede Dame sein.

The mockery makes amusing reading, but it made Berlin rather self-conscious: when Liszt played there again, a year later, people were so ashamed of their previous extravagance that they almost ignored him.

The vehement style in which the newer pianists were playing did not please everybody. "With these gentlemen," said Martin d'Angers in the *Gazette,* "striking accurately has been replaced by striking hard. Moreover, the pianos are now banded with iron and armored with steel, and still they often break under the feverish effort of a vigorous hand." He complains further of the violence, the complication, and the ugliness of modern piano music, saying some people are so revolted by it that they flee it like a plague.

Many pianists themselves were not in sympathy with the latest developments of pianism, nor with its more conspicuous practitioners. Moscheles in 1839, describing what he calls the "new school," says its leading features are:

> . . . a cultivation of amazing powers of execution, overwrought sentimentality, and the production of piquant effects by the most rapid changes from the soft to the loud pedal, or by rhythm and modulations which—if not to be completely repudiated—are only allowable on the rarest occasions. It is quite natural that I should not ally myself to this modern faction . . . In my school such a prodigal display of mechanical power was a thing unknown.

J. B. Cramer, late in life, said ironically: "Formerly piano playing was mighty good (*fort bien*), now it's good and mighty (*bien fort*)." Cramer's and Moscheles' attitude may be written off as the jealousy of older artists who had been left behind by a progressive development; the pianist Clara Schumann, however, was rather younger than Liszt and in the bloom of her repute when she said: "Before Liszt, people used to play; after Liszt, they pounded or whispered. He has the decline of piano playing on his conscience."

Her husband, Robert Schumann, was tireless in his fight against the fabricators of opera fantasies, galops and polkas, the facile variations with French titles, and the showy performers who garnered cheap applause by playing them. He opposed Herz, Thalberg, Czerny, and their like, called them Philistines, and encouraged anyone whose creations seemed to seek inward expressive truth rather than superficial effect. Many of his protégés nowadays seem to us to have been unworthy of his support, but he generously included all musicians of good will, as he deemed them, in his ideal "League of David." His campaign could be regarded as a championship of the more personal imagination, the more intimate sentiment, of the Germans as against the quickly titillating shiny shallows whose spiritual home was *nouveau-riche* Paris.

The exaggeration of public virtuosity was not the only objection to the pianoforte. In his article of January 17, 1847, reporting the instrument's wide vogue, Edouard Fétis reflects that this popularity has been dearly purchased with the obsolescence of other instruments: the violin, the flute, the cello, and the harp, "once cultivated by a large number of amateurs, have now fallen into disuse. . . . There was a time when large amounts of music were sold—overtures and entire opera scores—arranged for two flutes, two violins, two guitars, two flageolets." All this is much diminished in the provinces and completely gone in Paris, he says.

The long daily hours at the keyboard spent by girls in acquiring a dubious proficiency had their deplorers during the 1840's; we will, however, quote a bill of unpleasant particulars drawn up some forty years later by Louis Pagnerre in his curious book: *On the Evil Influence of the Piano upon the Art of Music.*

> The piano exempts a pupil from learning music. This is, from the educational point of view, the chief complaint against the instrument; all the other wrongs spring from it.
>
> A pupil, be he the most refractory toward any artistic feeling, be he the least apt to understand differences of pitch, their blend or their combinations, will succeed by a more or less obstinate mechanical labor in acquiring what is called "a pretty talent on the piano." In general this is the fate of young girls. At boarding school, at the convent, in certain courses, they learn the piano; sometimes they get to be quite good at it, and their families have made important pecuniary sacrifices to arrive at this result; the "talent" is obtained, and becomes a calculable item in the figure of the dowry. The father-in-law puts it into the bag: "My daughter is a good musician," he says, and the future son-in-law is obliged to hear with ecstasy such and such a brilliant piece, of which the front page is decorated with a pretty picture.
>
> In what does the young lady's "talent" consist? In making the little black and white circles of the page correspond with the keys of the piano. Nothing more. These circles carry with them no sense of intonation whatsoever; they indicate only the place where the finger is to strike. Notes printed one above the other are to be attacked on the keyboard simultaneously; that is the only harmonic, or even rhythmic, combination that is understood. Rhythm is only felt by the juxtaposition of beats on the two staves. The left hand guides the right, and reciprocally. Thus, the meter is no longer observed when it is a question of playing from a single staff. In that case, there are no more landmarks; when the subdivisions of the beat are no longer found clearly distributed between both hands, every idea of note value disappears. It is for this reason, too, that a piece for two hands, learned and played tolerably, becomes impossible of execution if it is written for four hands. . . .
>
> Pardon us this criticism, so uncomplimentary to the young ladies. The study of the piano is for them a compulsory adjunct to their education; whether they have aptitude or not, the lessons are imposed. . . . The young man, more independent, is able very soon to abandon the piano if he has no taste for it. The young lady, on the contrary, undergoes the study of the instrument in any event; she is riveted to it until marriage."

The author admits that there are some good teachers and good pupils. "But these are an elite, an exception . . ." he insists.

Such, then, were the complaints against the piano and its high vogue: it was often played with a revolting violence; its virtuosos became the objects of an absurb, undignified adulation; its spread encouraged a shallow style of music; its structure all too readily permitted unmusical persons to poke at it stupidly; its success provoked a neglect of other instruments. Furthermore, its ubiquity interfered with conversation and other mental pleasures; and finally, piano sounds could penetrate the ceilings, floors, and walls of apartments with distressing ease and thus often allow one girl's diversion to become another man's irritation.

We will call on Heinrich Heine to perorate for the prosecution. In his *Lutetia,* on March 20, 1843, he wrote:

> No one has comprehended the boredom that exhales from classic French tragedy better than the good burgher-wife from the days of Louis XV, who said to her children: "Don't envy the nobles, forgive them their arrogance; as a punishment from Heaven they have to bore themselves to death every night at the Théâtre-Français." The old regime has ceased, the scepter has come into the hands of the *bourgeoisie;* but these new rulers likewise have many transgressions for which to do penance, and the displeasure of the gods strikes them even more insufferably than their predecessors in the realm. . . .
>
> For its sins, the ruling *bourgeoisie* must not only endure old classic tragedies and trilogies that are not classical, but the Heavenly powers have vouchsafed them an even more horrible artistic treat, namely that pianoforte that one now can never anywhere escape, that one hears sounding in every house, in every company, day and night. Yes, pianoforte is the name of that instrument of torture with which present-day high society is pained and chastised for all its usurpations. If only the innocent did not have to suffer as well! This eternal piano playing is no longer to be endured! (Oh, my wall neighbors, young daughters of Albion, are at this moment playing a brillian *morceau* for two left hands.) Those shrill tinkle-tones without natural resonance, those heartless whirrings, that arch-prosaic rumbling and hacking, that fortepiano is killing all our thinking and feeling; we become stupid, dulled-off, imbecile. This predominance of piano playing, not to speak of the triumphal processions of the piano virtuosos, are characteristic of our time and bear witness to the victory of mechanism over spirit. Technical proficiency, the precision of an automaton, self-identification with

> wired wood, the resounding instrumentalization of the human being, all this is now praised and celebrated as the highest of things. . . .

The protests were in vain. The articulate antipianists were a feeble minority, powerless to stem the tide of the time. Not until a new century was well advanced did it turn.

SECTION

FIVE

Interlude: The High Plateau

THE HIGH PLATEAU

BY THE MIDDLE of the nineteenth century the piano infatuation had passed its peak. Somehow, the revolutions of 1848 seem to have had some connection with this phenomenon. In the Germanies and in the Austrian Empire the subversive movement, republican, democratic, or nationalist in spirit, was aimed at monarchical or foreign tyranny; but in France the uprising contained unmistakable proletarian, socialist elements. Already during the depression of 1846–47 there had been talk of *"les mauvais riches"*; the famous *Communist Manifesto* was dated 1847; and the heavy street fighting of June 1848, Paris' worst till then, was a battle in which the National Guard, acting for the businessmen, suppressed the riot of discontented wage earners.

Indeed, the burghers collectively speaking, or the *bourgeoisie,* the ancient European middle class, had for some time now been the upper class in France. In 1789 these people had been insurgents; but their grandsons in 1848 were the ruling group that stood pat on their millions, their machinery, their foreign connections, their control of the parliament and the executive. As it happened, the revolution did not begin to overthrow them; yet it gave them a significant jolt. They were permanently shocked by the emergence of a situation in which they had to gaze upon the awful spectacle of James de Rothschild, the greatest man in the world, losing a large amount of his fortune, having his castle at Suresnes burned and pillaged by an exasperated mob and himself escorted by a police guard to insure his bodily safety. Thenceforth their manners and their habits would tend increasingly toward the sedate, the conservative, or the sophisticated. After the Revolution the rich resumed their splurge, but now it seemed to be losing some of its innocence.

By reflection, the brave show of the piano virtuosos also lost its pristine freshness. For one thing, the actual violence of the Revolution, as well as the early uncertainties of the Second Republic, scared most of the pianists away. They flew off easily, for they were practically all foreigners anyway. Thalberg fled to England and after that toured the Americas. Charles Hallé also left for England, to make a permanent solid career there, chiefly as a conductor. Chopin's friends thought it prudent for him to make an English trip at that moment, and he died shortly after his return. Kalkbrenner, aging keyboard hero, also felt that a trip to England might benefit his health at that time; he also died in 1849. Herz, the lucky fellow, had left a couple of years earlier on a voyage to the United States; he was glad to extend it for several years during the critical Paris period. Liszt, king of them all, had quit resoundingly, even before being prompted thereto by any political storms. After his performance in Elizabethgrad, Russia, toward the end of 1847, when he was thirty-six years of age, he retired as a piano virtuoso; and apart from a trifling interlude a long time later, he no longer played piano solos in concerts of his own. He had begun to tire of the applause of fools, it seems. Here is what he wrote to his gifted friend Madame von Moukhanov, *née* Nesselrode:

> I have gone so far as to play that rumbling rumpus called "*Erlking*." Doubtless it is a masterpiece, but it has been spoiled for me by the public, which has condemned me to the perpetual gymnastics of storming octaves. What an unpleasant necessity that is in the virtuoso profession—that unrelieved chewing of the cud on the same thing!

Liszt presently ceased to make Paris his residence; he settled down as a composer, a conductor, and a teacher in the small German city of Weimar.

Never did the leading pianists of the time assemble again in Paris under the old atmosphere. With so many of them dead or departed from the city, Paris no longer remained Europe's central furnace of public pianism. This fact in itself tended to lower the prestige of the style of performance to which the city had lent its magical auspices. It was to Germany thenceforth that people looked for the creation of pianistic reputations; German notions of "good" music were to be those that gave the A to the rest of the Western world.

The climax of piano virtuosity was over, but in no sense did interest in the piano dry up. Merely, the piano, from teetering for fifteen years on the dizzy pinnacle of a craze, now slid down a few degrees to an endless high plateau of social esteem. There continued to be plenty of piano recitals, more than ever before; but the brilliant fantasies on opera tunes did not dominate the programs any longer so exclusively, while a greater sobriety and a better discrimination slowly percolated through the section of the public that had any care for concerts. By 1859 Eduard Hanslick, the keenest and wittiest of critics, wrote as follows in the columns of the old *Wiener Presse:*

> Quite a while has now elapsed since the time when an accomplished pianist could show himself off like a rare bird, or could even accuse himself of having robbed humanity if he refrained from blanketing city upon city with piano playing. The demand for piano virtuosos has been on the wane for a long time, whereas the supply —has seemed to increase in the same proportion.
>
> What are they driving at, these many pianizing youths and maidens, that makes them concentrate such heavy advertising fire from the street corners upon the unwary passer-by? A gentle anxiety comes over me at the sight of all those innocent white names: first concerning myself and then, much more severely and gloomily, concerning themselves! Do they really hope to lure paying mortals hither, and by playing the piano to inspire a public that itself consists of nothing but piano players? Do they really still envisage a position of brilliant distinction in the status of being a virtuoso—nowadays when half the population of Europe is suffering from the galloping virtuosity?
>
> In bitter seriousness: the sight of so many virtuoso announcements makes me sad. Sad, that still so many young people are sacrificing their time, their energy, their little fortune, their higher education, to make a life's aim out of skill on a stringed box. They are addressing their existence to a declining line of business, are producing an article in middling quality that only finds takers in the highest perfection. Having acquired some pretty little proficiency, they step before a public that has respect only for the highest technical achievement. And not even for that any more. Is there anyone still sought after or celebrated, may he be the supplest of acrobats, who, besides and before all technique, is not born to the true artistic nobility, with the most highly intensified capacity for thinking and feeling musically?
>
> Perhaps eight tenths of the young volunteers who annually make their raids against the public become, not generals of their art, but cannon fodder of the season. Presently the dream of gold and laurels will have been dreamed to a close, and those who had hoped to rock themselves on life's heights—we see them as obscure characters, going from house to house, inoculating younger generations with the virtuoso virus. . . .

The fact is, the virtuoso acrobat pure and simple was gradually becoming replaced by a performer who considered himself an interpreter, one who aimed to set forth as vividly and convincingly as he could the music of composers other than himself. During the fifties, the sixties, and later—instead of the Thalbergs and the Dreyschocks playing their own fantasies and dolled-up medleys designed to show off their special brands of skill—we get Clara Schumann and Hans von Bülow, who begin to devote their attention to presenting the works of Beethoven, Chopin, Schubert, Schumann, and Mendelssohn. The idea was indeed new: never before in the history of Western music did we encounter any considerable number of instrumental soloists who could achieve fame by confining their performances to other people's compositions.

It was at the end of 1837 that Clara Wieck, then a girl of nineteen, not yet married to Robert Schumann, made her debut in Vienna. On that occasion, and on a number of similar subsequent ones, she became the first person who dared offer Beethoven's sonatas to a concert audience, notably those in D minor, C-sharp minor, and the *Appassionata*. That was more than ten years after Beethoven's death. Clara was greatly acclaimed by connoisseurs, and Franz Grillparzer even expended some poetry upon her. Ultimately her example was followed, though not universally at first. Charles Hallé, fresh in London in 1848, was asked to play at the Musical Union. That was the name given to a series of select morning chamber-music concerts patronized by the Duke of Cambridge and other high denizens of the peerage. Hallé frightened John Ella, the musical director of the enterprise, by proposing to perform a Beethoven sonata at this occasion of his first appearance. Solo sonatas, protested Ella, were unsuitable for concerts and had never been played at such events in London before. He gave in finally; and when Hallé charmed his blue-blooded hearers with the swing and sweep of Opus 31 No. 3, the sonata was "in" as a concert dish.

From about 1850 to 1890 Anton Rubinstein enjoyed an intoxicating success that rivaled that of Liszt in many respects; yet he too was an interpreter, not an acrobat, and his own compositions were mostly far from being show stunts. We can perceive the nature of the best piano recitals of his time by inspecting two programs that he gave, on May 25 and 29, 1876, at St. James Hall, London. Practically everything Rubinstein played at these occasions was by composers resting in their graves; all the music was from twenty to a hundred and fifty years old, with that of the old masters predominating and Beethoven sonatas looming large. The wording of the printed program sheets seems to reflect a pretentious half-culture on the part of the audience to which they were addressed. For example, many compositions were referred to by generic name without further specification—such as Chopin *Nocturne,* Liszt *Rhapsodie,* and Bach *Gigue*—giving no identification by key or number. Great music and great pianists were, of course, properly non-English; thus it was considered interestingly appropriate to anoint the program with a hodgepodge of foreign tongues: a famous Bach work was called *Fantaisie Chromatique* in unaccountable French, while a well-known Scarlatti piece was given its dubious nickname of *Katzenfuge* in even more unsuitable German. A celebrated little theatrical excerpt by Beethoven was labeled *Marcia alla Turca* (*Des 'Ruines d'Athènes'*), in two different languages alien alike to the audience and to the composer; while Mendelssohn's melodies—so sweetly at home in many an English interior—were nevertheless distantly called *Lieder ohne Worte.* Moreover, the pianist himself, a true Russian and the Czar's own Concert Director, was referred to as Herr Rubinstein.

Programs consisting largely of time-sifted masterpieces may, of course, appeal more readily to people of wider culture and greater discrimination than those that dwell mostly in the froth of current fashion. Nevertheless, too persistent a preoccupation with the past, even with its glories, is an elderly posture, one of diminishing hope. Old music could seem new to the ever resurgent generations who had not heard it before; still, on the whole, what a "classical" program gains in "taste," it loses in living force. The essential contents of those Rubinstein programs of 1876 became the norm for piano recitals from that day to this. A few names of newer composers—not more than half a dozen—have replaced those of Field, Thalberg, Henselt, and Rubinstein himself; but those of Bach and Scarlatti, Mozart and Beethoven, Chopin and Schumann have remained even more rigidly rooted than before.

The change of piano-recital programs from modish bravura pieces to "classics" came about gradually. Liszt continued to make up operatic paraphrases during the 1850's and later, after he had stopped playing them himself. One of the most successful of these was based on the quartet from Verdi's *Rigoletto.* Still later he also made arrangements of excerpts from Wagner's music dramas.

Other music, not derived from operas, was made to serve as raw material for dividend-yielding concert-pianistic processing.

So long as the piano was still the thing of moment, other—non-pianistic—music had to be fitted to it somehow. Here again, Liszt was a pioneer. He had played his own transmogrified versions of Schubert songs in the programs of his glittering period; he followed them with elaborations of the songs of Schumann, Chopin, and Mendelssohn. It was Liszt, likewise, who started the vogue of concert versions of Vienna waltzes. About 1850 he put together his tasteful little flower arrangements based on Schubert waltzes, calling them *Vienna Evenings* (*Soirées de Vienne*). It was he, finally, who first transcribed some of Sebastian Bach's organ compositions for the piano. He did all these last-mentioned things after he had retired from concert playing, but other pianists were glad to take them up and shine through them. Liszt's gifted, short-lived pupil Carl Tausig followed his master's line: during the 1860's he constructed *New Vienna Evenings* out of the waltzes of Johann Strauss, as well as an arrangement of Bach's well-known organ *Toccata and Fugue in D minor.* These adaptations had long runs, more than fifty years, in piano recitals. Not until the second quarter of the twentieth century were concertgoers weaned from the habit of listening to pianists play music not originally written for their instrument.

During the middle of the nineteenth century, in truth, the *bourgeoisie* was slowly achieving a sophistication of artistic leadership. The showier purchasable habits of the rich could mostly be copied plausibly by people not nearly so rich, thus destroying their distinction. The principle had its musical analogy. Someone asked Thalberg during the 1850's why he no longer composed. "Alas," replied the pianist, "my imitators have made me impossible." Special groups of educated music lovers now became assertive, especially in German cities: they were mostly people of bourgeois background, imbued with intellectual rather than pecuniary snobbery. We may think of them as the spiritual descendants of the eighteenth century *Kenner und Liebhaber:* art pietists, worshipers of the audible God, grown bolder and more influential with Germany's remarkable economic and political rise, and breaking into outright arrogance after 1871. They were increasingly able to impose their standards of taste on larger circles of people; and partly through the prestige of thousands of emigrated German musicians, they even succeeded in persuading some of the rich and powerful of other nations to climb out with them on their not always comfortable little penthouse porch. Furthermore, they imposed a ceremonious solemnity, a kind of churchly decorum, upon the concert hall, replacing the "club" atmosphere of earlier German concerts or the "show" atmosphere of the Paris-heated virtuoso exhibitions. These were the people who formed the significant concert public of the later century, who tended to concentrate their enjoyment on the more distinguished masterpieces of a previous generation—especially on those of Beethoven and his immediate successors—and who even ventured to explore timidly the formidable relics of older masters such as Sebastian Bach. It was a sect of this narrow stratum of determined devotees that, with the aid of a lunatic king of Bavaria, succeeded after about thirty years in forcing the works of Richard Wagner upon its reluctant friends and neighbors. With this move a significant fraction of the *bourgeoisie* achieved a distinction that was not easily degraded. By submitting to being puzzled, bored, revolted—and occasionally thrilled—by these overbearing musical stage plays, their patrons made themselves safe from cheap emulation: they had achieved distance through suffering, had become difficult but not brilliant.

A drive toward distance, toward the assertion of personal distinction, also animated composers more urgently as the nineteenth century proceeded. Earlier musicians had been happy to fit their productions into situations where they were required—in church, theater, or drawing room. Handel and Bach, Haydn and Mozart were glad to allow the peculiar charm and power of their personalities to radiate unforced from works that were set in conventionally accepted formulas like the grammar and syntax of a current language. It was the commercialism of the nineteenth century, the domination of society by business habits of mind, that gave a morbid sting to some composers' egos. The spread of a small musical literacy through millions of people—the ease with which die-cut, patterned music could be sold to unconcerned hordes—seemed a degradation of the composer's always exceptional gifts. Formerly, if he wrote a claptrap string quartet to be played by the fiddlers of the Duke of Plaza-Toro, that still left him glowing with the tinge of the Duke's greatness. But to write claptrap polkas or romances for a welter of nameless grocers' daughters—that was somehow humiliating. At that rate, composing for the market seemed unworthy of a skilled, deliberate human effort; it seemed almost like something that could be equally well done by a machine. In point of fact, a music-composing machine was actually invented during the 1820's. It was called "Componium," appropriately enough; it operated on the pricked-cylinder-barrel-organ principle, turning up endless permutations of notes. Neat diagrams of the Componium's working parts can be seen in the English music magazine *The Harmonicon,* for 1824, appearing at just about the time Beethoven was completing his Ninth Symphony.

Furthermore, sensitive musicians and their sympathizers now expressed disdain for the habits of ordinary people by giving evil names to the kind of goods the latter were willing to buy and enjoy. The words mostly were equivalent to the notion of refuse: "trash" and "rubbish" were the usual ones; "junk" was a later American term, and other synonyms were rather more obscene. The Germans said *"Schund"* or *"Dreck."* The English word "trash" had been used in connection with literature already during the eighteenth century; the idea bobbed up in music, as we might expect, toward 1830. Musical "trash," like all other industrial production, multiplied enormously as the century advanced. Just as surely did some of the more self-assertive musicians revolt against it more and more emphatically, and insist on fishing in the remoter regions of their minds for what they wished to bring forth. The precious uniqueness of their persons was what they wanted to affirm most forcibly, their "individuality," and even more ardently their "originality." Without that, why bother to do anything so extraordinary as to compose?

Wagner's success gave great encouragement to these exquisite autoenthusiasts. It seemed, then, possible for a small bunch of zealous snobs, by much talk and insistence, to compel a considerable number of customers to accept something that made little sense to most of them. More and more composers became more and more "original" from the end of the nineteenth century on into the present one, addressing themselves to smaller and smaller groups of listeners. The ultimate ideal might seem to be the development of a class of generally and mutually unintelligible tone combiners, each speaking his completely original, unique, and inspired language to God alone. However, this radiant abyss of German art-idealism bids fair to remain eternally a mirage. The dedicated self-expressers all suffer from a fatal cleft in their own souls: they wish to be admired and loved by the very people whom they nervously avoid trying to please. As soon as one of them stumbles on a procedure that may be directly accessible to an appreciable number of people, it inevitably becomes imitated by others, running the danger of becoming marketable and thus again trash. On the other hand, if there were no ocean of trash, what would there be to have the fun of despising?

If this was to be the path of "art," then many otherwise intelligent, educated, well-to-do people, possessed of good eyes and ears, were glad to make detours around "art." If opera was going Wagner, many prosperous men and women of good will were going to get the sort of tunes they liked under some other heading, either as "*operette,*" "musical comedy," "comic opera," or "light opera." During the 1870's, '80's, and '90's many inhabitants of well-fitting evening clothes, who subjected themselves to being painfully edified by *Walküre* on Wednesday, were only too happy to spend Thursday, Friday, and Saturday dallying with the cozier charms of *Fledermaus, Belle Hélène,* or *Iolanthe.* For a generation after 1850, the *Gems from Martha* and similar cheaper grades of operatic medleys continued to thrive pianistically in living rooms; but they began to decline as new operas became scarcer and as those that did come out after *Carmen* (1875) rarely contained melodies that anybody cared to hear again in his own home. At the same rate, pianistically playable arrangements of tunes from musical comedies flourished increasingly; but mostly they were less amusing than those by Strauss, Offenbach, or Sullivan.

They were trash, by high-brow standards; and so was almost all other piano music of the century: *Skaters' Waltz, Pizzicato Polka, Czarine Mazurka, Flower Song, Shower of Pearls, Edelweiss, Dance of the Demons, Longing for Home, Alpine Maid's Dream, Simple Confession,* and *Monastery Bells.* Its fault was that it was pretty, that it gave mild, ready pleasure to a commercially profitable number of the less fastidious. It was an uncompromisingly homophonic music: its essence was a single all-important line of melody, supported by subordinate packages of tones called chords. (But this lone line of song with an occasional auxiliary harmonic strum had been the norm of all popular European music since ancient days.) Nineteenth-century commercial melody was always a rigorously symmetrical four-measure jingle. Accompanying chords were of limited assortment; some of their dissonances had once had some piquancy and charm, when they were first used, but constant reiteration of their progressions had made them commonplace, had insipidated their sugar and spice. In dancelike music the chords were naturally chopped into quick, regularly impinging chunks; but in suave, slower music they were rolled, folded, and draped in a variety of distributions.

The later nineteenth century produced a small quantity of piano music that transcended the commonest formulas of its time, and whose strength of conception gave it some staying power beyond its generation. I refer primarily to the works of Johannes Brahms and César Franck, much less positively to those of Camille

Saint-Saëns and Edvard Grieg. There was other piano music that was far from contemptible in the estimation of the day, that was approved and admired by the best contemporary musicians and regarded as safely and nobly over the heads of the Philistine herd. I refer to the compositions of Joachim Raff, Anton Rubinstein, Adolf Jensen, Adolf Henselt, Josef Rheinberger, Xaver Scharwenka, and a number of others. Alas, the repudiative rage of the twentieth century has swept them away; they are all trash now, if they were not then. But one could imagine, one or two hundred years hence—when most of the celulose that bears the notation of this nineteenth-century refuse will have crumbled to nothingness—that a generation of bright youths might discover the newly novel charm of the remainder, treat it with a profound respect, decorate itself with it assertively, pursue it for collectors' items, and make it the basis of Ph.D. theses. And if there will no longer be any pianos on which to play it, it will embody the additional lure of the unseizable.

In France, the Revolution of 1848 retarded piano manufacture for a year or two; but it picked up again soon and seemed for a time to maintain its old leadership of quality. At the Paris exposition of 1855 the Erards and the Pleyels both received the highest awards for their exhibits. However, both Pierre Erard and Camille Pleyel died that same year. Meanwhile, the Second Republic had fretted itself into a Second Empire: the Erards duly made a grand in a rosewood case, with angel caryatids for legs, and decorated with *"bronzes de Paillard,"* for His Majesty Napoleon III. Nevertheless, the successors to the managements of the two well-known firms seem to have relaxed the spirit of enterprise essential to commercial growth: they seemed to show a fateful tendency to coast on their established procedures and on their reputations. At the exposition of 1867 their regression was dramatically revealed, as we shall see later. The date may be definitely marked as the end of French supremacy in piano manufacture.

Supreme or not, however, the French makers continued to do a good business. Throughout the nineteenth century, piano sales increased at a far greater rate than did the population. French-made pianos rose from an approximate annual 10,000 in 1850 to 25,000 in 1910—a gain of 150%—while the total population during the period rose only from 32,000,000 to 40,000,000, a mere 25%. A somewhat similar but lower ratio could be observed in Great Britain, where piano production went from 25,000 units in 1851 to 75,000 in 1910—a gain of more than 200%—while the population rose from 27,000,000 to 45,000,000, about 66%. It is true that after the second third of the century, the French and English relinquished their leadership in the piano trade, both quantitatively and qualitatively, to the Americans and later Germans. This does not, however, mean that the business actually declined in France and England. The figures show merely that its rate of growth was overtaken by that of the other countries. Some time during the 1870's, as a consequence of Britain's traditional free-trade policies, it was possible for the comparatively new Berlin firm of C. Bechstein & Co. to open warerooms in London. By 1910, it and other German and American concerns were selling 20,000 pianos annually to England, once the world's champion in that branch of industry.

If new pianos were being made at a faster rate than new people were being born and new homes established, that must have meant primarily that more families could afford them. That, in turn, meant not only that more people became more prosperous, but also that the rationalization of the parts business made it possible to keep the price of an ordinary instrument down with respect to the general cost of living. On the other hand, our calculation must also allow for the fact that some of the bounding piano production of the principal European factories was absorbed by the enlarging export market. By the mysterious magnetism of success—whatever that word may be deemed to mean—people in other parts of the world felt urged to imitate the habits of Northwest European city dwellers. Southern Europe, Eastern Europe, Russia, Latin America, Australia, South Africa, India, Japan, and the Philippines bought pianos from France and England, and later, notably, from Germany, even though some of those areas supported a few smaller factories of their own as well. Well-to-do little lands such as the Scandinavian countries, the Low Countries, and Switzerland likewise provided "outlets" for the big houses in the big countries.

For nearly seventy years after the middle of the nineteenth century, then, the piano proceeded smoothly, levelly, on its voyage of destiny. The plateau of esteem on which it rode aloft had no more heady ups, and no perceptible downs; but its lateral expanse was immeasurable. Every family that considered itself above the "working class" level owned one, or aimed to own one and to let its daughters learn to play it a little. According to critic Oscar Comettant's estimate of 1868, Paris alone harbored twenty thousand persons occupied to a greater or lesser extent with piano teaching. But even unplayed, the piano had its positive meaning and value. The object was an unquestioned occupant of every *salon,* drawing room, living room, or parlor—whatever the shade of pretense with which the space was named. Its establishment in every school auditorium, theater, clubroom, hotel ballroom and banquet room, and ocean steamer was similarly taken for granted. Its fat carved legs, its curled openwork music rack, the bristling restless Gothic lettering on its name board were all made cheaply by machinery; yet that did not prevent them from giving an impression of assertive opulence, of expensive, detailed, useless labor, of a desire to be "fancy" rather than "plain." The candelabras built onto the sides of European uprights remained conspicuous long after the prevalence of gas lighting, and even of electric lighting, had made them functionless: they became a token of ostentatious idleness. The silk embroidered coverlet that women liked to drape over the instrument reflected their worship of surface appearances, their devotion to a cosmetic view of life.

By its presence, the piano betokened the self-satisfaction with which the well-to-do of the later century regarded themselves. It expressed their sense of progress achieved and maintained, their comfortable equation of moral with financial superiority, their tolerant disdain of laborers and "backward" peoples, their certainty of the exact location of "woman's place," and their general sense of security. "God's in his Heaven, Dinner's at seven, All's right with the world" was the silent counterpoint to much of the piano's music, and even to the piano's silence. The piano was safe, safe as the Bank of England; and both institutions seemed some how vaguely related.

SECTION

SIX

United States of America

1. RICH COLONIALS HAVE DAUGHTERS AND HARPSICHORDS

THE 25,000 English-speaking Caucasians on the North American continent in 1640 were clustered in small, feeble settlements, most of them in Massachusetts and Virginia. It is hard to imagine that their struggles with disease, Indians, and wilderness rigors left many of those people much time or energy for the pursuit of the polite arts.

By 1700 a vigorous native increase swelled by a dwindling immigration had caused the colonial numbers to rise to about 265,000, and the accompanying growth in wealth and leisure gradually created room for certain mental comforts and pleasures to exist more easily. We hear briefly, for example, from Anthony Aston—a mercurial English lawyer, actor, writer, and traveler—that he participated in theatricals in Charleston, South Carolina, during the winter of 1703–4, when that city had but a few thousand people; and that soon afterward he found an acquaintance in little old New York who had set up as a fencing master.

Among the communities of the time, Boston was pre-eminent in general literacy; and we are not astonished to know that in 1704, when it contained seven thousand inhabitants, it began to support a regular newspaper.

The Massachusetts Puritans, that is to say their ruling clergy, were sternly opposed to the use of organs in church; they did not, however, condemn the private exercise of music. For instance, Samuel Sewall, a Harvard divinity student, Boston judge, money lender, and politician—a pillar of society—noted in his diary for December 1, 1699, that he was "at Mr. Hiller's to enquire for my wives virginals . . ." What did she play on it, we wonder? Was she skillful enough to have managed the suites of Henry Purcell, or did she content herself with the simpler tunes in Playford's *Musick's Handmaid*?

All ruling cliques necessarily make opponents for themselves; and when these are rich and well connected, they may become hard to deal with. Thomas Brattle, one of Boston's wealthiest men and the treasurer of Harvard College, seems to have differed pointedly with the prevailing pontiff Increase Mather; for in 1699 Brattle and his friends issued a Manifesto and set up a dissident congregation called the Brattle Street Church, which departed from Puritan orthodoxy in such weighty points as the use of the Lord's Prayer and the occasional uncommentated public reading of the Bible. We must presume Mr. Brattle to have been a music lover; else why should he have troubled to import an organ from England for his own house, the first of its kind, some say, ever to have reached North American shores? Brattle never married; he may have had musical servants, yet it is not unreasonable to guess that he played it himself. In his will he left the organ to his Brattle Street Church; but that institution cautiously declined the devilish, subversive, and perhaps spiteful bequest. The will, however, anticipated this refusal and provided that in such case the organ was to go to King's Chapel. Mr. Brattle died on June 18, 1713, and we remember that Massachusetts had then been a royal province for nearly twenty years. The royal governor and his official train necessarily represented the Church of England; and that rite was now established, if not privileged, in Massachusetts as in all other royal domains.

King's Chapel coyly tried not to defy public opinion by seeming too brazenly eager: it left the "hot" instrument shivering in its wraps in front of the church for seven months. Thereafter it was taken inside to the churchly bosom, and a Mr. Price was hired to play it. Soon a more professional service was desired: the vestry persuaded Mr. Edward Enstone to come from London to be their organist, offering him a scant annual £30, but suggesting that he could piece out this stipend by giving lessons and selling musical merchandise. Soon Enstone's application for permission to open his music and dancing school was righteously refused by Boston's selectmen; but his self-assured King's Chapel backers apparently told him to go ahead anyway. They were the governor's crowd, and thus the royal sovereign's: Massachusetts was part of his domain. Anglicans might not now be hanged as Quakers once had been, nor kicked out like Roger Williams; thus, Mr. Enstone fiddled and led minuets while Cotton Mather and his fellow theocrats could only gnash their stomachs at the thought. Here is Enstone's advertisement in the *News Letter* for April 16–23, 1716:

> This is to give Notice that there is lately sent over from London a choice Collection of Musical Instruments, consisting of Flaguelets, Flutes, Haut-Boys, Bass-Viols, Violins, Bows, Strings, Reeds for Haut-Boys, Books of Instructions for all these Instruments, Books

of ruled Paper. To be sold at the Dancing School of Mr. *Enstone* in Sudbury Street near the Orange Tree Boston. *Note.* Any Person may have all Instruments of Music mended, or Virgenalls and Spinnets Strung and Tuned at a reasonable rate, and likewise may be taught to Play on any of these Instruments abovemention'd; dancing taught by a true and easier method than has been heretofore.

It seems clear that there were enough virginals in the town—now approaching the nine-thousand mark—to warrant his offer of these services.

Judge Sewall could still record a small rear-guard victory for the Lord. On November 29, 1716, two gentlemen "acquainted Mr. Bromfield and me that a Ball was designed at Enston's in the evening, pray'd us to prevent the Govr. being there. Accordingly, in the closet Capt. Belcher, Mr. Bromfield, and I spake to the Govr. and at last his Excel'y promised us not to be there." By 1720 Enstone was undertaking to board young ladies and have them "taught all sortes of Needle Work with Musick and Dancing etc."

The Pennsylvania Quakers were convinced even more thoroughly than the Puritans that music was an unholy vanity and a distraction from busy-ness. Yet they tried to be tolerant and peaceable; and they tended magnanimously to allow the German Lutherans, the Anglicans, the Catholics, the Jews, and the Deists in their midst to go to hell each in their own favorite melodious way. A relatively liberal atmosphere prevailed in Philadelphia through the eighteenth century, punctuated by a few suppressions of theaters.

Early in the century we may notice the English-born Dr. Christopher Witt. Though an avowed Pietist of the German coloration, his talents and his wealth nevertheless seem to have seduced him now and again into "setting the world on a level with the Saviour." He, too, had a large pipe organ in his home and was known to have bought and played a harpsichord after 1725, besides painting pictures and rearing a botanical garden.

Pennsylvania was a much younger settlement than Massachusetts, but its growth was relatively more rapid. In the columns of the *Pennsylvania Gazette* for March 5, 1730, a Miss Ball, "lately arrived from London," offered to teach "singing, playing on the spinet, dancing, and all sorts of needle work"—the orthodox young-lady-like package of arts. The city of Philadelphia then contained fewer than twelve thousand people.

Before the end of the century's first third, then, a steady small fraction of the colonial inhabitants were the kind of people who could and would afford their daughters the "accomplishments" considered proper to them.

Early in the 1730's we begin to hear of public musical performances, for money, advertised in advance in the newspapers. The colonies were not too backward a country in this respect: they were indeed half a century behind England, but well in time with Germany on this score. The first concert we know of—in Boston on December 30, 1731—was announced as "on sundry instruments." It took place in Mr. Pelham's Great Room, Peter Pelham being known as an engraver, dancing master, boarding school keeper, and instructor in painting upon glass, and thus a carrier-on of the work previously advanced by Enstone. It is hard to think that a harpsichord was not one of the "sundry instruments" played upon this occasion, if only for the accompaniments, seeing that Master Pelham was known to have brought up his own son to be a competent performer on it. The admission tickets cost five shillings; and we may not be amiss in supposing the audience to have contained a large representation of such people as had successively continued to patronize Messrs. Enstone's and Pelham's activities. These would be persons connected with the official British governmental establishment, whose red coats, gold lace, sword play, church organs, Christmas celebration, dancing, and general gaiety the Puritans had to learn to tolerate.

On June 24, 1732, an announcement of a concert in the *South Carolina Gazette*, of Charleston, promised "N.B. Country Dances for the Diversion of the Ladies," while an entertainment there in October of the same year advertised "A Ball after the Concert." In fact, colonial concerts, for the most part, seem to have been social assemblies with dancing to follow. This does not reflect unfavorably on the taste in the choice of programs, which compared well in quality with those of concerts in England.

New York's first traceable recorded concert took place in January 1736, when the future world metropolis harbored fewer than ten thousand inhabitants. The event was put on for his own benefit by Charles Theodore Pachelbel, late organist of Trinity Church, Newport, Rhode Island; "the harpsichord part performed by himself," he advertised, and "the songs, violins, and German flutes by private hands."

Concert performers were largely local teachers—who may have included dancing and fencing with music in their list of offered services—or worthy organists interested in forcing an occasional bolster under their incomes or their reputations. Competent gentleman and lady amateurs often supplemented the always variegated programs. It was inevitable, in any event, that a harpsichord be lent for the occasion—if only for the accompaniments; and at the Charleston concert of dancing-and-fencing-master Thomas Pike, on October 16, 1765, the program definitely announced a "Concerto on the Harpsichord."

Altogether, Charleston was perhaps America's most musically minded city during the later middle eighteenth century. Its long-lived St. Coecilia Society, organized in 1762, was necessarily exclusive, what with its yearly dues of £25. Its three or four annual private concerts, with an orchestra of mixed amateurs and professionals, must have been social events of considerable brilliance. Moreover, whatever wowsers the South harbored in those days exercised little influence, and the predominantly loyalist, Anglican social leaders had no prejudices against playhouses. Williamsburg, Virginia had one as early as 1722, and Charleston boasted of a "New Theatre in Queen Street" during the 1730's. At that time Charlestonians had an opportunity of hearing well-known ballad operas, such as *Adventures of Harlequin and Scaramouch* and *Flora, or Hob in the Well.*

New York, less religiously inhibited than Boston or Philadelphia, also enjoyed some kind of theater in the 1730's, probably some of it musical. By July 1751 Kean and Murray's troupe had given *The Beggar's Opera, The Devil to Pay,* and other favorite pieces there. Its singers' instrumental support must have included a harpsichord and may have consisted of that and nothing more.

The overpowering cultural fact of the time was the extraordinary population increase. The combined colonies had reached a million inhabitants by 1743, and numbered two million and a half on the eve of the Revolution. Actually, the American people was then doubling itself about every twenty-three years, continuing to grow at that rate until the outbreak of the Civil War. By comparison, England's population fell considerably short of doubling itself between one end of the eighteenth century and the other.

The multiplication of numbers involved a corresponding multiplication of all human resource, economic and intellectual. Everything became more, including such insignificant things as theaters, concerts, the private practice of music, and the sale of musical instruments. More boats plied between the mother country and the colonies, bringing more frequent news and fashions. They also brought more harpsichords, together with carpets, paintings, ladies' hoops, and fine cupboards, ordered by general merchants of the ports by special contract with customers who felt these polite luxuries essential to their self-esteem. Let us keep our picture in focus. We may remember that during the 1760's Shudi sold his cheapest harpsichords for £35, while he asked £84 for his most elaborate instruments. Freight, packing, and commissions would raise the American price substantially. It is clear that the small farmers, small tradesmen, indentured servants, and slaves that made up the overwhelming majority of the American population could hardly hope, by the furthest stretch, to swing such an expenditure. Large New York and Philadelphia merchants and factors, broad Virginia and Carolina planters were the likely purchasers of the article, as were also the lordly personnel of the royal governing establishment, the governor, the generals, and the colonels, the high judges and commissioners who constituted colonial high society, together with the expensive upper-class hangers-on and boondogglers whom they carried with them and foisted upon the taxpayers.

Apparently, a good many harpsichords were taken by Southerners, especially Virginians. We know a little about it from the diary of Philip Vickers Fithian, a Princeton theology student, an obscure fellow student of James Madison and Aaron Burr during the years 1770–1772. Fithian was engaged during 1773 and 1774 as a private tutor to the young sons of Colonel Robert Carter, one of Virginia's richest gentlemen. Colonel Carter ruled over an estate of sixty thousand widely scattered acres, worked by six hundred Negro slaves, centering in his great lordly ancestral residence in Westmoreland County, called Nomini Hall. There he brought up his large family and devoted himself to gentlemanly and scholarly pursuits. These last, Fithian tells us, consisted mostly of law and music. The young tutor was indeed impressed with Mr. Carter's theoretical and practical grasp of that art, his mastery of thorough bass (*i.e.*, harmony) and of transposition. "It seems to be his darling amusement—it seems to nourish as well as entertain his mind," he notes with astonishment. Elsewhere he admires his "good ear and vastly delicate taste" and says he is "indefatigable in the practice." The Colonel kept various instruments: a harpsichord, of course, as well as a guitar, several flutes, and a harmonica, which was Benjamin Franklin's radical improvement of the musical glasses. Fithian was charmed to hear Mr. Carter play *Water Parted from the Sea* upon it and said "the notes are inexpressibly clear and soft, they swell and are inexpressibly grand." Moreover, Colonel Carter was a member of the Virginia Council in Williamsburg, which he visited twice a year, and he kept an organ at his residence there for his delectation and practice.

Mr. Carter was undoubtedly exceptional in the extent of his care for music; however, Fithian also reports on lesser musical activities in the homes of comparable Virginia families in the neighborhood. On April 7, 1774, Fithian tells how he went with Colonel Carter and his son Ben to call on Colonel Tayloe, twelve miles away, from whose house "there is a good prospect of the River Rapahannock," two miles across. There the host's daughters Miss Polly and Miss Kitty "played several tunes for us, & in good Taste on the Harpsichord, and did the same for the guests the following morning, even before breakfast."

Fithian recounted a different sort of musical atmosphere when he told how on January 18 he had escorted Mrs. Carter and her daughters to a ball given by "Squire" Richard Lee, also of Westmoreland County:

> About Seven the Ladies & Gentlemen begun to dance in the Ball-Room—first Minuets one Round; Second Giggs; third Reels; and last of All Country-Dances; tho' they struck several Marches occasionally—The Music was a French-Horn and two Violins—The Ladies were Dressed Gay, and splendid, & when dancing, their Skirts & Brocades rustled and trailed behind them!—But all did not join in the Dance for there were Parties in Rooms made up, some at Cards; some drinking for Pleasure; some toasting the Sons of america; some singing "Liberty Songs" as they call'd them, in which six, eight, ten or more would put their Heads near together and roar, & for the most part as unharmounious as an affronted——

An affronted what? The young clergyman does not say. He is, however, proud to tell that he did not dance or game at this party.

On June 24, 1774, Miss "Jenny" Washington, aged seventeen, came early to the Carter mansion to join several other junior misses in a dancing class. "Jenny" was probably Jane, daughter of John Augustine and Hannah Bushrod Washington, and thus a niece of the future Father of his Country. Fithian was greatly impressed with her, her "agreeable Size," her "easy winning Behaviour," her refraining from "any Girlish affectation," the propriety with which she danced a minuet, and the absence of "any Flirts or vulgar Capers" when she danced a reel or country dance. "She plays well on the Harpsichord, & Spinet; understands the principles of Musick, & therefore performs her Tunes in perfect time, A Neglect of which always makes music intolerable, but it is a fault almost universal among young Ladies in the practice . . ." It is interesting to see the young theologian observe the musical phase of original sin. He reflects: "but most of the Virginia-Girls think it labour quite sufficient to thump the Keys of a Harpsichord into the air of a tune mechanically . . ." Alas, so it must ever be with compulsory "accomplishments."

The Marquis de Chastellux, Major General of the French Army under Rochambeau during the Revolution, later wrote an account of his travels through the middle states. In 1780 he was in Philadelphia, of which he tells the following incident:

> In the afternoon we drank tea with Miss Shippen. This was the first time, since my arrival in America, that I had seen music introduced into society, and mix with its amusements. Miss Rutledge played on the harpsichord, and played very well. Miss Shippen sang with timidity but with a pretty voice. Mr. Ottaw, secretary to M. de la Luzerne, sent for his harp; he accompanied Miss Shippen, and played several pieces. Music naturally leads to dancing: the Vicomte de Noailles took down a violin, which was mounted with harp strings, and he made the young ladies dance, whilst their mothers and other grave personages chatted in another room. When music, and the fine arts, come to prosper at Philadelphia, when society once becomes easy and gay there, and they learn to accept of pleasure when it presents itself, without a formal invitation, then may foreigners enjoy all the advantages peculiar to their manners and government, without envying anything in Europe.

2. THE PIANOFORTE FLOATS OVER AND STRIKES ROOT

As we have suggested, intercourse between London and the colonial cities became closer and livelier during the 1760's. Charles Dibdin's musical comedy *The Padlock* opened at Drury Lane in October 1768 and had a great run of fifty-three nights, whereupon the Old American Company, the foremost colonial troupe, was able to put it on in New York as early as May 4, 1769—about as rapid a transplantation of a hit as we are accustomed to in the twentieth century. It was that same Dibdin, we recall, who had first played an accompaniment between the acts of *The Beggar's Opera* "on a new instrument called the Piano Forte" a year and a half before; and we will also remember that it was in June 1768 that Johann Christian Bach gave the instrument a social boost by playing a solo on it in a fashionable concert. It was inevitable that some American visitor in London at this time would have one of the talked-of new-type keyboards sent back home to him across the Atlantic. Actually, the earliest American mention of it that we can find occurs in the *Massachusetts Gazette* for March 7, 1771. The issue contains an announcement of the postponement of a concert presented by one James Joan, or Juhan, as he sometimes spelled himself, a musician, a teacher of French, and a fiddle maker of some enterprise. In the intermission, says the card, Mr. Propert will play "select pieces' on the new instrument. The typesetter evidently did not understand the unfamiliar word and inserted an irrelevant comma, so that it read: "on the Forte, piano and guittar." David Propert had left New York; he had become organist of Trinity Church, Boston, and was said to have a "good hand" on the keys.

Later in the very month of this Boston "Forte, piano" performance, twenty-eight-year-old Thomas Jefferson, far away on his Monticello estate, thinking of marrying Mrs. Skelton, wrote to his agent Thomas Adams in Philadelphia, giving him a list of things to buy in Europe and offering two hogsheads of tobacco at £50 each in payment. Among the articles was a clavichord, to be presented to his fiancée—a curious choice of instrument, since it was hardly known in America and little enough known in England. In fact, Jefferson suggests that the agent secure it in Hamburg. Nine weeks later Jefferson wrote again to Adams, who was in England by that time:

> I must alter one article in the invoice. I wrote therein for a Clavichord. I have since seen a Forte-piano and am charmed with it. Send me this instrument instead of the Clavichord; let the case be of fine mahogany, solid, not veneered, the compass from double G. to F. in alt, a plenty of spare strings; and the workmanship of the whole very handsome and worthy of the acceptance of a lady for whom I intend it.

Where did Jefferson see a pianoforte in Virginia during the spring of 1771? Could it have been at Colonel Carter's? For the latter gentleman had one, which he used constantly. "While we supped, as he often does Mr. Carter played on the Forte-Piano," relates Fithian. "He almost never sups." Moreover, he made Miss Prissy, his eldest daughter, practice on the pianoforte each Tuesday and Thursday. Jefferson's Albemarle County home was rather far from the Carters' in Westmoreland; on the other hand, Jefferson may very well have met Mr. Carter in Williamsburg. Yet did the latter ever carry his pianoforte to the capital? It is a speculation.

In any event, occasional pianofortes were crossing the ocean in those years. For example, the ship *Pedro,* destination Baltimore, was wrecked, and some of its salvaged cargo was sold in New York at P. McDavitt's Auction Store, including "three hammer harpsichords slightly damaged"—so said an advertisement in the *New York Journal* some time during 1774.

The quarrels of the Colonies with England became acute in the 1760's, coming to a sharp crisis in the Stamp Act riots. The real Revolution may be said to have started then, some time before blood was actually spilled. Part of the discontent of some of the Colonies arose from the suppression of colonial manufactures. The resourceful Americans, for example, who had been so diligently proficient in shipbuilding might well feel irked at not being allowed to make hats. The spirit of independence made its perceptible reverberations even in the little world of music. In 1764 Josiah Flagg of Boston, in issuing a *Collection of Psalm Tunes, in two, three, and four parts,* announced that it was printed on paper made in the Colonies, saying in a curiously pointed way that he hoped that fact "will not diminish the value of the work in the estimation of any, but may in some degree recommend it, even to those who have no peculiar relish for the music." The publication, incidentally, was engraved by silversmith Paul Revere, soon to be better known as a horseman. In the same spirit James Juhan, afore-mentioned concert-giver, cried up his own violins a few years later as "equal in goodness to the best imported."

In a similar tone, the *Boston Gazette* stated in 1769 that "a few days since there was shipped for Newport a very curious Spinnet, being the first ever made in America, the performance of the ingenious Mr. John Harris of Boston." John Harris was not much of an American, having only arrived from London the year before; moreover, the statement was not true. Gustav Hesselius, of the Old Swedes' Church, had made harpsichords in Philadelphia twenty-five years earlier; and actor and stage carpenter Tremaine of the old John Street Theater seems to have improvised a harpsichord in New York ten years before the time of Mr. Harris. Yet those achievements did not seem worth boasting about in those less bristling days. By 1773 David Walhaupter, "at the upper end of Fair Street," New York, announced casually that he "makes and repairs harpsichords . . . and all sorts of musical instruments."

In this atmosphere of industrial self-assertion—we will not speak of self-sufficiency—it seems only natural to hear from John Behrent of Third and Green Streets, Philadelphia, who advertised that he had made "an extraordinary instrument, by the name of the pianoforte, in mahogany in the manner of a harpsichord," early in 1775. This, indeed, appears to have been the first American-made pianoforte, the single step that began the long journey to America's supremacy in this field of manufacture.

For the moment it had no sequel. The Revolution was breaking into war at that instant. The Continental Congress urged the separate legislatures to enact laws discouraging all manner of extravagance and dissipation, especially horse racing, gaming, and expensive diversions such as shows and plays. Pennsylvania Quakers and Presbyterians were happy again to outlaw theaters by 1778, while Boston's patterns of virtue had enthusiastically destroyed them in the embryo as early as 1750. Feminine fribbles and domestic luxuries were also being abated. The columns of the *New York Journal* for May 14, 1775, within a month of Lexington and Concord, were aflame with patriotic resolutions and also carried an advertisement of David Walhaupter's shop claiming that his "military drums equal anything imported."

Cornwallis surrendered, the red-coats evacuated New York, and the Treaty of Paris recognized the loosely united states as a sovereign nation extending to the Mississippi. Procreation, expansion into western lands, and transatlantic trade and commerce now went full speed ahead. Philadelphia was still the country's chief city, but New York was the up-and-coming town, the place where the people and the money were piling together the fastest. Perhaps this was happening because the opening of New York State's central and western regions and the city's incomparable harbor made a fortunate economic conjunction.

John Jacob Astor, a canny young German, obstinate and phlegmatic, evidently was aware of the trend. He had originally intended for Baltimore when he emigrated, but Manhattan Island seemed a more suitable vortex for the location of his own acquisitive talents. By 1786 he was doing business at 81 Queen Street, and in the *New York Packet* for May 22 he lists some of his recent imports:

> from London, An elegant assortment of Musical Instruments, such as pianofortes, spinnets, pianoforte guittars, the best of violins, Ger-

> man flutes, clarinets, hautboys, fifes, the best Roman violin strings, and other kinds of strings, music books and paper and every other article in the musical line, which he will dispose of on very low terms for cash.

Astor was probably acting in this business as the agent of his brother, who had a piano shop in London at the time. Pianos, however, were hardly a prime concern with Astor. Probably he had already discovered furs and their profits; soon he was also deep in shipping and banking—and finally in the real estate by which New York's fabulously burgeoning population was allowed to throw a fabulous fortune into his pockets and into those of his descendants. Early in his career he got rid of his small-change music business, letting John and Michael Paff carry it on during the 1790's.

Other persons sold imported English pianos in New York in those days; but, as in the case of Astor, the trade was still not extensive enough to be anything but a part-time business. George Gilfert, for example, played viola occasionally, was organist at the New Dutch Church, and kept a boarding house, in addition to selling pianos and other musical goods. Scotland-born Alexander Reinagle, a thorough and sober musician, taught the pianoforte and also offered to sell instruments to his pupils "at the same price as the shops"—and, of course, at the same markup.

Shortly after the Treaty of Paris, someone mentioned the recent "War for Independence" in Benjamin Franklin's presence. "Say, rather, the War of the Revolution," said Franklin; "the War for Independence is yet to be fought." Despite all yankee-doodling and fourth-of-julying, the country still remained an English province, culturally, for a long time. The ships came and went more and more frequently, but that made it all the easier for Americans to be quick and accurate in their slavishness. No styles of clothing or furniture, of literature or music, save those from London could flourish among the well-to-do of the eastern seaboard. During the 1780's the contest between the harpsichord and pianoforte was faithfully mirrored in the United States. When in England the grand pianoforte of the early nineties finally gave the harpsichord its quietus, the same process was obediently re-enacted on the other side of the Atlantic. It is hard to believe that any aesthetic consideration was involved here: anything the lords and nabobs did was the thing to do for the shippers, merchants, and landlords of Philadelphia, New York, Boston, and Baltimore.

Jacques Pierre Brissot de Warville, French lawyer, pamphleteer, libertarian, and presently revolutionist, was in the United States in 1788. There he remarked on seeing an occasional pianoforte in Boston drawing rooms. He evidently did not think the girls played it with much distinction or skill, for he said kindly:

> This art, it is true, is still in its infancy; but the young novices who exercise it are so gentle, so complaisant, and so modest that the proud perfection of art gives no pleasure equal to what they afford. God grant that the Bostonian women may never, like those of France, acquire the malady of perfection in this art! It is never attained but at the expense of the domestic virtues.

According to an estimate made in a newspaper of 1791, about twenty-seven Boston families owned pianos, all London-made.

Moreover, until the last decade of the eighteenth century, the music played by Americans was all printed and published in England, even when it had been originally composed elsewhere. The excellent libraries of contemporary sonatas that Thomas Jefferson and Francis Hopkinson accumulated—or the books of Vauxhall songs, ballad opera numbers, and dance tunes that were heard in genteel homes—practically all came from London. A number of psalm and hymn books had been domestically published, in Boston especially, during the century, and a few secular songsters came out during the eighties; but generally all printed notes were imported.

Native Americans seem to have been only faintly stirred toward the original composing of music throughout the century and well into the next. When Francis Hopkinson of Philadelphia published his *Six Songs for the Harpsichord or Pianoforte* in 1787, dedicating them to George Washington, he claimed in his preface that he was "the first native of the United States who has produced a musical composition." Granting his claim to be justified, these unpretentious efforts of a dilettante could point up the slightness of musical thought in the Colonies. The colonials were, indeed, true children of the English businesslike spirit that had triumphed in 1688: they enjoyed music, a little, while holding it in low esteem.

In this connection it is interesting to note how many of the traceable musicians functioning in America during the eighteenth century appear to have been of German origin: a Mr. Uhl and a Mr. Grunzweig both gave concerts in Charleston in the 1740's; Pachelbel and Knoetchel were organists in Newport; we hear of a German-born H. B. Victor in Philadelphia, a Stieglitz in Boston, and a Von Zedwitz in New York. After 1790 the German names increase. We know little about these men, but it is most unlikely that any of them came from the rather isolated German settlements in Pennsylvania and near by. They were probably all persons who, themselves or their parents, had first emigrated from Germany to England before crossing the ocean. A country that takes music seriously is likely to produce good professional musicians.

3. THE LIVELY YOUNG NATION SINGS SONGS HER MOTHER TAUGHT HER, WITH PIANO ACCOMPANIMENT

THE FIRST United States Census, that of 1790, revealed a redoubtable total population of 3,900,000. "A more perfect union" had been formed; moreover, the new government was promulgating a sound national currency, to remedy the monetary uncertainty of the immediate past. Businessmen, speculators, and landlords—money-handlers generally—were happy. They were the people who went to theaters and concerts, bought instruments, and had their daughters take lessons.

Numbers of musicians in crowded London felt that the larger cities of the new republic now would form a good market for their services. About 1792 Gottlieb Graupner came to America. Primarily an oboist, he was proficient on many other instruments, including the piano, and had played under Haydn in London. Eventually he settled in Boston, where he played, taught, published music, sold instruments, and was an important builder of musical organizations.

In September 1792 a whole bevy of "professors of music from the Opera House, Hanover Square, and Professional Concerts under the direction of Haydn, Pleyel, etc. London" arrived in New York and proclaimed a concert, with the customary ball to follow. James Hewitt, the ablest member of the group, contributed an original composition for the full band, an *Overture, in 9 movements, descriptive of a battle,* to which, however, he foolishly assigned no location. But Jean Gehot, violinist, later in the program, topped it by an *Overture, in 12 movements, expressive of a voyage from England to America.* These are the captions:

1. Introduction
2. Meeting of the adventurers, consultation and their determination on departure
3. March from London to Gravesend
4. Affectionate separation from their friends
5. Going on board, and pleasure at recollecting the encouragement they hope to meet with in a land where merit is sure to gain reward
6. Preparation for sailing, carpenter's hammering, crowing of the cock, weighing anchor etc.
7. A Storm
8. A Calm
9. Dance on deck by the passengers
10. Universal joy on seeing land
11. Thanksgiving for safe arrival
12. Finale

The London "professors of music" found a number of enterprising colleagues arrived in New York ahead of them. Alexander Reinagle, afore-mentioned, was a musician of serious purpose and a composer of more than ordinary thoughtfulness. Aided by fellow musicians, he had organized series of subscription concerts during the late 1780's in which—with the works of Haydn, Stamitz, Gossec, and J. C. Bach—he consistently commingled one or another of his own pianoforte sonatas, respectable works having a flavor akin to those of C. Philipp Emanuel Bach. One of his longer, more ambitious concerts included excerpts from the *Messiah*. Reinagle also ran his subscription concerts in Philadelphia, apparently commuting slowly between the two places. After a time he stayed permanently in the Pennsylvania city.

The Peter Albrecht van Hagens, Mr. and Mrs., were settled in New York in the late eighties. Thrifty and versatile, they supplied music in any way that it was wanted—whether in performance, instruction, instruments, or equipment. At their benefit concert on November 20, 1789, they made use of their offspring, eight years old, holding him forth as the performer of a concerto for the pianoforte. They published their terms: they would teach singing, as well as the violin, viola, cello, flute, oboe, clarinet, bassoon, and—of course—harpsichord, at "$6 a month (or 12 lessons) and one pound entrance." Somehow they did not seem altogether happy in New York, for a few years later we find them resettled in Boston, where they ran an "imported pianoforte warehouse."

Benjamin Carr, an able singer and pianist, came from England to Philadelphia in 1793 and there set up an establishment bearing the suggestively inclusive title of "Musical Repository." Here he published music and sold his "elegant assortment of pianofortes"; and from this center he further performed, composed, directed, and organized, becoming one of the city's leading promoters of music during more than thirty years. He was, like most others of the profession at the time, a musical grocer, cook, and caterer all rolled into one.

Within seven weeks of Washington's inauguration, the Bastille was stormed. The French upheaval aroused much vicarious agitation in the United States, and sides were taken passionately, as they were in England. Soon French refugees began to arrive, not only from France, but from the uprising in Santo Domingo. Some of them were professional musicians; others were gentlefolk anxiously hoping to make life rafts out of their musical "accomplishments." Their appeals to be gainfully heard often fell on compassionate as well as politically sympathetic ears, and French concerts became fairly frequent for a few years. Some new composers' names were thus brought to the general attention—for instance, those of Grétry and Dezède. Their music added to, but did not supplant, the predominantly English taste of the time.

Speaking of taste in concert fare, it was in many ways rather good so far as instrumental music was concerned: plenty of Haydn appeared on the programs, also of Pleyel, as well as works of other composers resident in London, such as Giordani. In addition to their own concertos, and concertos whose composers were not specified, the pianists played sonatas and other works by Dussek, Clementi, Cramer, Gyrowetz, Koželuch, Steibelt, Wanhal, and similar worthies of their time, mostly of direct London repute. Once or twice we notice the name of Mozart. One may still wonder whether the program selection did not represent the taste of the foreign-born musicians rather than that of the audiences.

Other program numbers look as if they could have been touted as "the latest scream from London"—for instance the *Ploughboy* Rondo, or divers variations on Scotch airs. Undoubtedly, the scream of the scream was *The Battle of Prague*. It raged up and down the young states—of course, through Boston, New York, Philadelphia, Baltimore, and Charleston, but also into the smaller nooks. For instance, J. H. Schmidt, elsewhere held up as "formerly organist of the cathedral in Schiedam, Holland," played it on April 18, 1797, at Angus' Assembly Room, Albany, New York, population five thousand. Earlier in the program he had performed "the celebrated Sonata of Dr. Haydn, for two performers on one pianoforte," with a man named Weisbecher, as well as his own variations on *The Heaving of the Lead.* On November 4 of the same year poor little Marianne d'Hemard, "only five years old, eight months from Paris," as her harp-playing mother portrayed her, offered *The Battle of Prague* to a kindly audience in Fredericksburg, Virginia, after having ridden it in triumph, as Mamma claimed, through Philadelphia, Baltimore, Richmond, and Alexandria. In Norfolk, too, on April 20 of that year, "A Divine Concert of vocal and instrumental music"—which was fronted with a Stabat Mater by Sacchini—wa nevertheless backed with *The Battle of Prague.*

The year 1797 was certainly a good one for battles. Prague was again refought at Mr. Poole's Hall, New London, Connecticut, on February 2 by "the musical family of Mr. Salter, organist of New Haven, late from England." Lest the audience drop into pacifist sloth immediately afterward, the program further concluded with:

Sea Engagement

Representing two fleets engaging, some sinking, others blowing up. Neptune drawn by two sea horses, emerging from the waves—Old Charon in his boat—A mermaid and dolphin—Between the music, Master Salter will speak the three warnings.

Each man mauls the thing he loves, and *The Battle of Prague* could not escape the manhandling of its affectionate friends. George Schetky of Philadelphia, an Austro-Scot like his uncle Reinagle, arranged the *Battle* for full orchestra, and Philadelphians did not tire of it even after hearing it three times over in one year in separate concerts. But the piece was also womanhandled; for Miss W. A. Wrighten, playing it in Boston, performed an Americanization-operation upon it by inserting the *President's* March—the later "Hail! Columbia" tune—after the "Cries of the Wounded."

James Hewitt, ready violinist, pianist, composer, and general music director, had, we recall, introduced himself to America with a futilely nameless battle-overture. In 1797, with Prague flaming around him, he tried to make up for lost showmanship by putting out *The Battle of Trenton* for the pianoforte, aspiringly dedicated to George Washington, the title page illuminated with the great soldier-president's portrait guarded by the Goddess of Liberty, flags, drums, and a spear. *Washington's* March and "Yankee Doodle" were appropriately incorporated into the score. It was a good spiel, but somehow it failed to captivate for long. The battle public remained unreasonably loyal to dear old Prague. Perhaps its very faraway suggestion was part of its charm.

Eight editions of *The Battle of Prague,* almost all for pianoforte, appeared in the United States between 1793 and 1800. A fascinating one was gotten out by Benjamin Carr: an arrangement of the piece for two flutes, without accompaniment, published as part of a collection called *The Gentleman's Amusement.* One wonders how the cannon shots were arrived at in this version. They might have been managed with the aid of an overturned dishpan, one of the gentlemen stopping to whack its bottom with his flute when the time came.

The trend of eighteenth-century European thought had become increasingly secularist, and the pervasion of this frame of mind inevitably reached influential circles in America. Progress, enlightenment, and man's control of his own destiny were the watchwords now beginning to be taken for granted, and God was being transformed from a close-snooping ogre named Jehovah into a cloudy, distant First Cause. Direct theological sanction for details of human behavior weakened. The old Brattle Street Church, for instance, some time later in the century finally changed its mind and ordered an organ. Boston and Philadelphia wowsers now could not resist the pressure of those who wanted to enjoy theatrical performances. Philadelphia, persuaded partially by the example of a venerated, playgoing Washington, repealed its laws against theaters in 1789. Boston, more obstinate, allowed them to go by default in 1793. The Old American Company, rejuvenated and reinforced by good imported actors and singers, flourished as never before. Musical pantomimes and musical comedies were among its most enjoyed presentations on its circuit from New York to Annapolis; and no fewer than one hundred and twenty musical shows were put on by the company during the years 1793–1800. These were, invariably, London successes, sometimes specially adapted for American performance. Their composers were the expert London practitioners—the masters of tried contemporary formula—of their time: Samuel Arnold, Charles Dibdin, William Shield, Stephen Storace, and Thomas Linley.

Inevitably, the Old Americans stimulated competition. This took one of its most formidable forms when a Philadelphia syndicate put up a great new theater on Chestnut Street, to house a permanent company. Thomas Wignell the actor and Alexander Reinagle the musician were its artistic directors, and long search was made in England to assemble a distinguished group of performers. The building was, naturally, a copy of an English theater—namely, the Royal Theater at Bath—and it was said to have held "2000 persons, or 600 pounds." Musical productions were to be emphasized, and for this purpose a band of twenty excellent instrumentalists was engaged, some of them Frenchmen; they undoubtedly formed the best orchestra that America had yet heard.

An old actor of the company, in his reminiscences, described Reinagle's dignified personality as he presided over the orchestra from his "grand square pianoforte"—probably a large square. The account tells how the musician seemed to be "investing the science of harmonious sounds . . . with a moral influence" and "adorning it with high respectability and polished manners." His imposing appearance was said to have even awed the disorderly of the galleries. Indeed, we can imagine that Reinagle's German parentage and tradition made him feel, and communicate, a kind of reverence for music unfamiliar to most Anglo-Saxons of the time. George Washington seems to have esteemed him and to have gone to his concerts; and we should not wonder if the report is true that the President had him give piano lessons to his stepdaughter Nelly Custis.

Henry Wansey, an English visitor, attended a performance at the Chestnut Street Theater in the summer of 1794. Writing about it later, he averred that judging from the dress and appearance of the people around him, and from the actors and the scenery, he could have thought he was still in England.

> The ladies wore the small bonnets of the same fashion as those I saw when I left England; some of checkered straw, etc., some with their hair fully dressed, without caps, as with us, and very few in the French style. The younger ladies with their hair flowing in ringlets on their shoulders. The gentlemen with rounded hats, their coats with high collars, and cut quite in the English fashion and many in silk striped coats.

Wansey also admired the stage scenery, but claimed that a good deal of it had once belonged to Lord Barrymore's theater at Wargrave.

New York had never been so repressed theatrically as had Philadelphia, and it too was swept along with the show-business boom of the end of the century. Its famous Park Theater was put up, after some delay, on Park Row and opened on January 29, 1798, at probably a total outlay of $130,000. The management hired a good permanent orchestra of fourteen, directed by James Hewitt; and we hear that the musicians' pay roll amounted to $140 a week, or an average of $10 per man.

City Americans also faithfully tried to imitate London in the matter of public pleasure gardens. Entrepreneurs in Charleston, Philadelphia, and New York several times built, and tried to operate, premises of the Vauxhall type—with music, shows, refreshments, lanterns, and promenades in green summer natural surroundings. Somehow, none of the earlier ones prospered for long; however, three or four of them came and went in New York during the 1790's and beyond. Perhaps the most successful was one at 112 Broadway, dutifully named "Vauxhall," run by Joseph Delacroix the caterer, who was understood to be particularly good at making that delicious new dessert called ice cream. He hired a band of fifteen musicians, James Hewitt again at their head, to give concerts there three times a week during the summer. Joseph Corré, hotelkeeper, also operated a similar "Mount Vernon Gardens," with musical programs and occasional complete musical shows. Favorite singing actors from the current theatrical companies, such as Mr. and Mrs. Hodgkinson, Mrs. Pownall, and John Tyler, were glad to make extra dollars by delivering their special hit-numbers at these popular concerts. They were also gladly available for collaboration in subscription and benefit concerts.

Boston had pushed past its crankier parsons and set up its Federal Street Theater in 1793. Englishman Henry Wansey visited it also in 1794; he paid a dollar to hear Arnold's *Inkle and Yarico,* looked at the dresses, and again felt very much at home, even though in the intermission the orchestra struck up the Jacobin "*Ça ira*"—as well as "Yankee Doodle"—by request. Soon the city could also boast of Bowen's Columbian Museum, where you could see exhibited "a large cat of the mountain" together with "the likenesses of President Adams and General Washington." It also installed a large organ whose manipulator played programs of popular songs on Tuesdays, Thursdays, and Fridays. On the opening night of the summer season of 1799 he led off with—you have guessed it—*The Battle of Prague.*

Musical shows, concerts, summer gardens—America was teeming with tunes as never before. Piano importers were steadily pushing their still rather expensive wares. A great demand arose for home-sung, home-played melody, and suddenly a flood of American publication arose to meet it. Carr, Blake, and Willig in Philadelphia, Paff, Gilfert, and Hewitt in New York, and one or two shops in Boston and Baltimore together brought out hundreds, perhaps thousands, of titles between 1793 and 1800. Practically all were reprints of English publications, and the vast majority were single songs "for the pianoforte." That meant they were printed on two staves, the right hand of the piano identical with the voice part—that is to say, carrying the tune—and the lower, left-hand staff representing the simple accompaniment. The words were usually printed between the two staves. The young ladies for whom these notes were intended evidently were mostly too awkward for singing one thing and playing another, and they could trust their voices better to stay on the pitch if they plunked each note simultaneously on the keys. Let us not forget that German publishers had shown the same tender consideration for their girls' ineptitudes fifty years earlier. Progressive Benjamin Carr, however, in his collection called *Musical Journal for the Pianoforte,* on December 1, 1800, included the new "very popular and beautiful Scotch ballad called *The Blue Bells of Scotland*" twice in the same volume, the second time in a more elaborate version on *three* staves. He explained: "N.B. The superior effect that will be produced by those who can sing one part and play the other as here adapted will make an apology unnecessary for the reinserting it in this form." It was a quarter of a century before the use of three staves in song prints was generally adopted.

The end-of-century songs usually covered two pages and were sold at twenty or twenty-five cents a copy. This was not exactly cheap when one reflects on price standards in other articles and when one compares it with later sheet-music prices. People of our day can remember buying two-page popular songs during the 1910's for ten or fifteen cents a copy.

The songs were largely taken from the current light operas of Shield, Arnold, Storace, and the rest; and many of them were the very ones being applauded that minute at the Park, the Chestnut Street, and the Federal Street Theaters. Many of them also were from the stout annual London packages of Vauxhall songs composed by James Hook. Their titles reflect the sentimental set of their customers' minds, prevailingly feminine. "Sweet" was a favorite titular adjective: "Sweet as Summer's Fragrant Gale," "Sweet Is the Balmy Breath of Spring," "Sweet Lilies of the Valley," "Sweet Echo," "Sweet Babes in the Wood"; or—more personal—"Sweet Girl by the Light of the Moon," "Sweet Myra of the Vale," "Sweet Nan of Hampton Green," "Sweet Poll of Plymouth." "Sweet" was sometimes varied with "lovely": "Lovely

Nymph," "The Lovely Rose," "Lovely Spring," "Lovely Nan," "Lovely Stella." Compassionate, protective, and maternal feelings were tickled: "Poor Black Boy," "Poor Blind Girl," "Poor Little Child of a Tar," "Poor Little Gypsy," "Poor Village Boy," "Poor Emma," "Poor Mary," "Poor Tom Bowling"; also "Little Ben," "Little Boy Blew," "The Little Sailor Boy," "The Little Singing Girl," "The Little Robin Redbreast." Anything Scotch was automatically cute: "Bonny Willy," "Bonny Charley," "Bonny Lem of Aberdeen," "The Highland Laddie," "The Lowland Laddie." The vapor of Rousseau was thick in the world, and rich city merchants could be expected to be stirred by lowly rustic images. "Cottage" was considered a delightful word, and we have "The Cottage Boy," "The Cottage in the Grove," "The Cottage on the Moor," "The Cottager's Daughter," "The Contented Cottager." One lyricist achieved a triple-decker ice-cream sandwich: "The Sweet Little Cottage." Too bad he did not work in "bonny" somehow.

There were other kinds of titles, some of them echolalic after the English manner: "Dilly Dally Shilly Shally," "Tink a Tink," "Fal lal la," "Robin a Bobbin a Bilberry Hen." One was fearfully British: "Tantivy Hark Forward Huzza: A Favorite Hunting Song." A few had arch suggestions: "She's Quite the Thing" and "No That Will Never Do." Some songs were decisively masculine, especially sailor songs with lots of Jack in them: "Jack at the Windlass," "Jack Clueline," "Jack Junk," "Jack the Guinea Pig." When it came to "Nothing Like Grog," it was published in a collection not for pianoforte—thus presumably for men only. On the other hand, "A Blessing on Brandy and Beer" came out femalely adapted for the keyboard, perhaps because the first line went: "When a man's drunk not a girl but looks pretty."

Dance tunes were, of course, symmetrical jingles and were given irrelevant if topical labels. *The Ball Room Assistant,* for example, a collection put together by William Francis, ballet master of the Chestnut Street Theater, and arranged for piano by Reinagle, contained cotillions and country dances, including "Speed the Plough," "The Constitution," "The Chesapeake," "The Lucky Hit," "The Virginia Reel," and "The Maryland Hornpipe." Coming out as it did shortly after 1800, we are interested also to note the inclusion of "Miss Smith's Waltz." The genial Alpine revolving step, then, was beginning to make its way on this side of the Atlantic at about that time. From New York we also get "The Prince of Wales's Waltz" from a *Ladies' Musical Journal.*

Marches, not illogically, were often named after well-known military commanders: we encounter *General Wayne's, General Knox's, Baron Steuben's, General Greene's, Colonel Orne's, General Wolfe's, General Pinckney's,* and of course *Washington's* March. European aristocratic appellations also looked well on title pages: the Marquis of Granby, the Duke of Holstein, the Duke of York, the Duke of Gloster, and Prince Eugene all had marches named for them in the American music press.

With so many more polite young girls now fingering the keys, there was a greater demand for piano lessons. The P. A. van Hagens moved to Boston in 1796, and we are glad to hear that there they raised their prices substantially. The lady of that house now offered to teach pianoforte and harpsichord, "with thorough-bass, if desired," as well as singing, at her pupils' homes at the rate of eight dollars for eight lessons, with a five-dollar entrance fee, according to her advertisement in the *Columbian Centinel* for April 3, 1799. However, "At Mrs. Von Hagen's house, the terms are only six dollars every eight lessons . . ." She also pointed out her advantage to prospective clients: "As motives of *delicacy* may induce parents to commit the tuition of young Ladies in this branch of education to one of their own sex . . . she flatters herself that she shall be indulged with their approbation, and the protection of a respectable Public." The $.75 to $1.00 fee per lesson may have been a large-city standard. On November 9, 1798, we read of a Mr. J. H. Smith—could he have been the J. H. Schmidt who had played *The Battle of Prague* in Albany the previous year?—offering to teach pianoforte and other instruments for 2s 6d ($.60) a lesson, in the small town of Portsmouth. As late as August 28, 1816, we read of a Mrs. Curtis advertising her girls' boarding school on Essex Street, Salem, Massachusetts, in a somewhat unpleasant beggarly manner and charging $.50 a lesson for pianoforte instruction, $6.00 a quarter for drawing and painting, while rating "Embroidery, per piece" at $3.00. All the prices for piano lessons seem humiliatingly low in comparison with those paid in London at the time; not only with the guinea a lesson exacted by such fashionable practitioners as Clementi, Cramer, or Dr. Burney, but even with the 10s 6d received by less well-connected musical characters. Evidently, no musicians in America—nor music itself—could achieve the prestige to elicit such an expenditure.

At that rate, piano teaching might represent a fair part-time living for a musician. Four lessons a day could earn him $18 a week; a tuning job might raise that a couple of dollars every once in a while; and if he were also playing, say, at the Park Theater, he could make nearly $30 in a week—not a bad little income when one reflects that a good house could be rented for an annual $350 and that $800 might defray a total year's expenses for an average well-living family. Those who printed and retailed copies of successful songs and sold an occasional guitar or imported piano probably did much better. Meanwhile, unskilled laborers working on roads or canals were getting about $.60 to $.80 a day.

In 1800, New York had about fifty gainfully employed musicians, out of a total population of sixty thousand. They were necessarily pluralists—as we have seen—but their side lines were sometimes far to the side of music. George Ulshoeffer, for instance, who had made a piano in 1785 and who played in the Park Theater at its opening, is listed in the New York City directory from 1789–95 as "musician," but as "musician & grocer" for the five years following. Isaac Samo, likewise a Park Theater orchestral house-warmer, is called "music teacher" in 1800, "grocer" from 1804–10, but reappears reconstructed as "musician" after 1817. Judging from the directory, the grocery store was the musicians' favorite city of refuge—quite understandably. But numbers of other occupations were pressed into the support of incurable musicians during the first quarter of the nineteenth century. We see them listed as "barber," "shoe store," "hairdresser," "French academy," "white washer," "morocco dresser," "mariner," "farmer," "segar-maker," "tavern," "money collector," and "turner." Victor Pelissier, one of the French refugees, was a clever arranger for many musical shows of the 1790's; but by 1802 and thereafter he is put down as "prof. of music and millinery store." We will not suppress a pang at reading the name of Henry Pier, "musician," at 64 Cedar until 1816, followed in 1817 by "PIER, widow, Judith, 64 Cedar, washwoman."

A candid opinion of the state of music in the United States in the year 1810 was given by a writer in a short-lived Philadelphia publication called *Mirror of Taste and Dramatic Censor.* He begins:

> In no country of the world is the practice of music more universally extended, and at the same time the science so little understood as in America. Almost every house included between the Delaware and the Schuylkill has its piano or harpsichord, its violin, its flute or its clarinet. Almost every young lady and gentleman, from the children of the Judge, the banker, and the general, down to those of the constable, the huckster and the drummer, can make

> a noise upon some instrument or other, and charm their neighbors with something which courtesy calls music. Europeans, as they walk our streets, are often surprised with the flute rudely warbling "Hail! Columbia" from an oyster cellar, or the piano forte thumped to a female voice screaming "O Lady Fair!" from behind a heap of cheese, a basket of eggs, a flour barrel, or a puncheon of apple whiskey; and on these grounds we take it for granted that we are a very musical people.

The writer draws an analogy from a remark of Dr. Johnson's. "Learning is in Scotland," the famous lexicographer is quoted as saying, "as food in a town besieged; every one has a mouthfull, but no one a bellyfull."

> The same may be said of music in America. The summit of attainment in that delightful science seldom reaching higher than the accompanying of a song so as to set off a tolerable voice, or aid a weak one, and the attracting a circle of beaus round a young lady, while she exhibits the nimbleness of her fingers in the execution of a darling waltz, or touches the hearts of the fond youths with a plaintive melody accompanied with false notes. Thus far, or but little further, does music extend, save in a few scattered instances.

He makes the ancient observation that feminine keyboard practice droops sharply after the mating season.

> Indeed nothing is more common than to hear a lady acknowledge it. "Mrs. Racket will you do us the favour." &c says a dapper young gentleman offering his hand to lead a lady to the piano. "Do excuse me, sir, I beg of you." she replies. "I have not touched an instrument of music half a dozen times since I was married—one, you know, has so much to do." Thus music as a science lags in the rear, while musical instruments in myriads twang away in the van: and thus the window cobweb having caught its flies for the season is swept away by the housemaid.

The writer deplores this as an evil and says it assumes all the frivolity, the coxcombry of music, without any of its benefits.

> That . . . which is supposed to be the language of saints and angels when they hymn their Maker's praise, ought to be a nation's care. . . . Not the miserable or the vitious levities of music . . . but harmony, such as befits the creature to pour forth at the altar

of the Creator; the sublime raptures of Handel; the divine strains of Haydn, and the majestic compositions of Purcel . . .

It is reassuring to think that some persons are always irked by the commonness of common human nature.

4. THE AMERICAN PIANO TAKES ITS OWN SHAPE

For the first thirty or forty years after the Revolution, American piano making progressed slowly. Behrent's early instrument was, perforce, an isolated phenomenon. So were the several pianofortes made here and there in New York and Philadelphia during the 1780's. From 1789 on, however, Charles Albrecht of the latter city, calling himself a "joiner," was able to make good instruments, pretty close copies of the English models of the time, and establish a custom trade over a period of more than twenty years. In general, the Revolutionary conceit that called home-made products "equal to anything imported" had subsided with the inauguration of the new government; for one thing, the rich people of the time were not likely to believe any such claims. The word "London" represented, as theretofore, a presumption of superior excellence. A New York maker of 1800 talked up his pianos as being constructed "on the best London principles," while Gilfert's New York shop regularly advertised a "consignment of patent pianofortes from London." Note that blessed word "patent," with all the suggestion of ingenuity, secret power, and privilege in which it allowed the customers to share.

Boston supported an active piano trade early in the century. About 1813 a group of piano makers named Appleton, Hayts, and Babcock got together and established a business, moving after a time to a large building at 6 Milk Street, a place said to have been the site of Benjamin Franklin's birthplace. After 1816 one John R. Parker backed the business financially and he called it the Franklin Music Warehouse, sometimes the Franklin Music Manufactory. The Franklin concern made pianos diligently and pushed its own product actively; nevertheless, it was glad enough to take money from the majority of customers who still felt safer with an imported article. The firm's lively advertisement in the *Columbian Centinel* for January 1, 1817, led off with a striking offer of two "horizontal Grand Pianofortes" brought from Vienna—of all remote places, practically Timbuktu! Moreover, they were described as having "six pedals, making a variety of tones, consisting of the Harp, Spinnet, Bassoon, Drum and Bell Stops." They were "for sale very low for cash." Just the thing for *The Battle of Prague* or *The Battle of New Orleans,* which had just come out. Having startled the readers with this exotic cry, the advertisement proceeded to impress them with a note of high expensiveness: it offered a fancy imported rosewood cabinet "inlaid with brass and brass mounted" for $750—quite a price for a piano, equal to a year's income for many comfortably-off families. After that the Franklin Music Warehouse subsided into telling of its great variety of uprights, grands, and squares made by Clementi & Co. of London, "forming the greatest assortment of Instruments ever offered for sale in this metropolis."

Broadwood's had always been the leaders of the piano trade in England, both in quantity and quality; nevertheless, they were not the preferred make in the United States during its English-dependent days. Clementi was apparently much more favored, for what reason it seems difficult to determine today. Perhaps it was that Broadwood's, with their great prestige, insisted on quoting American dealers too tight a wholesale price and that Clementi & Co. allowed them a more persuasive margin of profit. Quite a few old Clementi pianos are still lying about in various eastern American schools and museums. It is a Clementi that Oliver Wendell Holmes mentions specifically in his sentimental, nostalgic verses *The Opening of the Piano,* first published in the *Atlantic Monthly* in 1859.

An advertisement dated November 1821, of a musical instrument firm named Charles & Edwin W. Jackson, 64 Market Street, may give us an impression of how pianos were valued at that time. The prices are termed "moderate." Heading the list is an assortment of "Elegant Cabinet Piano Fortes by Clementi & Co." at $475, followed by "Elegant ditto ditto by Tomkison"—a relatively small English house—at $425. Broadwood & Sons does not appear until fifth on the list with an "Elegant horizontal mahogany" for $275 and a "Plain ditto ditto" for $250. Piano No. 7, at last, is an "Elegant horizontal, American, with drawers, $225" —and $200 without them. More humiliating than the low price is the offhand wastebasketlike use of the word "American," without the dignity of a maker's name. A year later C. & E. W. Jackson advertised themselves as a "Music Warehouse & Variety Store" selling "Ladies' indispensibles of every description, perfumes, soaps etc."

Despite lack of capital, and despite the lack of public confidence in them, early American piano makers showed remarkable persistence in their enterprise. One very early New York firm used exceptional intelligence in putting forward its product, when it persuaded a Mr. Kullin, a pianist, in announcing his benefit concert for March 7, 1791, to state that he would "perform on a Grand Concert Pianoforte, entirely of a new invention and just finished by Messrs. Dodds & Claus, of this city." Thus began the robust practice of advertising makes of pianos through public performances. The "entirely . . . new invention" spoken of may have been the English grand action—that is, the pilot-escapement-check action perfected by Broadwood and others during the 1780's to supplant the simple rebound mechanism of the little Zumpes that had been the norm previously. In that connection we could say that the word "grand" may at the time have been ambiguous, since it may have referred to the action as well as to the piano's shape. We recall the "grand square" at which Reinagle was described as presiding in his theater. It could have been a square instrument with the newer grand action.

On February 12, 1792, Dodds & Claus, of 66 Queen Street, put out a good advertisement in the *Diary or Louden's Register*. After generally recommending the pianoforte in itself, the firm proceeded to speak of its own improvements, including significantly "the means they have taken to prepare their wood to stand the effects of our climate, which imported instruments never do, but are sure to suffer from the saline quality of the seas." Here Dodds & Claus put their finger on the weak point of the European-made pianos, one that is brought up time and again for generations. The vagaries of the American climates—there are a number of American climates—proved to make perpetual trouble for imported pianos and, as effectively as any other cause, stimulated the development of specifically American piano building. Too bad Dodds & Claus faded away rather soon.

Presently there was further progress. A remarkable piano was made in Philadelphia in 1800, the work of a young Englishman by the name of John Isaac Hawkins, then resident in the city. Hawkins was not actually a piano maker at all, but rather a civil engineer with some special knowledge of the properties of metals. Unconditioned by any previous piano-making training, he was willing to stand the piano up unceremoniously on its tail—thus saving a lot of floor space—and have the strings struck upon by hammers from the front. In other words, he invented the upright pianoforte, almost at exactly the time when it was also invented, as we have seen, by Matthias Müller in Vienna. We will assume that Hawkins had the assistance of a practical piano maker in carrying out his ideas.

His "portable grand," as he called it, stood just a little more than four feet seven inches high and had a five-and-a-half-octave keyboard that could be folded back. This may have given rise to a conjecture that the instrument was originally designed for a ship's cabin; yet this was not evident from the way it was advertised in *Poulson's American Daily Advertiser* on March 20, 1800, where it was stated that it took up a quarter of the space occupied by a grand, stayed in tune five or six times as long, and was "an elegant piece of furniture" to be seen on display at Willig's Musical Magazine on Market Street. The staying in tune was due to several interesting features: the fact that the sounding board was suspended in a metal frame, which in turn was braced by iron bars; that the upper bridge was of metal; and that the tuning pins were true screws working in threaded sockets in a metal wrest-pin block. Furthermore, the bass strings were helically coiled into springs, thus substituting thickness and weight for space-consuming length in making the low pitches. These things were brusque innovations in their day, some of them twenty or thirty years ahead of their time, others too radical ever to have succeeded.

Thomas Jefferson, musically and mechanically alert, was on a visit to Philadelphia that year. Apparently he saw Hawkins' "portable grand," was pleased with its novelty and ingenuity, and wrote to his daughter that it "tempted me to engage one for Monticello." He never did so that we know of; anyway, he moved to the White House the following March. Interesting as Hawkins' piano was, it may not have had a satisfactory tone quality and it may have seemed too queer-looking a domestic object for fashionable people to take up. In any event, it made no headway. We do not know what became of Hawkins, though one account says he became the inventor of the ever-pointed pencil. It is important to understand, however, that the use of metal in pianofortes was in the American air from then on.

About half a dozen piano makers, in addition to the importers, are known to have worked in Boston during the first two decades after 1800. Probably the earliest of these was Benjamin Crehore, who began as a Federal Street Theater stage carpenter and a maker and repairer of small nonkeyboard instruments. He had a shop in

Milton, a village not far from Boston; and it said that P. A. von Hagen, from his store in Cornhill Square, helped him sell ten or twelve of his pianos per year. We bring him up because several generations later a curious statement was made, rather widely accepted, and even canonized in Grove's *Dictionary of Music and Musicians,* that Crehore was the first man to make a piano in the United States. The point is worth mentioning merely since it illustrates a tendency on the part of Bostonians to assume implicitly that anything that might have happened outside of Boston was unlikely to be of much consequence.

It is true, nevertheless, that Boston was the liveliest American center for the development of new piano-making ideas before the middle of the century. On February 23, 1819, John R. Parker had occasion to write a letter to the *New England Palladium* concerning his Franklin Music Manufactory. The firm had been making upright pianos, he said, since 1813 and had thus far turned out fifty of them. These were not, indeed, constructed along Hawkins' strange ideas, but were like the English "cabinets" of the time. The "cabinets" were quite new then, and for a Boston factory to be making them as early as 1813 shows a keen alertness on its part. Parker also spoke of the state of his business at the moment. The Franklin Manufactory was now finishing two pianos per week, he said, and falling short of the demand. If he was not indulging in routine business bragging, this meant that a Boston factory of 1819—while far behind the largest English plants—was comparing rather favorably in output with the larger and better ones on the European continent.

Despite Parker's enthusiasm, the upright piano did not become the standard in the United States for a long time. It continued to be made in small quantities, not quite so small as were the true wing-shaped grands; but it was the square shape that remained Americans' overwhelming preference for nearly three generations. Moreover, Parker had taken too bright a view of the vigor of his Franklin establishment as a factory. It maintained good prosperity as a music store for a number of years, but soon declined as a piano-manufacturing enterprise. Its personnel of piano makers broke up presently and formed other connections.

Among the former Franklin craftsmen the most interesting was Alpheus Babcock. He appears to have been highly respected in the trade as a fine mechanic; yet, after separating from his associates, he seems not to have been able to set up a shop completely under his own direction. Instead, we find him about 1821 working for John Mackay, a sea captain with money to invest and an interest in pianos. Babcock, in any event, took pains to scratch his name on all specimens of his work. He must have felt highly encouraged when the newly founded Franklin Institute of Philadelphia, organized "for the promotion of the mechanic arts," awarded him the first prize for his piano at its very first exhibit in 1824.

The question of metal bracing for a piano's sounding board, to support the higher tension necessitated by thicker strings, was agitating many minds in Europe toward 1820; while the problem of rigidity, of preventing the instrument's parts from sliding with the extremes of the weather, was a specially acute American concern. By 1825 Babcock, still with Mackay, was ready with a construction of far-reaching importance. On December 17 he was granted a patent on a complete iron frame, cast in one piece, for a square piano, uniting the hitch-pin plate and the bracing bars with the portion covering the wrest plank.

Somehow, Babcock was unable himself to promote his invention in Boston. Perhaps—like many another true craftsman—his heart was in his wood and his iron and he had little understanding of how to deal with people. At any rate, he was so ill-advised, or so unlucky, as to break with Mackay—or perhaps Mackay threw him over. He went to Philadelphia in 1829, and there he induced several piano makers to take up his idea tentatively. Indeed, one of them, much later, after it had vindicated itself brilliantly, tried retrospectively to claim it as his own. In any event, Babcock, even after returning to Boston, was unable to derive much profit from his important invention.

There could hardly be a question of the superior efficiency, from the manufacturing point of view, of the one-piece cast-iron frame. Surely it was more economical to make than a "composite" frame in which hitch-pin plate, bracing bars, and wrest-plank covering were all separate to begin with. Moreover, the full iron frame was the only practical solution of both the problem of tension and that of compensation. Babcock's patent gave direction to the particularly American form of contribution to piano construction; nevertheless, it took considerable time before the Babcock principle became generally adopted, even in the United States. It soon began to thrive in Boston; but New York manufacturers were slow at first in taking it up, preferring to string along with European makers who tarried for years with composite frames and partial frames. The latent ancestral distaste for metal in an indoor musical instrument could not be quickly overcome. Furthermore, there were persistent objections—perhaps not entirely unjustified for a time—that the excessive use of metal tended to make a piano's tone sound thin and tinny. American piano manufacturers, however, pushed the idea through to ultimate triumph, as we shall see.

At this point we are ready to announce the debut of a young man whose name was to become one of the two most famous in the American piano business and, through the distribution of his products, literally an American household word. Jonas Chickering began as a cabinetmaker in Ipswich, New Hampshire, and in 1818, at the age of twenty, sought his fortune in Boston by becoming an apprentice in one of the town's few piano-making shops. Five years later he was in the piano-making business with a partner, who, however, left him three years later. Soon after this came the Mackay-Babcock divorce, whereupon the solitary Chickering made a connection with the likewise fancy-free financial sea-captain in what was to be a most fruitful collaboration. Chickering was, like Babcock, primarily a craftsman; yet something in his nature must have allowed him to get on with the businessman Mackay harmoniously, for the partnership became outstandingly successful. During the 1830's the combination of fine workmanship, alertness to new mechanical developments, sound business methods, expansive enterprise, and—above all—ample capital enabled the firm of Chickering & Mackay to ride the fast-rising wave of American prosperity to a position of undoubted national preeminence. The wave broke a little during the panic of 1837, but the firm held; and by the time Captain Mackay was lost at sea in 1841, it was beyond easy damage either from competition or the fluctuations of the business cycle.

Chickering soon became convinced of the value of Babcock's full cast-iron frame and incorporated it into his own pianos, after having made some changes in its design. It is easy to think that this was one of the elements that gave his instruments their solidity and their durability. His partner Mackay expoited the new means of communication that the country was developing—the canals and the infant railroads—and Chickering pianos became distributed over a wider range of the United States than any make had been previously. Again, it may be that the full iron frame made his instruments better able to withstand long journeys, transshipments, and reloadings.

After some delay, Chickering was able to take out his own patent on an improved one-piece frame for square pianos in 1840. Presently he turned his attention to grand pianos, thitherto quite neglected in the United States; and his patent for the full one-piece iron frame for grands was granted in 1843. For some years after that he was one of the very few American manufacturers to make them.

A number of developments of the general music consciousness may be recorded in the Boston of the first quarter of the century. This was the time when a somewhat more serious attitude toward music could take root in New England, when an influential section of the population could begin to look upon it as something a little more than a slightly imbecile, though harmless, ladies' pastime. It was characteristic that in New England the elevation of music's value should take a religious form. The moral earnestness, as well as the respect for learning, of the original Calvinists persisted; and when many of the richer and more educated among their descendants evolved into Unitarians, it was natural that some of them could see something divine in music. It was not really paradoxical that the great-great-grandchildren of those who had all but forbidden music in church services should now become enthusiastic promoters of a kind of sacred music. Both the negative and the positive point of view implied an appreciation of the power of music.

Choirs became eager to amplify and improve their performances, and organs were installed: by 1815, it was said, five Boston churches had them. It was in the logic of the time that that year should witness the foundation there of the Handel and Haydn Society, America's oldest permanent oratorio society. The name was significant, both the patron saints of the organization being composers of nonliturgical sacred music who were especially known and admired in England. Those earlier decades of the century also marked a change in ordinary hymnody. The old "lined-out" psalms and "fuguing tunes" were declining in the polite churches; and congregations were now enjoying the singing of non-Biblical religious words to sweet symmetrical melodies with regular cadences—melodies in the common four-measure phrase pattern of contemporary European secular music, without polyphony, and harmonized with an undisturbing smoothness and simplicity. Some of the tunes were, indeed, taken and altered from the works of respected European masters.

Many collections of these hymns were now published. The most famous was the one compiled by young Lowell Mason, which contained numbers of his own tunes—as well as some adapted from Haydn, Mozart, and even Beethoven—and which he offered for publication to the Handel and Haydn Society itself. It came out in 1821, and its success must have been phenomenal if we can believe the report that after two years the books netted the society and Mason a profit of $30,000 each.

The Boston fondness for these easily singable, gently gaited religious songs took on the dimensions of a national movement. The New England hymnbooks spread all over the United States and, with copious subsequent additions of cognate material, indeed became the norm for all Protestant church service in America from that day to this. In later days, under Mason's indirect influence, snippets from all manner of "good" music were dressed up, or rather down, for church; and we find melodies from Beethoven sonatas, Mendelssohn *Songs without Words,* Donizetti arias, and Chopin nocturnes abridged and expurgated before becoming rhymedly Baptized, Methodized, or Presbyterianized as hymns. Mason's hymnbooks, and those of his numerous followers, early found their way into numberless parlors, there to be sung to the support of uncounted Clementis, Chickerings, and other instruments. Perhaps, when the leaves of the Judgment Book unfold, it will be revealed that during the mid-century years more hymns were played more often on American domestic keyboards than was any other music whatsoever.

Concerted instrumental music had a more difficult time than choral music in making pretensions to seriousness, let alone divinity, among Bostonians. Nevertheless, through the efforts of the devoted Gottlieb Graupner, a small band of amateurs stiffened by a handful of professionals managed to keep alive a Philharmonic Society, which gave more or less regular concerts. Its social standing was enhanced by the fact that it was expected to collaborate with the Handel and Haydn Society in productions of *Messiah* and *The Creation.*

A few competent female pianists—professional or on the verge of being so—lived in Boston during 1810 to 1820. One was Sophia Hewitt, daughter of James, the New York music director who had moved to the Massachusetts capital. She played publicly in Boston a number of times and—amidst the works of Wölfl, Kalkbrenner, and Gelinek with which she usually regaled her listeners—there seems to be the likelihood that on February 27, 1819, she achieved the distinction of performing Beethoven's *Sonata in A-flat,* Opus 26, the one with the Funeral March, at a Philharmonic concert. If so, it may have been the earliest public hearing of an important Beethoven piano composition in America. Another Boston pianist of the time was a Miss Eustaphieve, the daughter of the Russian consul, a girl wonder, some thought, who at the age of twelve occasionally treated her admirers to Steibelt's "Storm" Rondo or his *Burning of Moscow.*

Some parents were no doubt insisting that their children learn the piano, in the worst way. In the fall of 1817 J. B. Logier's Royal Patent Chiroplast and his system of wholesale lessons had barely invaded London; but it had already achieved a smooth transatlantic crossing, for on October 4, in the *Centinel,* we read of a Miss Brown, otherwise unidentifiable, who proposed to introduce that revelation to Boston, offering to sell a pamphlet describing the new gadget for twenty-five cents at her house in Court Street and also at the Franklin Music Warehouse, at Graupner's and other music stores, and at Callender's Shakspere Circulating Library.

In 1820 John R. Parker, encouraged by his success as the proprietor of the Franklin Music Warehouse, considered that Boston might now be ready to support a periodical entirely devoted to music lore, news, opinion, and chatter. Thus, he founded the first music magazine ever to appear in America, naming it *Euterpeiad, or Musical Intelligencer, Devoted to the Diffusion of Musical Information and Belles Lettres.* It carried reviews of local musical events and filled out its pages with abstracts of music history, reprints from other publications, as well as anecdotes and curiosities with a musical link. Every issue came out also with a supplement of actual music, almost all of it songs with piano accompaniment. A year's worth of response to Parker's venture seems not to have been too eager, and he therefore, for the future, tried to tone it up with a little more pungent feminine flavor—just as the Jacksons toned up their piano store with perfumes and soap. *Euterpeiad* now further subtitled itself *Ladies' Gazette* and began to incorporate pieces with piquant headings such as "Scheme for Getting a Husband" or "Pleasures of a Married State" or "An Illustrious Female." It did not avail, and *Euterpeiad* died in its third year. It was, however, the forerunner of a long line of similar publications that studded the following decades.

In inspecting *Euterpeiad's* music supplements, it is interesting to note that by 1821 Mr. Parker considered that his readers were big girls now and able to sing a tune while playing some other notes with the right hand, since he had most of the songs printed on three staves. However, he seemed to think—probably with reason—that his fair subscribers had little interest in the identity of the persons who were the authors of their little musical pleasure. In the supplements of Vol. II hardly any composers' names are mentioned. Instead we have: " 'Take This Rose,' arranged for the Pianoforte," " 'Love Has Eyes,' as sung by Mr. Phillips," " 'Is There a Heart That Never Loved,' a favourite Ballad," or " 'The Hungarian Waltz' as danced in the admired Ballet of Love Among the Roses." Parker showed the same unconcern in advertising the songs he had for sale in his own warehouse: " 'Belles without Beaux,' a new Overture," " 'Heart's Ease,' a Rondo," " 'Tis Thee I Love," "My Native Land Good-night," and so on—all anonymous. Under the circumstances, we are glad that he made an exception and gave Lowell Mason credit for a couple of hymns. He also advertised "Mr. Shaw's new song 'The Polar Star' is just published." He was referring to Oliver Shaw, a blind singer and organist from Providence, Rhode Island, who deserves our mention since he was one of the earliest native American composers worthy of the name; that is to say, he was not a casual dilettante, but one who composed with professional skill throughout a lifetime, making an appeal to a wide audience. Shaw's songs mostly breathed forth a faultless devotional sentiment, judging from their titles: "Nothing True but Heaven," "Arrayed in Clouds," "Home of My Soul," and "Mary's Tears."

In general, however, we may say that ordinary song consumers of 1820, and long after, were inclined to assume vaguely that music was generated anonymously by a kind of spontaneous combustion.

Leaving Boston aside, there were, between 1800 and 1820, about six or eight piano makers that we know of doing business in New York, about three or four in Philadelphia, and two or three in Baltimore. None of them, so far as we know, developed any remarkable improvements in the instrument, and all of them had to struggle against the prevailing predilection for imported pianos. A "DIGEST of Accounts of Manufacturing Establishments in the United States"—made under the direction of the Secretary of State in 1822—after tabulating various gross statistics pertaining to piano manufacture, added the sentences: "Demand and sales very limited, owing to importations. A duty of 50% would greatly benefit the situation." A duty of 30% on all cabinetware and articles of wood was levied in 1816; but whether it was construed as applying to pianos, and whether it was still in force in 1822, or whether it was high enough to be sufficiently protective we do not know. It does seem possible, however, that the government report may have been unduly depressed; moreover, it is true that accurate national statistics of manufactures are notoriously difficult to assemble.

It is a fact that piano making took a decided upswing between 1820 and 1830. The Philadelphia firm of Loud Brothers even claimed alone to have turned out 680 pianos during 1824—a very high figure if it could be substantiated. Forty years later J. Leander Bishop, a careful historian of American manufactures, estimated the number of pianos made in the United States during the year 1829 at 2500, with a total aggregate value of $750,000. Philadelphia, New York, and Boston, in that order, were named as the three chief producing-centers, with Baltimore a poor fourth. The country at that time had a population of 12,000,000; thus, if the estimate was anywhere near the truth, it meant that one new American piano was manufactured for every 4800 inhabitants. Put in other terms, it meant that a little more than eight persons went out every working day of the year to buy a new American piano.

Piano imports continued after 1830, but we are convinced that they were on the defensive from that time on.

5. A CHANGE OF APRON STRINGS

AFTER 1820 only a fast-dwindling fraction of the population could remember ever having lived as subjects of an English king. The national egoism began to reassert itself, with no revolutionary or hostile bravado, but on a broader, more self-assured basis, even among the intellectual classes. It was during the following decade, for instance, that Noah Webster considered that the lexicographer's function was "to *ascertain* the national usage" and then proceeded to bring forth his declaration of orthographic independence.

If England was no longer to remain the absolute monarch of the higher American tastes and habits, it was implied that Americans now felt encouraged to interest themselves directly in foreign cultures, notably those of the European continent. Wealthy, suave George Ticknor had returned from his long European sojourn as early as 1819. He had studied at Göttingen, had met Goethe and Madame de Staël, and had spent months in Madrid reading old Spanish literature. He shed his light upon generations of Harvard students and indirectly upon many others, becoming the father of modern language study in America. His friend, the ambitious Edward Everett, formidable Greek scholar, the future governor of Massachusetts and ambassador to Great Britain, was with Ticknor at Göttingen, becoming the first American to achieve the degree of *Philosophiae Doctor* there, besides also treating himself to a visit to Greece. Toward the end of the 1820's, James Fenimore Cooper—famous romancer about American wilds —was happy to bask in the sophisticated delights of Paris for some time during his long European stay. At about that time also, Horatio Greenough thought to betake his young sculptural talents direct to Italy. By the 1830's the *Knickerbocker Magazine* was regularly running reviews of articles on "German Biblical Criticism," critiques of Lamartine's *Jocelyn,* and essays on "Italian Historical Romances."

A share in the broadening of American horizons must be ascribed to the Baltimore clippers. Those trim-lined ships, designed for speed, were built during the War of 1812, proving themselves to be invincible blockade runners, since the British Navy was unable to catch up with them. After the war they were put into passenger service in regular lines, making it much more convenient than ever before for wealthy Americans to travel abroad.

It was while moneyed, leisured, and educated Americans were beginning to discover continental Europe that the tenor and impresario Manuel Garcia decided to bring his troupe of Italian opera singers to New York. They opened at the Park Theater on November 29, 1825, with Rossini's *The Barber of Seville,* the first time that an American audience heard an Italian opera sung in authentic style, in the original language. During the months to follow they also gave the same composer's *La Cenerentola, Semiramide, Tancredi,* and *Il Turco in Italia,* as well as Mozart's *Don Giovanni* and a couple of Garcia's own operas. We may suspect that the group's work lacked distinction and that some of its performances were actually ragged; nevertheless, its visit made an ineradicable impression on upper-class New York. We might go so far as to say that it left the fashionable world in a state of permanent shock, musically speaking.

Lorenzo da Ponte, Mozart's bubbling old librettist, was drifting out his protracted old age in America at the time. His charm of manner and conversation had made him influential New York friends, whom he needled and wheedled into trying to set up a permanent Italian opera establishment there. The second failure of such an attempt was indeed rather magnificent. A new Italian Opera House was built on Church and Leonard Streets at a cost of $150,000. Sixteen Knickerbocker aristocrat proprietors paid $6000 apiece, each to own his own blue-silk-curtained box in a tier; and even the "parterre"—no longer a vulgar English "pit"—had mahogany seats upholstered in blue damask. It opened brilliantly on November 18, 1833, with Rossini's *La Gazza Ladra;* but two years later this precocious vaulting ancestor of the Metropolitan was a financial wreck that had to be abandoned, while it cast up numbers of good foreign singers and instrumentalists on the American shore.

The failure of one or two organizations, however, no longer mattered: from those years on, secular music of the more evolved kind was, in the United States, definitively oriented toward the continent of Europe. Thenceforth, Italian, French, and soon German apron strings were proudly and permanently substituted for English.

Among the several musical associations active in New York during that period, one of the most enterprising was the Musical Fund Society. It was, like an older group of the same name in Philadelphia, an organization of mingled amateurs and professionals that aimed to provide assistance to superannuated musicians. It met regularly, once a month, for practice and preened itself annually in a couple of public concerts for which outside professional talent was engaged. In the program of its second concert of the season, at the City Hotel, on December 18, 1834, we can remark the overwhelming rage of the Italian opera. Signor Fabj sang a *scena* and aria from Rossini's *Edoardo e Cristina* and Signora Maroncelli delivered *"Di tanti palpiti"* from the same composer's *Tancredi.* The stainlessly Anglo-Saxon Miss Watson sang Rossini's cavatina *"Di piacer mi balza il cor";* while Miss Lewis, an American child of twelve, offered *"Una voce poco fa"* from *The Barber of Seville.* Signor Maroncelli sang a barcarolle from *Jean de Calais* and Signors Fabj and Ferrero presented a duo from *Elisa e Claudio;* shall we credit the artists with a note of variety because those operas were by Donizetti and Mercadante? In any event, the force of fashionable gravitation was not to be overcome, and the orchestra of thirty-eight played the overtures to *Semiramide* and *William Tell,* both by the overpowering Rossini. In the instrumental part of the program a few non-Italian numbers were able to survive, but their dissent was effectually buried under the Rossini landslide.

The current Italianitis had its influence on the music of the pianoforte. *Mosè in Egitto* was a stagy oratorio rather than an opera; still it was by Rossini, and a writer in the *American Musical Journal* for April 1835 expressed the "hope, however, that our young ladies will . . . leave the march in *Mosè* alone for some short time—an event devoutly to be prayed for by any man who has the misfortune to live in the neighborhood of a pianoforte in New York."

With all their lively sympathy for Italy, the more skillful pianists among the genteel girls tended rather to be swayed by the style that radiated from the City of Light. As early as May 10, 1830, the Musical Fund Society had given a City Hotel concert brimming with Rossini. In the course of its program, however, a Miss Sterling played "Grand Variations, Pianoforte, on *Ma Fanchette est Charmante*" by Herz. Regular newspapers were condescending to report musical events, it seems, in those days, for the *Mercantile Adviser* undertook to describe her performance:

> The keys of her piano seemed gifted with vocal powers, which addressed themselves to the inmost feelings of the auditory, in tones of stirring excitement, or of melting passion, of solemn grandeur or hurried breathlessness, at the will of their mistress . . .

Apparently, Miss Sterling was using her notes, for she:

> unlike the great mass of performers, was, while her quick eye was keenly observant of the language of her note book, listening with intensity to the articulation of her instrument, her practised fingers meantime flying from key to key with all magic celerity and unfaltering accuracy.

The *Adviser* was further impressed by her "double run on the chromatic scale," in which all the semitones were heard with perfect distinctness, and by her "skipping passages," which were said to have made some of the lady listeners envious. The weather was bad, we are told; but ten to twelve hundred persons came to this concert, to be made aware of Miss Sterling, Monsieur Herz, and a degree of piano virtuosity. On June 22 the same lady gave a concert of her own, in which she again played *Ma Fanchette*—and also Moscheles' *The Fall of Paris,* a "fugitive" if thunderous piece. "Brilliant," "majestic," "graceful," and "elegant," ran the adjectives in the review this time, and there was also a report of "transports of applause." During the next five years we imagine that Miss Sterling acquired a variety of new gowns, scarves, hats, and buckles for the occasions on which she went among people; yet we find her, on May 21 and again on May 26, 1835, continuing to adorn herself in public concerts with *Ma Fanchette* and *The Fall of*

Paris—to the audiences' "most rapturous approbation." Was she still using her notes, we might ask?

We have been dwelling on New York in this chapter and will continue to do so for some space. The rise of that city to a dominant position among American communities was accomplished during the first three decades of the century. After the completion of the Erie Canal and the vast expansion of Atlantic shipping, it achieved a lead over its nearest rival, Philadelphia—both in population and wealth—that could never be overtaken. English travelers now called it "the London of America," whereas thirty-five years earlier they had flattered Philadelphia with this metaphor. New York was where the big money was now, and where it was going to accumulate more and more: thenceforth, therefore, New York fashions and tads, however foreign in origin, were to be dutifully imitated by dwellers elsewhere in the country. By 1835 the *American Musical Journal* admits slyly that it "has heard much" of "an assumption that all talent must fail in America which is not imported *via* New York and makes its debut in this city . . ." Thus, we can understand that Philadelphia was happy to have New York's Italian Opera Company of 1833–34 condescend to throw off fifteen of its eighty-three performances to it, in the course of the season.

Similarly, if we assume that—as is likely—the new style of bravura piano playing was first brought to New York before 1830, we shall not be astonished to find it in full feather in Philadelphia in 1835. We have reports of several concerts given in the latter city during that year by a newly formed organization, of mingled amateurs and professionals, calling itself the Philharmonic Society. Apparently the events proved to be displays of the pupils of the society's professional members and instigators. On one occasion a young lady pupil, for example, of Mr. Darley, played Moscheles' *Recollections of Scotland*—not too well, it seems, since "she was evidently struggling against the tormenting monster fear." But on another occasion an eleven-year-old pupil of Mr. Meignen played Herz's variations on *"Non più mesta"* and also those on a tune from *Anna Bolena* with great "neatness . . . of execution." Another young lady, a pupil of Mr. Plich's, offered Herz's "difficult variation" on *La Parisienne* "in a style so perfect" and so on. Thereupon a different eleven-year-old female offered variations by Hünten in a duet with her teacher, Mr. Standbridge. Finally "one of the brightest gems of the concerts" was a Miss Darcy, a pianist, whose teacher, a Mr. Reinhart, nevertheless played violin with her in Lafont's and Herz's variations on *L'Enfant du Régiment.* One Moscheles, one Hünten, and four Herz's, then, were the pianistic offerings of the Philadelphia Philharmonic Society, at whose concerts sometimes fifteen hundred people were present.

In due course, a home-grown species of the Herz genus of bravura piece could not fail to develop. We hear of a concert from that same year 1835 in which Mr. W. A. King, a reputable New York pianist, performed his *Grand Fantasia on the National Air "Hail, Columbia."* A week earlier the New York Sacred Music Society had put forth a strong effort, an "Oratorio"—meaning a mixed sacred concert—with a program full of Haydn, Handel, Mozart, and similar loftinesses. Amidst it, Mr. King played *A Grand National Fantasie on the "Star-Spangled Banner" with Finale "à la Valse"* of his own composition.

The offerings of American music publishers reflect these trends, though not to an overwhelming degree. The Herz-players aforementioned seem to have done a good deal of their practicing from imported notes. During the early thirties, among the reprinted piano music advertised, we notice in addition to *The Fall of Paris* also Steibelt's *Russian galopade with variations* and Herz's *Galoppade à la Giraffe.* Favorite operatic "numbers" were of course published in legitimate practical arrangements. On the other hand, there seems to have been a kind of bootleg trade in these melodies. Enterprising Americans had a way of swiping well-known operatic tunes, changing a note or two, and having them published with plausible new labels as their own creations. A *Pastora* Waltz for the pianoforte—"composed and dedicated to a lady of New Haven, by S.P.R."—proved to be nothing but a melody from Auber's *Masaniello.* But that same tune was again published the same year, with new words, as a ballad, under the title of "Ah, do not forget, love." A waltz labeled *L'Amitié,* "to which Mr. Willson has attached his name as composer, is taken almost entirely from Rossini's Waltz in *Guillaume Tell* . . . the subject disguised by a few alterations," as the bright reviewer of the *American Musical Journal* perceived, in an article that also uncovers a theft of the same waltz on the part of a Richard L. Williams. The reviewer suggests a department called "The Counterfeit Detector."

During the 1830's, as theretofore and for a long time to come, songs with piano accompaniment formed the greater part of the music shops' stock in trade. The English type of ballad was still supreme, many, if not most, of the examples being composed abroad and popularized in America by visiting singers such as Thomas Phillips, Charles Incledon, and later Henry Russell.

Many, however, now were of domestic make. Their character was of the sentimental kind we have recounted for the preceding generation, but now an element of cold-blooded sadness seemed to take hold of the song confectioners and retailers. There seemed to be a growing notion that the picture of a depressing situation could arouse more emotion than that of an exultant one. Lugubrious titles became more frequent: "The Motherless," "The Dying Minstrel," "The Days of Joy Are Gone," "The Last Farewell," "King Death." Even "Hot Corn" turns out to be about a little girl peddler who dies because her drunken mother has maltreated her. It may have been that sad songs were safer than gay ones: the latter may have led to hilarity or frivolity of performance, a dangerous direction for nice young ladies to take; whereas sad songs naturally induced a respectable demeanor. In any event, the publishers were glad to multiply them as long as they could squeeze out dimes with the tears.

Another magazine called *Euterpeiad,* not closely related to the older Boston one, came out briefly in New York in 1830. On May 1, after chronicling and describing a number of recently published pieces and ballads, with and without variations, the reviewer burst out:

> It really puzzles us to discover why composers, as they are called, will risk their reputations in sending forth so many of their productions; for although the engraving of plates is cheap and paper low priced, still we cannot conceive that any good can be attached to the many tens of thousands of similar pieces that swarm forth. We cannot divest ourselves of the knowledge of the thousands that have preceded them, containing precisely the same phrases.

There seems truly to have been an overproduction of sheet music at the time, for the same periodical announces on July 15 that the principal dealers of the city have made an agreement to sell music at a reduction of thirty to fifty per cent from their former prices. Can this be the beginning, in America, of the silly custom of combining fictitious list prices with heavy discounts? It had come up in England before this. One of the enterprising reductionists was George Melksham Bourne, who successively ran a newspaper agency, a "depository of arts," and an "engravings and fancy store" at 359 Broadway. On June 1 he had announced: "For the PIANOFORTE: *'My bark shall tempt the seas no more!'* " the ballad was being "republished," said the *Euterpeiad* reviewer, "on violet, straw and other colored paper, embellished by a lithographic sea-scene vignette." Some changes were made from the original music, "which makes it nothing better except for the purpose of securing the copyright." But Bourne stepped up his allurements one notch further. A few weeks later the *New York Commercial Advertiser* reported: "*'She never blamed him, never.'* Bourne has just laid upon my desk an air to the above words, arranged by Mr. Boyle, which in addition to the usual attributes of good music pleases both sight and smell, it being printed upon lilac-tinted paper scented by some aromatic essence." That lady-vapor again.

6. OTHER AMERICAN PIANO TRENDS

DURING the later 1830's American piano manufacture took certain directions peculiar to itself. The latest European improvements were, of course, soon brought over. R. & W. Nunns, the leading New York makers of the time, received an award at the annual show of the Mechanics Institute in 1830 for "the best square pianoforte, with the grand or French action." This could probably be interpreted to mean a form of the Erard-type repetition action. It was something of a novelty at the time, for at the same show the Nunns' chief rival, Dubois & Stodart, got second prizes for the best squares "with the usual English action." We are safe in surmising that the use of felt for hammer covering was introduced into the United States during the earlier thirties. The Boston one-piece cast-iron frame, as we have said before, was slow in becoming established in New York, the local makers continuing for a time to use the "composite" frame. In general, for about two decades, New York pianos tended to resemble French instruments, while those of Boston were more assimilated to English.

The most distinctive thing about the American piano makers of the time was that—as the trend grew toward a heavier, tighter, more sonorous instrument of greater range—it was the square type upon which they primarily lavished their improvements. In Europe by 1840 the square was rapidly declining, becoming virtually obsolete ten years later. The upright had become the practical shape for the great majority of simpler homes, while the grand was the form designed for ostentation in ampler drawing rooms—and for concerts. On the other hand, in the United States the large, elaborate square was the thing now increasingly bought by families who could afford the best. Cabinet uprights, we remember, had begun with a certain *élan,* but they soon occupied a secondary position. After 1840, Chickering made some excellent grands with the aid of his newly designed frame; but it required quite some time before they became widely distributed.

It is not altogether obvious why American preference should have departed from the European at this point. It may be that the squares imported during the 1800's, 1810's, and 1820's gave momentum to a fashion, established a buying habit, which the rising American piano makers and their customers might feel like expanding and elaborating but not rejecting in principle. Then, too, in Europe from 1820 on—or even earlier—it was the concert virtuosos who implanted the most acute piano awareness in people's minds. Now, a solo concert pianist invariably wants to play on a grand, on the instrument that has the fullest length of string as well as a sound-projecting lid that can be raised toward an audience. It is understandable that upper-class Europeans with large drawing rooms would have wished to adorn their homes with instruments that looked like those the adored virtuosos used when they were actually doing their marvelous stuff. A countess or money lender whom Liszt or Thalberg might visit would prefer to have a piano on view that the artists might consider worthy of themselves. But the United States had no Liszts or Thalbergs, had not even seen or heard feebler examples of this species of performer before 1845. The piano was occasionally played as a solo instrument in concerts, it is true, but mostly as a subordinate contribution to a mixed program. Moreover, there is evidence that during the thirties and forties piano solos were often played in public on squares.

Thus, the American piano makers put their growing resources into producing bigger and better squares; and the great, massive, iron-braced, heavy-legged rectangular horizontal box became the normal American piano for nearly fifty years. Nor did ladies of the house regret this. Well-to-do living rooms were large; but as the century put on its middle-aged fat, they became cluttered with overstuffed love seats, hand-embroidered hassocks, onyx tables, cabinets full of carved elephants, and other little burdens of wealth. Despite all amplitude of space, simpler-minded American matrons may well have felt relieved to think that a square piano presented fewer geometrical complications than a wing-shaped one.

The art of the pianoforte was now trailing wide over the United States, even though it could not be said to be putting forth any rare blooms. After the great trek over and past the Alleghenies had been going on for fifty years, Ohio in 1830 recorded that it had 937,000 inhabitants, thus becoming the fourth most populous of the twenty-seven states. Mrs. Trollope, trying to keep her shop in Cincinnati during the late 1820's, wrote down how her delicate English eyes, ears, and nose were lacerated by the unconcern of occasional homicides, the debauchery of revival meetings, and the gush of tobacco juice that she was compelled to witness there. Still, the intensity of her revulsions may have allowed a few things to escape her. Shortly after the time of her departure, we learn that a couple of her countrymen, Mr. and Mrs. W. Nixon, were operating a "Musical Seminary" in "the Queen City of the West." By 1834, Mr. Nixon had written and had had published, right there in Cincinnati, a *Guide to Instruction on the Pianoforte.* Books on music were not common anywhere in the United States, all the less so when arising from the banks of the Ohio. It "presupposes the existence of a demand for musical information, or an author would scarcely print," as the appreciative and astonished New York reviewer said. Five years later the "Musical Seminary" held exercises at which thirty-seven young ladies received certificates, premiums, and medals for musical proficiency. The *New York Musical Review,* reprinting this news from the *Cincinnati Daily Gazette* of April 29, 1839, found it remarkable that the "West" had a whole music *school* that also *taught "theory"!*

How did the Nixons get pianos for teaching their thirty-seven girls, in the days of practically no railroads? Perhaps from New York up the Hudson to Albany, by barge through the Erie Canal, then along Lake Erie to Cleveland, and finally down the Ohio Canal to Cincinnati, reloading all along the line. Or perhaps by boat from Boston to New Orleans, then by river steamer up the Mississippi and up the Ohio, which only very recently had had its snags expunged. The Ohioans must have wanted their pianos very hard, for getting them was certainly much more troublesome than it had been for Bostonians to have their Clementis floated over from London in one scoop.

It is just possible that the "Musical Seminary" used some locally produced instruments. The afore-mentioned census of manufactures for 1822 does indicate that Cincinnati, population ten thousand, had a plant employing three men and one boy, making pianofortes to the total value of $250 to $400. "Little sale for the articles," the report added sadly; but there may have been some development in ten years. There is also a tale of an Englishman, William Bourne, who attempted to make pianofortes as early as 1837 in Dayton, sixty miles from Cincinnati. Since Dayton had only a thousand inhabitants at the time, we do not wonder that Mr. Bourne presently moved to Boston to work for the Chickerings.

7. THE GERMANS INVADE AND ESTABLISH A BEACHHEAD

AFTER 1820, improved shipping facilities allowed many more Europeans to realize the wild old dream of starting life over again in a new world. During the earlier 1820's the annual entries into the United States fluctuated between thirty-five hundred and eighty-five hundred persons; but they took a sharp rise after 1827, and by the end of the 1830's around sixty thousand people sought admittance to the country every year. The largest number of these were Irish, but Germans were running them a good second before 1840. The Irish were mostly of the poorest and most ignorant kind; apart from getting into small-time politics, they had little opportunity at first to become anything but unskilled laborers. Among the Germans, however, there were some who had gentler aspirations, who were possessed of some education—of musical literacy in particular, coupled with some devotion to the profounder essence of music. It is interesting to note that the first German singing society in the United States, the old *Männerchor,* was organized in Philadelphia as early as 1835.

Three German-born pianists came to live in New York during the 1830's: Henry C. Timm, William Scharfenberg, and Daniel Schlesinger. The first was a thorough musician of no showiness; the second a nimble, sensitive player who may have lacked fire; while the last was, by all accounts, a fine concert performer, a pupil of Ries and Moscheles, the best pianist yet heard in America, many said. At his concert at the City Hotel on February 4, 1839, he played one of Thalberg's fantasies and also delivered an improvisation of his own. However, he opened the program, assisted by young Scharfenberg, with an arrangement of Beethoven's *Egmont* Overture for two pianos. This was something comparatively new in New York. The name of Beethoven was indeed known among musicians at the time; in fact, there had been a long article about the composer in the *American Musical Journal* a few years earlier. Nevertheless, his music was, for most concertgoers, until then a legend rather than an experience. One finds his name with difficulty on programs, and one sees him on publishers' lists mostly in such guises as: "The Clara Waltz, Beethoven, For pianoforte, by S. C. Jollie" or " 'I Pity and Forgive!' The last words of Gen. Simon Bolivar; the music selected from Beethoven, the words by a gentleman of this city." It was a relatively small dose of Beethoven that Schlesinger administered at his concert, one that the late-comers could have missed. Later in the program—among the afore-mentioned pianistic *plats du jour*—he and Scharfenberg, reinforced by pianists Thibault and Etienne, performed Cherubini's *Anacréon* Overture for eight hands, the multiple pianism thus confirming one more Paris fashion.

Schlesinger's career was unfortunately cut short, for he died at forty—within a few months of the concert just described—after having lived in New York a mere three years. He had evidently aroused much admiration and affection during that time, for a memorial concert in his honor arranged on June 25, 1839, at the large Broadway Tabernacle drew an audience of two thousand persons. The Concordia, a German singing and orchestral society that Schlesinger had led, participated in the production of one of his works, while an orchestra of sixty players gave a rousing performance of Weber's *Freischütz* Overture. The sound must have been unusually impressive, and the editor of the *Knickerbocker Magazine* called it "the noblest musical performance ever heard in America."

The Schlesinger memorial was called a "solemnity"; actually, it was also a benefit, for it netted $3381.78 to the musician's widow. The outstanding artistic quality of the performance and the support given it by "the German element"—as well as its consequent pecuniary success—are what must have encouraged the forthcoming enterprise of Ureli Corelli Hill, a German-trained Connecticut Yankee violinist and music promoter. Heading a group of German musicians, Timm and Scharfenberg among them, he organized the New York Philharmonic Society, destined to become the longest-lived of all American symphony orchestras. Its first concert took place on December 7, 1842, the program including Beethoven's Fifth Symphony as well as Weber's Overture to *Oberon*.

There was much prejudice against the invading Germans, as

indeed there was against most immigrants; that was one thing that had helped delay the Philharmonic's definitive organization. With it, however, they had now won a firm beachhead in the realm of American music.

8. HUMBUG HUMS

THE UNITED STATES began to spurt high and wide in the years following 1840. Steamships had been crossing the Atlantic here and there during the late thirties, but it was in 1840 that Samuel Cunard first established his regular line of such boats plying between Liverpool and Boston. They did not always better the best speed of the sailing vessels; but partly through the Cunard principle of sister ships, the time of passage was now regular, and departures and arrivals could practically be guaranteed. Immigrants now poured out of the boats in unheard-of numbers, more than 1,300,000 in ten years, contributing as much as twenty-two per cent to the country's increase in population during that period.

In the West, expansion was prodigious. This was the decade that witnessed the annexation of Texas, the victorious Mexican War, and the consequent acquisition of most of the vast mountain and intermountain country including California. The discovery of gold there soon afterward created another social dynamism, another orgy of adventure; and meanwhile the huge Oregon country had also been added to the national territory, thus making it a fabulous empire covering the entire continent. Other enterprises were shooting up rankly: cotton mills in New England, for instance, with Southern plantations spreading far to feed them. Railroads were being built out everywhere, portending soon to quicken the entire nation within a tight net of iron nerves; and the first operation of that marvelous device the electric telegraph also falls within the decade.

The business boom and the real estate boom made everybody a little dizzy. It was all achieved by men, and they intoxicated each other with their dreams and ardors. Much had been accomplished that would have seemed fantastic to a previous generation; but who was now to say which schemes were crazy and which were pregnant with success? The line between fancy and truth was often blurred, and justly so; the general speech took on a tone of extravagance and bristled with superlatives, while wild promises and claims about all manner of things agitated the air. It was the age of what a later generation called "hokum," and what outraged and envious Britishers called "humbug." Germans, too, handed around that disdainful word a good deal, pronouncing it *"hoom-bock."* Poor Europeans! It was hard for them to partake of the exuberance that brought it forth: woe to the sober at a drunken party!

Humbug involved fraud very often, but the victims were often humbuggers themselves and could appreciate the comedy. It was the age of the early career of P. T. Barnum; and when he exhibited an ancient female Negro imbecile as George Washington's nurse, or the fused remains of a monkey and a fish as a dead mermaid, even those who didn't believe a word of it gladly paid their admissions to look—and got their money's worth smiling at the idea of the thing. Nobody asks for his money back after a good show merely because it does not happen to be "true"; moreover, the showman makes the show, as much as do the performers.

In the world of music, hokum had gotten to a good start well before 1840. We have an account of a contest between two musicians: an Englishman named Norton in the late summer of 1834 challenged an Italian named Gambati to a public musical duel with brass tubes. The affair was largely promoted by William Niblo, restaurateur and provider of light entertainment (called "pop concerts" at a much later date), New York's leading continuer of the old pleasure-gardens idea. He hired an orchestra of sorts—in which temporarily unemployed opera players, including Gambati, were glad to put in the slack season—also English-language vocalists of easy appeal. Niblo's musical premises were half outdoors and in close reach of the gin and brandy slings, wines, and "segars" from which much of his profit was derived. The trumpet contest was blown up with many preliminaries and anticipatory incidents. On the great day, twenty-five hundred persons crowded Niblo's Gardens and adjacent "saloon." The audience was encouraged to be violently partisan: cheering squads of Gambatinis and Nortoninis gave noisy vent to their enthusiasms, feeling was whipped high, and fisticuffs were imminent between the respective supporters of either of the high contending parties. Gambati played variations on a tune from Rossini's *Otello* as well as the famous "march in *Mosè*"; whereas Norton played his elaborations of "Robin Adair" and "The British Grenadiers." A solemn committee of three umpires awarded Norton the decision on points. The trumpeters garnered $530 apiece for their evening's efforts, and publishers proceeded to advertise "Signor Gambati's celebrated trumpet solo" in an arrangement for the piano. Everybody was happy, in varying degrees.

By the middle forties the United States was obviously more than ripe for a touring visit by a glamorous, currently waving European piano virtuoso. The first to arrive was Leopold de Meyer. Certainly the ways in which he liked to assert himself fitted rather well with the American atmosphere of the time. Some impressionable admirer had once referred to him as "the lion among pianists," whereupon he appropriated the personification—or rather bestification—calling himself officially the "Lion Pianist" and expecting others to follow suit. He arrived in the United States in September 1845, bringing with him a kind of manager, or *chargé d'affaires,* named G. C. Reitheimer. While in England, the pianist had had a sort of treatise written about him, a prettified biography recounting and embroidering his various past successes. We would call it a long blurb nowadays. Reitheimer hawked this book through newspaper offices, possibly using some pecuniary or alcoholic persuasion at the same time. The result was a number of glittering press pieces about the pianist, done in a style that a British correspondent called "the Yankee lyrical." Early during De Meyer's visit somebody made a cartoon of him, showing enormous elliptical mops of hair pointing out from either side of his head, a cigar holder in his mouth, a piano slung over his shoulder, and a bag of money in his hand. He liked it so well he had it reprinted at the head of all his programs, as well as on his stationery.

The "Lion Pianist" was an effective player in his way and succeeded in appearing in about sixty concerts during the course of a year, traveling as far as St. Louis, no small journey in those days. In Philadelphia the Philharmonic Society presented him with a silver cup, eighteen inches high, on which was engraved the figure of a lion playing the piano. We have reports of some of the things he played; they were what we might expect: his own fantasies on *Semiramide,* on *Robert le Diable,* and on the *Carnival of Venice;* his own well-known *Marche Marocaine* and an elaboration of "National Airs." Into these last he incorporated—obviously enough—"Yankee Doodle," sure to be interrupted by delighted applause. There were other tales about the construction of his successes. Numbers of bouquets were thrown at him at one concert and duly carried off into the artists' room, where a group of his hangers-on had gathered. Soon he counted his bunches of flowers and was angry to find several missing. "Well, he ought to know how many he paid for," said some one maliciously. And once, when the advance sale to one of his New York concerts was unsatisfactory—according to another story—he hired carriages to stand or pass slowly before the doors of the hall just before concert time, so as to give an impression of bustle, on the principle that a crowd draws a crowd.

Most of the hokum surrounding De Meyer's American tour would be understood nowadays as commonplaces of "publicity," but it was all new and outrageous then. Much of our information about it, we are sorry to say, comes from an unsympathetic British source, which summed him up thus: "The 'lion pianist' shall have achieved his mission, that of throughly humbugging a nation, the chief element of whose character is humbug."

De Meyer brought his own Erard pianos with him, probably two in number, not trusting himself to the unknown capacities of the American instruments. He had been in the country for fourteen months and was thinking lightly of leaving, when another piano virtuoso encroached upon him, speeding his departure. This was no other than Henri Herz, the celebrated, amiable Parisian multiplier of piano performances, piano pieces, piano lessons, and pianos. We are fortunate in that Monsieur Herz left us an account of his trip entitled *Mes Voyages en Amérique*, a charming book full of quaint anecdotes, shrewd observations, and a few tall tales. No American entrepreneur seems to have sent for Monsieur Herz: he came to America on his own, he said, to see more of the world and meanwhile to exercise his profession here and there if possible. Like any other genteel European hypocrite, he refrained from saying that he came chiefly to bag some of the famous dollars that he had heard were flying around so thick and fast across the Atlantic.

Herz embarked at Liverpool on November 2, 1846, on the steamer *Caledonia*, one of the four original Cunard sister ships; and eighteen days later he landed in Boston. He came armed with "my tool," as he called it: a grand piano, from his own factory we may be sure. Right in Boston harbor, with the boat in the dock, an American, probably a newspaper reporter, came on board and asked him: "How do you like America? Don't you think it's a wonderful country?" "Well, will you at least wait till I go ashore?" replied Herz. The old gag. At his hotel he was much impressed with American ideas of comfort: the hot and cold running water and the gas jets in every room, the good dining-room service, and the presence of carpets everywhere. In the public sitting room he saw for the first time an American piano, "so square, so heavy, that from a distance it could have been taken for one of those antediluvian animals that Cuvier has reconstructed." Europeans were not used to those big squares. Representatives of the musical world called on him in Boston, he tells, urging him to give a concert right away; but no, he evidently was well informed about prestige values in the American show business and insisted on making his debut in the "Empire City," as he says it was called.

Herz made his first New York appearance to the noise of some curious publicity. He burned his hand, he said, in grabbing a sheet of hot metal before a fireplace. The injury was so bad that he was on the point of postponing his concert when, providentially, an anonymous medicineman came to see him and plied him with a miraculous "pain extractor" salve of his own invention, which completely mended the hurt hand so that he could go on with the concert as planned. Of course, he felt duty-bound to acknowledge publicly the benefit he had received. There was a lot of talk in New York about the terrible accident and the wonderful cure, and he mildly suggests that some of his first success at the Broadway Tabernacle may have been due to the circulation of this story.

It seems pretty clear that Herz was rather well versed in hokum before he ever boarded the *Caledonia.* However, the kind he had thitherto handled was of the pale, puny European species, and he was soon to be startled by a more robust American variety. His debut had packed the house with extra chairs, and the smell of success attracted a very great fox indeed: the great P. T. Barnum himself came to call. The showman said he was thinking of making a contract with Jenny Lind for a series of concerts in the United States—would Herz consider being an associate artist on such a tour? Barnum further explained that he planned to advertise the Swedish singer as an actual angel come down from heaven. "You think you will make people believe that?" asked Herz. "They won't believe it at first," answered Barnum, "but I'll say it and have it repeated everywhere so often and so well, that they finally will believe it." After all, had he not already sold the public a mermaid? "And would you pass me off as one of the cherubim?" queried Herz. "No," said the Prince of Humbugs, "I'll have enough with one angel in my troupe." At that point Herz turned down the deal.

Meanwhile a Mr. Bernard Ullmann came to see Herz with a rather more modest-seeming proposal. He offered himself as the pianist's secretary, errand boy, representative, and factotum. Herz accepted, was delighted with the result, and soon declared: "I make it a rule always to obey Ullmann." The fact is, Ullmann was finding Herz a good wedge for forcing his own career as an impresario. Presently he amused Herz by saying: "*We will give* a concert in Philadelphia tomorrow." (The italics are Herz's.)

For launching that Philadelphia concert, or possibly a subsequent one, Ullmann thought up a unique scheme. On the billboards and advertising posters announcing it, the words that hit the eye with big letters were: "A THOUSAND CANDLES"—meaning that the hall was to be thus lavishly illuminated. Herz would not believe at first that such an irrelevance would draw people to a musical performance; but draw them it did, as he found. At the concert he complained of some commotion in the audience while he was playing his *Russian* Rondo; it came from people trying to count the candles. During the intermission a man got up and protested out loud to the stage that he was being gypped, that the count was eight candles short. Herz promised restitution and made a package of eight candles at his hotel the next day, to be left till called for; but no one came for them.

Something different had to be thought up for Philadelphia after that stunt. Here was Ullmann's next showman's creation:

FAREWELL

TO THE CITY OF PHILADELPHIA.

Grand festival in honor of the Declaration of Independence published in this city before the assembled people, amidst unspeakable enthusiasm, on the Fourth of July of the immortal year 1776.

PROGRAM.

1. *Homage to Washington,* cantata for eight voices, with solos and choruses, performed by five orchestras and eighteen hundred singers. *Note.* The bust of the Father of his Country will be crowned together with the last chords of the cantata.
2. *Constitution Concerto,* expressly composed for this solemnity by Henri Herz, played by the composer.
3. *Lecture* on the Genius of the American People and on the Rights of Women, by Miss ——
4. *Grand Triumphal March* dedicated to young America and arranged for forty pianists, by Henri Herz.
5. *The Capitol,* chorus apotheosizing the spirits of the Presidents of the United States.
6. The national song *Hail, Columbia,* performed by all the military bands of Philadelphia and surrounding cities, combined for this occasion.

N.B. The illuminations of the interior of the hall will form allegorical figures recalling the great events of our country's history.

Price of tickets: *Six Dollars.*

When Herz demurred at entering into this magniloquacious undertaking, Ullmann explained: "I have figured it out. Our expenses will come to $8,000, we will take in $16,000, and a profit of $8,000 will be the result. Will you consent?" "Never," answered Herz. "Your refusal proves that you do not know the American character," countered Ullmann. They compromised: for his "farewell" Herz wrote and participated in a piece for eight pianists on four pianos. The crowd was dense, and Herz said the pianists had practically to be carried into the hall. Suppose there really had been forty?

In Baltimore, Herz was persuaded to offer to improvise on melodies supplied by the audience. All went well so long as the themes were written out and handed up to the stage. But he had a tough time with one or two volunteers who could not write music and insisted on whistling to him in rather vague intonation.

The multiple-piano stunts—especially when they involved famous "national" tunes—were generally crowd drawers, and Ullmann called them "financial music." Still, the old mechanical principle held good with regard to them: namely that the more moving parts an apparatus has, the more opportunities there are for some of them to go out of order. In New Orleans, with Herz's and Ullmann's connivance, a performance was scheduled to be given by sixteen beautifully gowned lady amateur pianists, at eight pianos, for the benefit of the local poor. At the last minute one of the performers turned ill and did not show up. Herz gazed among the boxes, spied an appropriately attired lady, and courteously asked her to substitute for the missing member. When she protested that she did not know how to play the piano, Herz reassured her: the fifteen others would make enough sound; she needed merely to make plausible-looking silent motions with her hands on top of the keys. She accepted, for the sake of the poor; all went well until the composition came to a general pause of which the fair pinch hitter had had no previous inkling—and she kept right on through the halt, waving her hands gracefully over the keyboard, as a soundless solo. No harm was done, for there was much applause and many bouquets, and $4000 was taken in —thus justifying Ullmann's epithet.

As those of a successful music-businessman, Herz's remarks on the American music trades are worth noting. While viewing the rising interest in polite music with sympathy, he felt that American piano manufacture, qualitatively, left much to be desired. He excepted Chickering & Sons, whom he praised, saying that their instruments had *"éclat"* and that their concert grand models could compete with English grands, which they resembled in many ways. As for uprights, the type less emphasized in America, Herz said "the United States will probably be tributary to Europe for a long time" in that field. He confirmed the general impression that French pianos made for home consumption did not hold up well in America; and he blamed this not only on the extremes of climate, but also on the excessive furnace heat in American houses—which caused veneer and ivory to chip off. In the United States central heating indeed has long been considered an enemy of pianos, against which they must be protected from birth. Herz maintained that good French pianos, especially built for export, would withstand American rigors, and he deplored what he considered a budding prejudice against them. But here he was talking as an interested party, for we notice that he was trying to sell his own instruments in the United States. On October 6, 1849, an advertisement appeared in *Saroni's Musical Times* of dealers Firth, Pond & Co., saying they were the "sole agents for Herz's celebrated grand and semi-grand pianos and pianinos, which are manufactured expressly to meet this climate." Incidentally, the advertisement again prompts the following query: is that term "grand" a denotating qualifier, or a mere swearword?

Herz was also impressed by the extent of the American sheet-music business. Some publishers, he found, had a stock of 150,000 to 200,000 plates—which might be equivalent to 20,000 or 30,000 compositions or collections. This music, he said, "suffices to a great extent for the consumption of the country." On the other hand, he regretted the absence of a treaty that would prevent American publishers from reprinting European music—to their profit—without having to pay anything to the foreign copyright-holders. Herz may still have succeeded in flaking off a few little dollars from a publisher during his American stay. Within that time he could hardly have failed to design his own musical American souvenir card; and, sure enough, we discover his *Variations brilliantes et Grande Fantaisie sur des airs nationaux américains* published by Oliver Ditson of Boston. The *morceau* involved *General Jackson's* March—a tune now forgotten—"Hail, Columbia," and the inescapable "Yankee Doodle" worked up into a comic *fugato* as well as into some jumpy, jittery variations. It is a rather good piece of its meretricious kind, but much too hard for most girls.

It was Barnum, naturally, the greatest showman on earth, who scaled the Everest of American hokum in the concert business when he finally did bring over Jenny Lind in 1850. He gave up the "angel from heaven" pitch, but he hardly needed it. A Jenny Lind delirium was readily worked up among people who felt so bully that they insisted on doing something ridiculously and harmlessly reckless: for her debut at Castle Garden the general admission was fixed at $3.00, but the actual choices of location in the house were then auctioned off just before the concert. The prices realized were mostly between $10 and $100, but the crowning parsley of this contest went to John N. Genin—whose ticket cost him $225. Genin was a hatter, and surely mad that evening. We trust his glory helped him sell more hats.

The Jenny Lind debut has its interest for piano lore: two instruments were used at the occasion, announced importantly as "Chickering grands." There is some reason to believe, however, that one of them, at least, was a square. Thalberg's fantasy on themes from *Norma,* for two pianos, was offered as an entr'acte—one instrument played by Julius Benedict, the London-derived conductor of the concert's orchestra, the other by Richard Hoffman, a recently immigrated capable young English native. The *Albion,* a smart little New York weekly journal of comment, said of it:

> The piano duett was doubtless very well played, but as we could never hear more than one performer at a time, we cannot speak positively. Mr. Benedict, however, seemed to have a very brilliant touch. The pianos sounded to us like a loud guitar smothered in flannel.

Hokum naturally arouses antihokum, and in the United States this likes to take a humorous form. The suave, well-bred *Knickerbocker Magazine* presently indulged its readers with a regular humorous supplement called *The Bunkum Flagstaff and Independent Echo,* whereby "Bunkum" was to be taken as a significant pseudonym for New York. In September 1849 its redactor issued a burlesque account of a concert by a foreign piano virtuoso whom he calls "HERR SMASH." The caricature has a resemblance both to Herz and to De Meyer; but it probably was intended to apply to one Maurice Strakosch, whose debut took place at about the time the article appeared. The piece describes Herr Smash's hairy appearance, his musk-scented handkerchief, and his posey stance. The piano was secured to the floor by transverse timbers and a sidelong piece of iron, claimed the writer; one assistant fastened the pianist's coattails down with tacks, while another secured his body with ropes. Herr Smash began by raising his hands three feet above the keys, keeping them there for three minutes, then coming down with a furious crash that wrenched the brass plate off the piano and sent one leg scurrying across the floor. He played "Yankee Doodle" smothered in ornamental blankets, then he played a variety of "battles" ending with a "grand junction cannonade." Women waved handkerchiefs, infants bawled at the breast, sober men boohooed out of enthusiasm. The reporter glumly sucked his cane, he said, and applauded a little with his thumbnails.

9. MORE GERMANS COME—THEY MAKE AMERICAN PIANOS

THE WAVE of immigration rose higher and higher during the late forties and early fifties. The potato famine of 1847 sent over still greater hordes of shanty Irish; while the failure of the revolutions of 1848 uprooted many Germans less useful for hod-carrying or pugilism, but inclined to be literate, industrious, skillful with their hands, and musical. A number of unusually capable German musicians arrived in America during the late forties. Among them was Otto Dresel—a close friend of Robert Franz—an interesting composer who soon became the leading pianist of Boston. Theodore Thomas was a boy of ten when he was brought over, as early as 1845; he was destined to become the foremost leader and founder of symphony orchestras in America. Theodore Eisfeld came in 1849; he was to be the conductor of the New York Philharmonic for a long time. Karl Bergmann, thorough musician and cellist, arrived in 1850, to make a distinguished place for himself as a conductor and music director. In 1848 a group of twenty-four young Germans came, forming what they called the Germania Orchestra; they toured the United States and gave American music lovers a taste of a precision and expression in performance that set a new standard of excellence. Some of the Germania members remained in America after the group disbanded.

We have merely cited a tiny sampling. Hundreds, perhaps thousands, of German musicians, distinguished and mediocre, came to live in New York, Boston, and Philadelphia in those years, and also in Cincinnati, St. Louis, and the gangling village of Chicago. They made strong, permanent focuses of German musicality in the country; and from then on the higher reaches of instrumental music were to take on, for generations, a predominantly German physiognomy. Indeed, the United States became, on this musical level, a German province. The Germans did not merely promulgate their tastes and their melodic idiom; more notably, they brought a particular attitude toward music as an art, a devotion to it as a serious, infinitely valuable pursuit, one more akin to religion than to amusement, together with a profound reverence for music's saints and heroes. Some of the Anglo-Saxons—among the well-to-do, better-educated, urban groups—responded to it with some sympathy.

It was the Mendelssohn Quintette Club, organized 1849 in Boston—four out of its five members German—that first gave good performances of chamber music in America. Soon Theodore Eisfeld formed a group in New York that gave series of chamber-music concerts, while a few years later Karl Bergmann and some others started another such series there. It was during the 1850's then, that the quartets and trios of Mozart, Beethoven, Mendelssohn, and Schubert were first properly heard on this side of the Atlantic. So were the piano concertos of Beethoven and that of Schumann, while the Mendelssohn *Concerto in G minor* soon proved to be a favorite of its kind.

German pianists were likewise active; however, it was a Yankee of ancient, unblemished, boiled-dinner background who became one of the leading propagators of great German piano music. This was William Mason, third son of Lowell Mason the hymn writer and planter of musical literacy in endless American schools and churches. William, it is true, had done his significant studying in Germany and had become marked for life by the four years he spent there, which included ample time with Liszt at Weimar. It was William Mason who first realized many of Beethoven's greater sonatas, as well as much other important piano literature, in sound for the first time before audiences in America. Whether they were American audiences, in New York, is another question. Mason returned to New York in 1854 and was joined in his work of presenting piano "classics" five years later by a pianist with the suggestive name of Sebastian Bach Mills, English-born, but likewise German-trained.

The Germans and their English-speaking adherents played and taught Beethoven, Schubert, and Mendelssohn—and even a little Bach and Mozart, when their pupils would let them; and despite resistance and indifference, the ultimate influence they exerted was deep and wide. For one thing, they succeeded in changing the nation's habitual musical nomenclature in two points. They made Americans stop speaking of "minims," "crochets," and "quavers" —after the somewhat ritualistic English fashion—and got them to adopt the logical German way of saying "half notes" "quarter notes" and "eighth notes." Furthermore, the German piano teachers, through their pupils and grandpupils, were able finally to establish the universal practice of numbering the fingers 1 2 3 4 5—with 1 signifying the thumb—in place of the antediluvian English system of writing them x 1 2 3 4. According to the English scheme, 1 meant the index finger and the outlandish symbol x the thumb, thereby giving that difficult bumpy member mental aid and comfort in continuing to be bumpy. It required several generations for the old English fingering notation to become obsolete, and one continues to meet with it occasionally in music from the last quarter of the century.

The piano-manufacturing business was doing quite well during the 1840's; its spread was healthy if not spectacular. An estimate made by the United States Commissioner of Patents in 1852 stated that the output of pianos for the preceding year had been about 9000. With a population grown to 25,000,000, that would mean a new piano for every 2777 inhabitants. Contrasting this with the previously quoted figure for 1829, which gave one new piano for every 4800 inhabitants, we can see that the relative distribution of instruments fell rather short of doubling in twenty-three years. If we were able to add imports to our calculation, the relative rise would be even less, since the indications are that the number of piano importations declined steadily—despite the lowering of the tariff in 1846.

Chickering of Boston was the trade's undisputed leader in the mid-century years, probably making and selling nearly a thousand pianos a year by 1850. His iron frame gave his pianos solidity, high tension, and consequent tone power: they were exhibited at the great London Exposition in 1851 and there won favorable mention. After the failure of Loud Brothers in 1837, Philadelphia ceased to be prominent as a piano-making center. On the other hand, Albany—then a comparatively much more important city than it is now—began to make a stir with the establishment of Boardman & Gray, a firm that thrived for many decades, turning out a product of consistent good quality. Its instruments became associated with a patented device that consisted of a number of weights used to apply additional pressure on the sounding board, to be worked by a pedal. This lowered the pitch a trifle; but by jiggling the pedal rapidly up and down, a kind of vibrato could be produced. The thing was called *"Dolce Compana,"* a pleasantly suggestive gibberish, like most trade names. Like all special gadgets and attachments, it made a fine "talking point" for American customers. Baltimore began to grow, too, as a piano-making locality. A number of Germans were in the trade there quite early in the century; and after William Knabe helped to establish his firm in 1837, the city took on a regional significance, since his good instruments drew much of the southern market to them.

There were many piano makers among the mid-century German immigrants. The craft was an old one with them: actually, Germans were almost the earliest piano makers of all, far back in the first half of the eighteenth century; they were the ones who had taught the French and the English; they were the people who cared most for the instrument, even though economic and political conditions in Germany had not yet permitted a great modern industry to arise there. New York was where most of these new craftsmen landed and stayed, and they made that city the great piano-manufacturing center of the country.

In the thirties the Germans worked in older, established shops such as those of Nunns & Clark, or Raven & Bacon, or Dubois & Stodart. There was quite a prejudice against them, since plebeian Anglo-Saxons have always seemed to assume that anyone who speaks English haltingly or with a foreign accent must therefore be subhuman, or at least imbecile. The injustice with which the Germans were treated—probably by a discriminatory scale of wages—caused a general strike among piano makers in New York in 1835 and resulted in the formation of the first labor union in that trade, which attempted to fix fair rates of pay. We are told this by Daniel Spillane, whose valuable *History of the American Pianoforte* is nevertheless rather vague on many important matters. It was William Lindeman, however, Spillane says, who—after having mastered the crazy American-English language—was able in the late thirties to set up a prosperous piano manufactory of his own and thus force a certain respect from the native and English supermen.

A few years later, German piano makers were coming fast. Their names are remotely familiar to older New Yorkers today, for they can remember the names in gilt letters on the instruments of their youth: Albert Weber, Frederick Mathushek, Ernst Gabler, George Steck, John and Charles Fischer, Henry Behning, and Bernhard Shoninger. Later came Hugo Sohmer and Simon Krakauer. All went into business for themselves and prospered. All of them fade into insignificance, however, before the name of Steinway. The founder of the dynasty, Henry E. Steinway (originally Steinweg), an experienced piano maker from Braunschweig, came to New York in 1850, having been preceded by two of his sons who had reconnoitered the situation. Three years later the firm of Steinway & Sons was founded. It began manufacturing in a small way in a shop on Varick Street and presently moved to larger quarters on Walker Street.

Right in those early years father and sons must have worked out the distinctive features of piano construction that ultimately led to their glory. Evidently they started by assuming the basic necessity of the one-piece cast-iron frame, as successfully developed by the Chickerings. Without that firmness of support, no further progress in tonal volume could be made. However, the Boston-type iron-frame instruments were sometimes criticized for giving out a nasal, thin tone, for all their volume. The Steinways were set to remedy this quality: they made use of the principle of cross-stringing, not a new idea fundamentally, since it had been thought up for little uprights as early as the 1820's. The Steinways, however, combined it with a special kind of space distribution with reference to the sounding board. They lengthened the bridge by giving it more curve and brought it further away from the rim, thus utilizing the inner portions of the sounding board to a greater extent. Moreover, they strung the strings in a fan-shaped manner, again giving their vibrations the benefit of more sounding-board area. The Steinways, furthermore, gradually increased the general tension on the frame far beyond all previously set limits. We may recall that the total tension on all the strings of a European six-octave grand piano of 1844 was 10.9 tons. Twenty years after the Steinways began their operations, they were making grands with a total tension of about 30 tons. In order to make this resistance tonally profitable, the strings had to be struck more powerfully; and with this end in view, the designers had the hammers covered with much heavier felt than had previously ever been used—making for a more massive blow upon the wires. This, in turn, necessitated some adjustments in the action—Steinways used a modification of the Erard double-escapement action—so that pianists' fingers would not be subjected to a killing strain. These improvements took some time to be developed in their totality, and it may be that the complete modern Steinway piano was not fully evolved until the 1870's.

Henry E. Steinway and the sons with whom he came to America were men of good schooling; but it is uncertain whether in their first experiments they proceeded on calculated scientific principles or whether to a large extent their work was empirical—that is to say, a playing of educated hunches. However, after the eldest son, C. F. Theodore Steinway, came from Germany to join the firm in 1865, science became the guide, since he had been a special student of physics and acoustics and was in close touch with the great physicist Hermann Helmholtz much of the time.

The end result of the Steinway effort was a tone-producing tool of matchless strength and sensitiveness. It was a structure that could withstand the most passionate punches of the most furious virtuoso. No latter-day Liszt could smash it. All the muscle of the strongest man could now be utilized for tonal expression. Moreover, the unheard-of volume was combined with a noble quality of sound: it was a sound that embodied the nineteenth century ideal to the full—rich and ringing, and wrapped in billows of overtonal fuzz, especially in the bass. It was a tone that craved to stream out of itself, to blend with all other tone, to merge ecstatically into a universal ocean of tone. It was a marvelous kind of sound for the music that people loved then: thick, thundering piles of chords, booming batteries of octaves, and headlong, sizzling double jets of arpeggios. But the single Steinway tone, struck gently and held, also worked its ineffable spell, taking an endless, yearning time to die.

The speed of the Steinways' rise was remarkable. In the early fifties, the Chickerings were at their zenith, after thirty years of work and thought. Of the country's nine thousand pianos produced in 1851, they accounted for thirteen hundred. A devastating fire burned up their plant and most of their stock in 1852, the damage amounting to $250,000. The calamity hardly diminished their momentum. With hardly a year more to live, Jonas Chickering with his sons took advantage of the cleanness of the destruction they had suffered: they set about immediately to build a brand-new, modern super-factory. Little more than a year after the fire, they had put up the largest industrial building in the United States—five stories high, its front facing Tremont Street for 275 feet, its wings on either side extending 280 feet in length and 50 feet in depth. It had built-in elevators for the normal transportation of materials and was fitted with eleven miles of steam pipes for heating. At the time it was said that this factory had the greatest cubic content of any building in the entire country except the Capitol in Washington. Jonas did not live to see it completed, but that huge complex was where his sons George and C. Frank Chickering soon were to employ five hundred workmen to turn out two thousand pianos per year.

The year of this enormous enterprise, 1853, was the very year in which the Steinways began to operate their first little shop in downtown New York. Already in 1854 their instruments won a prize at a so-called Metropolitan Fair in Washington, D. C. The following year a rather elaborate local trade fair was held in New York, at a large building called "Crystal Palace" after the famous similar one in London. A member of the jury charged with making the awards for musical instruments later described how he and his colleagues, their minds almost made up, were walking among the exhibited pianos, trying them quickly, when one of their number lifted the lid of an unpretentious, sober-looking square and played a few chords. It gave a remarkable sound; the other jurors clustered around it, and it was soon evident, without a word being spoken, that this instrument with the unfamiliar name was the best one of the exhibition. All prior predilections were cast aside, and Steinways' were given the highest award for their overstrung square, unanimously and without argument.

The victory made a sensation in its little world. In 1859 the Steinways felt encouraged to apply their new overstringing principles to grand pianos; and when these began to come forth triumphantly from their early trials in the battles of the concert halls, their eminence was assured. By then Steinway sales had already mounted to five hundred a year, and the firm began to think of building its great factory on Fourth Avenue between Fifty-second and Fifty-third Streets. Extended in 1863, it finally measured an uninterrupted 631 feet of street frontage on three sides and was six stories high, rivaling the great Chickering plant in Boston not only in size but in the modernity of its steam-driven apparatus. Production soon rose to one thousand per year and to more than two thousand by the end of the Civil War. In 1869 the new company could boast that it was the foremost in the United States, having surpassed the Chickerings both in the quantity and the total money value of its annual output. In fifteen years then, the Steinways achieved a pre-eminence that had taken the Chickerings twice that time to reach.

10. NEW YORK HEARS A GOOD DEAL OF FINE PIANO PLAYING

New York, its population well beyond the half-million mark, was teeming with concerts during the 1850's. It was as much the professional music center of the country then as it is today, perhaps even more so. High-brow German affairs—such as those put on by the Philharmonic or by the William Mason–Karl Bergmann–Theodore Thomas combination in their chamber-music series—formed only a small portion of the city's total public musical performances. Mixed instrumental and vocal concerts were the rule, featuring one headlined principal seconded by a number of assistants. The principals were sometimes foreign celebrities, hoping to make their favorite hit-and-run play upon the dollar land; sometimes they were foreign noncelebrities who hoped that a naïve America would vouchsafe them an acclaim denied them at home. Some were resident teachers trying to build up local prestige for themselves. Magniloquence was evident in some of the announcements; for many a concert could not bear to call itself merely that, but insisted on being known as a "Grand Musical Festival," or a "*Grande Soirée musicale.*" A variety of halls was available in those days, more proportionately than today: Niblo's Saloon, the Astor Place Opera House, Dodworth's Hall, Castle Garden, Tripler Hall, and some others.

A great many of the concerts involved piano playing in some prominent way. Andrew C. Minor, at the University of Michigan in 1947, industriously compiled a most instructive listing of those that included piano solos, piano concertos, and two-or-more-piano numbers, between the years 1849 and 1865. From an annual average of twenty-eight during the early fifties, these rose to forty-three in the later decade, and touched sixty-five for each of the last years of the Civil War. Despite the ubiquity of the piano and the frequency of pianists, there were as yet, before 1870, hardly any piano recitals in New York. Even the more renowned virtuosos felt the need of being relieved several times in the course of an evening and of having opportunities for making fresh entrances. The music offered was predominantly of the Paris-fashionable variety, with the virtuosos preferring to serve their own, home-brewed musical cocktails. True, Gustav Satter, a conceited Viennese, did on March 10, 1855, play Beethoven's *Emperor* Concerto with the Philharmonic Orchestra "for the first time"; whereupon the *New York Times* reviewer, a couple of days later, censured the management for not detailing one of the sixty-eight orchestra men to turn the soloist's pages. It is true, too, that Arthur Napoleon, a brilliant teen-aged Portuguese, was the one to give Beethoven's famous *Waldstein* Sonata its first public New York airing during the spring of 1859, at a nondescript "Special Sacred Concert" at Palace Garden, Fourteenth Street and Sixth Avenue. However, much more in the main swim of things was Maurice Strakosch, a showy native of Poland, who regaled his audience at the Broadway Tabernacle on September 12, 1849, with a *Fantaisie dramatique* based on tunes from *Lucia,* the "Prayer" from *Otello* "executed with the *left hand* alone," besides a nocturne called *Spring of Love,* a *Flirtation Polka,* a *California Gold Fever Galop,* and a *Fantasie Caprice on "Yankee Doodle"*—all of his own decoction. Seven years later Strakosch was still aiming to please, as widely as he might. Assisting in a concert given by the singer Teresa Parodi, he first offered *A Tempest in a Teapot* of his own; but then, according to the *New York Times,* "in response to an *encore* rather surprised, and we fear offended the audience by playing a mild fantasia on the nigger melody 'Nelly Bly.' This is trying to be a little too popular." We observe that the *Times* was less chaste in its expression than it has since become.

Louis Moreau Gottschalk came back to his native America early in 1853, to be highly appreciated there. He gave a kind of preview concert for a few artists and newspapermen on January 24 at the small Irving Hall. The *Herald* raved, saying, "He makes the keys all but speak." "Making the piano speak" was getting to be a favorite critical *cliché,* one that is not entirely obsolete to this day. It seems to be an American homologue of the French "shower of pearls." Gottschalk's true New York debut took place at Niblo's Saloon on February 11, and to that occasion he drew a good-sized high-society audience that included ex-President Martin Van Buren and his son. There was no doubt of his success, since his appeal was many-sided, personal as well as musical. Eventually he gave no fewer than ninety concerts in New York during the seven seasons that he was active there. He understood the general predilection for multiple-piano performances and almost always got another pianist to play a few pieces with him, as one of his assistant artists. Usually this was a worthy performer of lesser prestige, who could only thereby enhance the principal's glory—in the manner of a five-star general who seems even grander when flanked by an escort of three-starrers.

Gottschalk's Negroid and Creolesque pieces, such as *The Banjo* and *Bamboula,* whose piquant distinctiveness had charmed the Parisians, were likewise greatly enjoyed by Americans. However, his droopy, dreamy eyelids induced dreams in many ladies; and these lady dreams, in turn, had a vapidifying effect on his creative impulses. Instead of resolutely pushing his best line, he pleased his feminine admirers by composing a lot of pink-lemonade pieces —such, for instance, as *La Scintilla, Mazurka sentimentale.*

Gottschalk's two best-liked titles were concerned with death. Death was a highly fashionable poetic and musical essence in the mid-century. A large proportion of best-selling songs and verses in those days were about people dying, especially people whose death it was too bad to contemplate, such as children, sweethearts, young sons, or mothers. An average song of the period began by extolling the beloved creature in the first verse, then killing him or her ruthlessly by unspecified disease in the second or third. Sometimes the last stanza was a graveside lament. The customers who bought and listened to these songs were not afflicted with temperamental pessimism, nor were they in the swamps of despair, nor were they imbued with perverse morbid tastes. Not at all: Americans of the time were the most buoyant, enterprising, and hopeful people on earth. This death stuff merely represented the lunatic outskirts of the old cult of "feeling" of which seventeenth-century German Pietism was an early outcrop. Extreme displays of emotion were, for many generations, valued as vaguely divine inspirations—just as they are to this day among certain charismatic sects in their "revival" meetings. To be so full of feeling that you lose control of yourself, that you tremble or weep or faint or drop dead, was wonderful, was a blessing, a thing to live for, to boast about, to pretend to. Now, nothing is an easier incentive to strong feeling than death, especially the premature death of a loved person. Thus, the cheapest way for an author to arouse "feeling" was to kill off a child or sweetheart. Like all effective procedures, however, this soon became a formula, a habit, without which writers and readers of poems and novels, and songs, would have felt unsatisfied. We may say that unseasonable death became a commercial literary staple.

In this way we can understand why *The Dying Poet* and *Last Hope* became Gottschalk's most widely known compositions. In ladies' mythology, poets are sweet, gentle creatures—a little like children or possibly canary birds—and it is delightfully heart-rending to think of them dying. Anyway, no matter how sad, their deaths must be beautiful. On the other hand, *The Death of a Salesman,* the title of a true mid-twentieth-century tragedy, would have seemed a grotesquely improper, revoltingly comic title to the world of 1855. *The Dying Poet*'s principal melody is first stated by the right hand, in the tenor region of the keyboard, while the left hand plays a regular accompanying figure by striking one note in the bass and then crossing over the right hand to deliver two further chords in the treble. It all proceeds slowly and soulfully, and Gottschalk's languid eye coupled with his languid hand-crossing must have been truly captivating. Ladies proceeding to purchase copies of *The Dying Poet* were then glad to find that its progressions were not beyond their moderate capacities and that the piece, though irresistible, was not insuperable.

Last Hope is concerned with a certain Cuban lady's ultimate moments—so says an explanatory essay that prefaces some of the older editions. It too consists of a sweet, slow, widely ranging melody; but this one is decorated by a profusion of detached, rapid little tinkling twiddles in the high treble. Later on, longer ornamental runs and trills occur. To one of these the composer has appended the expression mark *"élégante,"* to another *"scintillante,"* and finally—toward the end—the word *"brillante."* He cannot have intended these to represent the patient making a whirlwind finish; more likely they were a way of inducing the pianist to play those very high passages with great sparkle and thus to suggest the supernal refulgence of the heavenly next world.

Last Hope was enormously successful, even though not altogether easy for average tyro fingers to negotiate convincingly. Hundreds of thousands of pianos re-echoed it for generations, and it became, throughout the United States, one of the best-known, most-played pieces of the century. The Library of Congress now possesses specimens of it in twenty-eight different editions. What with its popularity and its pious front, its naturalization by the genteeler churches was imperative. It may be found, for example, in the hymnal published in 1907 by the authority of the General Assembly of the Presbyterian Church in the United States of America, where it has been officially nicknamed, like all American hymn tunes: it is called sometimes "Gottschalk," fairly enough, and sometimes "Mercy." Several sets of words have been adapted to it. One begins "Gracious Spirit, Dove Divine, Let Thy light within me shine"; and another "Cast thy burden on the Lord, Only lean upon His word." The melody, purged of all digital dross, has had its extreme range somewhat trimmed and folded in so as to be more accessible to ordinary churchgoing voices.

By the rarefied monastic standards of latter-day high-brows, *Last Hope* ranks as trash. However, if there is value in something because it has given satisfaction to a great many people for a long time, then *Last Hope* must count as an important piece of music.

The most celebrated and probably also the ablest and most effective concert pianist to visit the United States during the 1850's was Sigismond Thalberg. He came managed by Herz's old friend and promoter Bernard Ullmann, him of the "financial music." It being eight or nine years after the days of Herz, Ullmann was now an experienced impresario and he merchandized his new piano virtuoso most successfully. In New York, Thalberg played in fifty-six concerts during two seasons, from the fall of 1856 to the winter of 1858; while during the first season he played in Philadelphia thirteen times and in Boston fifteen. At his debut at Music Hall in the last-named city, on January 3, 1857, the receipts were a decent $1200, whereas two weeks later he drew three thousand people to the same hall. Thalberg gratified his hearers with the masterfully smooth, elegant figurations that he wove around well-known melodies from *Masaniello, L'Elisir d'Amore, Don Pasquale, Moses in Egypt, Lucrezia Borgia,* and a flock of other operas, besides also impressing his viewers with his aristocratic appearance, "wonderfully like a fox hunting squire of Merrie England," said the *New York Times*. The *New York Herald* stuck to the veteran phrase and said he "made the keys speak to the audience."

Since Thalberg was such an utter, utter gentleman, Ullmann figured that he might be good for a little special snob appeal. He announced several series of *"Matinées musicales,"* in fearfully smart French, to be given at 2 P.M. in a small hall, with subscribers limited to four hundred, at $5.00 a ticket for the set of three concerts. The advertisement stated:

> Nearly nine tenths of the tickets have been subscribed for by ladies belonging to the first families in the city. In view of the responsibility thus devolved upon the management a correct address will be required from every subscriber, determination of which will insure the utmost respectability of the audience, and will be appreciated by no one more than the subscribers themselves.

It appears that Negro waiters in knee breeches served chocolate and ice cream at these affairs. The scheme worked pretty well in

New York, also in Boston, though the address-giving requirement was withdrawn there. In Philadelphia the "*Matinée*" sales languished after about one hundred subscriptions had been sold, and these concerts were abandoned.

Thalberg played a few "classics" at some of these concerts, in addition to his own specialties. Actually, there were about three of them: Chopin's Funeral March, Beethoven's so-called *Moonlight* Sonata, and a few of Mendelssohn's Songs without Words. In those days these things were not so "threshed off," in German parlance, as they became later; still, for connoisseurs, they were showing evidences of heavy usage even then.

Like other visiting virtuosos, Thalberg wrote his autograph in America's album: he composed and had published two pieces while he was there, namely a party-dress version of "Home, Sweet Home" and also one of "The Last Rose of Summer." The former tune, transposed into a romantic D-flat major, he swathed and reswathed in great streamers of tulle—that is to say, rapid filmy arpeggios of the simplest chords. Their relative speed is represented by their being notated in thirty-second and sixty-fourth notes, thus making Thalberg's "Home, Sweet Home" the inkiest-looking harmless short piece ever printed. Brilliant—to gaze upon—but not difficult. The other tune appeared with its accompanying figures in small type, lest the girls become confused.

We cannot begin to enumerate the dozens of other good pianists who let themselves be heard publicly in the New York of that time. Very few of them achieved any noteworthy success, either in the shape of paying concert engagements or of wider renown. On November 17, 1853, a Mademoiselle Gabrielle de la Motte offered Beethoven and Mendelssohn trios in the course of a program in which she also played bravura pieces. The disillusioned reviewer of the *Albion,* while admiring the pianist's abilities, considered these offerings ill-advised, saying:

> No general auditory, unless it be that of the Philharmonic or of the Eisfeld Quartettes, will without uneasiness sit through a forty-five minute performance, even of a Beethoven or Mendelssohn trio . . . It is a pity, but 'tis true that our people generally would just as soon hear one pianist as another, provided he or she has a name or reputation (honestly acquired, or fictitious, it matters but little); and they have recently had a surfeit of all kinds. We are sorry to offer so little encouragement to so meritorious a young artiste, *mais c'est la vérité.*

11. LABELS ARE MORE POWERFUL THAN MUSIC

ALL THE CONCERTS added together, lofty and shallow, spectacular and dull, with all the opera performances thrown in, did not make up a tiny segment of America's musical life, or account for more than an infinitesimal fraction of the total use to which America's pianos were being put. Only a very restricted number of people, in the United States as elsewhere, conceived of music as a fine art or as an object of absorbed scrutiny. To most it was an easy pleasure, an entertainment that would defeat its purpose if it required a serious effort of attention; moreover, it was an amusement eminently suited to the home circle and to private gatherings of friends.

Songs for a single voice, designed in a familiar rhythmic symmetry and in well-grooved harmonic successions, with piano accompaniment, made up the chief musical fare in families of middling situation of life, as they always had. In the fifties and sixties, however, the amount of songs published increased prodigiously, the stimulants to sing new ones were more frequent, and the songs themselves had greater intrinsic resource than before, especially in their words. The green Irish brought over a few of their favorite songs to be naturalized—such, for instance, as "Garyone" and "St. Patrick's Day"; however, the days of the imported English ballad were now pretty well over. No more could English tunes such as "Home, Sweet Home" or "Columbia [*née* Britannia] the Gem of the Ocean" become American folksongs. American musicians were now making up the melodies Americans liked to sing: the fifties and sixties were the days of Stephen C. Foster, Henry C. Work, George F. Root, Septimus Winner, Will S. Hays, and many another widely successful tunesmith. Those were the days in which popular American song-and-dance performers— such as Christy's Minstrels and the Hutchinson family—aroused renewing interest in new song creations. As for the texts of most of these songs, nostalgia sirup pasted up a large portion of their pages—take-me-backs and far-far-aways; and tears for dead children and dead brides—who slept in the valley or 'neath the cold gray stone—drooled over a great many more, as we have already recounted. On the other hand, a new element had also entered the American songs, that of topicality. Songs were put out dealing with all manner of current events and interests: the California trek, the Jenny Lind mania, the oil boom, the Irish immigrants, the transatlantic cable, and of course the Civil War. In particular, the temperance movement called forth much lyrical effort, and "Temperance Songs" became a separate, numerous category in the publishers' lists. A topical song carries the sting of immediacy; it is an easy kind of song to go right out and buy just after you have heard it; and it may be that the progressing success of this type of song was moved along by a cozy collusion of singers with publishers.

All that, then, was what chiefly came out of the American family squares. Nonvocal piano music also throve cheerfully, perhaps with only slightly less vigor. Most of it was dance music. Waltzes and quadrilles had flourished for a long time, and the schottische —a gavottelike duple step of moderate speed—came into vogue with little fuss. On the other hand, the polka was rather controversial when its Paris success in 1843 made it a New York "must." A Mr. Korponay, retired officer in the Hungarian army, did indeed teach it to fashionable society there in 1844, and it was soon danced with confident swank at Saratoga and Newport. Its movements were quick and jerky and required the feet occasionally to be turned in an unusual way. This was enough to make the *New York Herald* call it "indecent, immodest, and scandalous" and castigate its "low" origin. Templeton Strong—lawyer, financier, and music lover, later President of the New York Philharmonic—was no cheap moralist, still he found the polka graceless. On December 23, 1845, he noted in his diary that he had spent the evening at Mrs. Mary Jones's great ball, where the new dance was "for the first time brought under my inspection. It's a kind of insane Tartar jig performed to a disagreeable music of an uncivilized character."

Nevertheless, the cultivation of a successful foreign fanciness reflected a measure of social glory; and to have money and time to waste on farfetched trifles was a mark of superiority. So the polka stayed for a long time, diverting the best people, then the next best people, and so on down. Ultimately it seems to have merged into the two-step. Pianos, then, became cluttered gaily with sheets of polkas, added to those of the older dances. Several subspecies developed, now mere words: the "polka-redowa" and the "polka-mazurka."

The essence of each of the few current species of dance music was its meter and rhythm; all else was formula: four-measure phrases; cadences and semicadences; the use of three or four harmonies, or of one or two modulations. It was hardly possible to find specific terms appropriately to characterize each of these thousands of differently same productions. Recourse was had to wildly irrelevant, extraneous words to distinguish one of these little pieces of goods from another. Thus, the title racket burgeoned into a lush jungle. Hardly a formable image or idea existed that was not tacked onto a piece of dance music, or of any other piano music. Titles that were topical had at least some momentary social meaning, if not a musical one. The famous lady's divided garment, put forward in 1851, gave rise to a *Bloomer* Schottische and a *Bloomer* Quickstep, each with a cover prettily illustrating both the garment and the wearer. A *Gaslight* Schottische and a *Baseball* Waltz probably likewise reflected some news items of the day. We have already met the *California Gold Fever* Galop. The *Yacht America* Schottische must have helped celebrate a favorite boat of 1851. Were there mysteriously radiant nights in 1849 that prompted the *Aurora Borealis* Polka? we would need an almanach better to understand the *Eclipse* Polka of 1856; however, we could place the *Sebastopol* March out of hand with fair accuracy in the latter part of 1854.

Geographical names aroused special sympathies: a *Rochester* Schottisch naturally pleased citizens of Rochester; a *Forest City* Waltz was pointed at the residents of Cleveland; a *Staten Island* Polka-Mazurka probably found a wider market across the bay; while social climbers were assuaged with a *Saratoga Lake* Waltz. A feminine cognomen on a title page could attract families that boasted a member of the same name. Emeline, Katie, Clara, Rachel, Wanda—we need not continue: no girl was safe from having her name harnessed to a polka or a waltz. An idyllic little story could be suggested by a succession of a few polka-labels of the day. We might begin unconcernedly with *Youth, Love, and Folly* Polka, subside into *Day Dream* Polka, brighten up expectantly with *Flirtation* Polka, proceed glowingly to *Magic Spell* Polka, which leads triumphantly to *Three Bells* Polka, comes to a climax in *Matrimonial Blessings* Polka, and ends with a happy coda in *Prize Baby* Polka. Most of the above titles were published by Oliver Ditson & Co. of Boston.

Ditsons' were, indeed, the largest house in the country, and we can get an idea of the profusion of music available for home entertainment by considering one of their catalogues as described in

1867. It was a closely printed volume of 360 pages, containing the titles of no fewer than 33,000 pieces of music—all playable wholly or in part on the piano. This zealous overproduction was, of course, a requirement of the business. It was true that sometimes a piece might sell as many as 100,000 copies, but that was the saving exception that made it possible for a firm to stay alive. According to the Ditsons' own statement, not one piece in fifty was a success and not one in ten paid back the cost of getting it up. At the same time, some items in the Ditson catalogue may not have appeared at the firm's own risk. The company offered, at the time, to publish anything for anybody who would assume the cost, which they calculated thus: for engraving, $3.00 per page; for paper, $2.50 per one hundred sheets; for printing, $1.25 per one hundred pages. At that rate, anyone who wanted the Ditsons to put out a four-page piece, requiring two sheets of paper, in an edition of one thousand, would have to pay them $112. The sum was not negligible, in those days, for people in ordinary stations in life; nevertheless, it seems to have been spent occasionally by teachers in a position to bully pupils into purchases or by amateurs overcome with the vanity of seeing themselves in print.

Never underestimate the power of a label. Merchants of soap, cigarettes, refrigerators, roofing, raincoats, shoes, ships, and sealing wax now understand this very well. Music merchants understood it long ago, before the business fraternity ever made a habit of hiring advertising agents to rub their noses in it. One of the most remarkable phenomena in the history of piano music was brought to the United States toward 1860. It was a piece composed by a Polish girl named Thekla Badarzewska, a person otherwise so obscure that we know nothing of her life save that she died at the romantic age of twenty-four, of consumption, we trust. The piece was called *The Maiden's Prayer*. It is difficult to imagine any intrinsic musical reason for the invincible appeal that this composition has had, for its unquenchable persistence, bordering on immortality. To a candid listener, it seems like the work of an awkward amateur: its tune is not catchy or easily flowing, and its initial arpeggio passage would be quite inconvenient to sing or hum. The piece has no interest or grace or distinction, the vapid melody and its rudimentary harmony being repeated monotonously four times over with changes so slight they can hardly be dignified by calling them variations. Moreover, its sentimentality has no cheap vulgar lure, no slick surface prettiness; nor is the piece showy or brilliant, nor are its octaves easy to play correctly. Actually, a poorer specimen of an attempted music—in form, content, and effect—would be hard to conceive. Yet edition after edition was brought out regularly and persistently, in many parts of the world, through the nineteenth century and far into the twentieth. A Melbourne music dealer reported that he sold ten thousand copies of it in 1924. In all the years since 1860 there have been any number of glamorous operas, sparkling musical comedies, impressive concertos like those of Anton Rubinstein, touching little tone poems like those of Adolf Jensen, as well as towering stacks of amusing, lilting, stirring popular songs, waltzes, marches, and fox trots that have spun brightly and profitably around the world and then descended into the dust; while *A Maiden's Prayer*—that dowdy product of ineptitude—has outlived them all. What is the reason for this perversity? Is it that *A Maiden's Prayer* is not so much a piece of music as it is a title, an ambiguously suggestive, ticklish, perennially challenging title? Never underestimate the power of a title.

We note that in the course of generations the maiden of the famous prayer changed her appearance, judging from the cover designs. The 1860 maiden is shown kneeling before a *prie-Dieu,* with solemn upturned eyes and a cheek of the purest vanilla pudding. By 1910 the maiden has become extremely attractive; her eyes are still upturned, but she may be dreaming as well as praying, for she has no unmistakable religious apparatus and the book she is holding might be a volume of poems. The 1936 maiden is a cocktail girl, standing in a sophisticated tight-fitting, form-revealing gown, turning a pert profile and holding her palms upward in a fashion-magazine pose. The music remains unchanged always, down to the very typography, unless one counts a few fingerings and pedal markings in the 1936 edition, applied by the eminent Chicago pianist Mossaye Boguslawski.

In time the words "maiden's prayer" have taken on a proverbial kind of familiarity, with humorous overtones: for a while an eligible male, or handsome youth, was occasionally facetiously referred to as an "answer to a maiden's prayer." Little did the glib repeaters of this adolescent smartness realize how unmodern they were. There *is* a real musical answer to *A Maiden's Prayer,* composed by the original Badarzewska herself. The piece *Prayer Answered* was marketed in the United States together with the "Prayer" itself, at the same price, back in the primordial 1860's. The "Answer" is no worse music than the "Prayer"—it couldn't be—yet it made no career. An answer has no swing: it drops dead and final, destroying the prayer's delicious strain and teeter. Save the label and you save all.

In the course of a year or two, well-brought-up girls often acquired a considerable number of take-me-back, dead-sweetheart, and demon-rum songs, as well as a fair amount of polkas and waltzes together with copies of *A Maiden's Prayer* and the *Last Hope*. Scattered over the piano, they would not "look nice" (that is, tidy); and even if kept in piles on a cabinet shelf, they might develop decrepit edges that would drop paper crumbs on the floor—a troublesome business in the days before carpet sweepers. Therefore, mothers very often gathered up fifty pieces of music or so, had them trimmed even and bound together in boards in a stout volume, had the young proprietress' name stamped in gilt letters on the front, and presented the package to her for Christmas. Many of these mid-century young-lady albums are still in existence and give us a good picture of home music in the days of Abraham Lincoln.

Charles Grobe is a composer whose name frequently recurs in these books. Born in Germany, he came to America in the late 1830's and held a position for many years teaching piano at Wesleyan Female Seminary in Wilmington, Delaware. His works sound like late, faint offsets of the Herz-Hünten stamp. Many are variations on opera melodies, many are piano versions of American songs. We find Lee & Walker of Philadelphia, for instance, advertising over his name: "*Bonnie Blue Flag,* with beautiful variations," "*Glory Hallelujah,* with brilliant variations," and "*Rock beside the Sea,* with charming variations"—all in the same blurb. Grobe's writing is competent if shallow, and it is interesting to contemplate a composer so well accepted in his day who has been so thoroughly forgotten that his very name is not to be found in any modern musical reference work. By 1860 the old vogue of battle pieces seems to have subsided; still Grobe thought the old flintlock could be given a new oiling, so he and his publishers put out *The Battle of Prague* again—"revamped, remodeled, and renovated," as they said, with a few extra octaves and a number of new captions. Soon the war broke out, and Grobe responded bravely with *The Battle of Port Royal* and *The Battle of Roanoke Island: Story of an Eye Witness.* But the ammunition was stale and failed to go off, even though fortified with colored lithographs. Apparently, Grobe's productivity was prodigious, exceeding that of any known composer. The prolific Czerny reached near to Opus 1000, but one of Grobe's pieces was numbered Opus 1995. On the other hand, nothing can be as phony as an opus number.

We get some feel of the home-music atmosphere of the time by reading the little pieces of advice on good musical behavior that were published in *Harper's Magazine* for September 1851 under the heading "Mems for Musical Misses."

> Sit in a simple, graceful, unconstrained posture. Never turn up the eyes or swing about the body; the expression you mean to give . . . will never be understood by those foolish motions which are rarely resorted to but by those who do not really feel what they play. . . . However loud you wish to be, never thump. . . . Aim more at pleasing than at astonishing. . . . Be above the vulgar folly of pretending that you cannot play for dancing; for it proves only that if not disobliging, you are stupid. . . . In performing simple airs, which very few people can do fit to be listened to, study the *style* of the different nations to which the tunes belong. . . . Although you must be strictly accurate as to time . . . it should sometimes be relaxed to favor the expression of Irish and Scotch airs. . . . Never bore people with ugly music merely because it is the work of some famous composer, and do not let the pieces you perform before people not professedly scientific be too long.

The underlining of music as a bland, decorous parlor pleasure—and a corresponding antagonism to it as a fine art—is evident from the foregoing. Boring, ugly, too long music by famous composers was under other kinds of handicap. A Ditson advertisement for 1856 offers "Carry Me Home to Die" and "My Mother's Grave" for $.25 each and the *Flying Cloud* Schottische and the *Mountain Maid's* Quickstep for as little as $.10 each. But down in the lower right-hand corner, under the smallest rubric of all, we find "Beethoven's Sonatas, 2 vols. . . . each $7.50."

12. THE AMERICAN PIANO WINS OUT AT HOME, THEN CONQUERS EUROPE. HOW "RUBY" PLAYED IT

THE DECADE 1850–60 marked the domestic triumph of the American piano. Importations from England began to decline after 1830 and apparently ceased to be a factor of any importance twenty years later. There was, however, some little stir of importation of French instruments during the late forties and early fifties.

Among the New York concerts of the fifties in which any make of piano is specifically mentioned, the name of Chickering is the one most frequently met with. Chickerings were the preferred instruments for public use, justifiedly so at the time. The firm's factory was, in fact, one of the very few that made grands at all. Even so, newspaper reviews occasionally complained of thinness and insufficiency in their tone, as witness the remarks after the Jenny Lind *première*. After their great fire and reconstruction in 1852–53, the firm evidently succeeded in turning out a concert instrument capable of more powerful and prolonged sound.

De Meyer and Herz had brought French-made pianos with them when they came during the forties, but this practice was gradually seen to be futile during the fifties. Gottschalk came to New York with a Pleyel and played it for a while, but after his fifth "Musical *Soirée*" he changed to Chickering and apparently never changed back. He even took a Chickering with him when he went on a tour of South America, years later. Thalberg brought an Erard; in fact, he was said to have brought over seven of them. He probably deposited them for sale at the warerooms of C. Breusing, 701 Broadway, who was the New York agent for these French instruments. Thalberg played Erards in New York for a while; but when he went to other cities, the expense and trouble of shipping the bulky object may have induced him to take potluck and consider playing pianos available in the places where he happened to be. In Boston the Chickering company had a small hall just suited to his *"Matinées musicales,"* where he played their instruments and seems to have been thoroughly well satisfied, for he continued the practice. In Albany a large concert was gotten up on January 27, 1857, at which both Thalberg and Gottschalk played, separately and together, on two pianos from the factory of Boardman & Gray of that city. Gustave Satter—who in 1855 had given the New York *première* of Beethoven's *Concerto in E-flat* on an Erard—was glad enough, in Boston the following year, to play an instrument made by the local firm of Hallet & Davis, Chickering competitors at a considerable distance.

We first notice the name of Steinway used at the series of six chamber-music concerts organized by Theodore Thomas and William Mason, given monthly at Dodworth Hall in New York between November 1858 and May 1859. Presently it occurs at the New York Philharmonic on February 11, 1860, when soloist S. B. Mills used one of the newfangled overstrung Steinway grands to play Moscheles' *Concerto in G minor* and Chopin's Fantasy Opus 49. The *Times* was impressed and said the instrument "ceases to be a machine. It breathes into the soul of an audience and animates it with the strongest delights." We feel pretty certain that Mills used a Steinway grand when he first introduced Chopin's *Concerto in F minor* to a New York audience with the Philharmonic on November 9, 1861; and when he first presented Beethoven's *Concerto No. 4, in G major* under the same auspices on January 31, 1863, his Steinway "new scale" grand struck the *Times* "as being one of the most majestic instruments we have ever heard in the concert room. Concertos like this, and the one in f minor by Chopin . . . have new significance when interpreted by such ample means." It was the high-brows, the Germans, the chamber-music and symphony coterie—that is to say, the people who cared profoundly for music and all its developments, and who were not merely content to like it passively—who most eagerly flocked to the Steinway piano. In 1866 the Steinways spent $200,000 to build a fine concert hall in New York, seating twenty-five hundred, and the Philharmonic immediately transferred its performances to that location. Americans in general distrusted high-brows, distrusted fine arts, distrusted Germans and other foreigners; nevertheless, a steady arrogance on the part of a few outstanding musicians, a faithful pressure on the part of a larger number of lesser musicians and teachers, and the support of a few rich Yankees and Knickerbockers, all contributed to building up a formidable prestige for the new-designed piano. The name Steinway soon became synonymous with the highest excellence of piano making.

In any event, the American piano had achieved complete victory on its own ground before the beginning of the Civil War. Barring utterly insignificant exceptions, no piano of foreign make has been heard in public concerts in the United States since 1860. The importation of instruments for home use has also dwindled to a trifling trickle since that time.

The fifties also marked a very large relative increase of distribution of pianos among the American population in general. The first official national statistics of manufactures—those of 1860—give an annual production of 21,000 pianos, a rise of 12,000, or 133%, over the estimate for 1851. The population meanwhile had grown from 25,000,000 to more than 31,000,000. In other words, after nine years of Chickering and Steinway, of Gottschalk, Thalberg, and Jenny Lind, of Stephen Foster, H. C. Work, and Christy's Minstrels, one out of every 1500 persons was buying a new American piano in the course of a year—instead of the one out of 2777 who had done so previously. Or—translating the figures—after nine years, seventy rather than thirty Americans bought a new piano every working day.

Having made their position secure at home, the leading American piano makers set about the conquest of Europe. The guns of Bull Run and Shiloh did not prevent Steinways' from sending instruments for exhibition to the London fair of 1862. There they won the interest and approbation of Dr. Hanslick, the distinguished Vienna critic and musicologist, who seems to have predicted their future supremacy in the world. Reports of the remarkable new American improvements of piano construction were floating around Europe during the middle sixties, and it may have been Dr. Hanslick's article in the *Wiener Musikzeitung* that helped to induce the old-established Vienna firm of Streicher soon to alter its designs radically in the American direction.

The decisive event was the great Paris Exposition of 1867. Both Chickering and Steinway made strenuous efforts to show themselves and their products off at their best. In addition to securing favorable conditions for exhibit and performance of their instruments, their representatives in Paris tried hard to create an atmosphere of good will toward themselves. It was said that the exhibition cost each of the American firms $80,000 during a period of two months, probably for brochures, for the engaging of pianists, direct advertising, entertainment, and the judicious insinuation of favorable anecdotes and references into newspapers. All this may have been competitively necessary, as between the American firms themselves, but it probably was hardly needed to affect the result of the awards. The jury was rather distinguished: it included Dr. Hanslick again; Ambroise Thomas, director of the *Conservatoire* and eminent composer of *Mignon;* F. A. Gevaert, an esteemed Belgian composer and music theorist; and Julius Schiedmayer, a German piano manufacturer. A couple of stuffed shirts, French and English, filled out the list. There was not an American in the group, thus making the American victory even more overwhelming. Steinways' received the first gold medal for the United States, by unanimous decision of the judges. Chickerings' also received a gold medal, though it was said that two members of the jury had dissented, wishing to award them only a silver one. On the other hand, C. Frank Chickering, head of the firm, was made a Chevalier of the Legion of Honor in recognition of his achievement. News of the American successes were among the early messages to be transmitted over the new transatlantic cable; and when the report was delivered in Boston, Chickering employees declared a holiday and proceeded to parade the streets waving French and American flags.

Steinways' immediately received some eminent tribute: Hector Berlioz, great composer, often a cranky and sarcastic critic, wrote them a fine letter of appreciation, calling their instruments "magnificent" and speaking of their "beautiful and rare qualities" and their "essentially noble" sonority. Furthermore, Rossini, who had long ceased to compose operas, did a good deal of playing and writing for the piano in his old age. On hearing a Steinway, he is said to have said: "It is a nightingale cooing in a thunderstorm."

Frank Chickering was not to be left behind. He went with his lieutenant Joseph Poznanski on a fishing trip across the Alps, aiming to hook a whale of a testimonial. The two took along their well-packed fresh bait: a fine new Chickering grand. Poznanski made a successful casting: he finally got permission to set it up at the worshipful Franz Liszt's apartments in Rome. The old master swept his hand over it in some fine octaves, arpeggios, and trills. "It's lordly!" he said, grasping Chickering by both hands; "I never thought a piano could have such qualities . . . I congratulate you." He said as much in writing presently; however, when soon afterward he made the acquaintance of a Steinway, he became equally enthusiastic and wrote the Steinways an appreciation likewise. Liszt was notoriously capable of many loves.

The Paris awards were a resounding vindication of the American principles of piano construction—of the one-piece frame first practically applied by Chickering, and the later developments of stringing and scaling worked out by Steinway. The American ideas had been vaguely discussed for a while past; but after the dramatic event of 1867, it was clear that a revolution had been accomplished. All future European development would now in some degree have to follow the lines laid down by the Americans. Revolutions are easier for the young, for they are less lazy and have less to lose. The old French houses of Pleyel and Erard, which had served Chopin and Liszt so well, had now traveled a long distance away from the creativeness of their original managements. They were quite in the shade at the fair, right in their own home town, and their exhibits were arranged to be *hors concours.* Broadwood's, indeed, also received a gold medal; but that was understood to be a token of respect for their age and their past performance. The exposition clearly revealed that they, too, had been marking time. It was the new German firms—especially Bechstein of Berlin and Blüthner of Leipzig—that were best able to profit from the Steinway success. They had as yet no names to coast on and they were eager to take advantage of any new ideas that could build up their prestige. Without imitating Steinways' literally, they steered their future construction down the American path. They prospered and grew and exported their pianos; and thus American principles, at one remove, set the world's standard after a comparatively short time.

Steinways', however, were not going to wait for self-willed independent followers to profit gratuitously from Steinway achievements. Already in 1868 they were reported to have entered into negotiations with the small, enterprising French firm of Mangeot Frères in Nancy, to found an agency there for the manufacture of Steinway pianos in France. The proposed instruments were to be —had to be—sold at half the American price in view of the disparity between American and European conditions of labor, procurement of materials, and standards of living. One of the Mangeot brothers went to New York and was said to have returned with various plans, designs, and models. Somehow, nothing further seems to have resulted from this premature project. The outcome of the Franco-Prussian War soon thereafter must have put a different face on many matters. In 1877 Steinways' opened branch warerooms in London. Thus, now American pianos, the most expensive ones at that, were being exported to England, once the undisputed leader in this trade. By 1880 Steinways' had built a factory in Hamburg, to make their own instruments on European soil under their own direction, and where they could be a yardstick for the rapidly growing new German piano industry.

At home in the United States, William, the next-to-the-youngest Steinway son, had a good understanding of the inveterate ooziness of the human mind. He would not have used such a word; nevertheless, he evidently had a keen appreciation of the universal belief in contagious magic: the willingness of the mind to let anything catch anything from whatever is next to it, or sounds like it, or is mentioned in the same breath with it—the fact that everything is known not only by itself, but by the company it happens, or is allowed, or is made, to keep. To keep a great, complex factory running, its product must be constantly sold in great quantities. If the product is one of unusual excellence, such as a Steinway piano, it must be sold to large numbers of people who have no judgment of how excellent it is and little basis on which ever to form one. The consciousness of its excellence can only be established contagiously—that is, by borrowing it from some other excellence. In the case of a piano, the obvious one—of course—is a musical excellence; and thus we have piano makers trying to attach their product in one way or another to famous musicians. It was an old practice when William Steinway took it up: it was what had brought Broadwoods to Dussek, Haydn, and Beethoven; Erards to Liszt and Thalberg; and Pleyels to Chopin.

If in America the consciousness of musical excellence took a longer while to build itself up, Steinways' would give it some accelerating help. Steinway Hall could be regarded as an educational center. We have already mentioned its treaty with the Philharmonic; soon it housed the concerts of Theodore Thomas' new orchestra, and presently Steinways helped pay for the Thomas Orchestra's tour.

In June of 1872, William Steinway guaranteed a contract made in Vienna, and signed also by administrative manager Maurice Grau, by which Anton Rubinstein—the most fiery, most fabulous, and most hypnotic of living pianists, the true inheritor of Liszt's crown—was to make a tour of the United States the following season. The contract called for two hundred concerts at $200 a concert—the condition, of course, being that the artist was to play Steinway pianos exclusively. Rubinstein had heard some tales about America, not all of them false, as a result of which he insisted that he be paid in gold and also that he not be required to perform "at any establishments devoted to other than artistic purposes," meaning beer halls or cafés.

Rubinstein's first appearance was at Steinway Hall on September 23, 1872. From then on Steinways' and Grau kept him hustling. His tour became "more difficult, more unbearable every day," as he wrote. He went to Buffalo, to Cleveland, to Detroit, to Toronto and Montreal, to New Orleans, and even to Central City, Colorado, the incredible mining camp. Sometimes he played several concerts in each place, sometimes he traveled every day. Coming back to New York in January, he gave a recital that took in $3100, to the managers' astonishment, following it with a Boston recital that grossed $2600. Then he was off again, for more touring. Finally, in the middle of May, he gave seven farewell recitals in a period of nine days at Steinway Hall before sailing away. During his American stay of 239 days, he had played in 215 concerts, more than six every week.

Rubinstein was a tremendous success. His playing had a compelling power and sweep, a zeal for expression and communication, such as Americans had not yet experienced. His predecessors Herz, De Meyer, Gottschalk, and Thalberg were shallow fellows by comparison. Moreover, the Steinway instruments could take him and give him back in all his fury, without rebelling or succumbing. Furthermore, his emotional capacity was put at the service of the great music he loved, the masterpieces of the piano literature. Bach and Beethoven, Chopin and Schumann was what he played, in addition to some of his own compositions. True, he also yielded fleetingly to the performer's universal vice of effect snatching; and he too, like all the other pianists, did compose and play his variations on "Yankee Doodle." But that was an insignificant lapse. On April 25, 1873, he—together with the worthy William Mason and S. B. Mills, and supported by the Theodore Thomas Orchestra—offered J. S. Bach's concerto for three pianos to a New York audience that never before had had a similar experience. He did stir it, later in the program, with his own sizzling *Concerto in D minor*. His farewell recitals were historically grouped and included old music hardly known in America; and one recital was all Beethoven.

With Anton Rubinstein, abetted by Steinway, the age of "classics" was established in American piano concerts. Mason and Mills had preceded him in this respect, it is true, but only here and there, and with no such all-overpowering, convincing emphasis. In his way, Rubinstein made a contribution to American folklore, apart from those of his compositions that became popular. George W. Bagby, a onetime Confederate Army clerk and spare-time newspaper correspondent, invented a backwoods character "half chaw-bacon cutup, half lachrymose poet," whom he named Jud Brownin. In the seventies the author told how "Jud Brownin Hears Ruby Play," in Jud's own words:

> Well, sir, he had the blamedest, biggest catty-corneredest pianner you ever laid your eyes on—something like a distracted billiard table on three legs. . . . When he first sit down, he peered to care mighty little about playing, and wished he hadn't come. He tweedle-eedled a little on the treble, and twoodle-oodled some on the bass—just fooling and boxing the thing's jaws for being in his way. . . .
>
> But presently his hands commenced chasing one another up and down the keys, like a passel of rats scampering through a garret very swift. Parts of it was sweet, though, and reminded me of a sugar squirrel turning the wheel of a candy cage. . . .
>
> I was just about to git up and go home, being tired of that foolishness, when I heard a little bird waking up away off in the woods, and calling sleepy-like, and I looked up and see Ruby was beginning to take some interest in his business, and I sit down again.

It was the peep of day. The light come faint from the east, the breezes blowed fresh, some more birds waked up in the orchard, then some more in the trees near the house, and all begun singing together. . . . Just then the first beam of the sun fell on the garden and it teched the roses on the bushes, and the next thing it was broad day. . . . All the leaves was moving and flashing diamonds of dew, and the whole world was bright and happy as a king. . . .

And I says to my neighbor, "That's fine music, that is."

But he glared at me like he'd like to cut my throat.

By and by the wind turned. It begun to thicken up, and a kind of gray mist come over things. I got low spirited directly. Then a silver rain began to fall. . . . I could smell the wet flowers in the meadow, but the sun didn't shine, nor the birds sing, and it was a foggy day, pretty but kind of melancholy.

. . . .

All of a sudden, old Ruby changed his tune. He ripped out and he rared, he pranced and he charged like the grand entry at a circus. Peered to me that all the gaslights in the house was turned on at once, things got so bright, and I hilt up my head, ready to look any man in the face. It was a circus, and a brass band, and a big ball, all going on at the same time. . . . He set every living joint in me a-going . . . I jumped spang on to my seat, and jest hollered—

"Go it, my Rube!" . . .

With that, some several policemen run up, and I had to simmer down. . . .

He had changed his tune again. He hop-light ladies and tiptoed fine from end to end of the keyboard. He played soft and low and solemn. I heard the church bells over the hills. . . . then the music changed to water, full of feeling that couldn't be thought, and begun to drop—drip, drop . . . falling into a lake of glory.

. . . .

He stopped a moment or two to ketch breath. Then he got mad. He run his fingers through his hair, he shoved up his sleeve, he opened his coat tails a little further, he drug up his stool, he leaned over, and, sir, he jest went for that old pianner. He slapped her face . . . he pulled her nose, he pinched her ears, and he scratched her cheeks until she fairly yelled. She bellered like a bull, she bleated like a calf, she howled like a hound, she squeled like a pig, she shrieked like a rat . . . He ran a quarter stretch down the low grounds of the bass . . . through the hollows and caves of perdition. Then he fox-chased his right hand with his left till he got way out of the treble into the clouds, where the notes was finer than the points of cambric needles, and you couldn't hear nothing but the shadders of 'em.

....

By jinks, it was a mixtery! He fetched up his right wing, he fetched up his left wing, he fetched up his center, he fetched up his reserves. . . . He opened his cannon—round shot, shells, shrapnels, grape, canister, mines, and magazines—every living battery and bomb a-going at the same time. The house trembled, the lights danced, the walls shuck, the sky split, the ground rocked—heavens and earth, creation, sweet potatoes, Moses, ninepences, glory, tenpenny nails, Sampson in a 'simmon tree—Bang!!! . . .

With that bang! he lifted himself bodily into the air, and he come down with his knees, fingers, toes, elbows and his nose, striking every single solitary key on the pianner at the same time.

. . . I knowed no more that evening.

This is the authentic vein of what was once called "American humor"; and Jud Brownin was contemporary with Josh Billings, Bill Nye, Petroleum V. Nasby, Artemus Ward, and Peck's Bad Boy. The little piece was much enjoyed and repeated in its day. Its climactic development and musical subject suggested a wide pathos of delivery that "elocutionists" liked to put forth; moreover, it was not political, satirical, or controversial. Those may have been the reasons why "How Ruby Played" was a favorite recitation at Sunday-school gatherings for thirty years.

13. THE AMERICAN PIANO'S LITTLE COUNTRY COUSIN

HERE we will amplify our subject, not unreasonably, by briefly discussing the instrument that, in the United States, became the piano's important rival as a keyboard for home use. It is the instrument variously known as the reed organ, harmonium (the favored European designation), melodeon (the specifically American term), or cabinet organ. Its basic tone-producing agency consists of gusts of air forced against "reeds," or blades of metal that support freely vibrating tongues of various sizes corresponding to differing pitches. It operates on much the same principle as the accordeon; and the earlier, small, portable American specimens were made so that the player, holding the instrument upon his knees, could work the bellows with one elbow while playing the keys with both hands. Soon, however, the reeds became encased in a larger cabinet, with the player seated before it, making the wind by pumping two levers with his feet. The force of the pumping, of course, affected the volume of tone; and thus the instrument was capable of general shading, though naturally not discriminatingly so with regard to simultaneous tones. Multiple ranks of reeds could constitute stops of varying tone quality and register, analogous to those of a pipe organ.

The melodeon first began to come up in New England before 1820, at a time when progressing religious liberalism was rapidly breaking down the old objection to organs in churches and when a need was felt for more amiable, harmonious music at church services. It was the time when metrical hymns were first being widely sung and when the hymn collections of Lowell Mason and others began to be copiously distributed throughout the country. The melodeon fitted into this frame of mind: not only was it suitable for use in many smaller churches that could not afford a large organ, but it also made an appropriate little instrument for the home. There it could agreeably provoke an informal religiosity among family and friends, any evening of the week; and with it, it was possible to feel virtuous pleasantly very often.

Melodeons seem to have been fairly common in the 1840's, when an important improvement was undertaken upon them. Noting that an accordeon sounds better when drawn than when pushed, the firm of Carhart & Needham brought out a device whereby the wind was sucked across the reeds rather than driven against them. The melodeon's quality of tone was rendered smoother and finer thereby, and more people found it desirable.

It was fitting that it should have been Henry Mason—another son of Lowell, and brother of William the pianist—who, meeting Emmons Hamlin, a melodeon mechanic, at Ditson's shop in Boston in 1854, decided to form a partnership with him for the manufacture of reed organs. Thus they founded the famous firm of Mason & Hamlin, which soon became and remained the foremost in the field. In addition to simple instruments, Mason & Hamlin built some of greater complexity and multiplicity of stops, culminating in a remarkable type that they called the "Liszt organ"—not inappropriately, in view of that master's capacity for combining interest in novel tonal sensualities with his religious aspirations. By 1867 the output of American melodeon factories was about fifteen thousand per year, that is, about forty per cent of the country's piano output, Mason & Hamlin accounting for about one fourth of the total.

Socially, the domestic function of the melodeon was similar to that of the piano; yet the surroundings in which it mostly lived differed in certain shades of flavor from those usually inhabited by the hammer instrument. Little atmosphere of fashion or of showiness hovered around a melodeon, few Parisian *odeurs.* This is not to say that only hymns and sentimental songs were sung to its guidance and accompaniment. *Carhart's Melodeon Instructor,* published in 1851, contains two hundred pieces, including quite a few polkas, waltzes, marches, and simple arrangements of opera airs. Nevertheless, one feels that melodeon families were more given to singing than to dancing, that they suffered music more gladly to hum and to whine than to tinkle and to plunk. The melodeon was sold largely to the residents of smaller towns and villages, and to rural people. In European phraseology, it was a lower, rather than an upper, middle-class instrument. Its price reflected this attribution: a fairly good melodeon could be installed in a parlor for $100 at a time when a cheap piano cost close to $300.

The melodeon factories and their product moved west from their New England beginnings; and as the new lands of Indiana, Wisconsin, Michigan, and Illinois filled up, the melodeon, it was said, often was the first musical instrument to arrive. By the end of the century, Chicago was the center of the reed organ manufacturing business.

14. A WHOLE IS MADE UP OF PARTS

THE PARIS TRIUMPH of the American piano naturally aroused comment at home, as well as reflections on the instrument in general. A number of writers were deeply impressed with the degree to which the piano had become a necessary-seeming element of households. James Parton, a popular littérateur and biographer of his day, in a long article published in the *Atlantic Monthly* for July 1867, declared that "almost every couple that sets up housekeeping on a respectable scale considers a piano only less indispensable than a kitchen range." Paran Stevens, reporting for the United States Commissioners at the Paris Universal Exposition of 1867, suggested that the piano "is in some sort taking the place in our homes of the family hearth" and is regarded "almost a requisite of housekeeping."

Parton and Stevens were exaggerating: they were thinking of the "nice" people they habitually went with, and—like many such "nice" people—they habitually threw all other people away in their minds. Actually, the subsequent history of the piano is largely a record of its purchase by great numbers of not so "nice" people. For the forty-five years after the close of the Civil War, we can chronicle a prodigious rise in the density of piano distribution. In 1870 about one person out of every 1540 bought a new piano in the course of the year; by 1890 the rate had gone up to one out of 874; while in 1910 it reached one in 252—pianos having crowded themselves more than six times thicker in forty years. Or, every working day of 1870 eighty persons bought a new piano; in 1910 twelve hundred persons did so, fifteen times as many, whereas the population had multiplied itself by no more than two and one half in the meanwhile.

This all came about because the price of the cheaper pianos was lowered still further, during a period in which many necessities of life became more expensive. At the same time, wider and wider groups of less moneyed people—spurred by their admiration of those richer than themselves—were encouraged to develop aspirations and pretenses toward fancier things. The cost of producing the instrument could come down after its various parts—action, sounding board, plate, and so on—could be more efficiently manufactured in separate specialized plants, and after a number of manufacturers became willing to use poorer materials and poorer workmanship for turning out their products. Furthermore, the upright, consuming less of materials, became the standard type of home piano, gradually replacing the bulkier square. Correspondingly, improved and more widespread music education, through private teachers and in public schools, as well as improved and more frequent public musical performances in concerts and theaters, all stimulated more frequent, more earnest piano-buying impulses among the population; while piano makers and dealers prodded these vague budding urges effectively with unremitting assaults of advertising, wondrous in their variety and their impudence.

As we have shown in a previous section, the component of a

piano first produced in separate factories, as a separate business, was the action. It is easily the instrument's most complicated element, consisting of more than six thousand little individual parts and made up of a great many different materials. The delicate machines that give these parts their evenness and precision pay for themselves best when they keep working as much as possible, far beyond the requirements of most smaller individual piano makers. Action making is troublesome, and any piano manufacturer would be most easily tempted to buy this portion of his assembly ready-made from a specialist, probably better and certainly cheaper than he could make it himself.

During the 1850's reputable middling piano makers, such as Boardman & Gray of Albany and Hallet & Davis of Boston, were still making their own actions. Some makers, however, were already importing theirs from Schwander of Paris, and at least one action maker was established on American soil as early as 1851. By 1866 the action business achieved respectability within the trade and the newly organized firm of Strauch Bros. saw fit to advertise itself in print. Only a few years later three Steinway employees quit their status as hirelings and went into the action business for themselves under the firm name of Wessell, Nickel & Gross. They soon became the largest in the field.

In the 1870's the parts-business breeze was blowing up fast and strong. About 1874 we find B. N. Smith & Co. established at Eleventh Avenue and Twenty-first Street, New York, devoting themselves exclusively to the shaping of piano legs. Two years later they were reported to be employing fifty experienced carvers and their capacity was stated to be two hundred sets of these fat, frilly supports per week. At that early time they claimed there were scarcely six makers—out of the eighty-odd throughout the country—to whom they were not furnishing the means of standing their pianos up. In 1880 B. N. Smith & Co., overrun with demands for their legs, were employing seventy-five men, could employ twenty-five more carvers if they could get them, and were using two specially designed carving machines. They were also beginning to make piano cases and were filling a single order for one thousand of them. At that same moment Behr & Peck, eight blocks further uptown on Eleventh Avenue, were employing one hundred and thirty men to make one hundred and forty cases a week for the trade. Moreover, ivory slicing, trimming, and beveling came to be a full-time specialty; and an expert estimate for 1880 stated that not more than half a dozen manufacturers were supplying the keys for all the pianos and organs made in the country.

When the full one-piece iron frame and the newer principles of stringing and scaling were generally adopted, it was seen that unusual demands were thereby made on the quality and the tensile strength of the metal employed. The smaller piano makers soon felt that the techniques of meeting these requirements were beyond their capacities and realized that they had to turn elsewhere for this element of their product. Thus, the casting of iron frames for pianos became a specialty of certain foundries. The earliest important one was that of Thomas Shriver & Co., which seems to have had little competition for some time after the Civil War. During the 1880's, however, the frame business became large enough to support a number of different firms. Of these the most notable was Davenport & Treacy, which, beginning in a small way in 1884, were able to report in 1890 that in their foundry and machine works at Stamford, Connecticut, they had made plates for sixteen thousand pianos—almost one quarter of the country's entire output—in the course of the previous year.

The most interesting and most extensive American piano-supply business, as it was called, was the great one built up by Alfred Dolge. He, too, was an emigrant from Germany and was first apprenticed to the Mathushek Piano Co. during the later sixties. Presently he became interested in felt and went into business for himself in this commodity. He was drawn into it, no doubt, because his employer, Frederick Mathushek, had been one of the two earliest American patentees of a machine for covering complete sets of piano hammers with felt in one operation. A German of Breslau had thought up such a device as early as the 1830's, when felt itself was a novelty; but possibly it was a vague lingering prejudice against machinery that prevented Europeans from adopting it until the success of the American pianos in 1867 swept many old notions away. Before a sheet of felt can be used in a hammer-covering machine, it must be tapered: that is, its thickness must be carefully graduated from one side to the other so that the bass hammers can receive a thicker covering, in the right proportion, than those intended to hit the treble strings. Until Dolge's day, this tapering was done by hand, to suit the whims of different piano makers. Dolge started his own factory in 1871 and first made his mark by the fine quality of his felts, which he was even able to sell in Europe. Soon he attracted special notice by inventing a process whereby the wool for his felt was fed into the cards in a way calculated to produce sheets of a correct standard thickness and taper from the outset. The Dolge process was able to turn out six full sheets of tapered felt in one operation, sufficient for one hundred sets of hammers.

Dolge had placed his factory in the village of Brockett's Bridge, Herkimer County, New York, where there was an excellent water supply for felt manufacture and where the nearness of the Adirondack forests formed an additional factor in his plans. Soon Dolge, with his profits, acquired large holdings of timberlands as well as sawmills, and we see him shortly in the business of piano lumber. Up until his time, according to his own account, raw lumber had been shipped to manufacturers straight from the sawmill, with knots and other imperfections, so that a maker of pianos could hardly utilize more than forty per cent of what he bought. Dolge went into the manufacture of ready-made sounding boards, which he sold to the piano maker, letting the latter season them at his discretion. His specialization again allowed him to use certain elaborate gluing and planing machines profitably. His cylinder planer with knives five feet wide, he said, enabled two men to plane three hundred sounding boards in the course of one ten-hour day, whereas the best workman using hand planes could not finish more than ten boards a day.

Dolge's own published statements reveal the growth of his operations. He began making sounding boards in 1876, turning out 260 during the year. In 1878 he shipped more than 9000 of them. The following year, 1879, must have been a critical one in the piano-supply business, for Dolge's production of ready-made sounding boards multiplied by four during the twelve months, reaching the extraordinary figure of 37,690. In 1880 it increased still further, to 41,585. Some of Dolge's products went to Canadian manufacturers, but the proportion must have been small. If we deduct these and reflect that the total piano output of the United States was no more than 45,000 at the time, we must then conclude that all except two or three of the largest piano makers in the entire country had decided, within a couple of years, to buy their sounding boards from Dolge. That same year, he estimated, he was furnishing the felt for about two out of every three pianos made in the United States.

Alfred Dolge's activities had, naturally, transformed the community of Brockett's Bridge, since the prodigious increase in its population and its wealth was mostly owing to him and his works. At some time during the eighties the grateful town council decided to change the place's name officially to Dolgeville, and it has been called that ever since, to the present day. Dolge was a remarkable man who managed to maintain, at least ideally, something of the craftsman's devotion to quality, as well as an appreciation of music, while at the same time developing his great capacity for imaginative, far-reaching business enterprise. He must have been painfully impressed with the numerous strikes and other labor troubles that he had witnessed in New York piano factories; and when he himself became a large employer, he instituted a liberal profit-sharing system, noteworthy for its time, with the people who worked for him. It is sad to have to report that eventually Dolge overextended his interests, especially in connection with a railroad built near his properties, and that some shrewd local schemers were then able to oust him from his business, shortly before the close of the century.

Meanwhile the American piano-making industry had become, to a greater or lesser degree, an assembly of separately, independently made parts. As early as 1880 Steinway & Sons advertised in a trade paper that they were "the only manufacturers who make every part of their pianofortes—including the casting of the full iron frames—in their manufactories." They continued making this claim for decades; it was never challenged as long as it was made.

15. PIANOS—AND STENCILS —FOR "THE PEOPLE"

WHEN THE YOUNG PIANIST Richard Hoffman, fresh off the boat from England in 1847, was taken to the Chickering factory, Jonas Chickering greeted him with his apron on and his tools in his hand. The man who had become the head of the largest company of its kind in the country had not therefore ceased to be a manual craftsman. This was likewise true of Henry E. Steinway and of many other successful piano makers of the time. Into their positions as executives these men brought with them the craftsman's devotion to workmanship, his happiness in knowing that he has used his own hands to do a fine job to which he is proud to affix his own name for all to read. We may say that many of the leading piano makers tended frequently to be more interested in their product than in their business. We can understand that some of them were inclined to yield reluctantly to the noticeable trend of making piano parts in specialized factories.

It was in the nature of the case that a pure businessman, one unhindered by any paralyzing artistic considerations, should first take fuller advantage of the newly forming situation. Joseph P. Hale was a canny Yankee from Worcester, Massachusetts, who had made himself a workable little capital of about $35,000 by peddling cheap crockery, probably eking it out with a few real estate deals. His mind was a complete blank on the subject of music and on the acoustical theories of piano making, but he saw that the piano business had possibilities of extension far beyond the notions of some of those soggy Dutchmen in New York.

Hale proceeded to take the piano apart, element by element, with the one thought of calculating how it could be produced more cheaply. He began by buying an interest in a smaller factory, then withdrew to start a small shop of his own on Canal and Hudson Streets, New York, as early as 1860. His precise transactions are hard to follow at this date; but it appears that he was soon able to buy some sort of cases, keys, actions, plates, legs, and so on at rock-bottom prices from specialists by paying spot cash on delivery. Moreover, he was able to organize his process of assembly more efficiently than had been done previously, thus making substantial savings on labor. Concentrating on the intrinsically cheaper uprights, he was able to turn out an instrument that, as the quantity of his dealings increased, could be sold at one half or one third the price asked by a maker of high-grade pianos and still make a good profit.

But Hale's sales methods were even more startling in their day. He discarded the prevalent practice of disposing of pianos through a system of agents, with exclusive rights to sell a given make within a given territory. On the contrary, Hale sold to anybody—private individual, dealer or jobber anywhere—who paid him. The notion of an exclusive agency is bound up with that of the prestige of a name—the association of the name with a peculiar, individual quality of excellence or serviceability, real or fancied. There can be no point to an exclusive agency for just another potato or pocket comb. Hale had no personal interest in his product and did not care whether his name was on it or not, as long as his bills were met promptly. But the public at large, especially its more ignorant sections, felt vaguely that a piano was something special, something exceptional that could not be thought of anonymously with the unconcern with which one regarded, say, a kitchen chair.

Somehow, the simplest customers needed some anchor of association, some suggestive name with a ring to it, to justify their choice of a dynamic, expensive piece of furniture such as a piano. Hale's own name was far from glamorous, as he knew, and he thought that putting it on the pianos he sold to competing dealers would only create confusion and clashing among them. Therefore, he started the stencil system—a practice that disturbed the minds of the piano trade for a generation. Under this scheme, Hale put any name on a piano's fall board that was desired by the customer. Dealers and jobbers forwarded their own stencils with their orders.

Thus, to invent a fictitious example—not therefore untrue in principle—let us suppose the thriving middle-sized town of Zoab, or Franklinsburg, in North-Southern Ohio, harbored two music stores: that of Hezekiah Hitchcock, and that of Benno Bimmelgieser & Son. Each would buy the same piano from Joseph P. Hale, differing possibly in the color of the varnish or in some detail of the leg carving; one, however, would have "Hitchcock" and the other "Bimmelgieser & Son" in gilt letters on the name board. Hitchcock, on the corner of Main Street and Broadway, would ask $350 for it, while Bimmelgieser & Son, housed in less glittering real estate, would sell it for $250 and still make a profit, since Hale sold these instruments indiscrimately for $160. Hitchcock's customers would be glad to pay the extra $100, feeling somehow that his nobler name and location were bound to make the piano better suited to their parlors. Or we can picture the hustling piano jobbers Twiddle & Bangs of Wampum City, the metropolis of Pennsyltucky. After making a reputation by selling Hale's pianos under their own stencil to small towns and villages, Twiddle & Bangs might want to clear out some remaining stock at a much lower price without injuring the prestige of "their" product. They might then sell the same old Hale pianos at a reduction of fifty per cent, but restenciled "Washington" or "Mozart" or "Rip van Winkle."

Stenciling was legal, but it could sometimes be used in attempts to circumvent the law. Leaving invented examples aside, the Canadian tariff schedule specified a valuation for Hale pianos that Hale tried to have lowered. Conniving with a Canadian dealer, he stenciled the strange name of "Thalberg" on a shipment of his instruments. The ultimate buyer, he figured, might recognize the name of the famous pianist and be attracted by that association, whereas an ignorant customs official might well imagine "Thalberg" to be a new and unfamiliar piano manufacturer and would then accept the Canadian dealer's low valuation.

The stencil had some imaginative variations: in deepest Georgia, during the seventies, some customers apparently could be less charmed with a name than with a term of endearment; thus, Hale's pianos—or those of his imitators—were sold there labeled "Southern Gem," "Parlor Gem," or "Conservatory." Hale and his fellow stencilers did not have much respect for names; nevertheless, they and their dealer-customers understood that the names of the makers of high-quality pianos were known, foggily, in quite remote circles. The population, like all populations, being mostly semi-literate, smart peddlers could often get away with stenciling on pianos a name that was similar to, but not quite identical with, that of a highly reputed manufacturer. Consequently, we find "Stein*m*ay," "Stannay," "Shumway," "Steinmetz," and "Stanley & Sons" on some of these bastard instruments; also "Pickering" and "Web*b*er" (for Weber); while the name of Decker Bros., an estimable New York house, was sometimes altered to "Decker and Bro." The trick often worked, among the rather large class of people who at the same time know nothing about a piano, cannot spell, and think they can get something for nothing.

Hale rose to prosperity rather rapidly. According to his own account, he soon moved away from his Canal Street beginnings and—with the Civil War and the New York draft riots raging about him—succeeded in raising his annual production to about five hundred pianos within five years. Thereupon he put up two five-story buildings near Thirty-fifth Street and Tenth Avenue, which gave him a capacity of twenty to twenty-four pianos per week. During 1869 his sales amounted to $207,000, ranking him seventh in dollar volume of business among the country's twenty-six leading manufacturers. Only Steinway, Chickering, Knabe, Haines Brothers, William P. Emerson, and Weber were ahead of him. The following year he further enlarged his premises with an eight-story building, and spread out again in 1872. By 1876 he was expanding once more; and presently he succeeded in assembling and selling over five thousand pianos a year—more than any other manufacturer—and accounting for about one eighth of the country's total output.

Hale's methods naturally aroused fierce antagonism, especially on the part of the older manufacturers of high-grade instruments. The *Music Trade Review* went on a kind of crusade against him, talking of his "bogus" pianos, caricaturing him in word and image. Hale was inclined to disregard the attacks on him; he did, however, once launch into self-defense in a long letter, dated December 17, 1875, New York, which the *Cincinnati Times* undertook to publish. The prices charged by the leading older firms, he asserted, were "disproportionate, fictitious, and fanciful" in relation to the real cost of the instruments. He spoke of the "indirect, circuitous, and irrelevant ways in the current routine of sales" practiced by those houses—by which presumably he meant the agency system, the extension of credit to dealers, the commissions and discounts given to teachers, and the paying of concert pianists. He also held the great firms guilty of an "enormous multiplication of manufacturing outlay." Either the whole thing is a humbug, he said, "or else . . . the monopoly of the piano by the upper ten thousand was a fraud on the lower ten millions." He claimed he had done the nation a vast service by contriving, through his computations and his unconventional methods of marketing, to build a piano just as good as the best, "in form, mechanical construction, component material . . . perfection of tone, and in the great matter of durability," at one third the price. His pianos had the same ash, maple, and rosewood as the others, he maintained, the same pins and strings, and "nine tenths of the component parts from the same hands at the same cost." Again he assailed "the enchantment or the tyranny of prestige and reputation."

Hale was pushing his hot-air pump a little hard when he said his pianos contained the same materials as the quality instruments, or when he boasted of their durability; moreover, he refrained from talking about workmanship. His enemies used to say that the best material in his pianos was brass. Still, when he said that his instruments were as good as the best, he was, in his way, almost sincere. For a man who knows and cares nothing about music, the nobility of quality of a Steinway tone—and its exquisite responsiveness to the smallest changes of finger impulse—mean nothing. He might honestly consider all talk about such things as the hallucinations of a music-deranged brain. His pianos had all the parts of any other pianos, therefore they must be just as good. Besides, it was quite true that some of the famed glamour-firms were, indeed, now buying some of their parts from the very people who sold to Hale.

Hale did, in fact, perform a valuable service by producing a playable piano at a price that multitudes of people could afford. If he was not able to tell the difference in tone between one of his instruments and a Steinway, or if he did not care about tone to begin with—why neither did hundreds of thousands of his potential customers. Although Hale's pianos were no great works of art, they were better than the pianists who were to play them—

or the music they were destined to bring forth. If Hale did not achieve the glory with his cheap product that Henry Ford did with his, forty years later, it was because of the stencil monkey-business, which deprived him of publicity while it also aroused an ethical revulsion against him. Still, he was not entirely to blame for that racket; for it was inherent in the very nature of the piano and of what it meant to its customers. In the 1870's a piano's value was almost entirely imponderable and its buyers, with few exceptions, needed to feel that its label lived up to their pretense in regard to it. Better for them a piano with the fairy slogan "King David," or "Parlor Favorite"—or with the sign of a well-known store fronted by a big sheet of plate glass—than one carrying the muggy name of a notorious cheap-John. It was a credit to Hale that he actually did consider altering his policy and putting his own name on his pianos. He promised to do so in his letter to the *Cincinnati Times,* but somehow it seems to have been too late for the reform.

The stencil corruption continued to exert its unholy attraction. It was one thing for dealers who made no pretense of manufacturing to put their stencils on a Hale piano; and little harm was done when small or marginal manufacturers, making an indifferent product, gave up their factories to sell Hale pianos under their own names. However, the stories would not down that some of the big boys, or near-big boys, were being seduced by the quick lures of the cheap piano trade. There were persistent rumors about Albert Weber, for instance. He was the winner of a high award at the Philadelphia Centennial Exposition and was a resolute promoter of fine concerts; nevertheless, it was said that some of his cheaper pianos were really Hale instruments with a Weber stencil. The same suggestion was made about the Chickerings. Perhaps it came from malicious competitors or disgruntled employees. The fact would be hard to prove now. The temptation would certainly be very great to sell a name expensively—without the quality that created it—to people who did not know any better. It is true, in any case, since after the days of Hale, that makers of expensive, high-grade instruments have also put out cheaper pianos under another label, registered as a trade-mark. The situation during the seventies, eighties, and nineties was confused—with some "makers" not manufacturing pianos at all, some cheap makers buying all parts prefabricated, quality makers buying some parts prefabricated from the same factories as the cheap makers, and only Steinways making everything themselves.

In time Joseph P. Hale made more money than any other piano

manufacturer of his day, but he also developed rivals in low-cost production who finally outstripped him. He died some time before 1891.

The stencil practice is another phase of the label racket that we have discussed previously, in other connections. It is no mere small abuse, one that a little righteous reform could cure. It springs from a fundamental quality of the human mind itself. Without labels, we could not deal with things; yet labels are futile attempts to establish fixities in a world in which all things flow. Sooner or later all labels, titles, names, and symbols become false and make idolaters of us.

16. PIANO FIRMS PLAY VIRTUOSOS, AND CONVERSELY

THE ASSOCIATION for mutual aid between piano manufacturers and concert pianists continued vigorously. The booming success of the Rubinstein-Steinway combination put spurs into the Chickerings: they too now had to have a fabulous virtuoso to rub off some of his fabulousness onto their product. They persuaded Hans von Bülow to play Chickering pianos exclusively on his forthcoming American tour, of which the bustling Ullmann again was the manager. The pianist was at the height of his artistic fame, also at the height of his scandalous prominence in connection with his marital affairs. He might well have posed appealingly as an injured hero whose wife, the daughter of the awesome Liszt, had been snatched from him by that unconscionable tonal and moral anarchist Richard Wagner. It was good "publicity"; but he hated reading it in a New York paper, and the incident provoked another of his many sneers.

Bülow made his American debut, as an exception to the rule, in Boston, the home of the Chickerings; and that was the occasion on which Americans first heard Tchaikovsky's new *Concerto in B-flat minor,* a composition that they have since taken generously to their bosoms. The Chickerings were building a new home, in New York—new warerooms at Fifth Avenue and Eighteenth Street, with a fine, new, elegant concert hall attached—and Bülow was appointed as the housewarmer on November 18, 1875, together with an orchestra conducted by Dr. Leopold Damrosch, in a program entirely devoted to Beethoven. Less than twenty years before, the great Thalberg had impressed American audiences almost exclusively with his own operatic fantasies; but now the Germans had created a new atmosphere, the electrical Rubinstein had ionized it, and great authentic piano literature was the fare expected from loudly heralded foreign virtuosos.

Bülow led off with great éclat, taking in $6000 during his first week of four concerts. But alas, the Germans also helped his undoing. He was frail, intellectual, quick-tempered, and arrogant; and the type of Germans he saw in America, drinking beer and getting blearily sentimental in their singing meets, did not please him. He made some sarcastic remarks, which were printed in an interview in the *New York Sun*. After that he lost a rather numerous group of supporters. In Baltimore he developed a spasm of pure-mindedness. At a rehearsal with an orchestra he spied the large gilt-lettered sign saying "CHICKERING" that had been hung on the side of his piano, facing the audience. He took it off, threw it on the floor, looked at it malevolently, and said furiously for all to hear: "I am not a traveling advertisement!" Presently, in an intermission, he picked up the offending piece of wood, hooked it on the tail end of the piano, and proceeded to give it a poke with his foot. Kicking his patron and collaborator Chickering in the behind, publicly, was not likely to gain him friends, even among disinterested parties. (Incidentally, hanging out a large sign that announced the make of piano became a standard American concert practice until the 1920's.) Bülow's audiences began to fall off in many places. Nevertheless, he kept on with his tour for a number of months, though he did finally give up after completing 139 of his scheduled 172 concerts. In part, he was a failure: his nature never could allow his playing to work up the intoxicating sweep of Rubinstein. Still, he afforded many music lovers rich experience of piano masterpieces they had never heard before and he inspired many an eager young musician with his impassionedly analytical performances of Haydn and Bach, Beethoven and Chopin—thus furthering the cause of great music throughout the country.

Another Chickering artist, in his early career, was Rafael Joseffy, an elegant, attractive young pianist—and a particularly delicious pianissimist—who came from Central Europe to make his debut at Chickering Hall in 1879. A great success, he decided to make New

York his home; but after living there for a while, he switched to the Steinway piano.

After that time, the Chickering management seemed to lose its grip. C. Frank Chickering, its head, moved to New York, forsaking the Boston that had nurtured his family and their works. Once he had been a piano designer; now he bought a Fifth Avenue residence, became a society man and clubman, and indulged other expensive tastes. The name of Chickering had weight, and its momentum rolled up large sales, especially in newer western regions; but fewer and fewer artists became interested in playing this piano. When Frank Chickering died in 1891, the firm was seen to be in severe financial trouble, despite its fair volume of business, and it required a thoroughgoing reorganization. Never did it regain its former prestige. Chickering Hall was sold in 1900; and the firm that had aroused Liszt's delighted enthusiasm and had helped Bülow bring Opus 111 to life, was now ignominiously boasting that it had sold a piano to Lillian Russell!

It had to be a large firm, with loose money to play with, one that catered to the quality trade—that is, to people who likewise had money to throw away—that could afford to go in for artist-concert-testimonial advertising, or that could profit therefrom. Albert Weber, a restless business mind, was the head of such a firm and was determined to sit in with Steinway and Chickering in that expensive game. He died prematurely in 1879, but his son carried on the father's plans. Weber junior backed a tour made by Constantin Sternberg—a pianist of good, though not scintillating, European reputation—hoping that the public imagination would blow him up iridescently long before his circuit of one hundred guaranteed concerts was completed. Somehow, this pianist's inflationary capacity was not high; but he remained in America, becoming a highly respected teacher in Philadelphia. His touring companion, the violinist August Wilhelmj, made a shorter but more reverberant success. Weber also induced Teresa Carreño—flashing, black-eyed, South American beauty as well as vigorously vivacious pianist—to play his piano. Like Liszt, she had a large and hasty heart: she rejoiced in the fascinations of three or four successive husbands and was impelled, as a pianist, to turn from Weber to Steinway and then to Everett in search of happiness and cash. Weber, having tried men and women, began to think of children. Eleven-year-old Josef Hofmann, already an extraordinary manipulator of the keyboard, amazed and delighted thousands of Americans during his first tour in 1887–1888; and it was on a Weber piano that his elders made him play so many concerts that year as to give anxiety to the Society for the Prevention of Cruelty to Children. But Hofmann, too, soon switched to Steinways, never to depart.

Albert Weber, Jr., like other makers, was often willing to hitch his box to a star of lesser luminosity. For instance, in 1880 he got Oscar M. Newell, a worthy New York pianist, to play recitals on his piano every evening for two months at the National Academy of Design and also at the principal Saratoga hotels during the season. He saw to it, moreover, that the pits of principal New York theaters were provided with Weber pianos and that the fact was conspicuously stated in the programs. At the Philadelphia Centennial in 1876 almost all the larger piano manufacturers hired reputable American-resident pianists as jockeys to trot out their exhibits. John Nelson Pattison, a greatly proficient Thalberg pupil, rode Webers; the estimable Frederick Boscovitz showed off the Steinway points; Charles Jarvis, one of Philadelphia's most memorizing musicians, displayed those of Chickering; while Decker Bros. used a lady rider, Miss Julie Rivé, soon to blossom as Madame Rivé-King.

The old-established firm of William Knabe & Co. also got into the concert business prominently. Well settled in Baltimore as early as 1837, the house became the leading piano maker for Southern customers. In 1864 it was easy for the directors to guess how the war was going to turn out, and they proceeded to open spacious warerooms in New York City. Prospering substantially, they too felt in time that their excellent instruments deserved to be perfumed with the incense that was being wafted to the higher musical art. In 1889 they supported Bülow on his later, much more successful, tour; while in the spring of 1891 they helped largely to defray the expense of bringing Tchaikovsky to New York, so that he might enhance the dedicatory concerts at the opening of Carnegie Hall with his services as a conductor. In return, the great composer bore pen-and-ink witness to the Knabe pianos' "rare sympathetic and noble tone color, and perfect action." Fifteen years later the Knabes paid liberally to let American music lovers see and hear the eminent composer Saint-Saëns, and to read the name of Knabe on his programs.

The most flaming pianistic glory in America's history broke out when the Steinways first put forth Ignace Paderewski in the autumn of 1891. He was, indeed, a performer of very high ability, an artist of unusual expressive powers; yet that was only one element of his peculiar appeal. His total personality was just what, in the American idea, a concert pianist's ought to be, if one were to marvel at him and respect him at the same time. His chrysanthemum of pale red hair, the feminine dreaminess and brooding of his look coupled with his aggressive solid muscularity—all this was strange and might have seemed ridiculous to Philistines. But the reserve of his bearing, the hypnotic deliberateness and lordly courtesy of his movements, were the signs of a profound inner dignity, before which a measure of awe could not fail to be felt. He seemed, verily, the prince of a foreign realm. No pianist has ever captured the American imagination as he did, keeping his hold over it for thirty years. He became a legend: his mispronounced name drew farmers from their barns, schoolboys from their baseball, real estate speculators from their offices—all manner of unlikely persons from their dens—into a concert hall to have a look and a listen at him. Paderewski played Steinway pianos first and also last; but in the middle years a quarrel with a member of the firm drove him for a while before the keyboard of another make of instrument.

From the piano manufacturers' point of view, the greatest difficulty in tying themselves up with concert virtuosos was that of keeping the creatures from straying. Any season one of those mercurial people might become broke or disgruntled, have an attack of swelled-headedness, peevishness, greed, envy, or softheartedness, and go off and play a competitor's instrument and write him a testimonial that in some measure lessened the value of the one written previously.

In the older days William Steinway was rather generous with musicians, especially those estimable ones who did not enjoy the most superstitious and pecunious kind of fame. For example, he was happy to give S. B. Mills, afore-mentioned, one piano for his home and another for his studio, knowing that Mills really preferred to play Steinway pianos and always chose them for important concerts, such as solo appearances with the New York Philharmonic. Mr. Steinway closed an eye when, in the fall of 1876, Mills accepted an engagement from a Mr. Hamilton, a piano dealer in Pittsburgh and agent there for the Decker Bros. pianos, to play two recitals at a local exposition for $239. (The $39 probably represented railroad and hotel expenses.) Mills naturally played the Decker piano at those occasions and was willing to give Hamilton a testimonial; but the Pittsburgh Steinway agent, inflamed with competitive ill will, published the fact that Mills was a Steinway man and had, in writing, considered the Steinway the best of pianos. An unpleasant situation occurred, which was aired in the *Music Trade Review*. It appeared that although Steinway was the choice of Mr. Mills's heart, he had in the past—glad of a few paying engagements—also written love letters to Decker, Knabe, Bradbury, and Weber. The Steinways wrote to the *Music Trade Review,* full of kindly sympathy for Mr. Mills, saying that he always used their pianos when he had his choice but that they understood that, for money, he would have to play others once in a while. The letter goes on with some patronizing remarks about a piano manufacturer "of limited reputation, who has no other chance of having his grand pianos played in public by a first-class artist, except by paying the compensation out of his own pocket." Just a little supercilious on the part of the Steinways, and not quite consistent, considering all the money they guaranteed Rubinstein.

When the piano makers paid artists to play their instruments, they did so, of course, as a matter of advertisement—since their ultimate aim was greater prestige and, therefore, greater sales and profits for themselves. A quip made at the time was certainly true: "Instead of saying 'Herr Wischer uses the Hammerschlag piano,' the announcement ought to read 'The Hammerschlag Piano Co. uses Herr Wischer.' "

On the other hand, the piano makers, at their risk, thereby afforded many people outstanding musical experiences that they could not otherwise have had; and by presenting such figures as Rubinstein, Bülow, Tchaikovsky, and Paderewski in person, they kindled musical enthusiasm and idealism throughout the country. Indeed, the great American piano manufacturers were a type of latter-day music patron, toward whom devotees of great music ought to have a feeling of gratitude. That they were animated also by self-interest does not lessen the credit due them. The old-world music patrons were likewise animated by self-interest, let us not forget. When European potentates, from Louis XIV and Duke Esterházy down, surrounded themselves with artistic genius, they did so partially for the enhancement of their own glory; and this imponderable prestige again was of help to them subtly, in making advantageous personal connections, raising funds for special projects, or forming favorable matrimonial alliances. Thanks, then, to Messrs. Steinway, Chickering, Weber, and Knabe—and later to Mason & Hamlin and Baldwin—for their share in our present musical awareness.

17. MANY AMERICANS STUDY PIANO MORE SERIOUSLY. SOME BECOME HADJIS, AND SOME DO GYMNASTICS

IN EVERY SIZABLE American city the mid-century German musicians persisted in their missionary work and soon converted many an exceptional American of the older stock to the enjoyment of the greater instrumental literature, to the gospel according to Saints Beethoven and Mozart and Saints Schumann, Chopin, and Mendelssohn. After the Civil War, numerous serious schools of music were founded, many of which have persisted to this day. In 1865 the Oberlin Conservatory was established, while in the same year Clara Baur founded the Cincinnati Conservatory of Music. Florenz Ziegfeld started Chicago Musical College two years later, while Robert Goldbeck began his Chicago Conservatory at about the same time. The New England Conservatory also dates from that period, while the Zeckwer-Hahn Conservatory of Philadelphia opened its doors only shortly thereafter. These schools are well known. But it may surprise some persons to be informed that the Iowa State Normal Academy of Music, teaching harmony and composition in addition to piano, organ, and violin, was established in Iowa City, sixty miles west of the Mississippi, as early as 1866; or that, the following year, a Western Normal Academy of Music offered eight annual terms of music instruction at three different smaller places—namely, Akron, Ohio, Adrian, Michigan, and Aurora, Illinois. William S. B. Mathews, a prominent music educator, found this institution an early field for his activities.

Clearly, a small but persistent, convinced minority of Americans were turning to instrumental music as an art. During the summer of 1871, for example, citizens of the small town of Binghamton, New York, were pleased to attend a series of five piano recitals, with accompanying lectures, by William Mason, in which he played some of the *Novelettes* and *Fantasiestücke* by Schumann and the *Etudes* and *Polonaises* by Chopin, besides Beethoven's *Sonata in E minor,* Opus 90, and the *Sonata in C major,* Opus 2 No. 3. In all this sprouting interest, the trans-Allegheny population was not backward; in fact, we might say it was relatively more eager than the inhabitants of the eastern seaboard.

Mason had been a rare specimen of his kind when he went to study music in Europe in 1849; more Americans, however, followed his example after 1860. It seemed a far adventure in those days and conferred a sort of hallowed distinction upon him who undertook it, as if he were a hadji among Moslems. By 1871 we read of American music teachers "going to Germany merely for a name." Amy Fay, a young native of Mississippi who had come East early, arrived in Berlin, a lone girl with no German, in November 1869. Her pianistic talents were positive, if moderate; and during the next six years she found herself taking piano lessons from Louis Ehlert, Carl Tausig, Theodor Kullak, as well as the less known Ludwig Deppe. Finally she had the opportunity of attending Liszt's classes in Weimar. While abroad, she described her experiences to her family in many letters full of vivid critical observations and easy warm enthusiasms—naïve and keen at the same time. Although extravagantly impressed with the wonderful music and musicians she encountered in Germany, she never went native but always retained her American sense of values.

When Miss Fay's letters were published in book form in 1881, under the title of *Music Study in Germany,* they aroused fellow ardors in unnumbered musically apt American girls. The volume went through twenty editions before 1912 and undoubtedly was influential in helping to propel a steady stream of music students across the Atlantic. In the fall of 1888 a correspondent of the *New York Sun* was astonished at the hundreds of earnest American "ladies" working at music in Berlin. Two years later the pianist Eugen d'Albert was quoted as estimating that twenty per cent of the concert audiences in any German city consisted of Americans; while New York's *Musical Courier* for November 25, 1891, assessed the American population of Berlin at two thousand, almost all music students. We will state confidently that the females were in the majority among them and that students of the piano outnumbered all other music students several times over. That same volume of the *Musical Courier* carried regular advertisements of German music schools in every issue: the conservatories of Leipzig, Dresden, Hamburg, Weimar, and Sondershausen all considered it profitable to take regular substantial space in this

American journal. After Paderewski's dizzy success, many talented Americans, in the spell of the same old contagious magic, flocked to Vienna hoping to snatch a few lessons from Theodor Leschetitsky, Paderewski's last teacher.

With all this flurry of higher music education on both sides of the ocean, it was only to be expected that a certain number of highly proficient native American pianists would develop. So they did, indeed. We have mentioned John N. Pattison, Charles H. Jarvis, and Julie Rivé-King. Presently there appeared William H. Sherwood, A. Victor Benham, and Fannie Bloomfield-Zeisler, the last brought to America from Central Europe as an infant. Mrs. King and Mrs. Zeisler did well, the former playing in about four thousand performances in the course of her career and the latter becoming a long successful, favorite concert artist. The men, however, had less appeal: somehow, the ancient established English equation of performing instrumentalist with foreignness thrust itself with invincible persistence into latter-day America, despite all growth of music appreciation. The American musicians were admired judiciously by those qualified to appreciate them; but they had no swing, no flash, they stirred no drunken thoughts. Some of Paderewski's charm seemed to reside in the fact that he was Polish. Years before his time, Amy Fay, in Berlin, had developed a little "crush" on the good-looking, young, German-born Xaver Scharwenka—partly because she thought he was Polish. "And indeed," prattled the usually sensible Amy:

> there *is* something interesting and romantic about being a Pole. The very name conjures up thoughts of revolutions, conspiracies, bloody executions, masked balls, and, *of course,* grace, wit and beauty!—I find myself looking at him and saying to myself with a certain degree of satisfaction: "He is a Pole." Why I should have this feeling I know not, but I seem to be proud of knowing Poles.

At that rate, the Pattisons and Sherwoods were at a disadvantage, for they were more likely to make the girls think of house agents or soap salesmen. It is too bad those pianists could not have had their revenge by living into an age when —owski names are just as likely to suggest coal miners or delicatessen storekeepers.

The Germans, too, found it disagreeable to think of American musical artists. Somehow, the concepts "musician" and "America" were paired in a profound incongruity in their minds. Miss Fay tells that Kullak was perpetually seasoning his adverse criticisms with sarcastic remarks about Americans, even though, she claimed, some of his more talented students came from the United States. It was probably not a congenital nastiness on the European's part; but he simply could not bear the thought of an American musician: it was a Mona Lisa's mustache to him. No mere fact, or evidence of his own senses, could destroy such a powerful preconception.

We can get an idea of the amount of piano study going on in the country toward the end of the 1880's by putting together a few not entirely unreasonable statistical guesses. The Music Teachers' National Association, founded in 1876 for its members' mutual support and improvement, held its annual convention in 1887 in Indianapolis. At that occasion a spokesman for the association publicly offered the informed estimate that there were 500,000 piano pupils in the United States at that moment. It is not an overwhelmingly large figure. The population of the country at that time was 60,000,000, of which about one third, or 20,000,000, was within the piano-lesson age-bracket—that is, between seven and twenty. At that rate, only about one youngster in every forty was taking piano lessons. We might guess at the number of pianos then in existence in the country: if we assume, perhaps rather generously, that all the instruments made during the preceding thirty years were in playable condition at the moment, that would give us an approximate figure of 800,000. If we multiply the number of current piano pupils by two or three (to account for those who had "taken" but had since discontinued) and if we also remember that the same family instrument was likely to be belabored by several different persons, we can conclude vaguely that about eight per cent of the nation's youth was playing the piano after some fashion, while still providing for a considerable number of completely idle instruments.

In any event, piano dabbling was far from universal, even though members of well-regulated family groups in cities, associating with each other exclusively, might have said in their fatuous way that "everybody" took piano lessons. There were, indeed, vast segments of the population—subsistence farmers, agricultural laborers, Southern Negroes, hillbillies, factory workers, mariners', fishermen's, and loggers' families, and hordes of city workers in service occupations—to whom a piano and its use were foreign. The piano was much bought and drummed; but it was not in 1887, nor did it ever afterward become, a possession of the "masses"—to use the blasphemous word with which many present-day writers enjoy referring to their fellow humans.

The greatly increased interest in the higher artistic developments of music gave those who offered to teach them an occasion for raising their prices. W. Eugene Thayer, a well-known Boston and New York organist, writing in *The Etude* for May 1889, said that the best teachers in those cities were now charging from four to six dollars per hour, American teachers thus now having advanced to a fee equal to that received regularly by Clementi and Cramer in London nearly a century earlier. On the other hand, the demand for "name" lessons had become so great during the last quarter of the century that it was generally found profitable to reduce their duration from the long traditional hour to a half hour.

Once Americans had set their minds on anything—say, the achievement of piano technique—it was impossible for them not to believe that the use of some kind of metallic mechanism would benefit it. The multiplication of advertisements for gymnastic apparatus for piano practice reveals the earnestness with which music study was pursued in the United States during the late 1880's. Theodore Presser, the editor of *The Etude,* put out a contraption having the old purpose of imprisoning the hands in a "correct" position. It forced the wrist into a vise and each finger into a tight ring supported from a set of metal rods curving over them. The picture of it looks terrifying, like a little ancient rack with multiple thumbscrews. Presser appropriated Henri Herz's old, forgotten name of fifty years previous and called his torture instrument "Dactylion"—price $3.50. F. L. Becker, a New York piano teacher, got out a contrivance "for the development of technique," which he described somewhat incompletely as "an apparatus of five keys with adjustable touch . . . combining . . . the greatest number of gymnastic appliances 'directly' useful to the hands of pianists . . ." He gave it the name of "Manumoneon," babbling and learned-sounding at the same time—price $10. On the other hand, C. H. Bidwell of 145 West Sixty-first Street, New York, thought up a modest "Pocket Hand Exerciser"—cheaply made with finger loops and rubber bands, and supported from the floor by means of a foot stirrup. Its stated aim was "to prepare the hands for the keyboard."

A particularly pretentious, elaborate-looking construction was put out for sale by one J. Brotherhood, who called it the "Technicon"—$22.50 in black walnut, $27.00 in mahogany. It was a wondrous complex of rollers, springs, levers, screws, and counterweights, plus a cushioned inclined plane to use as an elbow rest. The idea was to exercise the lifting and pushing power of all the muscles of the hand individually and consciously, against specially contrived resistances, so as "to concentrate the mental powers upon separate muscular details," something which ordinary practice at the piano fails to permit. His point seemed to be, in other words, that playing the music itself gets in the way of the finger exercise. A mere simple pianist could not be expected to understand the Technicon's maze of parts and functions unaided; accordingly, Mr. Brotherhood also offered an explanatory pamphlet to use with his machine—price $.75, to teachers $.50. The Brotherhood Technicon continued to be advertised for ten years or more, a fact that speaks for some success on its part. Its acceptance illustrated one direction that the musical ambition of many students took during the latter end of the century.

The most successful, and actually the best, of all the piano-practicing aids was the one brought out by A. K. Virgil; he called it the "Practice Clavier." It seems to have been a development of a rather smaller earlier device known as the "Digitorium." The Virgil Practice Clavier was a small box on a stand, fronted with a complete keyboard. It was first advertised as a "silent piano," but that description failed to do it justice. It was not a piano; and its virtue was that it was *not* silent, but that each key when fairly and firmly struck gave a click and also, if a certain lever were thrown in, a different kind of click when completely released. On the real piano, the easy musical sweep of a rapid arpeggio or scale passage might readily seduce a quick-fingered student into failing to give each of its component notes its proper force or even into leaving some of them entirely unstruck, thus producing a slovenly effect. On the Clavier, the telltale click, or its absence, having no relation to musical semantics, would inform him absolutely whether he had made his key stroke properly or not, thus inducing him to use more detailed care in his work. Moreover, the Clavier was useful in learning to play legato. If the back-click of one key could be made to synchronize exactly with the direct click of the next, it was certain that the sounds of the two keys had been connected cleanly, without either a gap or an overlap between them. Furthermore, the Clavier had an apparatus whereby—by turning the spokes of a small knob—the resistant weight of each key used could be increased or diminished, in a range of from two to twenty ounces per key. At that rate, a student able to play through an exercise cleanly and fluently at six ounces might find himself missing a number of clicks when the weight was raised to ten or twelve. Thus, it was a useful device for measuring the acquired growth of finger strength.

The Virgil Clavier was comparatively expensive, a full seven-octave model being priced at $60 in 1889; nevertheless, it found many takers. Piano virtuosos and teachers of great repute, such as Moriz Rosenthal, William Mason, and Rafael Joseffy, endorsed it sincerely, and it spread to a considerable vogue in the music profession between the years 1888 and 1913. Aftei that the naïve zeal for "technique" as a separate aim in itself—especially the striving for fleetness of finger articulation—seems to have subsided, and interest in the Clavier drooped along with it. It is interesting to contemplate the musical trend of which the rise and fall of the Clavier was a symptom.

18. LIGHT GOOD MUSIC—BETTER LIGHT MUSIC

As THE NINETEENTH CENTURY went into its last decade, the better-schooled girls among those who learned the piano for "accomplishment's" sake became less inclined to moon over the uneventful insipidities of the *Last Hope, A Maiden's Prayer,* or Lefébure-Wély's cognate *Monastery Bells.* After the ministrations of two generations of teachers of the German stripe, they were quite likely to beguile themselves with Chopin's *Nocturne in E-flat* or his so-called *Minute* Waltz, with Schumann's *Träumerei* or *Warum,* with Mendelssohn's *Spring Song* or *Spinning Song,* or with an arrangement of Schubert's "Serenade"; and they might occasionally even risk blunting themselves against the unladylike rigors and vigors of the first movement of Beethoven's *Pathétique* Sonata.

Even more probably, they would play certain favored pieces by respectable composers then thought modern. Anton Rubinstein, for instance, was regarded importantly as a creator in those days; and if the most splendid virtuosos chose to display themselves in his *Concerto in D minor,* why, tasteful young ladies were safe in indulging in his *Kamennoi Ostrow* and his *Melody in F.* The nonsense syllables of the former title (they make sense, of course, in incomprehensible Russian) helped render the piece easy to ask for in a music store; whereas the latter composition achieved the crowning American success of having words fitted to it and sung in elementary-school assemblies. Xaver Scharwenka composed quite a number of rather piquant Polish dances, but it was only the one in the somber key of E-flat minor, leading off with undifficult heavy chords, that captured the girls. Edvard Grieg's melodious, lyrical pieces—short and not strenuous—began to be seen as plausible fare for young ladies. Their occasional tangy harmony drew attention away from the flimsiness of their structure; on the other hand, the cut-and-dried symmetry and recurrence of their phrases gave them the advantage of being easy to learn. *Papillons,* one of the best, was a great favorite; likewise *To Spring* and *Albumleaf.* All this was curiously termed "classical" music.

There was, however, another kind of piece especially favored by the generation of 1890 to 1914, which evolved along a certain line from the mid-nineteenth century *salon-* or parlor-piece—but with somewhat altered ethical and aesthetic import. We refer to the compositions of Cécile Chaminade, Eduard Schütt, Maurice Moszkowski, and Benjamin Godard. The parlor pets of the 1860's were of the *adagio* type, their sentimentality tinged with an air of solemnity. Death and religion were frequently the subjects of their titles, and they gave forth a pretense of a heavy emotion that tried to believe in itself. The 1895 music played around with much the same chord succession, much the same harmonic texture; yet it was in a definitely lighter vein, its sentiment flirtatious, its gait and rhythm quicker. It took itself less seriously, and the pieces came rather closer to a *scherzo* type. Compare the languishing expression suitable to *The Dying Poet,* or to Leybach's Fifth Nocturne, with the euphoric little smile that naturally accompanies Chaminade's *The Flatterer,* or Schütt's *A la bien-aimée,* or Moszkowski's *Serenade.* Death and religion had lost their appeal as dainty refreshments for the drawing room, and in their places we have a *Scarf* Dance, a *Juggleress, Au Matin,* and quantities of fake Spanish dances.

Not that the older, more viscous, sentimentalism was extinct during the nineties. In 1893 there appeared a piece called *Hearts and Flowers,* published as the work of Theodore Moses-Tobani, a New York theater musician—though some persons have cast doubt on its ostensible paternity. By 1913 the tune appeared in what was called "Million Edition," which we presume to mean that a million copies had been sold in the course of twenty years. *Hearts and Flowers* is not a bad tune of its kind and has an affinity with one of Dvorak's *Slavonic* Dances; still, it seems to have no intrinsic quality that would call forth such long-term affection.

This seems to be another case of a triumphant title dragging a few notes behind it.

One indubitable American, a native of Pittsburgh, became an important supplier of young-lady music: his name was Ethelbert Nevin. His little set of five pieces called *Water Scenes* came out in 1891, in a highly feminine rig, with a pale-green cover and notes printed in smaller, daintier type-faces than were customary. The requirements of *Dragon Fly, Water Nymphs, and Barcarolle* were too nimble for most girlish fingers, while *Ophelia,* slow and low, failed to stir. But ah! number four, labeled *Narcissus,* set a quick fire. It too had the light, swinging amble that best expressed the mood of the time; moreover, it specified much hand-crossing, facile and fascinating. Nevin's publishers continued to emphasize the visual appeal of his works. His customers, however, being mostly carriage trade, could not be convinced by too garish an offering. A blank magenta-purple wrapper with silver lettering proved to be just right for the four-piece package called *A Day in Venice,* which appeared in 1898. On opening the book, the ladies found that free doilies were given away with each piece: there were two supernumerary pages—a few short verses of poetry glided about easily on the otherwise empty paper to the left, while the right was occupied with pale-chaste sepia drawings of carvels, gondolas, and lovers. For a decade or more *A Day in Venice* was amply represented in the parlors of the better neighborhoods.

This pretty turn-of-the-century parlor music may be judged an improvement over that of the previous generation. Certainly, it was put together with more skill and had more wit and grace. Nevertheless, it involved an element of decadence. The worship of "feeling," dominant for more than a century, was now subsiding. People no longer believed in pretenses to overpowering emotions. Swooning had gone out of fashion—that is to say, no one any longer found it praiseworthy to seem to have such capacity for "feeling" as to lose control of her senses. To anguish and languish, to rant and pant—all this was beginning to seem overwrought. The lightheartedness was a sign of skepticism, of a faith on the wane—a faith in foolishness, perhaps, but still faith. The way was paved for the cynicism of the generation to follow.

We hardly need to repeat, again, that all the parlor pieces and all the "classical" music added together and multiplied many times over did not equal the quantity, distribution, and frequency of vocal music, especially of songs for a single voice with piano accompaniment. In these productions, too, a distinct trend can be seen through the 1870's, '80's, and '90's, one that we might call a progressive plebeianization. Possibly it is more evident from the songs' words than from their tunes. The older ones that saw the light of print were largely of the sentimental ballad type and their language was, approximately, "correct" English, which occasionally even solemnized itself with conventionally "poetic" thees and thys, as well as word inversions. Minstrel and Negroid songs were indeed plentiful, but they were placed in an inferior category of their own. They were enjoyed in relaxed situations, but banished from occasions requiring best behavior. No lady or gentleman could seriously act or talk like a laborer, an immigrant, or a Negro. Stephen Foster allowed some of his best songs to be first published under the name of E. P. Christy, not wishing to make an off-color reputation as a specific composer of "Ethiopian melodies." It is curious to look through a publisher's list of the 1850's and find certain titles bearing after them the warning "comic" in parentheses. As the century went forward, song texts increasingly were set in the common manner of speech. "I Dream of Jeanie with the Light Brown Hair" was a fair parlor expression of amorous yearning in the 1850's; but in 1902 millions of people were mouthing "Bedelia, I'd Like to Steal Ya" unaffectedly, without stopping to call it "comic."

Not only the accent and the syntax—but the affective atmosphere of the lyrics—underwent a change. "Silver Threads Among the Gold" (from the early 1870's) and "Put on Your Old Gray Bonnet" (from the early 1900's) both deal with the same long-lived uxoriousness; yet it is not hard to appreciate the difference between the sticky, teary flavor of one and the pert, laughing mood of the other expression of the identical sentiment. Musically, too, a change developed, especially in movement: the older songs were slower, with less emphasis of beat, while the later ones were brisk, despite their verses' tender protestations, and were suitable for dancing as well as singing. The change was gradual, of course, and involved no sudden revolution, though it seems to have become accelerated in the nineties. As late as 1906 many people could still sing, with a straight face:

> I care not for the stars that shine,
> I dare not hope to e'er be thine,
> I only know I love you,
> Love me, and the world is mine.

The newer, gayer, quicker, more vulgar songs were marketed in special ways, largely through the agency of the rising vaudeville shows, which had their center in New York. The hits among them achieved sales that were enormous by any previous standards. "Silver Threads" may have sold a million copies during twenty-five years, but many of the newer songs arrived at an equal figure within eighteen months.

The new development of popular songs had its relationship to the piano: for one little thing, it was the piano that gave it a name. The publishers of these plebeian ditties coagulated in a certain neighborhood of New York's theater district. Their premises were liberally equipped with rather battered uprights, on which hopeful songs were fashioned, mended, and tried out all day long. The aggregate noise may have been notable, for the neighborhood got to be known as Tin Pan Alley. The words soon became the generic term for the entire popular-song business. In the social history of the piano, it is indeed a fact of importance that these common racy songs were all published with piano accompaniment as a matter of course. It meant that the millions of their purchasers, who talked these songs' language, were now assumed unquestioningly to have pianos in their homes. Tin Pan Alley songs, like their predecessors the minstrel and coon songs, were not welcomed in all families with equal eagerness. Even in 1900, "nice" girls were not supposed to use "slang" or even to understand it too surely—"slang" being a humiliating term used to designate the habitual speech of the lower classes. But the pressure from below was steady and wide, and hard to resist. Daughters of the gentry often went to the public schools, where they learned things they did not hear at home; their brothers, less socially reclusive, were even less unwilling to say the vulgar phrases and sing the tunes that eased them out. After a time, Tin Pan Alley—with its slick lurid front covers, its "vamp till ready," its "verse" and "chorus"—invaded many a well-bred parlor and there buried *A Day in Venice* and *Kamennoi Ostrow* under its sheer quantity right on top of the piano.

In the field of musical comedy or light opera, the United States of the 1900's still depended on London and Vienna for some of its best productions. A number of the most popular and most lasting successes, such as *Floradora, The Merry Widow,* and *The Chocolate Soldier,* were importations. The European pieces, however, now had to compete hard with excellent American-made shows, such as the earlier ones of George M. Cohan and Victor Herbert. Inevitably and promptly, the best show tunes, native and foreign, found their way to the home pianos. Musical comedy "numbers" were usually printed on more expensive paper, and in better type, than ordinary Tin Pan Alley songs, and they were looked upon as forming a sort of "quality grade" of popular music. Complete piano-vocal scores of entire musical comedies were also published and sold to many persons for home use.

The earliest auditorium devoted entirely to motion pictures was opened in Pittsburgh in 1905 and was called "Nickelodeon" in honor of the lowly admission fee that it charged. The lively shadows that were displayed there and in similar establishments soon seemed to crave some kind of audible accompaniment; and while the little theaters proceeded to multiply and to raise their admission to as high as twenty-five cents, it was generally a piano and a pianist that supplied this necessary sound. During the following years the motion picture business grew fabulously rich and pretentious, and for a time it went so far as to lavish symphonic ensembles and great, gaudy organs upon the larger city theaters; however, all along, in smaller communities and in multitudes of smaller houses, during twenty years, it chiefly was a jaded female beating a scarred upright whose duty it was to scare away the ghostly silence that otherwise enveloped the screen.

Other homely public places were now furnished with pianos as a matter of course. By 1900 they had pretty generally been introduced into urban public schools, there to encourage the children into assembly with the *Washington Post* March as well as to provide a bass and guide-rail for the National Anthem. Ten-cent stores had sheet-music counters in those days, dealing pretty exclusively in Tin Pan Alley products. Some of them installed a piano as a sales-hormone, hiring a pianist salesgirl to try over catchy titles and thereby hearten the teetering customer who could not hear the notes in his mind's ear. Meanwhile, other nearby customers—shopping for ribbons, candy, or hairpins—were made happier by hearing the little tinkle.

During those years 1895 to 1914, and perhaps a little later, informal home gatherings of adolescents were most likely to cluster around the piano. Usually it was a girl who played; but both boys and girls sang lustily, all the way from "Who Threw the Overalls in Mrs. Murphy's Chowder," "I Don't Want to Play in Your Yard," and "I Guess I'll Have to Telegraph My Baby," through "Whistling Rufus," "Under the Bamboo Tree," and "Everybody Works but Father," down to "I Wonder Who's Kissing Her Now" and "Alexander's Ragtime Band"—together with a thousand songs more, new every few weeks. Parodies were improvised and sporadic dancing engaged in, while silly-clever remarks and gestures sprinkled the air. This was the American heyday of the piano—the time when the instrument was most useful, most esteemed, and when it gave the most substantial pleasure of which it was capable to the greatest number of people.

19. THE KEYBOARDS GO WEST

THE EXTENT to which the piano was considered a household staple can be seen from an item in the *New York Times* from May 1891. Goaded by the persistent demand for steam heating, gas ranges, iceboxes, and other things called "modern improvements" on the part of prospective tenants, "a young Napoleon in flat architecture" thought up a novel attraction for his newly erected row of apartments on the West Side of Harlem. Into the wall of every one of his forty-eight parlors he built a good, strong upright piano, "just as other landlords build hat racks in the hall and china closets in the dining room." The idea did not spread, but its emergence was symptomatic.

Actually, most of the enormous expansion of the American piano market took place between 1890 and 1910. From 1870 to 1890 pianos multiplied only 1.6 times as fast as the population. But they increased more than 5.6 times as rapidly between 1890 and 1900, and from 1900 to 1910 the rate of piano increase was 6.2 times as high as that of human beings. New firms, naturally, accounted for much of the new production.

In the earlier days almost all the piano factories were located in the Boston, New York, and Baltimore areas. But by 1890 numbers of smaller plants were to be found in small inland cities: Auburn, Waterloo, and Jamestown, New York—in addition to Buffalo—all harbored piano factories in that year; so did Erie, Pennsylvania, Norwalk, Ohio, Richmond, Indiana, Grand Rapids, Michigan, and Rockford, Illinois. By 1893 one was being discussed for Sioux City, Iowa. It was the region of the Great Lakes and the Mississippi Valley that was growing the most rapidly, and that was where pianos were being sold most briskly.

The organ business likewise boomed while developing westward: for a time that instrument's intrinsically lower price allowed it to be sold rather more readily than a piano. According to a credible trade estimate of 1880, the average price paid for a piano that year was $200 and that for a melodeon $70, with the latter outnumbering the former by seven to four in the year's total output. General "rationalization" of organ manufacture, similar to that applied to the piano, succeeded in reducing the cost to an astonishing figure. In 1880 it was possible for one firm—not a very reputable one, it is true—to advertise a "$75 melodeon for $28."

Undoubtedly, the great center of the instrument trade—away from the Atlantic coast—was Chicago. William Wallace Kimball, an enterprising New Englander, decided to settle there during the 1850's, when it was a small city with an incalculably expectant future, and set himself up as a retail dealer in pianos and organs. In particular, he made profitable connections with Joseph P. Hale of New York and did a large business selling the latter's cheaply made wares under various stencils. Soon Chicago became the largest community beyond the Alleghenies, and the W. W. Kimball Co., growing with it, became a huge piano and organ jobber over a vast area—the largest in the so-called West. During the third quarter of the century, the exploitation of its wonderfully fertile soil and the building up of good means of transportation had raised up a substantial body of well-to-do farmers in the region. Prosperity made them self-confident: they knew they were as good as anybody, and some of them might be willing to buy a piano, or at least an organ, to prove it. A man likely to persuade them was Edwin S. Conway, W. W. Kimball's chief lieutenant and himself a person of rural Midwestern origin who understood his customers *ab intra.* He built up a great selling organization, inducing merchants in small Indiana and Wisconsin, Illinois and Iowa communities to take Kimball instruments on consignment. In many cases, the piano or organ was literally "brought to" the farmers by being peddled to them from a dray.

A Kimball salesman, writing in 1880, said that he had sold their instruments for fourteen years all over the "West" and that the name of Kimball was as familiar there as that of Grant. A vogue had sprung up at that time for a style of organ cabinet, built up high with wooden columns, up-pointing knobs, and shelves. "Three fourths of the buyers," said our salesman, "want a top that towers high above all the bedsteads in the country, and scarcely ever question the inside." It may be that the high-pointed melodeon structure gave a pleasantly appropriate ecclesiastical suggestion. Here and there at the time, upright pianos were also known to be made with an extra ornamental shelf above the top, handy for bric-a-bac. Incidentally, it may have been in those years too that a particular way of saying the word "piano" became customary in the Great Central Plain. To this day, in that section of the country, one often hears it pronounced "pie-anna."

Chicago went through an astounding development during the twenty years after its great fire of 1871: it more than tripled in population, and quadrupled, quintupled, and octupled in various forms of wealth and means of communication. By the early 1880's Kimball was ready to do away with the expense of hauling his instruments from the East. The capital, the labor, and the facilities for material procurement were now effectively available to him for starting his own manufacture on a large scale right in Chicago, so as to supply the great selling organization he had already built up. Kimball concentrated on the production of cheap, quick-selling instruments, both organs and pianos; and after a time he made all the parts of his pianos—cases, plates, actions, and keys—in his own factories. Ultimately he became, in the number of complete units put out, the largest piano manufacturer in the world.

Unlike the piano factories, when the organ factories also moved to Illinois and other points in the "West," they all but deserted the Atlantic coast. Apparently, Eastern organ business was relatively declining. Mason & Hamlin of Boston, leading makers of cabinet organs, felt the need of developing another line of industry—in view of the trend—and decided to embark on the manufacture of high-grade pianos. Their first uprights came out in 1882; and when their careful efforts went into the construction of grands, they succeeded in producing instruments of a rare quality of tone, with a treble of a remarkable femininely poignant, sustained sweetness. The unusual character of the Mason & Hamlin grands was duly recognized by musicians, and for the first quarter of the twentieth century they became the Steinways' closest rivals in the true preferences of concert artists. They were never turned out in large quantities; and during the fifty years in which the company made pianos as an independent concern, its total output did not much exceed thirty-five thousand, an average of seven hundred per year.

20. MARKET SCREAMING—WITH COUNTERPOINT, IMITATION, AND VARIATIONS

In 1865 the Chickerings' huge factory was driven by a 120-horsepower steam engine, Steinways' great Fourth Avenue plant had a 50-horsepower engine housed in a separate building to heat forty thousand feet of pipes, while the somewhat smaller factory of the Haines Brothers likewise turned out its thousand annual medium-priced squares by means of a 40-horsepower steam apparatus. Those expensive, fiery machines would only produce goods profitably if they were kept working all the time. At a distance they might resemble benevolent slaves, but at close range they became rapacious dictators. The directors of an undertaking that depended upon them had to worry away their nights to be sure the monsters always had enough to chug on, lest they eat the business' head off. The lathes and belts and mechanical saws must keep turning; and, therefore, customers had perpetually to keep acquiring their products. Innocent, susceptible people had constantly to be nudged and prodded into buying the factories' output, so as to insure that the engines would stay happy and solvent. All the manufacturers felt the same pressure, and each one's pressure added to that of all the others. Beset by their own machines and their overhead—and by that of their competitors—all the piano makers anxiously advertised their wares in print, most especially in publications such as theater programs, among whose readers the potential customers came the thickest.

Advertising copy is among the world's most instructive literature; and it reveals most, not about the advertisers, but about the minds of the readers to whom their appeals are addressed. It would seem that Americans worshiped their Constitutional principle of majority rule with consuming fervor, even in nonpolitical situations. Else why should each piano maker have been so eager to suggest that his particular brand had found the greatest number of takers? In a Boston program book called *The Opera Box,* dated January 9, 1873, four different makers attack the audience on separate pages. Chickerings' bark assertively that forty-one thousand of their pianos have been made and sold since 1823. Quite a reassuringly large army to join, they would imply. Steinways' utter a couple of snappier yaps from their platform page: *"One piano every working hour!! Ten pianos every day!!"* Haines' produce a loud high note in their turn: "Largest manufacturers of square pianofortes in the U.S. . . . As a proof we are now producing forty pianos per week." On the conspicuous back page, Weber lets out a longer but somewhat ambiguous yowl: "The sale of the *Weber pianofortes* has increased in four years 368 per cent, as per Internal Revenue returns, while the other leading Pianoforte Houses have increased by 20 to 25 per cent." So, quantity was the most important of all considerations: you could only be right if you agreed with hordes of others, and the only safe conveyance was a band wagon. To this day, the "fastest-selling" article— or "the one most people buy"—is still considered supremely desirable. At least, that is what many advertising men think people think.

Some years later, however, the Steinways must have felt that this boast of sheer muchness was rather incompatible with their rightful claims to a distinctive excellence of product. After they opened their London warerooms in the later 1870's, many high-society British persons found it proper to become their customers. Those people too traveled in herds, if not in hordes. Moreover, the Steinways' German origin was no detriment to the preferences of a court and an aristocracy that were connected with Germany in many intimate ways. A royal warrant dated May 29, 1890, appointed Steinway & Sons Piano Manufacturers to Her Majesty the Queen of England, the illustrious Victoria. Other royal warrants, issued shortly thereafter, similarly favored the Steinways as purveyors to the Prince and the Princess of Wales.

On the fourteenth of October 1891, Steinways' bought a large double-page advertisement in the *Musical Courier* announcing the above honors. It was a stupefying display, on special glazed paper, in purple and gold inks. The lower half of the legend was taken up with a suffocating list of 174 Steinway patrons, almost all belonging to the British or English-resident foreign nobility. The names were arranged in their correct order of precedence—heading off with five dukes and duchesses; continuing with twenty seven earls and countesses, nine marquesses, and marchionesses, descending thence to fifteen lords and barons, nine viscountesses, fifty-seven simple "Ladies," fourteen mere "Sirs," and thirteen paltry "Honorables"; and listing toward the end ten generals. admirals, and colonels. A few plebeian but learned-sounding institutions were allowed to parade in the lower echelons—for in stance, "The Principal of Brasenose, Oxford" and the "Oxford Musical Union." In the case, however, of the "Royal Amateur Orchestra Society," the advertisement is careful to append "Duke of Edinburgh, President." Two rudely jarring names occur near the very end: Agatha Gröndahl-Backer, and C. Villiers Stanford—the former a pianist, the latter a composer. What? Musicians? Outrageous!! Who let that rabble in?

After recovering from one's daze at perusing the above-mentioned document, one can begin to savor the overtone melody that it sings. "You too," it runs, "can be a duke—well, not quite, really. But you can acquire a tinge of the celestial dukishness by buying the same brand of piano as did His Grace. Then you can use its keyboard to play 'Nearer, My Lord, to Thee.' "

The snaky jungle of the human mind brought forth some curious piano-advertising iconography. In the later nineteenth century a widely used device for attracting favorable attention to a manufactured article was a picture of the factory in which it was made. Publications were filled with designs of large, rectangular, densely fenestrated buildings equipped with enormous, towering, fuming chimneys and shown with teeming horsecars and drays plying before their façades. One might wonder what in such an image would help induce anyone to buy a piano. The thought seems to have been: this is our great, bustling, whirring, hammering place; all this buzz means we are a success: buy our piano (or suspender buckle or hair tonic) and you, too, will partake of the same foaming wine of success.

Another lure to buying was a portrait of the proprietor. During the 1870's and 1880's he would be likely to look severe, conservative, and framed in heavy whiskers. Again, the idea was: you can be safe in buying something made by such a solid-looking citizen; moreover, by acquiring his product you will acquire some of his virtuousness. The most famous advertising portraits now remembered are those of the Smith Brothers decorating the boxes of the cough drops that bear their name. Piano advertisements almost achieved their own Smith Brothers, failing by a mere degree of consanguinity. An old firm of piano makers known as Bradbury later came into the hands of a Mr. Freeborn Garretson Smith, who carried on the business together with his son. During the 1890's one could observe Bradbury & Co. advertisements showing the conventional picture of a factory, with two medallion inserts bearing the bearded effigies of two Smiths—not brothers, alas, but merely senior and junior.

Americans have long tended to feel that mechanical ingenuity is the key to the conquest of the universe. With enough of that new thaumatite metal and that new lunium gas—and plenty of cams, brads, sockets, sprockets, and jockets—you might build a turbo-encabulator that could bore a glorious hole right through the middle of the earth. Many persons could find it plausible to think that a noble tone quality in a musical instrument was the result of a few mechanical tricks or—better still—that anything in the world was the better for a few jiggers, whether they accomplished anything worth doing or not. We have already discussed the intoxicating effect of the word "patent." There was quite a striving on the part of nineteenth-century piano makers to apotheosize their instruments, or parts of them, by the use of that word. Even Steinways called some of their early pianos "Patent Grand." In a collection of advertisements from the year 1890, we find Behr Brothers proffering a "Patent Cylinder Top" and a "Patent Piano Muffler." That was small stuff compared to Conover Brothers, who boasted a "Repeating Action Metallic Action Rail, Duplex Bridge with Auxiliary Vibrators, Telescope Lamp Bracket, Automatic Music Desk"—all patent, of course. This was topped, however, by Paul G. Mehlin & Sons, who arrayed a "Patent Grand Plate and Scale, Patent Touch Regulator, Patent Grand Fall Board, Patent Harmonic Scale, Patent Piano Muffler, Patent Endwood Bridge, Patent Finger Guard, Patent Steel Action Frame, Patent Cylinder Top and Tone Reflector." With all those patents, one would imagine Mehlin & Sons could have squared the circle, achieved perpetual motion, or at least raised the dead.

When it came to medium-grade or cheap pianos, little that was distinctive could be said about them. Within a comparable range of price, if honestly sold, they were all pretty much the same. "They bewilder competitors and delight customers," said Vose & Sons of theirs; but the statement is colorless despite its assertiveness. Mostly, the dealers in these lower-priced goods had recourse to a kind of kittenishness or clownishness in their advertising copy. If a woman could be lured into a store by some "cute" publicity, a glib, insistent salesman might then succeed in holding her there till she was a good many dollars lighter. The "cuteness" usually consisted in a set of words or phrases completely irrelevant to the article to be sold. "Go to Held" said a sign on the Brooklyn elevated, meaning the premises of George Held, a meek dealer in pianos. "GHOST STORIES" was a large heading in a San Francisco advertisement. It continued: "When you hear a man say 'We've got a PIANO here just as good as the IVERS & POND for a great deal less money,' remember that all the ghost stories have not been told yet"—and so on, with more of the same. The ghost motif seemed to be regarded as particularly scintillating, for soon another piano company put out a fanfare in a trade paper which read: *"ALAS, POOR GHOST,* said Hamlet," going on with "Whether there was a ghost or not makes no difference. *Hamlet thought there was.* Dealers who fail to secure the Agency of the BRIGGS PIANO but let their neighbors get it will not stand a *ghost of a show.* Whether you believe it or not does not alter the fact." This was even crazier and further-fetched than the previous advertisement, therefore even "cuter" or "cleverer." Another San Francisco paper printed an advertisement purporting to give a testimonial from a mouse. The little rodent is quoted as saying:

> One night I had been ousted from a warm nest where my wife and myself proposed to stay all the winter, by a hard-hearted servant girl . . . Oddly enough we had to remove to the drawing room, a place barren of food. . . . A home we had to have and my wife, who was always musically inclined, proposed the piano. . . . As she insisted I volunteered to gnaw a hole through it, but I found it tough work, as the independent iron frame and solid wood resisted my efforts. . . . The gas had been left burning . . . cautiously I surveyed the premises, when my dazzled vision gradually read the magic word STECK. I told my waiting wife that sacrilege was not included in my list of crimes, and we wintered in an adroitly made nest in a velvet lounge. . . . We never repented our virtuous decision, for night after night we were lulled to sleep by its dulcet tones, its perfect tone, and the very soul of music which seemed to dwell in its touch.

The frenzy to sell was manifested not only in advertising verbiage. On the lower levels of the retail trade, all manner of merchandising bait was tried. One concern offered to give away, free, every tenth piano. Another concern got up a lottery scheme whereby a "class" of 120 members was formed, each paying $1.00 a week for a maximum of 120 weeks. After a time weekly "drawings" were to be held; and the schemers suggested archly that, what with the persons who inevitably would drop out and forfeit their money, some member might get his piano for as little as $40. On the other end of the spectrum was an enterprise calling itself the Epworth Organ Co., later the Epworth Piano Co. It did business exclusively through Methodist ministers: selling low-grade instruments at somewhat too high a price; but securing the clergymen's influential co-operation by offering them a substantial commission, which those underpaid persons rather welcomed. The instruments were stenciled with that sanctified word "Epworth," thus letting the poor objects give off an aroma of righteousness, for which the excess price may not have been too high to pay. Another scheme was the fake auction. A newspaper advertisement would announce the public sale of the effects of an ostensibly deceased person, including a "magnificent" piano. By the use of "cappers" or "shills" and tall talk, an innocent person could be made to pay more for a poor piano than it was worth. The petty tricks of the petty peddlers were endless.

Competition among merchants who dealt in goods of approximately the same quality and price might still be fairly based on service. Nevertheless, some salesmen, excited by the spirit of the times, scorned such legitimacy and occasionally preferred to take their advantage unfairly. One of their feats was to acquire a piano bearing a stencil handled by one of their rivals, knock it out of tune or mutilate it in some not too obvious way, and then show off its sour clanks alongside the bright sounds emitted by one from their own line of goods. The customer is not necessarily victimized even if he is led by the nose, the tricksters might say virtuously, since he will generally get his money's worth of what he will pay for. All this was called "business."

The big barons among the piano manufacturers were quite as uninhibited as the retailers in their efforts to jostle each other aside. In October 1878 "Colonel" James Henry Mapleson, the English impresario, brought his company to the Academy of Music in New York for a season of opera, introducing a number of important singers. During the company's stay in New York, Steinways' supplied its members liberally with pianos, both at the theater and for their individual use. A testimonial letter was sent to Steinways', dated December 28 and signed by Etelka Gerster, Marie Roze, Minnie Hauck, Italo Campanini, Luigi Arditi, and other stars of the group, expressing their "unqualified admiration" of their pianos' "sonority, evenness, richness, astonishing durability of tone . . ." and their beautiful blending with the voice. The letter called them "the most desirable instruments for the public generally." When the company played in Philadelphia the following February, it was surprised to find that a fine Steinway had been placed in each member's hotel room. At this point, Albert Weber felt his business-manhood challenged. When the singers came back from dinner, they found that the Steinways had been put outside their doors and Weber pianos placed in their rooms. Now Steinways, too, felt the spur of honor and sent up their men to eject the Webers and reinstate their own instruments. The squads of rival piano movers met in the halls of the hotel, and a hot scrimmage was joined, the weapons being piano legs unscrewed from their cases. The Weber men had the advantage of weight, muscle, and position, and they routed their foes.

Mr. Weber, victorious on the field of battle, proceeded immediately to consolidate his success in the chambers of diplomacy. That same evening, after the performance, he gave a grand supper party for the entire company. Champagne was liberally unloosed; and on one of its later rounds, a paper was passed along with it for the guests to sign. After they had done so, giddily, Mr. Weber was able to claim that the great stars of Her Majesty's Company had now certified that his pianos were the best they had ever known. We doubt, however, that the Haines Brothers—some time later—had to use either bludgeons or knock-out drops when they, in turn, induced the same bunch of opera-mummers to sign a testimonial on behalf of their instruments: singers seem to have been recklessly impartial when it came to pianos.

These little piano wars appear to have been quite frequent. On June 16, 1893, the combined high schools of Cleveland, Ohio, held commencement exercises in the new Sängerfest Building. The music director of Cleveland's public schools, N. Coe Stewart, was to conduct a large chorus at the occasion. But just before the opening, an altercation took place. It seems that Mr. C. S. Kopell, of the local Sängerfest Committee, had made a special arrangement with Chickerings' whereby their pianos were to be used at all Sängerfest Hall entertainments; on the other hand, Mr. Stewart had, on behalf of the Board of Education, ordered a Knabe piano for the occasion that evening. A loud quarrel ensued, before a large and delighted audience of parents and children. Overt physical acts were probably committed, for the police were called to keep the peace. The *Musical Courier* was discreetly silent on the outcome, saying: "The accompaniments were played on a——."

That was the year of the great Chicago World's Fair. Its directors put forth their best effort to make it an outstanding display of American industry and of Chicago's industry in particular. The musical-instrument section was duly emphasized. Various important piano houses announced their support, and Steinways' made a substantial money contribution to the fair funds. However, as the plans went forward, misgivings began to arise. First, the selection of the committee on awards aroused the dissatisfaction of certain Eastern piano manufacturers. Dr. Ziegfeld, for instance, of the

Chicago Musical College, might have seemed a reasonable choice as a judge of pianos; but W. W. Kimball, the outstanding Chicago manufacturer, was on his board of directors. Could there be undue influence? Evidently, the most important Eastern piano makers thought there would be; in any event, it was suspected that those guiding the fair were anxious that as many awards as possible be slanted in the direction of Chicago industries. In the spring of 1893 important Eastern firms, notably Steinways', decided not to exhibit at Chicago.

Meanwhile, the directors of the fair were going through with an elaborate musical program, in which a great part was played by a fine orchestra under the leadership of Theodore Thomas, America's leading symphonic conductor. But now the manufacturers who had taken space at the fair went to Thomas, requiring him to guarantee that no piano by a nonexhibiting maker would be played at a fair concert. This was highly embarrassing to Thomas, since it was against all his artistic principles and also because he had already made engagements with Steinway-playing artists, including Paderewski. The embattled businessmen would listen to no compromises. They had spent a million dollars to exhibit there, they said; did Thomas suppose they were doing it for their health? They were entitled to the advertising that went with a soloist's appearance. Anyway, why couldn't the soloists play Chicago pianos? They were just as good as Steinways.

That was their line, and they took the matter up with certain fair authorities, who supported them. Four days before Paderewski's appearance, the "National Commission of the World's Columbian Exposition"—a Congressional creation with ill-defined powers —passed a resolution to the effect that "no piano shall be used on the Exposition grounds except those represented by firms that make exhibits at the Fair." To this was added: "If any Steinway pianos are announced for concerts at the Exposition grounds, the Director General is authorized to send teams and dump the pianos outside the gates." And, to be sure that they were making themselves understood, they stipulated further that "the bills announcing Mr. Paderewski's appearance at a concert with the Exposition Orchestra be taken down and Mr. Paderewski's name erased."

But it seems that the National Commission's high words were mostly histrionic; for not they but a board of directors were the real bosses to whom Thomas considered himself responsible. Paderewski did play his own concerto on May 2 with the Exposition Orchestra, on a Steinway piano that had been sneaked in under the label of "hardware" or some such thing. The concert was a great success, no teams appeared, and the piano was not dumped anywhere.

It was, indeed, a galling victory of art over business. Some of the newspapers felt honor-bound to line up on the side of the defeated angels; and now the *Chicago Herald* and the *Evening Post* went after Paderewski and after Thomas with salvos of mud. They accused the pianist of showing contempt for this country and the fair commission by playing the work of greasy foreigners such as Chopin and Schumann instead of honest American music. The *Herald,* in particular, made quite a target of Thomas, calling him "a small despot," "a dull and self-opinionated man," and "a pragmatic curmudgeon," saying he "should have been the leader of a barrack band in a mountainous camp in North Germany," and speaking of his "unscrupulous resistance to reasonable appeals." The *Herald* music critic, however, continued to be enthusiastic about Thomas' masterly interpretations. The *Herald* boss called him in and told him to roast Thomas or quit. He quit.

Ah, those were the great old days, when business was business and rejoiced in good old American fun. And to hear some people talk nowadays, one gets the impression they are craving to return to them.

21. HOUSEHOLD GOODS ARE ALL RELATED

WHAT CONNECTION is there between a piano, or organ, and a sewing machine? None whatsoever, say you scornfully if you are an Art fancier, as you turn your eyes soulfully toward the bust of Mozart. But an unprejudiced American merchant of 1880, not necessarily incapable of enjoying music, might have viewed the question rather differently. Both melodeons and sewing machines were moderately bulky objects that women liked to play with around the house; moreover, they were not incomparable in price. The same kind of woman could be a customer for either, and there seems to have been some logic in having them sold by the same dealer or peddler. The sewing machine was a triumph of American engineering and industrial organization, and was regarded as an unmixed boon by the country's female population. Its production had been organized so that it could be sold at a price accessible to large numbers of people at just about the time when reed organs and pianos, likewise, could be made cheaply enough to distribute widely.

The fact is, in the decades after the Civil War, sewing machines and keyboard instruments were habitually thought of together—in a harmonious bracket. Not only were they sold in the same salesrooms, but house-to-house canvassers in the more sparsely settled communities often carried both articles on their wagons. As late as the spring of 1891 we read of the incorporation of the G. E. Van Syckle Co. of Bay City, Michigan, capital $20,000, whose stated object was the manufacture of both musical instruments and sewing machines. If the thought of this association strikes you as ridiculous today, think of your radio set, which provides you with Tchaikovsky if you want it and which you might well have bought in the very store that sold you a refrigerator.

Will S. (for Shakespeare) Hays of Louisville, Kentucky, was one of the country's most successful song writers of his day, having sired such hits as "Oh, Let Me Kiss the Baby" and "Evangeline"—to whose death as early as the first verse 100,000 copy-buyers loved to listen. In 1869 he wrote, composed, and had published a "Song of the Sewing Machine." The front cover shows mamma at the machine, left, turning her face affectionately toward papa, center, who is fondling one of two little children; at the right stands a large square piano to complete the necessary elements of the domestic scene. The song is evidently an early example of a "singing commercial," advertising a special make of the article, for the refrain goes: "Sing a song, a song, of the beautiful FLORENCE machine." One verse says:

> But now she has her "household pet,"
> And one to which she'll cling;
> For labor is a pleasure now,
> And she can toil and sing.

The Wheeler & Wilson Co. of Bridgeport, Connecticut, the largest manufacturers of their kind, experimented with the idea of letting her not only toil and sing, but even play her accompaniments at the same time. During the sixties they put out a "novelty" in the shape of a combination sewing machine and melodeon; it had the form of a parlor sideboard. When opened, it presented a set of keys; whereas the sewing machine was revealed after the top was turned back. There were side doors below, containing two pedals—one for the musical and one for the sewing apparatus—and by changing her foot from one to the other, the fair operator could play at tones or at stitches as she felt inclined.

On Saturday February 7, 1880, the first number of a new periodical came out in New York. The publisher, Howard Lockwood, explained its purpose on the front cover:

> When in the natural course of trade two or three commodities are constantly associated with each other, it may be reasonably inferred that the association fulfills some useful purpose. Such an association exists between Pianos, Organs, and Sewing Machines. In thousands of salesrooms outside the larger cities of the Union these three commodities are kept on sale together. Obviously they are associated in compliance with the requirements of business.

He goes on to say that the relationship is "comparatively new" and that—"although clearly recognized for some time"—dealers have often been forced to take several papers to know what was going on in each of the piano, organ, and sewing machine trades. One paper could serve them all simultaneously, thought Mr. Lockwood, and thereby offered the *Musical and Sewing Machine Gazette*. The paper kept its word, carrying music trade news and features on the earlier pages, sewing machine news on the later ones, and including a column called "Needle Points." The contrasting advertisements of each were sometimes bedded together, and we find Singer and Steinway displays in friendly contact on the same page. After three numbers, the *Gazette* became dissatisfied with its title and changed it to *Musical and Sewing Machine Courier*. Somehow, the publication's attempt to harness itself to several trades abreast did not seem to work out: with the ninth issue, April 3, 1880, the sewing machine interest was dropped and the paper became simply the *Musical Courier*. It made a significant career under that name and still bears it to this day.

The *Musical Herald*, published in Boston, revealed the piano in its happy household habitat. The journal was a decent, informative supplier of music news and comment; and its editors were not cold-eyed businessmen who did not care what it was they sold, but on the contrary were earnest promoters of the best in music as they saw it. Eben Tourjée, the founder of the New England Conservatory, was their chief, and among his assistants were William F. Apthorp, the music reviewer on the *Transcript* and later the program editor for the Boston Symphony Orchestra, as well as Louis C. Elson, a reputable critic and historian of American music. Page 197 of Volume III of the *Musical Herald* for the year 1882 shows an advertisement for Guild Pianos (medium-priced instruments made by Guild, Church & Co.), as well as one for volumes of *Music of the Old Masters,* which included the nocturnes of Chopin and the sonatas of Mozart. After what we have already recounted, it may not be too surprising to hear that the opposite page is devoted to an illustrated spread extolling the qualities of the "light-running DOMESTIC sewing machine." It may be only slightly more quaint to see "Dunham's Technique" claimed as a "direct preparation" for Moscheles' Studies Opus 70 only one column away from "FANCY WORK. A book of instructions and patterns for Artistic Needle Work, Kensington, Embroidery, Crochet and Knitted work, patterns for Hand Bag, Scrap Basket, Tidy, Mat, Oak Leaf Lace, Piano Cover etc." But what are we to say to *Three Beautiful Sacred Pieces*—one of which is titled *Jesus, I My Cross Have Taken*—placed midway between "Wilbor's Compound of PURE COD LIVER OIL and LIME" and "DISEASES CURED by the Electro-Magnetic Treatment . . . by Dr. George W. Rhodes"? Turning to page 138, we are asked—if we are piano teachers or students—to purchase Mr. A. D. Turner's "SETS of SCALES . . . including *double thirds, double sixths,*" and so forth, on the right-hand side, while on the lower left we are encouraged to acquire the "STAR GAME of CITIES, *a new game* for Home and Winter Evenings' pleasure—similar to 'Authors' but more *instructive.*" The same page offers for sale the recently published *Comprehensive Analysis of Beethoven's Ninth Symphony, by Dr. George Grove,* and right above it is a larger space devoted to "THE COMFORT CORSET. For Ladies and Children . . . NO BONES TO BREAK."

Music in the home, centering around the piano, is cozy. The home's very warmth is partly derived from the variety of lowly objects in it—each carrying familiar and personal associations. The sentimental attachment that the piano could arouse was bound up with the things with which it lived: the parlor games, the embroidery, the sewing machine, and even the medicines and the corsets with which it shared the house. It may be we are hardhearted and priggish nowadays, to laugh at the *Musical Herald*'s reflection of the past century's domestic interiors.

After a few years the *Musical Courier* passed from Howard Lockwood's hands into those of two men by the rather differently flavored names of Marc Blumenberg and Otto Floersheim. By 1890 the mercurial musician, aesthete, and verbalist James Huneker was writing regular pieces for it. Advertisements were now strictly music-professional: piano makers, piano teachers, and publishers. All except one: a page near the front carried a steady card proclaiming Ehret's Lager Beer. Dutifully, the editors "took care" of their advertiser, and into an article about the composer Gounod sneaked in the statement: "After all, beer is and possibly always will be the liquid pabulum of the musician." After all—can there be such a thing as pure music?

22. SOMETIMES, BETTER IS NO GOOD

WHEN the Steinways in 1859 perfected their special scheme of overstringing together with the relocation of their sounding-board bridge and the increase of general tension on the strings, the piano gained its complete physical maturity as a music-producing implement. It was now capable of utilizing the full muscular vigor—as well as the quickest, most delicate alterations of finger impact—that a human being could put forth. Further improvements were either trifling, impractical, or of insufficient value. Among such as these may be mentioned a slight extension of the instrument's range. Seven octaves—from A to a''''—remained the norm from the middle of the century until the 1890's. At this time an additional three notes were built on to the highest treble of most pianos, giving the instrument its present standard range of seven and one third octaves, or eighty-eight notes. The highest B-flat, B, and C are rarely used and are certainly the poorest in quality of all the piano's tones.

In an earlier section of this book we stated that a device for keeping the damper lifted, at the will of the player, off any single string or strings, without affecting the other dampers, was constructed by a French piano maker and exhibited by him at a Paris fair as early as 1844. Little interest was shown in it at the time, and it seems to have been forgotten. In 1874 Steinways' perfected a mechanism for the same purpose, on a different principle, to which they gave the name "*sostenuto*" pedal. They made it into a standard piece of equipment on their pianos, on which it forms the middle pedal of three. Other makers followed the Steinway lead, and the *sostenuto* pedal is now to be found on most American-made grands. Its utility is rather limited, and some of the most outstanding virtuosos have refrained from using it altogether. Josef Hofmann ordered it removed from the concert grands the Steinways furnished him, saying he was afraid he might step on it inadvertently. Europeans, both musicians and piano makers, have consistently disregarded this apparatus. Even Steinways did not build it into the instruments they made in Hamburg.

The most important developments of later piano construction were those involving the instrument's over-all shape. We have already stated that the uprights eventually completely displaced the squares in American homes, a trend that began soon after the Civil War. Its cause probably lay not only in the intrinsic cheapness of the upright—based on the smaller amount of material it consumes—but also in the narrowness of living quarters among later generations of piano owners. This does not mean that in the 1880's wealthy people moved into smaller houses; it means, rather, that pianos were now wanted by more of the less moneyed people, who were already living in smaller quarters. The trend away from squares was noticeable at the Philadelphia Centennial in 1876, at which the most important piano exhibitors stressed their uprights and made relatively little of their squares. By 1890 the squares were about finished: a mere handful continued to be made during a further ten years, and they were obsolete at the beginning of the twentieth century.

Grands were quite rare before the middle of the century, as we have seen. Their shape seemed awkward with respect to American notions of drawing-room symmetry, and they consumed much more space than their actual linear dimensions indicated. However, they were favored by public performers; and as the many concerts of the 1850's and thereafter invested them with a certain prestige, they came into some demand. In 1876 Steinways' stated that grands constituted about one sixth of their output. That manufactory was probably uniquely high in this proportion; it would be safe to guess, therefore, that during the last quarter of the century not more than about four per cent of all the American pianos made were grands.

It was clear that many aspiring families would wish to own a piano having the artistic, concertlike look of a grand, but one of less ungainly shape and lower cost. As early as 1860 Henry Lindeman of the Lindeman Piano Co. devised a "cycloid" piano, of generally grand outline but considerably shorter and blunter at the tail. It could have been called a compromise between a grand and a square. The Lindemans were a small firm and they found it difficult to push its sales to any great extent. In the spring of 1879, however, Steinways' adopted a similar idea and put out a compact piano that they called a "baby grand." Steinways' had great prestige and large resources; moreover, feminine customers were likely to find "baby" a rather more attractive word than "cycloid." Thus, the "baby grand" came into a considerable vogue and became widely imitated; and, indeed, the words became a generic term.

We can record a few inventions involving more radical changes in the piano's anatomy. Early in the twentieth century Hungarian-born Emanuel Moór, otherwise known as a composer of skill, thought up his "Duplex Coupler Grand Piano." This instrument apparently consisted of two pianos in a single case, one tuned an octave higher than the other, with two manuals playable separately or capable of being coupled together by a lever. In other words, it was a sort of piano with an octave stop. It attracted some brief notice, especially when ably demonstrated in concerts by the excellent pianist Winifred Christie, the inventor's wife. However, it had limited musical purpose and was, moreover, bulky in shape and heavy to play.

A remarkable latter-day alteration of the piano is worth talking about; it is interesting in its very failure. The arrangement of semitones in two unequal ranks has been standard in keyboards, probably since the fifteenth century. The execution of the whole enormous body of organ, harpsichord, and piano literature—the totality of practice throughout the Western world for four centuries—has been on a keyboard that consists of "naturals" forming the seven tones of the scale of C major and of "sharps" forming the five remaining semitones, the latter produceable through sets of narrower keys raised and to the rear of the "naturals." During the years 1882–84 a Hungarian nobleman named Paul von Jankó, a graduate of both the Vienna Conservatory and the Polytechnicum, undertook to reform the ancient structure of the musical keyboard. Discarding the C major scale as a basis, he built two ranks, each having the same number of keys of equal width, striking alternating semitones. Thus, in one octave the lower rank went C, D, E, F-sharp, G-sharp, A-sharp, while the upper rank went C-sharp, D-sharp, F, G, A, B. Since each semitone succeeded the next in absolutely regular formation, it followed that all twelve diatonic scales could be played with the use of but two sets of fingerings—no small convenience, in theory. As a concession to old habits, Jankó had the keys for C-sharp, D-sharp, F-sharp, G-sharp, and A-sharp painted with an unfunctional black stripe. Moreover, let us remember that on a standard keyboard two of the semitones within an octave are taken up with full-width keys, whereas the narrowness of the "sharps" (black keys) saves no total lateral space. In other words, an octave span has the cumulative width of seven "natural" (white) keys. On the other hand, in Jankó's keyboard a full octave took up the space of only six white keys, thus giving the hand a far greater normal stretch.

All this was only one phase of the invention. Jankó felt that the standard keyboard has little consideration for the movements easiest to the natural configuration of the hands—in particular, that it allows insufficient maneuverability in the front–back dimension. Thus, he made his keys of much greater length and thickness, providing each one with three separate finger-striking places terraced behind each other. Each of these striking areas he covered with a separate piece of ivory, so that the Jankó keyboard looked superficially like a system of three keyboards or manuals. It was not that, as we have shown, but merely a single one, playable on three close levels.

Jankó, trained both as an engineer and as a musician, worked out his invention carefully and scientifically. There is no doubt that on his keyboard the arrangement of sharps and naturals can make the execution of many passages much easier, that the division of keys into playing levels facilitates an even articulation, and that the saving of lateral space makes for greater reaching capacity of the hands. Jankó's explanatory treatise *A New Keyboard* (*Eine neue Klaviatur*) was published in Vienna in 1886, after one of the smaller Vienna firms of piano makers had decided to go in for the device's manufacture. That same year Herr von Jankó himself gave a demonstratory piano recital on his new construction.

The Jankó keyboard aroused considerable interest and discussion—justly so, since it was certainly the most radical, most intelligently conceived, and most efficient innovation ever put forward in its field. Within a few years it was brought to the United States, and there too it made a considerable impression on musicians of the more thoughtful type. About 1891 the well-established New York piano-making firm of Decker Bros. decided to put the Jankó keyboard into commercial production, applying it to their own instruments. Even before then a center was established for giving instruction in playing it. It was called the Paul de Jankó Conservatory of Music, and after the autumn of 1891 it was located at 9 East Seventeenth Street. It was run by a man named Emil K. Winkler, whose serialized articles on the subject in the *Musical Courier* of that year were long and explicit and were probably widely read in the music profession. Moreover, W. Bradley Keeler, one of Winkler's collaborators, wrote a manual on *How to Play the New Keyboard.*

In vain! Professional musical interest, even when occasionally appreciative and well wishing, nevertheless waned. The great increase of material in the Jankó keys created a problem of balance in the action, resulting in a somewhat sluggish touch; but that was not a fatal detriment, and Paul Perzina, a piano maker of Schwerin, Germany, remedied it in 1910. Still, he could not impart social momentum to the invention. Even after Perzina devised a method whereby a standard keyboard and a Jankó could be folded up and set in position alternately for use on the same piano, the spread of the remarkable construction could not thereby be furthered.

The fact was that the Jankó keyboard, however practical and efficient in principle, could not overcome the pressure of accumulated habit and tradition of centuries, in which the practice of the keyboard players and that of the keyboard builders supported each other. Many a good pianist, thirty or forty years of age, might concede that the Jankó keyboard was a "better" implement than the one on which he had been brought up; still, hardly any practitioner would care to learn how to play his own instrument all over again, even if by a more favorable method. The few whose enthusiasm drove them to do so and to acquire the new technique were, of course, eager to impart the new skill to others and might be likely to find apt pupils among beginners and among the very young. However, a child could learn to use the new keyboard conveniently only if its parents gave up the old piano—on which mamma and the elder sister had played—and bought a new Decker. Moreover, even if Jane or Susan did learn to play and to accompany, and even to improvise, quite pleasantly on the Jankó keyboard at home and at her teacher's, she never could entertain anybody at her friends' houses, or at school or church, unless the queer new keyboard were also to be found in those places. Nor did concert pianists derive much incentive from the new invention. The keyboard did not affect the sound of the instrument, apart from permitting some greater stretches: it was a mere convenience to the player, costing him, however, great labor to be able to put it to use. It could mean little or nothing to the lay listener, or even to one who was a non-piano-playing musician.

Our complex, advanced civilization cannot upset itself for the sake of a facilitation of procedure that otherwise produces no immediate spectacular result. The British nation will not, in our time, become converted to the decimal system, nor the Japanese people to the Latin alphabet, nor the world of music to the Jankó keyboard. In the far future—after all the apparatus of our civilization, including its musical instruments, will have crumbled in disuse and the skills pertaining thereto faded away in discouragement—it may happen that newly simple people will again hit upon the idea of making music by means of keyboards, and then, possibly, may come to construct them regularly on the logical Jankó principle.

A good surviving specimen of a Jankó keyboard, attached to a Decker upright, can be seen at the National Museum in Washington, D. C.

23. IF YOU CAN'T FIGHT, JOIN

THE PIANO RETAILERS' strained efforts to sell combine into a colorful human picture: the lottery clubs, the give-away stunts, the "Epworth" spiel, the clownish advertising copy, the fake auctions, the suggestive stencils, and the mutilation of competitors' goods. Nevertheless, from their core, all these tricks give off an odor of despair: they are really wit's-end antics. In point of fact, there was no particular reason why anyone should have bought one brand of cheap piano rather than another. As industrial products they were all bound to be pretty much the same, since the parts of any one came from factories that also supplied the parts for many of the others: sounding boards by Dolge, metal frames by Davenport & Treacy (or later by O. S. Kelly), actions by Strauch (or by Wessell, Nickel & Gross) with ivory by Sylvester Tower and felt of standardized weight and taper again by Dolge. In other words, each of the competing merchants had little to compete with except the peculiar flavor of his own impertinence. It was conventionally pretended, of course, that this desperately comic game was one of the worthiest of human occupations; and no doubt there were some types of men who did find it intrinsically delightful. On the other hand, there were also interested persons who were beginning to have misgivings about it—not so much as to whether this feverish salesmanship was benefiting the public, but rather as to whether it was doing the piano business itself any good.

The one particular feature of the prevailing free-for-all fight about nothing that may have made some businessmen anxious was the overextension of credit. On the basis of an old merchandizing view of the wavering customer—"Get every dollar he has in his pocket, but don't lose a sale"—many salesmen, in their urgency, were willing to dispose of pianos on easier and easier installment-plan terms. Now, at $25 down and $10 a month, for example, a customer would require two years to pay for an instrument listed at $265. That is a fairly long time to wait for money. The dealer naturally passed this delay on to the manufacturer from whom he bought, the manufacturer being already beset by the fact that it may have taken him six months to make the piano in the first place. In the slang of modern business, the dealer "carried" the customer and the manufacturer "carried" the dealer. Then the banks "carried" the manufacturer, if they would, for a while. But sometimes they would do so no longer. In the face of hard times, overselling, lapses, and the hazards of "repossession," merchants and manufacturers may often have been tempted to leniency; but bankers were likely to be more inflexible. Businesses with large resources could hold out, but the smaller houses might have to go to the wall when the squeeze was put on.

Meanwhile a certain amount of decay was going on at the top. Some of the largest makers of the highest-quality pianos were losing their interest. We have mentioned the Chickerings, whose reorganization never could bring back their former standing. The Webers also stumbled and fell sometime during the nineties: control of the company and of the all-important name left the hands of the family that had created its value. Ernest Knabe, son of the original William, died in 1894. Both the Knabe business and its product were held in the highest esteem, and the momentum of their achievement kept their prestige at a high level for quite a while. Yet Knabe & Co. also subtly seemed to feel the lack of a boss man by the name of Knabe.

Somehow, the quality-piano business is bound up with family tradition and pride. At the base of a fine instrument is a man in an apron at a bench, a stolid-looking idealist with a sensitive understanding of materials and an unreasonable, scrupulous devotion to all finesses of workmanship. When he becomes a boss, he can make other workmen hew to his line, and he can often instill a vicarious form of his artistic conscience into his sons. Through their early upbringing, the younger generation could be made to feel that their own self-esteem was involved in the quality of their father's product, that they could not bear to do anything that would break the old man's heart. But if a firm's spiritual connection with that old craftsman was broken and it fell into alien hands, it would tend to become just another business—that is to say, a mere system of arithmetic.

With the makers of cheaper goods spending their energy pulling out each other's eyelashes, and even some of the lords of the trade getting sick, the situation was ripe for some sort of reform—which, in the general movement of the times, could only take the form of a merging of business interests. Regretfully, the chaotic ecstasies of unrestrained competition had to be abated. In the spring of 1892, fully eighteen months after the passage of the Sherman Anti-trust Law, the first attempt to form a piano trust was under way. A corporation was planned, to be capitalized rather extravagantly at $50,000,000. A great majority of the important piano manufacturers were expected to come into the combine, with the firms joining the trust to exchange their assets for the new corporation's stock. A loan of $5,000,000 was secured from a group of bankers, to help take care of firms that preferred to sell out for cash. The projected production plan was highly rational, aiming at a standardization of quality. Only three grades of instrument were to be put out: a high-grade, a medium-grade, and a cheap piano. To these would be added a special concert grand, suitable for artists for public work. Fair progress had been made in the consolidation, when the plan had to be suspended because of the financial crisis of 1893. So said Alfred Dolge, the great piano-parts manufacturer, in his account of the matter, in which he himself played a leading part.

Five years later negotiations were again resumed, but without success; and again on a different basis two years after that, with the same frustration of result. According to Dolge, it was the difficult state of the money market that prevented a satisfactory settlement, despite the willingness of several large companies to go into the scheme. Mutual jealousies and the efforts of certain firms to sell themselves for more than they were worth also had a detrimental effect.

A large combination of piano businesses was finally effected early in the twentieth century, but it was dominated by a group of men chiefly interested in putting out mechanical player-pianos. In 1903 the new Aeolian Co. was organized, capitalized at $10,-000,000. Among the subsidiaries that it controlled were a number of piano-making firms. These included the Weber company, George Steck & Co., and other companies named Wheelock and Stuyvesant. The idea of making pianos of different levels of quality in separate factories was carried out by the Aeolian Co., much as it had been thought out by the unsuccessful trust formers of ten years earlier. By 1903, Weber was a name without an essence—one that sounded rather better than the pianos on which it was stenciled. Nevertheless, the Weber instrument served the Aeolian Co. as a leader, as their particular brand of quality merchandise. The Steck, long known as an honestly made, good second-class instrument, served as their middling line; while the other names were used on their cheaper goods.

Not long after this organization, Paderewski had a great quarrel with one of the Steinways—about what, no one seems to remember—and broke off relations with the firm that had launched him so brilliantly. As he bounced out of the Steinway office, the Aeolian Co. was ready to catch him. What persuasions they used, we know not; but it is hard to think they consisted of nothing but money. At any rate, for a season or two the most glamorous of all pianists played the Weber piano. It was wonderful advertising while it lasted, and may have helped increase the sale of Weber pianos to the wealthy ignorant; but other pianists held back, hardly any following Paderewski's example. The Aeolian Co. presently built an excellent concert hall in New York, which came into great demand by recitalists and other concertgivers. Nevertheless, almost all of the artists preferred to use Steinway or Mason & Hamlin pianos, and Weber instruments were conspicuous by their infrequent appearance on their own stage.

Another large merger of piano interests was accomplished in 1908 with the organization of the American Piano Co., capitalized at $12,000,000. In this case, it was the Knabe piano—still enjoying some of its pristine vitality—that became the headliner; while Chickering, once the glorious pinnacle of American piano making, took an official second place in the trust's line of goods, since even the name's resonance was now fading. Haines Brothers, a solid firm high on the list of Grade B makers during the nineteenth century, lost its titular head in 1900 and was soon ripe to disappear in the whirlpool of the new combine. A number of other factories making lower-grade instruments completed the American Piano Co.'s table of organization.

With their enlarged capacities, these consolidated businesses could, and needed to, produce in much greater quantities than any of the older factories had done previously. Not long after its establishment, the American Piano Co. was putting out fifteen thousand pianos a year; whereas Steinways', at the height of their production, never made more than five thousand.

The Aeolian Co. and the American Piano Co. could be called

"trusts" in a loose sense of the word; yet they did not remotely approach the dimensions of a monopoly, even regionally or locally. Together, these two concerns did not account for one tenth of the total American output of 360,000 units in 1910. Their production was far exceeded by that of a few leading Middle Western firms such as the W. W. Kimball Co. and the Cable Co. of Chicago, and the Rudolph Wurlitzer Co. of Cincinnati. In fact, by the end of the first decade of the new century the Middle West, especially the Chicago area, had become the country's chief piano-manufacturing region. Needless to say, the overwhelming majority of instruments produced there were of the cheap, "commercial" grade. Professional musicians of the more cultivated kind rarely enjoyed playing on such pianos, yet the instruments were very serviceable articles in their way and more than amply adapted to the small skill of the millions of persons for whom they were made.

In those days professionals of the higher type—concert pianists, students, and teachers of the classics, as well as vocalists and other instrumentalists who needed proper pianistic support—almost invariably, when not prodded by a dollar sign, preferred to use the pianos by Steinway, or by Mason & Hamlin, and bought them for themselves when they could afford them. C. A. Gianelli, manager of Mason & Hamlin's retail store in New York, told this writer about 1920 that at the moment most of his customers were professional musicians. It is interesting to note that this firm affected a special brand of snobbery, not altogether unjustified: it boasted that its pianos were the most expensive of all. Perhaps this was not a gratuitous affectation, but merely an attempt to make a virtue of a necessity, since the company's small output made for high production costs.

Americans have long shown a propensity to exult in the contemplation of large quantities. This may be a reflection of the awe felt by early settlers before the vastness of an unexplored continent. In any event, the idea of thousands of miles, millions of tons, and billions of dollars has always made American hearts leap. To achieve a great amount of anything has generally been regarded as an equivalent of success. Yet that coy nymph Quality—whose charms cannot be measured in points per inch or revolutions per second—nevertheless has allured many an otherwise sharp-figuring American businessman. Quality: it is the sense of uniqueness in the world, the idea of a thing being itself and no other, of having a soul, a touch of divinity, of commanding an affection no merely similar thing could call forth.

Some piano makers, thoroughly solvent and comfortable, nevertheless envied whatever it was about Steinways and Mason & Hamlins that made musicians love them for themselves alone. During the 1890's, Hardman & Peck got pianist Victor Benham to try to make his listeners feel that their instruments had distinction; and the pianos made by the small, aspiring firm of Behr Brothers developed enough quality to allow the visiting Scharwenka to feel that he could do himself justice upon them. But these firms gave up presently. Frank Lee did better, with a piano to which he gave the fictitious name of "Everett," giving off a vapor of high-class New England glory. Aiming at quality, Lee prospered sufficiently so that for a short time Ossip Gabrilówitsch, Teresa Carreño, and Cécile Chaminade considered they were not compromising their work too seriously by allowing themselves to be persuaded to play it. But the "Everett" flurry subsided soon. The firm that persisted the longest and succeeded the best in the ascent from mediocrity to distinction was the Baldwin Piano Co. of Cincinnati. Founded during the days of the Civil War, its products made little stir until 1900, when it received an outstanding award at the Paris exposition. Presently that clownish eccentric and delightful Chopin player Vladimir de Pachmann—James Huneker had called him the "Chopinzee"—found that he could project his delicate effects satisfactorily on a Baldwin piano. So did Raoul Pugno, elegant black-bearded French pianist, during his short American sojourn. Most of the more important artistic history of the Baldwin rise, however, belongs to a later period.

SECTION

SEVEN

General Developments

1. "AN INSTRUMENT THAT GOETHE WITH A WHELE WITHOUTE PLAYINGE UPPON"

Clocks, operating by means of toothed wheels driven by springs, were built in Europe before 1300. From that time on, it was plausible to think that a musical instrument of fixed pitches, consisting of sets of either pipes or strings, could be activated mechanically or automatically. We hear reports of a barrel organ, for example, in fifteenth-century Holland. In a barrel organ a cylinder with pins sticking out from it is made to revolve by a spring, or may be turned by a hand crank. Each pin is so placed that it will engage a lever which will trip a valve opening a particular pipe. Meanwhile the force—either spring or hand—that turns the cylinder simultaneously works a bellows, creating the wind that blows through the opened pipes to make the tone. By appropriate setting of the pins, a tune may thus be played, or a succession of chords, or entire compositions, for the duration of a complete revolution of the cylinder.

Apparently, barrel organs had reached a high degree of development before the end of the sixteenth century. In 1593, Elizabeth I had an elaborate one constructed by Thomas Dallam, the most reputable of English builders, and had him take it to Constantinople as a present for the Sultan of Turkey, hoping thus to lubricate the activities of the Company of Merchants in the Levant. The machine struck the hours and went off by itself four times in twenty-four hours to play several pieces of music. By touching a certain spring, however, one could make it break into tune at any time. It also had keys, enabling it to be played by hand.

Barrel organs, or "musical clocks," were common during the eighteenth century. They were used in English churches, and on the European continent as amusements in divers situations. Handel, Haydn, and Mozart all wrote music expressly to be translated onto their cylinders. Mälzel's huge "Panharmonicon," for which Beethoven composed, was substantially the same kind of apparatus; and so was the little box carried through the streets by itinerants as a fig leaf for their begging. They "ground" their organs—that is to say, they turned a cylinder and squeezed a bellows simultaneously with the same crank.

In applying the cylinder principle to a harpsichord, of course, no bellows was necessary; an arrangement was merely needed whereby the projecting pins would engage the lever that was to activate its particular jack and quill. In the inventory of the effects of Henry VIII, taken upon his death in 1547, among the many virginals listed is included "Item an instrument that goethe with a whele withoute playinge uppon of woode varnisshed yellowe . . ." By the seventeenth century, references to such instruments become more frequent. A Lady Arabella Stuart, in a letter to the Earl of Shrewsbury dated June 17, 1609, writes: "But now from doctrines to miracles; I assure you within these few dayes I saw a paire of virginalles make good musick without help of any hand . . ." In August 1623 the Master of the Revels to James I issued a license to one Bartholomew Cloys to exhibit various devices, including "a Virginal with machinery." In a broadside announcing "Fireworks to be presented at Lincoln's Inn Fields on the 5th of November 1647," there is mention of virginals "musically playing of themselves." During the eighteenth century, the age of mechanical toys, self-playing harpsichords were likewise occasionally constructed. We have mentioned the complex automaton made by the Swiss P. J. Droz in 1774, representing a young lady going through all the correct finger motions and other appropriate bodily movements, of the performance of a piece on the harpsichord. We do not know whether the music was made entirely by the doll's fingers, or whether the harpsichord did not also contain a separate synchronized mechanism.

As the pianoforte became common, it was inevitable that the barrel-and-pin mechanism be applied to it likewise. In 1825 the learned musician Dr. Busby, in his *Concert Room Anecdotes,* described a "self-acting pianoforte" made by no less an agency than the famous firm of Clementi, Collard & Company. "This curious instrument," said the writer, "furnished with a horizontal cylinder similar to that of the barrel organ, and put into motion by a steel spring, performs without external force or manual operation, the most difficult and intricate compositions." He said the keys could be played independently, even while the automatic mechanism was working; and this seems to suggest that the machine was built in, inside the piano. "When the spring is fully wound up," continued Dr. Busby, "[it] will act for more than half an hour, and may again be prepared for performance in half a minute, and if required, stopped in an instant while in full action." Speed could be regulated at pleasure, while piano, forte, sforzato, and diminuendo were "produced by the slightest motion of the hand applied to a sliding ball at the side of the instrument."

In the same volume, Dr. Busby mentioned another instrument—put out in January 1825 by a man named Courcell—called the "Cylindrichord." (Those inventors would have had to shut up shop if deprived of their Greek dictionaries.) He dubbed it "an admirable and efficient substitute for a first-rate performer on the pianoforte." To judge by the description, it differed from the Clementi mechanism, though its basic principle may have been the same, for it evidently was a separate structure that could be wheeled up to a piano, striking its keys by means of a set of mechanical fingers. "In small family parties," expounded Dr. Bushy, "when dancing to the music of a pianoforte is practised, one of the company had always been necessarily engaged at the instrument; that unpleasant necessity became obviated; for by the aid of the Cylindrichord, a person totally unacquainted with music, a child or servant, may perform in the very best and most correct style *quadrilles, waltzes, minuets, country dances, marches, songs, overtures, sonatas, choruses,* or indeed any piece of music, however difficult." It must have been worked by a crank or a foot pump, else why bring in the child or servant. The description concludes: "it can be accommodated to the height or dimensions of any pianoforte, and when not in use for that purpose, forms a piece of elegant furniture." The "Cylindrichord" was in production and on sale, and all this latter verbiage has a flavor of peddler's wheedling, making us feel we are deep in the commercial age. Perhaps Busby, for all the oratorio he composed and his Oxonian Mus. Doc., was not above sneaking a vulgar advertisement into his informative book.

We mention this since we must observe that though the above-described contraptions are practically identical in purpose and function with the player pianos of nearly a century later, they nevertheless aroused little interest in their day. Again we are forced to reflect that inventions are not significant because they are mechanically practical, but because of the mysterious manner in which they affect the imaginations of the persons at whom they are thrust. The most important thing about a gadget is not whether it works, but whether it can be sold.

Apparently, genteel families of the earlier nineteenth century did not as yet care for machine-made music in their living rooms.

However, there was a social situation of the time into which the barrel piano was deemed to fit most agreeably. There is a claim that an Englishman, early in the nineteenth century, first made a street piano. Be that as it may, its true home proved to be Italy. It was an upright, worked by a cylinder mechanism turned by a crank, its hammer heads leather-covered and hard, suitable for a noisy outdoors; and it had no dampers, which could only have been a detriment to its purpose. For a century Italians pushed and pulled this music box through the streets of the world, especially the poorer, more populous thoroughfares, to the glee of their younger inhabitants.

Older city-Americans can remember it very well, with its large wheels, always in the roadway, never on the sidewalk, sometimes propelled by a man and a woman each holding one of its projecting wooden traces. They would halt at a suitable section of the curb; he would turn the crank, she would sometimes play the tambourine or sing, while delighted children danced, yelled, and threw pennies. More often a lone man was the whole show, acting as his own stagehand, virtuoso, and box office rolled into one. Mostly he was called an "organ grinder"—inaccurately, as we see, since his machine was really a piano. In the 1920's that obnoxious upstart Mussolini, suffering from the touchiness of the insecure, considered that the fame of his compatriot street musicians did not contribute to the image of nasty truculence that he was trying to build up for his Italy; and in a burst of stuffiness he called the music grinders back and abolished them. Perhaps it was as well in the long run, for street pianos do not move well among rows of parked automobiles.

In 1801, Joseph Jacquard first exhibited his famous improved loom in Paris. The way in which its perforated card on a cylinder permitted certain needles to pass while rejecting others gave the dreamers about mechanical musical instruments an idea. If perforated cardboard could "select" needles in a loom, it could "select" bursts of air from a bellows. In time, a Frenchman named Peytre came up with a perforated paper music roll, to be wound up on two cylinders, for use in barrel organs or, derivatively, in pianos. An Englishman worked out a similar idea a few years later. By 1851 Henri Pape, the protean inventor, was fooling with the notion.

The first complete pneumatic player-piano to be constructed seems to have been one on which a French patent was granted to a Monsieur Fourneaux of Paris in 1863. He called it "Pianista," almost a good name, but too human-sounding for a machine. It was an independent structure, of the kind later called "cabinet"—a wheel-up, crank-operated, artificial-finger machine, externally very much like one of those described by Dr. Busby nearly forty years earlier, apart from the pneumatic feature. "Pianista" was exhibited at the Philadelphia Centennial Exposition in 1876 and thereby seems to have boosted the temperature of some of the many Americans suffering from chronic mechanitis. It was not much of a success with people who cared either for music or for a conventional show of gentility—that is to say, with the only persons who could be expected to buy it. Nothing deterred, the gadgeteers now had a new line to work, and they were bound to make new pneumatic music boxes whether anybody wanted them or not. About 1880 there appeared several applications of the paper-roll idea to reed organs. One of them was called "Mechanical Orguinette," and we mention it because the firm manufacturing it later became the Aeolian Co.

During the eighties and nineties varying new species of pneumatic piano-playing mechanisms were being put forward with increasing frequency, chiefly in the United States, but also in England and Germany. Piano makers at first showed reluctance to build the machine inside the piano, fearing too great an internal complication; and most of the players were of the "cabinet" type. Acceptance was slow. One company presented a specimen of its machine to Anton Seidl, the eminent Wagnerian conductor of the Metropolitan Opera. He was injudiciously courteous enough to praise its ingenuity, and the company started boasting of his approval; but that did not prevent Dr. Seidl from relegating the contraption to his attic, out of sight and hearing, or from making sarcastic remarks about it in private. A San Antonio, Texas, newspaper of September 1891 described a wheel-up player piano as a novelty and said it "enables the cook to furnish music for her mistress's guests with exactly the same technic that is required to mash up the coffee for their dinner delectation."

Still, by the end of the century the American public was weakening. What with the nagging of salesmen and the general democratic craving to be ruled by the pretenses of the Joneses, American homes harbored a million pianos that nobody could play to amount to anything. The allurements of the player piano might begin to seem more persuasive, especially since the things could now be made with some control of speed and shading, at the discretion of the operator. The crank was out, however, for it had too many prosaic associations: a successful machine would have to be foot-pumped, like a melodeon.

At this critical moment E. S. Votey devised a pedal-operated cabinet-type of piano-playing machine, differing little in practice from a number of similar ones, for the Aeolian Co., which patented it in 1900. Some unnamed poetic genius, however, created a name for it so potent that Americans surrendered to it in battalions and regiments. The name was "Pianola"—indeed, a happy thought: not a set of nonsense syllables, not a vaguely allusive foreign hybrid, but a good naturalized-American word meaningfully extended. "Pianola" was, clearly, a piano and something more. The something more, the *ola,* sounded easily mechanical, playfully pleasant, and feminine. Moreover, the word's vowels and consonants were evenly and euphoniously distributed, and any sixth grader could read them without trouble. "Pianola" was a musical word for a musical object: quite perfect. Used in an aggressive advertising campaign, it was an invincible weapon. Three years after the granting of the patent, the Aeolian Co. formed its great new corporation, controlling the manufacture of tens of thousands of pianos onto which it hoped to attach its mechanical and verbal masterpiece. The word "Pianola" was the exclusive property of the Aeolian Co., and may still be so of its assigns. But the public took it up, spelled it with a small *p,* and made it into a generic term for all player pianos.

After the success of the Aeolian Co., other piano makers scrambled to get into the player business. The expert piano-construction technician William Braid White, writing in 1914, listed forty-two concerns making player pianos. Many of them strained hard to baptize their brands attractively: we notice "Amphion," "Auto-piano," "Autotone," "Playotone," "Manualo," "Air-o-Player," "Angelus," "Cecilian," "Apollo," "Euphona," "Artistano," "Symphonola," "Harmonola," "Peerless," "Simplex," "Humana," and some others. But to the man in the street, they were all pianolas.

The machine became much improved presently. Piano makers overcame their resistance to building them in; and, indeed, the "cabinet" player soon became obsolete. Control of speed and of shading was made more sensitive—and responsive to the action of neat hand levers. The shadings and other expression marks supposedly proper to a piece of music were indicated on the roll by a continuous line, for the operator to watch and to follow. An enormous amount of music was now punched out on rolls: the latest popular songs—with the words to be read on the roll as it unwound—dance music, classics of the piano literature, and arrangements of symphonies and other works.

"PERFECTION WITHOUT PRACTICE," proclaimed the Cleveland, Ohio, piano store of J. T. Wamelink & Son in 1905. "How many thousands of American parlors contain that shining monument to a past girlhood—a silent piano. Do you wish to enjoy your piano? This can be accomplished by owning a Cecilian Piano Player." Pumping pedals is easier—and therefore better—than playing keys; it is easier and better still to press a button and do nothing. With the spread of electricity, this capability was readily introduced into player pianos. In certain public places the button was made to be pressed by a nickel in a slot.

The player-piano habit grew furiously, once the pianola had broken down the resistance. At the time of the foregoing advertisement less than six per cent of all American pianos were being manufactured with pneumatic intestines. Ten years later the proportion was more than one out of every four. By 1919 the players outnumbered the straight pianos and constituted more than fifty-three per cent of the total annual output.

The player-piano was capable of one further development, which was achieved fairly early in the history of its success. A pneumatic playing machine that worked automatically and electrically—and was capable of rapid changes in the force of the air puffs it gave forth—might seem competent to reproduce the exact playing of a professional performing artist. The artist, playing on a specially built instrument, could complete an electrical circuit by means of contacts situated just beneath each key. In this way, a set of lead pencils could be activated to make longer or shorter marks on an actual player-piano paper roll as it revolved at the standard speed. The length and spacing of the pencil marks, then, would exactly correspond to the performer's own strokes upon the keys, thus giving the precise nuance of his rhythm and phrasing. His pedaling could be similarly recorded. His shadings would be more difficult, if not impossible, to reproduce, because the force of the key stroke—since it merely made a connection—could not affect the action of the recording pencils. The nearest solution was to have the artist's shading carefully noted in a copy of the music by another musician and then synthesized on the finished roll by the cutting of special perforations near both its edges, designed to control the force of the air puffs. Some of this synthesis of shading could be achieved with a high degree of plausibility and, when coupled with the authentic recording of the key strokes, often gave a close approximation to the artist's playing. Incidentally, this type of machine had a special advantage: any false note played by the artist could be rectified with complete smoothness by the simple process of erasing the pencil mark that represented it on the master roll and substituting an equivalent, correct one.

The first practical machine of this kind to be developed was the product of M. Welte & Co., a German firm located in Freiburg-in-Breisgau. Herr Welte first exhibited his instrument in 1904, giving it the pretty cognomen of "Mignon"; and it was marketed under the commercial name of "Welte-Mignon." Many interesting recordings were made for it, notably those of famous composers such as Edvard Grieg and Claude Debussy playing their own compositions.

The Welte-Mignon was soon introduced into the United States with some success, but Americans could not expect to feel happy for long with a foreign gadget. Native tinkerers got busy and put together American-made reproducing player-pianos embodying similar principles. In the fall of 1913 the Aeolian Co. came out with an automatic reproducing player-piano branded with the words "Duo-Art." The term may have had some farfetched significance; anyway, that syllable "Art" could be presumed to be worth a considerable retail markup. The illustriousness of the pianists who were expected to make recordings on it, however, seemed to demand an association with a more prestigious piano name than any of which the Aeolian Co. had the disposal. Its managers succeeded in getting together with the high and mighty Steinway & Sons, hitherto aloof from the subject of player pianos. They persuaded Steinway to make numbers of grands with great gaps in their abdomens, to be stuffed with the player action; and thus, Steinway-Duo-Art instruments were made and sold expensively for a number of years. Presently the other "trust," the American Piano Co., needed to get even with its rival. In 1916 it, too, brought out a reproducing piano—which it called "Ampico" after itself, by a commonplace fusion of initial syllables relished alike in the world of American business and in the bureaucracy of the Soviet Union. The "Ampico" was, of course, applied to the Knabe and the Chickering pianos.

For some years, about 1916 to 1925, almost every concert pianist of any prominence in the United States made record rolls for either the Duo-Art or the Ampico. The promoters of the machines were imaginative in their advertising; moreover, they had a lot of money for it. The point they always wanted to make was the equivalence of the record with the performance of a famous living virtuoso: buy our reproducing piano, and you can have Paderewski, Artur Rubinstein, and Leopold Godowsky right in your own living room on your own instrument. The Aeolian Co., for example, hired most of the country's leading symphony orchestras to give special concerts. The *pièce de résistance* of their programs was always a piano concerto, accompanied by the orchestra, the solor part delivered by an unmanned Duo-Art machine reeling off the record roll of an absent virtuoso. Walter Damrosch, Josef Stransky, Leopold Stokowski, Alfred Hertz, Nikolai Sokoloff, Ossip Gabrilówitsch, and Eugène Ysaÿe were among the well-known conductors who lent themselves to this commercial promotion.

On February 3, 1920, the American Piano Co. put on a large demonstration at Carnegie Hall, New York, before a numerous invited audience. Five eminent pianists—Artur Rubinstein, Leopold Godowsky, Benno Moiseiwitsch, Leo Ornstein, and Mischa Levitzki—each played one or two pieces, interspersed with renditions by the Ampico. For the final number, the program merely announced that Levitzki was to play Liszt's *Hungarian* Rhapsody No. 6. The pianist began it vigorously, arrived at the hold that ends the first section, and extended his hands expectantly over the keys before the beginning of the following slower episode. The music came forth gently—but Levitzki removed his hands and the sounds went on without him. The Ampico had taken up where the artist stopped, and just as skillfully! That would have seemed the proper moment for the audience to make some demonstration of admiration; however, the people remained silent and attentive. The rhapsody proceeded; at the top of its fast final furiousness, Levitzki jumped back into it and played the close in person. It was at his plunge that the audience became electrified, breaking into the music with a salvo of applause. To snatch up the thread instantly, anywhere, of a composition he has played innumerable times, is no great feat for a good musician; in fact, he would hardly deserve the name of professional if he were unable to do so. Yet at that moment many people felt that a man who had complete command over the succession of several thousand notes was more remarkable than any machine. Perhaps they were right.

The striving for finer musical culture was keen in those days. Concerts of high quality were being pushed into hundreds of communities that had not had them before, and the names of more virtuosos were becoming more widely known than ever before. The situation was, indeed, favorable for the sale of reproducing pianos. On the other hand, once the habit of passive home listening before a machine had become established, the Duo-Arts and the Ampicos became highly vulnerable to competition. In 1920 a Steinway Duo-Art grand cost more than $4000, while even a small Chickering Ampico upright retailed for about $1400. Their attractions were hard to maintain before the advance of improved phonographs and radio sets, which offered greater and more varied repertoire as well as more authentic reproduction, which took up less room, and which cost only a couple of hundred dollars or so. Before the end of the 1920's, the reproducing pianos were all but obsolete.

2. THE CASE OF GERMANY

THE VIGOR of piano manufacture, as we have stated before, is not primarily related to the higher cultivation of music, nor even to an intensive devotion to the handicraft of instrument making. It is, on the contrary, a phase of the development of machine technology, of large-scale industry and commerce. This thesis can be well exemplified by the case of Germany. The Germans, from the very beginning, had an affectionate interest in the pianoforte. It appeared to them at first as an improvement upon the clavichord, whose simplicity, cheapness, and sensitiveness had long suited both their poverty and their introspective bent. During the time from 1720 to 1760, the Germans took up the pianoforte and worked on it with persistence; while the Italians—in whose lands it had first been made—very soon lost interest in it. The German talent for cabinet making and the German fondness for music found a harmonious common ground in this craft. It was Germans who introduced piano making into England and into France, and who guided the trade there for a generation. Germans introduced the piano into Russia, and in the United States they were associated with its construction from the earliest time. Moreover, during the late eighteenth century Germans were producing most of the world's first- and second-rate literature for the instrument.

Yet as soon as the simpler developmental stages of piano making were passed, the Germans could not keep pace with the larger capital accumulations, the wider trading opportunities, the better communications, and the better factory organization of the people of the countries to the west. Any inventive impulses German individuals may have had tended to be discouraged by the lack of facilities for exploiting them on a suitable scale. The best of the German mechanical geniuses, such as Pape, were only able to make good careers by emigrating. During the early nineteenth century—despite Haydn, Mozart, and Beethoven, despite Weber, Hummel, and Schubert and a host of fainter lights—North German piano makers were boasting pitifully that their instruments were "like English," or "made on English principles." In Vienna, it is true, the Stein-Streicher dynasty of piano makers were able to achieve a certain local prestige; yet Beethoven himself felt that his English instrument was in a category superior to any of Austrian make he had previously had.

By the 1840's, German dependence in piano manufacture had shifted from England to France. Erards had then become the favorites with those Germans who could afford them, among whom we may name Felix Mendelssohn-Bartholdy. To a Cologne piano maker, Liszt offered the following advice: "Since you have to copy your designs, why don't you copy Erards'?" A competent Austrian observer at the great London Exposition of 1851 stated that the German pianos exhibited there actually were all more or less close imitations of Erards.

The economic rise of Germany, coupled with the political rise of Prussia, took a decided spurt during the 1850's. That was the time in which Germans began to exploit their thitherto neglected mineral resources, most especially their coal and iron. The world's supply of gold went up after the discovery of that metal in California and Australia, and Germany got her share of it. Moreover, theoretical science, thitherto pursued by Germans as a form of philosophical exercise, began to appeal to them as a basis for technology and practical engineering. Within not too long a period, Germany changed from a nation remarkable for its romantic poets, its idealist philosophers, and its musicians into one noteworthy for its steel makers, ship builders and owners, railroad and coal-mine operators, and industrial chemists; from a poor people two thirds rural and feudal in outlook to one increasingly urban and industrial, led on many fronts by wealthy bourgeois capitalists. In 1871 Prussia won her spectacular military victory over France, at the same time forging the congeries of little German states into a united empire. The event dramatically signaled Germany's metamorphosis from a backward country into a world power. The event, in turn, led to an even greater development of industry and trade.

In all this growth of wealth and power, the piano business played its modest part. The two piano manufacturers who became the most important in modern Germany were Julius Blüthner of Leipzig and Carl Bechstein of Berlin—the former establishing his business in 1853, the latter three years later. These German firms, then, were of about the same age as Steinways' or slightly younger, at least fifteen years younger than William Knabe & Co., and at least thirty years younger than Chickerings'.

Bechstein and Blüthner did moderately well during the 1860's; but it was lucky for them that their prosperity was not too overwhelming at first, since too great a momentum of production might have deterred them from making the adjustments on which their future pre-eminence was to depend. It is likely that Carl Bechstein was aware of the newer American ideas of piano construction—the one-piece metal frame, the overstrung scale, the increased tension, and so on—even before 1860. He attended the London fair of 1862, exhibiting a piano there that was said, at the time, to have been constructed on Chickering principles. Moreover, at the same exposition he had ample opportunity of studying the Steinway instruments displayed there. The decisive success of the Americans in Paris in 1867 undoubtedly convinced both him and Blüthner that all future piano-making progress was thenceforth bound to be along the path struck out by the Americans. Thus, it would be fair to say that the modern German piano industry is, in a sense, a derivative of the American. However, insofar as the American leadership was to a great extent that of Steinway, it is only fair to remember that the Steinways' success was one of German piano-making genius developing in the favorable American environment.

In any event, Bechstein—adopting American ideas with certain modifications and benefiting from the new German technological and metallurgical developments—was soon able to produce an instrument of very high quality, which presently became a favorite with the largest number of European concert performers. The firm, indeed, became recognized as supreme in Europe. When the Steinways started their Hamburg factory in 1880, they could stimulate Bechsteins to competitive effort, but could encroach very little upon their domestic business. The Blüthner piano, too, was a fine product; its tone on the whole was less virile but often sweeter in the treble than that of the Bechstein. The relationship between the two was somewhat comparable to that between the Mason & Hamlin and the Steinway tone qualities. A distinctive feature of the Blüthner piano was its use of a sympathetic, unstruck fourth string—of half length—for three full treble octaves. The pedantic Latin word "*Aliquot,*" given to this device, did not seem to estrange German customers.

Both Bechstein and Blüthner sought successfully to attach their repute to that of concert artists and both opened Berlin concert halls in which their instruments were in constant service—Berlin, the new capital and chief city of the new empire, being the place where virtuoso reputations were thenceforth to be created. The newer companies Bechstein and Blüthner became the German industry leaders, but other respectable German and Austrian piano makers also benefited from the general advance of prosperity; among these were the old houses of Rudolf Ibach Sons of Barmen, Schiedmayer & Sons of Stuttgart, and Ludwig Bösendorfer of Vienna—to say nothing of those who produced cheaper goods.

The point to be made is that the improvement and expansion of the German piano business was essentially a phase of the general German boom. When the country became a united empire, broke down the boundaries of its smaller component states, and established a uniform currency, it created a more accessible large internal market; and with the establishment of a strong stable government, Germany became a safe, attractive place for larger investments of capital. Moreover, the technology of iron and other metals created improved communications—larger and faster ships and a denser net of railroads. All this formed part of the piano business. Better and readier iron meant readier frames, wires, and pins for pianos; better steel and steam engines meant better tools and power for shaping piano parts; and better communications meant better procurement of materials, both domestic and imported, as well as better distribution of the finished product. Finally, it all meant more people—with wealth derived from all this industry—who could become piano buyers. The fact that Germany was a country with a great musical tradition was a minor element in the situation.

Germany's geographical limitations, like those of other European countries, produced their inevitable effects on her economy. Her factories could turn out more goods than her inhabitants could buy, yet her land could not produce enough materials to keep the factories running, or even properly to feed her fast-growing population. The export trade was a necessity from the moment the country became thoroughly industrialized. Thus, German pianos, like German toys and dyestuffs, were made to be sent to foreign countries. In 1890 it was reported that German manufacturers were dominating the piano markets of Switzerland

and Rumania; and by the end of the century they were supplying a considerable fraction of the piano demand of all Europe, in addition to doing a very sizable overseas business.

England, herself still a leading piano producer, proved, interestingly enough, to be an especially good customer for German instruments. In 1879, following the Steinways' example of a few years earlier, Bechstein established warerooms in London, besides also building a concert hall there. By 1900 one half of the annual Bechstein output of eighteen hundred grands and twenty-two hundred uprights went to Britain and its colonies and possessions. Other good German firms, such as Ibach, also kept London shops. On the cheap side, too, German goods could invade England successfully. A London publication named *Truth* complained in 1891 that floods of flimsy German pianos, offered at £16 10s (about $80) apiece, were being sent to London dealers, together with an assortment of stencils, some of which, alas, consisted of letters perilously close to the spelling of certain ancient and honorable names—for instance, "Br*a*dwood" or "Erar*t*."

England was, traditionally, a free-trade country. But some German manufacturers even made efforts to hop over the thirty-five per cent tariff wall of the United States. Early in the nineties we can see advertisements in American trade papers of a German-made thing called "Pianett." It was described as a four-octave iron-frame "check-repeater-action" miniature—three feet nine inches high, two feet eleven inches long, and one foot seven inches deep. Illustrations showed a single pedal. It was offered at from $25 to $40 including packing, F.O.B. Hamburg or Bremen. Even with freight and customs duty, it might have seemed attractive to price buyers. Yet, evidently, it must have been too toylike and too blatantly cheap-looking to appeal to Americans ambitious enough to want any kind of piano at all.

By 1910 Germany ranked second among the world's piano-making nations in the number of instruments produced. The United States was first, with an annual production of more than 360,000 units, while Germany turned out 150,000—of which two fifths, or 60,000, were exported. At that moment England's annual output was about 75,000, giving her third place, while France ran a bad fourth with 25,000. With all Germany's great industrial development and gain of wealth, its inhabitants, individually, could not approach the purchasing power of Americans. The 90,000 pianos absorbed within Germany during 1910 represent one new instrument for every 666 persons. By comparison, in that same year, one new American piano was bought for every 255 persons—more than two and one half times as many relative to the population. The fact is one indication of the generally lower standard of living in the European country. Great Britain's piano-distribution figure for the same year may be estimated as roughly equivalent to the German and, likewise, far below the American.

3. OTHER LANDS: THE PIANO *IN PARTIBUS INFIDELIUM*

Our study has been concerned almost exclusively with Germany and Austria, England, France, and the United States. These, indeed, are the countries whose inhabitants were overwhelmingly the most numerous buyers and makers of pianos, and among whose people the piano became most truly an institution. They were the countries in which the machine technology was most firmly and most widely established, and operated under the leadership of businessmen. They were the countries whose standards of living were highest and whose economic structures brought forth the largest number of comfortably well-to-do city-dwelling persons.

A number of smaller countries lying adjacent to the large ones afore-mentioned also were "modern," industrial, and prosperous. Holland and Belgium, Switzerland and the Scandinavian countries also believed in the piano as a household idol, bought pianos in large quantities proportional to their populations, and even supported a few smaller piano factories of their own. The same is true of Canada. We have omitted discussing them because their roles are subordinate and their piano histories embody no divergent principles. South European countries such as Spain and Italy, being less industrialized, have consequently produced few pianos; and their correspondingly smaller upper middle class has largely tended to import its instruments from Germany, England, and France. Characteristically, such piano making as there was in Spain was located in Barcelona, the country's greatest industrial center. The communities of Latin America, Iberian cultural derivatives, have likewise always been piano importers. That has not prevented the educated circles in these nations from encouraging their natives' keyboard-playing talents, and a number of superb piano virtuosos have emanated from among them.

A piano industry did grow up in Russia during the nineteenth century—on a small scale, indeed, by comparison with her enormous potential resources. Most of the Russian piano makers were located in St. Petersburg, and all of the early ones were Germans, or of German origin. Gebrüder Diederichs were established there as early as 1810, while Johann Friedrich Schroeder started his factory in 1818. One of the best and most successful manufacturers was Jakob Becker, a native of the Palatinate, who began his activities in St. Petersburg in 1841. A parallel with the United States might be observed: up to the third quarter of the nineteenth century, foreign virtuosos traveling in Russia were unwilling to trust themselves to the local makers, but brought their own instruments with them. However, Becker and Schroeder then succeeded in turning out good concert grands, whereupon Anton and Nikolai Rubinstein—influential heads of conservatories in St. Petersburg and Moscow—actively promoted the home product. Meanwhile the Russian makers were alert to modern developments and were applying American principles of cross-stringing to their instruments. After a time Josef Hofmann and Eugen d'Albert played Russian pianos on their Russian tours. Both Becker and Schroeder became purveyors to various royal families besides their own and received honors and distinctions abroad. At the Chicago World's Fair in 1893, Russian piano makers had a special exhibit of their own, which attracted much favorable comment.

The Russians were evidently able to achieve good quality, but their output was small. In 1891 Becker claimed to have made a mere 11,400 pianos during the past fifty years, while Schroeder was said to have turned out about 25,000 in seventy-three years. At that moment each of these leading firms was stated to be employing about three hundred men, indicating a production substantially below that of comparable contemporary American or German concerns. The Russian factories apparently did not suffice even to supply the home demand: in 1910 their total annual production was about 10,000 pianos, while another 10,000 were brought into the country annually from abroad. Thus, all the pianos the Russians made plus all they imported came to twenty per cent less than the output of France, the least industrial among the major Western nations, a country of less than one third Russia's population and of less than one fortieth its area. In 1910 Russian piano production and consumption amounted to less than six per cent of that of the United States, thus revealing the relative insignificance of the prosperous urban middle class in the vast empire.

Serious professional music education hardly existed in Russia until the establishment of the Russian Musical Society in 1859, through the efforts of Anton Rubinstein and his pioneer friend Vassily Kologrivov. Before that music teaching had consisted—in Rubinstein's own words—of "pounding a piano piece into a youth for father's or mother's birthday, or in honor of a [female] school principal." Under the circumstances, it is interesting to contemplate the numbers of remarkable composers for the piano, and the outstanding virtuosos of the instrument, that came forth from later Imperial Russia. We may mention Alexander Scriabin and Sergei Rachmaninov, both eminent piano-music creators and performers; and also Annette Essipov, Ossip Gabrilówitsch, Mark Hambourg, and Josef Lhévinne, distinguished interpreters pure and simple. Their emergence speaks well for the exalted artistic aspirations and the high standards of music education that became prevalent in the small part of the Russian world in which the piano could thrive.

In time, the piano spilled over the fringes of the Western world and was taken up with more or less conviction by some of the infidels.

Since the Renaissance, a portion of the technology and business enterprise of Western Europeans has been turned into fireams. When these were shot off at people of other cultures and races, they made a strong impression, since all human beings have a profound respect for the power and the willingness to kill. Little by little, and especially during the later nineteenth century, many Africans and Asians took on some of the Western man's ways, partly from compulsion, partly from convenience, and partly from an admiration of his superior magic and ruthlessness. A few even went so far as to adopt his ostensible Christianity.

In general, Western music made slow progress in the non-Western world, since a musical system or scale is a bodily habit, like that of speech, formed very early in life and very difficult to change thereafter. Nevertheless, a gesture toward European music on the part of a rich Oriental might help to buoy up his self-confidence. A Turkish magnate living on the edge of Europe could feel that buying an expensive piano would make him a little less inferior to those formidable Christian dogs who could build those terrific battleships. Not that he would waste his own time with it: he would have his women do that for him. The *New York Musical Review and Gazette* for November 29, 1856, quoted from a letter received from Constantinople to the effect that, as a result of the

Crimean War, the taste for European music was progressing in Turkey. The Sultan kept an orchestra, it said, composed of women alone, for the amusement of his harem. "Very few harems are now without a pianoforte and many of the Turkish ladies are excellent performers."

The Turkish Sultan had had some experience of the piano before that time. It appears that His Royal Highness Abdul-Medjid, early in the 1840's, had hired a brother of the composer Donizetti to teach music at his court, conferring upon him the honorary title of Bey, suitable to his closeness to the potentate's person. Moreover, the lively young Leopold de Meyer, who was spending the summer of 1843 in Constantinople, received—through the agency of Sir Stratford Canning, the British ambassador—a command to play before the Sultan on August 19. The pianist sent his Erard on ahead; but it seems that he was obliged to be at the palace at eight in the morning and had to wait in a great, beautiful gallery with mosaic floors, standing, all dressed up in court costume, for six hours before the time scheduled for his performance. Despite the repute of his finger-nimbleness, he had to "antechambrize," as the Germans called it. In the meantime occasional proclamations resounded through the hall, announcing the doings of His Highness: "He has risen!" or "He is going in to the bath!" —at every one of which, the entire company prostrated itself on the floor. At about 2 P.M. His Ethereal Impossibility appeared, mounted a dais, and ordered the Austrian pianist to fire away. De Meyer obeyed, playing his own fantasies on tunes from *Anna Bolena* and, later, from *Lucia di Lammermoor*—both offerings tactfully derived from Donizetti. Between these two offerings he exuded still more tact, delivering a medley on Turkish tunes supplied him by brother Donizetti Bey. The Inconceivable Panjandrum then had a barrel organ brought out and displayed more Turkish melodies to De Meyer. No low-class money could pass from Sultan to artist; instead, the virtuoso was awarded a golden snuffbox garnished with brilliants.

The Sultan's furniture movers evidently understood about pianos; those of the Prime Minister, however, seem to have been less well versed. When De Meyer, engaged to play at that worthy's residence, sent his grand piano on ahead, it was shipped, as is customary, with legs detached. The laborers, not taking notice of the legs and not imagining how the instrument was to be raised for playing, presented themselves before De Meyer, five of them supporting the piano aloft upon their backs. He indicated that he could not pound it while it was on the bodies of men; but the foreman of the gang, not grasping his humane squeamishness, thought he was complaining of some slant in the keyboard level and ordered a cushion inserted between the piano and one of the shorter Turks. Finally, things were made clear, the legs were brought forth and attached, and all turned out well. De Meyer told these stories himself, and they were retold in Paris and elsewhere with inessential modifications. That, unfortunately, does not prove their absolute agreement with fact. They were enjoyed because they nourished the prevelant European superciliousness toward the rest of the world.

Four years after De Meyer, on June 8, 1847, the incomparable Franz Liszt came to Constantinople, on a side trip from his Russian tour, his final one for a long while. But Liszt had a much higher electric potential than De Meyer ever could attain, for he had derived it partly from those French and Prussian magnates who had acclaimed him and whom De Meyer had never approached. No *antichambre* for Liszt: he was escorted immediately upon his arrival to the palace at Tcheragan, where it was the Sultan who was doing the waiting this time. Baron Resta from the Papal internuncio acted as interpreter, and a fine Erard piano had been set up and tuned. Liszt regaled the Grand Turk with his transmogrifications of an Andante from *Lucia,* the Overture to *William Tell,* and a garland of tunes from *Norma.* The monarch seemed pleased; but his imagination failed him in the expression of his gratitude, for he could think of nothing else than to present Liszt, too, with a golden snuffbox studded with precious stones. At any rate, that made him even with the Czar of Russia, the King of Prussia, and other high infantry commanders who had comparably honored the famous pianist.

The piano remained a Sultanese institution. Years after De Meyer and Liszt, one Guatelli, music teacher to His Majesty Abdul-Hamid's six-year-old daughter, suggested that the royal princess' hands might do better on a piano with narrower keys. Accordingly, in 1889, her august father ordered one from Pleyel, Wolff & Cie. in Paris, on which the stretch of an octave took up no more room than that of a sixth on an ordinary keyboard. The object was troublesome to construct; thus, the makers—considering the identity of the customer—were not averse to adding a few more costlinesses to it. It was provided with delicate and sober ornamentation in the style of Louis XVI, and its paintings were done in pink, sky blue, and tender transparent water-green tints, with bouquets of flowers and wreathed trophies representing musical instruments, the whole thing framed in a network of gold. It was all in "good taste," as Oscar Comettant tells us, that being the supreme praise of which a Frenchman is capable. He said also that this "sonorous jewel" had a pure melodious tone, "gentle to the point of making itself heard in a sick-chamber without disturbing the patient." Just the thing for a princess.

Turnabout was fair play. The Turks had lorded it over Hungary all through the seventeenth century and had even threatened Vienna. Presently, numbers of German princes found they could develop a sharp taste for the Janizaries' percussion instruments; and "Turkish" music became quite a vogue in Western Europe, as we have seen. Now, under the gleam of British naval guns and Paris bank loans, Turkish grandees could find something quite fascinating about a piano. It is clear that a gravitational field develops, culturally speaking, about those who control the land, the money, and the deadly weapons.

Acculturation by artillery also took place, with a somewhat different flavor, in Japan. Toward the end of the sixteenth century, the Japanese authorities became justly suspicious of the motives of the numerous Europeans, especially Spaniards and Portuguese, who were moving among them. They chased all the hairy barbarians out, suppressed the Christian religion, and forbade all intercourse with the West—accomplishing this by the simple process of putting to death any Caucasian trying to land or take refuge in Japan, as well as any Japanese who had sneaked out and was trying to return. The sealed-up paradise of cultural and national purity endured for two hundred and fifteen years, until Americans and Europeans blasted their way in again with steam-driven warships equipped with big guns.

Compelled to come to terms with Westerners, the Japanese saw little in them to admire, but felt that their peculiar arrogance was chiefly supported by their powerful gadgets. They hit on a scheme: if they, too, could learn to make and handle the gadgets, they might use them to maintain their own brand of arrogance. An elaborate re-education began in Japan, by order of the Emperor; and with Western help, the Japanese learned to construct railroads and telegraphs, bicycles and cameras, and a thousand other things—including rifles, of course. It is difficult, however, to keep cultural elements in impermeable compartments. The Japanese students abroad were bound to absorb other things beside the chemistry and engineering for which they had come—such things as drinking beer, sitting in chairs, wearing frock coats, and shaking hands. Westerners resident in Japan also taught many things unwittingly. The need for intelligent industrial labor, in turn, demanded a universal minimum literacy; thus, free public schools were established, on the American plan, since primary education was considered a pre-eminent American strong point.

If American schools taught music and class singing, the new Japanese schools could do no less. Thus, Western music came into Japan in a particularly systematic and effective way. In 1879, Luther Whiting Mason (no relation of Lowell Mason's), of Connecticut, went to Japan by invitation of its government and introduced the singing of Western scale modes to Japanese elementary teachers and pupils. By 1882, thirty thousand schools throughout the country were getting their children to sing *do re mi* in the diatonic major scale, to learn Western music notation, and to achieve simple Western tunes in that idiom. A generation later, official Japanese school music books contained about the same material as the American: Mendelssohn songs and "The British Grenadiers"—all with Japanese words—as well as "Home, Sweet Home" and "The Last Rose of Summer." In 1885, a few years before the Japanese began to enjoy playing baseball, a school of Western music was established, under government auspices, at Ueno, then a Tokyo suburb. Germans, mostly, were hired to guide Japanese students into the realm of the higher *Tonkunst*. Even previous to all this official inculcation, the Japanese appear to have been fascinated by the Western man's lively reaction to his music, as well as by the complication of some of his instruments. Before the founding of the Ueno school, even before the day of Luther Mason, a square piano made in Japan was exhibited at the Paris Exposition of 1878.

Thus, without totally repudiating their ancestral musical habits, the Japanese became Westernized musically. This came about not because their upper classes affected Western music as a fancy foreign fad, but because the practice of it was implanted systematically and generally in the very young of all ranks, three quarters of a century ago. We cannot here tell the story of its progress; we will content ourselves with saying that by the end of the first third of the twentieth century Japan supported every manner of Western musical institution and activity, and developed numbers of good performers and competent composers, much as did any smaller European country.

Under the circumstances, a demand for pianos was bound to arise, and the rapidly progressing industrialization of the country allowed it to be supplied at home. The limiting factor was the generally low standard of living, which meant that relatively few families could afford them. Furthermore, a piano, especially a grand, would seem like a rather brutal incongruity in a room of a true Japanese house. For one thing, it would ruin the floor mats. However, later in the nineteenth century many wealthier Japanese took up the custom of adding to their homes a suite of rooms built and furnished in Western style, with hinged doors, plaster ceilings, tables, chairs, and hangings. They did it primarily for the more convenient entertaining of European and American guests. These "foreign-style" apartments were often arranged in poor taste compared to the exquisite simplicity of the Japanese rooms, yet they could harbor pianos more fittingly. As time went on, and especially after the war of 1914–18, the appetite for "foreign-style" living sharpened among those who could afford it, becoming quite widespread in Tokyo and other large cities. Ownership of pianos went along with this trend.

When Konan Yamaha started his piano-making shop as early as 1880, he was likely to have built rather slavish copies of the pianos he was able to observe at home. The same was probably true of the organ he made five years later, the first to be constructed in Japan. It was in the same year, 1885, however, that he encountered competition; for that was when Nishikawa & Sons established their piano shop in Tokyo. Presently a number of Japanese went to America and to Germany to learn the piano-manufacturing business more expertly. During the 1890's Yamaha reorganized his company as a corporation, with himself as president, calling it *Nippon Gak-ki Seizō Kabushiki Kaisha* (Japan Musical Instrument Manufacturing Corporation). In 1907 its capitalization was increased to 600,000 yen ($300,000), and by 1911 the company was turning out six hundred pianos and eight thousand organs annually. Its rival Nishikawa & Sons also prospered, reaching an output of two hundred pianos that year. Japan enjoyed a considerable burst of affluence during and after the First World War, its manufacturing and shipping having been able, for the time being, to supplant that of the Germans in many markets. Foreign musical artists were invited to give concerts, the full cumulation of previous music education was beginning to be felt, enthusiasm for music ran high, and the instrument business boomed correspondingly. By 1932 the *Nippon Gak-ki Seizō* Corporation was a concern with a capital of 4,000,000 yen and with huge factories at Hamamatsu—midway between Yokohama and Osaka—employing 2050 persons of whom 1800 were actual factory workers.

A plant equipped for making and putting together various shapes of metal and wood could be adjusted or expanded comparatively easily for the manufacture of many different products composed of the same or similar materials. Thus, it is not astonishing that the *Nippon Gak-ki Seizō* Corporation, in addition to musical instruments, also manufactured articles quite unrelated to music. According to their statements of 1932, they produced in one year 4000 pianos, 20,000 organs, 240,000 dozen mouth harmonicas, 369,000 square meters of veneer, besides mantelpieces and airplane propellers—to a total value of 8,000,000 yen. Undoubtedly, much of this merchandise—especially the harmonicas—was exported.

The Nishikawa & Sons company continued to progress, on a much more modest scale. Meanwhile another piano firm, the Ono Co., had some success, putting out an instrument mysteriously labeled "Horugel," in Latin letters. It is a set of syllables impossible to the Japanese language and, consequently, is globally meaningless; nevertheless, "Horugel" pianos are met with rather frequently in Tokyo to this day. Until the early 1930's, the Ono Co. was considered sufficiently reputable for the Steinways to entrust it with their agency. Finally, the great Mitsubishi Trading Co. also had a piano department at one time.

The best Japanese-made grand pianos are quite good and compare favorably with American and German instruments of second or third quality. They give very satisfactory service for studio or home use, though, for the most part, they do not seem to have sufficient stamina or carrying power for playing in large concert halls. In Tokyo in 1946, piano soloists with the *Nippon Kō-kyogaku Dan* (Nippon Philharmonic Orchestra) at its Hibiya Hall subscription concerts almost invariably played on a Blüthner piano.

4. THE DUSK OF THE IDOL

THE FEW YEARS before 1914 marked the widest extent of the high plateau on which the piano had been riding for more than two generations. From then on its spread narrowed, and presently the honor in which it had been held began to diminish rapidly.

Beginning with the later 1920's it plunged down a dark, destructive ravine—to emerge in the late 1930's on the low plateau on which it is proceeding at present.

Subtle symptoms of decadence might have been discerned by 1910 or before. Somewhere about that time the Steinways, as well as some makers of low-priced instruments, altered a number of the visual aspects of their pianos, especially of their grands: the obese carved legs were replaced by straight, gracefully tapered underpinnings; the tortured-looking Gothic lettering on the name board was changed to calm serifed roman capitals; and the intricately carved openwork of the music rack gave way to a solid near-rectangular board.

The originators of these alterations may have thought they were intending them merely to be a welcome relief from a too-long prevalent style, a mere salutary movement of fashion without further significance. Yet no permanent change of fashion can be just that and nothing more. All notions and values jostle and infect each other, often in dim, surreptitious ways. The abandonment of a familiar object's old-fashioned physiognomy suggested a coming break with a previous way of life, the start of a loss of faith in a hitherto robust set of standards. The old legs, lettering, and lattice were visible points of a certain flavor of ostentation; and their frank air of elaborate uselessness was their reason for being. They did not, indeed, express a pointed, aggressive showing off, but rather gave a conventionalized, sedate effect of decent wastefulness. Now the instrument was to acquire a quieter, more functional look; but a functional look in a piano might vaguely signify that one of the important motives for owning one was losing its potency. If the palpable boast of the instrument's uselessness were abandoned—and it looked as simple and businesslike as a kitchen utensil—that could mean that it was presumed to be acquired rigorously for its musical value. But the growth of such an idea would end by greatly reducing the number of persons caring to buy the instrument.

On the surface, the piano business was in the ruddiest flush of health in 1914; and at that time a suggestion like the foregoing would have been dismissed as a morbid fantasy. Indeed, among the fresh millionaires, piano ostentation was putting forth some notably lush new orchids. Among the few who could afford them, custom-made "art pianos" were at their gaudiest and most frequent: there were pianos in "Gothic," "Renaissance," "Louis XIV," *"Art nouveau,"* or any other "style" in the dictionary; pianos armored with angels, carried by gryphons, lined with pastoral scenes, or plastered with wreaths, panels, medallions, and the names of all nine Muses in Greek letters. Somehow, this expensive wedding cake made no school of itself—it developed no wide following, no wave of cheaply made imitation: not many people really believed in it very much.

Nor could, on the higher layers of musical art—in the world of concerts, virtuosos, and serious music students—any evidence of a decline of the piano yet be discerned. On the contrary, the experience of musical masterpieces and the development of good musical taste seemed to be spreading more rapidly than ever before. Throughout the United States concerts, especially those involving piano playing, increased on a great scale. During the second decade of the century Manitowoc, Wisconsin, Sabetha, Kansas, Hood River, Oregon, and a thousand other small ambitious American communities made more and more regular opportunities for themselves to hear great piano music performed with skill and artistry upon the very finest instruments. Sizable crops of good American pianists grew up every year.

Yet, higher layers, as we are perpetually saying, cover little ground. As the country raised more good pianists and more discriminating listeners, the population bought fewer pianos. The figures tell the sad tale. According to the Department of Commerce, the piano factories of the United States put out 364,545 instruments in 1909, whereas the 1919 total was 341,652—showing a decline of 6.28 per cent during a period in which the population had grown by 14 per cent. By 1925 the output had again gone down to 306,584, a further loss of more than 10 per cent, while the population again went up about 8 per cent. That was the year in which the player pianos reached their greatest relative distribution: 55 per cent of the total of all piano units. A dramatic descent came during the following four years: the great depression began to brandish its threats only during the last two months of 1929, yet the pianos sold within the year showed a drop of more than 57 per cent below the figure for 1925.

Meanwhile another trend was interesting to observe. In 1909 a mere 2.4 per cent of pianos sold were grands; but by 1927, right in the sweep of the decline, grands constituted as much as 21.4 per cent of the total output. It is tempting to conclude that those who, decreasingly, did buy pianos were becoming more in earnest about playing them. Indeed, the cachexia of the piano business took place at a period of the most eager enthusiasm for the experience of the higher reaches of music. It coincided with the rise of a considerable number of new symphony orchestras, including some of the country's finest, such as the San Francisco, the Los Angeles, and the Cleveland; moreover, it was the time of the foundation of a number of highly endowed, superbly staffed music schools of exalted standards; it was the time, too, of the maturing and sophistication of the tingling complexities of jazz music. The year 1924 marked the establishment of the great Curtis Institute of Music; it also marked George Gershwin's famous Aeolian Hall *première* performance of his *Rhapsody in Blue* with Paul Whiteman's band. All this did not avail the piano business: it slid down, down, and down.

The vogue of the player piano was to blame, to a certain extent. It did, indeed, for a time pump a kind of plausible functionality into the ordinary domestic piano. That was, nevertheless, an effort of artificial respiration which eventually accelerated its decline. For the player piano defeated one of the piano's main traditional purposes, that of symbolizing a status of respectability, since the instrument's social value was bound up with the "accomplishment" of the girls who had learned, as well as might be, to play it. Reduced to a machine that could be turned on by a child or a menial, it lost what remaining prestige it had and became a music box, a mechanical convenience like a water faucet. That made it more useful, physically, than it had been before, but left it free to be supplanted at any moment by better, more varied, more convenient, and cheaper music boxes. The phonographs of the 1910's, though technically imperfect, made inroads on the piano market; while the rise of radio broadcasting and the widespread purchase of sets, beginning in 1921, shoved the piano down a sharply steeper slope.

Within a year or two, with the national production still hovering around the 300,000 mark, the piano's plight began to encourage a number of volunteer gravediggers. In the October 1924 issue of *The Antiquarian,* a magazine evidently devoted to domestic antiques, there appeared an article entitled "American Pianos"—probably by the editor, Esther Singleton—which said:

> In this age of victrolas and radios, the piano is fast becoming a rare article in the ordinary home . . . Few persons now strum the abused instrument . . . The once ubiquitous instrument is now silenced, for only students of real talent are encouraged. The piano, therefore, is in danger of becoming as rare now as a brougham, a phaeton or a dogcart for the banished horse.

This opinion is important because it comes from a presumably disinterested source, though it might be objected that the author could have been overeager to find a potential supply of old furniture.

On the other side of the Atlantic, the piano was faring no better. Walter J. Turner, music critic of the London *New Statesman,* wrote an article for his paper for August 29, 1925, entitled "The Passing of the Pianoforte." In it he quoted an interview with "a well-known English musician," who is reported to have said: "Wireless and gramophone have broken the head of the amateur, and I firmly believe that soon the piano and the fiddle will be as out of fashion in the average British home as anti-macassars and wax flowers." Turner was not really sorry that the piano was "passing," as he thought. He described its status in most British households:

> . . . more of an ornament than an instrument for daily or even weekly use. More pianofortes have rusted away in the British Isles than have ever been worn out with practice. . . . It would not surprise me if in another fifty years the pianoforte were an extinct instrument along with the viol and the harpsichord.

He envisaged a "concert of ancient music" of 1975, with the piano as the antiquarian *pièce de résistance.* Turner was a most enthusiastic repudiator at the time, saying that soon the music of the great piano composers—Beethoven, Schumann, Chopin, Brahms, and Liszt—would sound incredibly old-fashioned. The *New Statesman,* let us remember, has always been professionally "progressive," happy to cheer on the decay of old institutions. Nevertheless, thirteen years after writing the above article, Turner published a biography of Mozart.

Germany too felt the wasting away of the piano by 1924, even though the currency had been stabilized that year and business was generally better. Kurt Luethge, however, writing in *Die Musik* for September, did not deign to bother with economics or ordinary human nature, but placed the phenomenon in a true German fog-swollen realm of "aesthetics." The instrument, he maintained in his article "Concerning the Piano and its Future," has not proved itself suitable for the expression of modern musical trends. Its "rigid objectivity" has not allowed it to become pliable to the "art will" of our generation. It is finished, he thought.

In the United States, misgivings about the piano now began to creep into the concert world. The Curtis Institute, of Philadelphia, soon after its founding in 1924, came under the distinguished directorship of Josef Hofmann, the renowned piano virtuoso. Curtis was planned as a professional school, a training center only for musicians of the highest capacity. Presently, numbers of remarkable, capable orchestra players issued from its doors, as well as opera singers and conductors. Yet solo piano playing was consciously de-emphasized in the school's policy, and accompanying was rather taught—that is, the use of the piano in a subordinate capacity. The school's leaders evidently felt that there were already more excellent concert pianists at large than the shrinking market was likely to support.

The decline of the piano was reflected in numbers of business difficulties. The Mason & Hamlin Company needed more capital and got it from the Cable Co., large Chicago producers of cheap instruments. The Cable Co. probably owned control of Mason's, but did not interfere with their management or their factory operation; and the quality of the product was maintained for a considerable time. However, in 1924 the owners of the Cable Co., in turn, felt constrained to sell it out to the American Piano Co. That large concern was already glutted with piano brand names, but Mason & Hamlin was one with a ring to it. The corporation made it into its "leader" and made ready to stuff the Ampico machine into its guts, thus aiming to build up a still better competitor to the Steinway Duo-Art combination. But the time was late: reproducing pianos were losing their charm along with the others, and a fateful leukemia seemed to be consuming the entire business.

The American Piano Co., with all its factories, offices, stencils, and advertising magic, was indeed getting very sick. In 1926 it had still reported a large excess of sales revenue over operating expenses, depreciation, and taxes; but from 1928 to 1929 it showed an operating deficit of $235,000. The last dividend on its common stock was paid in October 1927; the last on its 7% cumulative preferred, in April 1928—whereupon that insecure security skidded from par down to 38, right during the full high jinks of the "Coolidge prosperity." The no-par common dropped from 43¼ in 1927 to 12¾ the following year. Fine American corporations are reluctant to go broke in the good old-fashioned way, with shattering bankruptcy proceedings; they prefer to save a little more wreckage by a shock-absorbing "reorganization" instead. On May 8, 1930, a new "American Piano Corporation" was formed to succeed the old American Piano Co. After arranging various sorts of exchanges of stock, the new company acquired the assets of the old for $1,348,167 (but where did it get the money?) as well as obligations of $2,500,000 "claimed by predecessor's creditors in court actions," as the neutral lingo of Moody's Manual states. The new American Piano Corporation drifted around for a while, an incapacitated cripple, doing little except to sell the Mason & Hamlin factory to the Aeolian Co.

But the Aeolian Co. was also being ravaged by disease. As of May 1, 1929, the dividends on its 7% cumulative preferred stock were 47¼% in arrears. That year the company showed a net loss of $743,119. The common stock, which had been dealt in at 27 or 28 during 1928, went as low as 4 the following year.

In 1932 the two tired octopuses decided to get married, pooling their salvageable resources and forming the Aeolian-American Corporation. Meanwhile the continuity of Mason & Hamlin production was interrupted. Musicians, uncertain of the fate of the piano's quality, deserted it, and the name never regained its former standing. It was more than a commercial casualty.

The great depression was now in swing. All through the preceeding boom, the piano business had been drooping fast. Many things soared during the late 1920's: automobiles, movies, cosmetics, Florida real estate, night clubs, and skyscrapers. Walking sticks were offered at $90, silk stockings at $500 a pair, traveling bags at $4000—and a choice pearl necklace at $685,000. Yet, fewer and fewer people wanted to buy pianos. Soon fewer and fewer persons were able to buy anything at all. Between the stock-market crash of the autumn of 1929 and the bank closings of March 1933, the piano business faded to the brink of annihilation. The player piano, including the reproducing piano, became extinct in 1932, no shipments being recorded for that year. The great Steinways, rich and honored, decided it was cheapest to quit manufacturing for a while: they shut down their plants for at least a year, while keeping most of the working staff together and on the payroll. Watch the piano makers drop off like autumn leaves: in 1909, the peak year, the United States counted 294 of them, all separate establishments; ten years later, before there was any radio, they had already dwindled to 191. By 1929 a mere 81 were left. Then the depression blew its icy blast, and the years from 1933 on proceeded with a subdued remnant of 36 companies that still persisted in hoping they could continue to fabricate pianos.

The ailment of the piano was a syndrome, a running together of various processes. One of the most influential among them was the change that came about in the standards of behavior considered proper to females—in particular, those of the genteel, pretentious sections of society. Through the first decade of the twentieth century many intelligent daughters of the well-to-do began to feel uneasy under the respectable restrictions within which their lives were expected to be contained. To earn their own living, to travel freely, to visit public places unescorted, to participate in masculine sports, to wear comfortable clothes—all these seemed better than to spend their lives painting china buttons, embroidering silk pansies, tracing wood-burning designs, and playing *The Robin's Return*. The feminine "accomplishments" of the previous generations now began to turn stale and trivial.

The feeling of restlessness smoldered indecisively for a while, but the general upheaval involved in the World War of 1914–18 pushed it into active flame. After it was over, "nice" girls worked usefully and gainfully outside their homes as a matter of course; moreover, they also went out alone in the evening, to any eating or drinking places they chose, played hockey, smoked cigarettes, voted for president, and discarded their corsets. They cared less about appearing "proper," about whether anyone might imagine they were "running after" men. Indeed, a few of them actually did so run. Under the sweep of this gust of emancipation, it was hard to persuade a girl of scant musical aptitude to submit to expensive, painful piano lessons for years in order at some time to be able to play a piece for "company"—a thousand-dollar piece, as ironical fathers were known to call it.

Another, related, enemy of the piano was the partial devaluation of the home as the significant center of living. Among the moderately well-to-do this was due in part to the increasing difficulty of getting domestic servants. Ostentation took on new forms that were focused outside the house. A younger generation considered a "front parlor" full of costly junk a dull way of showing off, compared to a troublesomely shiny, needlessly high-powered automobile of well-advertised make. A home party for a crowd of friends, with elaborate homemade refreshments and homemade music, became a bore when compared to a deafening evening spent among provocative strangers at a well-talked-up night club.

When women, passively abetted by their men, lost their faith in the kind of respectability by which their grandmothers had lived —and when the home premises had to share themselves self-denyingly with the automobile, the country club, the dance restaurant, and the moving-picture palace in the general affection—the piano lost its symbolical potency. There was no point in setting up a visible sign of something one no longer believed in. The home piano, naturally, also lost much of its musical usefulness with the wide spread of machines that could reproduce skillfully performed music at the touch of a knob. Yet the machines, with all their superior efficiency, could never by themselves have supplanted the piano if the ideal values for which the instrument stood had kept their hold on people's mind. The player pianos of 1825 were quite practicable, yet they could make no headway at the time against a strong faith in "accomplishments." But in the early 1900's, when the faith began to wane, the pianola could win out.

Thus, the piano can be seen as a feature in the physiognomy of a certain way of life, the way of moneyed middle-class people, of the *bourgeoisie*, whose habits dominated the Western world for a century and a half. In the middle eighteenth century, when these people first felt their importance and their strength, they believed mystically in "liberty," in unrestrained expression in word and tone, and in the emphatic utterance of humane sentiment: thus they wanted an instrument that could play any tone loud or soft from bodily impulse at the whim of an instant, that could reflect the free, incalculable play of "feeling" within their hearts. They believed in "humanity," in the right of all human beings, regardless of their birth, to an opportunity for their self-development: therefore they compelled their children to take music lessons, and thus they favored the piano—on which even the most slow-handed and dull-eared could produce some minimum of acceptable result. The liberty they prized the most was the liberty to engage in lucrative schemes, to pile up profits: they believed in money and in the palpable evidences of its assured possession, and that gave them a predilection for an instrument that looked solid and expensive in a drawing room. Their belief in business enterprise allowed them to think of music as a simple article of commerce and thus to encourage publishers to put out vast quantities of music that wallowed in identical formulas, so as to keep up a steady stream of buying and selling. They agreed with Rousseau that woman exists only with reference to man, and for his comfort and vanity, and that her place is in the home: thus they liked an instrument that she could play congruously with her aspect of chaste idleness. Presently they developed a great admiration for what they could, with some superstitious exaggeration, call individual achievement. They spun dreams about bold, crazy heroes; and they enjoyed looking up worshipfully—especially after his defeat and departure—to one man who could rise from artillery captain to European dictator, or to another who could climb from antique-peddler to world banker: thus they also liked to expend their hero worship upon piano virtuosos whose startling feats of loudness, speed, and agility commanded the attention of thousands, and who, humbly born, came to have their names linked with those of princesses. They believed in mechanical devices, which helped them to make more money; and that gave them affection for an instrument that had many moving parts. They believed in the iron of their steam engines and did not shrink from introducing its severity into their pianos, so that the virtuosos could play still louder without smashing them.

There was ethical fervor and imaginative aspiration in all the elements of this complex; but they all, too, had their false and fatuous phases. The piano sometimes rose to sublime heights of musical thought and execution, but often it appeared an inept and absurd thing. At the end of the nineteenth century, when the bourgeois faith seemed most unquestionably established, it began to tire. A younger generation began to be subtly aware of its insufficiencies and its inner discrepancies. Skepticism of the piano went with skepticism of the way of life that had nurtured it. The low point of both was reached in 1933, the year of the bank failures and of Hitler's rise. The idol had been tottering for a quarter of a century; now it fell from its little pedestal, its halo shattered.

5. THE LOW PLATEAU

THE PIANO was dethroned as an idol; but after a little time it was able to carry on a steady, modest, subdued civilian life. In the world of fine art—of concerts and virtuosos—the change was felt the least, and there were blissful permanent dwellers in that enchanted mountain meadow who may not have known that anything had happened. Piano recitals continued and so did piano concertos with orchestra as well as vocal concerts with piano accompaniment. Their devotees were a small band, yet paradoxically their numbers were somewhat augmented through the stimulation of the phonograph and the radio—the very agencies that had done so much to discourage home piano playing.

A more critical, discriminating atmosphere, however, now began to prevail at concerts. Pianists could still stir and charm and even amuse; but they no longer astonished, or inspired awe, for the sound and movement of first-rate piano playing had become too generally familiar. Modern mythology could create no new Anton Rubinstein or Paderewski, and the innocent response to great pianistic skill was lost. Instead, a greater purity of taste—one might almost call it prudishness—began to be evident in the offering of programs. Piano soloists now largely refrained from playing anything not directly written for the instrument. Transcription of Wagnerian scenes or of Bach organ fugues, and elaborations of Vienna waltzes, were all abated. On the other hand, the music of Debussy and Ravel, once considered to be left-bank naughtiness, now became respectable and pleasant. Furthermore, the transparent euphony and unvehement mobility of Mozart's works began to take on revived allurement. Duo-piano performances, in abeyance since the days of the Civil War, broke into fresh vogue during the 1920's, '30's, and '40's—with several pairs of pianists entertaining a considerable number of audiences. Indeed, a group of four pianists calling themselves a "Piano Quartet" made quite a success in concerts after establishing a wide reputation with a radio audience. Duo- and multi-piano programs were far less straight-laced than those of solo players. In their case, the athletics of the performance itself still could maintain interest and excitement; and thus all kinds of arrangements, masquerades, and mutilations of music were enjoyed when ping-ponged by one or another of these "teams." Finally, in the world of jazz a number of imaginative improvising pianists could make lively, if ephemeral, reputations.

As for the makers of concert pianos: the name of Knabe now disappeared from programs, and also that of Mason & Hamlin. That of Baldwin became more frequent. The Baldwin Piano Co. grew increasingly ambitious, making earnest efforts to improve its product and persuading a fair number of successful concert artists to play its instrument regularly. Since 1930, Baldwin has become Steinways' only mentionable rival in the quality and concert field. Steinways' soon resumed production after their short syncope and, after some vicissitudes, became stabilized at about 2500–3000 units per years, as compared with the 5000 of the piano's full flower.

After the nadir of the depression was passed, new pianos were again being bought by a certain number of ordinary people; and the object that had fitted harmoniously with overstuffed sofas, gilt carved picture frames, curio cabinets, plush hangings, and ormolu clocks could now again take its place, a little anachronistically, amidst the fluorescent lamps, the electric refrigerators, the high-fidelity radio sets, the portable bars, and the sundry constructions of bakelite and tube steel of a changed world and home.

The piano's decline and fall had thrown it into a coma, and the wiser doctors understood that it had a chance of surviving without a halo only if it underwent certain impromptu changes of shape. The direction which this saving operation was to take was enunciated as early as February 1931 by Carl Haselbrunner, in an article entitled "Is the Piano Still a Domestic Instrument?" appearing in the *Oesterreichische Musiker-Zeitung (Austrian Musicians' Journal)*, an organ of the Austrian musicians' union. After expressing his shock at the diminution of Vienna piano production, and after noting that eight firms had united into a "rationalization concern" so that they might continue to "vegetate honorably," the author said: the piano is too expensive and too loud; but it might be rescued by reducing its size, its tonal volume, and its price.

This was, indeed, the general line taken by the squad of thirty-odd American firms still contingently engaged in piano making. One of them, not the largest by any means, put out a redesigned model in May 1935, which the others took up with varying alterations. The new instruments were uniformly small, between two feet ten inches and three feet nine inches in height, with short strings and an action called "drop." Even dwarf models were put out, with only seventy-two keys instead of the standard eighty-eight. Straight "modern" lines formed the shape of the case, now called a "console." The tone emanating from the short wires and the condensed sounding board was correspondingly faint. At the time, these instruments were offered at retail at about $300 or less, about twenty-five per cent lower than the average price of a small upright of 1924. The new designs were not really new in principle. Small pianos three feet in height had been made in Europe in 1830. Moreover, even many of the new trade names were not new. "Console" had been the name of an elegant little piano, two feet nine inches high, designed by Pape in 1839. "Pianinos" were made by Pleyel in the 1820's and '30's, and the word had been common in Germany for a century thereafter. "Spinet," of course, was the ancient word for a small square-shaped harpsichord; but only persons eccentric enough to be interested in the past were annoyed by the misappropriation. American sloganeering genius did, indeed, bring forth "Mini-piano," "Vertichord" (there had been a "Vertegrand" a long time before), and "Acrosonic" as new creations under the sun. Noteworthy was tne trend toward gibberish labels in place of makers' names, as it had been under the old regime.

The new designs were successful. In 1937, 107,000 pianos were shipped in the United States—mostly of the little species. There may have been a slight increase by 1939, but the Second World War sharply reduced all piano making because of the need for critical materials such as steel and copper in defense industries. The business picked up, however, after the shooting ended. In 1950 the industry reported 175,000 pianos made and shipped, and the prognosticators for 1953 were jubilant about a likely 180,000. That is about equal to the piano production figure for 1903, fifty years earlier, when the country's population was half of what it is today and its wealth far less. It is half the production figure for 1909, when the nation had only three fifths of the people it has now.

The piano was a child of nineteenth-century social habits: first an article of luxury for the rich, then gradually made more and more cheaply so that the less rich could ape their betters. The imitatory process, however, had to stop long before it penetrated more than a fraction of the population. The piano's decline was the twentieth-century fate of any object—or any publication, or performance, or idea—that cannot be sold quickly to scores of millions of people. Pianos are made by machinery, but they cannot call forth the machines' fuller potentialities. At the height of the reign of technology, only those things that machines can make the fastest and in the greatest quantities can command the fullest respect. Good machines must give way to better, those that make things for a million are thrust aside for those that can produce for a hundred million, while the supplying of mere thousands becomes an act of charity or of eccentric devotion. The logic of the machine, then, colors all sense of values and all ethics of human relations. People acquire not what they might want for themselves, but what machines can most conveniently and profitably make in the largest amounts. A man no longer apes his betters; rather he strives to be one of a great majority, one of those for whom the machines can do their best. At the climax of the worship of technology, its priests say "mass"—using a word that pretends we are not men, but crumbs in a pile of the inanimate stuff that machines live on.

The piano was made in large quantities, but not in "mass" production; and the "mass" article defeated it. In 1920, at the cumulative height of production—before the instrument's social devaluation had too seriously lessened its output—the population of 105,000,000 owned about 7,000,000 pianofortes. (Again we are calculating that all the instruments made for thirty years past were extant.) That meant one piano for every fifteen persons. In

1953 it was reported that 154,000,000 Americans owned 110,000,-000 radio sets. That means five sets for every seven men, women, children, infants in arms, inmates of prisons, hospitals, and poor-houses, sheepherders, stumble-bums, lighthouse keepers, and Pueblo Indians. Here is the real "mass" production, the triumph of mechanical sameness, the victory of "the people" over people.

Fortunately, in the United States no trends ever reach their apparent ultimate destinations—since they are permitted to develop countertrends—and human currents are mildly tolerant of their saving stragglers and dissidents. Many persons still wear vests, read books, write their own Christmas greetings, go to the theater, shave with straight razors, and play the piano.

The piano is not obsolete, nor is it likely to become so in the appreciable future. Its intrinsic musical convenience is still effective: it still allows persons of moderate aptitude to realize simple harmony, melody, and figuration readily, while playing loud and soft in direct response to bodily impact; and it remains the most practical support for the human voice. Experimental and "serious" composers have continued to write for it. When one of them, a number of years ago, came out with a revelation of "tone clusters," he found the piano as made-to-order for those jolly smears as it had been for the brave "cannon shots" of a century earlier. The "twelve-tone" fraternity have found the piano almost the least ambiguous board on which to play their tonal dice games. Some time ago some of the young progressives leaned to the bright idea that the piano was really a percussion instrument. It was, indeed, a comforting notion for deep musical thinkers who had never learned to articulate their fingers properly. With their minds in this frame, numbers of young males liking to hack and to whack, after their kind, could take satisfaction in delivering the cheap, clumsy chunks that make up the concerto by Aram Khachaturian. On the other hand, the admirable Béla Bartók was able to create a remarkably stirring, powerful sonata by combining the sounds of two pianos with those of a group of actual percussion instruments, such as drums, cymbals, triangle, and xylophone.

The success of high-brow adventures, however, is less important to the viability of the piano than the fact that popular songs, including "numbers" from successful shows, are still being published with piano accompaniments as a matter of course and that the hits among them sell their hundred thousand copies—instead of their former millions—to persons who presumably have pianos available in their dwellings. Many children continue to take piano lessons, for the sake of such fun as they are capable of developing out of the result. Certain musicians continue diligently to set down quantities of innocuous compositions for these youngsters, so-called "teaching pieces," meanwhile burning up the dictionary to find sprightly labels for them. They vary this exercise with the making of facilitated mutilations of excerpts from "classics" temporarily in the public attention, such as Tchaikovsky's *B-flat minor Concerto* or Chopin's *Polonaise in A-flat.* The piano still seems appropriate in dance orchestras and maintains its proprietary spot in jazz combinations.

In the family, the piano competes manfully with the washing machine and the station wagon for the installment dollar, and rather more weakly with gardening, photography, and canasta for hobby time. As a source of passive musical enjoyment, it has been all but snuffed out by the phonograph, the radio, and the television set; but as an active musical exercise among the young, it runs not far behind the clarinet, the trumpet, the accordeon, and the guitar.

It is doubtful now whether the piano will be improved, in any fundamental sense. One wonders, however, why the electronic piano has never caught on. This is an instrument with very small hammers, low tension, and no sounding board—every string, however, being provided with a set of pickups from which the tone is then amplified through a loud-speaker. A special lever can regulate the degree of amplification. In this instrument, the agreeable feeling of dynamic stroke-responsiveness is not only preserved, but augmented, by electronic means. Several small companies were experimenting with it during the 1930's, but nothing further seems to have happened.

The low plateau has no slope that we can now see. Our tale is told.

BIBLIOGRAPHY

DICTIONARIES

Allgemeine Deutsche Biographie. 44 vols. Leipzig 1875-1898.

Biographie Universelle, Ancienne et Moderne. "Nouvelle Edition," prob. 2nd. Paris 1854 ff.

Biographisches Lexikon des Kaisertums Oesterreich. Dr. Constant von Wurzbach ed. 55 vols. Vienna 1856-1887.

Brenet, Michel (pseud. for Marie Bobillier). *Dictionnaire pratique et historique de la musique.* Paris 1926.

The Complete Peerage of England, Scotland, Ireland, Great Britain and the United Kingdom. By G. E. C(okayne). New ed. rev. etc. by the Hon. Vicary Gibbs. London 1910.

Dictionary of American Biography. Allen Johnson ed. New York 1929.

Dictionary of National Biography. Sir Leslie Stephen and Sidney Lee eds. Oxford Univ. Press 1917 ff.

Eitner, Robert. *Biographisch-bibliographisches Quellen-Lexikon der Musiker und Musikgelehrten . . .* Leipzig 1900-1903.

Encyclopaedia Britannica. 14th ed. 1929.

Encyclopédie Methodique ou par ordre de Matières. Par une Société de gens de lettres de savans, et d'artistes. Section entitled *Encyclopédie des Arts et Métiers.* Paris 1778.

Entziklopeditchesky Slovař. (Encyclopedic Word Book). Andreyevsky ed. St. Petersburg 1890 f.

Fétis, F. J. *Biographie Universelle des Musiciens et Bibliographie Générale de la Musique.* 2nd ed. Paris 1873-78.

Gendai Ongaku Daikan (Contemporary Survey of Music). Taiji Tsuruhashi ed. Tokyo 1927.

Gerber, Ernst Ludwig. *Historisches-biographisches Lexicon der Tonkünstler.* Leipzig 1790.

Gerber, Ernst Ludwig. *Neues Lexicon der Tonkünstler.* Leipzig 1813.

Der Grosse Brockhaus. 15th ed. Leipzig 1928 ff.

La grande encyclopédie, inventaire raisonné des sciences, des lettres et des arts. Paris n.d.

Grove's Dictionary of Music and Musicians. 3rd ed. 1927. 2nd ed. 1904.

The International Cyclopedia of Music and Musicians. Oscar Thompson ed. New York 1939.

Koch, Heinrich Christoph. *Musikalisches Lexicon.* Frankfurt 1802.

Mendel, Hermann. (Dr. August Reissmann compl.) *Musikalisches Conversations-Lexicon.* 2nd ed. 11 vols. Berlin 1880.

Meyer's Lexicon. 7th ed. Leipzig 1924 ff.

Michel's Piano Atlas. N. E. Michel comp. Contains names, dates and serial numbers of almost all makes of pianos. Rivera, Calif. 1953.

Moody's Manual of Investments. 1927-1932.

Moore, John W. *Complete Encyclopaedia of Music.* Boston 1876.

Music Directory of Early New York City. Virginia Larkin Redway comp. and ed. New York 1941.

Nouvelle biographie générale depuis les temps les plus reculés jusqu'à nos jours

. . . Firmin Didot frères publ., Dr. Hoefer ed. Paris 1858 ff.

Ongaku Nenkan (Music Year Book). Tokyo 1940.

Rees, Abraham. *The Cyclopaedia*. 39 vols. London 1819. Incl. articles: "Guitarra," "Harpsichord," "Ravalement," "Schroeter," all by Charles Burney.

Riemann, Hugo. *Musik Lexicon*. 2 vols. Berlin 1929.

Rousseau, Jean-Jacques. *Dictionnaire de Musique*. Paris 1768.

Scholes, Percy A. *The Oxford Companion to Music*. Oxford Univ. Press, 7th ed. 1947.

Walther, Johann Gottfried. *Musicalisches Lexikon oder Musicalische Bibliothec*. Leipzig 1732.

PERIODICALS

Allgemeine Musikalische Zeitung. Leipzig 1798-1848.

American Musical Journal. A Monthly Repository of Musical Literature. . . . Vol. I 1834-1835. New York, James Dunn, publ.

L'Avant-coureur. Feuille Hebdomadaire. Paris 1770-1773.

C. F. Cramer's Magazin der Musik. Kiel 1783.

Dwight's Journal of Music. Boston 1852-1862.

The Etude. Philadelphia 1886-1890.

Euterpeiad or *Musical Intelligencer and Ladies Gazette*. J. R. Parker ed. Boston 1820-1822.

The Euterpeiad. An Album of Music, Poetry and Prose. New York 1830-31.

The Gentleman's Magazine and Historical Chronicle. Vols. 58-77. London 1788-1807.

Giornale de' Letterati d'Italia. Vol. V. Venice 1711.

Godey's Lady's Book. Philadelphia 1854-1857.

The Harmonicon. London 1823-1832.

Harper's New Monthly Magazine. Vol. III no. 16. New York September 1851.

Fortune. New York, August 1939.

Hiller, Johann Adam, ed. *Wöchentliche Nachrichten und Anmerkungen die Musik betreffend*. Leipzig 1766-1770.

Journal de musique par une société d'amateurs. Paris 1773.

Knickerbocker Magazine. New York. Vols. 9-14 1837-1839. Vol. 34 1849.

Monthly Magazine of Music. London January 1, 1823. (No more published.)

Monthly Musical Record. London 1871 ff.

Musical Courier. New York 1880 ff.

The Musical Herald. Vol. III. Boston 1882.

Musical Quarterly. New York 1915 ff.

The Musical Review and Record of Musical Science . . . E. Ives ed. Vol. I, New York 1838-1839.

The Musical World. Vols. XXI and XXII. London 1846-1847.

Music Trade Review. New York 1875 ff.

The Music Trades. New York 1890 ff.

Musique et instruments. Vol. 25. Paris 1934.

New York Musical Review and Gazette. Mason Bros. eds. Vols. VII and VIII. New York, 1856-1857.

Piano Trade Magazine. Vols. 25-50. Chicago 1928-1953.

Putnam's Monthly Magazine . . . Vol. I. New York March 1853.

The Quarterly Musical Magazine and Review. London 1818-1828.

Quarterly Musical Register. A. F. C. Kollmann ed. London 1812.

Revue et gazette musicale. M. Schlesinger ed. Paris 1834-1848.

Revue musicale. F. J. Fétis ed. Paris 1827-1834.

La revue musicale. Henri Prunières ed. *Numéro Spéciale Chopin*. Vol. XII, Paris 1931.

Saroni's Musical Times. H. Saroni ed. New York 1849-1852.

The Spectator. By Joseph Addison, Richard Steele, and others. London 1711-1712. June-December 1714.

Zeitschrift für Instrumentenbau. Leipzig. Vol. XXIII 1903. Vol. XLVI 1925.

BOOKS, MONOGRAPHS, AND SPECIAL ARTICLES

Adam, Louis, ed. *Méthode de Piano du Conservatoire Adoptée pour servir à l'Enseignement dans cet Établissement*. Paris XII (1804).

Adams, W. H. Davenport. *Good Queen Anne. Men and Manners, Life and Letters in England's Augustan Age*. Introduction includes Gregory King's analysis of the distribution of England's wealth as of 1688. 2 vols. London 1886.

Adlung, Jacob. *Anleitung zu der Musikalischen Gelahrtheit*. Erfurt 1758.

d'Agoult, Marie, Countess. *Mes Souvenirs 1806-1833*. Paris 1877.

Amster, Isabella. *Das Virtuosenkonzert in der ersten Hälfe des 19 Jahrhunderts*. Wolfenbüttel and Berlin 1931.

Ancelet, ——. *Observations sur la musique, les musiciens et les instruments*. Amsterdam 1757.

Antrim, Doron K. "The Piano as a Barometer of Musical Conditions." Article in *The Musical Observer*, Vol. XXX no. 4. New York, April 1931.

Apperson, G. I. *Bygone London Life*. New York 1904.

Aswell, James R. ed. *Native American Humor*. New York and London 1947. Includes "A Piano in Arkansas" by Thomas B. Thorpe; "Jud Brownin' hears Ruby play" by G. W. Bagby; and "Advertising" by P. T. Barnum.

Auerbach, Cornelia. *Die deutsche Clavichordkunst des 18ten Jahrhunderts*. Kassel 1930.

Austen, Jane. *Emma*. (1st ed. 1816.)

Austen, Jane. *Letters to her Sister Cassandra and Others*. R. W. Chapman ed. 2 vols. Oxford 1932.

Austen, Jane. *Pride and Prejudice*. (Written 1796-97. 1st ed. 1813.)

Avison, Charles. *Essay on Musical Expression*. 2nd ed. London 1753.

Ayars, Christine Merrick. *Contributions to the Art of Music in America by the Music Industries of Boston 1640 to 1936*. New York 1937.

Bach, Carl Philipp Emanuel. *Versuch über die wahre Art das Clavier zu spielen*. Berlin 1753.

Balet, Dr. Leo. *Die Verbürgerlichung der deutschen Kunst, Literatur und Musik im 18ten Jahrhundert*. Strassburg 1936.

Baum, Richard. *Joseph Wölfl 1773-1812. Sein Leben und seine Klavierwerke*. Kassel 1928.

Beethoven, Ludwig van. *Neue Briefe Beethovens*. Ludwig Nohl ed. Stuttgart 1867.

Beethoven, Ludwig van. *Beethoven's Letters*. Dr. A. C. Kalischer ed. J. S. Shedlock transl. 2 vols. London and New York 1909.

Bishop, J. Leander. *A History of American Manufactures from 1608 to 1860*. 3 vols. 3rd ed. Philadelphia 1868.

Bitter, Karl Hermann. *Johann Sebastian Bach*. 2 vols. Berlin 1865.

Bowen, Catherine Drinker. *"Free Artist," the Story of Anton and Nicholas Rubinstein*. New York 1939.

Brancour, René. *Histoire des Instruments de Musique*. Paris 1921.

Brenet, Michel (pseud. for Marie Bobillier). *Les Concerts en France sous l'Ancien Régime*. Paris 1900.

Bricqueville, Eugène de. *Le Piano de Mme. DuBarry et le Clavecin de la Reine Marie-Antoinette*. Versailles 1892.

Bricqueville, Eugène de. *Le Piano à Versailles sous Marie-Antoinette*. In: *Revue de l'Histoire de Versailles et Seine-et-Oise*. 1906.

Bricqueville, Eugène de. *Les Ventes d'Instruments de Musique au XVIIIe siècle*. Paris 1908.

Brinsmead, Edgar. *History of the Pianoforte*. London 1877.

Brissot de Warville, J. P. *New Travels in the United States of America performed in 1788*. (First printed 1792.) Repr. in: *Great American Historical Classics Series*. Bowling Green, Ohio, 1919.

Brooks, Henry M. *Olden-Time Music. A Compilation from Newspapers and Books*. Boston 1888.

Brooks, Van Wyck. *The Flowering of New England 1815-1865*. Revised ed. Cleveland and New York 1946.

Bruford, W. H. *Germany in the Eighteenth Century. The Social Background of the Literary Revival*. Cambridge 1935.

Bruni, Antonio Bartolommeo. *Un inventaire sous la Terreur. Etat des Instruments de Musique rélevé chez les émigrés et les condamnés*. J. Gallay ed. Paris 1890.

Buecken, Dr. Ernst. *Die Musik des Rokokos und der Klassik*. In series: *Handbuch der Musikwissenschaft*, Bücken ed. Wildpark-Potsdam 1929.

Bukofzer, Manfred. *Music in the Baroque Era*. New York 1947.

Burgh, A. *Anecdotes of Music*. 3 vols. London 1814.

Burney, Charles. *General History of Music from the Earliest Ages to the Present Period*. 2nd ed. London 1789.

Burney, Charles. *The Present State of Music in France and Italy*. London 1771.

Burney, Charles. *The Present State of Music in Germany, the Netherlands, the United Provinces, etc.* 2nd ed. London 1775.

Burney, Frances. *Diary and Letters of Madame d'Arblay (1778-1840).* Charlotte Barrett and Austin Dobson ed. 6 vols. London 1904.

Burney, Frances. *Early Diary 1768-1778.* Annie Raine Ellis ed. 2 vols. London 1907. (1st ed. 1889).

Burton, Robert ("Democritus Junior," pseud.). *The Anatomy of Melancholy.* New York 1867 (1st ed. 1621).

Busby, Thomas. *Concert Room and Orchestra Anecdotes of Music and Musicians.* London 1825.

Byron, George Gordon, Lord. *Poetical Works,* complete in 1 vol. New York, n.d. ca. 1850.

Calmus, Georgy. *Die ersten deutschen Singspiele von Standfuss und Hiller.* In: *Publikationen der Internationalen Musikgeselleschaft,* supplementary volumes, 2nd series. Leipzig 1908.

Carner, Mosco. *The Waltz.* London 1946.

Chappell, W. *Popular Music of the Olden Time.* London 1859.

Chastellux, Marquis de. *Travels in North America in the Years 1780, 1781 and 1782.* In: *Great American Historical Classics Series.* Bowling Green, Ohio, 1919.

Chateauneuf, l'Abbé de. *Dialogue sur la musique des Anciens.* Paris (1725).

Chesterfield, Philip Dormer Stanhope, 4th Earl of. *Letters.* Bonamy Dobrée ed. 6 vols. London 1932.

Chickering, ——. *The Commemoration of the Founding of the House of Chickering & Sons—1823-1903.* Boston 1904.

Clemen, Otto. *Andreas Streicher in Wien.* In: *Neues Beethoven-Jahrbuch,* Adolf Sandberger ed. Vol. 4, Augsburg 1930.

Clifford, James L. *Hester Lynch Piozzi (Mrs. Thrale).* Oxford 1941.

Closson, Ernest. *History of the Piano.* Delano Ames transl. London 1947.

Clough, Shephard Bancroft. *France, a History of National Economics 1789-1939.* New York 1939.

Comettant, Oscar. *Histoire de Cent Mille Pianos et d'une Salle de Concert.* Paris 1890.

Comettant, Oscar. *La Musique, Les Musiciens, et les Instruments de Musique.* With documents "*qui se rattachent à l'exposition internationale de 1867.*" Paris 1869.

Corti, Egon Caesar, Count. *The Rise of the House of Rothschild.* B. and B. Lunn transl. (Vienna 1927) New York 1928.

Couperin, François. *L'Art de toucher le Clavecin.* After 2nd ed. 1717, with transl. by Anna Linde and Mevamvy Roberts. Leipzig 1933.

Crosten, William L. *French Grand Opera. An Art and a Business.* New York 1948.

Czerny, Carl. Complete list of his works to opus 798. In appendix to: *Czerny's School of Practical Composition.* 3 vols. London, Robert Cocks, 1848.

Czerny, Carl. *Letters to a Young Lady on the Art of Playing the Pianoforte.* J. A. Hamilton transl. New York 1868 (after London 1848).

Dale, William. *Tschudi the Harpsichord Maker.* London 1913.

David, Hans. "Die Crise unserer Tasteninstrumente." Article in *Melos,* Vol. 7, no. 2. Berlin, February 1928.

Dexter, Franklin B. "Estimates of the Population in the American Colonies." Article in: *Proceedings of the American Antiquarian Society,* New Series, Vol. V, 1887-1888. Worcester 1889.

Dolge, Alfred. *Pianos and their Makers.* Covina, Calif., 1911.

Edgeworth, Maria and R. L. *Practical Education.* 2nd ed. London 1801. (1st ed. 1798).

Ella, John. *Musical Sketches Abroad and at Home.* 3rd ed. London 1878.

Engel, Carl. *A Descriptive Catalogue of the Musical Instruments in the South Kensington Museum.* 2nd ed. London 1874.

Erard, ——. *Exposition Universelle de 1855. Notices sur les Travaux de Mm. Erard, Facteurs de pianos et harpes de leurs majestés imperiales et de sa majesté la reine d'Angleterre.* Paris (1855?).

Escudier, Leon. *Mes Souvenirs. Les Virtuoses.* Paris 1868.

Fay, Amy. *Music Study in Germany.* 16th ed. New York 1896.

Ferrari, Giacomo Gotifredo. *Anedotti piacevoli e interessanti.* London 1830.

Fétis, F. J., and Moscheles, I., eds. *Méthode des Méthodes de Piano. Traité de l'Art de jouer de cet Instrument.* Paris 1840.

Fielding, Henry. *The History of Tom Jones.* (1st ed. 1749.)

Findeisen, Nicolaus. *Die Entwickelung der Tonkunst in Russland in der ersten Hälfte des 19. Jahrhunderts.* In: *Sammelbände der Internationalen Musikgesellschaft.* Vol. 2 1900-1901. Leipzig.

Fischhof, Joseph. *Versuch einer Geschichte des Clavierbaues. Mit besonderem Hinblicke auf die Londoner Grosse Industrie-Ausstellung in Jahre 1851.* Vienna 1853.

Fisher, William Arms. *Notes on Music in Old Boston.* Boston 1918.

Fisher, William Arms. *One Hundred and Fifty Years of Music Publishing in the United States.* Boston 1933.

Fithian, Philip Vickers. *Journal and Letters 1767-1774.* John Rogers Williams ed. Princeton 1900.

Flood, W. H. Grattan. "Dublin Harpsichord and Pianoforte Makers of the Eighteenth Century." In: *The Journal of the Royal Society of Antiquaries of Ireland . . .* Vol. XXXIX Consecutive Series (Vol. XIX Fifth Series), 1909. Dublin 1910.

Flood, W. H. Grattan. *A History of Irish Music.* 2nd ed. Dublin 1906.

Flood, W. H. Grattan. *John Field of Dublin.* Dublin 1921.

Flower, Newman. *George Frederic Handel.* New York 1948.

Forkel, Johann Nikolaus. *Johann Sebastian Bach. His Life, Art, and Work.* Charles Sanford Terry transl. New York 1920. 1st ed. 1802.

Freytag, Gustav. *Bilder aus der deutschen Vergangenheit.* Vol. IV: *Aus neuer Zeit.* Leipzig 1904.

Friedländer, Max. *Das deutsche Lied im 18ten Jahrhundert.* Stuttgart and Berlin 1902.

Frimmel, Theodor von. *Beethoven Studien.* 2 vols. Munich and Leipzig 1906.

Frimmel, Theodor von. *Ludwig van Beethoven.* 6th ed. Berlin 1922.

Fritz, Barthold. *Anweisung wie man Claviere Clavecins und Orgeln in allen zwölf Tonen gleich rein stimmen könne . . .* Leipzig 1757.

Fürstenau, Moritz. *Zur Geschichte der Musik und des Theaters am Hofe zu Dresden.* Dresden 1861.

Gardiner, Dorothy. *English Girlhood at School. A Study of Women's Education through Twelve Centuries.* Oxford and London 1929.

Gerson, Robert A. *Music in Philadelphia.* Philadelphia 1940.

Goebel, J. *Grundzüge des modernen Klavierbaues.* Leipzig 1925.

Goehlinger, Franz August. *Geschichte des Klavichords.* Basle 1910.

Goethe, Johann Wolfgang von. *Sämmtliche Werke.* Reclam. reprint, Leipzig n.d. Vol. 15, *Leiden des jungen Werthers* (1774). Vol. 22, *Aus meinem Leben, Dichtung und Wahrheit* (1811).

Gottschalk, Louis Moreau. *Notes of a Pianist.* Clara Gottschalk ed. Philadelphia 1881.

Gray, Thomas. *Letters.* Duncan C. Tovey ed. London 1900.

Grillparzer, Franz. *Sämtliche Werke.* Dr. Albert Zipper ed. Vol. I. Leipzig 1902.

Guerard, Albert Leon. *Reflections on the Napoleonic Legend.* New York 1924.

Haessler, Johann Wilhelm. "Drei leichte Sonaten für Klavier." In: *Nagel's Musik-Archiv no. 20.* Hanover 1932. Contains reprint of composer's preface and autobiography appended to his *Easy Sonatas* publ. in Erfurt 1786 and 1787.

Hallé, Sir Charles. *Life and Letters . . . an Autobiography (1819-1860) with Correspondence and Diaries . . .* C. E. Hallé (son) and Marie Hallé (dghtr.) ed. London 1896.

Hanslick, Eduard. *Geschichte des Concertwesens in Wien.* 2 vols. Vienna 1869.

Harding, Rosamond E. M. *The Piano-Forte. Its History Traced to the Great Exhibition of 1851.* Cambridge 1933.

Harris, Clement A. "The Bicentenary of the Piano." Article in: *Musical Opinion–Music Trade Review,* Vol. 36. London 1913.

Harrison, G. B. *England in Shakespeare's Day.* New York 1928.

Hase, Oskar von. *Breitkopf & Härtel. Gedenschrift und Arbeitsbericht.* 4th ed. Leipzig 1917.

Haselbruner, Carl Maria. "Ist das Klavier noch ein Hausinstrument? Article in: *Oesterreichische Musiker Zeitung.* Vol. 39, no. 2. Vienna February 1931.

Hayes, Gerald, ed. *King's Music. An Anthology . . .* with an essay by Sir H. Walford Davies, Master of the King's Musick. Oxford University Press 1937.

Heine, Heinrich. *Sämtliche Werke in zwölf Teilen.* Paul Beyer, Karl Quenzel and Karl H. Wegener, eds. Leipzig.

Vol. 10: *Lutetia*, with appendix (1841-1844). Vol. 12, part 2: *Meyerbeer's "Hugenotten" und Rothschilds grosser Ball* (March 1, 1836). From: *Sechs Berichte für die Allgemeine Zeitung.*

Heine, Heinrich. *Französische Zustände I.* (1931 ff). In: *Werke*, Vol. 5. Heinrich Laube ed. Vienna, Leipzig, Prague.

Herrmann, Heinrich. *Die Regensburger Klavierbauer Späth und Schmahl und ihr Tangentenflügel.* Erlangen 1928.

Hertz, Eva. *Johann Andreas Stein. Ein Beitrag zur Geschichte des Klavierbaues.* Wolfenbüttel and Berlin 1937.

Herz, Henri. *Mes Voyages en Amérique.* Paris 1866.

Heuss, A. "Die Dynamik der Mannheimer Schule." In: *Riemann Festschrift.* Leipzig 1909.

Hipkins, A. J. *A Description and History of the Pianoforte.* London 1896.

Hobson, Johan A. *The Evolution of Modern Capitalism. A Study of Machine Production.* London and New York, rev. ed. 1927.

Hoffman, Richard. *Some Musical Recollections of Fifty Years.* New York 1910.

Humanus, P. C. (pseud. for Hartung). *Musicus Theoretico-Practicus . . . I. Theoria Musica . . . II. Die methodische Clavier-Anweisung . . .* Nürnberg 1749.

Huneker, James. *Franz Liszt.* New York 1911.

Israel, Carl. *Frankfurter Concert-Chronik von 1713-1780.* Frankfurt-a.-M. 1876.

James, Philip. *Early Keyboard Instruments from their Beginnings to the Year 1820.* New York 1920.

Jankó, Paul von. *Eine neue Klaviatur.* Vienna 1886.

Jefferson, Thomas. *Writings.* Pub. by Thomas Jefferson Memorial Association. Washington 1905.

Johnson, H. Earle. *Musical Interludes in Boston 1795-1830.* New York 1943.

Josephson, Matthew. *Jean-Jacques Rousseau.* New York 1931.

Juramie, Ghislaine. *Histoire du Piano.* Paris n.d. (ca. 1947).

Kapp, Julius. *Franz Liszt, Eine Biographie.* Berlin 1911.

Kapp, Julius. *Giacomo Meyerbeer, Eine Biographie.* Berlin and Schoeneberg, 1932.

Keeler, Walter Bradley. *How to Learn the New Keyboard.* Pub. by the Paul von Jankó Conservatory of Music. New York 1892.

Kelso, Ruth. *The Doctrine of the English Gentleman in the Sixteenth Century.* In: *University of Illinois Studies in Language and Literature.* Vol. XIV. Urbana 1929.

Kidson, Frank. *The Beggar's Opera, Its Predecessors and Successors.* Cambridge 1922.

Kidson, Frank. *British Music Publishers, Printers and Engravers from Queen Elizabeth's Reign to George the Fourth's.* London 1901.

Kirkpatrick, Ralph. *Domenico Scarlatti.* Princeton 1953.

Krehbiel, Henry Edward. *Chapters of Opera.* New York 1909.

Krehbiel, Henry Edward. *The Philharmonic Society of New York. A Memorial.* New York and London 1892.

Krille, Annemarie. *Beiträge zur Geschichte der Musikerzeihung und Musikübung der deutschen Frau (von 1750 bis 1820).* Berlin 1938.

Kuhe, William. *My Musical Recollections.* London 1896.

Lafontaine, Henry Cart de, ed. *The King's Music 1460-1700.* London (1909).

Langwill, Lyndesay G. *Two Rare Eighteenth Century London Directories.* Article in: *Music & Letters*, Vol. XXX no. 1. London 1949.

Lecky, William E. Hartpole. *A History of England in the Eighteenth Century.* 5th ed. London 1891.

Leibniz, Gottfried Wilhelm. *Philosophische Schriften.* C. J. Gerhardt, ed. 7 vols. Berlin 1885. Vol. VI. *Principes de la Nature et de la Grace, fondés en raison* (1714). Vol. VI. *"Monadologie"* (1714).

Liszt, Franz. *Letters.* La Mara ed. Constance Bache transl. 2 vols. New York 1894.

Liszt, Franz. *Pages Romantiques.* Jean Chantavoine ed. Paris 1912.

Das Lisztige Berlin. Anonymous collection of satirical anecdotes and verses lampooning Liszt's visit to Berlin. 3 vols. said to constitute nos. 9, 10, and 11 of a collected series called *Berliner Witze.* Berlin 1842.

Locke, John. *Some Thoughts Concerning Education* (1693). In Vol. III of *Works.* 2 vols. London 1768.

Logier, J. B. *Tracts on Logier's System of Music*. A collection of eight pamphlets on the subject, by Logier and various of his opponents, all published in London or Edinburgh bet. 1814 and 1824.

Longman & Broderip. *Catalogue of Music Printed and Sold*. London 1789.

Luethge, Kurt. "Vom Klavier und seiner Zukunst." Article in: *Die Musik*, Vol. XVI, no. 12. Berlin, September 1924.

Mace, Thomas. *Musick's Monument*. London 1676.

Mapleson, James Henry. *The Mapleson Memoirs 1848-1888*. 2 vols. Chicago, New York and San Francisco 1888.

Marpurg, Friedrich Wilhelm. *Abhandlung von der Fuge*. Berlin 1753.

Marpurg, Friedrich Wilhelm. *Anleitung zum Klavierspielen*. Berlin 1755, 2nd ed. 1765.

(Marpurg, F. W.) *Der Critische Musikus an der Spree*. Berlin 1750.

(Marpurg, F. W.) *Die Kunst das Klavier zu spielen*. Berlin 1751, rev. ed. 1762.

(Marpurg, F. W.) *Kritische Briefe über die Tonkunst*. Berlin 1764.

Mason, William. *Memoirs of a Musical Life*. New York 1901.

Mattheson, Johann. *Critica Musica*. Hamburg 1725.

Mattheson, Johann. *Das Neu-Eröffnete Orchestre*. Hamburg 1713.

Metropolitan Museum of Art. *Catalogue of the Keyboard Musical Instruments in the Crosby Brown Collection*. New York 1903.

Meyer, Leopold de. *Biography* (Memoir). London 1845.

Middleton, Thomas (ca. 1370-1627). *Works*. 8 vols. A. H. Bullen ed. London 1885.

Milchmayer, Johann Peter. *Die wahre Art das Pianoforte zu spielen*. Dresden 1797.

Minor, Andrew C. *Piano Concerts in New York City 1849-1865*. Master's thesis, typescript, University of Michigan 1947.

Mizler, Lorenz. *Neu-Eröffnete Musikalische Bibliothek*. Leipzig 1739.

Molière. *Le Bourgeois Gentilhomme, Comédie Ballet* (1670). In: *Œuvres de Molière. Avec les notes de tous les commentateurs*. Paris 1875.

Montal, Claude. *L'Art d'accorder soi-même son piano*. Paris 1836.

Mooser, Ludwig. *Gottfried Silbermann der Orgelbauer*. Langensalza 1857.

More, Hannah. *Complete Works*. New York 1857.

Moscheles, Charlotte. *Life of* (Ignaz) *Moscheles with selections from his diaries and correspondence*. A. D. Coleridge transl. from the German. 2 vols. London 1873.

Mozart, Wolfgang Amadeus. *Mozart's Briefe*. Ludwig Nohl ed. Leipzig 1877.

Mozart. *Letters of Mozart and his Family*. Emily Anderson ed. and transl. London 1938.

Müller, Gottfried. *Daniel Steibelt. Sein Leben und seine Klavierwerke*. Strassburg 1933.

Murdock, Kenneth Ballard. *Increase Mather*. Cambridge 1925.

Musikalischer Almanach auf das Jahr 1782. Anon. "Alethinopel" (Leipzig?).

"Musikalisches Taschenbuch." *Musikalischer Almanach auf das Jahr 1784*. Anon. Freyburg.

Myers, Gustavus. *History of the Great American Fortunes*. Chicago 1909.

Nef, Karl. "Clavicymbel und Clavichord." Article in: *Jahrbuch der Musikbibliothek Peters für 1903*. Leipzig 1904.

Nettl, Paul. *The Story of Dance Music*. New York 1947.

Newman, Ernest. *The Man Liszt*. New York 1935.

Nicolai, Friedrich. *Beschreibung einer Reise durch Deutschland und die Schweiz im Jahre 1781*. 12 vols. Berlin and Stettin 1784.

Niecks, Frederic. "Henri Herz and Stephen Heller." Article in: *Monthly Musical Record*, Vol. XVIII, no. 206. London February 1, 1888.

Niemann, Walter. *Klavierabende: Gedanken zu ihrer Reform*. Article in: *Die Musik*, Vol. 20, no. 9. Leipzig June 1928.

North, Roger (1653-1733). *Memoires of Music*. E. F. Rimbault ed. London 1846.

Nottebohm, Gustav. *Thematisches Verzeichniss der im Druck erschienenen Werke von Ludwig van Beethoven*. 2nd ed. Leipzig 1868.

Orel, Alfred, ed. *Ein Wiener Beethoven Buch*. Collection of nine articles on Vienna in Beethoven's day. Incl. "Die Stadt" by Johann Eugen Probst, and

"Die Gesellschaft" by Ludwig Böck. Vienna 1921.

Paesler, Karl. Preface to *Haydn's Klavierwerke,* Vol. I (Sonatas). Breitkopf & Härtel. Leipzig 1919.

Pagnerre, Louis. *De la mauvaise influence du piano sur l'art musical.* Paris 1885.

Papendieck, Mrs. Charlotte. *Court and Private Life in the Time of Queen Charlotte* (Consort of George III). Mrs. Vernon Delves Broughton ed. London 1887.

Paribeni, Giulio Cesare. *Muzio Clementi nella Vita e nell'Arte.* Milan 1922.

Parton, James. "The Piano in the United States." Article in: *The Atlantic Monthly,* Boston July 1867.

Pauer, E. "Henri Herz." Article in: *Monthly Musical Record,* Vol. XVIII no. 207. London March 1, 1888.

Paul, Dr. Oscar. *Geschichte des Claviers . . . nebst einer Übersicht über die musikalische Abteilung der Pariser Weltausstellung im Jahre 1867.* Leipzig 1868.

Peacham, Henry. *The Compleat Gentleman.* facsim. of 2nd ed. of 1634. (1st ed. 1622). Oxford 1906.

Pepys, Samuel. *Diary* (1660-1669). Henry B. Wheatly ed. 8 vols. London 1893.

Pichler, Caroline, née von Greiner (1769-1843). *Denkwürdigkeiten aus meinem Leben.* Emil Karl Blümml ed. acc. 1st ed. 1844. Munich 1914.

Pierre, Constant. *Les Facteurs d'Instruments de Musique, Les Luthiers et la Facture Instrumentale. Précis Historique.* Paris 1893.

Pinson, Koppel S. *Pietism as a Factor in the Rise of German Nationalism.* New York 1934.

Pinthus, Gerhard. *Das Konzertleben in Deutschland.* Strassburg 1932.

Pirro, André. *Les Clavecinistes.* From the collection: *Les Musiciens Célèbres.* Paris 1822?

Pleyel. *Exposition Universelle 1855. Médaille d'Honneur. J. Pleyel & Cie.* Paris 1855.

Poelitz, K. H. L. *Oesterreichische Geschichte.* Vienna 1859 (1st ed. 1817).

Pohl, Conrad Ferdinand. *Mozart und Haydn in London.* Vienna 1867.

Praz, Mario. *The Romantic Agony.* Angus Davidson transl. London 1933.

Preussner, Eberhard. *Die Bürgerliche Musikkultur.* Hamburg 1935.

Prod'homme, J. G. "Napoleon, Music and Musicians." Article in: *Musical Quarterly,* New York Oct. 1921.

Prutz, Robert. *Menschen und Bücher. Biographische Beiträge zur deutschen Literatur- und Sittengeschichte des achtzehnten Jahrhunderts.* Leipzig 1862.

Pulver, Jeffrey. *Paganini, the Romantic Virtuoso.* London 1936.

Quantz, Johann Joachim. *Versuch einer Anweisung die Flöte Traversiere zu spielen.* Berlin 1752. Rev. ed. Arnold Schering. Leipzig 1906.

Rebling, Eberhard. *Die Soziologischen Grundlagen der Stilwandlung der Musik in Deutschland um die Mitte des 18ten Jahrhunderts.* Berlin-Wilmersdorf 1935.

Reeser, Dr. Eduard. *The History of the Waltz.* Stockholm n.d.

Reeser, Dr. Eduard. *The Sons of Bach.* W. A. G. Doyle-Davidson transl. Stockholm n.d.

Reichardt, Johann Friedrich. *Briefe eines aufmerksamen Reisenden, die Musik betreffend.* Part I Frankfurt and Leipzig 1774. Part II Frankfurt and Breslau 1776.

Reichardt, Johann Friedrich. *Vertraute Briefe aus Paris geschreiben in den Jahren 1802 und 1803.* 3 vols. Hamburg 1804.

Reichardt, Johann Friedrich. *Vertraute Briefe aus Wien 1808-1809.* Gustav Gugitz ed. 2 vols. Munich 1918.

Rimbault, Edward F. *The Pianoforte, its Origin, Progress, and Construction. . . .* London 1860.

Roscoe, E. S. *The English Scene in the Eighteenth Century.* New York 1912.

Rousseau, Jean-Jacques. *Écrits sur la Musique,* incl. *Lettre sur la musique française* (1753), and *Traités sur la Musique* (Geneva 1781 collection). In vol. 9 of *Œuvres Completes.* Louis Barré ed. Paris 1857.

Rousseau, Jean-Jacques. *Émile, ou de l'éducation.* The Hague 1762.

Rubinstein, Anton. *Erinnerungen aus fünfzig Jahren 1839-1889.* Eduard Kretschmar transl. from the Russian. Leipzig 1895.

Russell, Charles Edward. *The American Orchestra and Theodore Thomas.* Garden City 1927.

Sauer, Dr. August, ed. *Stürmer und Dränger.* In: *Deutsche National-Litteratur.* Joseph Kürscher ed. Vol. 79. Berlin and Stuttgart 1883.

Scheibe, Johann Adolph. *Critischer Musikus.* Leipzig 1745.

Schering, Arnold. *Johann Sebastian Bach und das Musikleben Leipzigs im 18ten Jahrhundert.* Vol. 3 (1723-1800) of: *Musikgeschichte Leipzigs.* Leipzig 1941.

Schering, Arnold. *Die Musikaesthetik der deutschen Aufklärung.* In: *Zeitschrift der Internationalen Musik-Gesellschaft.* Vol. VIII April 1907.

Schiffer, Leo. *Johann Ladislaus Dussek, seine Sonaten und seine Konzerte.* Borna-Leipzig 1914.

Schiller, J. C. Friedrich. *Werke.* Ludwig Bellermann ed. 14 vols. Leipzig and Vienna (1895). Vol. I: *Gedichte.* Vol. II: *Dramen in Prosa.*

Schlesinger, Thea. *Johann Baptist Cramer und seine Klaviersonaten.* Munich 1928.

Schletterer, Hans Michel. *Johann Friedrich Reichardt. Sein Leben und seine musikalische Tätigkeit.* Leipzig 1879 (1st ed. Augsburg 1865.)

Schneider, Max. "Biographische Nachrichten" about Georg Philipp Telemann, in the introduction to Telemann's *Der Tag des Gerichts* and *Io.* In: *Denkmäler deutscher Tonkunst,* series 1, Vol. XXVIII.

Scholes, Percy A. *The Puritans and Music.* London 1934.

Scholes, Percy A. *The Great Doctor Burney.* 2 vols. London and New York 1948.

Schrenk, Oswald. *Berlin und die Musik. Zweihundert Jahre Musikleben einer Stadt, 1740-1940.* Berlin 1940.

Schubart, Christian Friedrich Daniel. *Ideen zu einer Aesthetik der Tonkunst.* Wien 1806.

Schumann, Robert. *Schriften über Musik und Musiker.* Dr. Heinrich Simon ed. 3 vols. Leipzig 1888-1889. (Written 1834-1853).

Schweitzer, Albert. *Johann Sebastian Bach.* Ernest Newman transl. 2 vols. London 1911.

Sewall, Samuel (1674-1729). *Diary.* In: *Collections of the Massachusetts Historical Society,* Vol. V, Fifth Series. Boston 1878.

Shakespeare's England. A collection of articles by various English specialists. C. T. Onions ed. Oxford 1932. (1st ed. 1916).

Shimizu, Tomosaburo, and Unno, Kazuma. *Modern Japan.* Chap. XX entitled "Music." Tokyo 1933.

Singleton, Esther, ed. Article: "American Pianos" in: *The Antiquarian,* Vol. III no. 3, October 1924

Sittard, Josef. *Geschichte der Musik- und Concertwesens in Hamburg vom 14ten Jahrhundert bis auf die Gegenwart.* Altona and Leipzig 1890.

Smith, Sir Thomas. *De Republica Anglorum* (1565). L. Alston ed. Cambridge 1906.

Sonneck, Oscar G. *Early Concert-Life in America, 1731-1800.* Leipzig 1907.

Sonneck, Oscar G. *Early Opera in America.* New York 1915.

Sonneck, Oscar G., William Treat Upton rev. and ed. *A Bibliography of Early Secular American Music (18th century).* Library of Congress, Washington 1945.

Spillane, Daniel. *History of the American Pianoforte.* New York 1890.

Spitta, Philipp. *Johann Sebastian Bach.* Vol. 2, Leipzig 1880.

Spohr, Ludwig. *Autobiography.* English transl. London 1865.

Steinway & Sons. *Pianofortes.* Illustrated Catalogue of 1875.

Steinway & Sons. *1876. Pianofortes.* Illustrated circular, probably put out in connection with the Philadelphia Centennial.

Steinway & Sons. *Prospectus for 1881.*

Stevens, Paran. "Report upon Musical Instruments." In: *Paris Universal Exposition 1867. Reports of the U. S. Commissioners.* Washington, Government Printing Office 1869.

Storck, Karl. "Das Klavier. Seine Geschichte und sein Bau." In: *Westermann's Illustrierte Deutsche Monatshefte.* Braunschweig April 1900.

Strauch Bros. *The Manufacture of Pianoforte Action, Its Rise and Development.* New York 1892.

Strong, George Templeton. *Diary.* Allan Nevins and Milton Halsey Thomas eds. New York 1952.

Terry, Charles Sandford. *Bach, a Biography.* London 1928.

Terry, Charles Sandford. *John Christian Bach.* London 1929.

Thackeray, William Makepeace. *Vanity Fair. A Novel without a Hero.* (1st ed. 1846-48.)

Thayer, Alexander Wheelock. *The Life of Ludwig van Beethoven.* H. E. Krehbiel ed. 3 vols. New York 1921.

Thon, Christian Friedrich Gottlieb. *Über Klavierinstrumente, deren Ankauf, Behandlung und Stimmung.* Sondershausen 1817.

Thureau-Dangin, P. *La Monarchie de Juillet.* Paris 1884

Trollope, Frances M. *Domestic Manners of the Americans* (1st ed. 1833). Donald Smalley ed. New York 1949.

Turner, Walter James. "The Passing of the Pianoforte." Article in: *The New Statesman,* Vol. XXV no. 644. London, August 29, 1925.

Unger, Max. *Muzio Clementi's Leben.* Langensalza 1914.

United States of America. 6th Census. *Compendium of Statistics of the United States* (incl. manufactures). Washington 1841.

United States of America. *Digest of Accounts of Manufacturing Establishments . . . and of their Manufactures . . .* Washington 1823.

United States. 7th Census 1850. *Abstract of the Statistics of Manufactures,* also *Comparative Populations of 30 Largest Cities.* Washington.

United States Department of Commerce. *Census of Manufactures 1905.* Washington.

United States Department of Commerce. *15th Census 1930.* Washington.

United States Department of Commerce. *16th Census 1940. Manufactures 1939. Musical Instruments and Parts.* Washington.

United States Senate. *Reports of the Immigration Commission. Statistical Review of Immigration 1820-1910. Distribution of Immigrants 1850-1900.* Vol. 3. Washington 1911.

Van Doren, Carl. *Benjamin Franklin.* New York 1938.

Voelcker, Dr. Heinrich, ed. *Die Stadt Goethes. Frankfurt am Main im XVIII. Jahrhundert.* Incl. *Das Elternhaus Goethes und das Leben in der Familie,* by Dr. Robert Hering, archivist of the Frankfurt Goethe museum; and *Pflege der Tonkunst in Frankfurt a. M.,* by Dr. Bodo Wolf.

Voltaire, François Marie Arouet. *Oeuvres Complètes.* Vol. 49. (*Correspondance* vol. XVII. 1774-1776). Paris 1882.

Walter, Dr. Friedrich. *Geschichte des Theaters und der Musik am Kurpfälzischen Hofe.* Leipzig 1898.

Weber, Carl Maria von. *Tonkünstlers Leben, eine Arabeske.* 1827. In: *Hinterlassene Schriften,* Vol. I. Dresden and Leipzig 1828.

Weckerlin, J. B. *Nouveau Musiciana. Extraits d'ouvrages rares ou bizarres anecdotes, lettres etc. concernant la musique et les musiciens.* Paris 1890.

Weill, Georges. *La France sous la Monarchie Constitutionelle (1814-1848).* Paris 1912.

Weitzmann, C. F. *Geschichte des Clavierspiels und der Clavierliteratur.* 2nd ed. Berlin (1887).

White, William Braid. *The Player-Piano Up-to-date.* New York 1914.

Whitehouse, H. Remsen. *A Revolutionary Princess. Christina Belgiojoso-Trivulzio. Her Life and Times 1808-1871.* New York 1906.

Wierzynski, Casimir. *The Life and Death of Chopin.* Norbert Guiterman transl. New York 1949.

Wingfield-Stratford, Esmé. *Those Earnest Victorians.* New York 1930.

Wroth, Warwick. *The London Pleasure Gardens of the Eighteenth Century.* London 1896.

Zachariae, Friedrich Wilhelm. *Poetische Schriften.* Braunschweig 1772.

MUSIC
(Selected List)

Albanese—"Musician du Roy." *La Soirée du Palais Royal. Nouveau Recueil d'Airs . . . Avec accompagnement de Forte Piano, ou de Harpe . . .* Paris (ca. 1775).

Beethoven, L. van. *Wellington's Sieg oder die Schlacht bey Vittoria. Für das Piano Forte. 91tes Werk.* Vienna ca. 1816.

Byrd, William. *My Lady Nevells Booke* (1591). Hilda Andrews ed. London and Philadelphia 1926.

Carhart's Melodeon Instructor. Boston 1851.

Dandrieu, François. *Pieces de Clavecin. Contenant plusieurs Divertissement, dont les principaux sont Les Caracteres de la Guerre, ceux de la Chasse et la Fete de Village. Dédié au Roi.* Paris 1724.

.ckard, Godefroy (Gottfried). *Six Sonates pour le Clavecin . . . les Oeuvre.* Paris n.d. (1763?).

nglish *Minstrelsie, A National Monument of English Song.* S. Baring Gould :oll. and ed. 8 vols. Edinburgh ca. 1895.

iustini, Lodovico, di Pistoia. *Sonate da Cembalo di piano, e forte detto volgarmente di martelletti.* Florence 1732. Facsim. reprint, Rosamond Harding ed. Cambridge 1933.

Jadin, Louis. "21st potpourri" composed on *Airs du Prisonnier de Dellamaria,* for pianoforte. Paris ca. 1800.

Jadin, L. Arrangement of Boieldieu's *Overture* to *De la Fête du Village-Voisin.* Paris ca. 1816.

Jadin, L. "*Ode à J. J. Rousseau.*" In: *Ouvrages periodiques de chansons et romances civiques 1794-1799.*

Parthenia. Virginal pieces by William Byrd, John Bull, and Orlando Gibbons. (1st ed. ca. 1612). Reprint, with preface by Otto Erich Deutsch. London 1942.

Reichardt, Johann Friedrich. *Gesänge fürs schöne Geschlecht.* Berlin 1775.

Sperontes (pseud. for Johann Sigismund Scholze). *Die Singende Muse an der Pleisse.* Vols. 35 and 36 of *Denkmäler deutscher Tonkunst,* series 1. Preface by Edward Buhle, ed. Leipzig 1909.

INDEX